CURRENT COMPETITION LAW

VOLUME III

CURRENT
COMPETITION
LAW

Volume III

Edited by

MADS ANDENAS,
MICHAEL HUTCHINGS
and
PHILIP MARSDEN

THE BRITISH INSTITUTE OF INTERNATIONAL AND COMPARATIVE LAW

Published and Distributed by
The British Institute of International and Comparative Law
Charles Clore House, 17 Russell Square, London WC1B 5JP

© *The British Institute of International and Comparative Law 2005*

British Library Cataloguing in Publication Data
A Catalogue record of this book is available from the British Library

ISBN 0–903067–93–5

Typeset by Cambrian Typesetters
Frimley, Surrey
Printed in Great Britain by Biddles Ltd
King's Lynn

CONTENTS

PREFACE

The third volume of *Current Competition Law* brings together for the first time, papers and speeches from the two main competition law conferences the British Institute held in 2003 and 2004. We begin with the proceedings of our 2nd annual Merger Conference, held on 2 December 2003. At this conference, competition officials and experts from the private sector engaged in a frank discussion of pressing policy issues: underpinning much of the commentary was the (then) recent change to the substantive merger control test in Europe, as well as the debate in the UK with respect to the test for merger referrals by the OFT to the Competition Commission. The second half of this volume is comprised of the papers delivered and discussion at our 4th annual Trans-Atlantic Antitrust Dialogue, held on 10–11 May, 2004. Amongst the many excellent contributions at this conference were key insights into the evolution of US antitrust law offered to us by the Assistant Attorney General for Antitrust, R. Hewitt Pate; important guidance on the consumer interest from Director General Philip Lowe of the European Commission; the first remarks on state aid from the Chief Economist, Lars-Hendrik Roller, and a fascinating roundtable discussion amongst the heads of various agencies.

Current Competition Law continues to evolve as the competition law programme at the Institute develops. Future volumes will include papers on competition litigation and some of the substantive submissions at our expert practitioner workshop series <http://www.biicl.org> and Competition Law Forum meetings <http://www.competitionlawforum.org>.

I hope you find this third volume to be a helpful research resource, and I thank all of our contributors for their time and effort. Research assistance was provided by our first Junior Fellow in Competition Law, Charles Smith. I look forward to seeing you at our competition workshops, meetings, and conferences, and look forward to all comments on this volume, and our programme at the Institute.

Dr Philip Marsden
Director, Competition Law Forum
and Senior Research Fellow, BIICL

PART ONE—BIICL MERGER CONFERENCE

CHAPTER 1

Transatlantic Cooperation

DR PHILIP MARSDEN

Good morning. I would like to welcome you to the second Annual Merger Control Conference of the British Institute. It's our second conference on merger control in December but it's our first at the delightfully named Goodenough College. I am the director of the Competition Law Programme at the Institute and I would like to thank our sponsor Shearman and Sterling LLP and in particular Chris Bright and his team for helping us out two years running with this event. The Institute as you may know, is a not for profit research centre. We focus on International and Comparative Law Issues, primarily Public International Law, Tort Law, Human Rights, Data Protection and of course Competition Law. Now within the Competition Law Programme, we have events, we do research and we make policy recommendations to Governments and to the European Commission.

With respect to our events, we have practitioner workshops every couple of weeks where I've tried, since I joined the Institute six months ago, to make sure that we have the leading counsel involved in various cases to describe them to us and to describe a little bit of the strategy and the ramifications of the case for the future of the case law. We have recently looked at *IMS Health* for example, the Safeway bids, and also we had a very good workshop last week on the Technology Transfer Block Exemption.

I am also the director of the Competition Law Forum which is something new here in London. It is a quarterly series of sessions in a closed meeting of leading experts on competition law and economists and officials. We have had 3 meetings this year already. Merger Control was one topic, Modernisation another and Price and Non-Price abuse was the third and next week we have our final meeting this year on Enhancing the Effectiveness and the Efficiency of State Aid Policy and that will be held in Brussels.

I mention all of this to you because it is those kinds of meetings and it is the kind of conference we are having today and it is membership of the Institute that allows all of this to happen, that funds our comparative research and allows us to make policy recommendations which, it would appear, have been very much appreciated particularly by the Commission representatives.

Our conference today obviously has an international and comparative theme. When Chris and I were discussing how to set up this conference, we wanted very much to make sure that we dug down quite deep and looked at what is really happening, not so much necessarily in terms of a know-how 'download of developments', or in terms of allowing people to have a platform to speak about all the excellent things going on, but to test them a little bit and to say 'What is happening? What are the ramifications of the Commission's new merger test?' That is probably a topic that will filter through most of the panels today. 'International Convergence: what are its extents and its limits'; 'International enforcement cooperation: what is its extent and what constraints are there still on such cooperation?' This topic is what we are kicking off the conference with today. 'What is really happening in transatlantic cooperation?'

Our chairman, and for the purposes of this morning's presentation, our genteel interrogator, Dr Irwin Stelzer, is the director of Economic Policy Studies at the Hudson Institute. He was the founder of NERA. He's familiar to may of you on this side of the Atlantic as a frequent political and economic columnist for the *Sunday Times* but you may be less familiar with one of his publications entitled 'The United States, a United Europe and the United Kingdom: three characters in search of a policy'. Now that book was primarily about defence policy but I wonder if it also applies to merger policy in some ways? We have four experts joining Dr Stelzer on the panel today to discuss this. They are all experts in the area. I would like to welcome Dale Collins who is a former senior official at the Department of Justice and is now a senior competition Partner at Shearman and Sterling. We also welcome Debbie Majoras who is the Principal Deputy Assistant Attorney General at the Department of Justice and is the Deputy primarily responsible for the Microsoft case. She is also the former Chair of the ICN's Merger Working Group. We also welcome Dr Frank Montag who is the Co-Head of Freshfield Bruckhaus Deringer's Anti-Trust, Competition and Trade group and is one of the leading European competition lawyers, and finally last but not least of course is Götz Drauz who is the Head of the Commission's Merger Task Force and very much familiar to all of you. We are very grateful for them coming and we are also very grateful for you coming today. Thank you very much.

A. Götz Drauz

Good morning. It's my great pleasure to share the podium with some good friends, if I may say so, and I am especially grateful to Philip Marsden for giving me the opportunity to provide you with my, or rather the European Commission's, perspective on transatlantic cooperation. I have to say I may disappoint you a little bit in that most of what you've heard from Debbie I am going to agree with, and you may later try to see where there are still some differences; of course there are and that is normal.

Let me start by just saying a few words about why we are cooperating. To state the obvious, business is becoming global and mergers are being concluded on a global basis, and of course competition agencies have to follow that up and obviously cooperation facilitates convergence in the treatment of mergers, which is very beneficial for business. When the same or similar approaches are adopted by regulators, this is clearly positive in economic terms, and is an approach likely not to hamper but to promote economic growth and expansion. Cooperation increases the chances that a) unwarranted regulator interference is minimized; and b) that of course legal certainty is enhanced. Seen from the perspective of the regulator, cooperation enables the agencies to learn from each other and even rather sophisticated agencies like the EU and US can benefit from such mutual education. As I will explain in a minute, this cross fertilization of ideas can come not only in the form of case-related cooperation, but also from the horizontal projects and work which we have done together. In individual cases, cooperation enables the agencies to pool case-specific information and expertise which increases the efficiency of the cooperating agencies' investigation and contributes again towards avoiding divergent incoherent outcomes including, and I think this is very important, remedial actions. Cooperation also helps to avoid that our respective enforcement gives rise to unnecessary political tensions, something which can be damaging to the overall credibility of antitrust policy on both sides of the Atlantic. Cooperation does not mean that we always agree: that would be unrealistic and, to echo the chairman, it would probably even be unhealthy. But instead, cooperation means striving to ensure that disagreement is confined within the narrowest possible area of policy diversion, and that when we disagree, the disagreement is managed, understood, and its detrimental effects are minimized.

Now what makes a successful cooperative relationship like the EU/US one? The single most important ingredient for the success of any bilateral relationship between law enforcement agencies, in my view, can be summed up in one word—pragmatism; and maybe you might add mutual respect as well, and that has characterized the relationship between the European Commission and its US counterparts over the last 13 years. And this success is not, as Debbie has said, primarily due to the existence of bilateral cooperation agreements or other formal arrangements. They have formed an important part of it, but what has counted most is a pragmatic result-oriented mindset on the part of our respective agencies, both in individual case cooperation and in relation to our more general policy dialogue.

Let me elaborate a little bit by explaining how we cooperate on these two fronts. On individual case cooperation we now have a strong history of success. Our staff know each other. They know when to pick up the phone and whom to talk to. This is cooperation which is anything but formal. Communication is by phone, by fax, by email, in face-to-face meetings, but of course—let me reassure you—it does not involve exchange of confidential information. Our people talk to each other about every aspect of a merger investigation. We share publicly available information; we share information on which we have received confidentiality waivers; we discuss our respective analysis at the various stages: market definition, competitive effects, theories of harm, empirical evidence, efficiencies; we may coordinate fact-finding sometimes by exchanging draft questionnaires; and we strive to ensure remedies accepted do not impose inconsistent obligations on the parties. And of course, although that is very important, we always keep ourselves updated on what each other is doing and we have a close watch on the timing of both sides on the investigation. But of course successful cooperation depends to a large extent on the good will of the merging parties as well. And I must say that this is not normally a major problem. In particular, parties tend to grant us confidentiality waivers with little difficulty. The coordinated timing of merger notification is something we will be further exploring, along the lines of our recent best practices, and I think this cooperative attitude of merging parties comes from the recognition that cooperation is ultimately in their own interest.

There are many successful examples of cooperation. Debbie mentioned the *GE/Instrumentarium* case. On the DoJ side, I would certainly also want to add the *Cruises* case, where we cooperated with the FTC and the UK Competition Commission. Of course there are some less shining examples or bad practices as well. Some parties may argue their cases differently over here and in the US. Some parties behave strategically in that they try to obtain an early resolution from the agency which they find may be 'easier going' and of course that's fair enough, but such strategies, in my experience, are not always successful. Debbie also mentioned that we have worked together in many horizontal policy areas and we are very grateful for the very informal input which we are able to achieve in our projects, either our remedies notice or more recently the Horizontal Merger Guidelines, which we have drawn up for the first time; and I think we have benefited quite a lot from that input. So I think what is very important is to avoid concluding overly detailed, cumbersome bilateral cooperation agreements, and how to avoid this is to make sure that competition agencies are in the driving seat for such initiatives and not trade officials or diplomats.

Indeed, I have to say that if you look more generally into the US relationship then I think the cooperation in the competition field is clearly an excellent example of what you can achieve if you keep politics out, so to speak. But of course we have to be realistic in our ambition. National sovereignty is a fact and that will not change any time soon. This means that, while substantive convergence is important and highly desirable, legislative harmonization or the promulgation, for example, of an antitrust code is neither necessary, nor realistic.

So, to sum up, what is essential on the side of the agency is that the leadership is fully committed, which is the case here; that the working level people know each other; that they are at ease in communicating with each other; and of course on the side of business and advisers, that they are fully aware of the advantages which can be derived from cooperation between agencies, and that they embrace those possibilities in a positive way. Thank you very much.

B. Dr Frank Montag

Good morning to you all. It is also a pleasure for me to be on this prestigious panel and I actually asked myself, 'Why me, what do I know about what is really happening in the US/EU relationship?' After all of the speeches this morning about more fundamental matters concerning the relationship, I thought I might discuss three or four more practical issues that have come up in actual merger cases and which do show that sometimes EU/US cooperation does have an effect on cases.

The first issue concerns the extent of information requests. The US system, as you know, is geared towards litigation. Therefore, a second request is very document-intensive, whereas the Article 11 requests of the Commission are generally much less document-intensive and more focused on obtaining specific information. However, in one case that went to Phase II in Europe, we found ourselves in a situation where suddenly we got an information request from the Commission, which asked for more or less the same documents as the FTC had asked for in its second request. We were told by the Commission's case handler that the Commission wanted to be on an equal footing with the FTC in terms of the documents that it had, which was why they required us to produce the same documents in Europe as had been produced in the US. I think that this issue shows that there can also be a negative impact, or negative effect, from cooperation when suddenly one agency requires the parties to provide or do something which they normally would not really need for their review of the transaction.

The second issue that we have experienced, also to do with documents, concerns another case where in response to a second request in the US, documents were produced which, on one view, could apparently have suggested some degree of contact between companies that could permit tacit collusion. Under the terms of a waiver given by the parties, these documents were then shared with the EU Commission and were relied upon by it in its Phase I decision to approve this transaction. However, the parties only learned that the Commission had received these documents from the decision—the parties were never asked to comment on the documents before the decision was adopted, because it was a first phase merger clearance with remedies. That is a point where I would suggest that cooperation could be improved, especially on the EU side, so that access to the file would be granted earlier to enable the parties to know when documents provided in response to the United States' second request have been provided to the Commission and could be used in its procedure.

Now I understand that maybe, going forward, there will be developments in providing access to the file even in Phase I, as was permitted to a limited extent in the recent *Alcan/Pechiney* case. Perhaps this is a point to discuss.

Another point I wanted to raise, also from practical experience, was joint meetings and conference calls. As you are aware, in the Commission's Best Practices for the Conduct of EC Merger Control Proceedings, it is suggested that it may be appropriate to hold joint conference calls between the agencies and the parties and the advisers on both sides of the Atlantic. Now I remember—and I see Hans-Jürgen Meyer-Lindemann sitting in the room, he will also remember very vividly—in the *Bayer/Aventis Crop Science* case, a meeting around your conference table, Götz, in your office, where you were sitting on the EU side with the parties and their advisers and then on the conference telephone we had the FTC and the US advisers sitting in the United States. I, at least, had the impression we were part of some kind of pre-arranged act that was then played back and forth between the FTC and the Commission in trying to talk each other up on which remedies were required to make both authorities happy.

So, my advice from this practical experience is, yes of course, in principle, it is good if everybody gets round a table and discusses the issues, if this will help one to resolve things more easily. However, merging parties need to think very hard, before agreeing to such a joint meeting or conference call, as to whether it could actually be used to pressure them into agreeing something that they would not want to agree.

My last point concerns the coordination of remedies. Dale Collins just mentioned, and Debbie Majoras also mentioned, that the *GE/Instrumentarium* case involved moving one step further in the cooperation on remedies between the US and the EU. I actually wanted to mention another case, *Solvay/Montedison-Ausimont*,[1] also a cooperation case, which concerned a worldwide (or at least European and North American) market for a particular chemical, called PVDF. Solvay and a competitor, Atofina, each had market shares in excess of 40 per cent on this market and Ausimont, the company to be acquired by Solvay, had about a five per cent market share. In the EU, the case was assessed as raising joint dominance issues. In the US, it was dealt with as a coordinated effects case (although this wasn't quite clear and it could also have been unilateral effects, but it doesn't matter). Remedies were agreed on both sides of the Atlantic. In Europe (where remedies were, in principle, agreed first), a Solvay plant in North America was to be sold. The FTC afterwards required the same remedy, but demanded a 'crown jewel' provision, which meant that if the

---

[1] Case No COMP/M. 2690—*Solvay/Montedison-Ausimont.*

Solvay plant couldn't be sold within a set period of time, then the trustee would be instructed to sell Ausimont's only PVDF plant. This could have resulted in a situation where, under the EU remedies, if there was no sale within the period specified, the EU trustee would have had to sell the Solvay plant, whereas in the US, the crown jewel provision would have taken effect and then, in the US, the Ausimont plant would have had to have been sold by the trustee. That would have meant that both plants would have been sold. It was therefore agreed with the Commission that, if such a scenario were to emerge, Solvay could use the 'speaking clause' provision in the commitments which enables changes to be made to a remedy in case of a fundamental change in circumstances. So there was a way to solve this.

Finally, I think that the approach taken in the *GE/Instrumentarium* case is a good step forward, in having a joint trustee or consultations about the trustee concerning the remedies.

Thank you.

C. Deborah Majoras

Good morning. It is a pleasure for me to be here this morning to give you the perspective from the US Department of Justice Antitrust Division and, in particular, for me to be on this panel with several good friends. Now, in preparing for today's programme I have to say that the title stumped me a little bit. 'What is really happening?' implies that perhaps some things you may have heard about US/EU cooperation in the merger context maybe are not quite right, or that there may be something more to it lying below the surface. While I may be missing something (of course, I do not know what all of you have heard), and I will count on the distinguished gentlemen on this panel to tell me later if I am, but I can only tell you what I know from the US perspective. Transatlantic cooperation on all of competition enforcement and policy, including in the merger area, is at an all-time high and, in substance, is quite constructive and efficiency-enhancing, if you will. The fact that enforcement agencies are working together cooperatively and that things are working well is not the stuff of headlines, but then good government should not be considered something that is particularly extraordinary. The importance of our working relationship with the Commission is reflected in the large amount of resources we expend on consultation. This is something that you would not see because it is going on every day, behind the scenes. The huge space that the US and the EU occupy together in the global economy compels the conclusion that we, as enforcers, must act cooperatively to reduce the risk of divergent outcomes, reduce the burdens on parties, and ensure that an agency's remedy, in a particular overlapping manner, does not conflict with the other. There are three primary ways in which we cooperate with the European Commission in our merger work. First, we cooperate on individual investigations. Second, we do it through bilateral consultations on matters of merger policy. And finally, we cooperate and collaborate through multilateral organizations which are also addressing merger policy, and each one of these in turn has an impact on the other.

Now, turning to merger specific cooperation, as you may know last year the Antitrust Division and the Federal Trade Commission in the US, and the European Commission agreed on best practices for merger review coordination. And while we drew on practices that we had engaged in for some time, by formally adopting them, we were hoping to increase transparency for parties and also to provide guidance to all agency participants. Obviously, these agencies are quite large, with employees coming and going, and we wanted to make sure that we were all singing from the same hymn book, if you will, as we proceed through common investigations. Since the adoption of these practices, a little over a year ago, their use has been somewhat limited by the relatively few mergers that we have had to review in this economic situation. To give you some perspective on this, in our fiscal year 2003 which ended on 30 September, we received only 2,000 Hart-Scott-Rodino filings. To give you a point of comparison, even in the fiscal year 2001, we had received 4,800 and this can be further compared with those received in 1999 and 2000 which amounted to nearly 10,000 applications in each of the two years. Granted, that was before the US increased its thresholds, but again, the thresholds were increased by 2001, and mergers are still way down. We keep hearing from the private bar that merger activity is coming back, but with a few large exceptions, we are not seeing a real increase in numbers. Notwithstanding these low numbers, cooperation on the individual mergers has become, in Commissioner Monti's recent words 'part of our daily routine'. In fact, when I enquire of my staff whether in a particular matter they have contacted their colleagues at the Commission to begin talking about a matter and cooperating on it, the response I receive is most often 'well of course', because it has become a quite natural part of what we do. A recent example of exemplary cooperation was in the *GE/Instrumentarium* US DOJ and EU investigations (which Shearman and Sterling was involved with so perhaps Dale can let us know whether he agrees with me).

We began coordinating earlier this year, on timing, theory, and evidence, right from the very start. We were aided in our coordination because the parties to the deal believed that in fact it would be to their benefit to waive any confidentiality and to allow the two agencies to cooperate, which was extremely important to what we did. We ultimately determined that the transaction would substantially lessen competition in the sale of critical care patient monitors and mobile C-arms in the United States market, and the Commission found competitive problems relating to the sale of patient monitors in the EU. So, the issues in the two jurisdictions overlapped but were not entirely identical. We coordinated closely in accepting and implementing our remedy in this matter. The EC reached their settlement first and they required divestiture of Instrumentarium's SpaceLabs patient monitoring unit. We then reached a settlement which also required divestiture of the SpaceLabs subsidiary, as well as one other divestiture for a competitive impact that only affected the United States. If you look at the proposed final judgment that we filed in this matter, you will see that it contains provisions in which we ensure that the SpaceLabs assets will be sold to a buyer that will maintain competition in both jurisdictions. We explicitly say, for example, that should it ultimately be necessary to appoint a trustee to sell these assets (if the parties cannot complete the divestiture in the requisite period of time), that we will consult in good faith with the EC on the appointment.

The decree also says that if the trustee decides on a sale that is acceptable to the United States, nonetheless GE can object to it if the Commission doesn't also agree. This may not sound monumental but it is, I believe, the first time that we have ever explicitly, in one of our consent decrees, laid out our cooperation efforts on the remedy with the Commission.

I will just quickly tell you about a couple of issues with respect to bilateral policy consultations. We have fairly consistent informal communications on matters of merger policy. It is something that has developed over time, and, of course, in the current administrations of both the FTC and the DOJ, we have been in place for a long enough period of time now that we know our colleagues at the Commission fairly well. It is a fairly simple matter to pick up the phone and have a chat. For example, on the remarkable number of reforms that the EU has undertaken, we have provided input when requested to do so—and this may not mean necessarily taking ultimate positions on what is good or bad, but just talking things through and relaying our own experiences. We intend to continue these consultations because we have a lot we can learn from the current reforms. We also work in a much more structured setting through the US/EU merger working group. Instituted in 1999 and then reinvigorated in 2001, it has produced the best practices, which I referred to a few moments ago, and has also worked through issues relating to such things as conglomerate merger theory, efficiencies, and remedies in merger matters. Through these discussions, we are increasing our understanding of each other's respective precedents and positions; where we agree and disagree. And finally, the US agencies and the Commission work cooperatively in global organizations like the International Competition Network. As you may know, in its first two years of existence the ICN has been quite active on the merger front, producing guiding principles and best practices for conducting merger investigations, exploring merger review doctrine in 14 different jurisdictions, and exploring techniques for effective merger review. Both the US agencies and the Commission have played instrumental roles in getting that work done. And I should add that in cooperating on the multilateral front, it becomes particularly apparent that our two jurisdictions have far more similarities than differences. Together with Canada, we also have far more collective experience in merger review than countries in the rest of the world, and so we are working together to exercise some leadership for the now 80 competition regimes in the world that have some sort of merger review schemes, most of which are quite new. With that, I will conclude my prepared remarks, and I will be happy to answer any questions you might have. Thank you.

D. Dale Collins

Good morning. It is a pleasure for me to be here on this panel with such distinguished colleagues.

You can think about agency cooperation in an individual case within four dimensions: the investigation timetable, the analytical approach, the evidence, and the relief. From an outsider's perspective, with the exception of relief, there appears to be little if any agency cooperation or coordination that has any effect. Perhaps the agencies are talking to one another a great deal—I can't tell one way or the other—but if they are talking, little comes out of it that has any operational consequence from the practitioner's perspective.

Actually, this should not be surprising. There are good, sound institutional reasons why coordination on the timetable, the analytical approach, and the evidence is difficult if not practically impossible.

Consider the timetable for the investigation. In the United States, the timetable for a merger investigation is largely within the control of the parties. The parties essentially are free to choose when to make their premerger notification filing under the Hart-Scott-Rodino Act. They can sign a definitive agreement and then wait for months to file, or they can sign a non-binding letter of intent and file weeks, if not months, before negotiating a definitive agreement. If the investigating agency issues a second request, when the final waiting period begins to run is completely within the control of the parties. The final waiting period (which is usually only 30 calendar days) starts when the parties make a proper response to their second request. Sometimes the parties respond in a few weeks or even a few days, while in other cases the parties can take many months, a year, or even longer to respond. Even after the final waiting period has run, the parties can agree, informally at least, to extend the waiting period for weeks or months to give the agency more time to review the transaction or to permit the parties an opportunity to make a better case. Contrast that with the EU, where the merger investigation timetable is much more rigid. Although there is some flexibility through informal pre-filing consultations between the parties and the Commission staff, once the filing is formally made, the timetable is essentially set. So where the timetable in the US is almost completely in the control of the parties, and the timetable in the EU is set by regulation, there is usually little, if any, ability for the agencies to coordinate on timing.

Coordination on the analytical approach is equally problematic. The analytical approach of a jurisdiction is a fundamental policy judgment, and there is no good reason for an agency to compromise on a matter of competition policy just for the sake of coordination. In the United States, the analytical approach is almost completely consumer-centric: will the transaction have an adverse effect on consumers? More particularly, the US authorities ask whether, going forward, customers will face higher prices, lower product or service quality, reduced rates of technological innovation, or product improvement with the transaction than without it. I am not an EU practitioner, but looking at things from across the pond, it appears to me that in the EU the question is somewhat different: will the merger either create or strengthen a dominant position that will impede effective competition? This standard is going to change a bit with the new Merger Regulation, but even so I suspect that the traditional means of analysis are going to continue for the most part after the new Merger Regulation becomes effective. As a result, EU analysis will continue to focus heavily on market structure, rather than the consumer welfare standards that prevail in prosecutorial decision-making in the US.

These differences in the analytical approach also lead to differences in the evidence the investigating agencies seek to gather. Not surprisingly in light of the customer focus of the US analytical approach, one of the most important types of evidence in a US investigation is customer evidence, especially the customer's identification of alternative suppliers to the combined company and the customer's predictions of the transaction's effect on price and quality levels and on the rate of technological innovation. What the competitors have to say, on the other hand, is largely discounted by the US antitrust enforcement authorities. Competitor interests are often contrary to customer interests—competitors, for example, dislike mergers that are likely to lead to significant efficiencies on the part of the merging firm, which can significantly benefit customers—and US agencies fear that they will be 'played' by competitors to oppose transactions that are in fact in the customer's interests. By contrast, the structural emphasis in the EU drives the evidence collection towards structural factors, especially geographic market definition, product market definition, and market shares. Commission investigators also appear to give considerable weight to what competitors have to say about the effects of a transaction, perhaps because competitors are likely to know more about the current structure and the likely effects of the transaction on the future structure of the market.

As an aside, I might mention that these differences in the evidentiary focus can create enormous problems for the parties, as the US lawyers seek to focus the client on the customer story, while the EU lawyers struggle to answer the structural data demands of the Form CO.

Finally, on relief, let me say quickly that I agree with everything that has been said by Debbie and Götz. Here there is real cooperation with real consequences. The nature of the cooperation is more to ensure that the relief being sought in one jurisdiction does not interfere with the relief being sought in the other jurisdiction, rather than to agree to fashion common relief to solve the problems in the two jurisdictions, but given that the problems in the two jurisdictions may be different for reasons of analytical approach or market facts, one cannot reasonably expect or ask for more.

E. Discussion

[DR IRWIN STELZER]

Thank you. I think it would be useful, since we've heard what I consider to be divergent presentations—that is that the people on the government side seem rather self-satisfied with their performance, whilst the people who are working, toiling in the mines, seem less satisfied—to hear from Deborah and Götz briefly on what's wrong with what Dale and Frank said, because we did hear that they think that cooperation is not having the practical effect in the field that was described by the government side.

[GÖTZ DRAUZ]

First of all, I vividly recollect this conference call that Frank was referring to. However, I had a slightly different perception of it. I thought that what we are regularly hearing is that companies are asking us: 'Why are you so complicated, your US counterparts they have no problem, they have clear indications, they will clear the deal without any problems, and yes perhaps they want to clarify some issues here and there'. And when we are talking to them, we have a quite different story, they tell us: 'No we are not, we are still looking at this and that, and so on'. On the question of giving access to documents which we may receive from the US, I think there may be a problem—maybe everyone wants to comment or think about it—which is, in the US you do not have the possibility of such early access because of the difference in our systems, and I don't think that it would be possible for us then to make these documents available to parties in Europe when they are not accessible in the US. This does not mean that we should always inform you about what we think these documents say but I think there is clearly a legal problem here.

And also, when Frank was saying that he was a bit surprised that we were asking the same questions, I don't think that is in any way worthy of criticism. Also, of course, asking for the same documents. Again, the difference would be that we would ask you for certain specified documents while in the US you have to disclose documents and we are not talking about masses of documents anyway. I think to avoid the problems with remedies, we have developed the idea of a speaking clause, whereby procedures ending here in Europe first, or the other way round, which encounter a problem of difference in remedies, should be able to exercise a speaking clause so that the remedy can be looked at, and perhaps aligned with the one secured in the second jurisdiction, once the second procedure or the later procedure is finished as well.

[Dr Irwin Stelzer]

We have, I think, a little time for some questions. Sir, would you identify yourself please?

[Simon Holmes, *SJ Berwin*]

I wanted to pick up on something which Dale raised, and that's the problem of the timing differences between the EU and the US, and Deborah made a comment on that. Perhaps I could ask Götz if he would like to comment on that? In particular, the difficulties that may arise in cooperating if in the US, the parties file first under Hart Scott Rodino, and again perhaps another pinch point is when the EU is coming to the end of phase one and the time is ready to reach a decision. How does that affect cooperation in your field?

[Götz Drauz]

Well, I think there is not much that can be done about it because our system, even after the modifications, is still a time-organized system, so if the parties have chosen to notify at a certain moment, then you know what the timetable will be from that point on. However, there can be exceptional scenarios where more information is needed, and the clock can then be stopped. Otherwise there is no way that we can stall the procedure. We then have to go in Phase II and I think that is exactly something we would advise you to think about beforehand because, at least on the EU side, once you notify, you know more or less exactly when the various steps are coming up and I think, as we assured earlier, we are quite happy to discuss between ourselves to give you all an indication of when the right time would be to notify.

[Dr Irwin Stelzer]

Is it fair to say that the US authorities give more weight to customer reaction in mergers and the EU authorities give more weight to competitors' reactions to mergers, or is than an unfair distinction?

[Götz Drauz]

I first want to clearly agree with Debbie. Competitors' input to fact finding—they being the ones who know the market probably equally as well as the merging parties, because they are competing on the same market—is an important input into fact-finding. We have come some way here as well, and make a clear distinction between what competitors tell us and what their interests are: I think that it is very important to take what you get from them with a pinch of salt. I think also in Europe competitors are starting to understand that if they are arguing against a merger, then this may turn against themselves at some point, and I can tell you we are also increasingly grilling competitors, probably very much in the same way as in the US, so I don't think this distinction 'US concern is consumers, EU concern is competitors' has any basis.

[DEBORAH MAJORAS]

Well, I'd just like to note for the record, first of all, that we toil too!

[DR IRWIN STELZER]

Yes, you said 'good government is not something we should consider unusual'.

[DEBORAH MAJORAS]

That's right. I was particularly interested in what Dale had to say about whether the cooperation has any impact on any of his four factors other than relief. I do not agree with that. I would say a couple of things. First of all, one of the reasons why I said that the various types of cooperation all have an impact on one another is because, the impact of our cooperation really evolves, as opposed to necessarily pointing to where we have had 'x' result. Now, I recognize that when you are a party to a deal, you do not really care about this evolution. What you care about is getting your deal done today and getting it done as efficiently as possible, unless it is ultimately blocked. But I do think that even in individual transactions, cooperation can have an effect. It is true that, for example, the timetables are set up differently in the two jurisdictions. We have managed, however, with the cooperation of the parties—and that is important when one or two weeks at the end of an investigation can make a difference—to coordinate appropriately and for one agency to perhaps step back for a little while to let the other catch up and so forth, so we do try to work on that. Also, with respect to evidence, one of the things that parties, as well as third parties, have tried over time, is telling slightly or not even slightly, different stories to different agencies. But by cooperating, we can compare notes on the evidence that we have collected and test the veracity and the durability of that evidence. So I think that's another way. And finally, regarding the analytical approach, that is obviously a lot more complicated, but I think the approaches have over time moved closer to one another. We do talk a great deal during the course of investigations about one another's theories and approaches and I think that it does have some impact.

[DR IRWIN STELZER]

Is it fair to say that the US authorities give more weight to customer reaction in mergers and the EU authorities give more weight to competitors' reactions to mergers, or is than an unfair distinction?

[DEBORAH MAJORAS]

I don't think there is any question that in the US we place a great deal of weight on customer reactions. Obviously, we are looking to see whether a merger will ultimately inflict consumer harm and the customers generally are something of a proxy for the consumer in our analysis. And frankly, not only from an analysis perspective do we think that the customer's reaction is a quite important market test, but also pragmatically it is important because, as you know, if we wish to block a deal, we have to go into court and prove that it should be blocked, and I think it would be fair to say that it might be difficult to go in and prove such a case to a judge when there is no one sitting on the witness stand saying here is how we will be injured by this and here is what we are concerned about. Now having said that, it isn't that we are not grateful for the input we get from competitors. That is untrue. Competitors provide very useful market information to us and their reactions can be quite helpful. Competitors, however, have to be quite careful, because one can argue that if, in fact, a competitor is unhappy about a deal, that may mean that that deal is presumptively pro-competitive and will make for a nice strong competitor that the complaining guy does not want. I know that there has been criticism of the Commission in the past that, 'Oh gosh, they are listening to competitors too much'. The complaints themselves often come from US firms, because many are trying to be very strategic in their use of antitrust investigations and take their complaint to whomever will listen. But I do not think it is fair to say competitor views are all that the Commission is relying on and I should let Götz have the final word on that.

CHAPTER 2

Cooperation with and amongst Member State Authorities—What is Really Happening

A. Christian Ahlborn

I've been asked to say a couple of words on cooperation on substance and the first thought I had was, do we really mean cooperation or do we now mean—given that we have a new test under the ECMR—a new sort of harmonization? I think what we probably mean is at least a harmonization in the analytical framework used at the EC level and at Member State level. The reasons for an agreed common analytical framework are pretty clear and I've listed them in my first slide. Given that we can now expect a more seamless referral system, from the EC system to the Member State system, it would be really embarrassing to draft a notification which fits one analytical system and then to realize that actually you end up in a completely different system. The reduction of competition among regulatory systems is well understood as well, but I would like to say one word about the sort of economies of scale, in the sense that I think there is a huge benefit in having a common analytical framework so that people in different Member States can actually work across the system. I think one reason why the Americans are so much more advanced in their substantive analysis is that they have a much bigger antitrust market. I think we would benefit from the sort of cross-border fertilization in that respect and that may also drive cooperation with the US. I think it would also benefit from importing a lot of know-how which is available in the US on substance. I am not talking necessarily about procedure, but on substance, what is currently available. Now if you look at the substantive test, it's not a very beautiful child. It's a bit of a mongrel, a sort of half way between the SLC test and the dominance test, which brings to mind a couple of jokes about European directives. But beauty is not really what we were really striving for and I think John is right in saying that from a substantive outcome, it's very much an SLC test with a little bit of dominance there as well for retrospective compatibility, and I will come to that probably in a moment.

Now one of the issues we have is that a lot of Member States, including the accession countries, very obediently adopted the dominance test, so we've got 17 Member States with the dominance test. What does that mean for them? Can we happily live with a dominance test side by side with the SLC test? Backward compatibility is there in the sense that you preserve the dominance test and you can look at past cases and they may still work reasonably well, although I am not sure that I think the value of precedence for past cases is really that great on the substantive side. But I have my doubts about the 'forward compatibility' of the dominance test with the new SLC test for two reasons.

The first one is that I think once the new test is in force there is really no need for the Commission to apply dominance, at least unilateral single-firm dominance, any more. The thresholds for significantly impeding competition are lower and encompass dominance. But they extend further so there is no point in really developing the dominance concept any more. And those Member States which still have a dominance test are suddenly stuck trying to enlarge their concepts of dominance to include what is, or possibly what is not, captured by the dominance test under the old view. So you will see a tension between how the dominance test was used in the past and how the SIEC test and the dominance test will be used, and so I think there's a benefit in my view, given that you have to change and harmonize a lot of things as well, to move to either the SIEC test or a straightforward SLC test.

Now if I could say a word about efficiencies, I think that is the other big aspect of the substantive analysis. I will deal with two types of efficiencies. There are efficiencies which are not really in conflict with the competition process, in the sense that they enhance rivalry. That is never really a big issue and could always be taken into account comfortably in the normal substantive analysis and even in the dominance analysis. But you've got another type of efficiency which lowers prices, although at the same time the transaction reduces competition in the sense of rivalry. Here you've got some sort of balancing act, which under the old dominance test I think you couldn't have for the simple reason that if you were below the dominance threshold you didn't need the efficiencies, and if you had established dominance, ie a restriction of competition so severe that you had a single dominant firm, efficiencies wouldn't help you. So the second type of efficiencies were not really 'workable' under the dominance test and I think a lot of Member States, if they don't have an explicit dominance test, will struggle with that point. Now if you look to the SLC test, in principle it's capable of taking into account both types of efficiencies. The question is really, when we say that efficiencies are only going to be taken into account if it does not lead to a significant lessening of competition or impediment of competition, what do we mean by this? There are two possibilities. Either we define substantive lessening of competition in terms of process (eg rivalry), as the UK has done, in which case the second type of efficiencies could not be taken into account under the ECMR, or we define SLC in terms of outcome (eg prices), as in the US, in which case these efficiencies could be taken into account under EC Merger Control. In this case you could still balance efficiencies against restrictions of competition.

A couple of words about the guidelines, clearly a key instrument for harmonization and cooperation. I think the ECMR draft guidelines in their form, suffered a little bit from trying to argue that the dominance test actually captured everything and we had new concepts suddenly popping up which had as their sole purpose the attempt to widen the scope of the dominance test. There was a little bit of re-writing of history on the side of efficiencies. You had a whole section on it without a single case mentioned, for the simple reason that it hadn't played a significant role as yet. So I think the next version of the guidelines hopefully, given that we now have the SIEC test, will not have to suffer these deficiencies. There's one inherent problem with the guidelines and that is obviously they are very good on areas where you had lots of case law but they are a little bit thin on the ground where there wasn't a lot. And that's mostly the areas where people are interested in; so if you look at the UK guidelines which talk about vertical and conglomerate aspects, there is not much there.

Finally, I will quickly run through merger control goals, and stop there. I think what is needed in Europe is an honest debate about what goals merger control is supposed to achieve and I agree with Götz Drauz when he said that it is certainly not the protection of competitors. I think there should be a debate about whether we are really talking about consumer welfare, very simply, or whether we talk about protection of competition as a process, because they will lead to different outcomes in certain circumstances. I think one should have a debate about it and see which of the two one would really like to follow. At the moment it's a bit of motherhood and apple pie. Yes we protect consumers, but we also protect the process and we protect all sorts of things, and I think until we have really articulated what we want to aim for, it is going to be very difficult to harmonize between the EU and the Member States.

B. Balázs Csépai

I'd like to move to a slightly different area in the field of international cooperation and that is cooperation between the European Commission and the
National Competition Authority (NCA) of a future European Union
Member State. I'd like to focus within this topic on a very specific problem
or question and that is the interesting dilemma which the national competition authority has to face in the case of a transnational border, which
affects both the EU and that future Member State of the European Union.
This dilemma is that, when the proposed merger is notified to it, the NCA
not only has to take into account the present economic situation when it
deals with a national market and with the effects of the merger on the
national market, but also it has to take into consideration that in some
years the country would become a Member State of the EU and it would
become part of a single European market and therefore the economic effects
of the merger, and its whole impact on the national economy or the economy on which this authority has the role of the watchdog, will completely
change. This might mean that an established dominant position created by
this merger on the national market would be eliminated due to the accession to the European Union or that negative effects would be balanced by
the effect of the opening up of the market. This means, from the point of
view of cooperation, that the NCA must analyse the effect of the merger on
an EU-wide scale. However, this authority normally does not have enough
information on the European market, on the structure of the market and
the possible outcome and effects of the merger, so it has to consult or cooperate with the Commission to get access to this information. Not only is its
source of information is limited, but its investigative powers are also limited
by the national competition law, so cooperation in this respect is very
important.

The second point is that at the formulation of the remedies, the NCA has
to take into account the possible outcome of the case on the EU level,
because if the Commission imposes structural remedies which have effect
on the national market as well as the accessing country, then it might mean
that another structural remedy applied by the NCA would be contradictory to the remedy applied by the Commission. So it should avoid applying contradictory remedies. The NCA should take into account the
possible outcome, or the outcome of the case in a merger case at the EU
level. This also requires some sort of cooperation with the Commission to
discuss what the Commission envisaged as a decision. However, these two
levels of cooperation might face some difficulties. The first is that the decision has to be taken in the present and not in the future; it's not always

easy to harmonize the information available at present with the information that will change after the accession, so the NCA might face difficulties in taking account future changes because the decision has to be taken now and not later in the future. The second problem is that optimal remedies for the pre-accession period might be contradictory with optimal remedies for the post-accession period. The NCA imposes a remedy on the parties in order to be able to clear the merger but after the accession in three, four, or five years, these remedies will be against effective competition in the changed enlarged market.

Another problem is that the date of the accession was uncertain for the 10 countries some years ago and is uncertain for many European countries like Bulgaria and Romania, so it is not easy to deal with a merger issue and forthcoming economic changes if you cannot see in advance when these changes will occur. Another issue is the problem with public administration. I think our discussion here today has shown which kind of problems could occur. This could be that a competition authority might not be able or willing to cooperate on an international field because of language issues, or because of other problems in the public administration.

The last problem I would like to refer to concerns the role played by the Commission. There isn't always a mutual interest in this cooperation because the Commission can arrange the case at EU level and it doesn't always take into consideration these kinds of problems faced by the NCA before the accession period.

C. Dr John Fingleton

For those of you who expected that I was invited here today to be controversial or to stir things up, I'm probably going to disappoint you, partly because—being very happy with the new Merger Regulation and the change in the substantive test—I'm probably going to poke at fewer targets than normal. What I am going to say is that cooperation happens at many levels and we have a diverse discussion in Europe. I am going to say that policy cooperation has worked well and that bodes well for cooperation on jurisdiction and on substance under the new merger regulation. Case cooperation has been constrained, but I think it will improve. The cooperation on substance will be improved both by the new test and by the widespread publication of guidelines, but then I'm still tempted to say that there are a few things we still need to do.

When I was asked to speak about this, I began to think, well, most of the cooperation I experience is actually what we might call vertical cooperation between an individual Member State and the Commission, but the title of the seminar seemed to be more about cooperation amongst the Member States which is largely in my experience, bilateral, although there have been some who describe it as network cooperation as well. Then I thought, in actual fact, a lot of the most important cooperation, particularly at the policy level, is actually between the ministries and the Commission as opposed to between the competition authorities and the Commission. On the Merger Regulation it is, generally speaking, government ministries that determine policy, not competition authorities. But the competition authorities are there in the background. We attend the Council working group on the reform of the Merger Regulation, but it's the ministry who votes and at the early stages, the competition authority and the ministry always agree, but as you get closer to agreement, ministries know the rules of reaching a political agreement at a European level and so divergences are more likely to emerge between let's say us and our ministry in the last days or weeks of the negotiation of the merger regulation. And then in terms of areas of cooperation, on cases, the working of Articles 9 and 22 of the Merger Regulation and the working of the Advisory Committee are the main focus there. On policy, there are things like the review of the Merger Regulation remedies, efficiencies and so forth, and the question of guidelines where Ireland and the UK were first off the block with guidelines—the Commission's guidelines, the draft were published around the same time; France and other countries are also producing guidelines.

And then we cooperate hugely in international fora as competition authorities, the OECD, the ICN, and obviously a forum like this, but also the private Bar, the International Bar Association, and others have played an important role in developing policy cooperation. I said policy cooperation has worked well and I think this is exemplified by the review of the ECMR and I think that the Commission is to be congratulated. If it didn't open up these issues for discussion, our discussions would be pretty useless and I think the fact that the Commission has been so open to listening and to change has meant those discussions are actually profitable. On the review of the Merger Regulation, the question of the test was very much led by the Member States. It happened at the Directors' General meetings and at the European competition authorities. I think for about four meetings in a row, or five, we discussed unilateral effects and it meant that the heads of the competition agencies were the most expert on oligopoly theory in the European Union. Similarly, the allocation of cases and the new rules for the application of Article 9 and 22 of the Merger Regulation happened both in the Advisory Committee and the Council working group, and they were very much led by those fora.

Again the question of ancillary restraints was hotly debated within the Council working group. And on the question of merger guidelines, there have been many Advisory Committee meetings on merger guidelines, but those have been supported, very strongly, by the work that has been done, both in the OECD and in the ICN, and very often the discussions we have at the OECD and the ICN enable us to short-circuit much of the discussion that we would have in the Advisory Committee. I think that these varied fora are the really positive story about cooperation at the policy level, and as you see there are some new organizations, like ICN and the European competition authorities. I've mentioned my own hobby-horse, the Association of Competition Economics (ACE), which we have just founded. In fact, I've been involved in quite a few of these new entrants to the market, but the traditional ones like the OECD and the International Bar Association have played a very important role. And transatlantic discussion has been very important. Our own agency has two American practitioners—Terry Calvani, Director of Cartels Division, and Edward Henneberry, Director of Mergers Division—as members of the Authority, and that's because we've been singularly unable to find any Irish lawyers or European lawyers willing to apply for jobs to work in the authority, so we are looking into competition in the professions to see if there are excess returns. That might increase the long-term supply of competition lawyers domestically, but I think it's a huge benefit to us and to EC merger policy to have US practitioners working with us.

On case cooperation, Articles 9 and 22 have been particularly cumbersome to use. We made, in our third ever merger decision this year, an Article 22 request, but it was almost impossibly difficult to form a view on competition, when we had so little information, and then the coordination aspects of Article 22 are crazy. So I think we expect much improvement there. The Advisory Committee is very constrained. The perception is that it is not taken seriously or properly used. I don't think that you could get a head of competition authority from another Member State to disagree with me on this. There's a free rider problem. Everybody thinks everybody else should do it and of course then, if the opposite happens, and people start to look at cases, there's a duplication of effort problem. And for some reason, and perhaps because it can be solved without changes in the law, this slipped off the reform agenda when the Commissioner spoke at the IBA conference in Brussels last year,[1] it was suddenly dropped from his speech as one of their headline issues and so the Member State competition authorities are probably going to continue to put pressure on the question of the Advisory Committee.

Bilateral cooperation is something that is beginning to come up as I think the reforms at the EU level are going to force other reforms at the Member State level. We are going to see changes in statutes and we've discovered that even though we in the UK work very well together, there are serious issues to do with timing and procedure. But I think overall on the allocation of cases, the new ECMR is going to improve things. On substance, I think that the new substantive test is going to assist us. One of the issues we have with both Article 9 and 22 requests at the moment is forming a view on dominance, even though we would then be applying an SLC test domestically, when the merger comes home—and I could tell you lots of interesting stories about that from our point of view and from the parties' point of view, but just suffice it to say that I think the new test, being more inclusive as a sort of a dual test, will work well with jurisdictions that have both dominance and competition based tests. I think it will also enable the guidelines to be better aligned. The new draft Commission Guidelines that we are looking at the moment are so close to the Irish and UK guidelines that I think that we are going to see, from our point of view at least, a very happy relationship there. I think that I've already made the point that the OECD roundtable work and the ICN work on merger guidelines and investigative techniques also assist convergence in this area.

In terms of having more to do, there is just one point I wanted to make: Dr Stelzer in his comment this morning talked about a cartel amongst competition authorities and interestingly enough, although the UK and Ireland are

---

[1] EC Merger Control Conference, Brussels, 7–8 Nov 2002, Commissioner M Monti gave the opening address entitled 'Merger Control in the European Union: a Radical Reform'.

very, very close on a lot of policy issues, there are quite stark differences in our merger laws. For example, our SLC test has to have the efficiency defence within it, whereas in the UK there's an explicit statutory efficiencies argument. Our procedure is very different: we have a single agency, you have two agencies with the OFT and the Competition Commission. We discovered in the *Ferries* case that the notification requirements in Ireland and the UK were very different so that we still haven't completed our Phase I, although the Competition Commission here has published what I think is probably called a statement of objections a few days ago. So we have big, big differences in timing and procedure despite very recent statutes; we are a long way off a cartel, but I think that is very useful experimentation. We will see over time which of those works well.

Finally, although things have improved—there have been big improvements at the policy level and I think there will be as result of the new Regulation, big improvements on case cooperation—there are still things to do: the Advisory Committee (and particularly here we will be focused on the role of the rapporteur and the earlier appointment of somebody as rapporteur perhaps when the case goes into Phase II), developing better local and bilateral cooperation, exchange of information, the time limits and the timing of notification in national law, continuing to use the variety of international fora to discuss cooperation, and I think one issue to watch is the question of consistency on ancillary restraints. There was a concern, when the Merger Regulation was being debated in the Council, that if the Commission didn't pronounce on ancillary restraints, it would be left to national courts to do so and national courts can come up with quite divergent views. The Irish and UK governments wanted ancillary restraints to be bundled in with the merger. Obviously that would have imposed a much higher burden on the Commission. The solution we've come to is, I think, somewhere between the two, but it is just something to watch and we may have to review it. But overall, I think there's a very positive picture; we've heard about transatlantic cooperation and I think the picture in Europe is much more positive than the picture in the US on merger review where the cooperation within and between the states and the Justice Department could probably benefit a lot from looking at how we do things in Europe. Thank you.

D. John Schmidt

I will talk about references both up and down (Article 9 and Article 22), and my first slide gives you my conclusion, so that just in case I'm not really finished in five minutes, you know what I think about it![1]

Broadly speaking, Article 9 has worked quite well both in terms of cooperation between the Member States and the Commission, but also in terms of achieving what it is designed to achieve, ie getting particular cases back to Member States that should be dealt with at Member State level. I have my doubts as to whether Article 22 has worked adequately, particularly because it was rediscovered for a purpose that it wasn't designed for in the first place, and it remains to be seen how much the reform proposals will improve the position.

The next slide gives you a brief view of statistics in terms of references and you can see that there has been a consistent increase in the number of references. There is particularly high referral activity in the years when there's a merger control review, and I leave you to decide what to make of that, but certainly I expect that the overall amount of references will increase in future, particularly under the new regimes.

Before looking at Article 9 and 22 on the next two slides, I just want to go back to what merger control aims to achieve, and how the reference systems fit into the system. Clearly, authorities aim to detect and prevent harmful mergers. Businesses have, I think, accepted that the process is a necessary process. Some call it perhaps a necessary evil, but on the whole they have accepted that they have to go through that process. One of the key advantages of the Brussels process is that it delivers a decision that is relatively predictable, relatively coherent, and pretty speedy. When we are thinking about increasing references or changing the reference system, I think we should bear in mind that, for the business community, any reference really has the opposite effect: introducing more uncertainty in terms of process, more uncertainty in terms of outcome, and certainly a longer process and perhaps, to a lesser extent, increased costs.

Article 9, as I said at the beginning, has worked well in terms of how Member States cooperate with the Commission and how the Commission cooperates with the Member States. That applies both in cases where the Commission refers a case to the Member State and retains part of the case—and you see a lot of cooperation and liaison between the Commission and

---

[1] Art 9: Generally works effectively; Scope for improvement. Art 22: Rediscovery; Does not work adequately.

the Member States there—but it also applies in cases where the Commission looks at one case and Member States look at another case: parallel cases, connected cases, or inter-connected cases. There I find that the Commission and Member States do come up with joint ideas about the analysis and about the remedies.

Two issues, I think, remain from the notifying parties' perspective. First, Article 9 really is a process between Member States and the Commission and sometimes, even the notifying parties become bystanders in the discussions, and I think that's where there is scope for improvement from a business' perspective. Second, there should be a more definite policy on references: when are references made and when are references refused? Particularly in instances where you have geographic markets that extend to the whole Member State but you have a number of Member States involved. I think there the policy should be that such cases remain with the Commission because that preserves the predictability and prevents an additional procedural step that adds uncertainty, delay, and cost.

Turning to Article 22, the story is in a way much more easily told because it really only started last year when Article 22 was rediscovered for joint references back up to the Commission. I think both cases are good examples for the actual problems involved and those other problems that John Fingleton identified earlier. Both cases involved markets that were larger than national markets, so they were cases that naturally would lend themselves to a reference up to the Commission, so that the Commission could then deal with the case and deal with any remedies that may span different markets. In the first case there is a clear timing issue in that it took some seven months from the first reference request until the final decision was reached. You had seven Member States involved, plus one country[2] outside the Community that the Commission had to liaise with. If you only look at the referral part of the process, it took some two-and-a-half to three months for all the authorities to refer the case to the Commission. That added a significant delay and a significant amount of uncertainty for the parties. In *GE/Unison*, in addition to the timing problem, the main problem was that although you had a reference from seven Member States, there were two Member States which applied their own laws, including the Irish Authority. The benefits of referring a case back up to the Commission didn't really apply in that case because you then have the possibility of additional national proceedings. Now I expect that will change in the future with the system of three or more countries that will automatically give the Commission jurisdiction over the whole of the case. Also, I believe that the pre-notification provisions from the new ECMR proposal will help to allow

---

[2] Switzerland.

the parties to force the issue right at the beginning. I think the same should be true in Article 22. You need to have a clear reference policy that spells out for the notifying parties in which cases you are likely to be able to succeed in a reference. You can then, at pre-notification, initiate and force the issue so that you are not left with potential delays and potential timing issues later in the process. Thank you.

E. Discussion

[MICHAEL KOENIG]

I am going to put one question to Christian because I think earlier, we saw or we heard that even in Europe there are some questions or some issues about the timing of notifications in allowing real cooperation, not least in the referral cases under Article 22. Do you see, even in Europe where systems are rather close, a reason why there could still be issues of the parallel timing of notifications to allow cooperation between the agencies?

[CHRISTIAN AHLBORN]

On the timing issue among Member States, as John has pointed out, I think clarity is the most important thing between the US and the EU. Götz Drauz made it clear that we'll have to live with whatever we'll have to live with. In Europe, I think there is scope for better timing and more clarity on the timing of referrals and the process as well and greater harmonization.

Previously I was not only referring to referrals but also multi-jurisdictional cases and the timing of the different notification, which would be filed in different Member States from the parties' point of view.

I think for Phase I we have anything from a month to six or seven weeks. I don't know if that is so dramatic? Yes ideally you would like to have a single Phase I duration so that parties come to the same decision at the same time, but then again you have different triggering events so you would have to harmonize that as well. Does it ultimately make a big difference whether you have got four months or three months, as some Member States have? Yes, ideally harmonization would be a good thing, but I think that would not be my first priority overall.

In a way, that gets me back to the problem I have with Article 22: how can you align a reference back up if the authorities think that is the most appropriate way to deal with the case? I think, in future, rather than harmonizing necessarily the national laws, I think the way ahead, although it may be quite some distance away, would be to have significantly lower thresholds at EC level and a very easy process, within clearly defined policy limits, of referring the case back to national Member States. Then you have the Commission effectively as a first step clearing house in deciding which cases are national and which cases are EC and then you have an easy process to send the cases back to national authorities. I think that would deal with the processes quite well although it obviously involves other policy issues.

[MICHAEL KOENIG]

Thank you very much. Before we move on to the next speaker, I just want to put one question back to John because to me it seems that we have some different perceptions on what the test will do to cooperation. On the one hand I understood from John that he says it's going to be much better and much easier, whereas Christian, I felt, was a bit more pessimistic and gave me the impression that it will be difficult for the Member States to talk to each other. John, do you think this is a problem? Do you think you can talk much more easily to your counterparts now?

[JOHN FINGLETON]

I think that it will be, but I think that where it's going to matter most is the referral system. The amount of times, when two competition authorities in neighbouring jurisdictions are deciding cases, where the tests are different is probably not going to be that great. If it is Ireland and the UK, we have the same test. The big issue is the referrals and I think that the new system of referrals is going to make it much easier. It is at that level that we are going to see the big benefits and I think that whether you have a dominance test or whether you have a competition test, it's going to fit quite well with this dual or broader test at the EU level.

[MICHAEL HUDSOUGH, *Davidson Company and Partners*]

I wonder if John Fingleton would discuss a recent case not to ask for a referral back under Article 9, and I am thinking here of the Royal Bank of Scotland offer to acquire First Active. If you could just tell us a little bit about the process and the decisions that went into the final decision not to ask for a referral, that would be very helpful, thanks.

[JOHN FINGLETON]

We issued a press release last week which said we wouldn't comment further on the matter until the Commission finished its process, but I would point out, without commenting on that deal, that this was the first Article 9 request since the competition authorities took over mergers. It raised interesting issues about the domestic procedure for making announcements publicly about what we are doing, and I am aware that the Office of Fair Trading has a policy of announcing that it's considering an Article 9 referral or request and inviting public comments. I think that is something that we are considering for the future because it would help us to get market information.

One of the problems we have with an Article 9 reference is that the notification is made to the Commission, but we have to form a view, and the notification is not made to us, so the question of how we get that information is important. I think what happened in the Royal Bank of Scotland case was that information was getting to the market from the parties and I think it probably would have been better, with the benefit of hindsight, if we had made an announcement, at an early state, that we were considering an Article 9 request and invited submissions. I suspect that we will do so in the future and we only decided that because we started to look at how the OFT does it, which is an example of how we do look to other competition authorities to see what their practice is when we are trying to do things better.

CHAPTER 3

ECMR Procedural Reform

[KAREN WILLIAMS]

The topic of the next panel is 'ECMR procedural reform—Is it working?' An immediate comment might be, 'well it has not had much of a chance yet to get going', but let that not deter us from considering the topic in general.

I have three eminent panellists here. On my far right, we have Frederic Depoortere from Skadden. We have Hendrik Bourgeois from General Electric, representing all General Electric's competition law and policy activities in Europe, and we have Annette Schild who is from Shearman & Sterling. They are all practitioners, in-house or external counsel. I am the only regulator here and I am the chair of the panel, not actually a panellist, but we have reflected a little bit on how to present this subject. We are going to have what you might call variations on a theme to begin with. Each of the speakers will talk for a maximum of 10 minutes on the various sort of hard law and soft law areas of procedural reform that we have had.

If you remember, we had the IBA conference just over a year ago, where the Commission sort of launched its package and then the proposal for merger reform followed soon afterward. That is what we are going to talk about now. I hope, though, that we will have some active participation from the audience. Some questions, thoughts and advice, maybe, for the future. But without further ado, Frederic, would you like to start?

A. Frederic Depoortere

I will try and stay brief so that there is room for discussion.

Basically, when looking at the 2001 Green Paper, I thought the Commission was a bit bullish on the topic of checks and balances, which is what I would like to deal with here. I just took a couple of cites from the Green Paper, and realized that at that stage the Commission was fairly confident that its procedure was working well.

Then you have the three judgments;[1] I have seen them referred to as the three musketeers. I do not know if that is very appropriate. That triggered more criticism and a more in-depth review of the Commission's procedures, which is a good thing I think.

One question which came about very frequently was whether we should move to a judicial system rather than an administrative system, so that basically we would have two different institutions investigating and adjudicating. The benefits of a judicial system have been commented upon frequently, so I think they are fairly straightforward. What I wanted to quickly say is that there may also be a certain number of disadvantages to a judicial system and I think the US system shows a couple of examples.

Everybody that has seen a Second Request from fairly close – luckily I have not been too close – has been able to see it can be an enormously burdensome system. I think the reason is that at a very early stage of the proceedings, what the US authorities are doing is actually two things: on the one hand they are doing the same thing as the Commission – that is investigating the case – but on the other hand they are also trying to build a case for court even though the case may never be brought before a judge. That can result in an extremely burdensome and resource-intensive document production exercise.

When one of the cases, which practically everybody here at the table was involved in, requires the companies to charter airplanes to bring the documents to Washington DC, it is easy to see how burdensome the system can be.

Luckily we are not there yet and it would be acceptable to stay where we are. But I do think that there would be a benefit to re-thinking somewhat the concept of how we see the administrative procedure. I would think that we need to see the administrative procedure as it exists today, not as an adversarial procedure, but rather as a cooperative process between the notifying parties and the Commission designed to find the best solution as quickly as possible. I will explain this a little bit further.

The procedures have been improved with the best practices guidelines and with the new draft Merger Regulations, so there are Commission internal checks and balances which I think are pretty good. I do not have any comments on them. I think the Commission is working towards improving its procedures.

---

[1] Case T-342/99 *Airtours v Commission* [2002] ECR II-2585, [2002] 5 CMLR 317; Case T-310/01 *Schneider Electric v Commission* [2002] ECR II-4071, [2003] 4 CMLR 768; Case T-5/02 *Tetra Laval v Commission* [2002] ECR II-4381, [2002] 5 CMLR 1182.

Judicial review has shown that it can be effective. There are still some questions there: is it too slow? Can it be improved? Do we need specialized judges, etc? I assume the future will reveal some answers.

What I think could be reinforced, going back to what I called seeing the administrative process as a cooperative process, is the habit of relying more on the parties as players in the process to come to the right solution.

The Commission has introduced some flexibility in the timing, or at least its proposals do. There are now the 'state-of-play' meetings, which I think are basically the formalization of existing practices; triangular meetings and earlier access to file. However, the Commission, in its proposals, does not go the whole way and I do not really understand why. So I would have two very pragmatic proposals in order to enhance the transparency and flexibility:

To give systematic access to file from the very start. What the Commission proposes, is to give access to file at an earlier stage in Phase II but not in Phase I, in which it would give access only to certain so-called 'key documents'. I do not see why we need to limit access to file in this way. Why does the Commission not simply send copies of all submissions it receives from third parties to the parties? What would be so wrong with that, again, under this concept of seeing the procedure as a cooperative process rather than an adversarial?

The second proposal concerns timelines. I have always understood that the predictability of the timelines is to the benefit of the notifying parties, so I do not see why the notifying parties could not deviate from them. The notifying parties, as a general matter, want to close a transaction as quickly as possible and obviously spend as few resources as possible on the review of their case, and they have an interest in expediting the procedure. So if they decide they need more time; it should be given to them. Under the current proposals, there is the possibility for parties to ask for an extension at the beginning of Phase II, but it needs to be requested within 15 days. Why is that? I do not really understand. Why not just give the parties the freedom to ask for extensions wherever they want?

Those are my two brief proposals.

B. Hendrik Bourgeois

Thank you for inviting me this morning. It is a pleasure for me to be able to participate in this morning's discussions.

Although we are still, obviously, several months away from the implementation of the procedural reforms contained in the new Merger Control Regulation, and although the best practices guidelines that contain important changes to the process, are already approximately a year old, but still in draft, notwithstanding these two facts I think that to ask ourselves today whether or not the procedural reforms are working is a valid question.

I think it is a valid question because as Annette [Schild] will explain in greater detail, the Commission has already started implementing some of the features of the process contained in the best practices guidelines and has certainly created the expectation with private parties that they are being applied, because Commissioner Monti has made several public remarks to that extent.

What is less clear, unfortunately, is whether or not, private parties can today derive rights of defence from these draft best practices guidelines. I believe there are not too many people at the Commission who would say so.

Having said that, what I would like to talk about very briefly this morning, and I apologize for stating something which might seem very obvious, is the question of procedural rules. This is not only a valid question to ask, but also an important one, because obviously procedural rules have a direct impact on the quality of the final decisions.

And this is so from a double perspective. First, it is clear that those who are called upon to enforce the substantive Merger Control rules need to have at their disposal sufficient tools, effective processes, efficient procedures that will allow them to comply with their mission of public interest. In the absence of procedural rules that permit them and give them sufficient time to apply these investigative tools, antitrust enforcement authorities would be faced with the risk of making, what statisticians call, 'type 1 errors': they would be risking clearing anti-competitive mergers, and so procedural tools are important in that respect.

However, there is a flip-side to it, in the sense that procedural rules need to be flexible enough to permit a real exchange of views between rival facts and rival views surrounding the particular case. They need to create, as it were, a level playing field where conflicting views and conflicting ideas might compete against each other in order to assure a better quality product. In the absence of such procedural rules which permit for exchange and real debate, competition authorities would probably be risking making 'type 2 errors': they would probably be prohibiting pro-competitive mergers or neutral mergers, so I think it is an important distinction to make.

Interestingly, when you look at the legislative changes, it seems to me that most of the procedural changes that have been incorporated in the Merger Control Regulation are actually changes that are designed to avoid type 1 errors rather than type 2 errors.

I just want to illustrate this, very briefly. The automatic extension of deadlines to 49 days in Phase I and 105 days in Phase II, in cases where remedies are necessary, is a change the aim of which is not to improve checks and balances, nor the rights or defence of the parties—although indirectly they may result in better checks and balances—but is clearly to give the Commission more time to make sure that when remedies are offered, the transaction may be cleared. So the aim of this rule is not really to protect the Commission from making type 2 errors, but to protect the Commission from making type 1 errors.

Even the new provision that permits private parties to ask for the extension at their option has been perceived by some as a de facto extension of the deadlines in favour of the Commission, for two reasons.

First, as a practical matter, private parties will be under tremendous pressure to agree to, or to ask for the extension, if the case team or others at the Commission suggest that it would be beneficial to the analysis of the case.

Secondly, as Frederic [Depoortere] remarked, it is interesting to see that the request for extension by the parties has to be made within the first 15 days after opening of proceedings, which has caused some observers to comment that these extensions will be actually used by the case team to prepare a more effective Statement of Objections, and not necessarily to engage in a useful discussion as to whether a Statement of Objections is necessary or not.

Another example relates to new procedural rules that need to be followed after annulment of a decision by the Court of First Instance, which provide that the Commission will review the case, taking into account the current market conditions. Arguably, somebody could say this could benefit the parties as well in situations where the annulment judgement annuls a clearance decision. However, I think that everybody will agree that those circumstances will be very few and that very often the aim of these procedures will again be to allow the Commission to review the cases *ex-novo* and *in-extenso*, in situations where the Commission decision was a prohibition decision.

The obvious example of new rules that aim at avoiding type 1 errors rather than type 2 errors are the new enforcement provisions which clearly provide for stronger investigative tools, and again it is difficult to see how those rules could be used to improve the process of checks and balances. Having said that, theoretically, the Commission could use them to ensure that complainants provide correct information.

If I still have time, I would like to say some remarks about the non-legislative reforms, in particular, those contained in the draft best practices guidelines.

I think you will agree that virtually all of the procedural reforms aiming at improving internal checks and balances and due process are contained in these draft best practices guidelines.

I am talking about early access to the files, state of play meetings, triangular meetings, etc, and I question why this approach was warranted. It seems to me that, obviously, if they are contained in soft law rather than in the Regulation itself, they are probably less enforceable than the provisions in the Merger Control Regulation and they are probably more prone to change.

I do not know whether this is legitimate or not, because it suggests that the Commission, after more than 10 years of experience in applying the Merger Control Regulation, is still more at risk to commit type 1 errors than type 2 errors. It is a debatable point, but jurisprudence can help.

There is the *Assicurazioni Generali* case, in which the Court of First Instance indicated that the rights of defence of the parties had to be protected even in proceedings that did not end up in a decision listed in Article 18 of the Merger Control Regulation.

In the recent *Lagardère/Canal+ v Commission case*, the Court of First Instance went even a bit further by stating and holding that the rights of defence of the private parties and of the notifying parties had to be respected in all proceedings, which were, if I am not mistaken, liable to culminate in a decision that may aversively affect the rights of the parties. The language I particularly enjoyed is 'liable to culminate', because I think it is fairly broad.

After having made this brief distinction, just let me conclude by saying that what is also very important is the manner in which the procedural reforms are and will be implemented, and that will vary from case to case and from case team to case team. I am sure there have been cases in the past where notifying parties were kept duly informed about where a particular case was going without the need to resort to formal state of play meetings.

At the same time, today the Commission can formally comply with some of the provisions and draft practices guidelines, without actually giving a lot to the notifying parties. For instance, in case of early access to the file, the Commission can comply by giving early access to the file but rely heavily on the rights of complainants or third parties in terms of protection of their business secrets.

So I do think that probably as important as this whole debate, is the manner in which, and the spirit with which, the procedural reforms will be implemented. I would like to finish on a positive note by just saying that the mere fact that the Commission has taken the initiative to make those changes suggests to me that the process is working better and will be working better, although at the same time I think that more progress could be made. Thank you.

C. Annette Schild

Good morning, it's a pleasure to be here. I believe that we will not have to spend much time on the background of the proposed reforms because everybody in the audience is informed.

The general overhaul of the system did not start with the CFI judgments.[1] There had been a long debate about the effectiveness of the checks and balances in the process, and then it was time for some reforms. Nevertheless, the judgments probably did help in speeding up things.

We also know what these reforms were. We have the OR, we have the ECMR, the draft best practices, and certain internal measures. As was probably the case for everybody on the panel, my first reaction when I saw the topic was: 'What on earth am I going to talk about?' because none of these measures have been formally implemented. Then I sat down and reconsidered.

Are there really so many novel things in the making that it would be premature to talk about the reforms or isn't it true that a lot of reforms have already happened? Aren't here many measures that have been presented as new but that have really been practiced quietly for some time?

If we look at the ECMR, we do have a new text, and it is not yet implemented. However, we quietly accept some of the future procedural elements as existing. It is true that we cannot notify an agreement that has not yet been signed. At the same time, I would like to see the colleagues who have notified an agreement within seven days after signature. I would venture to say that the vast majority of us have filed notifications significantly later. As far as early notifications are concerned, we have all had significant pre-notification contacts at much earlier stages than the signature.

The stop-the-clock provisions, in the sense of the new Merger Regulation have not yet been applied. At the same time, it seems to me that the Commission has taken advantage of Article 9 of the implementing Regulation which permits it to stop the clock if no sufficient responses have been obtained from the parties. Of course this provision is meant to apply only when the parties have not fully responded to the Commission's questions. On the other hand, it also depends on how many questions you ask and how much time you give, and I expect that some of the parties who have been subject to 'stop-the-clock' would say that the Commission has

---

[1] Case T-342/99 *Airtours v Commission* [2002] ECR II-2585, [2002] 5 CMLR 317; Case T-310/01 *Schneider Electric v Commission* [2002] ECR II-4071, [2003] 4 CMLR 768; Case T-5/02 *Tetra Laval v Commission* [2002] ECR II-4381, [2002] 5 CMLR 1182.

asked a tremendous amount of information that could not possibly be submitted in the time provided. There have been several cases recently where this was applied, among them *Lagardere*.[2]

Then we come to the investigative powers of the Commission. Fortunately those have not yet been applied and they could not be applied before we have a new Regulation.

Now as we come to the new rules relating to referrals to and from Member States (Articles 4 (4) and 4 (5) and revised Articles 9 and 22), again they are not yet in force and cannot formally have been applied. Nevertheless, in the last years we have seen more of cases that were referred to the Commission from Member States. I have counted three reactions: *Promatech/Sulzer*,[3] *GEES/Unison*,[4] and *GE/Agfa*,[5] although there maybe more. Clearly there is an increased willingness by Member States to refer and Member States did not wait for the new Regulation.

Now, as for the best practices, which are also still in draft form, pre-notification contacts are taking place and they have been taking place for a long time. While there is a lot to object to looking at the Commission's ideas as to when a draft form CO or a paper should be supplied, I think the system has worked quite well for many years. The Commission has been open to discussions about cases prior to formal notification and the parties have an interest in supplying a draft form CO because they want their notification to be considered as complete on the date when it is formally notified.

State of play meetings: again I think this has been working for a long time and to some extent it almost seems artificial to say 'Now you have a formal right'. I have not seen a case where you have not had access to the Commission and had a meeting where, depending on the case handler, you extracted more or less information. In almost all cases you came out better understanding the Commission's current thinking.

Tripartite meetings: these also have been encouraged for a while. In *GE/Instrumentarium*,[6] the Commission actually got pretty close to having a tripartite meeting, but my understanding is that this did not take place because the third party did not want to participate.

Access to key documents before the SO is issued: again I just obtained access to a key document and this after less than one month into Phase II. There have been other cases where access to such documents has been given

---

2 Case No COMP/M.2978 LAGARDÈRE / NATEXIS / VUP 07/01/2002.
3 Case No COMP/M.2698 PROMATECH / SULZER, 24/07/2002.
4 Case No COMP/M.2738 GEES / UNISON, 17/04/2002.
5 Case No COMP/M.3136, GE / AGFA, 05/12/2003.
6 Case No COMP/M.3083, GE / INSTRUMENTARIUM, 02/09/2003.

and that is extremely helpful. I would strongly agree with Frederic [Depoortere], that this should happen automatically and do not understand the Commission's objections. Discussing with people, you hear, 'It's too complicated to get non-confidential versions of things; competitors and customers will not want this and they are scared'. I can just say, that I have one case that is not a merger case, where the case handler regularly calls me and says, 'Annette, you haven't responded' and I say 'Well, yes, we filed the response', 'No, your client didn't send a non-confidential version, didn't you read the questionnaire?' It is true that everybody constantly ignores this sentence in the Commission's questionnaires. If we had some serious enforcement, people would just automatically send two versions and the non-confidential version could be passed on. I think that would work.

Now the internal reforms. We have had the first steps of the dissolution of the MTF although it is still not quite clear how the distribution of labour works. We are still seeing case handlers that we would suspect in some other industry. The Chief Economist's office and the Peer Review Panels are very new, but already in October this year, the peer review panel had been used in 10 cases. I can personally say that all the reports I have had were extremely positive and that the parties to these proceedings considered that, indeed, there was a fresh pair of eyes. In spite of the fact that the members of the Peer Review Panel are also internal and also administrators their requests seem to trigger debates.

Now there are a lot of things that have not been addressed. We clearly still do not have a division between the investigative power and the one taking the final decision. Who knows whether we will ever get there? We have the same case teams in Phases I and II, which was another element of the procedure that was objected to by many practitioners. We do have a rather complete lack of transparency as far as the competition economists and the Peer Review Panels are concerned and, quite frankly, also as far as the Hearing Officer's internal report (the somewhat more interesting one than the one that is published) is concerned. We also do not have any deadlines for the Commission's issuing of SOs, so there is still a lot of flexibility on the part of the Commission rather than for the parties. As to the access to documents before the SO, I understand the draft Best Practices will be even more restrictive than they are now and so, as Hendrik [Bourgeois] has said, it is rather up in the air as to what rights we will have. And yet, I am not sure all these things matter.

I would like to add a few more things about the procedure. I have talked to many colleagues about this, and we all have the impression the Commission is taking the 2002 judgments so much to heart that it has gone overboard. Huge questionnaires are sent in cases where there is no competitive concern; the collection of evidence on market definition may go back 10 years, even in markets where the Commission has taken a clear decision only recently. More and more customers are being questioned, and so there is a tendency to go towards the gathering of more evidence. We are not always sure what the evidence is for; what legal theory might be proven by it in the end. Also, this can always lead to (unnecessary) stop-the-clock situations.

So the concern is really that the Commission seems to have started reforms for really difficult cases where more time is needed, more flexibility is needed, more possibilities to gather evidence are needed, but those are not the majority of the cases. They are certainly not the majority of the cases right now.

So I end with an appeal: please let's not lose the benefits of the system that we have. I have been in the unfortunate position of participating in several second requests and I do not wish for this system to cross the Atlantic. I think we have a very good system that benefits from efficiency, from good timelines, so let's not use the tools that are given, as Hendrik [Bourgeois] says, for the complicated cases, to avoid type one errors in easy cases.

D. Discussion

[KAREN WILLIAMS]

Thank you very much Hendrik. Just one question before we move on. Coming back to the parties having the right to extend the deadlines, but within the 15 days, do you think that, given that the Commission can also extend the deadlines with the agreement of the parties, parties should really feel so bound to kowtow to the case team, if that is what they think the case team wants?

[HENDRIK BOURGEOIS]

Well I read the final text that was adopted a few days ago and I was puzzled by the distinction between on the one hand parties asking for an extension within the first 15 days and on the other hand the Commission being able to extend, but with the agreement of the parties, any time they want. It is not clear to me why this distinction has been made and I think it was made fairly recently, at least I did not catch it when the initial draft regulation was proposed.

I do not think it makes a lot of difference because, from a practical perspective, there is always a tremendous amount of incentive on behalf of the notifying parties to be cooperative, and unfortunately, when problems are identified by the Commission, to find settlements, because the deal is important and because what is on the parties' mind is, as has been said before, to close the deal as quickly and as efficiently as possible.

[QUESTION FROM THE FLOOR, UNIDENTIFIED]

I had a couple of reflections and a question for you, Karen. I suppose that it is not very often that people complain about access to the Commission. The Commission is always very open to meetings throughout the process in Phase I and Phase II. Triangular meetings in principle are a good idea, but my guess is that in practice people will resist it.

What is in practice much more useful is to see these key documents, because sometimes the notifying parties do not appear to know what it is that the complainant is objecting to. So the perception that all the parties have, I think, is that the final oral hearing, if and when it happens, comes a little bit late in the process. It comes at a stage in Phase II when the case is very developed and views are, to a certain extent, entrenched.

So I think one of the areas in which most work should be done is to have access to these key documents, and I think parties will get some comfort from an involvement of the Hearing Officer and their office at an early stage.

I was wondering whether you thought that there could be some sort of involvement, perhaps, through a report to you at a later stage—you as a Hearing Officer—about the documents that the parties have had access to in earlier stages of Phase II to see whether they really had the opportunity to submit their comments to the Commission and the Case Team.

I think it would be a process that would benefit everyone. It would benefit the Case Team, which sometimes sits in between two different comments and it is difficult to sort one from the other; it would give some comfort to the notifying parties who know that eventually there will be scrutiny by the Hearing Officer regarding the degree of access they have had to these key documents at an early stage. But there are some procedural difficulties and that is, in a way, the link between soft law and hard law, because the Hearing Officer will only get involved at a much later stage.

So I was wondering whether you had any views as to how these this balance could be squared between the intention of the Commission to give access to key documents and the procedural difficulties of the Hearing Officer only really taking an active role much later on in Phase II?

[KAREN WILLIAMS]

I think you had better stop otherwise I will not have time to answer! We have always said that as Hearing Officers we will get involved in, or at least will respond to, requests made to us at whatever stage in the procedure if there is a genuine and substantiated issue involved.

Hendrik has already stated that, in a sense, rights of defence exist throughout the whole procedure, and are not just limited to the later stages when there has been a Statement of Objections. So from that perspective, there is nothing stopping parties writing to us, or raising an issue and we will respond to that and we are very open to it.

At the same time, one has to see that the scope of what we can do varies to some extent according to the time. What I see in the best practice guidelines is that when these are adopted they should state specifically what is available. If there appears to be a problem then people should be able to write to us, and we can then address the DG and say, 'What is going on?' They should have parameters in their internal guidelines to be able to give us an answer to then enable us to make a value judgement for ourselves.

That is the way it will have to work. We are not auditors: we do not have the resources to go in and investigate the whole of the file, so to that extent we have to rely on the parties indicating that there is an issue. Then we will look into it.

The only thing that I do not like, and occasionally it happens, is where parties are, in a sense, also using us. Sometimes you have parties who are building procedural cases, maybe not initially, but at a certain point and they may write to us really just from a formalistic or a procedural perspective to get us to say something, I suppose, to get an answer. I have to say, I do not like us being used as a tool in that respect and sometimes I pick that up and I will not respond to it in that way either. But, where there is a genuine issue then we will look at it because ultimately we all have the same interests at stake.

There appears to be acceptance and general approval of the administrative system rather than the judicial system of the US, but clearly there is also concern as to how this is actually going to pan out in practice and I think to some extent the proof is going to be in the 'eating'.

We will, perhaps, have some cases where things will not work well, others will. From my personal perspective I would just like to make a couple of points. On hard law and soft law, I am very interested in your analyses, as I mentioned earlier, but I am also conscious that in fact once the Commission adopts a practice, it really becomes a practice that binds it. This has been made more evident in recent years since the courts have actually told the Commission this. So I think the Commission is very aware that it was stuck to what might have seemed as quasi-guidelines before. So I am not so sure that the difference is so huge.

What they also do is to provide a hook, and in particular it provides a hook to checks and balances. People like me and other regulators are able to say 'well if you are not doing this in a satisfactory manner, then we can maybe look into that in more detail'. But I think what we have had in the course of this year, looking from the perspective of the Hearing Officer, is that the language of the best practices has been really trying to establish what the significance is of some of the practices within the DG; whether the balance is right; and understanding that when it comes down to actually adopting these rules, then they will be stuck with them.

It has been a little bit of transitional year, a little bit of a difficult year for parties in some cases, but it has also been a learning curve for the Commission internally to think how these will operate in the future. On the 15 days, I do not know whether Götz [Drauz] has got anything to say on that in particular or whether he has got any other comments? I also want to see if people have got some questions or reflections of their own, but Götz, I do not know if you have something you want to say particularly?

[GÖTZ DRAUZ]

Well on the 15 days, to start with that point, first of all, I have to say that this is a Council Regulation. It is not the Commission who has made it and I think the Council is concerned about the planning of the Second Phase. They are concerned that we know, relatively early in Second Phases, how long it will take so that you do not have a completely open ended procedure, which is quite important if you think about how many people are involved in the process, not least the Advisory Committee as well.

You rightly said that, with the agreement of the Commission, there is the additional flexibility, so I do not think in practice this will be a real problem, because I do not think the Commission will reject your request or your suggestion, if you think, for some reason, more time should be given. I should say that I personally will be watching carefully to monitor where we are going, but in all cases this will require more time because we like to keep our system very predictable and rather short.

On some of the other issues mentioned here, first of all, what is important is to get the right balance between public interest and private interest, and I have also to correct the speakers a little bit here, because we have never said in the draft Best Practices that we are providing access to the file. So if you look at the text, it is very clear where we talk about early access to documents. We have made it very clear that this is not access to the file, because in Europe, access to the file is called a right of defence. Anything which we want to use against you must have been seen by you at some stage and it is clear that we are going to stick to that. We are trying to make sure that access can be given as soon as possible after the Statement of Objections, or on the same day, by providing you with a CD or something like that. But it is very important to make the distinction between access to the file and the possibility commented earlier, as we have said, in the interest of the procedure.

Also I would like to say that in the European system, the parties have a very strong and influential role. From the beginning they show us their way of thinking, from the pre-notification contacts over the Form CO and continued contact, often daily, with the Case Team. It would be difficult to say that they have not sufficient possibility to make their point. You need to see that the Commission, like any authority, at some stage has to build their own case. We need to have some time, some reflection of our own and you know how very capable law firms can occupy you from morning to night by submitting you comments on anything which you have offered them or showed them. There is no limit to that. I think you have to understand that at some stage we have to work on our case to build a case, or if there is no case, to say that there is no case, but we need some control over the system. Actually that is the reason why we introduced or formalized the state of play meetings, because we want to focus debate for some of the time on the issues at stake, for instance after the six months and before the Statement of Objections and so on.

Let me just pick up one other point, which are the type one and type two errors: actually, when we looked at the Chief Economist candidates, we found that two of those candidates had written an article precisely about type one and type one errors, and they came to the conclusion that there is little evidence that the Commission has made a lot of type two errors, but there may be a number of cases in which we have not picked up. This actually comes also out of some comparison we have made, with the DOJ or Bill Kolasky at a certain conference when he pointed out that actually the level of intervention in some types of cases, by the DOJ, was beyond the level of our own intervention. I think we have to be a bit balanced there. Of course, we have not selected the Chief Economist for that reason, but instead to tell us where and when those cases may arise, and I hope at some stage, this will show. Maybe, I am taking too much time, but maybe

One last word about about tripartite meetings which Annette [Schild] was referring to. This is something the Commission is offering to the process. We cannot force it. We cannot oblige parties and third parties to sit together with us and argue their point. This is something we can induce them to do in the formal hearings, but if you do that then of course the third parties and the parties themselves would like to see some kind of documents, some kind of documentary argumentation and again, this is not in our hand. We can only invite, we can only give our hand to that process. But then both sides have to play the game and I can see that when it did not happen it was frequently due to the lack of agreement on the type of documents to exchange. So we still are committed to that kind of meeting, but there we really are in the hands of the parties and third parties.

CHAPTER 4

New UK System—A Blueprint for the Future

RICHARD WHISH

From the Olympian heights of the Merger Regulation in the Community we descend into the Stygian depths of the Enterprise Act 2002, asking ourselves the question 'does it provide a blueprint for the future?' I am not sure whose future we are meant to be contemplating here but of course there are about 150 sovereign States around the world that don't yet have a system of merger control so I assume that we are making a pitch to the governments of Central Equatorial Guinea in Tuvalu. The Enterprise Act started from a very simple proposition: 'let's remove the Secretary of State from decision-making in merger decisions.' Once that very simple idea had been widely accepted, it was necessary to re-think every aspect of the Fair Trading Act's system. For example, what should the substantive test be for the control of mergers? If you remove the Minister you can't really have a public interest test, so what test should we have put in its place, and we looked widely around different systems in the world and alighted upon SLC.

Obviously it was necessary also to consider procedurally what the consequences would be if the Competition Commission itself were to make decisions and how the remedy- setting phase of merger investigations would need to be adjusted, and of course what system of judicial review or appeal one should have. We ended up with a system of appeal by way of judicial review and the first judgment under that new system will be delivered by the Competition Appeal Tribunal tomorrow morning so that's going to be a very interesting moment in the evolution of the system.

The way that we are going to handle this session is first to hear from Simon Priddis, head of mergers at the OFT who will give a fairly brief presentation as to how he sees the new system, what are its virtues and how is it bedding down in practice? We will then hear from Simon Baker of RBB Economics and from Nigel Parr of Ashursts. Each of them will limit themselves to about 10 minutes maximum and then hopefully we can draw questions and comments from the audience. So Simon, over to you.

A. Simon Priddis

Thanks very much Richard. As happy as I am to be likened to the underworld, I'd like to assure everybody that it's not really like that dealing with the OFT. What I would like to do for you this morning is to try and shed some light into this dark world that Richard paints for you. I thought I would try and do two things: first of all, try to explain what I see as a blueprint for a sound merger control regime; and then to explain why I think the UK regime, or the new UK regime, is an exemplar of that blueprint. Finally, in conclusion, I'd just like to offer a couple of thoughts as to why I put this forward as a blueprint. As Richard says, when the Enterprise Act was in its genesis we did have the opportunity to look widely across merger control systems around the world and take very much of what we saw as being, if one likes, the best of the breed, and to shape that into an effective domestic merger control regime.

I think how I would like to start is to advance this proposition for you this morning: the Enterprise Act is a good blueprint because it features three key characteristics. The first is that it has a competition-focused substantive test; it's applied in a sound legal framework and indeed a sound institutional structure. I suspect a lot of you are thinking, 'Well, that's really rather uncontroversial isn't it? I'm sure we'd all sign up to that'. But I would like to go on to explain that the devil here is truly in the detail. With your indulgence, I'll just work through each of those ideas, as Richard said, rather briefly. Let me kick off with our competition test. As Richard explained, what we've adopted in the UK is the substantial lessening of competition test: a pure competition-focused test. No public interest or broader industrial policy elements are taken into account. But the key points I would like to emphasize this morning include the fact that the substantive test is 'effects-oriented'. We are not really interested in broader structural issues like structure of markets; we are very focused on the effects of transactions. That's not to say, either, that the SLC test is the only formulation that could be adopted. There may well be other equally effective sets of language that achieve precisely the same aims. But a key part of the substantive test, of course, is to ensure that it covers all conceivable anti-competitive outcomes, briefly put: both non-coordinated and coordinated effects. I think you can already see this need to cover the range of conceivable competitive outcomes in cases that the UK authorities have pursued in the course of the past eight—nine months; just to pick up a few, the *Safeways* references, for example, from the OFT to the Competition Commission were based, very largely, on a non-coordinated effects analysis. More recently, references in the *P&O Stena* transaction were based, again, on a non-coordinated effects approach. One of the key benefits here, I think, is that the SLC test quite clearly covers these sorts of anti-competitive outcomes. There is no debate as to whether or not the test is broad enough or is sound enough to catch these sorts of issues. That in itself, I suggest, is a good thing, both for the authorities and for users of the system—that is you and your clients— because it brings a great deal of legal certainty to the process. You understand what is likely to be caught.

The development of a theory of competition harm, of course, takes place not just in the legislation, but also in the OFT's and the CC's guidance. Both agencies have published not only substantive guidance, but also procedural guidance. But just to focus for a moment on the substantive guidance, I think what one sees looking at both documents, from the OFT and the Competition Commission, is an acknowledgement of two important issues. The first is that competition review, and merger review specifically, is based soundly on economics: one has to have in mind the economic regime that one is applying when one looks at the effects of mergers. I think two points in particular arise there for you.

- The first is incentives. I think one can look at historic cases, both in the UK and in other regimes, that stray away from looking at the economic effects of a merger to look purely at whether or not parties have an ability to engage in particular action, and not necessarily whether they'd have the economic incentive to believe in that way. I would like to pick up on one recent UK example, the *Centrica/Dynegy*[1] transaction, which involved purely or largely vertical effects. There was extensive consideration in both the OFT's assessment and the Competition Commission's assessment of whether, post-merger, the merged entity would have not just the ability, but also the incentive to engage in the sort of anti-competitive conduct that was being mooted. That really is the thrust of the analysis in front of both authorities.

- We are also sensitive to efficiencies. We have to remember, I think, as authorities, that we're here for policy reasons: to ensure that markets work well for consumers, and that's why there is an explicit efficiencies defence built into the Enterprise Act. We, at the OFT, look at efficiencies at two levels as part of the SLC test and then also as an explicit defence if we think that the merger would nonetheless deliver consumer benefits. I think that is an important part of an effective merger regime, and it is a recognition of what we are actually trying to achieve.

The second overarching point arising from guidance is that sound theory, I

---

[1] Centrica plc and Dynergy Storage Ltd and Dynergy Onshore Processing UK Ltd <http://www.competition-commission.org.uk/inquiries/completed/2003/centrica/index.htm>.

am afraid, is not enough. It's important that the theory is applied in a sound legal framework and this is actually one of the key things I would like to draw out from my presentation this morning. I see the sound legal framework as based on essentially two key principles; the evidence-base for decision-making and the level of transparency that one brings to the process. Other beneficial side effects of a merger regime, for example predictability, certainly efficiency of the process, in large part I think flow from these two fundamental principles.

Just to take them briefly, evidence-based decision-making is a corner stone of the Enterprise Act, both for the OFT and for the Competition Commission. Indeed the language of the statutory test in the Enterprise Act bears testimony to this. The OFT has to have a reasonable belief that there may be an SLC before it makes a reference, and in the guidance we describe that as belief in a significant prospect of an SLC. Equally, the Competition Commission, before it proceeds to an adverse finding against a merger, has to have reached the belief that an SLC is more likely than not to result from the transaction. So everything, both in the legislation and the guidance, points towards this objective evidence-base for decision-making. But of course that evidence comes from both the merging parties and from third parties, and that evidence has to be properly weighed as part of the decision-making process. Part of that weighing process, too, I suggest, is pragmatism; an understanding of what transactions are actually about and why they are being conducted. Part of that consideration too is the recognition that we are there to protect consumers, to ensure the mergers don't harm consumers, whether that's through increased prices, reduced innovation or reduced service levels.

Let me turn to transparency. I think that the UK process has undergone a dramatic shift in the level of transparency over the past two years. If one looks back even to, say, mid-2000, mid-2001, certainly at the OFT level, there was remarkably little transparency. There was little published guidance on the principles we applied, there were few Advices actually published, and even at the CC level all one could look to for guidance as to the substantive principles applied, was the actual reports. There was no separate underlying theoretical guidance. And now we have moved from that end of the spectrum to completely the opposite, to a case where you have extensive guidance published by both the Competition Commission and the OFT. And just to skip to my last bullet point, you have publication by the OFT in particular of something in the order of 200 decisions a year. The metamorphosis from a situation two years ago where it was about 10 to a situation, to now where it is around 200, is just a dramatic change in the level of transparency and that, I believe, is a good thing. It allows you and your clients to understand the principles we apply. It allows merging parties and third parties to hold us to account against our guidance and against our legislation and I suggest it also serves a broader educative function in explaining how we will handle not just substantive issues, but also process issues: the sorts of evidence we will look for and how we will weigh competing types of evidence.

I suggest we've also gone quite a long way in improving the process in terms of giving parties a good chance to understand what the case is against their merger. At the OFT level, we have institutionalized the issues letters and issues meetings process that we've developed over quite a long period of time now, but that's now built into our merger control process. Parties at first phase in few other jurisdictions have an opportunity to comment as explicitly on the reasons why we would consider recommending a second phase in a particular case. The Competition Commission itself too has gone a long way beyond its previous process and now publishes provisional findings in merger cases. Those of you who read the UK press will have seen that at the end of last week, the Competition Commission published its first ever set of findings in the *P&O/Stena* case, and that's a very substantial shift in the level of insight into the decision-making process.

But again I'd say, even with sound theory and a sound legal framework, that's still not enough. You need one further element in a sound merger control regime and that's the institutional structure and I'd like to suggest that the UK (I say this rather self effacingly of course) is the paradigm of that institutional structure. Not only do we have at the OFT a first phase screen, we have the CC which acts, effectively, as a second pair of eyes carrying out an in-depth investigation into transactions. We've removed ministerial involvement so there's no risk of political issues interfering in the process. But perhaps most importantly, not content with introducing a second pair of eyes, we've gone even further and introduced very effective judicial oversight in the shape of the Competition Appeal Tribunal. As Richard said a moment ago, the very first merger appeal was actually heard last Friday. Just to give you an indication of how important I think this is, I will flag a couple of points for you. First, what is being challenged is not a reference but a clearance decision. It's being challenged by a third party, so that's a big change from the world we were in even six months ago. Second, I suggest, is the timing point. The notice of application was filed a week ago last Friday; the tribunal made procedural orders on Monday and Tuesday; and the full substantive hearing was all day Friday. So in seven days we went from notice of appeal to full hearing and in 10 days, ie tomorrow, we will have judgment on the matter, so the OFT's decision will either be upheld or we will be back to review the same transaction again. I venture no opinions as to which way it will go. Just the third point to raise on the appeal, by way of showing how important the CAT is as a constraint on the

OFT: just to take a look at the issues that are raised in this appeal. First the court has to decide whether this is on the facts judicial review (although nominally the legislation says this is an appeal); what is it that the court actually has to do; and what's the standard that the OFT has to apply? The tribunal is looking at that again, so as of tomorrow afternoon we may find ourselves with a materially shifted balance of work between the OFT and the Competition Commission. Further, what's the level of reasoning in OFT decisions? Bearing in mind we publish 200 a year, what do we have to include, what by way of reasoning and, more particularly, what by way of evidence?

So to conclude, I've put before you my reasons why I think there are three key features of the blueprint merger regime and in particular why I think the UK is an exemplar for that. But just to finish, why do I think this is important? Well I think it is important for three fundamental reasons. The first is simply that it is fair, not just to merger parties but also to third parties, to have an opportunity to put their case, to be heard, and to understand what the case is against the merger. The second point is predictability and certainty. You as advisors need to have a good sense of the principles that we would apply and the standards that we would apply. And finally, we should not lose sight of the overall policy goal of merger control, which is consumer protection and everything we do should be conditioned by that goal. With that, I hand over to Nigel.

B. Nigel Parr

When I was asked to give the lawyer's perspective, it was a bit like asking a competition lawyer to tie one hand behind his back because we are all amateur economists. But I've done my best. First I asked myself what is the ideal from a lawyer's perspective, and set that out in almost theoretical terms, and then I've seen how the OFT and then the Competition Commission measure up against those standards. I've then gone on to look and perhaps speculate a bit on the role of the Competition Appeal Tribunal. I've identified a number of standards or bench marks against which to assess the UK regime. The first one was hinted at by Simon: predictability and consistency, and what that seems to me really to involve, is the application of generally accepted principles and standards in relation to jurisdiction and assessment. We should all know where we are, it should be relatively easy to spot what's caught and what's not caught, the process in terms of how a merger will be assessed substantively should be known, and remedies is an important area in this regard that we shouldn't lose sight of. I think predictability and consistency also implies consistency from case to case and as Simon said, we have now had about 200 published OFT decisions and it is important that we as advisers are able to identify where the themes are, where the danger areas are, and when references and prohibition are likely to arise. In a nutshell, there should be no 'bolts from the blue'; there should be no real surprises in a properly structured system. The second standard I've identified is transparency, which in essence is knowing the case against you and having a fair opportunity to respond; and what most lawyers would say that involves is some sort of statement of objections, a reasoned statement of the case against you to which you can respond, and some sort of access to third party views, access to the file for example. The third standard is fairness which really means open minds, with no pre-conceptions. I think a separation of powers between the first and second stage really goes to the question of fairness, together with reliance on fact and evidence backed up by effective judicial control which I think ultimately is about encouraging discipline and thoroughness on the part of the primary decision makers. And lastly, I've inserted an additional standard in terms of cost and efficiency and some of those elements are clearly inconsistent with each other. We all want speed, as we heard this morning, but we want thoroughness and we may want to stop the clock and have an opportunity to put additional arguments in when it suits us, but all of that involves cost considerations.

So if we look at the OFT and see how they measure up, in terms of predictability and consistency, I think they do pretty well. Simon has spoken about the guidelines and I suppose my observation is; everything is in there. They are very broad and ultimately they don't really tell you what you didn't know or suspect already, but it's useful to have them nonetheless. The confidential guidance process which is relatively unique to the UK means that you can make a formal application in connection with a merger that is unannounced. The OFT will assess it in the normal way, subject only to their inability to speak to third parties, and that can be very valuable. In addition there is a less formal and rigorous version of that where the case team will look at a request for informal advice, again when the merger is confidential, and that is also very valuable. I think it's highly valued and welcomed by UK businesses and advisers. Moreover, what we experience with the OFT is a collegiate approach. You don't get the feeling that one unit or one or two case officers are pursuing their own theory on this case or that they are ploughing their own furrow, and I think that is supported by the structure of decision- making within the OFT in terms of case review meetings and then full decision meetings. Publication of decisions, again, facilitates predictability and consistency, but one area I would flag up, which I think is becoming increasingly difficult, is in relation to the notion of geographical jurisdiction: what is a substantial part of the UK? We have a House of Lords decision that says it is substantial if it is worthy of investigation for the purposes of the Act, which gives a lot of discretion to the OFT, but in terms of whether or not a small village in Yorkshire, for example, is a substantial part, there's not a lot of guidance.

Likewise, when considering local mergers; my own view, and Simon may disagree with this, is that local mergers have got an awful lot harder to figure out in the light of the *Safeway* report. If you read that report carefully and you look at the local fascia rules, you will find that there are about four or five cumulative tests for defining local geographic markets. If that's how you define a one-stop supermarket, what about a small convenience store, what about a betting office? We've got a history of looking at mergers between betting offices in the UK. What about pubs? We always used to think that pubs were defined in a slightly different way in terms of their catchment areas, but I think that means now that more mergers will be referred to the Competition Commission simply because it's all rather complicated and the OFT can't get to the bottom of it during the first stage investigation.

Transparency, I think, is good. The production of an issues letter by the OFT, and an issues-meeting works well. One area that I think could do with a little bit of further thought is the concept of undertakings in lieu of a reference to the Competition Commission. One of the benefits of changing the regime at the CC level was to introduce much more transparency in relation to remedies. What we have now at the CC stage is provisional findings being published and then the parties being invited back in to have a hearing, to sit down and discuss whether any of those adverse findings can be remedied. At the OFT stage with undertakings in lieu, you're still obliged to engage in a form of shadow boxing. You have the issues letter, you have the issues meeting, you don't know whether or not to suggest that you might sell something off, the OFT just sit there shuffling uncomfortably and they don't come back to you and say 'Yes we are minded to make an adverse finding in this case, it's looking like a reference, so now let's sit down and seriously work out whether or not that reference and all that cost and time can be avoided by giving some appropriate undertakings in lieu'.

Fairness: I feel that the merger parties get a fair crack of the whip when they are before the OFT. Consistent with the first stage investigation, there are not really bolts from the blue but obviously you don't get access to the file, you get the usual 'It's been put to us by a third party that X, Y & Z might follow', and you do your best to answer that.

In terms of cost and efficiency, I think the OFT score highly. Don't forget we have a system of voluntary filings. We also have a system of voluntary submissions. You don't have to use a merger notice. The whole system is pretty pragmatic and it is a lot easier to make filings to the OFT than it is, for example, to fill in a Form CO. Now obviously you are only dealing with one Member State rather than 15, but there is a real focus by the OFT on the key issues. They will not request a lot of unnecessary data just in case they might need it, so I think the OFT score quite highly in this area.

The Competition Commission, of course, is in a much more difficult position than the OFT. The OFT is just a first stage filter. They take a look at a merger and if they have doubts they can make a reference. It's an obvious point, but the Competition Commission has to sit down and reach a decision. Is the glass half full, or is it half empty? They can't sit on the fence. They've got to come up with a decision and they've got to adopt remedies if they reach an adverse finding, so it is a much more difficult job. We are just in the process of moving, as regards the Competition Commission, to the new regime. The OFT, I think, have looked at 70 mergers under the Enterprise Act. They've only referred three, and two of them have been abandoned, so the only one that's really proceeding at the moment is *P&O/Stena*.[1] The provisional findings were issued on Friday. There is a summary on the web site but when you look at them, they are about five centimetres thick. There is a serious amount of work that has gone into writing the adverse findings.

Regarding predictability and consistency, one always used to get the feeling that you were up against a theory of the case quite early on in the process. What's the theory of this case? What should economics be telling us? Let's see then how the facts fit in to that, rather than starting with what the facts are. Now that might be slightly unfair, but it's certainly the impression that one used to get. A key strength of the Competition Commission is that there are expert members. They are not full time officials, apart from the chairman and deputy chairman, but you do find that whoever the chairman is does matter. Who is chairing the inquiry is an important factor. They have particular interests, they have particular backgrounds and you need to understand that, and it's therefore less collegiate in that sense than the OFT. Remedies are again a difficult area where consistency is sometimes hard to spot and I don't have time to go into this in detail but one might look for example at *GWR*[2] which was a local radio merger that required divestment and *Carlton Granada*,[3] arguably much more significant in its effect, where a behavioural remedy was adopted.

---

[1] <http://www.competition-commission.org.uk/inquiries/current/stena/index.htm>.

[2] Acquisition by Scottish Radio Holdings plc and GWR Radio Group plc (through the joint venture company Vibe Radio Services Limited) of Galaxy Radio Wales and the West Ltd <http://www.competition-commission.org.uk/inquiries/completed/merger_refs/2003_2002/index.htm#merg2>

[3] Carlton Communications Plc and Granada plc <http://www.competition-commission.org.uk/inquiries/completed/merger_refs/2003_2002/index.htm#merg2>.

I think there is an issue concerning transparency. There's been no access to the file. There's no statement of objections as such unless the provisional findings become the statement of objections and people start saying 'Well now we know the case against us, let's roll our sleeves up and take issue with all of these points'. I think that would be unfortunate from a process and timing point of view. By the time the provisional findings are served on the parties, there should really be no surprises. We used to have the 'put-back' process under the old regime where you had to check material prior to the publication of the report, right at the end of the process, and there were occasions where you found new matters, new material, new arguments, and it seems to me that if one had access to the file that sort of difficulty would be overcome.

Fairness is well addressed. You have at least two almost full day hearings with the actual members of the Competition Commission who are the actual decision makers rather than the staff, and that is important. It is highly valued and you can have a genuine dialogue with them, but the difficulty is, of course, ascribing weight to conflicting evidence. That is a problem that the CC will always have. They are not looking for clear and compelling evidence, the standard under the Competition Act: for example, has this infringement taken place? Instead they are obliged to consider what is likely to happen; but what is the standard of proof there? What the statute says is 'May be expected to result in an SLC'. If you look at some old MMC reports, the Commission's task is to work out what may be expected to result; they are not concerned with mere possibilities. In terms of cost and efficiency the process is really quite time consuming. It's lengthy and it's getting more so. If one looks at the cost of these inquiries over the last five years, the cost is generally going up, and my suspicion is that the cost will go up under the new regime compared with the process under the Fair Trading Act.

Very briefly, because Simon has already explained the *IBA Health* case, it is clear, if one were at the hearing, that a lot of the submissions were in relation to the material errors of fact and assessment, not the usual sort of High Court judicial review type principles based on procedural irregularities. We wait to see the judgment tomorrow as to what it is that the Tribunal will decide. One suspects, like some of its early Competition Act judgments, that the CAT will want to set the scene a little bit, as to what judicial review in merger cases should focus on.

The final comment I will make is that there was a lot of debate at the time when the Enterprise Act was going through Parliament as to exactly what the standard of review should be. Should it be a full merits appeal? Should it be judicial review? The argument was that because we had a separate second stage with the Competition Commission, we already had a fair degree of procedural safeguards built in and therefore there could be more light handed judicial scrutiny rather than a full merits appeal. The IBA Health case involved a take-over bid under the Takeover Code. Time is of the essence and Simon described the very swift process that the Tribunal made. I think we would all applaud that, particularly as we're acting for the bidder. However, you have to ask yourself 'Is that always going to be the case?' What about a completed merger at the end of a full five months CC inquiry? Is the CAT going to say 'Well actually we are going to look at this rather quickly, as we set out in the IBA judgment?' But let's just step away from mergers for the moment. The same provision effectively is contained in section 179 of the Enterprise Act in relation to market investigations where the remedies can for example require the divestment of existing businesses. Now it would seem to be slightly odd that if someone is fined £250,000 under the Competition Act for breach of Chapter I or Chapter II, they have a full merits appeal. Look at the amount of judicial scrutiny that was expended in relation to the *Aberdeen Journals* case in relation to what, in overall terms, was a relatively low fine. But if for example, Microsoft were investigated by the Competition Commission and ordered to divest themselves of half their business, they would only be entitled to a High Court style judicial review, with no full re-appraisal of the facts, or consideration of the merits by the Tribunal. That's where I will finish.

C. Simon Baker

My first point will be to look at the objective of merger control. I agree largely with what Simon had to say. The UK regime is now explicitly focused on the maintenance of competition which de facto has been the case for many years now, but I think it is useful to finally clarify that and eliminate any possibility of broader considerations and to take out of the system the overt political element and the reduced risk that that brings of feeble argumentation and irrelevance. One thinks back to the Lilly Doctrine where mergers were referred where the acquirer was a state-owned foreign enterprise, for example. I assume that is now a thing of the past. So we have a well-focused objective which is clearly on the maintenance of competition. Is the scope of the regime wide enough? I think it is wide enough. It seems to capture absolutely everything, as Simon said, so it clearly captures all of those mergers raising unilateral effects potentially, including that class of non-collusive oligopoly that, it has been claimed, a straight dominance test may not, or historically has not captured. It covers all your coordinated effects concerns and it covers your vertical concerns which lead to foreclosure.

Clearly wide enough, but is it too wide? Simon argued that it was desirable for the merger regime to cover everything that could possibly be anti-competitive. I am not sure that I agree with that. It's a bit like optimal leakage theory in water pipes. Is it desirable to have zero leakage at all times? Well no, because you're continually digging up the road, with all the enforcement resources that involves and you're inconveniencing innocent passers-by. Does it make sense to have conglomerate mergers routinely assessed by the authorities, or should there be a very strong presumption that they are benign? I am not sure that there are many conglomerate mergers that raise serious anti-competitive issues and therefore putting everyone through the process of filing a defence for them and opening a door to vexatious complainants to rustle up some half-baked tying theory may not be a useful way to expend public or private resources. However, that said, I think the new regime clearly covers everything of potential concern and assuming that the authorities can efficiently avoid too many type-2 errors, then that is probably a good thing.

So, what about the quality of the analysis? Well I think the legal framework can facilitate it but it cannot guarantee high quality analysis and in my view, the quality of the analysis is the most important factor in the success of a regime. The wording of the substantive test can clearly influence the way that analysis is conducted, even if the formal scope of the tests are the same, so a dominance based test can clearly lead to an overly structural mode of analysis, too much focus on market shares, Herfindahl Indices and all the rest of it. The SLC test may usefully focus the analysis back on what really matters, which is the effects of the merger, specifically where the merger is likely to lead to price rises afterwards and I think the UK regime, again, passes that test pretty well and encourages an effects-based analysis, as Simon was suggesting.

So what of the relevant theory? Well that's clearly central to the quality of the analysis and I think the OFT and CC guidance do go a long way in clearly and usefully describing the theory of horizontal mergers that the authorities will apply in the UK. I strongly agree with something that Christian Ahlborn said in his presentation earlier, namely that the theory of vertical and conglomerate mergers is very thinly, one might say poorly, articulated and it's entirely unclear from reading of the guidance exactly what you are up against, what arguments you should be trying to develop and deploy in defending a vertical or conglomerate merger, so I think there is some scope for improvement in the guidelines there. Also, I think, looking at the underlying theory that underpins the horizontal guidelines, a very purist interpretation would imply that any horizontal merger will lead to some price increase, absent efficiencies, and that is potentially offset by the explicit consideration of efficiencies at the SLC stage, whether the merger will increase rivalry, and also at the post SLC stage where the cost reductions could lead to price reductions, notwithstanding a reduction in rivalry. So I think there is some useful guidance on that point. But, nevertheless, under this test, we have wide scope for intervention and no real bright lines or safe harbours emerging from the theory, and non-collusive oligopolies, as I mentioned earlier, are clearly at risk. So I think the UK guidelines clearly articulate the relevant horizontal merger theory and it is clear what hypothesis one generally needs to test and what constitutes relevant evidence, and I think that is useful.

As to relevant evidence itself, I think that's paramount in a system with such wide ranging discretion for the authorities. I think the onus is on all parties to set out their hypothesis of how the market operates, and to test that against the evidence, in particular explaining why a given piece of evidence is relevant to the theory in a particular case. So for example in the *Safeway* merger report, one could ask, was the evidence presented in that report uniquely consistent with the emergence of the effects that were discussed? Could a coordinated effects hypothesis have been falsified? Is there any set of evidence the parties could have presented to the Competition Commission in that case that could have falsified the hypothesis that there would be a paradigm shift following a reduction from five to four supermarkets? Could the same evidence have been written up differently to support the opposite conclusion? From my reading of the report and my involvement in that case, I think the answer is yes, I think it is very hard to know what one could have put before the Competition Commission by way of evidence that could have clearly refuted their hypothesis. I have to say as a sort of aside, it's not clear to me always that it will ever be possible to refute an allegation that there will be a paradigm shift following a structural change. Rather different to unilateral effects concerns, but that's something of an aside. I think when considering 'relevant evidence', despite the focus on effects which the UK regime clearly has, there is an unhelpful over-reliance on structural indicators in both sets of guidance and in current practice, particularly the discussion of HHIs, which I find unhelpful. Nowhere is it explained why these are relevant, particularly unilateral effects in differentiated product industries, or why the threshold is set at their current level? Do we really think that a market with 10 firms each with 10 per cent is a concentrated industry? It strikes me as rather un-concentrated, so what is the point of these thresholds? I can see they may have some value set at a suitable level for the OFT in dismissing the trivia, sorting the wheat from the chaff, but by the time a case has reached the Competition Commission, what really is gained by having a discussion of whether the HHIs are 2047 or 2547? The whole debate should have moved way beyond that by the time the case reaches the Competition Commission. So I think the evidence and the guidelines are basically sound. I think in practice, and this applies as much to practitioners as to the authorities, there is temptation to rely on check-lists and easily available structural evidence when you are trying to build a case one way or another and I think that's a danger the authorities must seek to avoid in Simon's evidence-based brave new world.

Clearly there are a number of drivers of quality independent of the guidelines. In quality of staff, the OFT has made great strides in recent years to expand its staff with more professional and in-house training, and I think the quality of the resources at the OFT is now higher than it has ever been. They have a clear understanding of the theory and of the empirical techniques. I think the division of the responsibilities between the OFT and the CC is useful. I think the requirement to publish reasons in advice reports, the transparency and timing talked about, is all pushing towards putting pressure on the authorities to raise the quality of the analysis, as does the possibility of judicial review, more of which we will find out about in Nigel's talk and tomorrow in the IBA case. So in conclusion, I think we have a broad test which captures all of the conceivable problems. Whether that is entirely desirable or not is a debatable point. I think the nature of the substantive test is important but the main determinant is the quality of the analysis. I think a key grasp of the theory is critical primarily for an appreciation of what is relevant evidence and theorising alone without that evidence, without both parties putting forward a hypothesis that they can support with relevant evidence, and a hypothesis that can be rejected is key to moving the world forward. Thank you.

D. Discussion

[MARK CLOUGH QC]

Just a quick question. We've spent the last year looking for a gap in Europe between dominance and SLC and I just wanted, with this panel here, to see whether we can find a new gap. In particular do any of you see a gap between 'a lessening of' and 'an impediment of' competition?

[SIMON BAKER]

No I don't think there is any gap. I think that SIEC and SLC are essentially synonyms. I think they are intended to achieve the same objectives, essentially, a lessening of competition. They can be interpreted in the same way as an impediment to effective competition. I think the two work along side each other rather well.

[NIGEL PARR]

I have been assuming that it will be operating as an SLC test otherwise we are presumably back where we started with the dominance test (as amended) versus the SLC test. As a lawyer goodness knows what it means; I suspect we will have to wait until the courts have told us, but I suppose it is possible to suggest that a substantial lessening of competition is looking at reductions in existing competition. An impediment to competition seems to imply some sort of barriers to entry that can't be overcome in the foreseeable future and beyond. Whether that's right or not, I don't know. My hope is it's the same because I think we do need some clarity and consistency as to what we are applying.

[RICHARD WHISH]

I think it's meant to be the same but I don't think it is. Anyway, any other questions or comments from the audience on anything that we've heard? On Nigel's point about the local market definition problem, of course there are difficulties and what we have to remember with this legislation is that the OFT has a duty to make a reference. That's the thing that is so different from the old law. So, in an area of uncertainty, and if there was ambiguity over a market definition, I think that there would have to be a reference and if there is not a reference then that is something that can be judicially reviewed and that is why we might get more of these kind of cases that we've had already.

[SIMON PRIDDIS]

Can I just reply to Richard's point a little. I think there are two issues. A lot has been made of the fact that the Enterprise Act now contains a duty to refer as opposed to the discretion under the old Fair Trading Act regime and it has been suggested that that is going to make a material difference to the number of references. The reason I simply think that isn't the case is twofold. First, we are still applying the same test as we were in the past so in order for the discretion to make any difference you would have to consider that there are currently cases that we think raise a competition issue that are not being recommended for referral. I can assure you that that wasn't the case. We haven't had any of those. The second point is just in relation to the operation of the pure duty under the Enterprise Act. The duty is really a duty contained within quite a substantial discretion because the duty only kicks in where the OFT has a reasonable belief that SLC will result. So the OFT, I suggest, has to go through the mechanism of gathering the evidence, weighing the evidence and arriving at it's own reasonable view as to what that evidence shows, and it is only where the OFT holds the belief that there might be an SLC, that the duty kicks in. Having said that, that is one of the issues in appeal under IBA. More of this tomorrow afternoon.

[SIMON BAKER]

Actually on Nigel's point, in relation to the local marketing licence and the *Safeway* case, I thought that was something that the Competition Commission actually did extremely well and I thought they moved the world forward from the analysis in the supermarkets report previously and actually started to try to apply some unilateral effects theory with real evidence and real data in local markets. I certainly wouldn't want to see us retreating from that in the name of giving the OFT an easier job.

[NIGEL PARR]

No I think it was thorough, certainly. My only observation is I think it is almost impossible for the OFT to apply. That's my worry that you end up with more local mergers being referred so that the Rolls Royce mapping system of the Competition Commission can be cranked into gear.

CHAPTER 5

Unilateral Effects—Cross-Atlantic Convergence

DR PHILIP MARSDEN

I am a lawyer chairing a panel of economists discussing, essentially, an economic concept, that being the concept of unilateral effects and whether there is any convergence of analytical approach particularly across the Atlantic. Now I think that any introduction that I may make of this topic would only introduce an added degree of confusion which hopefully the panel would clear up, but I would say that one way of approaching this discussion is to pose the question of whether the concept of unilateral effects—whereby the merged entity has the ability and incentive to raise price short term—is really all that different from where coordinated effects analysis is taking us, in the sense that we are looking at whether coordination amongst the remaining players means that there is room for them as a group to interact in a way which may keep prices up over the short term? So basically, we are ending up in both with a test of consumer welfare. Or, in the case of coordinated effects, is it really something much more amorphous, a test of rivalry and constraints on rivalry?

I think I have just proven in about 15 seconds that a lawyer can certainly confuse the issues, so I will quickly introduce the panel of economists. First off, wearing his hat as a Professor of the London Business School, is Paul Geroski who will clarify a few things about unilateral effects and coordinated effects analysis. After that, we have Dr Greg Vistnes from Charles River Associates. He is also former head of economics at the US FTC, where he supervised over 40 PhD economists, and he will offer us even more clarity. And then we have Dr Cristina Caffarra, Director of Lexecon in London and Brussels, who will actually bring us down to earth with a few examples and some cases to make the debate a bit more practical, and then, just before opening up the discussion to all of you, we will go back to Paul, wearing his hat this time as Deputy Chairman of the Competition Commission (but of course speaking in his personal capacity) who will react to Greg and Cristina's presentations. Then we will open up the discussion to the floor. So Paul, after you.

A. Paul Geroski

I've not really attended many conferences of lawyers, but I have noticed that there is an increasing tendency in these conferences to hold a session in which a group of economists are invited to come along and play with their toys in public, and this seems to be that in this conference session. I also notice that such sessions are often scheduled immediately after lunch. I presume this on the basis that it is impossible to disturb the digestion of a good, hardened competition lawyer, and next to impossible to imagine that a mere economist could do this!

This is an interesting session because unilateral and coordinated effects are concepts that have come into very wide currency. When I agreed to talk about them, I thought I knew what they were. I am not so sure anymore and what I am going to explain, very briefly, three things: what I think they are; where the difficulty comes, I believe, in making the distinction between the two; and then I am going to conclude by saying why it is, nonetheless, very useful to make this distinction, imperfect as it is.

I think it is easiest to start with coordinated effects. These describe pricing situations where firms act collectively to set a price at or near monopoly levels. This might occur if they explicitly collude, but it also may occur if they do not. The hallmark of tacit collusion is a sense of common interest which encourages firms to override the short run gain available to them by undercutting rivals through increased prices. It's been suggested that the key feature of this kind of behaviour is that it is essentially multi-period behaviour, in which the future is being used as a hostage against cooperative behaviour in the present. I myself use the phrase conscious parallelism in this context since it contains the essence of it for me, namely that when firms act they are conscious of their rivals' likely responses, and they try to act in a way which will promote parallel responses by their rivals.

Unilateral effects are a little bit more difficult. They are supposed to refer to situations where prices can get close to monopoly levels, even when firms act unilaterally and have no need to second guess their rivals. At first sight, this is rather difficult to understand, since it seems hard to think of situations where it makes sense to simply ignore rivals or at least not to try to persuade them to be cooperative. For those familiar with the simple static models of pricing that populate economics textbooks, by which I mean Cournot models of quality competition or so-called Bertrand models of pricing models (with differentiated products), unilateral effects are a little less mysterious. A firm will be quite confident that its rivals will not undercut a price rise that it pushes through, if those rivals are constrained by capacity or cannot otherwise increase output when it raises prices, or when their products are quite imperfect substitutes for those of the firm that is raising prices. And at a more common-sense level, a large well-established market leader is unlikely to be too concerned about what smaller fringe players in its market will do if it raises prices, either because it knows that they are too scared to undercut it, or because it knows they'll be more than happy to follow along any price increase that it initiates.

There is a natural, if slightly rough, mapping from concepts of dominance and collective dominance into unilateral and coordinated effects. What exactly do we mean when we say a firm is dominant? In plain language, this means that the firm is able to do pretty much what it wants and is not subject to the ordinary constraints of competition. If this is the case, then what we expect from dominant firms are unilateral effects. Almost by definition, their position of dominance enables them to increase prices without taking too much account of their actions or responses of their rivals. On the other hand, when there are several firms who are collectively dominant, unilateral effects are much less likely (although not of course impossible), not least because each is likely to be of sufficient size and strength to inflict considerable damage on attempts by any of the others to raise prices unilaterally. Instead, what seems much more likely in this case is that these firms will perceive their common interest with some clarity and act in concert, one way or the other. What is likely to emerge, then, are coordinated effects.

The problem with the distinction between unilateral and coordinated effects is that it turns on things which are fundamentally unobservable. The reactions of rivals to a proposed price rise always matters in pricing situations, and the distinction between unilateral and coordinated effects hinges on how those reactions are viewed by the firms initiating price increases. Coordinated effects arise when firms care a lot about the reactions of their rivals and, in addition, are able to act strategically to influence them. By contrast, a firm that can initiate unilateral effects makes no attempt to persuade its rivals to cooperate, and may not in the end even care how its rivals react to its pricing policies.

However clear all of this is in theory, in practice it rapidly becomes a bit murky, and a distinction which turns on attitudes that cannot be observed directly is always going to be one that is very hard to use with a great deal of precision. For example, when the smaller fry in an industry that hosts a dominant firm elect to match the leader's price increases, are we observing a coordinated effect or a unilateral effect? Similarly, if one of a group of firms which are collectively dominant acts unilaterally to increase its prices, and if, for some reason, the others in the collectively dominant group do not undercut the leader's price, then once again it is hard to work out whether what one is observing is a coordinated effect or a unilateral effect. In fact, both concepts really describe pricing paths that lead to the same end. A market in which either unilateral or coordinated effects are present is a market likely to display prices at or approaching monopoly levels.

One might well ask then why it's worth making a fuss if in principle a coordinated effect lessens competition just as much as unilateral effects do? The answer is, in my view, that there are perhaps two reasons why it's worth keeping this distinction in mind. First, the two concepts describe two different ways to the same end and recognizing this helps to ensure that examinations of whether a particular merger substantially lessens competition are thorough. That is, to properly consider the likely effects on prices, one must consider all of the ways in which these adverse effects might arise. Thus, the distinction between unilateral and coordinated effects is helpful because it suggests that there are two questions that one must ask when exploring the possible consequences of a merger. The first question is: will the merger result in the creation of a firm which will have the power to initiate unilateral effects? And the second is: if not, will the merger lead to an industry structure which is more conducive to the exercise of coordinated effects than it was pre-merger? As you heard this morning, there are now several sets of guidance which have been developed to help answer these questions, and I don't propose to go through them here. Those of you who are interested in the guidelines that have been developed at the Competition Commission and how they have been used in practice might well have a look at the decision in *Safeways*.[1]

The second reason why the distinction between unilateral and coordinated effects is important to make is that it is sometimes as important to know how something happened as it is to know what exactly has happened. If, for example, one is examining a market in which prices appear to be too high, it is important to know whether this is because one firm has the power to cause unilateral effects or because several of them are able to exercise coordinated effects. The gain to answering this question comes in the discussion of remedies because the appropriate remedy to an adverse effect depends on exactly how that effect is created. In particular, undoing the conditions which give rise to unilateral effects may require rather different remedies than undoing those that give rise to coordinated effects. There are, perhaps, three main differences. First, adverse effects caused by unilateral effects can be traced mainly to the actions of a single firm, while coordinated effects arise from the actions of several firms and may therefore require a rather wider remedy than one just applied to a single firm. Second, most people believe, rightly in my view, that coordinated effects are likely

---

[1] <http://www.competition-commission.org.uk/rep_pub/reports/2003/index.htm>.

to be more fragile. They are more likely to collapse in the face of market pressures than unilateral effects would be. If this is true, it means that remedying coordinated effects may well require less intrusive remedies than remedying unilateral effects. Third, and finally, it may be more straightforward to impose behavioural remedies on a dominant firm that exercises unilateral effects than it is to disrupt the conscious parallelism of a group of collectively dominated firms.

The bottom line then is that there is a distinction between unilateral and coordinated effects that's worth making, although it's a distinction that always blurs at the edges. The distinction is worth making partly because in making the distinction one ensures that one has set up a systematic way to explore possible paths by which competition may be substantially lessened, but in my view, even more important, because it's important to understand these effects when one comes to think of remedies.

Thank you.

B. Greg Vistnes

I was asked to talk on the extent to which there is a convergence of views on unilateral effects analysis on both sides of the Atlantic. As I began putting together some notes on this, I came to the realization that I couldn't figure out the extent to which there was convergence between the two sides until I first figured out where are we are on this topic in the US. That is, what does the US think about unilateral effects? I quickly realized that, even within the US there is still quite a bit of uncertainty and flux as to how unilateral effects should be incorporated into anti-trust analysis. There's certainly been flux over time regarding the extent to which the two anti-trust agencies in the US have been embracing unilateral effects analysis, and so I wanted to start out and focus on why there is this difference and why there is flux, that is, why is there uncertainty on how unilateral effects should be incorporated in to anti-trust analysis?

This is a fascinating question because, to an economist, unilateral effects embody all that is science about this wonderful profession—rather than being social scientists, here with unilateral effects we have the opportunity to do mathematical modelling and econometric estimations. We can move from being social scientists to pretend that we are real scientists, but therein lies what I think is much of the danger of unilateral effects. In fact, much of the reason why there's this tension or this uncertainty about what do we do with unilateral effects is because once these economists have been set loose in the field of unilateral effects I think there's a real danger that, at times, perhaps we've gone too far. We've become seduced by the magic of these econometrics and these mathematic simulations. But I think that's, to a large extent, what is causing this uncertainty as to what we do with unilateral effects, whereas the economists in one sense would say 'This is the best thing that's happened since sliced bread, there's no reason to hesitate, we should fully embrace it and use it in all our anti-trust analysis'. I think that is going too far in two regards that I want to talk about.

First, by trying to turn unilateral effects into a science, one runs the danger of imparting too much precision, too much science to what's actually going on out there. This has the result that we are trying to do more than we actually can do, and that leads to retaliation from the other side, from the realists, who say: 'You can't really put the whole world into this nice simple model that you are trying to create'. Second, some of the predictions coming out of unilateral effects are, in a sense, too good to believe. One of the things with unilateral effects is that, in almost every case concerning horizontal mergers, the end result is that the model will predict that prices go up. That's an awfully powerful argument but it can't be right. It can't be that any merger is going to be anti-competitive, so what's wrong with this theory? This is the other source of the tension; the detractors of unilateral effects analyses argue that it can't be right, it's just too mindless in its predictions, and that we should move on to something else. So that's what I want to talk about: how do we resolve these differences?

So before I get into some of the meat of this, let's talk a little about what these theories are and what form some of the applications of the theories take. There is in a sense a kind of the ying and the yang of anti-trust analysis when analysing coordinated effects and the unilateral effects. To an economist, coordinated effects are always a little bit frustrating because they represent the whole science of people coming together and coming to agreements, albeit unilaterally, even though it's potentially in their own self-interest to break that agreement, and so the whole analysis centres around the question of how do you keep these people doing something when they really want to cheat, when they want to break up? And that's turning us not into economists talking about incentives and optimisation but instead into sociologists. How do you get people to agree? Unilateral effects analysis is a whole different world. This is the world I was talking about earlier where you get to model, you get to optimise, you get to estimate, it's a wonderful area to be in if you are an economist. So that's what unilateral effects is, in a sense, all about. It's so much more conducive to modelling. That's why you see this big gravitation towards the unilateral effects analyses by economists, and I think nine out of 10 economists you talk to will tend to indicate that unilateral effects is where the action is at and that's where anti-trust should be going.

What kind of analysis can you do with unilateral effects? I could talk all day about the different types of models—theoretical models, merger simulations, econometrics galore, all sorts of fantastic bidding models. Most of these things, things like portfolio effect models and other things I am sure you are all familiar with, are all very interesting, but again virtually every single one of these models in its simplest form comes to the same powerful conclusion. The theory in a nutshell is, if you merge, you have one less rival, and if you have one less rival you have less competition. What else could prices do but go up? That's unilateral effects, in a nutshell. Prices are going to go up with a merger in this simple model, but it's the consistency of the result that, as I said before, is really causing the problem.

Now the problems with most of these models and these theories, concerns the degree of precision. You can estimate the price effect as a 2.73 per cent price increase, and I've seen people predict price increases for mergers to that degree of precision, but underlying all of these predictions are a huge degree of assumptions, so there's a lot hidden behind all of this. What are consumer preferences like? Is demand linear, is it constant elasticity, is it just downward sloping, are preferences nested? All these questions that, to a lot of economists don't really make a whole lot of sense, and probably to the attorneys out there, make even less sense. What do firms' costs look like? Are they constant costs? Are they going to go up or are they going to go down? Are they just kind of funny-shaped? Most business people would probably say they are funny-shaped. Are there capacity constraints? Probably, but most models don't incorporate those assumptions into it. How do firms compete? Well, we've got all sorts of crazy notions for Bertrand versus Cournot competition, we've got all sorts of super games, all sorts of funny concepts of equilibrium, all very interesting, all very fascinating, and all of them I will virtually guarantee can give you very big impacts on your estimated results.

To illustrate how these different assumptions can yield different results, here is a fantastic equation that will tell you the effects of a merger. All you need to know are two things, and with this equation, you can then predict the price increase. You need to know the firm's margins, pretty easy thing to come up with, at least as a ballpark figure and you need to know this thing called the diversion ratio. Diversion ratio is if I raise my price, how much of my demand, what percentage of it, will go to my merging partner. If you know those two things, there's your formula to estimate the price increase. For example, with a margin of 25 per cent and a diversion ratio of 25 per cent, this formula tells you that the merger's going to lead to a price increase of 12.5 per cent. That's pretty easy. But what if demand isn't constant elasticity? What if in fact it is linear demand? Well you get a different formula. Using the same margin M and the same diversion rate D, your predicted price increase drops by a factor of three. Now all of a sudden your price increase is only 4.2 per cent.

Well maybe that's not so much of a problem, I just need to know whether I've got a linear demand or constant elasticity. Unfortunately, every single time I've asked a business person which one of those curves reflects his industry, he can't tell me, and sometimes again he gives me a very funny shaped demand curve. Now, granted, some econometrics can help figure out what this demand curve looks like. It can help me figure out what assumption to put in to my formulas, but unfortunately my econometrics estimations, every single one of those, has its own assumptions embedded in it. So we've got this problem of despite all this wonderful precision, it's not very robust. It's very sensitive to all these assumptions and I don't have a good idea what's going on.

Now actually I have a different slide that I don't transport over the Atlantic too often entitled: 'models are just models'. If models could have everything in them, they wouldn't be a model; they'd be a full blown picture of reality. But you can't do that in a model. A model by its very nature has got to focus on the most important aspects of reality. You've got to embed some assumptions into it. That's a problem with reality. Perhaps more importantly, models are typically static. They aren't reflecting dynamic changes in the economy and that I think more than anything else that helps explain why we have that really powerful result that, if you merge, prices go up. It's because it's a result from a static model. It's assuming nothing else is changing, but in reality, we tend to have entry. We tend to have expansion by firms. We tend to have product repositioning. If Kellogs and Frosted Flakes merge, after the merger one of them may add a little bit more sugar. Maybe the product will be taken off the market; maybe they will do something different than what used to be the case. Most of the models don't have that in there and I've given a fair amount of thought to how difficult it would be to actually try to, since we love to optimize as economists. Let's figure out the optimal repositioning of products. How much would they want to move apart or change their differentiation after the merger? I've spent an awful lot of time and an awful lot of clients' money, unfortunately, trying to figure that out. You can't do it. Figuring out the re-optimization of firms' positioning is an awfully difficult problem. What do you do? You can't do a whole lot.

The other slide I've left out, probably because of my bias coming from the US, where we talk a lot about efficiencies but often don't fully adopt them into the analysis, is on efficiencies. If you go back to the formulas I was talking about earlier, if you allow for cost savings as a result of the merger, then the prediction that prices always going up after a merger doesn't necessarily hold any more. So this incompleteness of the models and the fact that they aren't incorporating efficiencies or the product repositioning goes a long way I think to this issue about this prediction that prices always go up under unilateral effects models.

So what do we do? We could just throw the model out. Alternatively, we simply recognize that a model is just a model—it's simple but don't throw it out; just recognize that it's not incorporating all these other factors. The other criticism is, 'Well you've just told me all these problems with the model so what good is that if it's got all these problems?' And again I'll go back to saying that we shouldn't throw the baby out with the bath water, because these models are still awfully important. They provide a tremendous amount of information for a number of reasons. One is they help with the intuitions of what's going on with the merger. They help you understand why prices may be going up. They help you understand who is competing with whom. They help you understand who are the strongest competitors with each other. Some of the models may also help because they give you a better sense of relative effects that may be going on. You may be able to calibrate them or 'baseline' them to state that even though every model predicts a 4 per cent price increase, so long as we know that we can take a base line merger of say 10 firms going down to nine, then if that merger predicts a pricing increase of 3.5 per cent under our models, we can go on to say that any price increase under 3.5 per cent can be ignored. That one can't be a problem.

But I think in a sense what is most important, ie the real value of unilateral effects analysis, is that it helps you understand competition today. Now for a merger analysis we need to understand what competition is going to look like in the future but we can't make predictions about future competitions unless we understand today's competition and today's competition isn't necessarily about current coordination, it's about understanding who do I compete with? If I raise my price, to whom do I lose my sales? Who am I most afraid of competing with? Who am I positioning my product against? What is driving my decisions today, because until we know what's driving my decisions today, we can't possibly know what's going to be driving decisions and pricing and competition tomorrow. And so in that sense I think unilateral effects has to be looked at for any type of a sensible merger analysis whether you are focusing on coordination or unilateral effects.

Now I started out this talk with 'be careful what you wish for'. What I want to change that to is 'don't be careful what you wish for, wish for unilateral effects'. But that's a very powerful genie. So be very careful with what you wish for—be careful once you let that genie out of the bottle. Because that genie is awfully powerful and it can do both good and evil. Know how to use it and interpret it correctly and once you do I think it will be very much something you can use.

So finally, switching back to the question of what we have in terms of convergence between US and European on unilateral effects, I think what we have is neither convergence nor divergence. There's still a tremendous amount of learning and understanding going on both across the oceans, both among economists and among attorneys. Even within the field of economics you don't always have people understanding the same things so what I think is tremendously important is we need to continue sharing our experiences. I think, certainly for this reason, that what the British Institute is doing here today, just bringing people together to talk about unilateral effects, to talk about experiences, is tremendously useful and through that we will move towards convergence and towards understanding how, in essence, to best tame this genie that we've let out of the bottle. Thank you.

C. Cristina Caffarra

Thank you and good afternoon. It has been a fascinating run-through of the current thinking in the US where, of course, they have the benefit of a much longer experience on unilateral effects than we have in Europe. My focus is going to be naturally European. I would like to chart briefly the rise of unilateral effects, particularly in European Commission merger review. I wanted to talk about what kind of behaviour we are concerned about when we talk about unilateral effects, and then to share with you a few thoughts on how we measure whether there is really a problem, and finally pick on a few cases in Europe and also in the UK which can be illustrative of where we have got to with unilateral effects analysis.

I think that it is fair to say that in terms of unilateral and coordinated effects, the trajectories which are being followed in Europe and in the US are in some way opposite. In the US, we started with a systematic focus on unilateral effects with all of the current deep thinking that's gone into it as illustrated by Greg. Coordinated effects have been marginalized. In Europe, to the contrary, we've paid much more intense attention to coordinated effects with unilateral effects really being acknowledged only about a year ago in the draft Notice on the Assessment of Horizontal Mergers published by the Commission. This was a Notice, as you are all aware, that followed a period of soul-searching by the Commission after the *CFI Airtours* decision.[1] A period that also included a number of discussions about the 'test', on the merits of dominance as a test vis-à-vis a different one. A great part of that debate was 'the gap'. Is there a 'gap' in the Merger Regulation? And the kind of questions that were very much debated were: bearing in mind that *Airtours* has told us that what we really mean when we talk about collective dominance, is it tacit coordination collusion, where we place market-wide price increases following a merger that do not arise from coordinated market behaviour, but simply from the reduction in the number of competitors? The classic examples in here have been the *Lloyds TSB/Abbey National* case[2] with market shares of 25/27 per cent and the *Heinz/BeechNut* case in the US, putting together number two and number three. Do we need to change the test then? Is a 'significant lessening of competition' in any way better than what we had before? The initial position of the Commission has been to retain dominance, but really the Notice has set out what forms of competitive harm really underlie the concerns we have. Now we have a new hybrid version of the test, 'significant impediment of effective competition'.

---

[1] Case T-342/99 [2002] ECR II-2585, [2002] 5 CMLR 317.
[2] See <http://www.competition-commission.org.uk/inquiries/completed/2001/index.htm>.

What's really important, though, is that however you change the order of these words—'significant', 'dominance', 'competition', 'impediment'—at the end there is some common ground on the type of harm that we are trying to capture. The Notice has tried to be quite explicit and didactic in identifying all of the aspects that we need to worry about. On the one hand there are mergers that facilitate coordination, 'coordinating oligopolies'; and then there's a dichotomy between 'paramount market position' and 'mergers that significantly reduce competition' without creating that monster. And it's obvious that the reason why the Notice includes this distinction is to make it as clear as can be that mergers which do not create a single leader can still be problematic and can still be subject to scrutiny. The mapping of these categories into 'unilateral' and 'coordinated effects' is pretty much as in the slide, with 'paramount' and 'non-collusive oligopoly' as pretty much the equivalent of 'unilateral effects', and separate from that there are 'coordinated effects' stories.

The reason why economists like this unilateral/coordinated effects distinction, although 'unilateral' is really a terminology that comes out of the Merger Guidelines, is because it maps quite well into two very distinct types of effects that arise from horizontal mergers. On the one hand there may be an increase in the market price due to the incentive of the merging parties to raise their price following the merger. Very distinct is a situation in which the merger relaxes one of the previous constraints that prevented coordination from succeeding, for example, by eliminating a maverick in a market, so it may become more feasible to sustain this collusive beast for the coordination. But what's important to economists is really that these are distinct mechanisms. One is about what are the short-term best responses. Another one is about maintaining and being able to achieve a certain type of outcome through a system of threats and promises over time. I will not spend very much on this because this is pretty much the substance that's been dealt with by other speakers. The key point for unilateral effects analysis is that certain assets are being combined, be they brands or capacities. The firms that are merging do not need to worry as much about raising prices, because the merged entity will capture part of the demand loss. This will *always* give the merged firm an incentive to raise prices. But by how much will prices go up? Under the dominance test, we didn't need to worry too much about it below 40 per cent. In fact the reality is that price effects can be quite appreciable even below that threshold and depend entirely on capacity constraints and substitution, on whether there are opportunities for repositioning. One observation, though, is that while it is the incentives of the merged firms that change (and that's why we say their prices go up), the other firms in the market can also find it optimal to raise their price. This is the reason why we hear sometimes reference to 'multilateral effects' as being probably a better way of describing this. It's not that the other firms in the markets stay still; they just jump on the increase that the merging parties have made. The reason why unilateral effects, as Greg has amply illustrated, appeal so much to economists is precisely due to the issue of measurement. In contrast, 'coordinated effects' is a slippery concept. We don't know how to reliably predict the changes of coordination occurring in a market, apart from with fairly 'soft' arguments. There are models out there that do that, but they are extremely sophisticated, delicate, and difficult to implement in the context of an investigation. Unilateral effects are a different thing. At least in principle it opens up this Aladdin's cave of wonderful treasures that you can explore; you can get this data, you can estimate, you can do all these fancy things and it would be good to start 'playing' with these in Europe, at least for a while.

I will not spend any time talking about this in detail, but certainly the one that's most seductive is the merger simulation, and Greg has spent quite a bit of time talking about its pros and cons. I wanted to conclude really with some thoughts on a few of the cases. By definition, because it's such a new development, there isn't an awful lot of practical case experience on unilateral effects in Europe. The earliest example, which is best known, is *Volvo/Scania*.[3] The Commission retained a number of academics to estimate a model of demand, and the outcome was a pretty good illustration of the kind of problems that Greg was mentioning. The model was predicting a certain type of price increase but there was great controversy at the time about the assumptions of the model. The predictions that were made seemed pretty unreliable: 25 per cent price increases, 90 per cent margins in some countries. There was a lot of debate on its reliability and the Commission in fact did not rely on that unilateral effects analysis in the decision when it prohibited the merger. I think the more recent example which is of interest is the *GE/Instrumentarium* case,[4] where the market was becoming more concentrated and the question really was whether the brands involved in the merger were the closest competitors. The Commission, together with the parties, did a detailed econometric study of bidding data trying precisely to assess how closely the brands of the two merging parties were competing.

Other than that, my experience is that unilateral effects analysis in Europe is pretty much still subordinate to the market definition question. However one of the advantages of unilateral effects analysis, in principle, is that it should allow you to do away with market definition altogether. You don't need to define a market and then get the market share as a proxy for the competitive effect indirectly: you can simply go to the point. In fact there's

---

[3] Case No COMP/M. 1672.   [4] Case No COMP/M. 3083.

still quite a lot of focus on the market definition question rather than the key question of what is going to be the impact of these particular brands coming together. The *Carnival/P&O* case is such an example. Admittedly this was before the Commission issued the Guidelines on Horizontal Mergers, but this was clearly a case that lent itself extremely well to unilateral effects analysis. Much of the analysis was implicitly about closeness of competition between brands, but it was very much couched in terms of 'What is the relevant market?'; 'Is there a market for British-style cruises as opposed to American-style cruises?', and so on. Other recent examples—I won't go into detail—have focused on highly differentiated product markets. Is competition being eliminated between brands? In fact the question is really pretty much put in terms of 'Is there a high price market as opposed to a low price market?', so we are still in a bit of a twilight world in which unilateral effects analysis is still too closely dealt with in terms of market definition.

The *Centrica/Dynegy* Competition Commission investigation is a case I don't have time to talk about, but if you have an opportunity and want to look up a case in which there is a very detailed analysis of unilateral effects, fully set out and presented as an annex to the report, this is it. The reason why this is interesting is because, prima facie, this was a merger that created the classic unilateral effects question and had all the reasons why one should have been quite sceptical. What this report shows is through very careful measurement of the costs and benefit of increasing prices, you could conclude that there was really no incentive to do so.

I think we are certainly unquestionably getting closer to an economic approach. This is extremely welcome. Obviously as we have heard, all of it has to do with quality of implementation. My expectation is that, while in the past we had certainly an over-expansive use of collective dominance without systematic nailing down the effects, we shouldn't hopefully see the same over-expansive use of unilateral effects as an opportunity to object to mergers without a careful measurement in so far as possible of the effects.

Thank you.

D. Comments

[GREG VISTNES]

One thing I want to add. There seems to be, both in the comments and in the questions that are coming up, some, at least in my mind, confusion as to what unilateral effects analysis consists of. So much of this discussion has been equating unilateral effects analysis with sophisticated models and simulations. That's an end result, that's an end conclusion of unilateral effects, but the very notion of what is unilateral effects can be extraordinarily simple. It doesn't require massive amounts of data to embrace the theory of unilateral effects. Unilateral effects is simply, 'Hey, if I'm going to lose a lot of my business to you pre-merger, but after the merger I don't need to be afraid of that any more, I'm going to raise price because all of a sudden that constraint is no longer there—boom'. That's the basic nutshell of unilateral effects and so to to answer the question, can we 'do' unilateral effects without massive amounts of data, the answer is clearly yes, you can do unilateral effects analysis without those data. In a sense what I was trying to drive across, is the power of unilateral effects; the intuition. Whether or not you take it to the end stage of the massive simulations and data intensive resources is a whole different question.

[PAUL GEROSKI]

Perhaps I could just pick up on one thing from each of the two presentations and then I'll leave you with some words of wisdom from one of the great American thinkers of our time.

Let me preface the remarks by saying every case is different. Every case is special and one has to look at things on a case by case basis. That said, I think I disagree with Greg that unilateral effects is where the action is in mergers and I think I disagree for three reasons. First of all, as Greg has made very clear, the amount of work that has to be put in to building a model that could simulate the effects of mergers is considerable. The amount of data that you require to do that is also considerable. In Europe we have very tight timescales and deadlines, and it's very hard to believe that in the vast majority of cases we would ever manage that. Second, typically when a merger comes to a competition authority you are typically down to your last two or three players in a market. Mergers don't come when there are still 35 players left in the market. When you get down to your last two or three players, the question about coordinated effects is always there, at least on the fringes of your peripheral vision. And third and finally, I think my personal experience is that in the vast majority of cases where there are unilateral effects or coordinated effects, these are not felt across the board. In many cases these effects arise because the merger facilitates the development of price discrimination. This means that certain parties have to bear most of the adverse effects and certain 'don'ts', and much of the unilateral effects analysis that Greg was talking about is just simply not sophisticated or detailed enough to unravel that.

Cristina made a suggestion that unilateral effects were rather easier to measure than coordinated effects and I'd like to disagree with that as well. I don't have to say much because I think Greg has made plain just how difficult it is to measure unilateral effects, and that is the first half of the answer. The second half of the answer is I think that several competition authorities in Europe have become very, very clear, partly thanks to the *Airtours*[1] decision, but partly thanks to their own thinking, about just how to uncover coordinated effects in the market. I don't agree with the speaker who said this morning that it was impossible to flunk these tests. I think a careful reading of the *Safeway* decision makes it absolutely plain that it is quite possible to flunk these tests. Although list-like in character, they are pretty exhaustive and the people who use them know what they are looking for, and so I don't think it is all that difficult. Nonetheless, there is some truth here, and that is that good economics is an art not a science.

Perhaps a quote from one of the deepest, wisest thinkers in the American political scene sums up much of the difficulties that we have been discussing today. His name is Donald Rumsfeld and this is what he had to say:

Reports that say something has or has not happened are always interesting to me because we know there are no knowns. There are things we know we know. We also know there are no unknowns; that is to say that we know that there are some things we do not know, but there are also unknown unknowns. The ones we don't know we don't know.

I think unilateral and coordinated effects fall in the category of known unknowns. Thank you.

---

[1] Case T-342/99 [2002] ECR II-2585, [2002] 5 CMLR 317 annulling the Commission's prohibition decision in Case IV/M.1524 *Airtours/First Choice* OJ [2000] L 93/1, [2000] 5 CMLR 494.

E. Discussion

[MICHAEL HUDSOUGH, *Davidson Company and Partners*]

You were talking about all these models and wondering whether they are predictive or not. My question is, is anyone actually looking at the deals post-merger and looking at empirical evidence to see whether the models were accurate or predictive in any sense?

[PAUL GEROSKI]

I have a very small answer to this. There is a woman in the UK named Margaret Slade who has spent a fair amount of time exhuming the corpses of various cases and she's built a number of models like this and published results, usually some years after the merger. There is a broad (but not perfect) congruence between what her models predicted and what the then Monopolies Commission felt was likely to occur as a result of the merger (although the Monopolies Commission wasn't making as precise a prediction as she was). I think if she were here now, she might well say there's been no fundamental disagreement between what her methods suggested and what our somewhat different methods produced. There's been a little bit of what you might call this retrospective work also on the US in this vein, more ongoing than complete. Whether this work will give us anything like as comprehensive an answer to your question about accuracy and predictability remains to be seen. These models try to calculate price increases and try to figure out what the likely consequences of various proposed mergers have (or would have) been.

[ANDREA APPELLA, *Time Warner*]

I would be interested to hear the views of the panel on a couple of issues that usually come up in unilateral effects analysis. One characteristic that is quite relevant is whether the products are differentiated or homogeneous, and also another area that usually comes up is whether the merging parties are the closest competitors or one of the closest competitors. I would be interested to hear your views as to how the modelling analysis reflects these types of characteristics and how less likely or more likely unilateral effects are likely to be present when these characteristics are there. Thanks.

[GREG VISTNES]

It's a tough question as to how the modelling analysis reflects these types of characteristics. These are, as you say, are they homogeneous or are they differentiated? How differentiated may they be? To some extent, that is captured by the basic elements of what you see. If you see very low margins out there, the chances are fairly good that the products are fairly homogeneous, because it means there is a lot of competition going on. If, when one firm raises price it loses a tremendous amount of business to another rival; again that is more suggestive of homogeneity. Now whether or not you need to answer directly, are they homogeneous or differentiated, or whether instead you look to some of these basic data elements, what are margins, what is the amount of diversion, how much sales do I lose, I think you want to be focusing on some of those indicators of the theories or these questions that you are asking. I hope that makes sense.

[JOHN FINGLETON]

Just on that last question, the competition authorities have discussed the question of making data more available to academics to do this type of work which is, I think, a constraint. I was going to ask two questions. One was, does the absence of zip codes in Europe mean that a lot of the type of econometric research that's best done in the US is unlikely ever to be done at a pan-European level? The second question is, is it best to have two sets of analysis done, one by the parties and one by the authority, or should the economists from the competition authority and the parties be working together on the discovery of truth, if I can put it that way, in these data type analyses? I should say by the way that I am very sympathetic to what Paul said about the lower likelihood of this work being done here. Not just because of zip codes, but most of the smaller authorities in Europe do not have, and I think are very unlikely ever to have, the capability of doing this type of empirical work.

[CRISTINA CAFFARRA]

I think there is no question that the availability of data remains a major problem. From experience, however, there are circumstances in which the data can be generated and although probably not as rich as in the US, I think it's enough to work on. On the second question as to what's best, my experience is that it's unquestionably best to work with the authority on a model, perhaps building it up first and then presenting it and exchanging ideas. *Centrica*[2] is a good illustration of that because it is a

---

[2] <http://www.competition-commission.org.uk/inquiries/completed/2003/centrica/index. htm>.

case in which the work done was shared with the Competition Commission. The Competition Commission questioned it in detail, developed a number of questions on the model, but eventually accepted it, so it's the best way to work, there is no question about that.

[ANDREA APPELLA, *Time Warner*]

I would be interested to hear the views of the panel on a couple of issues that usually come up in unilateral effects analysis. One characteristic that is quite relevant is whether the products are differentiated or homogeneous, and also another area that usually comes up is whether the merging parties are the closest competitors or one of the closest competitors. I would be interested to hear your views as to how the modelling analysis reflects these types of characteristics and how less likely or more likely unilateral effects are likely to be present when these characteristics are there. Thanks.

[CRISTINA CAFFARRA]

I think much of the attention historically has been focused on differentiated products. The point is really that there are two types of assets out there. There's 'capacity' and there's 'brands', and depending on what's really being consolidated, you'll be looking at models in which you want to analyse the homogeneous goods aspect, and models in which you are more interested in understanding how the coming together of brands impacts on competition. What you are doing in each case is trying to put forward a model that best captures these different ways in which firms compete.

[PHILIP MARSDEN]

Any last questions? I just have to quickly ask one of my own which is if, as Cristina said, 'At least let us play for a while with unilateral effects analysis', does the new SIEC test provide any rules for that playground, any guidance?

[CRISTINA CAFFARRA]

I think that there isn't any explicit guidance at all in the new test. It does clarify that mergers will be looked at even if they lead to shares below the conventional 'thresholds for concern' that we were used to before, but there isn't any further guidelines built into that.

CHAPTER 6

Judicial Remedies in Merger Cases—
Three Case Studies

[RICHARD WAINWRIGHT]

I tend to talk about judicial review myself but I guess that must be the same thing. I am a director in the legal service of the Commission and I am now Head of the Competition Team in that service, and one of our jobs, not the only one but probably the most important one in a sense, is to represent the Commission in legal proceedings before all courts in the competition field. That means mainly in front of the Court of First Instance where we win a few and we lose a few, as, no doubt, you will be hearing about later on. We have a strong team here in the green corner. We've got Malcolm Nicholson, who practices in London for Slaughter and May. In the blue corner, Martin Smith, practicing also in London for Simmons & Simmons and on the outside left, just to mix the sporting metaphors, we have Hans Jurgen Meyer-Lindemann, who practices with Shearman and Sterling both in Dusseldorf and in Brussels. I'll perhaps introduce the discussion because we are moving from high science—in a sense, unilateral effects, economics, econometric studies—to low law, arguing a case before the court. I'll start with a small anecdote. I was doing a case a few years ago before the EFTA Court,[1] which probably none of you have ever heard of, which in those days practiced in Geneva. What was at issue was a reference from Finland to the EFTA Court, this was before Finland joined the European Community, and of course it was an issue of an alcohol monopoly, and one of the questions was whether the Finish customs board, which made the reference, was a court for the purposes of the equivalent of what was then Article 177 in the EFTA Treaty, and we didn't know anything about that and I didn't really want to answer. So, I started my speech to the EFTA Court by quoting a small anecdote of the judge who is faced with a case being argued in front him and he hears first the counsel for the plaintiffs and he turns to his clerk at the end of that intervention, very impressed, and he says to the clerk 'I think he's right you know'. So then he listens to the argument for counsel for the defendant. Very impressive, very convincing,

---

[1] European Free Trade Association—EFTA. The EFTA Court, which sits in Luxembourg, carries out the judicial control regarding the EEA Agreement, operating in parallel to the Court of Justice of the European Communities. The EFTA Court has jurisdiction with regard to the EEA EFTA States. More info go to <http://www.eftacourt.lu>.

and at the end of that intervention he turns to his clerk and he said 'I think he's right'. So then the clerk, who is a bright young man, and realizes that his judge is getting out of control says to him, 'well look judge, you've got to decide this case, you know'. And he thinks seriously and he turns to the clerk, he says 'yes, you are right, too'! So with that anecdote, I'll introduce us to the mysteries of pleading cases before European Court before the national courts in Britain and Germany and we will start of first with Malcolm Nicholson, who will tell us about a case, which some of you may have heard of, called *Airtours*.[2] Thank you, Malcolm.

[2] Case T-342/99 [2002] ECR II-2585, [2002] 5 CMLR 317 annulling the Commission's prohibition decision in Case IV/M.1524 *Airtours/First Choice* OJ [2000] L 93/1, [2000] 5 CMLR 494.

A. Malcolm Nicholson

Thank you. I remember speaking to an audience like yourselves at BIICL a couple of years ago and the subject was 'Future Challenges of EU Competition Policy' or something of that sort. And this was at a time after Airtours had launched its appeal but someway before the judgement, and the conundrum I posed was this: the European Court has traditionally adopted an approach involving limited review when the Commission was exercising its discretion in the economic sphere. This dates back to *Consten and Grundig*.[3] In *Consten and Grundig* 1964, the court held, and I quote because its still a good quote, 'the exercise of the Commission's powers necessarily implies complex evaluations on economic matters. A judicial review of these evaluations must take account of their nature by confining itself to an evaluation of the relevance of the facts and the legal consequences which the Commission deduces therefrom'.[4] Now that was articulated in the context of Article 81(3) of the Treaty, but the same approach applies in merger cases, and you will see similar references in *Gencor/Lonrho*[5] for example. How, I asked my audience, were the European courts going to deal with proper judicial review in merger cases? After all, merger control is inextricably linked with the economic valuation of the facts and the competitive effects. A strict adherence to the policy of judicial non-intervention would effectively mean that merger decisions were not justiciable on substantive as opposed to procedural grounds. And I think at that time I was not alone in this fear, at a stage when the Commission Merger Task Force was running amuck, seeming to carry all before it. Now the court in *Airtours* and the subsequent *Schneider/Legrand*[6] and *Tetra/Laval*[7] cases, and I think you need to treat them as a trio, showed that the CFI was, in appropriate instances, prepared to review merger decisions of the Commission in some depth.

What are the principles that emerged from those cases? I think I can group the comments under three headings and just touch on each of them. Firstly, to what extent is the court prepared to engage in economic analysis? Secondly, what is the extent of review of the Commission fact finding?

---

[3] Cases 56 & 58/64 *Consten and Grundig* [1966] ECR 299.
[4] ibid, 347.
[5] Case No IV/M.619 OJ [1997] L 11/30, [1999] 4 CMLR 1076.
[6] Case T-310/01 *Schneider Electric v Commission* [2002] ECR II-4071, [2003] 4 CMLR 768 (annulment of prohibition decision); Case T-77/02 *Schneider Electric v Commission* [2002] ECR II-4201 (annulment of divestiture decision).
[7] Case T-5/02 *Tetra Laval v Commission* [2002] ECR II-4381, [2002] 5 CMLR 1182 (annulment of prohibition decision); Case T-80/02 *Tetra Laval v Commission* [2002] ECR II-4519, [2002] 4 CMLR 1271 (annulment of divestiture decision).

Thirdly, what is the burden of proof applied? Starting with economic analysis, I've neither the time nor the inclination to go into the *Airtours* case in any detail. It will be familiar to most of you, but suffice it to say that the argument related to the meaning of collective dominance and in particular whether this corresponded to the economically familiar concepts of tacit collusion or coordinated effects, I use the two interchangeably. The CFI, in *Airtours*, and also in *Tetra/Laval*, showed that it was prepared to engage with, and try and understand economic theory, at least to the extent necessary to undertake its function of judicial scrutiny and review. Now, without overstating the proposition, it seems to me that the CFI will do so in at least two situations. The first is where the legal and economic contexts are so inextricably intertwined that you cannot deal with the law without some reference to the economics and actually, the meaning of collective dominance, which is after all a legal concept, is a pretty good example of this. Secondly, where the court needs to articulate and state in it's own words the economic proposition contended for, before it can then move on to its more familiar task of seeing if the Commission's fact finding and evidence stacks up against the proposition it is trying to substantiate. And this is the technique that they used in *Airtours*. The Court didn't deal with the theory of collective dominance in terms, it simply said, 'that's theory, I've got to deal with the facts of the case. Facts of the case are this, collective dominance means this, I've got to see whether the facts stack up against the theory'. And that's how it dealt with it and it did the same thing in *Tetral/Laval* but it was talking about leveraging theories. But of course in doing this the Court has to articulate the economic proposition that it's contending for, and give its own expression to that and the idea of competitive harm before it can undertake its normal review function, and the court showed itself prepared to do that.

Secondly, review of fact finding. The CFI is always engaged in analysis of the facts on which the Commission has based a particular decision but I think the three CFI judgements show an intensity of review which makes an appeal to the CFI more akin to a full re-hearing on the merits rather than a mere supervisory review of whether or not the Commission has erred in its application of the law. And this sort of detailed review was very apparent in the Schneider case but it also lay at the core of the *Airtours* case. The CFI's review of the Commission's case on collective dominance in *Airtours* was about 250 paragraphs. The court identified 10 key planks that the Commission was contending for, supported by underlying evidence and looked, examined and found against the Commission on every single aspect of that. It was a pretty ruthless demolition job. That's pretty satisfactory for the lawyer acting for the client when that happens, though to balance that, I have to say that I was in the CFI a couple of weeks ago on an entirely different case. Same panel of judges, same detailed review of the facts and they found against me on every single one and for the Commission, so it doesn't always go your way. Now that intensity of review to which the CFI is, in appropriate cases, subjected to, is a matter of some concern to the Commission. The Commission, you know, is appealing *Tetra/Laval* to the full European Court of Justice, and one of the stated grounds, at least from the press release, is that the CFI has, quote, 'exceeded its role' by substituting, quote, 'its view of the case for that of the Commission's', so there is an area of debate over the degree of judicial review of fact finding.

Finally the burden of proof. The starting point is a concern felt, I think, in some quarters that whilst mergers are presumptively lawful (I say this, although I think Enrique is in the audience and he's argued to the contrary with me before now) sometimes the Commission has sought to prohibit them, really, on somewhat flimsy grounds that involve more speculation as to the resulting competitive harm, than hard fact. And I think what the CFI appears to be saying in its three judgements is that the Commission cannot merely state that a particular consequence may flow from a merger. It must demonstrate that there is a sufficiently high degree of likelihood that that competitive harm will occur. Reliance on assertion and presumption is not sufficient to ground a merger prohibition. And that has a particular resonance in merger cases where the analysis is necessarily predictive, actually perhaps particularly so in my collective dominance case, because collective dominance relies on inferring conduct and behaviour from a series of surrounding circumstances. Again I think the Commission is concerned about the level of proof to which it is being put because again on the *Tetra/Laval* appeal the disproportionate standard of proof sought by the court is one of the factors of that appeal. So that I think sets the background for where I see judicial review in Europe and we can come back on some of those points if necessary.

[RICHARD WAINWRIGHT]

Very good, thank you Malcolm. Now we will turn straight to Martin to talk about the UK experience.

B. Martin Smith

Thank you Richard. If I may, I'll exercise a degree of 'speaker/artistic licence' by not only focusing my remarks on the *Interbrew* case,[8] because in fact although the *Interbrew* decision of the High Court[9] in the UK was decided only just over two years ago a lot has happened in the UK in the intervening period, but I'm going to also comment briefly on where we've come from, where we are and where we are going, and to quote the advertising slogan, the future's bright, the future's orange and the future's tomorrow because, as you already heard this morning, the Competition Appeal Tribunal in the UK will be hearing or giving judgement in its first case brought under the Enterprise Act in relation to a merger and we wait with baited breath to see what the president and his colleagues will decide in terms of the nature of judicial review in this first test case.[10]

In terms of where we've come from, as was remarked this morning, the test under the Fair Trading Act, the predecessor to the Enterprise Act of 2002, was this broad public interest test, interpreted in latter years, very much from the point of view of focus on competition issues, but nevertheless couched in very broad terms and competition issues were occasionally not the basis of a referral decision to the Commission. Equally we didn't have duties to refer. Instead we had discretions to refer and a combination of those factors meant that the authorities had a very, very broad discretionary role. That was then set against the traditional grounds of judicial review in the UK, familiar to all of you, procedural unfairness, error of law and then the famous Wednesbury test, the irrationality test, the 'no reasonable regulator could have done this' test, and as a result a) there were very few cases of judicial review brought in the UK under the Fair Trading Act of 1973, I think in total around 16 or 17, and the success rate of the UK authorities and essentially of the Competition Commission as the second phase body making recommendations to the Secretary of State, was a phenomenal one. Prior to the *Interbrew*[11] case it was a no cases lost record and I think it reflected the factors that I just referred to. The courts were singularly reluctant to get at all involved in the substance of the case. They saw a large area of discretion. They saw, essentially, economic factors at play, economic assessments being made and the courts were therefore really looking to see

---

[8] See Competition Commission website; <http://www.competition-commission.org.uk/inquiries/completed/2001/index.htm>.
[9] Dated 25 May 2001, Queen's Bench Division, Administrative Court before the Honourable Justice Moses.
[10] Case No 1023/4/1/03 *IBA Health Limited v Office of Fair Trading*.
[11] <http://www.competition-commission.org.uk/inquiries/completed/2001/index.htm>.

if there were any procedural grounds on which a challenge could successfully be brought and in none of the cases prior to *Interbrew*, was that the
case. Very briefly on *Interbrew* itself, the case started in Brussels. It was an
EC merger case. It was referred back to the UK by the Commission under
Article 9. There were limited elements outside the UK which were in fact
cleared by the European Commission, but the principal effects of the
merger were on the UK market. The matter was referred back to the
Competition Commission and the Competition Commission issued a prohibition recommendation which was followed by the Secretary of State. That
decision was taken in January 2001. Interbrew had to move quickly if it
was going to move and identified one area of the report in which it believed
that there had been procedural unfairness which was to do with the remedial recommendation, the basis on which one possible remedy which had
been floated with the company had been rejected, had not been aired with
company. That was the company's case and it was that very narrow focus
on which Interbrew brought its application. Whatever its views may have
been on the substance of the case, it was clear that there was no basis, under
English judicial review law, in which to challenge the substance but it
believed there was a procedural case to answer and the judgement of Mr
Justice Moses, delivered in May of 2001, found in favour of the company
on that point. The matter was remitted, in fact, to the Office of Fair
Trading. I think remittal there rather than to the Commission because the
substantive findings were not in dispute or not the subject of the application at least, and the Commission's role on remedies was advisory anyway
in those days, and so the matter was remitted to the OFT to advise the
minister and in the event a remedial package, as it were, was the ultimate
upshot of the case.

I think if you contrast with what Malcolm has been saying about the
European situation, I think there emerges a very significant contrast in two
key respects and they are flip sides of each other. There was no prospect
whatsoever, in realistic terms of having any form of substantive review of
the substantive findings of the Commission. That just wasn't possible under
traditional English law, but on the other hand, what was possible was swift
review in relation to the procedural aspect. I think *Airtours* took three years
from start to finish. What is, I think, notable in the context of *Interbrew*
was that the application was made in February of 2001 and the judgement
was delivered in May, three months later and relief had a tangible effect.
Unlike in the *Airtours* case, where the deal was well and truly dead and
buried by the time it got to the CFI, the remedial relief in the *Interbrew*
context did have some tangible effect. So, limited scope for substantive
challenge, but swift review on procedure.

Now, what are the main changes of relevance under the Enterprise Act of

2002, relevant from a judicial review perspective? I'll go through these fairly quickly because some have been touched on this morning in other contexts. As we all know, we now have a substantial lessening of competition test in the UK and therefore we have a test with a much sharper focus than the public interest test under the Fair Trading Act. Secondly, as we have already heard, the Office of Fair Trading now has a duty to refer to the Competition Commission if it believes there is or may be an SLC. I think Simon Priddis, this morning, said, and I think he is right in saying so, that albeit cast as a duty, there is inherently an element of discretion there because it is a duty to refer something which the OFT believes to be the case, and therefore there is inevitably an element of discretion there. We will come back in a moment to how that element of discretion may be tested by the Competition Appeal Tribunal, but nevertheless, a duty. Thirdly, the Commission is now a decision making body. It's not merely a recommending body and I think that is significant in a judicial review context because one of the features of the UK system and one of its singular elements of opaqueness was that the one person that you never had a chance to get close to was the ultimate decision maker, the Secretary of State. Granted, the Secretary of State's discretion was fettered to some degree if the Competition Commission found something not to be against the public interest, he or she could not decide otherwise, but if there was a finding of something being against the public interest, the Secretary of State's remedial rights were really unfettered, and there were a number of cases in which the remedies recommendation of the Commission, not many but a number, where the Secretary of State did not follow that and the reasoning for not following was set out in very short order in a press release, in very short order indeed. Now we have a decision making body, the Commission, which will have to publish its findings, as it has done in the past, but whose findings will also be the basis of the decision being taken. And then fourthly, and importantly, judicial review is now in the hands of a specialist tribunal, not the administrative court. So those I think are 4 key features of the new legislative model, and the key in the context of judicial review.

So what can we expect? And as I say I am in, I think all of us are in, a luxurious position today that we can simply engage in informed speculation. Tomorrow (after the release of the *IBA Health* judgment) we will know rather more. How much more we must wait to see but we will know at least a little more. So what can we expect in terms of substantive approach? Well a number of factors. First, as I say, a numbers of factors in my view which take us towards a more intensive review. Where exactly that may be is a matter still to speculate upon but certainly a more intensive review, perhaps closer to the CFI model. First, we have judicial review vested in a specialist body—a Competition Appeal Tribunal—that is only dealing with competition matters, be it under the competition act, be it under the Enterprise Act. Secondly, the first president of the CAT, Sir Christopher Bellamy, is himself a former judge of the CFI and I think his EU pedigree, his CFI background is clearly coming out in his role, admittedly a full appellate role, but it is an appellate role under the Competition Act, and I think that background is inevitably going to inform his approach when it comes to judicial review applications on mergers. Thirdly, we have this sharper much more sharply focused test that I've referred to which gives the reviewing body something more to get a grip on. And fourthly, and I think in the context of remedies it is worth noting that the Enterprise Act imposes a duty on the Commission, when considering remedial action, 'to have regard to the need to achieve as comprehensive a solution as is reasonable and practical to the substantial lessening of competition and any adverse effects resulting from it'.[12] The word 'reasonable' is expressly used in the statute and that I think provides something of a handle on which to rest a proportionality approach and proportionality is a well-known EU tenet but one which the English courts, traditionally in judicial review contexts, have been reluctant on the whole, and I say on the whole but reluctant on the whole, to embrace.

And then finally just an observation. I think we can expect to see in terms of substance a difference of approach between review of decisions of the OFT on the one hand, and decisions of the Competition Commission, and therefore I don't think necessarily that tomorrow's decision will tell us a huge amount about the approach to review of a Competition Commission decision issued after 5–6 months of extensive review. What is interesting about the case tomorrow is that it is a case brought by a third party in relation to a decision not to refer, and therefore that decision was conclusive for the case. There was a final decision not to refer. In a situation where the OFT refers, that decision is not final. It may be conclusive for the transaction of course for commercial reasons, but it is not final for the case. And I think one of the arguments, one of the many arguments, in front of the tribunal is that it may be that the nature of review in relation to those two types of OFT decision are not the same. I've already commented about the swiftness of judicial review in the English Law context against the European model but the down side appears to be one in relation to substance. Under the Enterprise Act, applications for judicial review in the merger context will have to be made within four weeks. Thereafter, the process is not spelt out and it's down to the CAT. It is remarkable, I think, that even in relation to a relatively narrow focus case, with not a huge amount of papers necessarily, the CAT is basically proposing to deliver judgment about ten business days

12 Section 35(4), Enterprise Act 2002.

after the application was made for review. I think that is quite a remarkable feature. Now whether the tribunal can keep that up as its case law grows and in relation to much more complicated factual matrices, for example at the end of a Competition Commission enquiry where there will be potentially much more for the tribunal to look at, is I think an open question, but there's no doubt that the CAT wants to start off as it means to go on and to move things along very speedily.

My final comment, before I briefly sum up, is in relation to the impact particularly on the Competition Commission procedures. It was noted this morning that the OFT has come a very long way in the last couple of years in relation to its procedures and that is true. Even two years ago, it was the case that parties before the Commission had to comment on remedies in what was called a hypothetical way, with no knowledge, maybe some reasonable bases for suspicion, but no knowledge as to what the Commission's likely findings were going to be on the substance. Now we have a situation, and this was coming about even before the Enterprise Act, whereby the Commission now, and the *Stena AB/P&O*[13] cases is the first one in which this has happened, is issuing the parties, and indeed making public, provisional findings before remedies are addressed. So there are considerable changes already under way. In relation to the vexed issue of access to file or access to key documents, I think access was something of an anathema in Commission corridors. The chairman of the Commission in July issued guidelines in which he has taken the Commission further than has ever been the case before in terms of indications that third party material will be put to parties.[14] Those guidelines I think are still slightly ambiguous. They talk about summaries, not simply non-confidential summaries, but genuinely summaries and I think the jury is still out as how fully the Commission is embracing access to key documents, but I think things are afoot and my guess is that the Commission in some degree is trying to anticipate what might be the approach of the tribunal.

Now to sum up my view in terms of what judicial review should be about is this. I believe that judicial review in the competition context should be about ensuring that the regulator has applied rigorous scrutiny in the course of its decision making. It should ensure that its substantive findings are adequately reasoned and should ensure that it operates a fully transparent system. I don't believe that judicial review should be about essentially just another hearing in front of another body at the behest of, as it were, a losing party. I don't think judicial review should be something that one has to resort to very frequently. Ideally the knowledge that judicial review is

[13] See <http://www.competition-commission.org.uk/inquiries/current/stena/index.htm>.
[14] See <http://www.competition-commission.org.uk/rep_pub/rules_and_guide/index.htm>.

available and the knowledge of its intensity should be the key elements that cause the decision maker to do the right thing in the first place within the margin of discretion that it has to operate within if the system is going to work properly at all.

[RICHARD WAINWRIGHT]

Very good. Thank you Martin. We will go straight on now to Hans Jurgen to tell us a little bit about the German experience.

C. Hans Jürgen Meyer-Lindemann

Thank you and good afternoon. Yes I will just talk about one case here, the *E.ON/Ruhrgas* case, but I am sure if I can lead you through this case then you will know almost everything about the judicial remedies in Germany. But before I come to the judicial remedies I should talk about the facts and the facts are somewhat simplified here. I start in Summer 2001. At that time E.ON had the opportunity to take over Ruhrgas, the big German gas supplier. It applied to the Bundeskartellamt for clearance of its intended acquisition of a 60 per cent majority of the gas company. E.ON intended to purchase Ruhrgas shares held by the companies Gelsenberg and Bergemann. The merger would make E.ON/Ruhrgas Europe's biggest energy company by combining Ruhrgas' strength in the gas sector with E.ON's strong position on the electricity sector. All shareholders in Ruhrgas were prepared to sell their respective shares, so Exxon, Shell, BP, the Gelsenberg shares, and the shareholders in Bergemann were also prepared to sell their shares to E.ON. The most important shareholder in this respect was RAG AG, the big German coal company and majority shareholder. RAG asked for an exchange of shares. RAG wanted to acquire the shares of Degussa-Hüls AG, a chemical company, and E.ON agreed with this deal. I mention this because this swap was very important for the timing of the whole transaction because the Degussa transaction had to be completed by 31 January 2003, so in other words, the parties had 18 months approximately to go through with this transaction and needless to say that the whole transaction was reliant on the Degussa acquisition.

What happened? It was a three-stage acquisition. First of all E.ON acquired 51 per cent of Gelsenberg AG and this was subject to German merger control. Why was it not subject to EU merger control? Because of the two thirds rule—this changed later on after the acquisition of Powergen in the UK.[15] The second step was the acquisition of Bergemann which was also subject to German merger control. The Degussa transaction was subject to European merger control,[16] but did not raise serious doubts as to its compatibility with the Common Market and with the EEA Agreement, and the Exxon and Shell transactions were not subject to merger control because E.ON would have acquired control beforehand. We know the merger control result of all this here. The federal cartel office in Bonn came back and said no, and so the Gelsenberg and the Bergemann transactions were prohibited.

---

[15] Case No COMP/M. 2443—E.ON/Powergen.
[16] Case No COMP/M. 2854—RAG/Degussa.

And that's where I have to talk about the judicial remedies. So the federal cartel office said no, and normally what you then is you go to the competent court of appeals which is the Court of Appeals in Dusseldorf, and then you go to the Federal Supreme Court. All that takes about 15 months for the Court of Appeals, but in this case it would have taken longer and for the next instance it will take another one and a half years, so this would have taken three years. This was of course too long because the transaction was reliant on Degussa. But, nevertheless, in order to protect their rights, E.ON lodged an appeal with the Court of Appeals in Dusseldorf. But there was another alternative and they could do this in parallel. They could go to the German Minister of Economics and ask for clearance. The test there is different from the test to be used by the Federal Cartel Office. It is, of course, a political test, and allows the Ministry of Economics as a special cartel office to overrule a decision by the Federal Cartel Office if 'the restraint of competition is outweighed by advantages to the economy as a whole following from the concentration, or if the concentration is justified by an overriding public interest'. So the question is, is the alleged restraint of competition outweighed by the advantages for the economy as a whole or justified when overriding public interest? The Minister of Economics had four months to think about this issue and then to come back with an answer. Before that, he was obliged under section 42(4) GWB[17] to ask the Monopolies Commission but its opinion is only a recommendation and thus not binding. The Monopolies Commission judged the intended merger negative for the German competitive situation but the Minister of Economics cleared the transaction.

Now third parties came into play. Nine complainants appeared on the scene and lodged an appeal against the ministerial decision. This appeal also went to the Court of Appeals in Dusseldorf. This appeal had no suspensive effect so in addition the complainants had to ask for injunctive relief which is what they did. The Court of Appeals suspended the merger on 2 August 2002 on a procedural basis due to procedural faults. The Minister of Economics read these decisions and thought he could do better and therefore tried the whole thing again. He set up another hearing and went back to the Monopolies Commission. The Monopolies Commission again said no but then he just amended the first decision and came back with a new amended first decision subject to certain remedies and that was the decision the Court of Appeals had to decide upon. On 16 December, the Court of Appeals again said no, we still need the suspensive effect. Everybody has to wait until the 31 January 2003, the very last possible date for a successful transaction, and the closer this date came, the more the parties were afraid

<hr>

[17] Gesetz gegen Wettbewerbsbeschränkungen (Act Against Restraints of Competition).

of a possible negative decision and in all likelihood it would have been negative. So E.ON tried to talk to the complainants, but the complainants were not interested in a negative decision. They were not so much interested in competition, they were more interested in getting something out of this here. So the parties met, and met several times, and finally on 30 January, they entered into a settlement agreement. E.ON paid, allegedly, €90,000,000 and helped these nine complainants. It helped a Finish complainant to build a pipeline from West Siberia to Finland and things like that, so these were very private remedies and had nothing to do with competition in Germany, but as a result of all this, the complainants withdrew their appeals. So there were no appeals anymore and the ministerial decision became effective, literally, at the very last minute and E.ON could then take our Ruhrgas.

So what do we learn form all that? We have different remedies from the cartel office; you can go to the Court of Appeals, to the Supreme Court. All that takes very, very long and from a practical point of view it very often doesn't make sense. There is, of course, this political recourse but it's also very risky. We have had 18 cases, six ended positively for the parties of the appellants, so the chances of success are relatively small in this regard but this is a possibility and we have very far reaching third party rights. They reach even too far according to the legislators. They want to change this and we will see that they will cut back on these third party rights in the next amended Act Against Restraints of Competition. So that's the system and that's how *E.ON/Rurhgas* worked. It had nothing to do with unilateral effects or sophisticated theories. It had a lot to do with simple, procedural steps but that's the way sometimes things happen also in Germany. Thank you.

[RICHARD WAINWRIGHT]

Thank you Hans Jurgen for bringing us back to earth with that cliff hanger. It was a bit like a Buster Keaton movie sometimes. I think I will try and round up by perhaps asking each of my colleagues to comment on a statement which was made, I think, by one of the interventions this morning, which suggested, and they can have this reflected either at the Community or the national level, that after the *Airtours* and the other judgments which we don't talk about, the Commission, to some extent, went overboard and started asking lots of irrelevant questions and far too many people and digging far too far back and in a sense over reacting. There was a suggestion that this was a negative reaction to too much judicial review and I'd like to ask each of the panellists, perhaps starting in the reverse order. Hans Jurgen do you have anything interesting or wise to say in relation to that intervention?

D. Discussion

[HANS JÜRGEN MEYER-LINDEMANN]

Sorry I don't think I understood you correctly. Was it whether there is too much judicial review?

[RICHARD WAINWRIGHT]

The question is, in the relation to the effect that judicial review can have on the behaviour of the regulatory authority, whether judicial review is benign or not benign or has no effect at all. Do you have any thing to say about that?

[HANS JÜRGEN MEYER-LINDEMANN]

In Germany it has a big impact and since E.ON Ruhrgas I think the situation has changed completely because of the president or the judge who presided over this panel of the Court of Appeals in Dusseldorf. He really went into all these procedural issues and made this very, very clear, and in the future I think it will be very difficult to comply with what the expectations of the Court of Appeals Dusseldorf were and are. This presiding judge is no longer there. Now his successor is an expert of medical law but nevertheless I think the standard will still be a high one and it will not be easy for the competition authorities to comply with the standard and they will work very thoroughly after this decision and other similar decisions I think.

[[MARTIN SMITH]

I think there is that risk. If you would like for me to comment from the UK perspective, I think the risk is slightly less in the UK because of the split system, but if the proposition was far too much information being sought in a case which didn't really justify it, I think a lot there will depend on how the tribunal interprets the role of the OFT. If it takes a slightly different view in terms of review of the OFT as compared with the Commission then I think the risk is lower because I think cases before the Commission will require a very significant amount of information, so I think there is that issue and the danger obviously is that a regulator essentially becomes obsessed with how to make itself 'judicial review proof', which is not the purpose in my view of judicial review but you can see how it becomes a chicken and egg situation. That's the regulators focus in life and that will be an unfortunate consequence of greater intensity of review. So there is a risk but I think it requires the system to be played sensibly.

[MALCOLM NICHOLSON]

I think there is a risk. I would like to think that that risk was actually obviated or reduced with intelligence brought to bear by the people running the enquiry as to the lines of investigation that they feel they need to pursue. I would like to think that something of a constructive dialogue frankly between the people whose merger is under examination and the regulator, and I suppose third party complainants, can help identify what these issues are. If you were getting deeper and more intensive questioning then this must be relevant questioning. Like all these things, the system is as good as the people who I think are playing the system, using the system at that moment in time.

CHAPTER 7

Managing the Antitrust Risk in Global Deals

Francisco Enrique Gonzalez-Diaz

After the technicalities of economic analysis of unilateral effects and the intricacies of judicial review both at European level and international level, we are going to have a relatively cosy panel this afternoon on the hands-on problems of how to go about multi-national filings. To have this discussion we have today both Bill Baer and Chris Bright. They are both very experienced lawyers with a lot of prior exposure to relatively or highly complex cases on both sides of the Atlantic and they are going to give us their views on how to go about these types of complex transactions. Chris you are going to start with the presentation on this.

A. Chris Bright

Thank you. We really wanted, I think, to go from the world of theory to the world of practice and talk a bit about what all this means in trying to do deals. Most of us, whatever capacity we are here in today, are really only here because, in my case, my clients, certainly corporations out there, are wanting to do deals, and I think we should spend some time thinking about the interaction of all of these processes with the deal-doing process. There clearly are a whole range of other tensions in commercial transactions in M & A deals other than the antitrust issues, and I'm just thinking briefly about things such as integration planning, protection of the goodwill of the company being taken over and other issues like that. We do need to be mindful of those as we go forward and one of the things that has emerged from this morning's and this afternoon's debates is a tendency to go for perfection in our antitrust reviews. We have, I think, in Europe and certainly in the UK, a sort of process of permanent revolution as we try and re-think, to improve the processes, and that has a lot of consequences in terms of doing deals and we will come on to those. But we do need, at some point, to stand back and say this is but one part, albeit a part that's important in protecting the public interest, of a process which is driven by other considerations. So I wanted really to start by saying what are we trying to achieve when we are doing this work and I think from an adviser's point of view, certainly, life is very simple in terms of what we are trying to do.

We are trying to deliver a deal within a time frame and within the commercial parameters set by the client and I think it is important to focus on that. That is the goal and we shouldn't forget it. I think one thing that is worth commenting on here is the tendency, as we have these debates particularly with regulators present, to be antipathetic to the regulatory process and to say 'you could do it better this way, you could do it better that way'. One thing we should recognize is that there are some deals that are not 'doable' from an antitrust perspective, but I think, when we talk about delivering a deal within a time frame and within certain commercial parameters, one of the responsibilities we have, certainly with the client given that ultimately it's the clients choice though, is to identify those cases which are either very difficult to do or probably 'un-doable', and hopefully part of the job of managing antitrust risk is actually screening those cases out. There are always going to be cases which are in the grey area which you cannot predict very well and there are going to be cases which, for strategic reasons, for instance where companies with maybe one last chance to do a deal before they know they cannot go any further, want to identify where their regulatory limit is. People will go and test the limits, which is fine, but we do need to be sensible about what is doable and what isn't. The one question, and I think others will come back to this I am sure and there are certainly people in the audience who are concerned about it, is how big is the grey area and what is the consequence of the developments that we've seen over the last couple of years, in terms of making predictability less certain? If we are going to spend time both on the theory and on working it out in practice, looking at modelling and so on and so forth, that is one area where the grey area is going to be quite large for a while but nonetheless that's life. We have to get on with it.

Moving on, I particularly wanted to concentrate on four areas: the selection of jurisdictions and the management of filings and timetable. Today we've been focusing mostly on the EU, the US and Member States. Clearly there are powers of other jurisdictions out there to additionally consider, some of which have more meat on them than others these days. I will talk about terms that must be included in transaction documents, the consequences of using such terms and conclude with a discussion about document preparation by the parties and by advisors and the implications they have for the regulatory process.

So, starting with the selection of jurisdiction and management of filings and timetables, I think the first point to say is we all have devised mechanisms for collecting information on multiple jurisdictions, but how ever much information you collect, I think you find that you don't have enough and that as you go into these transactions, particularly large international deals, you find that you can never be absolutely certain about every jurisdiction in terms of 'do you qualify for investigation in that jurisdiction or not?' The level of certainty needed does have a cost implication, and we will come back to that as we go through this process, but it is not infrequent that you will find now that you have more than 10, maybe 20 jurisdictions to think about in terms of 'do I have to file, and if so, what am I to do about it?' I think the question that I really want to get to by making this statement, 'multiple reviews may appear necessary', is to go on and ask whether all these filings are inevitable? I do think we need to develop as practitioners certainly a pragmatic approach to these filing requirements. The idea that you identify twenty countries and then spend your life dealing with them is great at one level in terms of business generation from a law firm's perspective, but on the other hand it is not necessarily terribly productive, and I think there are a whole range of areas where you can cut down on the jurisdictions that you really do have to deal with, up front, as you are dealing with a transaction.

So, just picking from three issues, voluntary regimes. Voluntary I think in two senses. In the UK we have a voluntary regime, you don't have to file if you don't want to file. It may be that one day someone will catch up with you and send you a bill for processing the case but in cases where there are clearly no competition issues, and as we all know the majority of cases are like that, you don't have to bother with the system. So the question in voluntary jurisdictions is, is this one that you have to make? We'll come on to the documentation, conditions precedent for doing the deal if there's really no risk. The other aspect of voluntary regimes, I suppose, is that although some countries, Brazil is one, have mandatory filing requirements, they don't have mandatory suspensory provisions. What are you going to do about those jurisdictions? There are a bunch of countries where, although there are mandatory regimes both in terms of filing and suspension, should you be dealing with transactions that are largely foreign to them, they will turn a blind eye. What do you do with those jurisdictions? Do you file in them? Don't you? And then there is the issue ultimately that if you decide that there are some jurisdictions that you have to deal with but which are not really commercially significant in the transaction, and which may be delaying factors, can you try and ring-fence them in the deal and have a sequenced closing for them. Actually it's something that happens also in relation to employment law, particularly in France where consultation requirements tend to be difficult to meet. So we can narrow down the number of jurisdictions that we file in and ultimately the risk profile of both parties, and they may have completely different risk profiles. Typically the tension in negotiating these things is that the purchaser wants maximum legal certainty and will try and do as many of these jurisdictions as possible. The vendor, obviously, is after getting the money, whatever it is, pretty quickly and is trying to reduce the list of these filings, and so we have to find what the balance is and what the overall risk profile is. There are companies who will say certainly that if there is a mandatory filing anywhere, they will do it and they will wait because they have large international profiles and they don't want to offend anyone in these jurisdictions. Other people will take different approaches and one of the big issues in all of this is simply the issue of cost. The cost of going through all of these filings is huge and some people will decide that the balance is in favour of not dealing with all of them.

The big issue though, really, when you get to the end of all of this, having decided which jurisdictions you are going to go to, is the issue of coordination and scheduling. From the point of view of doing a deal, the issue of when you file in any particular jurisdiction is an issue that needs to be looked at from the convenience of the parties not the convenience of the agencies. I think the discussion this morning was very much about trying to align timetables which may be convenient for agencies but it seems to me there are a limited set of circumstances where that is really necessary from the parties' point of view. In most cases you are dealing with markets which are not global; however, even so, if you are going to have a review by two agencies of the same markets within the same time frame, maybe you want to coordinate timetables. If you want to coordinate remedies, you may want to coordinate timetables, but in many situations you are going to be looking at what is the advantage to the parties of moving forward, and typically the advantages that you want to get—certainty into the transaction and uncertainty out of the transaction. We have people here who spend their lives looking at deal risk along the way in transactions, not the parties but people who are intermediaries dealing in shares along the way, and the fact that that market exists and that people can turn a buck on how much uncertainty is out there, just goes to show the importance of trying to close down these issues as quickly as you can in most deals.

So, going on to the documentation, just to start off covering the area that we've just been talking about, the first thing that you are going to need to identify is what jurisdictions need to be put into the agreement as conditions precedent to closing. We've discussed that a little bit already. We are going to need to look at interaction where the take-over rules apply obviously, in the UK for instance. The UK Take-over Code has some limitations on what you can do with conditions precedent and in terms of the overall bid timetable, the UK system is recognised as a possible intervening jurisdiction. Where intervention happens, you can extend your timetable—with other jurisdictions you cannot. Those things need to be taken into account. We've had the wonderful events coming out of the French system with *Schneider/Legrand*[1] and *Tetra Laval*[2] where difficulties have arisen. Clearly in France, those things have changed but there are other jurisdictions with similar problems. The issue of when do the parties want to close and how does this relate to filing is one of the key issues. I think as we all sit here and talk about the Brussels process, we think of it as a 5-month process. The truth is that this is not so in any case of significant competition interest. The reality is you look at filing dates, notifying dates against announcement dates. Typically it's taking probably around two months in a significant case for people to file their COs, sometimes more, sometimes less, so you are talking probably about a seven-month process possibly longer if you get a stopping of the clock, and it does seem that as we go out into these more adventurous areas of economic analysis, the likelihood of stopping the clock is going to increase, simply because the parties are unlikely to have delivered the information necessary for the modelling up front, and in the form CO there's going to need to be information requests, Article 11 requests. These are going to take time to comply with. So you are seeing, I think, these deadlines running out. In the UK we've become very accustomed to the Take Over Code as a 80-day time limit for a deal and we're unfortunately moving well away from the concept of doing deals in a contained time and much closer to the American model where for a long time you've had deals which have hung around for a year or so but nonetheless have managed to complete. Making a realistic assessment of what is going to be needed is really important in terms of managing expectations of the client and certainly making sure you can deal with agency expectations as well.

That takes us on to what contractual obligations you are going to have in these agreements in relation to Merger Control filings and into a whole bunch of issues on risk. One of the things that really is absolutely essential is the issue of what the parties agree to in terms of the efforts they are going to use to get clearances. Now, in a take-over situation in the UK for instance, this is academic because you cannot actually agree to these things. In the US you can have a merger agreement and you can agree to these things and obviously for market transactions as well, but, as you know, we all spend hours haggling over 'best efforts', 'reasonable best efforts', 'reasonable efforts', 'commercially reasonable efforts', all these different

---

[1] Case T-310/01 *Schneider Electric v Commission* [2002] ECR II-4071, [2003] 4 CMLR 768 (annulment of prohibition decision); Case T-77/02 *Schneider Electric v Commission* [2002] ECR II-4201 (annulment of divestiture decision).

[2] Case T-5/02 *Tetra Laval v Commission* [2002] ECR II-4381, [2002] 5 CMLR 1182 (annulment of prohibition decision); Case T-80/02 *Tetra Laval v Commission* [2002] ECR II-4519, [2002] 4 CMLR 1271 (annulment of divestiture decision).

phrases, but ultimately the issue is a liability issue in these situations. We often go into transactions: we know there's regulatory risk, and from a vendor perspective, you are wanting the purchaser to assume the risk. From a purchaser perspective you are wanting to be able to walk away if things don't turn out all right without having to do things you don't want to do, and so these words have become to have a very significant importance. In the US, now, we have a bunch of cases developing in different state courts in terms which seek to define the meaning of these words, and how far people have to go: if you say 'reasonable efforts', are you required to sell maybe up to 5 per cent of what you are buying?

And there are further related issues. For example, risk shifting provisions, where the purchaser will sell A, B, and C. People don't like them for obvious reasons—they provides a route map for the agency—and then you go back to relying on your best efforts, 'reasonable efforts' wording. How far do you have to go in defending transactions if you get a reference to the Competition Commission or a Phase II? Can you walk away? Typically you wouldn't want to but in the US for instance, you may get your negative decision and then you have to make a choice, are you going to oblige the purchaser, if you are on the vendor side, to go through with a challenge? It is worth noting that if we ever get to the point, for instance, where the Court of First Instance does things in 3 months, let alone 10 days, it may be that we will want to do the same in Europe. Corporation covenants are a big issue, I think, in these deals. In hostile take-overs typically you've got the target obviously not being cooperative and it's really then down to the agency. I'm sure Enrique has had these situations where you get half the file, in a sense, from the bidder. You have to get the target to cooperate with the agency through the agency, but in other situations there is the opportunity to tie down the vendor to cooperate in what they are doing. There is a mutuality of interest in this because I think for many, as we are moving into these situations of greyness and not being able to know where the risk is and so on, the vendor is going to want to have a significant presence in the processing of the case and so there is some debate to be had there.

Undoubtedly people can spend quite a long time negotiating these things. Break-up fees—something we haven't really been familiar with historically. But we are finding that people in the sale process are reluctant to sign up unless there is some benefit to them should things fall apart for regulatory reasons. So you see break up fees becoming more common; they are not common, but becoming more common.

As you are all aware, we all spend ages negotiating warranties and covenants and indemnities in sale and purchase agreements. Typically, nothing much comes out of them but there have been at least three cases recently where, as a consequence of the increased cartel investigation activity, deals have fallen apart post-signing/pre-completion, even though we have not done anything wrong in terms of entering into a cartel kind of covenant. You get an agency investigation announcement 'disclosed' and people then feel very diffident about obviously closing the deal, and we have had a number of cases that have collapsed as a consequence. It's important to have them in there to get them right. I just wanted to move on to a couple of other things: partly I put these other issues in because Enrique and I had been talking about them in the context of a deal.

Confidentiality agreements: it's very difficult to do these things on a unilateral basis. If they are going to be meaningful, you need to pool information between the parties; you need economists to be working through the information; you may need people in the companies to be working through the information to be able to make any sense of the task in hand. So it is obviously critical that people involved in those processes have confidentiality agreements. In the US there is a practice, and Bill may speak more of that, of Joint Defence Agreements which go further down the road in terms of trying to protect against agency intervention, in terms of exchange of information if it was thought to be too aggressive. One of the issues that has come out, and is an issue that is there for debate in the European context particularly, is the role of in-house counsel in these arrangements. We still have this issue open, although the courts are obviously beginning to look at it again, but where will they get to? I do not know of in-house lawyers in Europe not having protection of privilege and that sort of filters into this whole process. To what extent can they then be involved in your Joint Defence Agreements? Lastly, and this really goes back to the issue of risk allocation, one of the things we do find is that people do not want to set up an agreement whereby they are going to do A, B, or C if the agency asks them to do it because the belief is, rightly or wrongly, that the agency is more likely to ask you to do it if you said you will and they can see that. So the practice of having some sort of side letter has developed in some instances and there are interesting issues which we can talk about a bit more, about how side letters work; the extent of your obligation to the agency in relation to disclosure, how you protect side letters from being discovered, and so on and so forth.

Moving on, I just wanted to touch on this issue because it is an issue that I think is increasingly problematic. Obviously, in the US, we've had the experience for a very long time now of heavy document discovery by the agencies. In the European systems I think that has been there to an extent, but not to the extent it is now and I think there are issues that people should be focused on in terms of preparing for these cases. The first thing obviously is to recognise that these are processes that require disclosure, and increasingly higher levels of disclosure, of documentation. In addition it must be recognised that non-privileged documents of the parties and the advisors, and it is important to focus on particularly the investment bankers who do a lot of the preparatory work in these cases, are going to be reviewed and that care and attention and preparation of all of these things is really important. Not just the board presentation on what the benefits of the deal are, but in strategy papers lying behind that and actually in financial models as well. I think there is a lot to be learnt by the agencies from financial models, and care and attention is needed in the way these are developed. The last thing to say, really, which I think probably is important and I think is increasingly an issue for the agencies, is to look at historic documentation of the companies and see how consistent that is with the current argument. Of course we are used to the idea that we can go in as advisers, newly engaged with no real history in any of these markets, and argue from the point that we think is right, even though it is often the case that the historic documentation of the company is not supportive. So we do need to be very conscious of that. I think if we are in positions where we are arguing cases which have the history, then the record supporting what it is, is actually a good piece of evidence in itself.

[FRANCISCO ENRIQUE GONZALEZ-DIAZ]

Well thank you Chris. I think that was a very thorough tour of the complex and technical issues which go on in the back ground. I have a number of questions that I will put to you, if you don't mind, later on, but Bill is going to continue now.

B. Bill Baer

Thank you. I want to pick up on a couple of points that Chris raised that go to issues one has to worry about in getting the deal through. I'll go through these briefly and then we can turn it back to Enrique to ask his question. First, and this is based on some experience I had at the Federal Trade Commission in the late 1990s before returning to Arnold & Porter, you have to assume in a way that there is inter-agency transatlantic cooperation to an extent and at a level we did not see ten years ago. It used to be there were meetings twice a year between senior officials. They talked a little bit about broad policy issues. Today, in a merger, and it will vary from transaction to transaction, and among the staff at the FTC/DOJ and at DG-Comp, the likelihood is they will be speaking with each other. You have to assume they will be sharing information, talking about timing, talking about substance and talking about how they view the issues. It may be the issues in Europe and the US differ, and they often do, but there are often theories, timings, remedies (which I'll come to in a minute) which are matters that are focused on, so one can no longer assume that you can develop your arguments in Europe divorced from the substantive arguments you are making in the United States. One can no longer fail to get counsel together well in advance of the deal, whether you are using one firm or multiple firms to deal with the major transaction. They need to understand what they are going to say and how they are going to say it. Chris talked a little about squaring your story with your documents and he is absolutely right, and I think, to some extent, it is even more important in Europe than it used to be because of the potential for the massive second request discovery that comes about in the US. If you've waived confidentiality, there is the opportunity for documents that were disclosed in the US to be made available to your European counterparts. I was in a deal, not *GE/Instrumentarium*,[3] but a deal within the last year where documents that the US authorities discovered during their second request review were brought to the attention of the DG Comp authorities the very day they were focused on by the US. Questions were raised in the US that afternoon. A request was made for copies of those same documents. So the degree to which there is coordination by the investigation staff is very high and a risk you run is failing to anticipate that and to coordinate appropriately.

The second issue relates to this whole question of timing. As Chris appropriately stated, the job for the lawyers, inside and outside, is to get the job done in the right timeframe and there is tremendous pressure, when a deal

---

[3] Case COMP/M.3083.

is announced, to do a number of things to reassure the markets that whatever problems may exist are manageable and can be taken care of in an
appropriate time frame. But in addressing that risk, one of the best things
we can do, in advising our client, is to avoid strong pre-emptory statements
about whether there are any anti-trust issues to worry about and how
quickly the deal is going to get done. On the one hand one needs to offer
market assurance that we've anticipated these risks, but to say it's a 60- or
90-day process and no undertakings, no divestitures or nothing substantial,
actually transfers leverage, I think, to the investigators, because suddenly
counsel is under pressure to deliver within that timeframe and under those
conditions. That tendency to want to be affirmative and positive to the
marketplace is a legitimate desire but it has to be tempered by being realistic and avoiding creating a situation where the pressure to meet the expectations you have created, creates pressure on you to make concessions you
otherwise might not have to make, or fails to give you the opportunity to
develop arguments on the merits that you otherwise would be able to
develop. Indeed I was speaking last week with a colleague who is a senior
official at one of the US anti-trust agencies who said the biggest mistake she
sees in deals from a number of years handling mergers is the up-front statement of optimism that at the end of the day then comes back to haunt the
company because management needed to deliver on an expectation they
unilaterally created.

Chris also covered issues relating to risk allocation and how it is deal-
specific. One has to make an assessment about how to get from here to
there. I did want to talk very briefly about this question of identifying, in
the merger agreement, the divestitures that would be required to be made
as part of any resolution with the anti-trust authorities. In effect, specifying
the undertakings. That is obviously something one is reluctant to do. It
gives a road map to the government as to how far to push and one hates to
do that. There has been a tendency that has developed in the US, and I
believe in international deals as well, Chris alluded to it, to develop a side
letter between attorneys, which is claimed as a privileged document, that
specifies, as a matter of resolving the joint effort to get the agencies to agree
on undertakings, how far the parties will go with respect to divestitures.
There is a serious risk, I think, about whether or not that document is privileged, and indeed I think the US authorities, informally, are strongly of the
view that it is not, and it is a practice that is engaged in not infrequently and
often without challenge. The only point I make is that if that's the way one
is going to go in an effort to deal with risk allocation and the fear of discovery, the notion that something that is part and parcel of the agreement
between the parties but can be separated out is unlikely, at the end of the
day, to be swallowed by the anti-trust agencies. Nor do I think it will be

supported by the US courts. It does not mean one might not try it: it is privileged if you honestly believe it is until otherwise determined, but there is a risk there as well.

The final point I would like to make relates to the need to focus very early, on remedies. If you are going to need to potentially resolve horizontal issues, waiting until you are halfway through the investigation is problematic for two reasons. In Europe there's often the ability, with an early offering of undertakings, to negotiate an early resolution, so one needs to have that strategy in mind. In the US, there is, at least at the Federal Trade Commission though less so at the Justice Department, a tendency where there is going to be divestiture of assets, to demand that there be a buyer identified and actually under contract to purchase the assets or the division or the subsidiary, at the same time that the underlying transaction is closed. If you had not anticipated that and are confronted four or five months into your investigation with the prospect of putting together an offering memorandum, going through a sale, negotiating definitive terms, all to meet the FTC's timetable, you put yourself seriously at risk of not meeting one of the client's legitimate objectives, which is to get it done in real time. So identifying those areas early on and coming up with a strategy for dealing with them is critically important. With that I turn back to Enrique.

[FRANCISCO ENRIQUE GONZALEZ-DIAZ]

Thank you very much Bill. If you don't mind, and with the permission of the audience, I would like to ask a couple of questions to the panellists. The first one is a relatively general one. I would like to know whether you think that the recent reform of the Merger Regulation has had, or is likely to have, any impact on the issues that you have raised today, and if you could both comment briefly on the substantive and procedural aspects of the reform that would be very welcome I think.

C. Discussion

[Chris Bright]

With regard to the substantive reform, the test being relatively new, there has obviously been a long and energetic debate about the wording. In my opinion, the result is actually a sensible result in that it does fill the gaps in a Brussels context. It also embraces the now two traditions we have in Europe in terms of SLC or dominance tests. Is it going to make a difference? I think the reality is the paths, that have already been set from some years ago certainly going back to the beginning of the Monti era, are one of exploration and development and experimentation, to some degree, and that was ongoing and is ongoing to some extent. I suppose this new test makes it easier, but the reality is the European system and the international merger control 'system' is on a voyage of discovery and that is going to go on for some time. I'm not sure that, in terms of what we are talking about, the uncertainties in the system, that is the way you have to deal with the agencies, is going to change an awful lot as a consequence of that. We've had long debates again about the procedures that should be in place in these different systems and what you see in Brussels is encouraging. I think the whole range of different things that have taken place, the different ways of dealing with access; all of these different things are going to help the Chief Economist over time. Hopefully it will produce some more clarity about the economic and substantive issues. The other changes in the procedures are going to make people feel that they are more engaged in the process and give them a better opportunity to make their contribution in the process.

[Francisco Enrique Gonzalez-Diaz]

On the timing for example?

[Chris Bright]

I do not think the change in the regulation is *the* important point. I think the timing issue has been resolved largely through stopping the clock rather than the formal application in the phase 2 remedial stage to deal with getting some extra time. So again I think the changes in the regulation are not definitive in that, but the system in any event has developed a safety valve on timing which allows people to get where they want to. The changes, I think, are going to be helpful for us but the major issues pre-date and continue with the system.

[BILL BAER]

A couple of quick comments. I'm obviously the last person to talk in depth about European procedure and substance for that matter. On the substantive change, in some ways the degree to which it is a step towards convergence and having a common standard has to be a good thing in terms of framing issues in the US and the EU merger guidelines. Having a test that is closer, substantively, makes a lot of sense. At the same time, any change has uncertainty and cost with it. We don't know how the Court of First Instance is going to interpret it. Now they do not deal with every case. They deal with a small percentage. In the meantime, DG-Comp will be able to apply that test and develop an internally and externally articulated approach which I think will be helpful. It may not change dramatically what is going on today. This may be more evolutionary.

On procedure, I think the thing that is most interesting to me as a distant observer is watching how the reforms have taken place in light of a series of adverse rulings from the Court of First Instance in the last 18 months. I've heard at conference after conference how the difference between the US and Europe is that Europe lacks meaningful judicial review: the US has judicial review; therefore the case that is prepared in the US has to be more factually and legally intact than in Europe. Whether that was once true or not, it certainly seems to me, as a result of these three rulings on mergers in the Court of First Instance, that what Commissioner Monti, Enrique, and others have done is to tighten up that process so the cases really are better prepared, the decisions are better prepared to withstand judicial review. There has been, I think, a significant evolution. Reforms such as peer review and an opportunity for the theory being articulated by the case handler and staff to be vetted and looked at independently for the purpose of asking and answering some of the tough questions: these are all reforms that procedurally end up bringing the process in Europe and the process in the US closer together. I suspect that, at the end of the day, the changes will result in decisions that are likely to be more easily defended before the Court of First Instance.

[SIMON HOLMES, *SJ Berwin*]

I would like just to touch on a question which I think Chris raised, and that's the question of confidentiality of information which is exchanged by the parties. I've sometimes had the impression that the parties to a potential merger are over cautious in relation to the exchange of necessary information purely and solely for the purpose of getting the notification made to the competition authorities. I know there have been such concerns in the US, and I got the impression that US practices drive the European practices here. My question is this: how much has that been a real concern of the European authorities and how much are we simply reading over from the United States concerns that have been felt there?

[CHRIS BRIGHT]

I would see it the other way round actually. I think the American practice is much more liberal than our practice has been historically and I think we have been very cautious about exchanging information in these situations. I think the US approach, and Bill can speak more informatively about it than I can, is to be much more collaborative. I think this is partly because they see it as a litigation process in the sense that you are there and you are going to have to either potentially defend the case or at the very least see off the agency. You optimize your evidence, you optimize your argument and you do that together under the veil of this Joint Defence Agreement. I think certainly from what I've perceived historically in practice both in the UK and in the European Community, we tend to be much more uncomfortable with the degree of mixing of information.

[FRANCISCO ENRIQUE GONZALEZ-DIAZ]

Chris, when you refer to exchange of information, are you referring to exchanges between the legal teams or to exchanges between the actual parties to the concentration?

[CHRIS BRIGHT]

Between the legal teams, but I think even amongst the lawyers here we have been somewhat reluctant, whereas in the US they are almost setting up shop together really.

[SIMON HOLMES, *SJ Berwin*]

And that's the point I need to make: in the US, my experience is that they've been very conscious to put it within a tight legal framework, the Joint Defence Agreement, in specifying exactly what can go to the lawyers, what can or cannot go through to the underlying companies, whereas I would agree with Chris that historically we've been less developed in that sense. But in my experience it's been more precise because there has been more exchange without the need for that legal framework, and that legal framework has now been read over from the States.

[BILL BAER]

Chris, there is a consistency to the points both of you make in the sense that what is different in the United States is the anticipation that there may be litigation with the government, or that there may be litigation with private parties. Such cautions support the idea of having some sort of Joint Defence Agreement that states what will be shared, and more importantly, who will see it, to make sure there is privilege in place. Once you have that in place, Dale Collins and I are quite comfortable in sharing a lot of information with each other to run our effort to jointly get the deal through. The caution that I have heard on occasion relates to in-house: there's always a question about whether in-house counsel can be trusted to see documents and usually that can be worked out. But then there's this issue of whether there is in-house counsel privilege here in Europe and how that factors in. In my experience, I've never had an issue where either the European Commission or a Member State authority was attempting to get hold of documents that were exchanged between the lawyers, whether in-house or external lawyers. So I think there is, in a sense, a technicality we observe in the United States to preserve our litigation position but once that's in place, it's pretty free-flowing amongst the lawyers.

[JOHN DAVIES, *Freshfields*]

I'd like to pick up a point that Bill was touching upon, which is this issue of side letters between the parties or probably perhaps between the lawyers, about what the response of the parties will be to a regulatory problem, and Bill was questioning whether or not that document formed part of the agreement and therefore would it be ultimately subject to disclosure? I would like to ask the panel and perhaps invite others here to comment. It certainly is becoming much more common in Europe for there to be some similar kind of document and one means of doing that is for the lawyers to exchange views on, for example, what 'material concessions' means in the actual agreement. Now I think, and I have had reason to look at this quite recently, my understanding is that in a number of European jurisdictions, that is either regarded as being privileged or not forming part of the disclosure obligation under the relevant notification regulations. But I would just like to throw the point out because I think it's becoming a more regular testing question for all of us. Perhaps the panel could give us their views to begin with. Thank you.

[CHRIS BRIGHT]

I think it is easier in Europe in many ways than in the US. On one level, one has to be pragmatic about these things. Enrique will have a view on this I am sure, but it seems to me that it is not something the Commission in a European context is going to be running after you looking for. So that's the pragmatic view. In terms of defending it legally, clearly there are a range of issues: is an interpretation of a clause of an agreement part of the agreement itself? Can you claim privilege over it? The US practice comes in here to some extent because the side letters tend to be letters done either in the context of anticipated litigation or with the agency obviously conducting an investigation, or protected through the privilege claim as outside counsel. You know, maybe those privilege claims work in Europe as well, but I know the issue in the US is that much more difficult because of the extent of the second request disclosure obligation.

[BILL BAER]

It seems to me that at the end of the day, it's a difficult argument to make that something that the parties contend is a binding interpretation of the agreement and enforceable in a court of law, is not in fact part of the agreement. That strikes me as a fiction. There is an argument, though, as a matter of policy, that the US government and the European Commission ought to encourage people, as part of the negotiation process, to allocate risk and to work out how this will get done. There is efficiency associated with that and the reason, I think, the lawyers have moved to the side agreement, is in an effort to deal with legitimate concerns about how to allocate those sorts of risk and to keep the deal moving without basically handing a road map to the investigating agency on how far they can push before litigation will ensue. So there are conflicting public policy concerns that need to be addressed and the concern I raise is whether at the end of the day the letter will be held as a privileged document.

[JOHN DAVIES, *Freshfields*]

This is a follow up question for both Enrique and Bill. If the regulators get their hands on that kind of document in one way or another, to what extent do you think it would actually influence their thinking? I know there are different views on it but I would like to have your views.

[Francisco Enrique Gonzalez-Diaz]

Well, to the best of my knowledge and experience, the Commission has not been confronted with this situation.

[Bill Baer]

You never get to see the letters.

[Francisco Enrique Gonzalez-Diaz]

The Commission has requested this type of letter and the exchange of documents and so on, and so I think that the experience at the Commission level is very limited. One day the Commission will decide to explore these avenues. The Commission is in the process of considering, for example, requesting documents produced by the investment bankers, which is something which, in the past, has not been done systematically. I think, as Chris has mentioned before, that these may be requested on a more regular basis in the future and who knows, maybe one of these days, the Commission may consider at least raising the question and then of course the legal teams will have to put forward reasoning underlying the refusal to hand over the documents. But for the moment I would say there is no meaningful experience that I know of which could guide you in the future in advising your clients.

[Bill Baer]

Just a couple of thoughts. In my experience, the agencies look closely at the contract, at what agreements exist which address how risk will be allocated and that's legitimate. Is there a drop-dead date? Is there a break-up fee? I remember once, a couple of years ago, when I was still in the government, someone came in and argued with me that if a second request was issued, actually if any divestiture whatsoever were required, they would litigate. That's it, that's the end of it. I just pushed the agreement across the table to the guy, which said you have to divest up to 20 per cent of the assets. It was an argument that was inconsistent with the plain terms of the contractual understanding. It was an unfortunate argument to have been made. At the end of the day the terms of the agreement between the parties regarding possible undertakings will be taken into account by the government. While it might be better to divorce this so that the assessments were made solely on the merits, if the government has that information in its possession, it will consider it.

PART TWO—FOURTH ANNUAL CONFERENCE:
THE TRANS-ATLANTIC ANTITRUST DIALOGUE

CHAPTER 8

Keynote Speeches

Dr Philip Marsden

I would like to welcome you all here to our fourth Annual Antitrust Conference and particularly those here from the ten new Member States. Welcome to London. For 10 months or so, we at the Institute, and with some good friends of the Institute, have heaved the great big boulder that is this conference up to the point on 10th May when we launch it, and then we let it roll down and break over you for two days. But there is no sense of futility in this exercise because the conference itself has an incredibly dynamic series of panels, particularly this year, with a lot of panellists commenting on each other and role play. All sorts of research comes out of the conference and is published in our *Current Competition Law* volume every year. We are also launching a new journal, some of the promotional material of which is on the chairs. It's called the *European Competition Journal*, from which we hope to capture a lot of the papers that are produced at these kinds of conferences and indeed our Practitioner Workshop Events throughout the year. We are of course not a commercial conference organization, we are a research institute and that is why we really appreciate the high level of debate that happens at this conference and at our workshops all of which bleeds into our research programme, from which we try to produce policy proposals. And that's why last year we launched our Competition Law Forum. This consists of about 50 experts, officials, private practitioners, economists and other experts, who meet together quarterly to discuss certain issues, many of which are on your programme today, and no doubt all these issues will incite further debate I am sure.

Today and tomorrow we have a series of excellent papers that have been put up on our web site for the last week or two. Some are still being loaded up as well today. You've got some papers in your packs. We've got a lot of very interesting topics as I say on the programme and very dynamic panels. I'd like to thank Mary Clements in particular and her events team for ensuring that this conference got off as well as it has. I'd also like to thank the sponsors of the conference: Lovells, Clifford Chance, Shearman & Sterling, Virgin Atlantic and Freshfields who sponsored the Speakers' dinner last night. I'd also like to thank the organising committee Mark Clough, Margaret Bloom, Philip Collins, Deirdre Trapp, Derek Ridyard, Stephen Walzer, and Michael Hutchings. Now I'd like to introduce Michael, who is not only a member of the Organizing Committee and one of the main driving forces behind this conference, the fourth, as I say, that we've done, but also is a founding member of the Competition Law Forum itself and the Chairman of the British Institute's Executive Committee.

MICHAEL HUTCHINGS

Thank you Philip. In that latter capacity, I would like to start by making one small plea. We are a members' Institute. The Institute survives solely for and is supported by its members and any of you who are not already members of the Institute, I do urge you to join. You save the subscription in one event, so it is worth joining and then you have access to not only one of the leading international journals, the *International and Comparative Law Quarterly*, but you have a lot of other publications, you have a lot of events, so please do join. I am sure there are plenty of application forms outside.

My role this morning is, I am delighted to say, to introduce Francis Jacobs, who is well known to you. I think it is very important to recognize the contribution that has been made by the European Court over the years, by David, who you will be hearing from in a minute, and Francis as well from the UK point of view. The reason that we are able to have this conference is because European competition law has achieved a status in international law terms which is really remarkable and we are able to lay on this Trans-Atlantic Dialogue, which really means a global dialogue, about competition law, because we have a *corpus* of law built up over the years by the European Court and that has obviously filtered down into the Member States. So it's a tribute to our representatives in the Court and in this case, Francis in particular, for the contribution he has made to this *corpus* of law, so thank you Francis. I really just want to say we hugely appreciate your contribution to the Institute. Francis has chaired the European law section of the Institute for many, many years. He's a founding father of this conference and I am delighted he is here to set us off this morning. Thank you Francis.

FRANCIS JACOBS

Well thank you very much, Michael, for that very kind introduction and may I add my warm welcome to all of you to this conference. I am delighted that it has now become an established feature of the scene. When we launched it four years ago, we were hopeful that would happen, and I think it now has happened. Might I also, perhaps, underline Michael's message to those of you who are not members, to join the Institute. I can speak from

personal experience as I have been a member of the Institute from approximately the year dot! I have benefited over many very decades from
membership of the Institute and its excellent activities and publications.
When I say very many decades, I'm exaggerating just slightly. It is something which I warmly encourage you to join if you're not already members.
I've been asked just to say a word or two about the programme for the
conference, but of course you already have the details. You will see that we
have once again assembled a wide range of expert speakers, including representatives of the judiciary, representatives of practitioners, representatives
of business and indeed high level competition officials. We have speakers
from different jurisdictions and the fact that so many experts have come
together for these two days is in itself of course recognition of the great
importance of competition law. Something which it would be difficult to
exaggerate, I think, in relation to the needs of the modern economy, and
something that has been recognized from the outset in the European
Community treaties in which, of course, competition plays a vital role.
Whether completion and the other community policies should continue to
feature in the European constitution, is perhaps a matter which will be the
subject of continuing debate. Whether the constitution, which is being
drawn up for the European Union should be limited to matters of the kind
which one more regularly finds in the constitution, whether the policies
should continue to feature is another question, but it is not a question for
this conference. This conference we already have enough exciting topics to
discuss. We have the interface of Intellectual property with competition, we
have mergers, we have abuse of a dominant position, we have state aid, we
have a regulatory round table, we have the consumer perspective, we have
the very topical subject of modernization, and we have the subject of cartels
and leniency. So we have a great deal to keep us engaged and we are going
to get off to the best possible start with a keynote address by my former
colleague David Edward, who is, I think, still at this very moment putting
the finishing touches to his address! His timing is perfect. As they say,
David Edward needs no introduction. He will be known, I am sure, to all
of you, certainly be reputation if not personally. Advocate of the Scottish
bar for many years, who appeared in competition cases before the
European Court of Justice, Professor, for a time, at the University of
Edinburgh, Judge at the Court of First Instance, of the European
Communities, and most recently, Judge of the Court of Justice, and my
colleague thereof or many years from 1989 until his retirement earlier this
year. But when I use the word retirement in relation to David, it has to be
understood, I think, in a particular sense. David is not a retiring person and
he will continue to keep us informed, entertained and maybe perhaps a little
wiser for many years to come. So it is a particular pleasure to call upon
David Edward to give the keynote address this morning. David, thank you.

A. Keynote Speech by Sir David Edward KCMG QC

This is a particularly apposite time to be having a trans-Atlantic dialogue about competition law. On 1 May 2003, Regulation 1/2003 came into force and ten new Member States joined the European Union. At the same time, for various reasons, we are faced with the risk, if not the reality, of a loss of mutual confidence between the two sides of the Atlantic. Let's take these three themes in succession.

Regulation 1/2003 involves a substantial but incomplete transfer of responsibility for antitrust enforcement from the Community authorities to the national authorities, including the national courts. That has unforeseeable but potentially serious consequences in various respects: first, for the uniform application of competition policy in a union of 25 Member States; second, for the caseload of the Court of Justice and the Court of First Instance; and third, for the continuing efficiency of Article 234 EC procedure and, consequently, for the existing, and I hope continuing, mutual confidence between the national courts and the Court of Justice.

Accession, in its turn, brings into the frame a galaxy of new and untried actors, as well as new problems of competition policy as it comes to be applied in the new Member States. It is important in this connection to remember (and this relates to Francis' remark about the content of the new constitution) that European competition law is treaty-based. To the extent that the treaties are (for the time being) the constitution, the law of competition has a degree of constitutional validity, not just because it appears in the treaty, but because it appears in the treaty to serve political and social as well as economic ends.

As we know, market integration was seen as the route to political integration. The purpose of Articles 81 and 82 (ex-Articles 85 and 86) was to ensure that market integration promoted by the four freedoms in respect of State action would not be prejudiced or nullified by the anti-competitive conduct of economic operators. Those were the political and economic purposes of putting the competition provisions into the original treaty. But there was also a social purpose, as is demonstrated by the words of Article 81(3), which talks of improving the production and distribution of goods and promoting technical and economic progress, while allowing consumers a fair share of the resulting benefit. The new competition policy for Europe was not simply for the benefit of economic operators or economic efficiency but also, and expressly, for the benefit of ordinary people as consumers.

The third theme is trans-Atlantic confidence. At the best of times, there is bound to be a degree of tension between economic regulators operating in two markets as large, and with such global influence, as the markets of the United States and Europe. That is particularly so when those economic regulators are applying different texts and proceeding to some extent from different political, economic and social assumptions. It is in that respect that there is the potential risk of difficulty between us. The market in Europe has certain specific characteristics which are not present in the US market: the problem of language which affects any form of decision-taking in the European Union, administrative or judicial; the continued existence of the boundaries of nation States conscious of their own independence and their own sovereignty; and in many cases considerable differences in our systems of law and procedure that are rooted in a long historical tradition. By comparison, in the United States, there is a relatively uniform legal system, particularly in the field of economic regulation. In addition, the European market now covers Member States of very uneven development, and the new Member States have only had a little more than 10 years to emerge from a State-regulated economy to a market economy.

So, as regards competition enforcement, there are differences, some going a long way back, about the proper procedure to adopt and also about the assumptions underlying that procedure, since one's views on procedure are liable to depend very much on national history and national characteristics.

While there are many differences, and important differences, between the United States market and the European market, it is absolutely essential, if there is to be fair and efficient regulation of the market on both sides of the Atlantic, that there should be mutual trust and confidence between the regulators on both sides. Comity is not as easy to manage in practice as some people appear to suggest, and one can see this in the reaction of the Department of Justice to the Commission's *Microsoft* decision. It is easy enough to talk about comity; it is much less easy to put it into practice. That is why this kind of dialogue is particularly important and particularly apposite at this time.

Having suggested an overall context for today's conference, Philip Marsden suggested that I might now speak about the role of the courts in competition enforcement, with particular reference to the situation in the European Union and with more particular reference to the courts in Luxembourg.

As you know, the Community system has hitherto been based on a twofold approach. First, measures taken by the Community competition authorities are subject to judicial review by the Luxembourg courts, essentially according to the canons of French administrative law. The procedure is concerned with the annulment of administrative acts on limited grounds, going to the lawfulness and procedural propriety of the administrative decision (including in procedural propriety a broad notion of 'fairness'). There is limited scope for resolving issues of fact or opinion and there is no question of re-forming the decision or of taking a new decision, substituting the decision of the court for the decision of the administrative authority, except as regards the amount of the fine if a fine has been imposed.

Second, as regards national measures, these remain subject to the jurisdiction of national courts and tribunals which have the opportunity to refer questions to the Court of Justice under Article 234. Under this procedure the Court of Justice is called upon to interpret the Community texts so far as they are relevant to enforcement in a national context. This has given rise to a number of very important decisions, particularly in the early days—for example, *Consten and Grundig*.[1] More recently, there have been a number of cases concerned with the procedural safeguards demanded by Community law (and also by Strasbourg law) in the enforcement of competition law by the national authorities. But looking at it very broadly, I think one would have to say that, comparatively speaking, the Article 234 procedure has been rather little used in the competition field.

The Community system offers very limited scope for economic assessment, even in direct actions. There are three reasons. First, review of the lawfulness of a decision is a quite different question from review of whether the decision is a good decision, far less whether it is the correct decision. Within the context of the lawfulness of the decision, the correctness or otherwise of the economic assessment is not necessarily of great importance. Second, by comparison with the situation on the other side of the Atlantic, where the courts hear expert evidence tested by examination and cross examination, European court procedure does not lend itself to testing divergent economic points of view or their application to particular cases. Third, the caseload of the Court of Justice has not been conducive to detailed discussions of economic theory. The consequence has been that the approach has tended to be somewhat legalistic, concerned more with the legal proprieties than with the quality of the decision.

The picture has changed somewhat in the last ten years because of the creation of the Court of First Instance and will change further with Regulation 1/ 2003.[2]

When the Court of First Instance was set up, the Council Decision was quite explicit that it should undertake an examination of the factual basis of the

---

[1] Cases 56 and 58/64 [1966] ECR 299, [1966] CMLR 418.
[2] Council Regulation (EC) No 1/2003 on the implementation of the rules on competition laid down in Arts 81 and 82 of the Treaty, OJ [2003] L 1/1.

Commission decision under review. There was no change in the system of remedies and the basic procedural assumption remains that we are talking about annulment of an administrative act on limited legal grounds. Nevertheless, the Decision mentioned, as a reason for setting up the new court, the need to improve 'close examination of complex facts'. The Court of First Instance has evolved a system of procedure which enables it to do that, involving much longer oral hearings and very substantial question and answer sessions, which were not possible in the Court of Justice for very simple reasons of caseload and time. The Court of First Instance can be said to have grown in confidence and the alleged cosy relationship between the Court and the Commission is certainly no longer a characteristic of the Community system (I can see that Richard Wainwright agrees with that proposition!).

The responsibility of the Court of Justice has been limited to hearing what are called 'appeals' in English, but the procedure is one of *cassation* rather than appeal. The review conducted by the Court of Justice is a review, not of the original Commission decision, but of the judgment of the Court of First Instance. So the question is not whether the Commission decision was right, nor whether the Court of First Instance was right in its analysis, but whether the Court of First Instance was right in law? The Court of Justice has been pretty consistent in holding to that point of view.

Looking to the future, the caseload of the Court of Justice and of the Court of First Instance is bound to increase and I am not sure that the Court of First Instance will, in the longer term, be in a position to devote as much time as it currently does to the examination of complex competition cases— at any rate, not without a substantial increase in the number of judges and, perhaps in the longer term also, the creation of a specialist competition chamber. But there is the other suggested possibility of a judicial panel for competition matters, which would devolve what is currently done by the Court of First Instance to a lower specialist chamber.

More particularly, I think the situation is going to change because of the effect of Regulation 1/2003, as to which the Commission seems to me to have displayed a degree of sublime optimism. For example, in his report for the forthcoming FIDE Congress, Wouter Wils says:

The fact that the application of Article 81(3) may require complex economic assessments should not pose any particular problem. Indeed, Article 81(3) is not different in this respect from Article 81(1), Article 82 or Article 86, the application of which equally requires complex economic assessments to be carried out by national courts. National courts also deal with many other problems and areas of law, which are not less complex or technical than the application of competition law, where necessary with the help of experts.[3]

Perfectly true! But the question is which court, operating in what context? If I simply look at the courts of my own country north of the border, I don't see them being immediately ready to tackle the complex economic assessments which will be involved in assessing the interaction between Article 81(1) and Article 81(3).

As Wouter Wils himself points out, the effect of putting Article 81(1) and 81(3) together is that Article 81(1) is no longer self-standing since the answer to the question whether there has been a breach of Article 81(1) will depend on whether the agreement in question is entitled to benefit from Article 81(3). The two go together. It is true that Regulation 1/2003 provides that the burden of proof for 81(1) is on the party who claims there has been a breach of 81(1), while the burden of proof for 81(3) is on the party who claims the benefit. But at the end of the day, the national judge will have to assess whether the criteria of 81(3) make 81(1) inapplicable. That is an exercise that most national courts, other than specialist courts, have not had to undertake before.

We must therefore think how the national courts can best be prepared to balance the conflicting interests implied in 81(1) and the various criteria of 81(3). And because the national courts have to enter what is for them a new field, the Court of Justice will have to enter this new field too, because national courts will refer questions and the Court will have to guide them how to conduct this balancing exercise.

There are two ways of approaching this problem. The first is to say that we must, if necessary, restructure the national systems and find new ways of dealing with these cases. For example, it might be said that in the United Kingdom competition cases should go to specialist competition courts or tribunals, such as the Competition Appeal Tribunal. But, as we know from Community law in other contexts, competition problems don't arise in that kind of way. In particular, problems of Articles 81 or 82 arise in the context of ordinary civil litigation as one element, but not the only element, in the dispute. So I don't think it is realistic to say: 'We'll refer it all to specialist tribunals and they will cope'.

Also I am inclined to think that it is not very helpful, either in the Community context or in the national context, to discuss this in terms of separation of powers, saying: 'This aspect is for the judges and that is for the administration or the executive', nor in terms of the distinction between

---

[3] PJW Wouter 'Community Report' in D Cahill (ed) *The Modernisation of EU Competition Law Enforcement in the EU* (CUP Cambridge 2004) 695 para 92.

investigation, prosecution, and adjudication. The reality is that, at the administrative stage, there is an element of adjudication—a quasi-judicial element—in taking a regulatory decision and deciding between the conflicting claims and the conflicting political, economic and social priorities implied in competition law. This is illustrated in Federal Trade Commission procedure, which may involve at a certain stage the intervention of an administrative law judge, and at another stage the intervention of the FTC itself, acting in a judicial or at least a quasi-judicial capacity.

What we really need to discuss is, not so much who should take the decision and in what capacity, but what is the best means of arriving at what I would call the 'best decision'. What checks and balances are required to ensure that, one way or another, we arrive at the best decision? In that context, it is important to recognize that what is the best decision will involve some consideration of procedural propriety and fairness, because a decision will rarely be the best decision if all the relevant interests and points of view have not been taken into account. Procedure is not just about human rights or about legalistic points dreamt up by lawyers: good procedure should have the effect of arriving at the best decision by ensuring that, at the right time, everybody has had an opportunity to put their point of view and that the person taking the decision, whether an administrator, quasi-judicial officer or a judge, has the opportunity to weigh up all the conflicting interests and arrive at the best decision. The best decision also is one that is taken within a reasonable time, so we shouldn't overload the procedural system so that it delays unacceptably the taking of the decision. And we have to have a way to get the best information and the best opinion evidence before the person taking the decision.

In that context, the Commission has put in place for itself a system involving a process of peer review, with different teams looking at the problem once the investigation team has made a proposal. I believe that that system is at least better than the old one, and may turn out to provide a sufficient guarantee that the best decision will be taken within a reasonable time.

I am not satisfied that the Community courts should be called upon to play a more active role in decision-making in competition questions for the reason I've already mentioned. As long as you assume that the procedure before the European courts is a procedure for annulment on legal grounds, then I am not sure that you can ask the courts to play an active part in adjudication of the merits of the decision. There are others who take a different point of view, but I think it would involve a restructuring of the system based on new and different assumptions about what the system ought to be doing.

In the national context, much will depend on the national system. In the

United Kingdom, as in the United States, the notion of 'evidence' (including expert evidence) is very well embedded in the system and we shouldn't forget that, at least in the common law system, the concept of what is a fair decision depends to some extent on the evidential process, the adversarial evidential process. That may not be true in other countries but it is something that we have to take into consideration in the United Kingdom. In that context (and here I return to where I began), it seems to me that the dialogue between British and US competition practitioners, administrators and judges is particularly valuable, because we share the same procedural assumptions, the same assumptions about how courts ought to work, how decisions ought to be taken and the place of the expert, especially the economic expert, in the process of decision-taking.

That seems to me to be the justification for a dialogue of this sort and I hope very much that the conference will advance it considerably in the course of the next two days.

[FRANCIS JACOBS]

Thank you very much David for that extremely thought provoking overview and I think there has to be, because of the importance of proper procedures, an opportunity to put some questions in a moment to David Edward. Perhaps I could, while you are collecting your thoughts make just a couple of comments of my own. First, from the perspective of the courts, there is indeed much to be debated on the scope of judicial review in the context of competition appeals. I would also like to emphasize the significant role of the court in giving preliminary rulings on references from national courts in particular because that role will of course increase as a result of modernization where national courts will be faced with more problems and will be lead to refer more questions to the Court of Justice. I myself think, although it is difficult to quantify, that the Court of Justice has played a more significant role in the rulings which it has given on references from national courts than it has in dealing with appeals against competition decisions, and there have been many cases in recent years—I can think of several of my own but of many others too—where the Court of Justice has given guidance in general terms on such matters as the application of the competition rules to social security and pension schemes, on the scope of abuse of a dominant position in relation to such matters as essential facilities, in the wider context of state aid, the *Altmark* litigation[4] and many other areas where the court has given guidance to the national courts. And that role, as I say, is likely to grow.

---

[4] Case C-280/00, judgment of 24 July 2003.

On the question of judicial manpower and the problems of the limited resources of the two courts, we have of course a relevant development in that tomorrow in Luxembourg, the 10 new judges, the judges from the new Member States, will be sworn in before the Court of Justice and the 10 new judges, the following day, before the Court of First Instance. All of those judges are now fully engaged in the process of taking up their duties. They have appointed experienced *référendaires* in their departments/cabinets. They will, I am sure, make a very valuable contribution to our work and we are all very much looking forward to working with them. I think in the immediate future, the additional judge power of the courts will certainly outweigh any new cases likely to come in the immediate future from the new Member States. So that, to some extent, the problem of overload will lead to some alleviation for the time being. But finally it is of course perfectly true in the Court of Justice and the Court of First Instance that there is less opportunity for the examination and cross examination of witnesses which are a familiar feature of common law systems, but those of you who have appeared in the courts in Luxembourg will know that from time to time there are questions put by the judges, and Judge Edward in particular has played a notable part in that process. Today, you have the opportunity of putting equally acute questions to Judge Edward, and I would not suggest that we turn the entire process into a forensic dispute, but I would welcome, and I am sure Judge Edward would welcome, one or two questions from some of you on the subject of his address or indeed ranging even more widely. So is there anyone who would like to start the ball rolling?

[STEPHEN KINSELLA, *Herbert Smith*]

The Judge spoke with some approval, I think, of two initiatives. One being the devils' advocates' panel and the other, the introduction of the chief economist, as things that may contribute to arriving at a better or even the best decision. I think that might be laudable. I'm not sure it's actually the aim of the Commission or DG Competition; in fact they have made it very clear that both of these are intended actually just to make the decisions less *appealable*. They are not viewed as part of the rights of defence; they are there to eliminate some of the more obvious grounds of attack in the court. So, perhaps the Court is actually going to assist us here by clarifying that these are not only intended to be for the benefit of the defendants, but that they are actually intended to improve the achievement of a better decision.

[DAVID EDWARD]

I don't know that I can comment on that. It does seem to me that it is not just about rights of defence. The question is whether the decision is a good decision. One of the ways of seeing whether it is a good decision is to have somebody else look at it. If that person comes from within the same structure or context—and that's the criticism—at least you have a fresh eye thrown on the substance of the decision and, to that extent, it may make it less appealable because it is not a bad decision. It seems to me that it is important not to get hung up on particular notions of procedure and instead try and work towards something which will produce a better decision within a reasonable time and that seems to me to be one of the ways.

[PHILIP COLLINS, *Lovells*]

You made the comment that harmonization and the 10 new Member States will increase the workload. One of the concerns that the practitioners have is that the caseload will be so large that a court will not be able to operate within a 'reasonable time'. I just wonder whether there are some relatively simple steps that could be taken by the Court to speed up the process, certainly in cases which involve fundamental issues about harmonization.

[DAVID EDWARD]

I am sceptical about speeding up. I think you have to accept, particularly because of the language regime, that a certain period of time is necessary but this is going well beyond the topic of this lecture. In the context of what the Court is going to have to do, if one is looking at priorities for speeding up, one has to consider the Brussels II Convention on custody of children and so on and also the second pillar problems of visas, asylum and so on. These are going to be the real priorities I think and therefore one must either devolve responsibility for some Article 234 procedures, which is one of the options, or perhaps move toward some degree of specialization of the chambers. But I am not there and the one thing that I think retired judges should not do is tell those who are there how they ought to run their ship!

[FRANCIS JACOBS]

However, as one who is still there, I can tell you that we have been conducting a very intensive examination in recent months on how we can improve our procedures. If, as you suggest, there may be some simple methods by which we can speed up our procedures, please do, in the coffee break, tell me what they are. I will be extremely pleased to hear!

[DAVID BAILEY, *trainee, Linklaters*]

The Judge spoke about the standard of review under Article 81 and histor-ically it seems from the case law there has been almost a limited standard of review under Article 81(3) that dates back to *Consten* and *Grundig* and the Court has more comprehensively reviewed decisions, admittedly under Article 230, under 81(1). I would like to know what Judge Edward has to say about the impact of Regulation 1/2003 on the standard of review. As you were saying, if you have to apply 81(1) and 81(3) together, to what extent is it sustainable to have different standards or different scope of review under 81(1) and 81(3)?

[DAVID EDWARD]

We cannot foretell with precision how this is going to work out. Because the decision about 81(3) has been devolved or transferred from the Community authorities to the national authorities, one supposes that there will be less discussion of Article 81(3) in the context of direct actions under Article 230. What I was trying to suggest is that a consequence of the trans-fer is that those problems are going to come to the court under the Article 234 procedure and at that stage the Court of Justice is not conducting review of a decision. All the Court of Justice is doing is telling the national court how to apply the texts and how to apply competition law. It is the national court that is going to be reviewing the decision. As I see it, the intensity of review may very well differ from country to country. So, for example, in Germany the review may be much more intense at the judicial stage than in some other countries, and therefore the role of the Court of Justice is going to differ to some extent depending on where the case comes from. But I think it is very important to realize that under Article 234 it will not be a process of review as such, at all.

[FRANCIS JACOBS]

Unless of course there is a possibility for the Court of Justice to give guid-ance to the national courts on what the appropriate standard of review should be when they are reviewing the decisions of the national authorities. The Court of Justice has, in other contexts, given guidance to the national courts on the scope of review of administrative decisions. So that may be an area where there is a possibility of some guidance under Article 234 but that remains to be seen.

[DAVID EDWARD]

I think it is a stony path, all the same, because if the reference is from the Competition Appeal Tribunal for example, the context may be a very different from that of a reference from the Court of Appeal, because the Court of Appeal is not conducting the same kind of review as the Competition Appeal Tribunal. And to say 'this is how it should be done' in such a way that it can be applied both in the United Kingdom and in Slovakia is not self evident to me.

[FRANCIS JACOBS]

Although one can point to areas where there has emerged a certain common approach, at least a principle common approach in relation to judicial review. For example, the introduction of the principal of proportionality, in general terms, for reviewing administrative action. So the possibility I think cannot be excluded that there may be some guidance from the Court of Justice in that area. Of course it remains to be seen. It may be at this stage that we should conclude this opening session and it only remains for me to thank on your behalf David Edward for giving us a very good start to our conference, a great deal to think about and I am sure that some of the themes will be picked up in latter sessions. So, thank you very much again, and that concludes the opening session of this conference.

B. Keynote Speech by Philippe de Buck
Secretary General of UNICE

First of all I will start by saying that we fully support the policy of the EU Commission and we endorse what was said in the recent communication on a pro-active competition policy for a competitive Europe, namely that some competition policy is indeed a key Community policy to foster the competitiveness of Europe's industry and to obtain the goals of the Lisbon strategy. I won't go into those details. And we support also the needs of the consumers. Competition in markets is stronger than it has ever been and the implementation of the single market imperative, and even deregulation on the one hand, but also the development of global markets have contributed to this situation. As I listened this morning to Philip Lowe and his colleagues, advocating and presenting the Liaison Officer for Consumers, I would really ask also and plead for a Liaison Officer for enterprises. It is always said that enterprises have a lot of means and possibilities, but it is not always true and I think that it would be better to have a good organized relationship between DG Competition and the Commission and companies.

UNICE, representing European business through national organizations, not only from the 15 but already from the 25 Member States of the European Union and even larger, has argued for years that in a competitive market the role of competition rules should be limited to cases where there is a significant restriction of competition and where markets will not provide a sufficient competitive mechanism. Agreements and behaviour that has only an insignificant impact on competition should not be subjected to rules and procedures that take up the resources of competition authorities and businesses, and as we all know, the call for change has been heated. The Commission and Member States have embarked, as we have heard at length, on revolutionary reforms to move competition policy away from fairly formalistic and legalistic rules to a more economic approach which does justice to the actual competitive situation in a market: the reform of rules regarding distribution, R&D, and licensing agreements. The decentralized application of antitrust rules by national courts and competition authorities and the changes to the Merger Regulation, which to some extent strengthened the one stop shop but on the other hand increased the risk of national authorities applying their own rules to important mergers, will dramatically change, and have already changed, the world for companies and also for competition lawyers. Amidst all these changes we should not forget what companies really need. They should be able to compete with each other on a level playing field and develop their capabilities as they drive for long-term success.

We have just come back with an important UNICE mission from the United States and have assisted the John Hopkins Institute in a presentation of the importance and the links between businesses in a transatlantic context. We have come to the conclusion that we can of course speak about a national company, we can speak about a European company, we can speak about a state company in the United States or a US company, but increasingly large companies will have to look at least at an international transatlantic market and we will perhaps, have to develop the concept of the transatlantic market and the transatlantic company. But I come back to the capabilities which drive the long term success of a company. They include specifically the ability to first innovate, develop and exploit your projects, services and operating processes to maximize operating efficiency and produce goods and services of the highest quality at the lowest cost with the maximum flexibility and, of course, to satisfy the needs of the consumer: also to make structural adjustments to respond effectively to changes in the competitive environment and to enter into cooperation agreements with certainty of the legal status and effects, and that is really of importance because you will have heard about the famous notion of cooperation and competition between the same companies and that is becoming in the modern economy even a business model. We will continue to fight for a legal environment which helps companies to develop these capabilities. Fortunately, also the Commission is dedicated to maintaining and devising a Community competition policy that induces firms to engage in competitive and dynamically efficiency-enhancing behaviour.

I would like to touch briefly on one important aspect of a sound competition policy, namely the need for a level playing field. As I have understood it, the Commission also acknowledges the importance of a level playing field and stresses that competition strategies of enterprises should be, to the largest possible extent, submitted to a unified legal framework throughout the whole European Union. This is of vital importance, but more work needs to be done to create a real level playing field. We all know that the new rules of antitrust and market policy now in force still leave ample scope for divergence, and that there is a real risk of re-nationalization of competition law to the detriment of a level playing field. 15 plus 10 national judges and authorities: even if I heard all the good information and elements about internal coordination, it seems to me, at least from a business perspective, to be quite complicated. But they will have to deal with the complex arguments that arise when an agreement needs to be assessed under the European antitrust rules and I guess they will not always be comfortable with doing this. Many of the decisions taken by national courts in the past related to agreements that had not been notified to the Commission. Only a limited number of those judgments had to include a substantive economic assessment of both the anti and pro competitive aspects of the arrangement concerned, but now numerous tribunals throughout the EU will have to assess complex competition law issues, which augment significantly the chance of conflicting and perhaps erroneous decision making.

The new merger rules pose a problem too. They make it easier for national authorities to review a merger that has been notified to the Commission. Referral of merger cases to the Member States may lead to uncertainty and cause procedural difficulties and delays because the Member States concerned will apply national law. Any increase in such referrals again increases the risk of conflicting decisions, and a similar danger exists in the area of State aid. UNICE has always been worried about allowing Member States more flexibility in the area of State aid, but self assessment by Member States of State aid measures amplifies the risk of distortions. It is very important, ladies and gentlemen, that the Commission carefully monitors the implementation of the various block exemption regulations that are in force in the State aid area and continues to compel the Member States to notify aid measures that are not covered by the exemption regulations, otherwise we will have more aid and less equal treatment. We should just be careful to endorse recent proposals of the Commission to facilitate approval of State aid measures which can be expected to produce only limited effects on intra-Community trade. These proposals will give Member States more flexibility to give aid to certain activities that are considered non-tradable and I have listened carefully to what Jim Murray has said. It will be all about the discussion about service liberalization.

The discussion is now open for an open market for services. We have had, at length, discussion on services of general economic interest and to a large extent there is still a temptation for governments to maintain the dominant position of some incumbent operators. We have there a relationship which is a square relationship between governments, business, trade unions and consumers and we will have to look, or some others will have to look to some dominant positions of national regulators. Activities traditionally thought as public sectors, as was in the past for telecom, railway transport, postal offices, will now be more and more available privately in the field of, for instance, health and education which will be a big debate in Europe.

A few words (and I will stop at that), on State aid for research and development. It is widely acknowledged that in this area market failures exist which hinder private investment in R & D and innovation. This negatively affects growth and competitiveness. Recently, the European Spring Summit again has raised concerns over the relative weakness of European investment in R & D and that, we know, is the key element of the competitiveness of Europe and also the reason why the European economy is lagging behind the US. As I said, I have come back from the United States and we will have to discuss and perhaps look differently when we see how the Department of Defence on the one hand, and NASA and other authorities, give some support to research and development activities, whilst we here in Europe don't have that kind of support at all. It is also related in a certain sense because we cannot expect everything from the Commission. It is also a duty for national governments to implement a more structured and more combined economic governance in Europe.

So to sum up, a level playing field and predictability are key for European business. They should be ensured by actively pursuing uniform and predictable application of competition rules and strict control of State aid. Without this we will not have a genuinely proactive competition policy and there is also no competitive Europe. It will be, I think, a very difficult balance between different interests but if we want to be competitive in Europe we need to have competitive small, medium sized and large sized companies and therefore the activities of this conference and the conclusion of this conference will be very important for the future, and we do hope that the competition policy of the Commission will be really proactive. Thank you very much.

C. Keynote Speech by Lars-Hendrik Röller*

Thank you very much. I'm delighted to be here. My subject today, State aids, is a slightly different issue but nevertheless my main point today will be that it's very important and in fact, since having the pleasure of being at DG Comp, there have been quite a number of important decisions and cases in the area of EU State aid control. Actually it strikes me as an area where quite a bit of important strengthening of the economic performance of DG Comp can also be done, so I want to use a little bit of time to talk about some important issues about State aid control at the EU level. I will talk a little bit about where I would like to see economic analysis being used, and in fact there have been some very important steps and reforms taken. I would like to also argue that of course Commissioner Monti has said, when he took office, that this is going to be an area into which he is going to put a lot of effort and, in general, he has been arguing that State aid in Europe is too high and therefore we should reduce levels. Of course there are many different areas of State aid and I think we should be sensitive to the economics behind it, which is also quite different. But generally, the policy objective put forward is that we should control State aid.

Some of you might know these trends and I'd like to give you a little bit of the legal perspective, the legal framework we have at hand in terms of tackling that; I actually do believe that the legal framework is rather flexible, even though I am not a lawyer, but my interpretation is it's rather flexible for economic arguments and analysis and in particular empirical analysis in this area. I'd like to also talk a little bit about why I believe it is important; what is the rationale? Why do we need a supra-national institution like DG Comp to control EU state aid? There are two schools of thought and in fact it is very important which one you belong to. I'll say how I fit in with all of that and, as you will see, there is the so-called significant impact test which is a test largely based, but not exclusively, on an effect of trade concept; whenever there is an effect of trade there is a potential for the EU to get involved, so it is a priority-setting exercise, as has been stressed by Philip Lowe. We need to set out our priorities and a significant impact test is I believe one important step forward in terms of prioritizing what sort of State aid cases we should look at. Clearly it is a difficult issue to think about and I want to say a few words about that.

Then, of course, the assessment, whereby once you have prioritized which cases you put your resources into from an economic point of view, or

* European Commission

perhaps an internal resource point of view, then you need to assess state aid and you need to ask yourselves, 'is this aid compatible or not?' There are two steps to that. The first step is to define what an aid is, which is already a difficult task. Once you have defined aid you assess whether it is compatible or not and, as in any of the antitrust areas, whether there are benefits: in some areas it is called efficiencies. You also have distortions and in some areas that might be called restrictions, and we need to somehow think about whether it makes sense. How much analysis do we want to do of the benefits? My answer is that it is a difficult one to do. How much analysis should we do in terms of how distorted State aid is? I think there perhaps we can strengthen the analysis. Then you have to come to some sort of assessment. So that's the difficult part, although actually I don't regard the assessment as that different from some other areas even though State aid is, in the economic sense, more complicated than perhaps in other areas of antitrust. This is of course not to say it is easy in other areas. There is much debate and many issues involved and it is decision-making with imperfect information, but I think in State aid it is a rather difficult thing to think about.

Then I want to say a few words about the rescue and restructuring part which is one area of State aid which is of course very important with some important cases going on right now, and then I would like to close with some perspectives on how I see economic analysis in the area of State aid control at the EU level. It is important that we realize we are talking about DG Comp and not about a national agency. So let me start with some general facts and I will go through them very quickly because they are rather simple and very macro-oriented. Generally there has been a decline— we are excluding for example railways, transportation, agriculture—but generally it has been claimed there is a trend downwards, so there is some success. It shows in the data even though the data is of course difficult, but generally, as we have been publishing also on our scoreboard report, the trend has been downward. The second effect, and this is again a declared goal of the Commission in the area of State aid control, is so-called horizontal objectives, which you might argue are less distortive horizontal objectives, such as R&D or support to small- and medium-sized enterprises to whom we have been directing aid at the national level.

Now there is always a question of how you define a horizontal versus a more targeted approach in terms of supply aid to a firm or to an industry. There are some issues behind that but I think generally one can argue we have been moving in that direction. I believe that the service has been very careful and there has also been a declared policy by the Commission to move more into a horizontal area and from an economic point of view, I might argue that makes some sense. The third one, and again it's not clear how the statistical officers respond to it, is in terms of the movement towards horizontal objectives, which is something that is rather different at the Member State level. Now there might be some definition. I know there are some definitive issues behind that so we can argue about that another time, but there is some heterogeneity across different Member States. There are some Member States which have more of a horizontal objective than other ones. So generally, if you think about applying economic analysis to this, we have been successful in reducing State aid. We have been moving towards more of a horizontal objective but clearly not all Member States, according to the statistics, have done this in an equally successful way. We regularly discuss this and of course you might also argue about enlargement. That is another subject of interest which I don't have time to get into, but these are not the enlargement countries.

Moving on, the legal framework is essentially Article 87 and as I told you, there are two steps for us, if I understand this correctly, to analysing State aid. The first step is to define what is and what is not aid and there are four criteria which are typically used for such purposes. The first one seems reasonable: it is a grant. It is an advantage which the State grants, so that is part of State aid. The second one is the so-called very important selectivity criteria. Is it selective or not? Does it benefit certain firms for example? And quite a bit of analysis is done in terms of what is a selective aid and what is not and I think this is actually a very important aspect of the work we do and can be used later on when we come to more economic analysis and thinking about distortions. Speaking of which, you will see the third aspect is in fact distortion. These are the negative effects of competition; and the final one is the trade aspect. Normally what happens is that the last two objectives are assumed, or most of the time are assumed, so essentially we don't necessarily check the last two in the definition of aid. The aid definition is primarily: is it given through a Member State and is it selective? And if those two conditions hold, the chances are very high that we will call it aid and we do not therefore do any distortion analysis at this step. Step number two is also Article 87: once you have decided that aid is actually present, you can declare it compatible with the common market. Here you essentially do an economic analysis and Article 87 and the case law define certain conditions where the presumed benefits of that aid may be economic—as you can read in Article 87(3)—or even social or regional goals. Of course the question is; can we really quantify those very well? There are certain ways to declare the aid compatible and the approach which has been taken in the past, which I think is a reasonable approach at least in terms of direction, is that we have specified a number of block exemptions and regulations, which essentially have defined when the potential benefits are relatively large and they've also put certain limits and rules on the type of aid you can give to achieve those benefits.

Now we can clearly argue that in some of these areas you have market failures, which means that perhaps the aid corrects those market areas which increase the benefit to society, and therefore perhaps makes some sense. We also have other areas. I will talk about that in rescue and restructuring where there is a question about how much market failure should be allowed to work in those markets, or perhaps it's not a market failure argument? Perhaps there are other arguments, economic or social, which justify declaring aid in rescue and restructuring as compatible? There is regional aid and there are sectoral aid packages, so we have an approach which says 'define aid' and then we have the possibility of declaring it compatible and we have developed a number of guidelines, and we are revising some of these, which fit into the picture of addressing where the benefits are potentially large with some of the costs.

Now let me move on and talk a little bit about why I believe that in the EU State aid control is a good thing. Clearly this is a supranational organization and there are essentially two arguments that can be made. The first one is that we are there because there is a regulatory failure at the Member State level, so here you could argue we can use State aid because essentially aid leads to inefficiencies. Aid shouldn't be given at the national level. We declare the aid incompatible because the governments don't do what is good for their countries. Clearly we are talking about governments at least to a large extent and not about firms doing bad things. Given that, if you believe in democracy and governments doing the right thing for their country you might argue we should not interfere in such areas. Clearly you can argue about that. You can also wonder whether governments have a problem with commitment. There might be what economists sometimes call soft budget constraint problems and we might be able to help them resolve those. There are some economic studies—and I don't claim that they are the ultimate answer—which actually have looked at how effective State aids are in terms of raising benefits at the national level. Do they actually achieve those objectives which I talked about earlier? And there is some question as to how effective State aid is in certain areas; for example, whether rescue and restructuring aid has worked or not in the past. Clearly it's an interference in the marketplace to some extent, and then you have to wonder about what would have happened if the aid hadn't been given to that firm and to that market, which is difficult because it is a dynamic issue to analyse. But I would argue that clearly this is still an open debate.

The other argument is to refrain from mucking around in the domestic business of governments. What you can argue is the important effects of the aid on other Member States, and you can very easily make the argument that it has an effect on everybody else even though sometimes it's not that consistent an argument. You can argue we come in because there's a problem between Member States and we somehow resolve that issue. This is of course an important issue in DG Internal Market, in the internal market programme. If you are more of the second school then really we should get involved only if there's a significant spill-over across Member States. And essentially, if you believe that that is the reason then the priority setting exercise—ie where we should get involved in terms of balancing the benefits and the costs, economically speaking—should be based largely on the aspect of effect on trade which you actually also have in some other areas of antitrust. It is interesting to make the link between other areas of antitrust and State aid. So DG comp has developed the significant impact test which essentially says those cases in which we get involved are those where the trade is affected when there is an externality.

So we've defined a set of criteria, which can easily be criticized, but we've spent over a year thinking about the sensible criteria for determining when trade is involved, when you have aid, whether there is a significant effect on trade, and what is the amount involved, which is of course also what's really significant. We've been using and will continue to use the significant impact test to prioritize cases, which actually does make sense if you believe the externality across Member States is the mandate of the supranational institution.

So in terms of case allocation the significant impact test is a wonderful thing which is also in other areas of antitrust. There is a certain parallelism here. Suppose now we have a case, the bigger question is: how do you make that assessment about potential benefits of aid which gets you down into all sorts of slippery slope arguments and potential distortions of trade and that's essentially what we need to do. It's not that different actually from looking at efficiencies and restrictions in other areas of antitrust, but of course it's a different context. Again one would have to look at potential benefits, and each one of those guidelines you might argue looks at that. In R&D you might claim there are some benefits for doing it and we do it to a certain extent. I'm not sure one cannot do more there but clearly it is consistent with this approach. However on the distortion side you can ask yourselves, can you take this aid? And again there are some cases where we do that and the question is shall we strengthen that or not? And I think on both sides you can use economics. The question is only whether using economics makes it relatively easier and leads to better results?

Of course you also have the last two points. You have here, in terms of benefits, all these social considerations which people might argue are important, especially in Europe. They are much more strongly rooted here than in other areas of antitrust and there are also issues in terms of fairness—for example in the rescue and restructuring guidelines, the compensatory measures are often also argued as measures of fairness—so you need to compensate competitors for an advantage someone else has gained. This is another issue which from an economic point of view is something one can think about. Now I am asking myself, can we do more in terms of making that very difficult decision on a case by case basis or should we have more general rules and guidelines and try to just lower State aid as much as possible? It's a bit of a trade-off here as well, so if I look at the benefits: first I would argue that the approach we take here is in terms of moving towards horizontal objectives, mentioned earlier, and defining general rules and guidelines, which presumably are linked to market failures, which this aid presumably is correcting. I think this is not an altogether unreasonable approach. There is a question of whether we cannot strengthen that a little bit more, for example if the aid is rather large in terms of intensity or other measures. Should there be more justification in terms of analysing market failure? Now market failure is very difficult to analyse and you can justify just about anything with market failures, so there is a danger of making it extremely soft. I am not saying we should make it soft, I am just saying that maybe for very, very high levels of aid one might want to look at it.

Now on the other side we have these distortions, and we can do a little more here in the sense of strengthening the analysis. I think we have the right approach. Again if we look at distortions we typically look at intensities and types of aid, so there is quite a bit of work which goes into the precise guarantee versus loans and what sort of aid firms might actually be getting, so it's useful to think about the economics behind it in terms of distorting competition. There is this issue of selectivity. The more selective aid is, the easier it is actually to do a market-based analysis. The problem with horizontal aid is it becomes very difficult, but the more selective the aid is the easier it is to do a market-based analysis to assess the distortions, and of course the more selective the aid is the higher the likelihood of those distortions, so it all works in the same direction. So in terms of assessing State aid, I think it is rather difficult to analyse market failures and I looked at some of these cases. Sometimes it is easier to make that argument than others. If we want to use more market failure assessments we should have strengthened criteria and clear rules as to what sort of market failures and what sort of evidence. It's a little bit reminiscent of an efficiency defence argument in mergers. Yes, it is theoretically correct, but how do we do it in practice and we don't want just everybody claiming efficiencies. There has to be an effective means of enforcement and the same thing has to be true with market failures in many different areas.

On the market distortions, I do think it's possible if you have selectivity to move more toward a market-based analysis and there is a very similar sliding scale even though it is more difficult here. Social issues come into play as well which we don't have in some other areas, but it might be based on this sort of analysis in certain cases, where in fact the distortions are likely to be very high, so that we actually do more in terms of market-based analysis here. So I think this is something we more naturally know how to do, whereas assessing market failures is really a bit more difficult. I will skip the rescue and restructuring, even though that is one of my favourite topics. Let me come back to the last point just very briefly which consists of the so-called compensatory measures, which as I said are measures which are imposed to compensate competitors. You can argue that this makes economic sense if you believe in dynamic incentives, so you punish a firm hopefully creating the right incentives. Of course they hurt. Clearly I believe they are legally sound and I think there is an economic argument for having them but I actually do believe that we have other instruments, also legally sound, which we can use and which are more consumer-oriented, and these would actually be market-opening measures. If you have a closed market you might want to use compensatory measures; again that doesn't mean we have to change anything in terms of the law, and again it is an empirical question of how you can do that.

Let me close by saying I do think that economic analysis should also be strengthened in the area of State aid. We have already, because of the Commissioner and Philip Lowe, taken a number of steps which strengthen the economic analysis in this area. I think that the significant impact is a sensible thing if you believe in the externality argument. I do believe that we can move forward in terms of market-based analysis. In this area I do believe it is also important to think about the objectives of State aid. Now clearly I didn't talk very much about that and I know you have had, I think, an Irish competition conference, and even here I think you have a session about consumer orientation. This is a lot in a short period of time. It's a large area. It's very exciting and I think that economics can really be a useful tool in this area. Thank you very much for your attention.

[MICHAEL HUTCHINGS]

Well I apologize for cutting you short but I would like two minutes for questions. Would anyone like to raise a question?

[ADRIAN MAJUMDAR, *RBB Economics*]

Supposing you had an international market, say all the Member States, and one Member State wanted to have a national champion. It subsidized one firm a lot and as a result all the other firms in the market had lower prices. Here you'd have a situation where there's one national champion in one market leading to lower prices across all Member States. How would you weigh up that situation?

[LARS-HENDRIK RÖLLER]

I should say fine, that's great because you have a positive externality on other Member States, which is your argument there. That's what I've been arguing; that we should look at the spill-over effects. Now clearly I am not convinced that your hypothesis behind the question is correct. That is, in a way, my answer to your question. In the sense of creating national champions leading to necessarily lower prices across the board, we've been having some cases which look at this issue and I think the economic analysis which we are following is consistent with that regard. To answer your question: if there are positive externalities to other Member States and if you believe national governments are doing a proper job—and that's a big 'if' again in your case—then I've been pushing this. Now let me also say that there are plenty of people who believe, not incorrectly, that national governments sometimes aren't doing their proper job and we should use our powers to help and to improve the situation. This is clearly the other school of thought and I also accept that argument, even though I think that the significant impact test doesn't fully address that second concern as well as the first one, and that's why I have been following that line of reasoning. I am not sure I have answered your question but I tried!

[MICHAEL HUTCHINGS]

Well I am going to call this session to an end and thank Mr Röller very much indeed for those words. For those of you who weren't here last year, this all arises from a discussion we had with Mario Monti at lunchtime on the first day of the conference last year and he said he would particularly like us to give more time to the issue of State aids. We did hold one Competition Law Forum session specifically on that subject and I am very glad it has come up again today. So thank you very much indeed.

D. Antitrust Law in the US Supreme Court

R Hewitt Pate*

In considering my topic for a forum on comparative law, it occurred to me that it might be useful to focus on the special role of the United States Supreme Court in making American antitrust law. The topic is especially timely because our Supreme Court granted review in four antitrust cases this term, each of which is the object of intense study by US antitrust practitioners. The Supreme Court, unlike the intermediate appellate courts of the federal system, has discretion to choose the cases it will hear, and its choices have a profound effect on the development of antitrust law.

Little has changed over the last century in terms of the wording of our antitrust statutes. The Sherman Act was enacted in 1890, and the Clayton Act in 1914, and the legislative amendments since that time have been minimal. Yet US antitrust law has come a long way indeed in those years through judicial interpretations of the law. Congress chose not to enact detailed prescriptions for antitrust enforcement, relying instead on the courts to apply the broad statutory principles to particular fact situations. As former Assistant Attorney General William Baxter has observed, this 'common law' approach may lack the certainty provided by a more detailed statute, but it 'permits the law to adapt to new learning without the trauma of refashioning more general rules that afflict statutory law'.[1] Our Supreme Court has described the antitrust laws as having 'a generality and adaptability comparable to that found to be desirable in constitutional provisions'.[2]

American antitrust law began to take shape only when the Supreme Court began to build the basic framework of antitrust analysis in its decisions. In 1911, it decided the landmark *Standard Oil* case, in which the United States sought to break up the famed oil conglomerate.[3] Observing that the standards of the antitrust law must be developed by the courts deciding each case 'by the light of reason, guided by the principles of law and the duty to apply and enforce the public policy embodied in the statute',[4] the Court announced the Rule of Reason, under which the Sherman Act is deemed to

* Assistant Attorney General, Antitrust Division, US Department of Justice.
[1] W F Baxter, *Separation of Powers, Prosecutorial Discretion, and the 'Common Law' Nature of Antitrust Law*, 60 Tex L Rev (1982) 661, 666.
[2] *Appalachian Coals, Inc v United States*, 288 US (1933) 344, 360.
[3] *Standard Oil Co v United States*, 221 US (1911) 1.
[4] ibid at 64.

prohibit only 'unreasonable' restraints of trade. In another decision that
year, *United States v American Tobacco Co*,[5] involving a conglomerate in
the tobacco industry, the Supreme Court emphasized the Rule of Reason's
fundamental grounding in competition concerns. This standard proscribed
'contracts or agreements or combinations which operated to the prejudice
of the public interests by unduly restricting competition or unduly obstruct-
ing the due course of trade or which, either because of their inherent nature
or effect or because of the evident purpose of the acts, etc., injuriously
restrained trade . . .'[6]

In 1918, *Chicago Board of Trade v United States*[7] made clear that the Rule
of Reason encompasses all the relevant circumstances. To determine
whether a restraint is illegal, a court must 'ordinarily consider the facts
peculiar to the business to which the restraint is applied; its condition
before and after the restraint was imposed; the nature of the restraint and
its effect, actual or probable' and the 'history of the restraint, the evil
believed to exist, the reason for adopting the particular remedy, the purpose
or end sought to be attained'.[8]

Around the same time, the Court was also developing the doctrine of *per se*
illegality, which provides bright-line guidance as to certain clearly anticompetitive practices. In *United States v Trenton Potteries Co*,[9] the Court held
that a price fixing agreement among competitors is an unreasonable
restraint 'without the necessity of minute inquiry whether a particular price
is reasonable or unreasonable'.[10] In 1940, in another landmark case
brought by the United States in the oil industry, *United States v Socony-
Vacuum Oil Co*,[11] the Supreme Court repeated that price-fixing agreements
are illegal *per se* and that 'no showing of so-called competitive abuses or
evils which those agreements were designed to eliminate or alleviate may be
interposed as a defense'.[12] The *per se* rule underpins the Antitrust Division's
criminal prosecution of collusion among competitors.

The Supreme Court's pre-1950 decisions set the stage for the late 20th
century developments in antitrust law. They established the fundamental
principle—consistent with the modern approach worldwide—that antitrust
laws prohibit only conduct that unreasonably restricts competition, to the
detriment of consumers. And the Court established that the type of inquiry
required depended on the nature of the particular conduct at issue.

That auspicious beginning did not mean that the course of American
antitrust analysis always ran smoothly through the last half of the century.

[5] 221 US (1911) 106.   [6] ibid at 179.   [7] 246 US 231 (1918).
[8] ibid at 238.   [9] 273 US (1927) 392.   [10] ibid at 397.
[11] 310 US (1940) 150.   [12] ibid at 218.

A consequence of the common law approach is that when antitrust thinking veers from the path of promoting consumer welfare, the Supreme Court may follow. We experienced that effect in the 1960s and 1970s as our Supreme Court issued decisions emphasizing artificial presumptions not soundly grounded in economic reasoning. In *Brown Shoe*, *Pabst*, and *Von's Grocery*, the Court ruled that mergers could be found unlawful based on extremely small increases in market concentration.[13] In *Schwinn*,[14] it abandoned its formerly cautious approach to vertical practices,[15] holding exclusive dealer territories unlawful *per se*. Similarly, in *Albrecht*,[16] it held vertical maximum price fixing illegal *per se*.

As the sophistication of economic analysis increased, our Supreme Court began to reexamine some of these precedents and return to fundamental principles of competition and consumer welfare. In *GTE Sylvania*,[17] the Court overruled *Schwinn*, and in *State Oil v Khan*,[18] it overruled *Albrecht*. The Court adopted a significantly different approach to mergers in *General Dynamics*,[19] refusing to find a violation, despite current high market shares, in a case where those market shares did not reflect a realistic threat to future competition. And in *Matsushita*,[20] the Court poured cold water on theories of liability that make little economic sense, and it expressed scepticism of liability theories based on price cutting, which is often 'the very essence of competition'.[21]

Of particular note is the Court's decision in *Brunswick*,[22] in which it rejected the theory that a private plaintiff could obtain treble damages as compensation for continued competition resulting from a merger that prevented a firm from leaving the market. This may be one of the Supreme Court's lesser-known decisions outside the United States, but it is of fundamental significance. Private treble damage litigation is an important tool in the US antitrust enforcement scheme, and the *Brunswick* decision mandated that it, like government enforcement, be firmly anchored to pro-competition, pro-consumer principles. The Court emphasized that private damages must be based on conduct causing injury of the type that the antitrust laws were intended to prevent. Plaintiffs may not prevail unless they are harmed

---

[13] See *Brown Shoe Co v United States*, 370 US.294 (1962); *United States v Pabst Brewing Co*, 384 U.S. 546 (1966); *United States v Von's Grocery Co*, 384 US (1966) 270 .
[14] *United States v Arnold, Schwinn & Co*, 388 US 365 (1967).
[15] See *White Motor Co v United States*, 372 US 253 (1963).
[16] *Albrecht v Herald Co*, 390 US 145 (1968).
[17] *Continental TV, Inc v GTE Sylvania Inc*, 433 US 36 (1977).
[18] 522 US (1997) 3.
[19] *United States v. General Dynamics Corp.*, 415 U.S. 486 (1974).
[20] *Matsushita Elec. Indus. Co. v. Zenith Radio Corp.*, 475 U.S. 574 (1986).
[21] ibid at 594.
[22] *Brunswick Corp v Pueblo Bowl-O-Mat, Inc*, 429 US 477 (1977).

by *anticompetitive* consequences of a defendant's conduct, for the antitrust laws were enacted to protect competition, not competitors.

In the last quarter of the 20th century, the Supreme Court began hearing fewer antitrust cases. In part this reflects a general trend in the Court's practices. In its 2002 term, it issued 81 written opinions, having issued only 71 the year before.[23] In contrast, 30 years earlier, the Court issued 164 written opinions in its 1972 term and 151 in 1971, including full opinions in ten antitrust cases during those two terms.[24] A litigant's chance of obtaining review today is quite low. In the last complete term, 2002, the Supreme Court considered 8,340 petitions for review by writ of *certiorari*, but granted full review to only 91 cases, or 1.1 per cent.[25] Even if the unpaid, *in forma pauperis*, petitions are left out of the calculation, the odds improve only to 4.5 per cent.[26]

A change in the statute governing appeals in civil antitrust cases brought by the government has also had the effect of limiting the number of Supreme Court opinions in antitrust cases in recent years. Until 1974, appeals in these cases went directly to the Supreme Court under the Expediting Act. That statute was amended in 1974 to provide that these appeals go to the intermediate appellate courts unless the district court certifies that immediate Supreme Court review is of 'general public importance in the administration of justice'.[27] Even then, the Court retains discretion to remand the case to the court of appeals. District courts have certified only three such cases for direct appeal.[28] One of these was *Microsoft*, but the Supreme Court declined to hear the case and remanded it to the court of appeals.

Because there are so few Supreme Court antitrust decisions each year—and because each one sets precedent that will govern the application of the antitrust laws in the lower courts for decades to come—each decision is an event of major significance for antitrust enforcers and the antitrust bar. Every phrase is studied with care, and every future case is evaluated in terms of the Court's reasoning process.

Because of the central role of Supreme Court jurisprudence in the develop-

[23] Table I: Actions of Individual Justices, 116 Harv L Rev 453, 453 (Nov 2002); Table I: Actions of Individual Justices Granted Review, 117 Harv L Rev 480, 487 (Nov 2003).
[24] Table I: Actions of Individual Justices, Table III: Subject Matter of Dispositions with Full Opinions, 86 Harv L Rev 300, 304-05 (Nov. 1972); Table I: Actions of Individual Justices, Table III: Subject Matter of Dispositions with Full Opinions, 87 Harv L Rev 303, 307-08 (Nov 1973).
[25] Table II: Cases Granted Review, 117 Harv L Rev 480, 487 (Nov 2003).
[26] ibid.
[27] 15 USC § 29(b).
[28] *See Maryland v United States*, 460 US 1001 (1983); *California v United States*, 464 US 1013 (1983); *United States v Microsoft*, 530 US 1301 (2000).

ment of the law, antitrust enforcers devote significant effort to advising the Court as it chooses the few antitrust cases that it will hear. The government has filed briefs in all four of the antitrust cases the Court selected for review this term, even though only one actually involved the government as a party. The Court sometimes issues a formal invitation to the Solicitor General to express the views of the United States before it decides whether to hear a case. In the 2002 term, for example, the Court requested the views of the United States in 24 cases. Over the last 20 or so years, it has been typical for perhaps one of these invitations each year to involve an antitrust case. The Court has issued two such invitations in the current term—in *LePage's*[29] and *Andrx*.[30] On very rare occasions, the Solicitor General will file a brief urging the Court to hear a private antitrust case without such an invitation, as it did last term in *Trinko*, a fact that presumably figured in the Court's decision to hear that case on the merits.[31]

The government takes into account a variety of factors in deciding whether to recommend that the Court allocate one of the limited places on its docket to a particular case. In addition to discussing the legal merits and any split in authority, we try to give the Court our perspective on factors that may not be apparent on the face of the petition. We discuss the practical importance of the legal issues presented, in terms of their impact on enforcement, on judicial administration, on consumers, and on the business community. We consider whether the case before the Court presents a good vehicle to resolve the questions or whether the facts or the procedural posture might interfere with the Court's ability to give useful guidance of wide applicability. Finally, we consider whether it would be wise to allow the case law to develop further in the lower courts so that the Supreme Court may have the benefit of that additional experience before enunciating a general rule.

The government is by no means the only party interested in the Supreme Court's choice of cases, of course. Academics, public interest groups, and private entities affected by the issues file briefs urging the Court to hear particular cases. Indeed, even foreign governments do so occasionally, as they did in two of the cases currently pending before the Supreme Court. This brings me to the current Supreme Court term and the four antitrust cases before it. The Court has already decided two of these, *Verizon Communications Inc v Trinko*[32] and *United States Postal Service v*

---

[29] *3M Co v LePage's, Inc et al* (Sup Ct No 02-1865).

[30] *Andrx Pharmaceuticals, Inc v Kroger Co, et al* (Sup Ct No 03-779).

[31] In general, the success rate of the Solicitor General's recommendations at the petition stage is quite high. For example, recommendations to grant certiorari have been followed by a grant in five of six cases in 2000, five of six cases in 2001, and 11 of 11 cases in 2002.

[32] 124 SCt 872 (2004).

Flamingo Industries Ltd, [33] while the two others, *Intel Corp v Advanced Micro Devices, Inc,*[34] and *F Hoffman-La Roche Ltd v Empagran SA,*[35] have been argued, but remain undecided.

Trinko deals with fundamental questions about the nature of monpolization. The Telecommunications Act of 1996 requires incumbent telephone companies to assist would-be competitors by providing access to the incumbent's facilities. Congress intended our 1996 Act to bring competition to the telecommunications industry, including the market for local telephone service. The plaintiff alleged that the incumbent telephone company sought to discourage customers from using a competitor's telephone service by filling its competitors' orders on a discriminatory basis. The court of appeals upheld the plaintiff's antitrust claim on so-called 'essential facilities' and 'monopoly leveraging' theories.[36] The United States urged the Supreme Court to hear the case and reverse the appeals court. We argued that the 1996 Act neither restricts the antitrust laws, nor expands antitrust liability by creating new antitrust duties that did not exist before its passage. And, we argued that a failure to share monopoly power—without more—is not exclusionary. Rather, a refusal to assist rivals cannot be exclusionary unless it makes no economic sense for the defendant but for its tendency to reduce or eliminate competition.[37]

Earlier this year, the Supreme Court reversed. It concluded that 'just as the 1996 Act preserves claims that satisfy existing antitrust standards, it does not create new claims that go beyond existing antitrust standards'.[38] Considering the policies of the antitrust laws and the risk of chilling the very competition they are intended to protect, the Supreme Court emphasized the need for caution with respect to government intervention against single firm conduct, especially in imposing antitrust obligations on firms to assist competitors and share resources. The Court's opinion strictly circumscribed or eliminated expansive theories of antitrust liability under the labels of 'essential facilities' or 'monopoly leveraging'.

The other case already decided, *Flamingo Industries,* addressed the question of whether the United States Postal Service is subject to liability at all under the federal antitrust laws. The Supreme Court unanimously held that the Postal Service is not subject to suit under the federal antitrust laws. The

---

[33] 124 Sup Ct 1321 (2004).
[34] Sup Ct No 02-572.
[35] Sup Ct No 03-724.
[36] *Law Offices of Curtis v Trinko, LLP v Bell Atlantic Corp,* 305 F.3d 89 (2d Cir 2002).
[37] Brief for the United States and the Federal Trade Commission as Amici Curiae Supporting Petitioner, *Verizon Communications, Inc v Law Office of Curtis V Trinko,* (Sup Ct No 02-682) (filed May 2003), at 7, available at <http://www.usdoj.gov/atr/cases/f201000/ 201048>.
[38] 124 Sup Ct at 878.

Court explained that Congress is not presumed to have subjected the federal government itself to liability in the absence of clear evidence of such an intent, which is lacking in this statute.[39]

The two antitrust cases awaiting decision by the Court, *Intel Corp v Advanced Micro Devices, Inc* and *F Hoffman-La Roche Ltd v Empagran SA*, reflect how the growth in antitrust enforcement has made it in many ways an international undertaking. Each case asks, in different ways, what role US courts will play in addressing antitrust violations taking place outside of the United States.

The *Intel* case began when Advanced Micro Devices, or AMD, filed a complaint with the Directorate-General for Competition for the Commission of the European Communities, alleging that Intel was abusing its dominant market position. AMD then asked a US district court to order Intel to produce materials in the United States under a US statute, which authorizes a district court, upon the request of a 'foreign or international tribunal or upon the application of any interested person', to order production of testimony, documents or other things 'for use in a proceeding' in the tribunal.[40] The court of appeals held that production was authorized under the statute.[41] Intel successfully sought Supreme Court review. And in an unusual step, the Commission of the European Communities participated as amicus curiae and asked the Supreme Court to reverse. It argued that the statute should not be interpreted to apply to the proceedings of the European Commission and that such an interpretation 'would directly threaten the Commission's enforcement mission in competition law and possibly interfere with the Commission's responsibilities in other areas of regulatory concern as well'.[42] The United States also participated as amicus curiae, arguing that the statute gives the district court discretion to grant or deny AMD's application. The government urged the Supreme Court to send the case back to the district court to consider the points raised by the European Commission and others 'that may provide persuasive reasons for the district court to decline to compel production in this case'.[43] We expect a decision by the Supreme Court by the end of June.

---

[39] 124 Sup Ct at 1327.

[40] 28 USC § 1782(a).

[41] *Advanced Micro Devices, Inc v Intel Corp*, 292 F.3d 664, 668-69 (9th Cir 2002).

[42] Brief of Amicus Curiae the Commission of the European Communities Supporting Reversal in *Intel Corporation v Advanced Micro Devices, Inc* (Sup Ct No 02-572) (filed 15 Nov 2002).

[43] Brief for the United States as Amicus Curiae Supporting Affirmance, *Intel Corp v Advanced Micro Devices, Inc* (Sup Ct No 02-572) (filed Jan 2004), at 13, available at <http://www.usdoj.gov/osg/briefs/2003/3mer/1ami/2002-0572.mer.ami.pdf>.

Finally, just two weeks ago, I had the pleasure of appearing before the Supreme Court to argue the United States' position in *Empagran*. *Empagran* involves the global price-fixing and market-allocation conspiracies among American and foreign manufacturers and distributors of bulk vitamins. This cartel sold billions of dollars of vitamins in the United States and other countries around the world at fixed prices. The United States' investigation and prosecution of the cartel resulted in the criminal conviction of 12 corporate defendants and 13 individual defendants and the imposition of criminal fines exceeding US $900 million. American private parties sued the vitamin companies seeking treble damages under American antitrust law based on the conspiracies' effects on US commerce; they have obtained a settlement in excess of US $2 billion.

The plaintiffs in the *Empagran* are foreign corporations who purchased vitamins abroad for delivery abroad. They brought suit in a US district court under the US antitrust laws. The district court held that it lacked subject matter jurisdiction over their claims under the Foreign Trade Antitrust Improvements Act of 1982. The 1982 Act provides that the Sherman Act shall not apply to non-import foreign conduct unless it has a direct, substantial, and reasonably foreseeable effect on U.S. commerce and that such effect gives rise to a claim under the Sherman Act.[44] The court of appeals, however, reversed and held that the 1982 Act allows foreign plaintiffs injured by anticompetitive conduct to sue whenever the conduct's harmful effect on US commerce gives rise to a claim by anyone, even if not the foreign plaintiff who is actually before the court.[45]

The United States, joined by Germany, Belgium, Canada, Japan, the United Kingdom, Ireland, and the Netherlands, participated as amici and urged the Supreme Court to reverse.[46] Our position is that the 1982 Act's requirement that the effect on US commerce gives rise to a claim means that the effect must give rise to a claim by the particular plaintiff before the court. We also argue that the expansive reading by the court of appeals is 'highly likely to have the perverse effect of undermining the [United States'] efforts

---

[44] 15 USC § 6a.

[45] *Empagran SA v F Hoffman-LaRoche, Ltd*, 315 F.3d 338 (DC Cir 2003).

[46] Brief of the United States as Amicus Curiae Supporting Petitioners in *F Hoffman-La Roche Ltd v Empagran* (Sup Ct No 03-724) (filed 3 Feb 2004), available at <http://www.usdoj.gov/osg/briefs/2003/3mer/1ami/2003-0724.mer.ami.pdf>; Brief of the Governments of the Federal Republic of Germany and Belgium as Amici Curiae in Support of Petitioners in *F Hoffman-La Roche Ltd v Empagran* (Sup Ct No 03-724) (filed 3 Feb 2004); Brief for the Government of Canada as Amicus Curiae Supporting Reversal in *F Hoffman-La Roche Ltd v Empagran* (Sup Ct No 03-724) (filed 3 Feb 2004); Brief of Japan as Amicus Curiae in Support of Petitioners in *F Hoffman-La Roche Ltd v Empagran* (Sup Ct No 03-724) (filed 3 Feb 2004); Brief of the United Kingdom of Great Britain and Northern Ireland, Ireland, and the Kingdom of the Netherlands as Amici Curiae in Support of Petitioners in *F Hoffman-La Roche Ltd v Empagran* (Sup Ct No 03-724) (filed 3 Feb 2004).

to detect and deter international cartel activity' and to impair similar efforts by foreign nations.[47] Again a decision is expected by the end of June.

The Supreme Court's decision to hear these two cases is a sign of its recognition that the increasingly globalized nature of commerce makes controversies like these more prevalent and more important. The Court's decision to hear these cases also reflects its concern that the extraterritorial reach of US jurisdiction not be unreasonable. Certainly, the participation of foreign sovereigns as amici curiae has only heightened this issue with the Court.

Our Supreme Court is currently considering petitions for *certiorari* in two more antitrust cases: *3M (Minnesota Mining and Manufacturing Co) v LePage's Inc*,[48] an *en banc* decision of the Court of Appeals for the Third Circuit,[49] and *Andrx Pharmaceuticals, Inc v Kroger Co*,[50] a decision of the Court of Appeals for the Sixth Circuit in an interlocutory appeal.[51] As I mentioned, the Supreme Court often invites the views of the United States on whether a case is worthy of *certiorari* and it has done so in these cases. Because the United States has not yet filed briefs in these cases, it would be inappropriate for me to comment beyond a brief description of the cases. *LePage's* involves appropriate standard to be applied to 'bundled rebates' and 'fidelity discounts'. *Andrx* involves the antitrust implications of an agreement among parties to patent infringement litigation.

American antitrust law has come a long way since 1890. At every stage of the journey, the most significant mileposts have been decisions of our Supreme Court. This common law approach has led us on some detours. But this approach also provides the flexibility for the law to develop in light of sound economic principles. My hope is that the Antitrust Division's efforts will assist our Supreme Court in keeping us firmly on the road to sound economic policy and increased consumer welfare.

---

[47] Brief of the United States, above n 36, at 8.
[48] Sup Ct No 02-1865.
[49] 324 F.3d 141 (3d Cir 2003) (*en banc*).
[50] Sup Ct No 03-779.
[51] *In re Cardizem CD Antitrust Litigation*, 332 F.3d 896 (6th Cir 2003).

Questions and Answers

[DR PHILIP MARSDEN]

Thank you very much Hew for that fascinating summary of some of the past, present and increasingly pressing cases at your Supreme Court, and ones that have ramifications here. Doubtless there will be increasing interest and I look forward to questions from the audience here for a few minutes.

[DON BAKER, *Baker & Miller, PLLC*]

I have two questions for you. First, do you have any statistics on the *certiorari grants* where the Solicitor General has offered opinions on whether *he grants cert or not?*. You gave very low statistics for normal one. The second question I had, is whether *Intel v AMD* is the first case we've had where the European Commission and the United States have ended up on the opposite sides of the Court?

[HEWITT PATE]

Well I don't have a precise statistic. I have talked to the folks in the Solicitor General's office about it and all I can say is that where the Solicitor General supports a grant of cert, the grant rate is much higher than in cases on the average.

[DON BAKER]

That's why we come running into you and the Solicitor General.

[HEWITT PATE]

Yes. What I ought to do is announce that the text for the programme will be on our website and before I put it up I will find that statistic and so it will look like I told you about it today! I don't accept the premise that in *Intel v AMD* we were on the opposite side of the Commission. I should point out that the Civil Division was the lead Justice Department Agency on it, not the Antitrust Division. It was a general purpose discovery statute issue as opposed to an antitrust one. Be that as it may, it was not our view that this sort of discovery was an appropriate thing for plaintiffs to get in this type of Commission proceeding. We did end up on the other side with respect to some specific construction issues but I think not on the practical outcome. There are people here who could tell you more about it than I could. I'm not aware personally of other cases where the Commission has filed as *amicus* at the Court but may be there are some.

[PETER ROTH, *Monckton Chambers*]

Now I ask this question out of complete ignorance. We hear a lot about US federal antitrust law. How important or not in practice is state antitrust law? And if I can just give a context for that, I remember reading about the Supreme Court decisions in *Illinois Brick Co* and *Hanover Shoe* and the indirect purchaser rule, and thinking that makes it rather difficult for consumers to claim. I put this to a US plaintiff antitrust attorney and he said, 'oh no, we just bring our class actions under state antitrust law'.

[HEWITT PATE]

I think that's right. The answer is that it can be quite important. Our Supreme Court has a decision called *American Stores*. This was controversial for a time but it is now quite well established that the Court will not find state antitrust statutes to be pre-empted by the presence of a federal statute and that this is the case even if, under the federal statute, the Court has reached a decision such as the *Illinois Brick* decision for closing liability to a class of plaintiffs or on a particular theory. It remains open, within certain limitations, for state courts, or not just state courts but state law to provide a remedy to those plaintiffs and a large number of states have actually passed legislatively so-called *Illinois Brick* Repealer statutes which allow indirect purchasers to claim. I think it simply states a fact that the application of state law has taken a back seat in terms of the type of national tending toward global antitrust question that was at issue in *Microsoft*. There were state law claims, for example, in that case but they were really dealt with much in the background and they did not differ from federal law, but this is one aspect of what I had to say at the Roundtable with the Authorities session yesterday. In an increasingly national and then global economy, it is a very important to try to begin to think about how we do cohesive antitrust enforcement in the United States, so your question is a good one and as of right now though the role for state law is certainly there as part of the system.

[RICHARD WAINWRIGHT, *European Commission*]

Just to answer the question and then to put a question. Yes it is the case that this is the only antitrust type action before the Supreme Court that we have intervened in. We did strongly debate the issue of putting in an *amicus* in the *Empagran* case. In fact, the Member States did it for us. My question is perhaps slightly provocative although along the same lines. Has the United States government ever considered intervening in a case before the European Court of Justice?

[HEWITT PATE]

Not to my knowledge and I am certainly not aware of any antitrust case where that has been considered. To be honest, I don't know anything about the rules for *amicus* participation in the European Court system. I'll have to wait for this CLE programme that I am envisioning where I learn about that, but the answer to you question is no we have not. Our Solicitor General has control over all briefs filed in the Court of Appeal and Supreme Court levels in the United States. I'm not sure that there is a clear answer to what happens if an agency has an interest in making a filing in a foreign judicial system. Rest assured I would ask before doing it but I don't know the rules for it.

[OLIVER BRETZ, *Clifford Chance*]

It was quite interesting what you said about the effect that treble damages might have on your leniency programme, especially if the *Empagran* case went the wrong way. I know there has been some discussion about whether de-trebling would be an appropriate action to take as part of the leniency programme in the United States. Could you just fill us in on whether this debate has gone anywhere yet?

[HEWITT PATE]

The whole question of how civil liability dovetails with our amnesty programme is a very important one to us. It would be hard to come up with a precise prediction of what the incentive effects will be. In *Empagran* it was as much the unquantifiable nature of the potential liability. Another thing that's important is we don't look just at our own amnesty programme as part of the cartel detection system in which we participate, because for amnesty programmes in countries who don't have treble damages liability in the first place, it's an even more potentially severe impact. It's one thing on the margins for us to worry about the incentives for potential amnesty applicants who already know they are going to face some degree of treble damages litigation as a follow on: it's another thing entirely for companies who might be thinking about applying, say in Europe under an amnesty programme, to now learn for the first time that what may come with that is treble damages based on Ukrainian vitamin sales or something of that

nature, so it's a big deal. As to de-trebling, I don't know if you are familiar with it, there has been a legislative proposal in the United States that
would at the same time increase our criminal penalties from 3 years maximum prison sentence to 10 and then from a $10 million maximum guide-
lines fine to $100 million. Those increases would be put in place at the
same time as a provision that would say that for the successful amnesty
applicant who meets all of the qualifications of our programme and then
who, in addition, would agree to provide information to private plaintiffs
in the follow-on compensatory actions, such an amnesty applicant would
be relieved from treble civil damages liability and would instead pay only
single damages on its own conduct. So a dramatic difference. Single
damages on own conduct verses joint and several liability trebled, and so
the status of that is that it has passed our Senate 100 to nothing and that it
is pending in the House of Representatives, so that is something where we
may see a change in US law depending on how that goes.

[JIM GRIFFIN, *US Department of Justice*]

And would that just apply to the federal level or would it, coming back to
Peter's question, apply to the state level?

[HEWITT PATE]

Excellent point. As drafted, the legislation would, in that particular case,
excuse the defendant from treble damages liability based on any statute and
if you think about why that would have to be so, Peter's question reveals it;
otherwise the plaintiffs would simply step into a different statutory scheme
and then get around the potential de-trebling provision. Whether that
comes to pass we will see. We don't have an official administration position on it. It was a bill that was introduced on a bi-partisan basis by
Senators Kohl and DeWine, Chairman of the Anti-trust Subcommittee, but
in concept it is something that we and Jim Griffin, who is in the back of the
room would confirm, think has potential to have a very invigorating effect
on amnesty applications.

[DR PHILIP MARSDEN]

Well thank you very much Hew for those insights into the regime and thank
you all for your questions.

F. The Consumer Interest in EC Competition Cases

Philip Lowe*

[PHILIP MARSDEN]

Welcome to you all. We had a very interesting series of sessions yesterday and I hope we can surpass that today. We are very grateful to Philip Lowe, the Director General of DG Competition for joining us this morning. He is a great friend of the British Institute and helped us launch our Competition Law Forum last year. He is going to speak about 'the Consumer interest in Competition cases', which is actually the subject of the first panel and then he will be joining the first panel afterwards as well. Thank you very much Philip for coming.

[PHILIP LOWE]

Thank you Philip for that introduction and good morning everyone. Every two years, I think, in the life of any Institution its members have to go and revisit holy shrines. We've spent so much of our time in DG Competition over the last two years changing procedures and changing laws, but it's quite a delight to actually be able to go back and ask, why are we doing this all this? Why are we pursuing a competition policy? What are its benefits? This is very much linked to the theme of this next session on consumer interest in competition cases. It's not always evident. Many said, well are you intervening simply because you get complaints from competitors. Well, sometimes it looks as if we are. Are we allowing or disallowing State aids because of consumer interests? It is not at all clear in some cases. Maybe, State aids in the short term actually lead to lower prices. So, what is this competition policy of which you speak Director General? This is why we've been looking again at the way in which we ourselves articulate and advocate competition policy. Therefore, I want to take you through one or two aspects of our thinking on this, and it goes right the way back to why we say that competition is good for the economy and society.

The EC Treaty, which we occasionally look at, says the EU system is based on the principle of an open market economy with free competition and we generally say that competition leads to better resource allocation, leads to more productivity, and more growth. On the other hand, there might be someone who could say to you, well are you sure about that? If you have

---

* Director General of DG Competition, European Commission.

20 competitors does that mean that you are necessarily going to produce a better result than with five competitors? If you have a merger of some major corporations with competitive advantages in different fields it could quite well be that you would increase competition by having fewer players. The issue of competition as rivalry is not necessarily equated with the idea of more players as such, but underlying the notion of competition there seems to be a question of the capacity of that competition to produce better results in terms of price, quality, choice, and ultimately, for whom? Clearly it is for consumers. Therefore we as a competition agency tend to concentrate, contrary to what economics on the whole does, on consumer welfare as against on consumer surplus, more narrowly as against producer surplus. Is that something that we can measure in the short term or the long term? Well, we would argue that it is absolutely necessary not just to look at cost reduction, immediate price effects, immediate access conditions, but also the dynamics of competition which produces results which are better or worse for the consumer. The competitive process is what we are ultimately trying to improve in order to produce in our view better results for consumers. Does that mean that the issues of fairness of free and fair competition are totally absent from the underlying objectives of the policy? No, because the predictability, the equity achieved through competition on the basis of fair rules, generally speaking, gives more confidence, more predictability for business to compete on the merits. While we could say from an economic point of view that concentration on consumer surplus is rather narrow—even consumer welfare is rather narrow—we should look at the effect on productivity, ie producer surplus as well.

The general view taken by competition agencies and by governments has been that there is enough representation of business and producer surplus in the economy and society. What competition law enforcers should look at are the benefits to the consumers and the representation of consumers. This is what we see underlying the rules in EU antitrust and merger law. For example, efficiency claims can be taken into account only if consumers are not made worse off. Now coming back to the issue of what is consumer welfare, what is the measurement? It must be a measurement of dynamic effects. It must not simply look at price. It must look at the overall benefits to consumers. This is why we have to even encompass in that definition of a consumer orientation for competition policy also a factor such as health and safety, and indeed the consumer protection elements, which would be regarded as fair competition in certain jurisdictions.

Now let me turn to some of the examples of where we can see an immediate tangible impact of competition law enforcement policies on consumers. We talked earlier this morning at breakfast and elsewhere about fight against cartels and other illegal agreements. Quite clearly here one can say that if there is empirical evidence to be gathered about the damage to consumers, it is most tangible, most measurable where you see prices or output restricted specifically in the context of a cartel. During the last three or four years you have seen not just in the EU but elsewhere, a tremendous increase in our activity against cartels through leniency and amnesty programmes in the States. This is an activity which certainly does not necessarily need an input from consumers to assist competition law and enforcement agencies but certainly results in a benefit to them. On the other hand, in the area of abuse of market power by dominant firms, we have to measure, generally speaking on a rule of reason basis as one would say it in the US, what the ultimate effect for consumers in the short and longer term is. The issues which have, for example, arisen out of our recent *Microsoft* decision go to the heart of the debate which must take place when you look at cases, such as that concerning the Windows media player, as to what the ultimate effect on consumer welfare will be.

People have asked us to give consumer welfare a more tangible form. Why have you asked for the company concerned to market a product which is incomplete without a media player in it? Our point of view on that is if you want to have competition on the merits, with functionalities being developed and innovation taking place, then you have to create a context in which competition can result from alternative offers from different suppliers. We would expect that those who are selling media players like Realplayer or Quicktime to be competing to do deals with the original equipment manufacturers to integrate a media player into the operating system on to the hard disk of any PC. How do we ensure that the consumer gets a complete product with all the things he or she needs, and at the same time, how do we ensure that innovation is not chilled by the integration of any innovation based only upon one supplier? That is the basis for the orientation which we took as far as the remedies imposed for the media player. Incidentally I sincerely hope that having spent the last 18 months writing guidelines on virtually every concept in the EU Treaty on competition, we actually finally get round to saying something public about the kind of analysis we will apply to abusive market power cases. Whether we call that guidelines yet or not, I don't know. We are just about to have a regime change in Brussels in November. We have new members from the new Member States. We will have a new Competition Commissioner in November and he or she will have to review the work programme. However, we are, as you know, actively working on trying to synthesize what we regard as our practice, whether it is to do with exclusionary or exploitative conduct or indeed whether it is focusing on specific abuses such as tying and other abuses mentioned in the Treaty. Of course if you look at the benefits of competition for consumers it would be wrong to focus simply on the application of antitrust and merger rules. There are a host of other regulatory instruments used by EU, by the Commission, by national authorities through EU legislation, through national legislation, to promote competition with benefits for consumer welfare and we tend to forget what has happened sometimes in sectors where regulation has promoted competition. One of them is telecoms. We are always lamenting the non-unbundled loop, but we tend to forget that in August of last year for example, a third of EU subscribers used an alternative provider for their long distance international calls and 25 per cent were using them for local calls. We know that the incumbents with their guardians, the regulators, still retain a large market share of fixed voice telephone services but there are new entrants coming up and some of them get a foothold. Over the period 1998 to 2003 the average cost of an international call has been further reduced by 42 per cent for residential users so there are, irrespective of what we do in the specific area of antitrust and mergers, advocacy tasks for a competition agency to ensure that regulation is actually applied and enforced in a way that is going to produce benefits for the competitive process and for consumers.

We have also gone on in that context beyond issues of liberalization of utility sectors like energy which is a big challenge for increasing consumer welfare. Consumers are just about getting used to being helped to switch. Certainly in the UK it goes much faster than elsewhere, but it is something which is equally going to have a tremendous effect across Europe. The capacity of the alternative gas and electricity producers and suppliers to market their services throughout the European Union should in principle, if we make sure we apply the antitrust rules to them as well, result in further benefits for consumers. Beyond these sectoral liberalization processes there are other areas where regulation has played a huge role. One of them is the professional services area and the liberal professions or as John Vickers calls them, the illiberal ones. They have always based the need for regulation on protecting consumers from unscrupulous solicitors or estate agents or tax accountants etc, and yet we know that studies which we have launched and which other national jurisdictions have launched show quite clearly that in many areas regulation is holding back benefits which could be presented for consumers.

What about the area of mergers and State aids? We say quite clearly in the Merger Regulation that a merger can go ahead if it does not significantly impede effective competition and you can see increasingly in our practice as well as in the practice of our sister agencies throughout the world, the search for remedies which actually help consumers to have more choice in not just the longer term but in the short term. That is particularly the case, for example, in the air transport industry. We believe the European

Commission has said it many times that efficiencies are there to be grasped through greater consolidation in the passenger transport field of aviation in Europe and there are probably too many operators still on the market. That is something which we are tackling both through our aviation policy but also through State aid policy to ensure that no one who cannot survive does survive. Yet when there are mergers such as between Air France and KLM recently, it is absolutely essential to ensure that what is gained in efficiencies results in some benefit being passed on to consumers. In that case, as in many others, the analysis of point to point routes and the indirect effects of the concentration led to us asking Air France and KLM for a large number of concessions in terms of slots, frequencies, in order to give new entrants the critical mass to offer alternatives to Air France and KLM and not just on obvious routes like Paris and Amsterdam, but actually in the French domestic aviation market.

In the area of State aids this is, as I mentioned earlier, one category of our work where one could almost argue that the objective of eliminating distortions of competition from State subsidy is not immediately connected with the issue of consumer benefit. It is much more connected to the concepts of fairness and equity in competition. When we, for example, do have a rescue and restructuring scheme which is presented to us, as we frequently do these days, there are two stages to the analysis. One is to ask, is the aid sufficient but no more than sufficient to enable the company to become viable again? Secondly, what are the compensating measures on the market which the company can offer and which will allow competition to be, in some sense, restored to its pre-subsidy situation? Therefore, in rescue and restructuring it is almost more about transferring producer welfare back to those who were entitled to it, because they had been competing on the merits, from those who had an undue advantage from State aid. Does that mean that we should look only at restoring the competitive process? Could not there be, for example, in our policy other ways of reaching compensation for State aid which might actually be more beneficial to consumers? One possibility for example is that a government would open up markets which were previously closed. Therefore, instead of asking the company concerned who had benefited from the government aid to artificially reduce their market share by offering less or by divesting, one could actually ask the government concerned to say, well don't ask for compensation directly from the company but instead abolish these regulations which prevent other people competing against it. So, there are more creative ways of looking at State aid policy which we have not been doing up to know. Just as the caricature of European competition policy is being more about competitors than competition, in State aids concentrating entirely on competition and not thinking about the ultimate benefits for consumers is something which we need to change if we have not changed already.

When we actually go on to what the role is which consumers can play in competition enforcement, well of course, they play a crucial role. But, if you then look at the record of the involvement of consumers and consumer associations in the way in which we carry out investigations, the answer is they have a very weak role. Is that because there is too little money around in consumer associations? Well that depends. In many of them, there is quite a lot of money but they do not really believe that one way to actually advance their cause is to intervene in particular competition cases. There are exceptions to that. The UK Consumer Association made a very important contribution to our revision of the Car Block Exemption Regulation and indeed in the latest merger in France in the book publishing field, when Lagardere went to acquire Vivendi Publishing, consumers protested in their ranks because of course they believed that the choice of books and other publications, certainly in the provinces and away from the main centres, would be severely limited and the effects on price could have been considerable. The result of their intervention was that the ultimate grouping created by the merger after divestments was actually smaller than the original size of one of the companies concerned which is rather surprising. It shows that in these situations, where you are looking for remedies which are benefiting consumers, you may have to go quite far to develop the alternative force necessary to contest the new entity.

Of course if we can get consumers to intervene more regularly in investigations, it is a very good counterweight to the intense political pressure which the Commission and national authorities are often under. Equally it is a good counterweight to the interests of the parties which are forcefully represented. I think we have here the possibility to listen more to consumers which gives us direct guidance for action and also which helps us to support new action. As far as our own response to the need, at a practical level, to involve consumers more in the context of the merger review and in the warm-up to the date of the 1st of May, we thought it would be a good idea first of all to appoint a consumer liaison officer, which we did last year. Juan Riviere y Marti is sitting here and his role is an important one, although for the moment modestly described. The first and essential condition for involvement of consumers is that they know what is going on and they know who to contact first if they have a problem and that is why he will act as a primary contact point. He can alert consumer groups to competition cases. Therefore if we are making information requests it is a very good preliminary enquiry to make as to whether consumers are interested in taking part. Of course there is also now a network of consumer oriented officers in each of the national authorities.

How should we frame our approach to the consumer orientation which must be at the centre of the policy? I think the modernisation regime gives us the basis on which to do it because we move away from essentially a business oriented notification system to a proactive system where we have to concentrate our attention and our resources on those infringements of competition which actually are going to do damage to the consumer. One of the new disciplines we have placed on ourselves inside DG Competition is that from now on, when we look at whether we are going to investigate a case or not, we no longer analyse it simply on the basis of whether there has been an infringement. Instead we are going through the discipline of saying, yes there is an infringement, but if this infringement is there, what in our view, even before we start investigating, is the probable, the potential harm to competition and consumers? What is the likelihood, too, that we can achieve a result which is positive for them? In line with that, you have seen that inside the Directorate General we have moved away from an instrument based organisation to a sectoral organisation where our teams involved in merger and antitrust work pool their knowledge of what is going on in markets and have a much more natural dialogue, not just with national authorities, but with the sector and indeed with consumer groups who are following problems in particular sectors on a day to day basis. The sectoral focus, the concentration of our activities on potential areas of competition harm and the capacity to relate our work to market realities all goes along well with the idea of a much greater role for consumers. That will also involve our colleagues in the national authorities and of course there is a very important role for the courts.

What are some of the practical things that we can say that may happen or could happen in a more effective context to involve consumers? We have given some guidelines on how complaints should be dealt with and we have made it clear in notices what information is required. We have also said that, if that information is there, then we will be happy to give an answer on it within four months, which is quite a discipline for any administration when we have other deadlines to respect as well. We have also created a new web site to invite consumers to provide information on suspected infringements which would not be classified as any official complaint, but at least is there as a possible destination for any complaint or any suspicion of an infringement which may arise. Of course we have, in the new modernisation context, quite a complex network of authorities involved in looking after the interests of competition and consumers across many sectors of the economy. We tend to think that we are only talking about the competition authorities. That is true for the purposes of defining the European Competition Network but, if you are looking in a holistic way about how consumers are going to benefit from any particular action, well, regulation is relevant and the regulators are relevant too. So, if we are going to look at a problem of competition in the telecoms sector or in the energy sector, for example, where regulators have a key role as far as price is concerned and access, then we cannot ignore what they are doing. We believe that we will have to do a lot more work to bed down the relationships which are establishing themselves between authorities to see how we can mobilize our different efforts to achieve a particular result. I'll give you one sort of frustrating situation which can arise, again in the telecoms sector, which is the wholesale and retail price for broadband access. We have had complaints from consumers and indeed from competitors, but particularly in one country from competitors, who said that they were unable to provide services because of a squeeze between the retail and wholesale price of the broadband offer. What was the conclusion? The telecoms incumbent concerned said, well, I'm sorry Commission we cannot do anything about it, the wholesale and retail prices are fixed by the regulator; and then when we talk to the regulator they say, well, it is a bit difficult you see because we have employed an expert to model the industry and they have come up with these prices and if we are going to ask them to alter those prices we have to alter our whole methodology and we will have to start it again with a new system of how to fix prices in the sector. I think in the end we will arrive at a good solution in this area and we have scope for widening the gap between the retail and wholesale price. However, one nightmare scenario was that the company concerned would have gone to the press and said quite openly, well we have been asked by the Commission to increase the gap between the wholesale and retail price, so we are going to increase our retail price to consumers by 15 or 20 per cent. Now as you can imagine that would not have been a very good thing from the point of view of consumer orientation and thankfully we have not got to that situation and we have had more effect on the wholesale price, but it is the sort of issue that can arise and it is an example of where it is clear that simply cooperating between the competition authorities alone is enough.

When it comes to consumers acting on their own, if they have no joy from any competition agency in Europe, maybe they would like to take the matter in their own hands and take a complaint to a national court which could conceivably arise but it still remains very difficult to do. We believe that the victims of infringements of competition law need arguably to be given a much greater, much easier framework for taking up cases. As you know we have launched a study on the conditions under which under national law allows claims for damages for infringements, and if there is a second phase of modernization after we have digested this first phase, I am sure it will be in that direction as well as in procedural simplification and approximation between what's happening in the different jurisdictions.

Now let me finally turn to the issue of mergers which is outside the modernisation regime but is covered by the recast Merger Regulation. The wording on efficiencies and benefits to consumers in the Regulation have stayed the same but the guidelines which we have produced on horizontal mergers give much more prominence to the issue of merger efficiencies and the need to take them into account in the overall competition assessment if the benefits are passed on to the consumers. That is something that is very easy to judge if the benefits are clear in terms of cost reduction in the short term but it is extremely difficult to measure. That is where most competition agencies disagree with parties when they come to them and say, well we are going to create a new dynamic innovative force in the market which is going to revolutionize things. That of course is very difficult to measure and very difficult to reach a judgment on, balancing other anticompetitive effects. So, consumer is at the centre of the debate on the effects of a merger but those who would claim consumer benefits as a direct result of the merger, which has in principle some restraining effect on the process of competition, will have a hard job proving it with any competition authority.

I end up with the State aid field because I know that very few of you are actually probably actively involved in dealing with State aids. We had a very interesting case recently which was actually not dealt with as the lead service by my department but by the transport department. It was the question of whether there should be aids to a particular airport somewhere near Brussels. Now you can argue about other examples; Stockholm South, Frankfurt Hahn. This one is a very successful operation and we undertook with the Transport Department an in-depth analysis and we debated very hard this whole issue of what is the ultimate benefit for consumers. After all you can say with quite a good degree of force, as indeed the Chief Executive concerned said, I am delivering a better product for everyone and if a local government wants to help me do that, why can't I/they? It's perfectly all right. Just to clarify one or two things in this case, which is quite interesting, it was a complaint by two low cost airlines against another low cost airline. This is not always pointed out in the press. Both these other airlines were very annoyed about the way in which the subsidies were given. In practice we approved 75 per cent of that aid and on the competition side we said, well we like low cost airlines and we like the idea that airports, if they are run as autonomous businesses on a commercial basis, can offer promotional incentives to airlines to come in to new locations. That is a good thing from an aviation policy as well as from a transport policy, particularly because we have some very saturated hubs in Europe which some of our major airlines work out of and they want to make sure that the maximum amount of traffic goes through those hubs.

Therefore the low cost airline alternative is a very interesting one. It solves the problem of infrastructure shortage and also avoids any monopoly rents accruing to those who are actually sitting on that shortage. Then we have to ask, can we nevertheless allow airports to give those aids without any sort of restriction on the aids at all? We thought about that quite a lot. We thought that it was probably a good idea that something like a reduction on a landing fee to the airport should be a promotional offer which is available to other participants and not just simply one airline, but there must be a regime. There could be different levels of promotional offer against the landing fee but the airport must not be allowed to restrict any particular benefit to one particular airline. That is why we, despite everything, approved most of the aid but what we asked the Belgian authorities to do was simply to look back at the way that they are actually applying their policy, applying the aid. Instead of simply writing a cheque, there should be an attempt to set up an account, an accounting centre, a cost centre, profit centre for the airport, whether it is in public hands or in private hands, so that we can really see that the offers made are done on a commercial basis.

But of course the case in itself raised two wider questions. Were we concentrating only on that small airport because we could see what was going on there? We could see the cheque emerging from the pocket of the Belgian Minister and being handed to the airline. Do we know how the accounts of other public airports work? For example, if you go to Frankfurt, which is in public hands, it is not clear that we have the same transparency and accountability that we have now in Charleroi. In the Commission's decision there is a commitment to produce a framework which includes both public, large airports and small airports, for the way in which money is handed out in promotional offers when the authority is not in private hands. The other question is of course the wider question which I think the tabloid press raised: why don't we just let this happen? There are no negative externalities, or in other words, they are not doing anyone any harm, why don't you just let them give these aids? Well, this is an interesting question. I don't think the jury has come back on it yet. It the mayor of Turin or Coventry were giving vouchers for new cars €2000/£2000 off, if you bought a car that was manufactured in Coventry or Turin, I think people would not actually like that very much and they might see that there could be a distortion of competition which would actually undermine the competitive process and ultimately be bad for consumers. In the airline industry, are we in that kind of situation? It is certainly very interesting that, as I have said before, the low cost airlines can actually exploit infrastructure which is under-used and offer tickets to ordinary consumers at a much lower level. I think there is a good argument to say that a certain amount of distortion of competition in the interest of consumer benefit is tolerable and that we don't have to be too strict on these things. Nevertheless, free and savage use of subsidy is not a good thing even for the consumer in the long term.

So, that's some idea of where we see the consumers coming in and I would not say that we are half way down the road to a fully rigorous analysis of consumer orientation in our policy but we have started because we went back to look at the catechism of competition policy. Thank you.

[PHILIP MARSDEN]

Thank you very much Philip for that insightful examination of such an important issue. Of course it's an issue that the next panel is going to be talking about and you will have an opportunity to ask questions obviously on this subject during that panel. I'll take a couple of questions for Philip at this time and then we will move straight on to the next panel.

[DAVID AITMAN]

You mentioned the role of consumers specifically in a couple of cases, the acquisition by Lagardere of Vivendi and also the Car Block Exemption and, as I recall, in both of those cases the consumers had a limited role if you compare them to, say, the roles of trade associations such as CCIA or ACT in *Microsoft*, or even more so the role of third parties such as Sun in *Microsoft* or say Rolls Royce in *GE/Honeywell*. I've thought about the reasons for this and I wonder if it's because some of the trade associations and the rivals bring more to the table? They provide you with information that's unavailable to the consumer groups and so the consumer groups, as the decision gets closer, and I think this was the case in both the Lagardere acquisition and also the Car Block Exemption, begin to feel excluded in a way that the industry groups have not been quite as excluded from some of these other decisions. Do you see this as inevitable? Do you think this is going to change? Is it what you want to see?

[PHILIP LOWE]

I just want to say that I think all of us who have ever participated in any kind of antitrust or merger investigation would not dismiss the intervention of competitors as something totally unrelated to the consumer. The one thing which is always very interesting to listen to is how different firms view what is happening on the market. What is the market definition? What are consumers really interested in? What is the product substitutability? I remember having this particular argument years ago on *P & G Schickendanz* and it was a very embarrassing case because we were all males but it was on feminine sanitary towels and tampons. The parties claimed that the tampons and pads were in the same market and there was a certain degree of counter intuition in this. We did not believe them as men, so we asked our female colleagues, and others, and they of course all said, unanimously, that they existed in separate markets and this is why we got them to divest. As a matter of fact in that situation the competitors delivered some very, very hard empirical evidence supporting the market definition which we had and we swallowed immediately the views of the competitors. This is what we read in the papers. But there is, as you rightly say, a genuine information need there and the resources needed to find out what consumers want are not normally provided by those who are in that business. After all, the firm wants to sell its product and services and therefore would like to know what is best for consumers. This is the way to compete on the merits so I don't think that the caricature of looking only at competitors evidence and which they are going to paint to create a picture the way they want to look at it, is fair as long as we have counter checks against each of those who are intervening.

Regarding the role of the consumers themselves, the problem is, who are they representing first of all? Are we talking about individual consumers? Are we talking about class actions? Are we talking about consumer groups? Some consumer associations, as I said at the beginning, show no interest whatsoever in certain investigations in certain markets and yet in an area like cars or supermarket cases they do have a very, very strong view, but it is not always a uniform view. It is possible that as we develop this contact with consumer groups and consumer associations we will actually have not one consumer voice but several consumer voices. But the resource question is fundamental and I think that, coming back to the basic question of whether we should we be looking at, as the Canadians tried to, total surplus or consumer surplus, I think it is not just right from the point of view of ease of investigation but right politically and democratically, that an enforcement agency should try to represent consumers in the larger sense of the word, the largest majority of people who could buy or have bought the services concerned. They are going to be less strong in their voice themselves, so it is our role somewhat to correct that but that does not mean that the competitors' information and the dialogue we have with them and with the parties is not really educating us to reach a good result as it has done in recent cases too.

CHAPTER 9

The Consumer Interest in Competition Cases

[PHIL EVANS]

Well thank you very much everybody. We are going to have five minutes for each of the presentations and because we have the benefit of Philip Lowe joining us at the end, I'll ask him to make some comments in response to the other presentations and to borrow from the Frédéric Jenny school of chairing, we are going to try and keep it to bullet points and headlines only, seeing as we've only got five minutes each, to then allow us for some discussion thereafter. And in the spirit of consumer protection we'll be going by the list as it is on the agenda. So without further ado, I will hand over to Juan.

A. Juan Antonio Riviere Marti*

Hello. Well, I will be very brief. As Philip Lowe has already introduced the policy, I am the Consumer Liaison Officer. My duty is to receive all the information I can get from consumers all over the European Union, which number around 450 million. There is also the nice duty to have contact with the consumers associations represented here by the BEUC; there are others too, but the Bureau is a very important one. Then we are also in contact with national competition authorities because some of those authorities have a better knowledge or more experience in certain respects with relations with the consumers. My duty inside DG Comp is first to have good relations with other departments, especially with SANCO, which is in charge of consumer protection policy and also with other departments that specialize in certain economic sectors; secondly, to guide or to coordinate some of our action inside DG Comp where we have a group of *functionaires* from each unit and we try to coordinate the awareness of consumer protection and consumer welfare in all our cases. So that we enhance the quality of our decisions, as was mentioned yesterday by Lars-Hendrik Röller, our Chief Economist.

We have some control of impact on consumers in each case, but this would not be enough because it is not case by case that we are going to succeed.

---

* European Commission

What is useful is that we have a new organization in DG Comp, a structure by economic sectors that helps very much. At present it is not only necessary to improve the quality of our decisions, but also to prevent situations and for this we have a constructed a dialogue with consumers associations. We will list a number of issues that we can develop with them to have a broad vision of the problems that are arising. I have already started with Jim Murray some days ago. At the same time we are cooperating with the European Consultative Consumers Group, where all representatives of consumer associations around the Community are present. This is an important institutional group to work with, plus of course the work done at international level in the OECD with our national competition authorities in connection also with the national authorities related to consumer protection. This is the broad vision that we have. We hope that we will be able to multiply this objective to all our officials and take what is our level of responsibility, I would say the European dimension, because many things and many problems related to consumers and competition are national and even local. We have a very good prospect for work and I hope that we will get some support also from lawyers and economists by offering their advice to consumer associations, not only companies, to enable them to benefit. In the long term that will be very beneficial for our policy. Thank you very much.

B. Peter Freeman*

Good morning ladies and gentlemen. I am going to speak about the consumer with particular reference to my own Competition Commission. To begin with the present, in terms of evolution there is a clear and explicit recognition of the consumer interest in everything that we do now. It is fair to say that that may not always have been the perception. At some time in the past, authorities—I'll use the term in the generic sense—may have given the impression that they were in some sense pro-efficiency and in that sense more pro-industry. Now first of all I would like to make the obvious point in reply to that; that the split between the two is not all that clear. Businesses, particularly small businesses, can be the focus of anti-competitive harm and to that extent they are both consumers themselves and they also act as a proxy for consumers.

Now some quick points about procedure and institutions. These are always extremely dull, but they have a sacramental quality in that they are the outward and visible sign of an inward and spiritual thing. The Enterprise

* UK Competition Commission

Act has made the UK authorities determinative and has encouraged both the Competition Commission and the OFT to be much more transparent about their methods and objectives. Now this transparency helps to tell consumers what we are doing and how we go about it and in that sense how they can help. Specific measures like the Super-Complaints procedure and also the recognition of the importance of private actions in court procedures also give the citizen the chance to raise competition issues, and in one particular respect, obviously in the merger control and market enquiries regime there is express recognition of customer benefits at the remedy stage.

Now if we can go on quickly to doctrine, I mentioned the perception of a possible pro-industry bias in the past. This probably comes from a series of reports by the MMC, our predecessor body, in the early 1990s. These include *New Cars*, *Fine Fragrances*, *Ice Cream*, (I use those words with some trepidation sitting next to Malcolm) and *Recorded Music*. Now those were cases where the OFT referred complex monopolies to the Commission who, to all intents and purposes, found that there was no detriment to the public interest. Now I have no doubt there were excellent reasons for those decisions, but it is worth noting that they all involve vertical restraints in one form or another and it may well have been that the MMC was not so much focusing on doing down the consumer in that sense but was perhaps, how can one put it, leaning a bit to the right in vertical restraints theory and genuinely believed the consumer's interest was better served in that way, so the dichotomy might be a false one. Now if you contrast those cases with recent ones, some of which you will know about, I don't want to engage in ice cream wars as I've said, but you should note that in the 2000 *Ice Cream* report, the Commission did not take the retailers' and consumers' interest to be the same and did not take the view that the lack of shopping around or switching meant that consumers were necessarily happy. Similarly, in the *SME Banking* enquiry, a lack of customer switching was not taken as evidence of customer satisfaction and it's worth noting that that's a case where the customer was a business and the remedies that the Commission recommended were intended to empower those businesses and to make it easier for them to change suppliers. And you get the similar emphasis in the extended warranties report last year which shows that the Commission, having identified various detriments such as lack of choice, insufficient information, excessive pricing, and the sale of extended warranties at the point of sale, went for remedies intended to empower consumers to make better informed decisions about these warranties rather than taking or recommending direct measures to prohibit the availability of products, or that sort of thing, which would of course directly limit consumers' freedom of action.

So in short, I don't know how I am doing on time, but my view is that UK competition law is now very much focused on the consumer. As to the past, it might be said either in reproach or with approval that things are not what they were but then, as a philosopher said, things never were what they were.

C. Jim Murray*

Working for a European organization, and indeed since this is an EU/US forum, I should say something about the European situation. It's all different. Eleven days ago, there were only 11 languages and 15 national competition authorities, 15 different markets, 15 different cultures, but that is very much expanded now and so there are different ideas about competition and culture, not just among consumer organizations but also in different national cultures where competition and consumer policy have grown in different ways. I remember when I first came to this field being surprised to hear that the directive on misleading advertising was seen as a pillar of fair competition policy, whereas I had thought it was a pillar of consumer policy. In my own organization we are known to be pro-competition and pro-liberalization. There are some who merely dismiss us as being Anglo-Saxon (and in those quarters, by the way, to be Anglo-Saxon is a bad thing to be). It's a bit rough for an Irishman of course to be dismissed as being Anglo-Saxon, but we do the best we can. We have been as active as we can be in competition cases. You've heard already from Philip Lowe that the consumers' associations are our biggest members. For many years we worked together to change the block exemption for motor cars. This, by the way, wasn't so much a question of analysis, but simply a question of political pressure. In the end certainly there was analysis and we were fortunate to have an enlightened Commissioner in the shape of Commissioner Monti, but it was intriguing that, apart from, I think, some national competition authorities, the only other voices raised in support of any drastic change were from the consumer organizations. There were some private voices from some car dealers, but they were afraid to express that too publicly. We were also active, as indeed as you heard, in the Lagardère acquisition. We stayed well away from the Ryanair issue, despite pressure from Michael O'Leary and indeed some sections in the media, but we did see it as a question for analysis of State aid and not a question of whether consumers could have cheap flights or not. We felt also, and pointed out to the media, that Ryanair was famously against subsidized airlines and so were we.

Our problem, again Philip Lowe was right in mentioning it, is a question of

---

* BEUC.

resources, and because of the fact that bringing a consumer voice to competition policy or to other policy areas is not just a question of bringing consumers to these areas, it's bringing an analysis and an approach, but above all a serious analysis. It may be consumer advocacy. It may be providing information. It may be to exert pressure on the authorities. It may be to undertake consumer-oriented research. It may be a whole series of different things, but above all what it's not is just bringing in consumers to the process in some particular way. It's bringing a particular kind of orientation, but that orientation itself must be based on a great deal of expertise. We have, I acknowledge, sometimes not intervened as much as DG Competition would like us to do but we do feel that we shouldn't intervene unless we have something distinctive to contribute and some kind of analysis to bring to it and not just to come in with 'We represent the consumers and therefore…'. We have been helped in recent years through the Transatlantic Consumer Dialogue, of which I am co-chair, and they have helped particularly when we intervened in the *AOL/Time Warner* case. Our friends on the other side of the Atlantic had a great deal of information and analysis and market data to give to us and we were able to intervene in that case, which in passing, raised interesting questions, for example, about transfer of personal data when mergers arise. If you have given your personal data to one company, do you really expect then that data should be passed on to another company when a merger arises? There are interesting questions there which needed to be considered.

What would help us? I do hope indeed that there will be a 'Phase II' in the work of DG Competition looking more at the issue of consumers and competition. There is the question of resources. There is also the question of access to data and access to market data which, unless you actually intervene in a case, is difficult to achieve at European level. Here in the UK, as I understand, the advice of the OFT to the Competition Commission is published, but there isn't really an equivalent access to information and access to market data. We need market data for the purposes perhaps of intervening simply for the purposes of offering a countervailing voice to what some of the operators are saying. We need market data and other information for private enforcement apart from any other things and it's also needed for redress. There was a particular problem when DG Competition, rightly I believe, condemned the cartel among the Austrian banks. Our Austrian consumer organization wanted to go further and apply to the courts in Austria for redress for consumers in those cases but, of course, they needed to have more details than are publicly available about the cartel and the participants and the numbers involved.

For the future, and to conclude, I think competition policy itself, but also competition principles, are going to become more and more important on the

European level, both directly and indirectly, and also of course more important at national level with the move toward national enforcement. We hope that national authorities will have an open door to consumer organizations. It's not always the case, let me say immediately, in some Member States, but we hope that will change. It seems clear too there will be much freer movement of goods and services. People are upset about the slow progress in this area, but progress is being made, for example, in the new Directive on services in the internal market that is likely to open the market much more.

So we are going to be dealing with two things. More free movement but also, as we all know, with much more emphasis on the economic importance of services. We all buy more and more services as time goes by so we have to deal with the problems, or the issues, arising from freer movement and also the issues arising from promoting competition in the services area, which is a great deal more complicated than doing so in relation to goods. Another huge area where competition is, and must be, applied directly, but also where competition has been used as an instrument of social or political policies, is in relation to the liberalization of utility services. This is happening, of course, all around Europe at the moment to a greater or lesser extent, but here one of the most important aspects of policy in relation to utility services is universal service provision. These services in particular must be made available to all the population at affordable prices. So here we need to use competition, albeit regulated competition, to try to achieve universal service and also to make sure that the necessary conditions for investment are created in order to make sure that universal access will continue (In the TACD, we found that European consumer organizations seemed rather more favourable towards liberalization of utility services than our American counterparts and we wondered indeed if they had seen the future and found that it didn't work. But the I think one of the reasons why, and Bert Foer has many other reasons, is that in Europe we tend to think of liberalization side by side with regulation, whereas liberalization was perceived in the US as being deregulation and the signal to let in pure market forces).

I'll finish on the question of redress for consumers. This is a need to do something here. Some of us look at the fairly large fines which are levied from time to time in certain cases and wonder if some proportion of these might not be diverted to pro-consumer activities of one kind or another since it is rarely possible in these cases to identify individual consumers or to allocate the loss which they may have suffered. There is an argument, we believe, for trying to put resources into pro-consumer pro-competitive activities, to bring a consumer-oriented perspective, consumer oriented research and expertise to competition. Thank you.

D. Malcolm Nicholson*

When Philip Marsden asked me to do this session I said, 'Why me?' I don't do consumers and he said he wanted a little bit of grit put in the system; so grit in the system, spanner in the works is what I am going to do. We've had clearly explained to us by Philip Lowe and indeed by Peter Freeman that competition policy is very much about the protection of the consumer. It lies at the heart of the law. The consumer is a very important part of it so the administrators are on the side of the consumer. The role of the consumer bodies is to enhance that position and to bring value added. To my mind, I think they are failing in that role. They succeed some of the time but some of the time they fail which is why I thought I'd come and speak over here rather than sit down there! There are four points I want to pick up. They all come from real life experience.

First, beware the single issue fanatic trading as a consumer lobbying interest. At the *Airtours* oral hearing we had a consumer body represented at the hearing, not actually either of those two so they are safe, but what they did is they showed a film about an Airtours holiday in the Dominican Republic. It was originally made for a TV programme, you know, 'Horrible Holidays' or something like that. It wasn't shown, probably because it was defamatory and it was absolutely ghastly. It was all about open sewers and rats running around right next door to the food preparation areas. Horrible stuff, but it had absolutely nothing to do with collective dominance and whether Airtours should have been allowed to buy First Choice. That's one dramatic example, but there are other examples where single issue fanatics get into the process.

Secondly, consumer bodies need to beware the temptation to grandstand. Everyone enjoys grandstanding. I'm doing it now because I've been asked to do it to provoke some debate, but it seems to me that more caution is perhaps required from the consumer bodies when they are given the floor. There is a very obvious example in the public hearings that have over recent years been organized by the Competition Commission as part of their enquiries. This has provided a platform for consumer groups to lambaste whichever category of business institution was under investigation, motor manufacturers, high street retail banks, supermarkets, whatever. The industry can't talk back on those occasions. It's not that sort of forum. Now it plays well, gets extensive press coverage, you get on the Today programme, but does it actually deepen the debate? No, on the whole I think it doesn't.

Third problem; beware the tendency to recycle special interest pleadings as

* Slaughter & May.

being the considered consumer view. Because of the consumer orientation of competition policy those caught up in enquiries will often approach the consumer interest groups seeking their support and, in effect, offering briefings, data, information, even copies of the pleadings that they put into the regulator. Now this is very flattering to the consumer body; it's also very helpful to the consumer body because they suffer regrettably from an information asymmetry. They just don't have the data readily available. They don't have the resources to do the research quickly. But what it does mean is that from time to time the consumer view as put to the regulator is liable to be influenced by which lawyers or PR advisors did the best job of briefing them beforehand and that I regard as a tricky situation.

The last problem is that I do think sometimes the consumer groups tend to submit to the regulator research submissions that are not fully thought through, not fully reasoned. Some of the super complaints, I think, that are made under the UK system fall into that category. The one I have in mind comes not from one of these bodies, but a consumer representation in a sectoral industry and it looked on analysis as if they'd tried to put together a Chapter II case, found a Chapter II case wouldn't run, so they bashed it off as a super complaint to see what came out of the system in consequence. Now consumer groupings are not alone in making complaints that are less than fully thought through or properly balanced. Competitor complainants do it the whole time, but there is a difference here. Competitor complainants are doing no more than pursuing their own naked self interest. The consumer body is seeking to wrap itself in the flag of looking after the public interest and the public good and I think people need to be careful about that consideration.

They also do a lot of good work. I haven't been concentrating on the good work they do. They do do a lot of good work but they need to do more. They need to forgo the status of 'vox pop' all-purpose commentator. They need to recognize the information asymmetries. They need to concentrate their efforts on carefully targeted issues that are really important to consumers where they can conduct their full analysis and take the case through thoroughly. If I was looking for what a consumer body should be, actually the template I would be looking at would be the sort of reasoned, well-thought out reports that you get from a House of Lords Select Committee, possibly some of the House of Commons Committees. That's where I think they should be and that is where they are currently lacking. Thank you.

E. Albert A Foer

Thank you. Let me compliment the Institute first of all for having a forum on the consumer interest. I've never seen such a forum in the United States and in fact I am more used to being attacked by the Chairman of the Federal Trade Commission for what we do rather than being recognized as an important participant in the process. Yet I think, as Mario Monti said to the American Bar Association several years ago, the need for the political support and almost the spiritual support of consumers is terribly important to the infrastructure of the antitrust endeavour. I see a very real political need for consumer organizations to be part of the process to understand the reasons for antitrust and why it's in their benefit to play an active role. I don't have time to tell you all the things I would like to tell you. Please read the paper which goes into a great deal of detail and raises what I think are some interesting questions, some of them answering or recognizing the points that Malcolm just made. One piece of information I would love to impart with you is my website. It is *www.antitrustinstitute.org* and you can find there all the details that you might be interested in. The American Antitrust Institute, which is now over six years old, I would describe as a virtual public interest network. Unlike many other organizations, we are not a membership group. We are very small. It's really an elite approach rather than a membership or grass roots approach. I have an advisory board of roughly 70 of the top people in the United States from economics, law, and even a few from the business school background, so we are multi-disciplinary in our approach. We have an attitude. The attitude is what I would describe as post-Chicago and I would say that everything that Philip explained this morning, we would adhere to, which is one reason why we get criticized by the Chairman of the Federal Trade Commission. There are some differences and it is very important to know that in the United States everyone is not of one mind, unified behind the Chicago School approach, and we represent an alternative. So we have an advisory board that plays an important role often through communications over the internet. We have a website that is really our exclusive publication. We put on the website several times a month, maybe more often than that, the work product. The site also has a very user friendly research facility. The other things that we do are those things that a think tank or an advocacy organization does. We have participated in litigation. Generally speaking, consumer organizations have a difficult time doing this because of the expense, the time, the expertise, so we find that there is a preference for engaging in *amicus* briefs rather than litigation.

We involve ourselves in regulatory and law enforcement intervention, not only at the federal level, but at the state level. We try to influence case selection and outcomes in some cases. We participate in coalitions. We do a little bit of lobbying as a non-profit. We are limited in the kind of lobbying we can do, but we testify and present things to Congress. All of this goes up on the website. One of the areas in which we have been helpful in the past to the government, I think, is by providing briefings to the House and Senate on the budgetary needs of antitrust, something that hadn't been done in the past. We see ourselves as supportive of the antitrust interest. We do a lot of research in public education, conferences for instance. On the table you will see an advertisement for our conference in Washington on 22 June 2004, regarding buyer power and antitrust. One of the keynote speakers, Dr Röller, will address buyer power. Another keynote speaker will be the Chairman of the Board of Walmart, so I think we are going to have some interesting discussions about buyer power. Part of our objective is to raise issues that aren't otherwise being raised and to try to look to the future as to where antitrust can be useful.

Let me say that it's not always a question of saying antitrust can do this or that. I think one of the things that we bring to the process is occasionally talking about the limitations of antitrust. We've had an energy forum every year and one of the things that has gradually come out, as we repeat these workshops on electricity restructuring, is the limitation on what antitrust can do in a transitional deregulatory framework, such as electricity. Generally we would be advocating a lot of competition rather than regulation, but not always. It's not always in what we perceive to be the consumer interest. And that gets back to the basic question of; who does speak for consumers? What is the consumer interest? I talk about that in the paper. The bottom line is you cannot pay attention just to the name of the organization or who the organization says it is speaking for. We have a rich mix of advocacy and think tank organizations in the US, almost all of them saying that they speak for consumers. Some are speaking from a Borkean welfare analysis. Some libertarians will claim to speak for a pro-competitive competition policy. So what do you do when you hear the words 'consumer interest'? I think you have to look at the patterns of the positions that are being taken in order to reveal the underlying purpose, constituency, and philosophy about economics, politics, and law. I know that we have to maintain a level of consistency or I would lose the support of this advisory group if they thought that we were selling out to a particular interest or to a funding interest, and that's another question that deserves some discussion: where do consumer groups get their funding and, where should they get their funding and, where should they *not* get their funding? These are some of the questions raised in the paper. Given the time limitations I think that's all I can get to right now and I thank you very much for having me here.

[PHIL EVANS]

Thank you very much Bert and thank you very much to the panel so far for adhering to their time restraint admirably well. I'm now going to ask Philip to respond with any thoughts that he's got on what he has heard from our panel so far.

[PHILIP LOWE]

Just one brief comment. No one group anywhere can say that they represent the ultimate view, the final view on what the benefits for consumers are. On the other hand, a process which does not include consumer groups is unlikely to be fully informed of what is going on, and Bert and Malcolm and others have said with so many people who say they know what women and men want, the aim of an investigation is actually to arrive at a studied balancing of the effects of a transaction on consumers and benefits for consumers. So, our orientation here towards consumers is not just consumer groups, it is ultimately to arrive at the nearest thing we can do to truth. So it is not unnatural that you could have single issue guys or other groups who are actually misrepresenting the situation and you do need a lot of evidence in order to verify your conclusion. But finally on the other side, and more positively vis-à-vis consumer groups, as Jim says, without the advocacy which they do, we would not get anywhere with some of our antitrust cases.

F. Discussion

[JULES STUYCK, *Katholieke Universiteit Leuven*]

I have two questions for the panel; integration of consumer policy and competition policy. I think that most of the speakers have stressed that the consumer's interest is at the heart of competition policy. Rightly so, this is also a constitutional principle of the EC Treaty. Now of course there is also a consumer policy in its own right according to the Treaty. I heard that there is now, within the institution, within the Commission, liaison between the different services also with DG Sanco (the Directorate General for Health and Consumer Affairs). Now in that regard, integration of consumer policy and competition policy, I have two questions. The first one is consumer redress and actions in court. I understand that according to the modernization programme, the Commission also wants to increase actions in national courts. One of the reasons for modernization is that in national jurisdictions you have other forms of redress than you would have before the European Commission. So it might be interesting also for actions of consumer organizations. Now we do have a Directive from 1998, Collective Actions for Consumers for Injunctive Relief, and that Directive has an annex which refers to a certain number of EC directives on the basis of which consumer organizations should be able to act in a national jurisdiction and also across borders. We do not see Articles 81 and 82 in that annex, so one of my questions is whether you could add Articles 81 and 82 so as to enable private enforcement of antitrust law in Europe by consumer organizations? In the 12 years that we've had a competition act in Belgium, there has been one successful action against a cartel in the hospitalization insurance sector which was brought by the Belgian consumer association before a court.

My second question is about a possible conflict between some of the views on consumer policy and possibly antitrust law. The idea, which I think still exists within DG Sanco, is that it would be a good idea to have collective agreements between producers and consumer organizations in certain issues, which of course may be a problem. We all know the *Albany* judgments on the social exception to the EC Treaty. I don't think there is a consumer exception so I would like to have the views of the members of the panel on the possibilities and the antitrust problems which would exist if the Commission would also encourage consumer organizations and producer organizations to conclude collective agreements. Thank you.

[JIM MURRAY]

Yes of course we would like the possibility of consumer organizations being able to act under the Injunctions Directive. I think in some Member States they can because they are so recognized under national law. While we do engage in negotiation by codes of conduct of one kind or another, and are ready to do so, we remain sceptical and think that the attraction, which many people in the Commission and elsewhere in the industry find in negotiated agreements and in codes of conduct, is really irrational. It's as simple as that. It represents the triumph of hope over experience. We objected very strongly, for example, to DG Enterprise negotiating new rules with the motor industry on pedestrian safety as they have negotiated a voluntary code of practice with the motor industry on reducing emissions. Indeed I was present once when the motor industry pointed to the fact that cars pollute less than they do in the past. This is true, but the industry then claimed that this was due entirely to the fact that they had concluded an agreement with the Commission to reduce emissions: it didn't have anything to do with price or economies or market forces or anything like that—no, it was because they had voluntarily agreed with the Commission to reduce emissions that these wonderful results had been achieved. I believe those who promote negotiated arrangements and codes of practice are not giving enough attention to the ways in which they can facilitate anti-competitive behaviour. We've always argued that, more generally, DG Competition should be more active internally within the Commission on issues such as new forms of regulation because many of the new forms of regulation which are being proposed have, in my view, anticompetitive dangers within them.

[PHIL EVANS]

Has that prompted any more questions? If not I'll throw one last one at the panel: I always go for the 'on the one hand and on the other' approach to final questions and I want to ask everyone on the panel what they think the top two issues for the interaction between consumers and competition policy really will be over the next coming 10 years?

[ALBERT A FOER]

I wish you had prompted me on that. I haven't thought about that, but I think a truly important issue is: where does the money come from to make antitrust advocacy possible by consumers? This is a big problem in the US. It's a much bigger problem, I think, elsewhere, particularly now that we have 100 countries doing antitrust, lacking the basic resources in many cases just to enforce the new law, and lacking the infrastructure that will support antitrust institutions. There is an organization that Phil is well aware of called INCSOC, the International Network of Civil Society Organizations on Competition, which was propelled largely by the consumer organization in India. It's met a couple of times already and the objective is to help to create an international grouping of civil society organizations that will advocate antitrust policy. We need something like this, along with needing better training for antitrust enforcers in the rest of the world, developing Bar support for antitrust and other infrastructure supports. So I think possibly infrastructure support may be a critical topic of which funding is one element and I'll leave those as my points.

[MALCOLM NICHOLSON]

Two quick points. It will not surprise you from listening to what I said earlier on that I think that the level of advocacy of the consumer interest needs to be improved. I think that is a major challenge over the next years. I think there is a further issue which is the interface between competition policy and consumer protection, in the more traditional sense that consumer protection is understood. The OFT has responsibilities in both areas. I am unclear as to how joined up the two sides of the OFT are in dealing with the competition issues and the consumer policy issues. There are those sitting at the back of the audience who may disagree with me but that seems to me to be an issue.

[PETER FREEMAN]

Can I just first make a preliminary comment? Listening to the discussion, I would just like to echo what Philip Lowe said. There are two quite separate questions milling around here and it is important not to confuse them. One is as a matter of doctrine: is the consumer interest the actual interest that the authorities and the courts are trying to promote? That's an intellectual question. The next question is, how do you ascertain that? That's a question of method and what we have been talking about is whether the consumer groups contribute to that method and I would certainly say that in the evidence gathering process consumer groups have to be there giving evidence. Their evidence has to be tested, it has to be credible, but is it important, yes.

I think there are just two top issues. One I think is the need to be able to measure and quantify consumer benefits from the work that the antitrust authorities do, and the other I think is the point made by Professor Stuyck, which is the need to improve the crossover from the work of the authorities to private enforcement. We can free up the market but we cannot compensate people for what's gone wrong in the past. That has to be done by private action and there are still more things that can be done. Thank you.

[JUAN ANTONIO RIVIERE MARTI]

For us the best thing to do first is to promote a good competition policy. A good competition policy would show the benefit for the consumers. The questions of the problems in competition are not only in the international or European stratosphere, they are also local because citizens are everywhere. So we have to assure that competition policy reaches every citizen. That will be very important for us. Now we cannot do that without all the input we can get not only from the consumer associations but also from lawyers, economists, judges, and all the national competition authorities. As the Commission has already said some years ago, it is increasing the dialogue with the civil society. Now the associations of consumers are more or less representing all the consumers and the message they are passing, if it is a good message, is very good for our policy because then we understand their views. So we need also consumers associations to structure themselves in a way that they are able to give us more input for our work. In this manner, I think we can support much the consumer welfare, which is our goal.

[JIM MURRAY]

For me the big issue, as I mentioned before, is the liberalization of basic services, because if that goes wrong, and Europe now is going to be a gigantic test bed for this, not only will liberalization itself be opposed in the future, but even ideas of competition and using competition policy in other areas too will be seen as bad. You already have this feeling to some degree here in the UK. If liberalization goes wrong people will not want more competition but a good deal less. This therefore is one of the biggest issues, as well as services more generally. I hope we will bring a stronger consumer voice to the area. I've never, by the way, claimed to be the leader of Europe's 450 million consumers or anything like that and I would accept entirely all the 'don'ts' that Malcolm mentioned, not least because we know we would be very effective if we did those kind of things. Sometimes, 'grandstanding' is needed because competition is not a pure intellectual analysis; it can get very political at times and to bring political pressure can also be important.

If we are going to take consumer benefits seriously as the core of competition policy then there are two challenges. One is that the agencies, and others including ourselves, have to stop thinking simply about antitrust and merger rules and start developing a wider concept of what is the best response to a particular problem that hurts consumers. Is it regulation, is it using the antitrust rules, is it advocating more legislation in a certain area? We have got to widen our view of the world in order to be more effective in achieving the result. As far as consumers themselves are concerned, I think, if we take consumer benefits seriously at the centre of competition policy, that we will have to develop a system for private enforcement,. We have to learn from the US experience, not to go as far as some of the extremes, which the corporate world would not thank us for introducing in Europe, but nevertheless give an opportunity for raising problems and getting redress when the enforcement agencies themselves aren't able to do it.

G. The Consumer Interest and Antitrust Advocacy

Albert A Foer*

In the abstract, everyone is in favor of 'competition', even monopolists like Mr Gates who in the virtual absence of live rivals professes to benefit from the competition that resides in his anxiety closet, that is, competition that may possibly visit from the future. In the crunch of day-to-day existence, however, the intermixed worlds of politics and economics are driven by interests rather than by altruistic conceits, and each interest group tends to bestow on the concept of competition its own meaning. I once heard the late Henry Luce, founder of Time Magazine, answer an angry question from the audience about how he dared call Time a 'newsmagazine' when it was clearly anything but an objective source of news. 'I invented the term "newsmagazine"', Luce memorably responded: 'I can make it mean anything I want.'

I begin this discussion of the consumer interest and antitrust advocacy, therefore, with some comments on what we may mean by 'the consumer interest' in competition. From there I will turn to the other phrase in my title and speak briefly about the varieties of 'antitrust advocacy'. In the final part of this discussion, I will marry the parts of the title and offer some comments on the consumer interest and antitrust advocacy in the international context, raising three questions for further thought.

I. THE CONSUMER INTEREST IN COMPETITION

It is necessary to begin this conversation about consumers as antitrust advocates by ascertaining about whom we are talking. The Joe Public who buys a cheeseburger at McDonald's is of course a consumer—indeed, by my lights, having chucked out the cash, he is a consumer even if he doesn't actually consume the sandwich—but so, in a sense, is McDonald's itself a consumer when it purchases the cheese from its supplier, and so on down the line of distribution. Should one who wishes to represent consumers on antitrust matters distinguish between end-use consumers and other buyers? And what about the fact that most consumers are also producers?

Traditional consumer protection advocacy organizations probably have no trouble in saying that their constituency is the end-use consumer in his or

* President, the American Antitrust Institute.

her role as consumer.[1] An antitrust advocacy organization like the American Antitrust Institute,[2] however, may very well find itself advocating for the competitive process in the name of consumers generally, and in so doing may find itself supporting through antitrust the opportunity of entrepreneurs to compete on the merits. In other words, consumer-oriented antitrust advocates may support the competitive opportunity for businesses to compete on a level playing field, although this support will be tied into what it is intended to do for consumers, directly or indirectly, rather than as a protectionist strategy for small business.

Identification of the consumer interest can be muddled in some other ways. First, we have the problem of what I call the 'Borkean Appropriation'. In his influential book, *The Antitrust Paradox*,[3] Robert Bork postulated that consumer welfare is the goal of antitrust, thereby gaining a symbolic victory for the Chicago School by co-opting the role of consumer advocate. But it is crucial to apprehend that Bork and the associated Chicago School are not talking about what is immediately good for the man on the Clapham omnibus (if that particular mode of transportation still functions), but rather what is gained for society as a whole, including producers, when free markets operate efficiently. The difference may or may not be important, depending on circumstances. Advocates of antitrust continue, even now, even after years of Chicago School domination, to disagree over the purposes of antitrust. While Chicagoists and post-Chicagoists, as well as populists and some libertarians, would all agree that horizontal price-fixing is bad for consumers,[4] they might disagree on precisely why it is bad; and more importantly, they will likely disagree on their evaluations of other types of activities that sometimes receive antitrust scrutiny.

There is general agreement among those who advocate for antitrust in the name of consumers that competition has four principal deliverables: (1) *an efficient economy*, because competition allocates limited resources efficiently and minimizes waste, which has the potential, at least in the presence of appropriate distributional policies, of expanding the overall pie so

---

[1] eg, 'Consumers Union, publisher of Consumer Reports, is an independent, nonprofit testing and information organization serving only consumers . . . Since 1936, our mission has been to test products, inform the public, and protect consumers'. <http://www.consumersunion.org/aboutcu/about.html>.

[2] The AAI is an independent non-profit education, research, and advocacy organization headquartered in Washington, DC. Background and work product may be found at <http://www.antitrustinstitute.org>. The author is grateful to Ryan Kriger, a law student at New York University, for allowing him to draw on his unpublished draft survey paper, 'The Use of Antitrust by the Consumer Protection Advocacy Community'.

[3] RH Bork *The Antitrust Paradox, A Policy at War with Itself* (Basic Books NY 1978) 405: 'The only goal that should guide interpretation of the antitrust laws is the welfare of consumers'.

[4] At least they agree as to the fixing of minimum prices.

that all members of the society may benefit; (2) *prices that are relatively low*, because competition reduces the gap between a seller's cost and a buyer's price; (3) *an innovative economy*, because competition gives the incentive to innovate or risk becoming a loser;[5] and (4) *a range of consumer choice*,[6] because suppliers will diversify the variety and quality of their offerings in order to satisfy consumer demand. There is less agreement over whether competition is desirable because (5) it *redistributes resources* (known as monopoly rents) away from monopolists and toward consumers; and (6) *it reinforces democratic institutions* by controlling the degree of economic concentration, which is seen as closely related to political power.[7]

Obviously, different weights can be given to each of these four, five, or six goals. Put this together with the different visions of what goals are appropriately in play, and it is evident why it is difficult to say exactly what '*the consumer interest*' is or, for that matter, who represents it.

Yet another reason for this difficulty is that different groups that purport to speak for consumers may actually have more complex agendas, based on their particular history, ideology, and funding. For example, some major US consumer advocacy organizations receive substantial funding from organized labour, and they see themselves as speaking for workers, and perhaps the poor generally, as well as for end-use consumers.[8]

---

[5] See the terrific but underutilized book by BH Klein *Dynamic Economics* (Harvard University Press Cambridge 1977), which makes a case, in the tradition of Schumpeter, that dynamic efficiency is far more important to a civilization than the static efficiency promoted by neoclassic economics.

[6] RH Lande is a leading proponent of consumer choice as not only a consequence of, but a justification for antitrust policy. See his article 'Consumer Choice as the Ultimate Goal of Antitrust', in (2001) 62 *U Pitt L Rev* 503.

[7] See CE Lindblom *Politics and Markets* (Basic Books NY 1977) and his uneasy connection of market systems with democracy in a later work, *The Market System* (Yale University Press New Haven 2001) 226–50. Louis Brandeis was one who believed 'that the proposition that mere bigness can not be an offense against society is false, because I believe that our society, which rests upon democracy, can not endure under such conditions'. His support of small units of production was ultimately contrary to the consumer interest. See TK McCraw *Prophets of Regulation* (Harvard Univ Press Cambridge 1984) 108–9.

[8] Particularly close to organized labour is the National Consumers League, the oldest consumer protection organization in the United States. Its mission is 'to identify, protect, represent, and advance the economic and social interests of consumers and workers . . . NCL provides government, businesses, and other organizations with the consumer's perspective on concerns including child labour, privacy, food safety, and medication information'. See National Consumers League website, available at <http://www.nclnet.org>. Query: what position should such a group take when a unionized oligopolist that manufactures yachts proposes to buy a non-unionized yacht-builder? The antitrust question might very well take second place to other considerations. It can get even more complicated if the consumer group also sees itself, like Dr Seuss' Lorax, as protecting the environment.

Organized labour, in my experience, has not been a noteworthy friend of antitrust, except in a few cases where a merger threatens to harm union members through anticipated post-merger layoffs. Despite the expected disagreement between management and union perspectives, labour's stand-offish attitude toward antitrust is not surprising for two reasons. First, in the early days of the Sherman Act, the US government used the antitrust law to break up labour unions, which, after all, reflect the anti-competitive collaboration of competing labourers. That attitude has been eliminated by statutes and judicial interpretation.[9] But secondly, think about the comparative ability of firms in highly competitive industries and firms in relatively non-competitive industries to split the profits among stockholders, management, and labour. Labour often comes off best in the least competitive industries.

Interestingly, small business has not generally been supportive of antitrust advocacy organizations. In another paper,[10] I have suggested a variety of reasons for this, having to do with limited resources and limited attention, domination of their trade associations by relatively large players, and the fact that the US government by the late 1970s had stopped bringing the kinds of vertical cases that were perceived as most useful to small businesses. In particular, while small business has been politically strong enough to protect its favourite antitrust provision, the Robinson–Patman Act, from formal repeal, it has not been able to convince the government that enforcement of this antidiscrimination law is pro-consumer, rather than protectionist, with the result that Robinson–Patman enforcement is no longer an antitrust service offered to small business by government. In consequence, small business in general seems to have given up on antitrust as a political priority. This does not mean, however, that small businesses or their associations (like larger businesses and associations) will not utilize the antitrust laws from time to time when it is in their advantage to do so.

Some advocacy organizations, not limited to those that claim to speak for consumers, like to describe themselves, more generically, as 'public interest' organizations.[11] This implies such characteristics as not-for-profit status,

---

[9] See LA Sullivan and WS Grimes *The Law of Antitrust: An Integrated Handbook* (West Group St. Paul 2000) 716 et seq. The current labour exemption is the product of two statutes, secs 6 and 20 of the Clayton Act, 15 USCA ss 17 and 29 USCA s 52, and the Norris-La Guardia Act of 1932, 29 USCA ss 101-10, 113-15. A non-statutory exemption was created by the National Labor Relations Act and the Labor Management Relations Act, which establish a national policy favoring collective bargaining.

[10] AA Foer 'Small Business and Antitrust: Why the Little Guys Left the Fold and Why They Should Return', in Office of Advocacy, US Small Business Administration, *The Invisible Part of the Iceberg: Research Issues in Industrial Organization and Small Business* (Washington DC 2000), available at <http://www.antitrustinstitute.org/recent/87.cfm>.

[11] eg, 'The state PIRGs created U.S. Public Interest Research Group (US PIRG) in 1983 to

independence, and having an intent to speak for the public good. Being for the public good, however, doesn't necessarily suggest how anyone will come out on specific antitrust issues, where the defining question may well be: 'In the context of the complicated and disputed facts at hand, together with a variety of conflicting predictions about the future impact of a governmental intervention—where lies the public interest?'

This brings me to my particular organization, the American Antitrust Institute. We describe ourselves as an independent education, research, and advocacy organization focused on antitrust law and institutions, with an attitude that is favorable to more rather than less intervention. We come at antitrust with a multidisciplinary post-Chicago mentality[12] and try to advocate policies and positions that use competition and the competitive process in the interest of consumers.

One of the purposes of the AAI is to serve as a focal point for those who agree that antitrust is important and who want, in a general way, to see more of it. This requires identifying potential supporters of antitrust and bringing them into the AAI's network. With labour, big business, and small business not especially available as allies, it is especially important to look to consumers as a key element in any pro-antitrust coalition. Other likely allies include those who earn a living in the antitrust community: lawyers, economists, and academicians. Finally, there are special interests including certain trade associations and second-tier businesses that recognize antitrust as being in their short-term tactical interest or (more rarely, alas) in their long-term strategic interest.

Unlike many consumerist organizations, we are not based in a formal membership, either of individuals or of organizations, but constitute a network (actually, a virtual network) of experts.[13] We have three directors, an advisory board of about 70 professionals (lawyers and law professors, economists and economics professors, business people, and business school professors), and many hundreds of 'friends' that we are linked to by email and the internet. Our only in-house publication is a website <http://www.antitrustinstitute.org>, which not only publishes our work product and from time to time the work product of our advisers, but also

act as watchdog for the public interest in our nation's capital, much as PIRGs have worked to safeguard the public interest in state capitals since 1971'. See US PIRG website, available at <http://www.uspirg.org/uspirg.asp?id2=10115>.

[12] Among the sources with useful discussions of the difference between Chicago and post-Chicago approaches, one could consult the introduction to JE Kwoka, Jr and LJ White (eds) *The Antitrust Revolution* (4th edn Oxford University Press NY 2004).

[13] For a detailed history and analysis of the structure and work of the AAI, see AA Foer 'The American Antitrust Institute: The First Five Years of a Virtual Public Interest Network', available at <http://www.antitrustinstitute.org/recent2/275.cfm>.

provides a user-friendly tool for antitrust research.[14] Our advisory board undertakes a great deal of pro bono work, in addition to the work product of our three full-time equivalent professionals on payroll, and their own writings are published quite extensively.

AAI's funding comes from a fairly wide variety of sources without an especially heavy reliance on any one source or type of source. Our desire is to avoid reliance on any particular interests that might impede our independence or appearance of independence. Funding sources include various law firms and lawyers (both plaintiff and defendant oriented), some businesses and trade associations, *cy pres* or settlement funds arising from antitrust cases,[15] foundation grants, and individual gifts. Nothing comes from labour and relatively little from small business. One of the surprises has been to find that there are large but non-dominant businesses that are willing to contribute un-earmarked funds to our general treasury because they appreciate our direction and activities. Some of the contributions are for sponsored tables at our annual conference.

The only other public interest organization that is very similar to us is the Loyola Consumer Antitrust Institute in Chicago. Affiliated with a law school and funded largely by *cy pres* money, it conducts symposia and conferences, but is precluded from playing a blatant advocacy role. Its board and AAI's Advisory Board have many overlaps.

AAI cooperates with and sometimes assists various consumer groups, the three most important being the Consumer Federation of America, National Consumers League, and Consumers Union. These groups only occasionally participate in antitrust cases or regulatory proceedings that involve competition. CFA has been particularly active in issues relating to food. Consumers Union, because its funding is tied to the Consumer Report magazine, generally stays out of advocacy situations relating to specific companies, although it has participated in many competition policy questions involving telecommunications. When they do get involved in an antitrust matter, CFA and CU often work closely together.

All of the above organizations share a sense that markets are quite capable of failing and that government is capable of providing useful remedies, which distinguishes them, at least in degree, from public interest advocates of a more conservative bent. It is fair to say that they and some other organizations that represent a consumer perspective come from a tradition that often had substantial doubts about free markets. In an ideal world, some of

---

[14] The second section of this paper will provide examples of the AAI's activities.

[15] See H Miyakawa, 'Promotion of Antitrust and the Public Interest Through Cy Pres Distribution', <http://www.antitrustinstitute.org/recent2/283.cfm>.

their members might prefer considerably more government regulation, but recognize that we live in an era in which regulation has relatively little political support, leaving antitrust and competition as important tools for consumers.

We need also specify that there are many well-funded non-profit organizations that are ideologically devoted to free markets and will often participate in cases or regulatory proceedings that involve competition issues. They tend to present themselves as speaking for consumer welfare in the Borkean sense. The most influential examples are the Heritage Foundation, Cato Institute, and American Enterprise Institute. As advocates of laissez faire, they are often aligned with the interests of the largest corporations. Cato distinguishes itself by its opposition to the idea of antitrust.[16]

Who speaks for the consumer interest on antitrust? There is no simple answer. It is not enough to claim ownership of such words as 'consumer' 'consumer welfare', or 'consumer protection'. A fair test would be to look at the positions taken by any advocacy organization to determine whether there is a consistent pattern that reveals the underlying purpose, constituency, and philosophy about economics, politics, and law. How well does this pattern directly or indirectly serve the interests of end-use consumers?

II. VARIETIES OF ANTITRUST ADVOCACY

Like other forms of policy advocacy, antitrust advocacy can involve (a) litigation, (b) regulatory intervention, (c) coalitioning and lobbying, and (d) research and public education, each of which has many variations. What makes antitrust different from other types of advocacy is the amount and quality of expertise required. This is important because very few consumerist organizations have lawyers and economists at their disposal who are familiar with the doctrines, methodologies, and procedures of antitrust. Consequently, consumer organizations often lack the self-confidence to step into an antitrust matter, even though on occasion it would clearly serve their interests.

---

[16] Articles published on the Cato web site argue that antitrust laws should be repealed, see eg. DT Armentano 'Myths of Antitrust Progress', available at <http://www.cato.org/pubs/regulation/ reg20n2a.html>; RA Levy 'Antitrust: The Case for Repeal' available at <http://www.cato.org/dailys/01-11-03.html> (last visited 23 Mar 2004), or at the very least are no longer relevant to the 'new' economy, See, eg, CW Crews 'Jr 'The Antitrust Terrible 10: Why the Most Reviled "Anti-competitive" Business Practices Can Benefit Consumers in the New Economy' available at <http://www.cato.org/pubs/ pas/pa-405es.html>; RA Levy 'Rewriting the Rules for High-tech Antitrust' available at <http://www.cato.org/dailys/11-03-99.html> (last visited 23 Mar 2004), among other arguments. The Cato Institute alone published more about antitrust in the past five years than the combined six consumer groups that R Kriger (n 1) surveyed.

To put flesh on the bone, let me offer some examples of the AAI's experience in antitrust advocacy. One point that will come through is the difficulty in assessing the impact of anything we do. If our reasoning is poor, we will likely hear about it. But it is usually almost impossible to determine the linkage between anything we say or do and what actually happens. The faith of the public interest think tank/advocacy group is that in the long run, at least, and sometimes sooner, your voice makes a difference.

1. Litigation

Consumerist organizations do not often engage in antitrust litigation, for a variety of reasons including the expense, the time, the amount of expertise needed, and the relatively unfavorable chances of success.

The AAI has been an actual party to litigation, rather than a 'friend of the court', only one time. Toward the end of the historic *Microsoft* case,[17] there was an opportunity to file what is known as a Tunney Act comment, in response to disclosures about the settlement entered into by the Justice Department and Microsoft.[18] We filed a lengthy comment, but also wanted to get before the court in order to argue that the statutory disclosure requirements had either not been followed or were being interpreted too narrowly and that the public's right to comment was unduly constricted by these shortcomings. We brought a separate suit even as we filed comments.[19] The court issued some negative rulings and we ultimately dismissed the suit, but by that time the court had agreed to give us time as *amici* to make oral arguments during the statutory hearing on Tunney Act compliance, during which it was to be determined if the settlement was in the public interest.

Our lawsuit probably had the following effects. (1) We gained the opportunity to make our arguments. (2) Our arguments were unsuccessful with the court, but highlighted the need to reform the Tunney Act. A useful amendment to this law recently passed the Senate and is expected to pass the House.[20] (3) The Justice Department (DoJ) is still piqued by our audacity in suing it. We generally tend to be on the side of law enforcement and lost some goodwill at Justice, which can be valuable to an advocate. This example raises the necessity of weighing the possible downside of litigating directly (rather than participating as amicus) against a government agency that a public interest advocate often considers an ally.

---

[17] *United States v Microsoft Corp* 84 Supp 2d 9 (DDC 1999) and 87 F Supp 2d 30 (DDC 2000) and 253 F 3d 34 (DC Cir 2001).
[18] *United States v Microsoft Corp*, 231 F Supp 2d 144 (DDC 2002).
[19] See <http://www.antitrustinstitute.org/recent2/164.cfm>.
[20] HR 1086, 108th Cong, 2d Sess (Information in text as of early April 2004.)

In quite a few cases, we have filed briefs as *amicus curiae*.[21] Usually these are in the Supreme Court or a federal appellate court or a state high court, where antitrust policy questions are presented and the role of facts is minimized.

2. *Regulatory Intervention*

We have participated, sometimes formally and sometimes informally, in investigations before the FTC and the Antitrust Division, the Federal Energy Regulatory Commission, and the Federal Communications Commission, among others. Sometimes these are 'quick hits' and sometimes they require quite intensive preparation.

Our work on the Alcoa–Reynolds aluminum merger was detailed and painstaking.[22] We presented our analysis to the six-person DoJ staff doing the investigating, about six months into their investigation. In conversations with DoJ after the case was over, we learned that our factual and analytical understanding was approximately the same as theirs at the time of the meeting and that our communications with them helped focus their inquiries and reach a policy decision that, they say, would have been the same even without us. Who knows? As it happened, DoJ approved the merger, conditioned on the sale of certain key assets, but the settlement did not say who would buy the assets. Because of our deep understanding of the case, we believed that there was only one satisfactory buyer who could preserve competition, and DoJ knew we knew. Whether or not this was relevant, they made the right decision.[23]

In the Nestle–Ralston pet food merger, we raised issues that the FTC had not considered, relating to the newly emerging role of category captains and how this factor could be changed in anticompetitive ways by the merger.[24] We had unusual access in that merger to information that the FTC staff did not obtain, because of a company that wanted to oppose the merger, but was unwilling to risk being identified unless other companies in the industry

---

[21] Examples are easily found in the archives section of <http://www.antitrustinstitute.org>, by searching for 'amicus'.

[22] We assigned an economic consultant with an MBA degree to spend four months on this, working half-time. He read what was available on the internet and elsewhere, but gleaned much of his information from conversations with investment analysts. See <http://www.antitrustinstitute.org/recent/56.cfm>.

[23] We wrote a Tunney Act comment making the point that the public could not intelligently comment without being informed of who would buy the divested assets. <http://www.antitrustinstitute.org/recent/75.cfm>. DOJ's knee-jerk response denying an obligation to disclose this information generated an AAI interest in transparency, which is discussed in the paper.

[24] See <http://www.antitrustinstitute.org/recent/138.cfm>.

would also come forward. The staff did not issue the subpoenas we drafted (without invitation, but in great detail) to help them obtain relevant information and the Commission did not take the action we recommended. Nonetheless, several Commissioners privately communicated their hope we would keep developing the category captain issue, and we later co-sponsored with the Journal of Public Policy and Marketing a Roundtable on Category Captains and Antitrust, and published articles and reports on this subject.[25]

Before the Federal Communications Commission, we filed a series of comments in a rulemaking that will affect the shape of the digital TV and related industries.[26] While many other organizations filed comments, including quite a few consumer groups, we were the only one to focus on the competitive implications, which turned out to be quite significant. Our comments contributed to the FCC's decision to postpone certain aspects of its policymaking and caused many of the other participants to begin addressing the questions we raised.

Advocacy within the government may be one of the highest priorities for antitrust advocates in nations that are relatively new to antitrust. For example, where privatization is occurring, a very high priority would be to try to assure that a public monopoly is not being exchanged for a private monopoly.

3. Coalitioning and Lobbying

From time to time the AAI is consulted on an informal basis by consumer organizations, state enforcement officials, and congressional staff for advice on antitrust matters. The brain trust of our Advisory Board is also available for quick reactions to questions.

The AAI sometimes works in coalition or close coordination with consumer organizations that share our views on particular antitrust matters. In the Nestle-Ralston pet food merger, for example, we held a joint press conference with the Consumer Federation of America, National Consumers

[25] The Report is at <http://www.antitrustinstitute.org/recent2/270.cfm>. Also see DM Desrochers et al 'Analysis of Antitrust Challenges to Category Captain Arrangements' (Fall 2003) 22 J Public Policy & Marketing, reprinted with permission at <http://www.antitrustinstitute.org/recent2/293.cfm>.
[26] The filings are all in the archives at <http://www.antitrustinstitute.org>. Our most recent intervention was a detailed letter to the FCC, DoJ, FTC, and European Union urging them to get together in a mutual consultation because we believe the various agencies are heading in different directions, with trouble ahead. See <http://www.antitrustinstitute.org/recent2/314.cfm>. The FCC is only one of many federal agencies that have authority to regulate competition within specific economic sectors and are therefore appropriate targets for antitrust monitoring and intervention.

League, the Consumer Alliance, National Grange, and the Organization for Competitive Markets, in order to talk about the negative impact of this merger on consumers and farmers. Our statement was delivered to the relevant congressional committees, accompanied by a dog bone wrapped in a ribbon, to call attention to the message: 'This merger is a dog!' (The merger was approved by the FTC, with conditions that did not alleviate our concerns.)

When we opposed the Orbitz joint venture among most of the nation's air carriers, our petition was signed by 25 organizations and we visited the Antitrust Division along with representatives of the leading consumer organizations (both the DoJ and the FCC investigated Orbitz, but neither ultimately challenged it).[27]

As a 501(c)(3) organization, our tax exemption is conditioned on doing no more than a minimal amount of lobbying. Testimony and statements to Congress or to regulatory agencies, however, do not count as lobbying for exemption purposes.[28] I will mention three of these activities. The earliest was our first effort to affect the appropriations process. We knew that Congress rarely heard from outsiders in regard to the budgets of the FTC and the DoJ, and we knew that the appropriations staffs were not particularly well-briefed on antitrust. So we provided a 40-page discussion of the history of antitrust, antitrust budgets, and antitrust performance, emphasizing all the activities that needed to be done and the urgent need for more funding.[29] We convinced a large number of organizations to sign a letter conveying this report. Suddenly, and for the first time, there was a public display of support for an antitrust budget increase. And an increase occurred. (We are not claiming causation. As noted previously, one of the difficulties of this type of advocacy is that it is rarely possible responsibly to take credit for a victory. There are always other factors. And because we try to focus our resources on raising new issues and taking positions that egg onward a reluctant administration, we will appear to lose a high proportion of our initiatives, even as we build for the future.)

In June 2000, I testified before a Senate committee on the proposed acquisition by United Airlines of US Airways. Through something of a fluke, I

[27] '25 Consumer Groups Ask Justice to Modify Orbitz Launch Vehicle', <http://www.antitrustinstitute.org/recent/121.cfm>.
[28] Public charities may engage in lobbying to an insubstantial extent, generally no more than around five per cent of the organization's activities. Direct lobbying is defined as efforts to influence Congress, their staff or Executive Department personnel in the drafting and enactment of specific bills or bills that contain a specific provision. Some types of grassroots lobbying, ie efforts to influence members of the public about pending legislation, are also limited for a tax exempt organization.
[29] 'The Federal Antitrust Commitment: Providing Resources to Meet the Challenge' <http://www.antitrustinstitute.org/recent/23.cfm>.

ended up in a discussion with a full panel of senators for approximately an hour, during which I was able to talk at length about merger policy, the evolution of the airline industry, and why the proposed merger seemed anti-competitive.[30] (Under substantial political pressure, the DoJ stopped this merger from occurring).

A third example of an AAI effort to influence Congress came in September 2002, when we presented a written statement to the Senate's Antitrust Subcommittee, which was conducting oversight hearings.[31] We examined in detail the records of the FTC and DoJ in the Bush Administration and found that the FTC was performing far more productively than the DoJ. Not long afterward (though we are not claiming responsibility), the Assistant Attorney General for Antitrust resigned.

4. Research and Public Education

While all of the above activities involve research and public education, I want to focus on several other ways in which we attempt to influence thinking about antitrust. These may be categorized as (1) the website, (2) conferences and workshops, (3) other publications, and (4) assisting the media.

(a) Website

The AAI is the offspring of new economy models of business development, eg Internet-based communications, globally dispersed 'production' nodes, etc.[32] At the centre of our network, linking the nodes, is the Internet. We were fortunate to be able to develop an excellent website quickly and cheaply. The website is accessed from all over the world. In our second year, the *Legal Times of Washington* reported that ours was the best one-stop website for antitrust information. One of our features has been a daily

---

[30] Testimony before the Commerce, Science, and Transportation Committee of the US Senate, 22 June 2000. <http://www.antitrustinstitute.org/recent/74.cfm>. The fluke was that I showed up on the appointed date, but the Committee had also scheduled the CEO's of the airlines ahead of me and running out of time, commanded me to return the following day. The only other person testifying with me on the next day was the General Counsel of the Transportation Department (DoT) and she was conflicted from answering most questions because the merger was before both DoT and DoJ. I ended up conducting a seminar on merger policy in the presence of a dozen senators and a person involved in the formal decision-making process.

[31] <http://www.antitrustinstitute.org/recent2/203.pdf>.

[32] There are network economies present. The larger the number of experts having in-put (within limits), the more valuable is the AAI product to users. Additionally, the more materials we place on our website (eg archives of our activities and research sources), the more valuable the network is to users. Presumably, the more users, the more influence the AAI has and the better its chances of fundraising success. The network aspect of our structure is emphasized in the paper cited above (n 10).

report on antitrust in the news, which has been dredged up automatically at no cost by a search engine.

Our website has several other features to note. Most importantly, we post every new activity that the AAI undertakes. After some time, this is moved to our archives section, where materials can be searched on the basis of any word in the text. Our Who's Who in Antitrust contains contact information for the Federal Trade Commission, Antitrust Division, National Association of Attorneys General, and others. Our Links section provides what we think is a very complete, user-friendly way of finding information about antitrust. Finally, the website offers ways for readers to sign up as (1) a 'Friend of the AAI', which costs nothing and entitles them to be alerted by email to what we post; (2) as a journalist, with the self-same benefits; or (3) to make contributions by credit card, using a free system provided by an organization called Network for Good. The latter has unfortunately not proved to be productive.

(b) Conferences and Workshops

We have hosted four annual national conferences; four annual electricity restructuring workshops; and co-sponsored with universities or public interest groups workshops and roundtables on network access, defense procurement, supplier joint ventures, category captains and category management, and marketing and antitrust. In June 2004, we will host our fifth national conference and co-sponsor a workshop on combining horizontal and vertical analysis in antitrust. At our national conferences, we present the AAI Antitrust Achievement Award, an opportunity to reflect our values through the selection of the recipient.[33] And we present an award for outstanding antitrust writing.[34]

(c) Other Publications

Our national conferences give us the opportunity to generate publishable articles, and these have been published in symposium issues of law reviews.[35] In addition, articles and monographs we generate have been

---

[33] Recipients of the AAI Antitrust Achievement Award have been J Klein (outgoing Assistant Attorney General for Antitrust), R Pitofsky (outgoing Chair of the FTC), FM Scherer (industrial organization economist), and A Kahn (economist known as the 'godfather of deregulation'). The recipient in 2004 will be L Constantine, an attorney who was instrumental in building up the states as an effective mechanism of antitrust enforcement.

[34] The Jerry Cohen Award for Antitrust Scholarship is worth approximately $8000. Last year's recipient was Professor John M Connor for his book, *Global Price Fixing*.

[35] Law review symposium issues thus far are (2001) 62 U Pitt L Rev, (2001) 52 Case W L Rev (2003) 47 NYLS L Rev, and (2003) 51 Buffalo L Rev. In this way we are gradually building a substantial body of academic material that is generally supportive of our perspective on antitrust.

published in a variety of law reviews, economics journals, and other periodicals. We periodically write the 'AAI Column' for FTC:WATCH, a subscriber newsletter, and re-print it on-line. In 2004, we are completing a book consisting of papers written for our 'network access project', to be published by Routledge. Whenever possible, anything we publish is also made available on our website.

(d) Assisting the Media

It is difficult to speak of a trade press for antitrust. Only a handful of journalists are assigned to an antitrust 'beat'. Much of the relevant media consists of journalists assigned either to 'business' generally or to 'legal affairs' generally, and they usually have a very limited understanding of antitrust. Our website is geared, to a large extent, to help these journalists. When we post new materials on our website, we send email notices to our media list. The media frequently phones or sends email inquiries. Often, this results in referrals to members of the Advisory Board or to others with relevant expertise. Occasionally, we conduct press briefings or issue formal press releases.

III. THE CONSUMER INTEREST AND ANTITRUST ADVOCACY IN INTERNATIONAL
    CONTEXT

So far, I have talked about the consumer interest and antitrust advocacy in a domestic (ie US) context. There are two especially important reasons, however, for thinking more globally. First, antitrust issues increasingly cross national borders and the consumer interest requires understanding of international implications and perhaps suggests activity on a transnational level. Second, with approximately 100 countries now having market economies and competition policy laws, a great deal depends upon getting competition policy right in states that have very little experience with competition policy.

I will talk more about each of these points before addressing some questions that arise.

1. Understanding and Action Globally

The large amount of economic activity that crosses national borders generates situations in which antitrust and regulatory activities (governmental or private) within one country may affect one or more others. The AAI, for example, found that its interest in curtailing anticompetitive strategies of Microsoft within the US led naturally to an interest in the cases brought against Microsoft by the European Union. We have tried to keep US antitrust critics of Microsoft as well as the US media apprised of developments in Brussels and we have written articles and op-eds and spoken in public, explaining the recent European Commission decision within the US. We have urged US authorities and politicians to moderate their criticisms of the European decision.[36]

A second example involves the FCC's regulatory effort to shape the emerging digital TV industry. As mentioned earlier, we filed a series of comments to the FCC raising competitive questions. During our research, we became aware that the European Union was moving in a different (and, we would argue, more consumer-friendly) direction. We recently wrote a letter to the FCC, DoJ, FTC, and two of the directorates of the European Union (Information Society and Competition) calling on them to consult with each other in order to consider the ramifications of their going off in different directions.[37]

Antitrust advocates have traditionally supported free trade and international institutions to promote both free trade and antitrust mechanisms that can work across borders. One of the most encouraging developments in this regard has been the creation of the International Competition Network, a forum for the exchange of information and ideas, and the development of 'best practice' documents. The primary members of the ICN are enforcement authorities from around the world. While private parties and consumer organizations are invited to participate, the role of consumers has been small. The ICN must be encouraged to reach out to be more inclusive. It should be noted, however, that participation in international activities like the ICN is expensive and beyond the reach of most public interest organizations, unless special support can be obtained.

Having said this, however, we must begin to come to grips with the fact that increased international trade has created a backlash, particularly within the US. Some consumer organizations arguably allow their interests in labour and the environment to overcome their interest in the American consumer, per consumer, and they have become increasingly hostile to multilateral trade agreements and such institutions as the WTO. In other words, a dangerous split is opening between consumer organizations and antitrust advocates.

---

[36] See AA Foer and RH Lande 'No Wonder They Dislike Us: US Admonishes Europe for Protecting Itself from Microsoft's Predation' at <http://www.antitrustinstitute.org/recent2/311.cfm>. This was widely distributed on Capitol Hill.

[37] See <http://www.antitrustinstitute.org/recent2/314.cfm>.

Antitrust advocates will need to pay more attention to the linkage between a market economy and trade. Both depend on voluntary exchange as the fundamental mechanism. Both work in the interests of low prices, choice, and innovation to benefit consumers. Yet the very dynamic of competitive markets creates—and is intended to create—ongoing change, with winners and losers inevitably being generated. The pace of change at this point in history is frenetic and the insecurity that the threat of change is generating is widespread. 'Outsourcing' has come to the professional classes for the first time, which means that the fears of job loss and status loss have a new and forceful voice. Antitrust advocates have to understand and explicate the linkage between trade and antitrust. For example, a reduction in trade should logically require an increase in antitrust because of the diminution of competition from abroad.

Additionally, and this would constitute an innovation for the antitrust agenda, antitrust advocates must begin to speak to the need for systemic institutions that will deal with the insecurity and fear that are inherent in both domestic capitalism and international trade. Markets are not the gift of nature; they do not exist in a vacuum but are embedded in institutions. To push for ever-freer markets without also having sufficient positive government programs in place to deal with social insecurity is a recipe for destroying the political commitment to a market economy.

2. Getting It Right Where Antitrust Is Relatively New

The revolution that has occurred across the world in the past quarter century[38] bets the collective farm (so to speak) on the ability of markets and democratic institutions to work side by side in the widest variety of national contexts. This will be a tremendous challenge and it must be mastered. Nations at all stages of development will need to grow and perfect the basic institutional infrastructures, ranging from private property laws to honest judiciaries.

In the context of antitrust, several tasks are paramount: pass intelligently conceived laws; provide adequate funding for law enforcement; train bureaucrats in the proper enforcement of these laws; mold the procedures and values that will give substance to the laws. But laws without institutional support can evaporate. Somebody has to care enough to make the laws work. Additional infrastructure is also needed: media to explain the value of competition policy to the people; a bar association dedicated to making competition policy work; and other civil society organizations (eg,

---

[38] See, eg, D Yergin and J Stanislaw *The Commanding Heights* (Simon & Schuster NY 1998).

consumers; professors; research institutes) that can help shape as well as support competition policy.

In 2003, the International Network of Civil Society Organizations on Competition (INCSOC) was launched in Geneva, Switzerland, bringing representatives of civil society organizations from around the world for the purpose of assisting in the infrastructure-building task.[39] Thus far, INCSOC has met twice and has created a website and listserve, as well as initiating a project to create and publish a data base on civil society involvement in competition policy worldwide. The idea is right. Whether there will be funding to keep initiative going remains to be seen.

Funding for something like INCSOC or for antitrust advocacy within the world's nations is a critical issue. Creative thinking and selling will be needed at both levels, if activities are to go beyond the sporadic and voluntary.

Although approaches have been made to a variety of international and national competition agencies on behalf of INCSOC, to date the only one to respond with funding has been the UK Department for International Development, and this has been within the context of a pre-existing program enabling an Indian consumer organization, CUTS, to study competition policy in seven countries (the chair of CUTS is co-chair of INCSOC).

Continuing efforts must be made with government agencies, multinational organizations (such as UNCTAD, World Bank, WTO, OECD, EU), foundations (such as Ford, Open Society), universities, international bar associations, labour unions, consumer organizations, business associations, multinational corporations, wealthy individuals, law firms and economics consulting firms to fund operations, special events, and special projects.

3. Three Questions for Antitrust Advocates

(a) Who Will and Will Not Fund Antitrust Advocacy?

One question that antitrust advocates must deal with is whether there are private or governmental sources from which funding should not be accepted. In some countries, consumer organizations receive funding from their government. AAI made the decision not to solicit funding, for example to conduct studies, from any of the federal agencies that it wants to be able to criticize or praise. We have also made a strong effort to be non-partisan.

---

[39] See <http://www.incsoc.net>. The author co-chairs the INCSOC Capacity Building Working Group.

On the other hand, we do accept contributions to our general treasury (ie, non-earmarked funds) from private companies and trade associations, not as a quid pro quo but as a voluntary expression of gratitude or recognition when AAI takes a position that the private interest approves. Because both independence and the perception of independence are important, AAI has set up a policy committee to prescreen projects where conflict of interest claims might be raised. AAI feels constrained to maintain consistency in its positions at the very least because catering to the wants of private contributors would cause its esteemed Advisory Board members to depart.

This is a tricky situation and not necessarily desirable. However, in most antitrust cases there are at least two different viewpoints and one is likely to serve the consumer interest better. Laissez faire 'public interest' organizations have long been able to represent the ideological interests of the largest corporations whose donations (often through their foundations) make it possible for the organizations to act. As long as there is transparency and a consistency in policy, it is illogical to criticize a pro-consumer, pro-competition antitrust advocacy group for accepting private funds. The AAI makes its list of contributors (though not the amounts contributed) available on request. Many public interest groups refuse to do this, for fear of retribution to contributors. This consideration may be even heavier in other countries. Thus far, however, funding transparency has been a workable policy for the AAI.

(b) What Should Be the Role of Transparency in Antitrust Advocacy?

Transparency for the antitrust advocate is important because, as the AAI has found, transparency is one of the best policies to be argued for by antitrust advocates and it is difficult to advocate transparency without being transparent. AAI may have had its strongest impact to date through its advocacy of greater transparency in the enforcement process. This has been accomplished through a series of comments to both the FTC and the DoJ, evaluating their work in particular cases and raising questions about the adequacy of what they disclosed to the public. Building on this experience, we made transparency the topic of one of our national conferences and a law review issue is now devoted to this topic.[40] Perhaps as a result of our pressure, both the DoJ[41] and the

---

[40] 51 Buffalo L Rev (fall 2003), available at <http://www.antitrustinstitute.org/recent2/292. cfm>.

[41] See US Dept of Justice, Antitrust Division, 'Issuance of Public Statements upon Closing of Investigations', <http://www.usdoj.gov/atr/public/guidelines/201888.htm>. Also see AAI's statement following the DOJ closing of its Orbitz investigation, <http://www.antitrustinstitute.org/recent2/258.cfm>.

FTC[42] have made notable steps forward in both the frequency and the detail of their disclosures.

Transparency should be especially important to countries with new antitrust laws, for the following reasons:

• Without facts about a case, it is very difficult to evaluate how well the investigation was executed or whether the enforcement agency performed reasonably. Agencies need to make case-related facts liberally available to the public, even while protecting that which is truly proprietary;
• Getting appropriate rules in place while agencies are young and malleable can have huge impact over time, as enforcers learn to expect the public to watch over their shoulder and evaluate their work;
• Pushing for appropriate transparency rules requires relatively few resources and relatively little expertise;
• This is a good issue around which to develop relations with the media, who are direct beneficiaries of transparency;
• Transparency is part of the solution to the problem of potential corruption that can undermine effective antitrust enforcement.

At AAI, we feel that our role has been to round out the debate and put issues on the plate that otherwise might be ignored. The agencies still make the decisions, of course, but we try to add a dimension and depth to the consideration that might otherwise be lacking. After a decision, our commentary can contribute to a broader oversight and criticism that will help to shape future policy decisions, but intelligent commentary depends heavily on what the government chooses to disclose about the case.

(c) Should Antitrust Advocacy Be Separate from Consumer Protection Advocacy?

As nations go about establishing their antitrust systems, one of the decisions that is often controversial is whether to combine antitrust and consumer protection under the same administrative umbrella. Good reasons can be given for and against either choice. A similar decision arises with respect to antitrust advocacy. Should it be placed under the aegis of a consumer protection advocacy organization or should it stand alone?

There are many considerations that might attend this question, including considerations of personality and interests of the limited universe of people

---

[42] See the AAI's praise for the FTC's statement upon closing its investigation of the cruise mergers, <http://www.antitrustinstitute.org/recent2/217.cfm>.

both interested in public interest careers and qualified to be antitrust advocates, not to mention funding availability. Based on the experience of the AAI, I support the idea of a separate antitrust advocacy function that is both independent and expert-based. Such an antitrust-focused organization should coordinate with and assist other consumer and public interest units, providing expertise and an informed policy perspective, but it should also be free to pursue its own agenda with or without additional civil society support.

Within a consumer organization, there may occasionally be a protectionist agenda that is less comfortable with markets than antitrust advocates might prefer. Thus, structural independence is needed to assure that the antitrust agenda does not get smothered within an organization that has different priorities and to assure that the antitrust advocate is viewed by the world as independent and thus more credible with respect to antitrust issues.

As a practical matter, there always are a large number of potential worthwhile consumer-based initiatives that are compelling, immediate, and straightforward, at least compared to most antitrust projects, which are more likely to be equally compelling, but longer term and more complicated. Without a separate antitrust unit the advocacy group might well succumb to the path of least resistance and spend all of its resources on consumer protection matters, and rarely or never do antitrust. This problem could be especially acute because antitrust is so specialized that, as a practical matter, it is extremely difficult to do high quality antitrust work unless someone does a lot of it.

Often, consumerist organizations are the creative force behind reform legislation. An independent review by an antitrust advocate might help sharpen the focus of these legislative proposals, helping them avoid unnecessarily regulatory approaches and projecting market responses. This activity, which may often be perceived as negative, is more likely to be objective over time if it comes from without rather than within the consumer organization.

Typically the consumer organization has a lobbying and grassroots capability that far exceeds that of an antitrust advocate. The antitrust advocate organization more likely will be expert-based with a limited membership or following and with a network of connections primarily in the narrow world of antitrust. To reach beyond that confinement, it can try, through education and persuasion, to convince the other public interest organizations to bring their resources to bear on specific antitrust issues. This effort should bring forth the strongest effort to explicate complicated antitrust issues in terms that are meaningful and motivating to consumers. Too often, antitrust lacks salience with the public. The marriage of the consumer interest and the antitrust advocacy interest should result in a level of communication that makes apparent the value of competition not as an abstraction but as a tool for improving everyday life.

H. Competition Policy: Complementarity's Link with Consumer Protection

Juan Antonio Riviere Marti*

Competition Policy pursued by the European Commission has a direct impact on the daily life of the European Union citizens: requiring firms to compete with each other fosters innovation, lowers costs and prices, and increases choice and quality. This benefits each consumer. The consumer welfare-oriented approach has been reflected both in the enforcement activity and policy field.

It is the Commission's duty to fulfil the obligations imposed under Article 153 of the EC Treaty:

1. In order to promote the interests of consumers and to ensure a high level of consumer protection, the Community shall contribute to protecting the health, safety and economic interests of consumers, as well as to promoting their right to information, education and to organise themselves in order to safeguard their interests; 2. Consumer protection requirements shall be taken into account in defining and implementing other Community policies and activities.

During the latest Competition Day in Dublin, Commissioner Mario Monti recalled how:

On my appointment as Commissioner for Competition, I pledged that I would give central importance to the consumer. The competition authorities have a role to play in taking account of input from consumers. Public awareness of the importance of vigorous competition policy is a valuable ally. The competition authorities throughout the world need support and understanding from consumers of the interest they have in healthy competition. Awareness of this is gradually increasing in Europe . . . The Commission is committed to a proactive, modern and effective competition policy. Not only will this ensure that the market functions in such a way as to maximise benefits for consumers, but it also gives consumers an unparalleled opportunity to participate in the fight against violations of the competition rules.

The new regulatory framework from 1 May is more efficient because competition authorities will intervene when consumers are affected negatively. The Commission also gives consumers the opportunity to participate in the fight against violations of competition rules. Competition authorities have to take account of input from consumers. It is important to have active consumers and consumer associations which provide market information.

* Adviser, Consumer Liaison Officer; and Directorate General for Competition, European Commission.

A complaint submitted by a consumer association can provide the Commission with a basis to open an investigation.[1]

The Commission is also examining how private enforcement of the EU competition rules could be encouraged: it is not currently enjoying the degree of such it hoped for in its efforts to promote public enforcement and very little case law exists. Private parties, including consumers, could ask national courts to apply Articles 81 and 82 to grant damages resulting from illegal behaviour or to order the termination of illegal behaviour. The legal practice and economic consultants have a chance to enter into a new more active arena, this time looking to see how consumers' rights could be brought into Competition enforcement.

Also in the new Guidelines on assessment of horizontal mergers,[2] it is stated that mergers may bring about various types of efficiency gains, and efficiencies, when considering the case, should be substantial and timely and should benefit consumers in the relevant market studied. The concept of consumers covers intermediate (customers) and ultimate consumers.

In order to take account of consumers' interest, the function of the Consumer Liaison Officer (CLO) within DG Comp, already announced during the reform package in 2002, started in January 2004. The CLO will ensure a permanent dialogue with European consumers and consumer associations, of which BEUC[3]—European Consumers' Organization—is the

---

[1] Market information and Complaints: <http://europa.eu.int/comm/competition/antitrust/others/>. The Commission wishes to encourage citizens and undertakings to inform it about suspected infringements of the competition rules. There are two different ways to do this: (a) lodging a complaint pursuant to Art 7(2) of Regulation 1/2003. Complaints of this type must fulfil certain legal requirements. In particular, to be admissible, a complaint shall provide the information required by Form C. Exhaustive information on the handling of complaints by the Commission under Arts 81 and 82 of the EC Treaty can be found in the Commission Notice <http://europa.eu.int/eur-lex/pri/en/oj/dat/2004/c_101/c_10120040427 en00650077.pdf> on that subject. Complaint Form 'C' <http://europa.eu.int/eur-lex/pri/pt/oj/dat/2004/l_123/l_12320040427pt00180024.pdf>. It explains how to make a complaint regarding antitrust matters. It can also be found as an annex to Commission Regulation (EC) No 773/2004 of 7 Apr 2004 relating to the conduct of proceedings by the Commission pursuant to Arts 81 and 82 of the EC Treaty. *Official Journal L 123, 27 Apr 2004, 18–24*; (b) *Providing* market information in any forms and does not have to comply with the requirements for complaints pursuant to Art 7(2) of Regulation 1/2003. For the latter purpose, the Commission has created a mailbox that can be used by citizens and undertakings and their associations who wish to inform the Commission about suspected infringements of Arts 81 and 82. Such information can be the starting point for an investigation by the Commission).

[2] <http://www.europa.eu.int/comm/competition/mergers/legislation/regulation/#implementing>.

[3] <http://www.beuc.org> 'BEUC: the European Consumers' Organization is the Brussels-based federation of 36 independent national consumer organizations from the EU, accession and EEA countries. Our job is to try to influence, in the consumer interest, the development of EU policy and to promote and defend the interests of all European consumers'. BEUC is always very active in presenting their points to the Commission services. During the consulta-

main representative. The CLO is assisted by a group of Consumer Correspondents from all Directorates, and units within DGCOMP, that meet regularly and ensure that affected consumers in cases under examination get the assured benefit of fair treatment. The CLO is also responsible for improving contacts with other European Commission Directorates Generals, most notably with the Health and Consumers Protection DG; coordinating with national competition authorities regarding consumer protection matters; supporting the European Competition Day organized during each Member State's presidency; and participating in the activities of international organisations (like OCDE or ICN) related to consumer protection and competition issues.

This is, in brief, where we stand today and how far we have come towards fulfilling the guiding objectives to enforce Competition Policy in the Commission for the benefit of European citizens.

tion, a green paper on services stated: 'Access of all consumers to essential services of a reasonable quality at an affordable price shall be guaranteed. Consumers' expectations in that regard not only encompass physical and geographical access at an affordable price, but also choice; transparency and full information, quality, safety, security, reliability, fairness, independent regulation, representation, and active participation, redress.'

CHAPTER 10

Vertical and Conglomerate Mergers

[GAVIN ROBERT*]

I'm pleased to welcome to the panel Cristina Caffarra on my left who is a director at the economics consultants Lexecon. On my right we have two regulators. We have Bill Kovacic, General Counsel at the US Federal Trade Commission and Simon Priddis, Director of Mergers at the UK Office of Fair Trading. I think by now as a result of the release of in particular the EU guidelines and also a number of other guidelines around Europe there is a considerable degree of consensus on the appropriate frame-work for analyzing horizontal mergers. However, I think there is less consensus on the topic of vertical and conglomerate mergers. The European Commission's own guidelines on that topic are eagerly awaited and at the same time there are a number of cases before the European court where we are waiting to hear what the court has to say about those issues and it is with this in mind that we thought that this particular panel might be of interest. Just to tell you the format for the panel, rather than having set presentations by each of the speakers, what we have decided to do is to have a form of question time format where I will pose a number of ques-tions to each of the panelists and there will also be an opportunity for ques-tions from the floor. We are going to split the session into three parts. We will start with setting out what the frame-work for analysis may be, so a more general more analytical session. After which we will then see if we can have some questions from the floor. We will then more on to look at enforcement practice by the UK authorities, the EU and in the States and then finally we will consider the way forward. In between each of those sessions I will invite some questions from the floor and hopefully we will certainly try to keep to the allotted time of one hour. So first I think before we engage in this debate it is useful to define our terms. The words vertical and conglomerate are used very often and I think it is useful for us to under-stand exactly what we mean by those terms when assessing mergers. So first I am going to turn to Cristina and ask her to give us some idea of what we think we mean by conglomerate merger.

---

* Linklaters.

A. Cristina Caffarra*

Well in the most obvious sense mergers that are 'conglomerate' are mergers that are not vertical and not horizontal. But what should be put under that category? In Europe over the last seven or eight years we've seen a considerable expansion in the concerns and issues that have been looked at under that broad umbrella. We've had the rise of the 'portfolio' doctrine which has a number of strands but really is about the concern that a company acquiring different brands, albeit competing in separate markets, may be acquiring market power in excess of the sum of its parts. We've had the 'indirect effects' doctrine. We've had a lot of focus on cases where the concern was the potential for exclusion arising from practices that the merging firm would adopt after the merger, for example bundling and tying. I don't need to mention *GE/Honeywell* and *Tetra Laval/Sidel* as well as *GE/Amersham* in this context.

And then we've had stories to do with financial constraints, stories to do with creating barriers to entry and so on. So to an economist looking at this body of cases the impression is pretty much that there is a very heterogeneous set of issues that have been grouped under one broad term. And when you look at it carefully, perhaps there are issues that do not really quite belong to the same group of concerns, or could be looked at in a different way, through more conventional glasses. One useful way perhaps to organize our thoughts on this is to think about the relationship between the products that are being combined through the merger; and the way in which economists think about it is really looking at 'substitutes', or products that are 'unrelated' or products that are 'complements'. The reason why I think this distinction is important is because the efficiencies that flow from mergers that combine products with different characteristics in this way are also very different, in the same way as the competitive effects are very different.

We've had a number of cases where really the conglomerate effects were about 'weak substitutes' and in these cases it does not seem legitimate first to exclude formally a horizontal concern on grounds that the substitution between two products is weak, but then resurrect the concern at a latter stage by saying somehow when you look at it there is still some sort of interaction—however weak—and the products are in 'contiguous markets' or are 'close'. I'm not saying there are never concerns that arise about weak substitutes. It's perfectly possible that if you are bringing together a lot of weak substitutes, you have an appreciable price effect; but I am saying that this is an entirely horizontal issue and it doesn't help calling it a conglom-

* Lexecon.

erate one. Then you have products that are 'unrelated' in demand: people don't buy them together and they don't appear to have a relationship. That's really something that doesn't happen frequently but the only way you can generate concern is to build stories about the merger somehow creating asymmetries in financial constraints between the firms. This is an area which is extremely difficult to make tight economically. Then what you are left with is the big body of the 'complementary products' - the cases where what you are combining through the mergers are products that either go together or where consumers have a preference for one as well as for the other. Now there, and we go into that later in greater detail, the analogy with verticals is quite close in that it's conceivable that when you have market power in one product and are integrating into a product that's a complement, you may be able to do something that affects your rival's profit and ability to compete. So I would contend that this clearly has got to be the focus of concerns: there are various ways in which you can affect rival's ability to compete when you are combining complements, and the focus ought to be how in the particular merger that may arise.

[GAVIN ROBERT]

Thank you Cristina. Bill, how would you characterize a vertical merger?

B. Bill Kovacic*

I think the traditional approach has been to classify as a vertical transaction again a combination of assets or operations that are not in the same market and at least colloquially to speak about the unification of operations that are up steam or down stream of each other, for example a merger of a petroleum refiner and a firm that owns retail stations: the combination many years ago of MCI's long distance operations and a joint venture with BT's local operations in the United Kingdom This has been the traditional classifications scheme. I think increasingly what we see happening in practice though is a movement from these types of categories to concepts where perhaps in the future the basic divide will be between horizontal transactions and non-horizontal transactions or even more generally, a more unified scheme that really focuses on three basic issues. First, do the parties in some sense have market power, second, what is the theory of any competitive effect or harm that flows from the transactions: specifically, by what means might the merged entity exclude rivals to exert power over price or

---

* US Federal Trade Commission.

other dimensions of competition, or by what means or process might the transaction facilitate the coordination of behavior amongst direct rivals in the post merger market, and third, what efficiency claims or stories can be told about the practice? And I think, given the array of transactions that we see today that often combine a number of different features, it is increasingly likely that we will see analysis move in the direction away from reliance on a classification scheme that batches transactions within specific categories because in many ways those categories have been a shorthand form for identifying, or at least connoting, different theories of competitive effects and efficiency stories, towards an analytical methodology that asks about the existence of market power, focuses in detail on the anti-competitive effects story which can encompass a number of different approaches and lastly asks about the efficiency property. So, in many ways we still use the traditional classification scheme but I think in many respects we are moving in the direction of an approach that looks more at the analytical concepts behind the scheme and less at the labels themselves.

[GAVIN ROBERT]

Thanks very much. I'll ask both Simon and Cristina to comment on that. Simon, do you agree that the labels of vertical and conglomerate are less useful? Are they considered together just because they are non-horizontal or is there some genuine common ground between vertical and conglomerate mergers?

C. Simon Priddis*

I think that there is some common ground between vertical and conglomerate mergers. They don't simply exist as a miscellaneous category of non-horizontal theories of competition harm. I think though that Bill's point is absolutely right. We are moving to a point where we are looking beyond a traditional categorization of theories of competition harm and look more at the underlying concepts. And I think when one reaches that stage of analysis, one sees that, as Cristina mentioned earlier, there is quite a lot of common ground, or at least close analogy, between vertical and conglomerate merger assessment. Of course there is some overlay with horizontal analysis, as Cristina mentioned, in cases like *Tetra Laval/Sidel*. The Commission was essentially running a sort of 'weak substitutes' conglomerate analysis. But I think if one looks purely at vertical and conglomerate merger analysis, what one is really dealing with are theories of competition

* OFT.

harm that give rise to consumer detriment in a more indirect way than is the case with horizontal mergers. I think that is underpinned by looking at the key concept that normally lies behind vertical or conglomerate merger decisions and that, as we all know, is normally foreclosure. That has underpinned most of the vertical and conglomerate cases certainly in the EC and the UK over the past few years. So at that level, one might say, in a relatively simplistic way, that there is a good deal of common ground because these cases are often built on foreclosure analysis.

But I think one does have to delve a little deeper and I think Cristina was right on this point. If one looks at the conceptual underpinnings of foreclosure analysis in vertical and conglomerate mergers they are often relatively different. In a vertical merger there is quite a natural story one can tell about foreclosure. A firm in an upstream market is a supplier of an input product that is directly used in the downstream market: it is quite an easy foreclosure story to tell. In conglomerate mergers that is often much more difficult to do. It's a much less natural story. As a regulator one has to think much more carefully about the theory that one is applying in a conglomerate case because that foreclosure may have a much more indirect effect even than a vertical case. I think just to sum up on that, it is worth actually looking at a case that was reviewed on both sides of the Atlantic, the acquisition by Synopsys Incorporated of Avant! Corporation two years ago. It was looked at in the US and looked at in the UK. It's quite interesting. The UK looked at the case at the OFT stage only. We cleared it on essentially a vertical foreclosure analysis. The Federal Trade Commission at the time opened a second request, allowed the companies to close and then opened a third phase which most of you probably did not know even existed in US merger analysis. However it was used in the *Synopsys/Avant!* case. It's interesting because the analysis that the FTC Commissioners seemed to use when ultimately closing the case is essentially based on the underlying concept of foreclosure. They really seemed to have moved away from a label saying that this is a vertical transaction or this is a conglomerate transaction. Indeed the language of the closing statements isn't wholly clear whether they thought about it as vertical or conglomerate. What is clear is that the underlying concept is one of foreclosure and that is something very much in common with the UK analysis.

[GAVIN ROBERT]

Thanks. What I would like to do now is to ask Cristina if she can set out for us the current state of economic thinking on what is the theory of competitive harm that could flow from vertical or conglomerate mergers. We will allow Cristina a little bit of time to explain that to us.

[CRISTINA CAFFARRA]

It is an ambitious agenda and I am sure I won't be able to do it justice in a few minutes. Let me start with vertical mergers. I think that there is no question that in many vertical mergers you can construct a story that, given the vertical structure, it is possible for a firm with market power at one stage of production to somehow raise the price of an input or reduce the quality of that input to rival downstream producers, whichever way the integration goes, in such a way that shifts market share to itself and take it away from others. That is a story that can be constructed. The real question is where is the competition concern? If it is just about shifting market share but there is no increase in price to final end consumers then it is not clear what the competitive harm is. The firm that is integrating may have a larger market share, and its rivals downstream may have a smaller market share, but if final prices don't change there is no harm. Indeed because of efficiencies that vertical integration brings to pricing it is even possible that the prices that the integrating firm sets will be even lower. So it is not clear that just shifting market share takes us there at all. What you need to have is a further step that says not only will you shift market share, but you will actually foreclose or exclude the downstream rivals and there the big stumbling block for economics is really to explain why and in what circumstances it would be rational, credible for the integrating firm to really exclude the down stream firms and why would it make profit sense for them. The point is, in a very simple way, the one that was raised many years ago by the Chicago school, which of course has been overtaken by further analysis, but in many ways has got still a very compelling logic. If the upstream firm is making profit selling to downstream rivals, then even if it's a monopolist, it is not clear that it is in its interest to foreclose these rivals because it is making the monopoly profits selling to the rivals anyway. He may exclude them but what would he gain?

Economic analysis has moved on and it's clear that the kind of simple setting of the 'one monopoly profit' story of the Chicago school is oversimplified, but there is still this kind of fundamental question that one has to grapple with, and what economic analysis has done over the last 20 years is to try to come up with stories that overcome this fundamental stumbling block. There has been a great deal of analysis and we've had a great deal of theories that have been developed and there as been a lot of debate in the literature about some of these models: some are criticized; they are added to; some models are contrived; they only work under certain circumstances. But the reality is there is to date still no big over-arching principle that allows us to say in what specific circumstances a vertical foreclosure is rational and therefore likely as a result of the merger. We have a few examples where even in theory you think you've got fairly robust results, but typically it is not very easy to construct models and to predict situations in which shifting market share in the short term will make it profitable to foreclose.

And I think there is some fairly close analogy there with the conglomerate mergers. The circumstances are not dissimilar: again you can build a story that the firm with market power in one particular product that's integrating into a complement may be able, through actions that affect directly the quality or the profit of rival producers of that complement, to affect their ability to compete. That is certainly true. The question very closely analogous to verticals is, in what circumstances is it credible that there will be a link between actions that this firm takes in the short term and long term reduction of competition? In what circumstances is it really plausible? Is there a plausible mechanism, an economic mechanism, that links actions that may be taken just after the merger to long term exit from the market or reduction in R& D incentives that means that rivals will not be able to compete longer term?

Let me just give an example which is to do with bundling. Bundling is an area which has received a lot of focus because of cases like *GE/Honeywell* and cases like *Tetra/Sidel* where the concern was very much about the possibility that post merger bundling would marginalize and exclude competitors. Now economists have analyzed bundling extensively. There is extensive literature on that and really what you take out of the literature is one big strand of arguments that says the reason why firms bundle is because it helps them achieve price discrimination. It's just a way for them to offer consumers a menu of choices and consumers self-select and that is a way in which firms make more profit. Now that may certainly increase competition in the short run because firms without a bundle will have to reduce their prices in order to compete with the bundle, but what is bad about that? In these kinds of models you never price the bundle below the marginal cost of the bundle. There is no exclusion in the short term, where is the harm?

There is also literature about circumstances in which bundling can lead to exclusion and we have a number of models that show us that, but they tend to rely on relatively specific assumptions: the ability of the firm to commit only to sell as a bundle after the merger. But unless you think of a 'technical' bundle, which means the products are somehow physically combined, technically it is difficult to make that commitment credible; and if you remove that assumption, the whole thing starts shaking a bit. Another circumstance in which it is possible that you may achieve that effect of intensifying competition in the short term and then ending up with much less competition in the long run is really to do with special industries in which it is plausible that acquiring market share today will really turn into a permanent advantage. But that is limited to certain types of industry, software for example, industries where there is a kind of 'network effects' that has the potential to lead to snowballing. Software is one example in which you have the network effect generated by proprietary standards and if you are able to shift a lot of market share today or in the near future to yourself, it is possible that that may be quite difficult for rivals to recover from in future. However, it is not enough to say there is *going* to be more competition, there are *going* to be smaller cash flows available to competitors, *therefore* R&D incentives will be affected. We really need to understand how R&D is funded, how current cash flows affect R&D. So the number of statements of general application that we can take out of these theories is quite limited.

Let me make a final point, I think, on conglomerates. Economists have taken time to study certain phenomena when we see them in markets. What does it mean when we see bundling taking place? What does it mean when we see certain pricing practices taking place? How can we understand them? It is always difficult, even in an abuse case, when you actually have data in front of you about bundling taking place or about market share being undeniably shifted to be really clear that there is some abuse going on. In a merger where you are trying to look at this, and I accept that of course you have to be predictive in a merger, it demands a very big leap of faith to assume that you are going to be able to make reasonably robust predictions when your powers to predict these behaviors, I would suggest, remain very, very limited.

[GAVIN ROBERT]

Thank you very much Cristina. So there we've heard about what the theories of competitive harm might be and some of the difficulties that exist in actually constructing, as it were, the story of competitive harm. I guess the other side of the coin is on the efficiencies which is something that we mentioned at the outset. There is quite often if not a presumption, then some form of an assumption that vertical and conglomerate mergers may actually be pro-competitive and create efficiencies. I want to turn to both Bill and Simon and I want to ask you whether you believe firstly that vertical and conglomerate mergers may create efficiencies and indeed go further, and whether you think that there should be a presumption in favour of vertical and conglomerate mergers which may differ from the way in which horizontal mergers are usually treated. Bill, can I ask you first?

[BILL KOVACIC]

I think that compared to horizontal transactions the theoretical observations that Cristina referred to before have certainly led my agency to regard vertical and conglomerate transactions as being comparatively more benign or pro-competitive than horizontal transactions as a group. This is evident in any number of ways but I'd caution that I think there is a generally broader receptivity to efficiency concerns and the formulation of enforcement policy even for horizontal transactions. One way to think of it is to compare analytical methodologies of say 25/30 years ago to the present. Simon was referring before to the use of foreclosure data in older US jurisprudence, but cases that have not been repudiated by our Supreme Court. The last time our Supreme Court had something to say about substandard merger standards was in 1975. They have been quiet since then. For those of you keeping score at home that's nearly 30 years. In the past in some of these cases you had an assumption, almost a conclusive assumption/presumption of the existence of anti-competitive effects from vertical foreclosure where the market share increase was in the nature of 2–4 per cent and not necessarily by a firm where the verti- cally related firm had significant market power. Today the tendency is to make much more generous assumptions about efficiency possibilities so in general terms I would say that there is a tendency which reflects obser- vations from the theoretical literature to regard non-horizontal transac- tions as having either greater efficiency possibilities or to be comparatively benign.

But I'd add again as I mentioned before that I think this characterizes the treatment of horizontal mergers as well. We released data set from the FTC in early January that covered enforcement experience going from 1996 up through 2002 and that data set documents in a fairly stark way how the threshold of concern in a typical horizontal merger for us has shifted considerably to the point now where 4/3, 3/2 is the zone of concern not 6/5, 7/6, 8/6, and this again reflects a greater sensitivity to efficiency considerations across the board. Another thought that perhaps we will come back to later is that I think to analyse exactly how we take these things into account and to see whether these assumptions are warranted demands a greater investment than we make now in going back and assessing the consequences of actual enforcement choices.

[SIMON PRIDDIS]

I think that I would like to start off actually from the same point that Bill did which is to emphasize that in general the UK regime does regard mergers at a general level as being efficiency enhancing. You have to recall that we have a fairly permissive merger regime in the UK where we don't even have a mandatory notification requirement. In order to refer a transaction to the Competition Commission, the OFT itself has to reach a particular standard of belief. The burden rests on the OFT to show that belief. And that applies to all transactions, not just to vertical or conglomerate mergers. So the question I think really is, is there or should there be a stronger recognition for vertical and conglomerate mergers that they may be efficiency enhancing than normally applies in horizontal cases? To that question I think I would also answer yes. I say that for three reasons.

First of all we've explicitly recognized this ourselves in the OFT's substantive guide on merger analysis. We've gone so far as to explicitly recognize there that vertical and conglomerate mergers may well be efficiency enhancing. How does that recognition actually manifest itself in practice? I think it does that by informing the question of whether we've reached the relevant standard of proof to make a reference to the Competition Commission. That itself works in two ways. First of all when deciding whether the gathered evidence actually meets the relevant standard, which is much harder when one is trying to make a trade off between what one recognizes as potentially efficiency enhancing effects and the evidence one has gathered as to potential anti-competitive harm. A good case to look at for an explicit recognition of that trade off is the *Hilton/BSkyB* case which was late 2000/2001 where you see the OFT very clearly setting out a clear trade off. There was evidence that the merger might give rise to the sort of 'snowballing' effects that Cristina referred to earlier but also recognition that the merger would actually bring a whole new product to the market that didn't exist before, so there was a very difficult balance to be struck between the pro-consumer and the anti-competitive effects of that transactions. I think that this recognition also plays in relation simply to looking at the level of evidence that is needed when one is looking to show to the relevant standard of proof that a more uncertain and less clear theory of anti-competitive harm is actually soundly based in the facts of the case in front of us. Now as we touched on earlier, and I think all of us recognize this, theories of vertical and conglomerate harm are more uncertain, more difficult to show than the more natural story of horizontal anti-competitive effects, so the evidence one needs I think does have to reach a higher standard. Of course the legal standard itself doesn't change but one needs to be more certain, I think, that the anti-competitive story that one is seeking to tell is soundly based in the facts of the case. I think that is the second point where this recognition plays in.

The other two points that I wish to make very briefly are, first of all, that of course under the Enterprise Act we can take efficiencies into account expressly either as part of the SLC analysis in itself, which might pick up the point Cristina raises about the merger overall reducing the prices being charged to consumers downstream, or we can actually take into account even in a potentially anti-competitive merger, customer benefits and we can make an explicit trade off under the Enterprise Act of the anti-competitive effects one might expect and any customer benefits that we nonetheless feel that the merger may deliver. The Enterprise Act expressly allows us to do that. Now I think it goes some way towards addressing a concern here that the legislative framework in the UK expressly allows for and recognizes that one might need to make this sort of trade off.

[BILL KOVACIC]

Gavin, can I add one thought? I would also underscore how not only are our decisions informed by some general assessments of likely efficiency effects, but, in thinking as Simon was saying about the way in which we will be held to show a theory of any competitive effects, increasingly we approach both vertical, non-horizontal and horizontal transactions with a greater expectation that our courts are going to require us to spell out how that theory of anti-competitive effects will unfold. That means in the case of foreclosure not only must we identify the capacity to foreclose but also the likely incentive to foreclose, and I think indirectly we expect to see more and more of the approach taken by the *Airtours* tribunal in the horizontal context in which it was shown to be no longer enough, if it ever was in recent memory, to simply lay out structural factors of considerations and then expect that strong inferences would be drawn from those alone. My interpretation of *Airtours* is that it is, in a sense, a command to all competition authorities to do what one might do in a mathematics exam which is to show your work and lay out the intermediate steps by which coordination will take place. Tell us the story step by step to its conclusion. I think this again reflects a more demanding approach taken by the tribunals before whom we have to appear. They are likely to test our own theories of any competitive harm so not only is there a more generous set of assumptions about efficiencies but the expectation about the theories of harm is going to be tested by a more demanding approach in the courts before whom we appear.

[GAVIN ROBERT]

Thank you. I think that is a very good point and a good one on which perhaps to open some questions up to the floor. We will be going on to talk about enforcement practice so perhaps leave questions on individual cases and practice to then, but if anyone has got any questions to raise on the analytical framework that we've discussed so far?

D. Discussion

[MARGARET BLOOM, *Kings College London and Freshfields Bruckhaus Deringer*]

I want to ask Bill a question if I may. Bill, you referred to the change in time in the Federal Trade Commission being more permissive or less restrictive in terms of the way you approach mergers. What are the main factors that underline that change? Why has the FTC moved in this direction? Perhaps I could just give one other. You talked about showing your work when you have to present it before a court or third party. Will the FTC think about publishing more on actual cases which were resolved by consent decree as opposed to the very interesting work that you publish in terms of analysing series of cases?

[BILL KOVACIC]

I think two forces worked to change the approach. One is we grew weary of losing cases and I think if you were to map out our experience with the recent experience of DG Comp and the Commission itself, there is nothing like a few stinging appellate defeats to cause you to re-assess, and we went through precisely that experience in some of these areas. I reluctantly draw your attention to them but you can find Federal Trade Commission decisions in the 1960s that took the following approach when parties would raise arguments. They would say in vertical cases, for example a cement industry merger, that this is going to reduce costs and we'd say that's just what we thought, it counts against you, and you can find lines of text in our formal decisions in which the efficiencies offence is recognised and is counted against them. And we grew quite fond of pushing the use of talismanic foreclosure data down as close to zero as we could. You can find FTC cases where the requisite foreclosure crept below 2 per cent. It never got quite below 1 per cent but we tried. Our appellate courts, increasingly, started to push back aggressively so unless one had a genuine taste for further defeats, that was an occasion for re-assessment.

Secondly, I think that the developments in the commentary and the literature did begin to have a powerful influence internally as well, and indeed in many ways those forces actually converged to produce an internal re-assessment. But I guess the larger question going forward as you look at practice at any one moment is what mechanisms do you have in place to ensure that you don't get trapped in the wrong model, whatever that model may be? Certainly our courts provided a powerful bit of feedback on that front as well as an internal re-assessment. I think, Margaret, the goal of further revelation of the decision not to prosecute is entirely appropriate. Several of us who had written about this before we came to the Federal Trade Commission had staked that out as being an area of considerable improvement. On 12 occasions in the past 32 months the FTC has had something to say about a decision not to prosecute: that is a staggering number. But in the previous almost 30 years there was one such revelation and that was *Boeing/McDonnell Douglas*, so in a relative scale, at least, going from 1 to 12 and indeed 12 in 34 months is a significant adjustment. I think the norm for us ought to be, and it will take a while to get there, that every time we do something significant and don't act, and I consider the issuance of a second request to be quite significant, we ought to say something about why we did not finally intervene.

[SIMON PRIDDIS]

Could I make just one extra quick point on the same theme which is that we've talked a lot about the sorts of evidence that one needs; we've talked about the analytical framework. Linking that to transparency I think it is interesting to look, for example, at some of the recent Competition Commission publications in vertical and conglomerate mergers and to see the level of detailed evidence that is laid out in those reports with regard to the way in which the incentives would work. For example in the *Centrica/Dynergy* case which Cristina was involved with, there was a phenomenal level of detail in the published report as to the way in which the foreclosure incentives were analysed and ultimately the transaction was cleared subject to some behavioural remedies on other points. There is a very high level of detail there and again, only a couple of weeks ago in the first *Scotrail* case,[1] although I hate to use labels given what I said about them earlier, one can look at that transaction as a conglomerate type transaction where the risk was that two forms of public transport might well be bundled together. The Competition Commission's provisional findings lay out an extraordinary level of economic evidence and analysis all focused on incentives.

[GAVIN ROBERT]

Thank you. Well there is an awful lot of consensus on this panel, at least so far. True that the European Commission isn't on the panel but that doesn't prevent me asking the next question that if there is this amount of consensus, and perhaps contradicting what I said at the outset that there was less

[1] See <http://www.oft.gov.uk/nr/rdonlyres/3163c4be-e0e1-4f4a-9d93-d1c32b916f4a/0/scotrail.pdf>.

consensus in this area, why did the European Commission and the Department of Justice reach what were clearly different decisions on the basis of the same facts in *GE/Honeywell*? Bill, if would you have a go at answering that first, I would be grateful.

[BILL KOVACIC]

As you can tell by my affiliation, I didn't participate in that transaction, but from the outside let me give you my own assessment and I base it in part on roughly comparable experiences I had when I was an academic. Occasionally when I was serving as a truth seeker I acted as a shameless advocate for McDonnell Douglas in that transaction so you are hearing the views of someone who worked for one of the parties in that transaction. In that transaction, if I can superimpose some perspectives on to what I think took place in *GE/Honeywell*, there are some different assumptions about the appropriate calculus for decision and let me simply identify a couple of them. These are both rooted I think in assessments of how one's own economic system operates and perhaps some institutional characteristics of both of the reviewing bodies. One to touch on the point that Gavin asked us to address before, I think in many respects in looking at non-horizontal mergers, you do have an assumption within the US agencies that non-horizontal transactions tend to be benign or pro-competitive more often than not. That injects some bias in the direction of assuming that certain efficiencies will unfold and particularly where one assumes that this will happen in the relatively near term and middle term to regard those as more tangible and more likely to manifest themselves. You might recall there were a range effects argument of sorts raised in *Boeing/McDonnell Douglas* too, especially about the amalgamation of assets and possible use of the amassed assets of the merging firm to engage in various forms of predation, so that partly informs my thinking about the perspectives. Second, I think there is a difference in the way in which long term and short term effects are traded off. I think there tends to be a more robust expectation in the US agencies that rivals will be able to reposition themselves to cope with potential exclusionary strategies somewhat more readily than DG Comp might assume; that buyers will engage in counter moves that also will tend to protect themselves and that possibilities for new entry and expansion are somewhat more robust, and there is perhaps a greater faith, and I don't know if it is a mirage, but a greater faith that you can use *ex-post* tools to control abuse of dominance concepts to fix problems that may materialise if you made the wrong assumptions about the possibilities of competitive harm. So the calculus that I'd distil that comes through in the US is that there is an inclination to accept the presumed short term efficiency benefits or gains, to regard the competitive harm scenarios as being more long term, more speculative, more indeterminate and therefore to discount them more heavily. Take the short term gains now, worry about the long term gains later and yes we will use an abuse of dominance context to deal with possible problems.

[CRISTINA CAFFARRA]

I was involved in the case, but I will be brief. I agree with what Bill has said. I think that the most unsatisfactory part of that decision, and we are coming up to an oral hearing in Luxembourg in the next couple of weeks, is that this decision is really an example of a case that was decided based on a 'hunch' on the ability of potential practices in future to shift market share, and chain of further assumptions on the potential for these shifting market shares to lead to foreclosure. As I discussed earlier, these are things that are very difficult to make tight. Now in the case, there were attempts sponsored by third parties to put some structure around this question, and try and provide models that were going to help take a rational decision on this. The unsatisfactory part was that these modelling efforts were controversial, and in the face of that controversy the Commission simply ignored the economic models altogether, and effectively didn't rely on any formal economic analysis in the decision. There was never a very constructive dialogue about the assumptions of these models, what they really meant, whether we should believe them, whether the parameters that were assumed were realistic in the context of the industry? I am in favour of a rational exploration of the incentive question in a way that builds on models. Why not? If we have data that we can plug into these models to simulate the effect, let's do it. Simon mentioned *Centrica/Dynergy*. That was a case in which modelling was done, data was there, we tried to look at the incentive to shift market share in practice. I would like to see much more of a systematic analysis of this than happened in that case.

[GAVIN ROBERT]

And I think in fact, Simon, you do already talk about the vertical conglomerate mergers in the guidelines that were published at the entry into force of the Enterprise Act. You talk about modelling techniques and that the Office of Fair Trading will try to use and develop modelling techniques. Has a lot of work been done in that area or is that still to do?

[SIMON PRIDDIS]

We are still doing a lot of work internally but I think part of what the guidance is getting at is we are trying to use the sorts of techniques that Cristina described, looking for quantitative evidence that actually backs up the sorts of stories that either the parties or indeed third party complainants are telling us about the way in which the merger might have anti-competitive effects or the way in which the incentives might unfold. Certainly in the way that Bill described. That is certainly something we very much move towards. We do try to press parties, both merging parties and complaining parties, to provide that sort of evidence at that level of detail.

[BERT FOER, *American Antitrust Institute*]

I'm increasingly hearing on both sides of the Ocean almost presumptions in favour of efficiencies and I understand where that comes from, primarily in Chicago School economics, but there is also a large and increasing literature primarily from the business schools and business press that questions how efficient mergers actually are. How many have turned out as positively as was predicted? One also hears at various times that the types of efficiency projections and claims that are offered are if not unserious at least somewhat incredible. So the question is, how theoretical are we in danger of becoming as imposed to empirical?

[BILL KOVACIC]

I think one difficulty that Bert identifies in the entire field is that in many instances we don't have a great deal of empirical data to draw on in this area. One idea that we've been testing increasingly in the last few years that I'd like to see us do more of over time, is to devote more effort to looking at the effects of transactions where we've challenged and where we have not challenged. There have been a couple of incidences where we've allowed deals to go through making one set of assumptions. I'd like to see us devote more resources to an actual examination of how those episodes turned out. Another approach that is closely related is to look at the effectiveness of remedies that we've actually taken in specific cases where we've modified a transaction to permit it to go ahead. If you read our press releases you'd think they are all perfect successes (and I'm sure they are at least since I've been there), but I've looked at this and I've never seen a press release from any of our agents who said that this is a very close call. We think we've got it right but we are fallible human beings. Maybe we didn't, but we are carefully going to go back and take a look later to see if our assumptions proved to be right, so my main comment on Bert's intervention is that I think a necessary ingredient, not just a luxury of policy making here, but a necessary ingredient has to be a commitment to devote at least some resources in every budget cycle to go back and ask how did things actually turn out?

[SIMON PRIDDIS]

Just to respond to the same question as well, I think there is also a point which we have touched on a little bit as to how one's thoughts about the efficiency benefits of mergers are actually played into the analysis. It's not for parties essentially to come to us and prove that their merger is going to be pro-competitive or efficiency enhancing in order to get clearance. The burden lies the other way round. Now we can take an expectation of some efficiency enhancement into account but ultimately what we do have to show is that the merger is going to have or may be expected to have some sort of anti-competitive effect. One's overall view about efficiency enhancement may colour one's approach to that analysis in the way that I was describing earlier with conglomerate mergers, but I don't think that what we are doing is saying to parties that they actually need to come in up front with a strong efficiency enhancing story in order to obtain clearance.

[CRISTINA CAFFARA]

At the cost of recasting this in a slightly different way again, I think the reason we are focusing on efficiencies in this particular panel is because of the obviously very different role that they play in these type of mergers. The reality is that in horizontal mergers the economics of competition tells us that however small there will be a price increase as a result of horizontal mergers if there isn't a cost reduction. That is a simple starting point. Now in vertical and conglomerate mergers where you start from is really that you are putting together complements and there are pricing efficiencies that come into play. There are investment efficiencies. You can eliminate the 'coordination problem' that has held back investments. So I think it is an important point in these mergers where we have on the one hand theories of harm that are a lot more delicate and on the other hand more clear-cut efficiencies. Therefore the trade off is somewhat different.

[BERT FOER]

Over time in America the merger policy had become a little more liberal partly because there was a view taken that *ex-post*, if we'd got it wrong, one could deal with abuses using competition law and that's very similar to what has been said in the *Tetra Laval/Sidel* case as well, although currently on appeal. I just want to specifically state that in the US context, for both vertical and conglomerate mergers, some of the theories of competitive harm don't involve short run profit sacrifice. In the context of and following *Verizon Communications v Trinko* I wonder whether one can still be so lenient with mergers on that basis?

[BILL KOVACIC]

I realize that in our jurisprudence one always asks two questions about Supreme Court decisions. One is what is the core holding and observation, and second is how will it emanate? Will it creep beyond the institutional bounds in which the decision took place? In research that I have done with a couple of colleagues and looking at the papers of several of our justices in the Supreme Court, it's clear that they think of their decisions in exactly this way too, that is, the narrow observation and the larger possibilities. I realize that *Verizon Communications v Trinko*, because it has the fairly florid ebullient commentary that fills up the last few pages of the Scalia Opinion, is certainly going to be quoted. That's the sort of thing that brings the wet glistening look to the defendant bar's eyes. I expect 20 years from now in the class room to see students whose names are Trinko and I'll know exactly what their parents do for a living, but I find it difficult at the moment to ignore the unique setting in which *Trinko* took place. Very specifically, the intersection of an extraordinarily complex and elaborate regulatory scheme that imposed a requirement that antitrust courts acting on their own typically would not have imposed is basically a mandate to provide a service set, by some measure, less than its cost. A concern that had been echoed for over a decade—it's a Scalia Opinion but it's Steve Breyer really writing in the background was first echoed on the case called *Town of Concord v Boston Edison,*[2] in which Breyer is saying, well in this extraordinary thicket of regulatory policy and competition policy who am I to say that an antitrust court is better to solve this problem than the public utility regulators? The traditional view is that the public utility regulators were either captured or ignorant, the phrase used in one article being 'Tools or Fools'. And by contrast antitrust courts were prescient, all knowing and perfect in their intervention. Breyer's commentary in *Town of Concord,* reflected in Scalia's remark, says maybe we've got the institutional balance wrong here. So my initial thought, and ten years from now I will be proven wrong I suspect, but my initial thought is that it's a mistake to read that case outside, in particular, this extraordinary combination of factors, and for those who are thinking about a theme we addressed last year at this conference, please note that it's a private treble damage class action law suit that is driving the case to the Supreme Court. This is not intervention by a public competition agency. Part of what's running through the court's mind I suspect is the thought that the local bail operating companies are going to

---

[2] 915F2d17 1990.

be besieged by billions of dollars of liability and in our system that's created a tendency to draw lines a bit differently too. So I think that you may be entirely right that *Trinko* swallows the world with an extremely non-intervention minded approach but I find it hard to read that without taking into account the special context in which the case came up.

E. The UK's Analytical Framework for Vertical and Conglomerate Mergers*

Simon Priddis[1]

I. INTRODUCTION

I.1. In June 2003, the Enterprise Act 2002 (the Act) came into force in the UK: in substantive terms, its principal effect was to replace the UK's old 'public interest' merger test[2] with a new substantial lessening of competition (SLC) test.[3] The Act was accompanied by publication of OFT guidance, which explained not only how mergers would fall under the OFT's jurisdiction but also how the OFT would apply the SLC test to such mergers (the Guidance).[4] The Guidance discusses the application of the SLC test to horizontal, vertical, and conglomerate mergers.[5]

I.2. This paper explains the analytical framework applied by the OFT when assessing vertical and conglomerate mergers.[6] The paper begins by explaining the main elements of the UK's legal framework for merger control and, in particular, the scope for application of that framework to vertical and conglomerate mergers. Then it considers the information provided in the Guidance on the application of the SLC test to vertical and conglomerate mergers, and places that information in the practical context of examples of the OFT's analysis of such mergers.

I.3. Experience of analysing vertical and conglomerate mergers under the Act is so far limited, so this paper also refers to cases examined under the Fair Trading Act 1973 (FTA, which the Act superseded). These cases remain

---

* Paper presented at British Institute of International and Comparative Law Competition Conference, 10 May 2003, London.

[1] Director of Mergers Branch, Office of Fair Trading. The views expressed are those of the author and do not necessarily represent the views of the Office of Fair Trading. I am indebted to David Ruck for his detailed input to this paper, and for comments and thoughts from John Vickers.

[2] See Fair Trading Act 1973.

[3] For the SLC test in the context of the OFT's duties under the Act, see s 22 (completed mergers) and s 33 (anticipated mergers).

[4] OFT publication OFT516, *Mergers—Substantive assessment guidance*, which can be downloaded from <www.oft.gov.uk>. The Competition Commission has published similar guidance concerning the substantive application of the SLC test, which can be downloaded from its web site, <http://www.competition-commission.gov.uk>.

[5] Vertical and conglomerate mergers are described in general terms at para 3.8 of the Guidance, and then more specifically in chs 5 and 6, respectively.

[6] This paper closes follows the layout and approach of a paper presented at the IBA's competition law conference in Fiesole on horizontal mergers.

a good guide to the assessment of vertical and conglomerate mergers under the Act since, in practice, the OFT applied a competition-based test (akin to the SLC test) under the FTA.[7] The paper than offers some comments on the wider policy issues raised by vertical and conglomerate merger analysis, before concluding with a short summary of the main policy positions that underpin the OFT's analytical framework for vertical and conglomerate mergers.

I.4. Before turning to the UK's legal framework for merger review and its application to vertical and conglomerate mergers, one general point should be mentioned by way of introduction. The discussion in this paper on the application of the OFT's Guidance touches on the kinds of evidence useful in vertical and/or conglomerate merger analysis. In *IBA Health Ltd v Office of Fair Trading* (*IBA*), the Court of Appeal emphasized the importance of evidenced-based, robustly constructed, and well thought out merger analysis.[8] While the *IBA* appeal was framed largely as a horizontal merger case, the Court of Appeal's dicta are of broader relevance. The underlying theory and analysis of vertical and conglomerate mergers can be significantly more complex and less well understood than the more established principles of horizontal merger analysis. It is therefore important to bear in mind, when approaching vertical and conglomerate merger analysis, the need for particularly clear exposition of the law, theory and facts.

II. THE LEGAL FRAMEWORK OF MERGER CONTROL

II.1. Robust merger control regimes are founded on a solid legal base.[9] In this respect, the implementation of the Act in June 2003 brought the UK's legal framework for merger control into line with OFT practice by introducing the SLC test into the UK law (As noted above, the OFT had applied a competition-based test under the preceding FTA public interest test).[10] There is no need in this paper to dwell on the respective merits of different

---

[7] These FTA cases are possibly not such a good guide to the standard of concern necessary for reference. In *IBA Health Ltd v Office of Fair Trading*, the Court of Appeal noted that it might be risky to place too much reliance on FTA cases as a guide to the application of the Act.

[8] Of course, this does not relate only to the OFT. There is a greater onus on companies and their advisors to provide solid supporting evidence to their arguments.

[9] Sound merger control regimes are in reality comprised of three elements: (i) a legal base; (ii) guidelines; and (iii) application of the principles to cases.

[10] This was a position recognized by successive Secretaries of State for Trade and Industry, who had emphasized that decisions on reference were taken on the advice of the then Director General of Fair Trading and, save in exceptional cases, on competition grounds. See, for example, the announcement of Stephen Byers, then Secretary of State, on 26 Oct 2000 that he would in all, bar very exceptional cases, follow the Director General's advice and refer on competition considerations alone.

formulations of the substantive merger test. It suffices to emphasize that the SLC test, which is rooted in economic analysis and which focuses attention directly at the change in competitive conditions that flows from a merger, is particularly well suited to analysis of vertical and conglomerate mergers.

II.2. For present purposes, this paper touches on two aspects of the UK's legal framework: first, under what circumstances does the OFT have jurisdiction to review vertical and conglomerate mergers; and, secondly, how does the substantive test apply to vertical and conglomerate mergers (As to the latter question, it is important to note that, because the OFT is a first-phase authority, the 'substantive test' in OFT terms means the test for reference of a merger to the Competition Commission for in depth investigation).

A. *OFT jurisdiction to review vertical and conglomerate mergers*

II.3. In order to review any transaction, the OFT must believe that:[11]

(a) two or more enterprises (ie, ongoing businesses) have ceased to be distinct; *and*
(b) one of the two following criteria must be met: either -
  (i) the UK turnover of the company being acquired exceeds £70 million; or
  (ii) the merger must result in a share of supply of more than 25 per cent being created or strengthened in the UK or in a substantial part of the UK.[12]

II.4. There are no different jurisdictional tests for vertical or conglomerate mergers. In practice, this means that pure vertical and conglomerate mergers need to meet the turnover test in order to be susceptible to review. This is because the absence of direct overlap in the parties' activities means that pure vertical or conglomerate mergers do not generally give rise to increases in the share of supply (of course, mergers qualifying for investigation on the share of supply test may raise both horizontal and vertical competition issues).

II.5. In some cases, a reasonable description of the goods or services subject to the share of supply test may catch vertical mergers (eg, by including several stages of production) or conglomerate mergers (eg, where the prod-

---

[11] This is not a complete list of jurisdictional criteria. There are separate considerations in respect of rail, water, and newspaper mergers which this paper does not cover.
[12] It is important to note that this share of supply test is a legal test and does not rely on any market definition exercise. For a more detailed explanation of this point, see Guidance, para 2.24.

ucts are closely related). For example, the *Synopsys/Avant!* merger qualified for investigation on UK shares of supply of software tools for the electronic design automation industry.[13] The competition issues raised in that case (and discussed in detail below) are perhaps better characterized as vertical or conglomerate in nature rather than horizontal.

B. Application of the Act's substantive test to vertical and conglomerate mergers

II.6. Where the OFT believes that it is or may be the case that a relevant merger situation may be expected to give rise to an SLC, the OFT is under a duty to make a reference to the Competition Commission unless one of a limited set of exceptions to the duty is applicable.[14] The Act formulates the test for reference in the following way: the OFT is under a duty to make a reference where it believes that:

> it is or may be the case that the relevant merger situation may be expected to result in a substantial lessening of competition.

II.7. The OFT considers that the SLC test is particularly well suited to analysis of vertical and conglomerate mergers. It is rooted in economic analysis and focuses attention directly at the change in competitive conditions that flows from a merger. The SLC test itself appears to be sufficiently flexible to accommodate all ways in which a merger can lessen competition.

II.8. In practice, the central question in the UK's legal framework for merger analysis is not whether the SLC test extends to vertical or conglomerate mergers, but instead whether the economic story of harm being portrayed is supported by the facts. This is because, when considering the standard of proof to be met by the OFT in making a reference, the Court of Appeal in *IBA* made clear a number of points, of which three are particularly relevant to the discussion in this paper.

(a) The Court of Appeal emphasized the OFT's discretion in deciding whether a merger might have anti-competitive effects. Where the OFT believes that the merger is more likely than not to result in an SLC; then

---

[13] See Director General of Fair Trading's advice of 22 Aug 2002 concerning the *completed acquisition by Synopsys Incorporated of Avant! Corporation.*

[14] Those exceptions are set out in s 22(3) and s 33(3) of the Act for completed and anticipated mergers respectively. They relate to: (a) mergers of insufficient importance to warrant reference; (b) mergers that are insufficiently advanced to warrant reference; and (c) situations where the customer benefits of a transaction outweigh the expected SLC. In addition, the OFT is precluded from referring a merger to the Competition Commission when it is considering whether or not to accept first-phase remedial undertakings to address the competition concerns instead of making the reference.

the test for reference is met. If the OFT does not hold such a belief, but the prospect of an SLC is more than fanciful, then the OFT has a 'broad discretion' to decide whether it 'may be the case' that the merger may be expected to result in an SLC.

(b) In reaching its view, the OFT must base its decision on evidence and facts, and in so doing must act reasonably.

(c) The Court of Appeal also discussed the role of 'uncertainty' in arriving at decisions on mergers. In essence, where the evidence on a case is less extensive then the test for reference will be lower than in a case where the available evidence is more thorough.

II.9. Applying these analytical principles to the assessment of vertical and conglomerate mergers, a number of points can be made.

II.10. First, the ways in which competition may be harmed in vertical or conglomerate mergers are less direct than in horizontal mergers. In horizontal mergers of course, it is the overlap between the activities of the merging parties that directly leads to a loss of competition. In vertical and conglomerate mergers, there is no such direct loss of competition. So any loss of competition from such mergers arises only in more indirect ways. For example, in vertical mergers one can examine the possibility of foreclosure, but that entails more than a straightforward examination of overlap activities and surrounding competitive constraints. Establishing a credible theory of competitive harm in vertical and conglomerate merger cases requires examination of a broader range of evidence (such as the likely incentives of the merged entity to engage in foreclosure) than is generally needed in horizontal merger analysis.

II.11. Second, the nature of vertical and conglomerate merger cases often means that obtaining the evidence to ground or disprove theories of harm is difficult. This is in part due to the sorts of theories of harm typically encountered in such cases. Although all merger analysis is forward looking and therefore to some extent involves assessing an individual firm's incentives, evidence demonstrating a likely 'step change' in commercial behaviour is often hard to come by. In respect of vertical and conglomerate mergers it is therefore less likely that the OFT will be in a position at the end of a relatively short investigation to conclude that a merger is more likely than not to result in a SLC. Vertical and conglomerate cases are more likely to fall within the OFT's broad discretion to decide whether it may be the case that they may be expected to give rise to anti-competitive effects.

II.12. Third, exercising a discretion as to when 'it may be the case' that a merger may be expected to result in an SLC is also inherently more difficult in cases where there is a trade off involved between the possible pro- and anti-competitive effects of a merger. Vertical and sometimes conglomerate mergers can involve significant efficiency gains for the merging firms that can benefit consumers and intensify rather than lessen competition (see, for example, the elimination of double marginalisation in vertical mergers).[15] Assessment of the evidence is obviously much more complex in this situation.

II.13. In sum, the application (even in the abstract) of the legal framework for assessment of vertical and conglomerate mergers itself raises a number of real questions and challenges, both for the OFT and for merging parties. To see how these questions and challenges play out in practice, we turn now to consider the second and third elements of the OFT's analytical framework: ie the substantive guidance published by the OFT and the way in which that guidance has been applied in individual cases.

III. INTRODUCTION TO THE SUBSTANTIVE GUIDANCE AND OFT ANALYSIS

III.1. The Act requires the OFT to publish guidance on the application of the substantive test. The OFT did so in May 2003, covering jurisdictional issues as well as the substantive analysis of horizontal, vertical and conglomerate mergers.[16] Before turning to the detailed content and application of the Guidance to vertical and conglomerate mergers, we should first consider whether the traditional distinction between horizontal mergers on the one hand and vertical/conglomerate mergers on the other is either real or helpful.

A. Characterisation of horizontal, vertical and/or conglomerate mergers

III.2. Characterisation of mergers as horizontal, vertical or conglomerate in real life cases can be difficult. But if precise characterisation of the competitive effects may in certain cases be difficult, does that really matter? Or is it the case that the fundamental economic analysis of each type of merger is so closely related that distinctions are artificial and unhelpful?

III.3. There are reasons for suggesting that the economic analysis of vertical and conglomerate mergers may be closely related. In this sense, precise differentiation between the two may not necessarily be crucial in specific

---

[15] These are not the only possible efficiency enhancing aspects of vertical mergers and this could involve lower transaction costs, assurances of supply or elimination of externalities to name a few.

[16] At the same time, the OFT also published guidance on its procedures for conducting merger reviews. See OFT publication OFT526, *Mergers—procedural guidance*. The OFT also has an ongoing research programme that regularly publishes reports: see, for example, OFT Research Paper 12, *Vertical Restraints and Competition Policy*, Paul Dobson and Michael Waterson, Dec 1996. In addition the Department of Trade and Industry has published a report on conglomerate issues: Nalebuff, *Bundling, Tying, and Portfolio Effects*, Feb 2003.

cases: ultimately, analysis of both sorts of mergers turns primarily on questions of foreclosure, whether that takes the form of refusals to supply, raising rivals' costs, bundling or portfolio power.

- The competition issues in *Synopsys/Avant!* could be described as horizontal (overlap in the supply of front-end software tools for electronic design automation), vertical (risk of downstream foreclosure as the front-end tools were considered an essential input to the back-end tools) or conglomerate (the tools could be considered to rest in adjacent economic markets and thus complementary to each other).[17]

III.4. Although *Synopsys/Avant!* was ultimately treated as a vertical merger, there appears to be little at first sight to distinguish the framework of the analysis from a conglomerate foreclosure case: both turn on the ability and incentive to foreclose. However, cosmetic similarity may obscure underlying conceptual differences. For example, in conglomerate mergers, competitive harm from foreclosure generally arises even more indirectly than in vertical mergers, where a foreclosure story can more naturally be told given that one firm may supply an essential input to downstream rivals. In the conglomerate context, the foreclosure theory may require that: a firm must be able to commit to tying goods; this must have an exclusionary effect; the exclusionary effect must marginalize rivals and force their exit; and then the merged entity must be able to increase prices.

III.5. As to the distinction between horizontal and vertical/conglomerate mergers, there are less good arguments that distinctions between the two are cosmetic. As discussed above, vertical and conglomerate mergers, unlike horizontal mergers, do not directly eliminate competition. Nevertheless, the end impact of those rare vertical and conglomerate mergers which are anti-competitive is to create horizontal market power. In that sense vertical and conglomerate mergers may involve some analysis that is akin to horizontal mergers. In practice, mergers in the UK with significant vertical issues have tended to combine horizontal and vertical integration and raised issues at both levels.

- In *Nutreco Holding/Hydro Seafood*, horizontal concentration at the level of fish feed and salmon farming raised horizontal concerns aggravated by vertical concerns. In effect, the vertical linkages between salmon feed and salmon farming were identified as reinforcing market power at each level of production.[18]

---

[17] The US Federal Trade Commission's decision to close its investigation into this merger can be found at <http://www.ftc.gov/os/caselist/0210049.htm>. Closing statements from the FTC Commissioners talk variously about a merger of complementary products leading to foreclosure concerns or vertical concerns.

[18] See Competition Commission report: *Nutreco Holding NV and Hydro Seafood GSP Ltd.: A report on the proposed merger*, Cm 5004, Dec 2000.

- In *Centrica/Dynergy*, the OFT was concerned by significant concentration in gas storage by a firm with a leading position in gas trading and gas supply. Increased market power in gas storage could distort downstream markets through access to market sensitive information and reduce competitors' access to gas at times of peak demand.[19]

III.6. In both of these latter cases, the vertical competition concerns articulated were themselves a function of separate horizontal concerns. In this sense, an artificial distinction between horizontal and vertical concerns does not really assist in understanding the competitive effects of the merger. This is also the case in mergers where the underlying concern relates to increased risks of horizontal coordination as a result of increased vertical integration. Such concerns are rarely identified by competition authorities, but are in reality no more than a reflection of the close analytical relationship that can exist between horizontal and vertical concerns.

III.7. Conglomerate mergers may also involve mergers of weak substitutes. Analysis of these mergers may be more akin to horizontal merger analysis than vertical merger analysis. For example, a number of products that individually place only a weak constraint on products sold by one of the merging parties may—when purchased as a bundle—represent a more significant constraint.

- In *Capital Radio//Virgin Radio*, the concern was whether the acquisition of an important independent radio station which provided advertising airtime might deprive competitors of the merged entity of the opportunity to offer a bundle of advertising airtime across radio stations that could compete with the bundle offered by Capital.[20]

III.8. In short, application of a strict delineation between horizontal, vertical, and conglomerate mergers may not be warranted. However, as a matter of practice, it is often useful for competition authorities to retain such a strict delineation, if for no other reason than for the advantageous intellectual discipline that such an approach entails.

IV. THE OFT'S ANALYTICAL FRAMEWORK FOR VERTICAL MERGERS

IV.1. Chapter 5 of the Guidance sets out the OFT's analytical approach to

---

[19] See Director General of Fair Trading's advice of 11 Feb 2003 concerning the *completed acquisition by Centrica plc of Dynegy Storage Ltd and Dynegy Onshore Processing Ltd*; see also Competition Commission report: *Centrica plc and Dynegy Storage Ltd and Dynegy Onshore Processing Ltd: A report on the merger situation*, Aug 2003.

[20] See (as it then was) Monopolies and Mergers Commission Report: *Capital Radio plc and Virgin Radio Holdings Limited: A report on the proposed acquisition*, CM 3817, Jan 1998.

assessing the competitive impact of vertical mergers. Before explaining that approach in detail, it is important to put it in context.

IV.2. The OFT's approach to merger control is informed by its overall corporate goal: making markets work well for consumers. Markets work well for consumers when they are sufficiently competitive that firms compete with each other to win customers' business. The Guidance explains:

This process of rivalry, where it is effective, impels firms to deliver benefits to customers in terms of prices, quality and choice. When levels of rivalry are reduced ([eg] because customers have fewer firms among which to choose or because of coordinated behaviour between firms), the effectiveness of this process may be diminished to the detriment of customers.[21]

IV.3. The analytical framework applied by the OFT is therefore focused on identifying transactions that so reduce the level of rivalry among firms in a market so that the firms are no longer impelled to deliver benefits to customers in terms or price, quality and choice. At this point, the OFT may refer the transaction to the Competition Commission.[22]

IV.4. In this context, the Guidance recognises that vertical mergers are often pro-competitive and competition concerns arise only in certain circumstances:

Mergers between parties which operate at different levels of the supply chain of an industry, though often pro-competitive, may in some circumstances reduce the competitive constraints faced by the merged firm by foreclosing a substantial part of the market to competition ([eg] through refusals to supply, enhanced barriers to entry, facilitating price discrimination raising rivals costs) or by increasing the likelihood of post merger collusion. This risk is, however, unlikely to arise except in the presence of existing market power at one level in the supply chain at least, or in markets where there is already significant vertical integration/restraints.[23]

IV.5. The above comments on context and approach show that the OFT brings to analysis of vertical mergers an inherent recognition that they may well be pro-competitive. They also clarify that, in considering whether a vertical merger may have anti-competitive effects, the OFT focuses on harm to the process of competition, not on harm to particular competitors. It is

[21] Guidance, para 3.5.
[22] Note that the Act recognizes that there may be cases in which the merger may be expected to substantially lessen competition in the way described, but is nonetheless still expected to deliver customer benefits. In these cases, the Act allows the OFT to trade off the expected loss of competition against the expected customer benefits in deciding whether to refer the merger to the Competition Commission (Guidance, para 7.7). This is in addition to the more usual treatment of possible merger-specific efficiency gains as part of the overall SLC analysis (Guidance, para 4.29).
[23] Guidance, para 3.8.

not always easy readily to separate the two, but the OFT's focus is the former. In these circumstances, a key objective of the Guidance on vertical merger analysis is to focus attention on the economic analysis needed to underpin vertical theories of competitive harm.

IV.6. Although the Guidance identifies two primary theories of competitive harm that might arise from vertical mergers (foreclosure and increased risk of collusion—see above), this paper focuses on the analysis of foreclosure.[24] This is simply because, of the two theories, foreclosure arises as a concern significantly more often than increased risk of collusion.[25]

IV.7. Two concepts are central to economic analysis of any foreclosure theory: ability to foreclose and incentive to foreclose. Treatment of vertical issues in submissions to the OFT (whether from merging parties or complainants) is often limited to assessment of a firm's ability to foreclose competitors. Assessment of incentives is not only crucial, but in practice more complex and time-consuming. In line with these objectives, the OFT typically approaches vertical mergers by asking three fundamental questions: (i) what is the theory of competitive harm; (ii) is there pre-existing market power at one or more levels of the supply chain; and (iii) would the parties' economic incentives to engage in a foreclosure strategy change as a result of the merger?

IV.8. Before looking at each of these points in turn, an added practical reason for subjecting all possible suggestions of vertical competitive effects to particularly stringent analysis is that vertical mergers tend to prompt significant competitor complaint. It is important to distinguish between harm to competition (which is the focus of the regime) from harm to competitors (which is not, provided that competition overall remains effective). Absent such a rigorous evaluation process, there is a risk that complaints relating to harm to competitors may gain undue weight in the assessment of a merger. Such complaints may be well founded, but this does not necessarily entail a detriment to customers. For example, even where there is a loss of intra-brand competition, this need not entail a loss to consumers if the remaining intra-brand competition or existing/new extra-brand competition is sufficient to ensure an effective process of rivalry.[26]

---

[24] The OFT uses the term 'foreclosure' to cover not simply outright refusals to deal, but also subtler forms of foreclosure behaviour, such as raising rivals' costs or raising barriers to entry.

[25] The OFT has considered vertical mergers where risks of coordination in upstream or downstream markets were considered: see OFT decision of 26 Feb 2004 concerning the *completed acquisition by Milk Link Ltd, First Milk Ltd and Dairy Farmers of Great Britain Ltd of assets of United Milk, namely the Westbury Processing Plant.* The OFT found the concerns to be remote as any coordinated output restriction by the firms would likely result in reduced profits for the firms concerned.

[26] This is an issue familiar from analysis of exclusive vertical supply agreements.

A. *What is the story of competitive harm?*

IV.9. While seemingly a basic point, requiring articulation of a clear theory of how a merger might ultimately result in anti-competitive harm (provided of course that the appropriate factual evidence is available) is a useful discipline as a starting point for an investigation.

• First, articulation of how the merger may be anti-competitive focuses the later investigation on the sorts of evidence required. Absent this stage, experience suggests that one runs real risks of investigating the wrong point—particularly when it comes to assessment of incentives—and hence missing key evidence;

• Second, until the way in which a merger is believed to be anti-competitive has been clearly articulated in a decision, there is little prospect of the merging parties understanding the decision reached, and less prospect of the broader competition law community doing so. Hence, in *Synopsys/Avant!*, the OFT's advice explains the foreclosure concern that was at the heart of the investigation.

IV.10. To assist in formulating the theory of competitive harm, as discussed earlier, the Guidance sets out two main theories of competitive harm that might flow from a vertical merger: market foreclosure and increased risks of collusion (where the post-merger vertical integration increases the extent of market transparency so facilitating collusion). However, the Guidance notes that concerns under either of these broad theories are likely to arise only if 'market power exists or is created in one or more markets along the supply chain'.[27]

B. *Is there pre-existing market power at one level of the supply chain?*

IV.11. Without existing or newly created market power at one or both stages of supply, it would be highly unlikely that a merger will have any adverse effects.[28] In this respect, concerns generally arise only at a higher level of concentration than for horizontal mergers.[29] This is a function of,

---

[27] Guidance, para 5.1.

[28] This was the position taken by the OFT in *Vodafone/Project Telecom*, where—following OFTEL advice—the OFT concluded that Vodafone lacked significant market power and so it was '*highly unlikely that it can leverage its position in the supply of wholesale airtime to influence the supply of airtime to retail customers*', ie, raising the costs of its rivals at the retail level. The decision also concluded that the increment to Vodafone's share of retail mobile telephony was so small that the transaction was unlikely to increase the possibility of foreclosure at the retail level. See OFT decision of 18 Sept 2003 concerning the *anticipated acquisition by Vodafone Group plc of Project Telecom plc*.

[29] This approach mirrors that in the 1984 US non-horizontal merger guidelines, where the HHI indicators for concern are much higher than in their horizontal guidelines.

for example, the ability for firms at the lower level of the supply chain to switch to an alternative supplier (or suppliers) in order to defeat any foreclosure strategy from an upstream supplier.

IV.12. So in order for such a strategy to be effective, a firm needs to control a very significant proportion of supply of the product/service in question. In *Synopsys/Avant!*, the merged entity would have accounted for between 50–60 per cent in one of the software tools and 20–30 per cent in the other. The published advice stated:

> We have, considered whether Synopsis is already capable of exercising market power in respect of logic synthesis tools, the principal type of logic design implementation software. In this segment, Synopsis's current and historic share of sales has been estimated at over 80 per cent. There are other suppliers (such as Cadence and Magna) of logic design implementation tools—that compete with those of Synopsis. However, it does not appear that either company has made significant inroads into Synopsys's position.

IV.13. In that case, the OFT concluded that the merged entity would be able to exercise some degree of market power in the upstream products as a result of the proportion of sales it already accounted for and the relative inability of new entrants to constrain its competitive behaviour. From this analysis, the OFT reached the view that the merged entity may well have a post-merger ability to foreclose competitors by tying together the supply of their various software products.

IV.14. It is worth noting here that the analysis of upstream market power in this case was considered separately from the analysis of incentives to engage in the alleged foreclosure strategy. This need not always be the case, depending on the dynamics of the markets in question. Indeed, it may well be that in certain cases views on the ability and incentive of the merged entity to foreclose may arise from the same analysis. This would always include examination of 'traditional' constraining factors such as entry, expansion or buyer power.[30]

C. *Would the parties have the economic incentives to change to a foreclosure strategy as a result of this merger?*

IV.15. Where a merged firm might have a post-merger ability to pursue, say, a foreclosure strategy, that situation will not give rise to any competition concern unless the merged entity would actually have an incentive to behave in this way. In other words, would it be profitable for the merged

---

[30] Guidance, para 5.6.

firm to have in this way? If it would not be profitable, then there is a strong assumption that the merged firm would not engage in the conduct.[31]

IV.16. The examination of incentives to engage in activities depends on the circumstances of individual cases and upon the particular concerns involved. For example, where the theory of competitive harm being investigated concerns foreclosure through raising input costs or refusing to supply, the OFT investigates the following sorts of issues.

- For what proportion of final costs does the input in question account? This allows investigation of the likely effect of any increase in the price of the input in question. For example, where the input in question represents only a small proportion of the total production cost of the downstream product, an increase in the price of the input might not have vertical foreclosure effects;
- What is the potential for increased profitability downstream versus the potential for foregone profits upstream?[32] And how easy is it and what incentives exist for competing upstream suppliers to increase capacity and expand supply? These questions target issues familiar from horizontal merger analysis, but now the question is not whether an increase in price will be profitable in the same market, but whether the sub-optimal price in one market would be offset through benefits in the downstream market.

IV.17. In *Convatec/Acordis*, the OFT referred a merger to the Competition Commission for further investigation, which had a strong vertical foreclosure element.[33] The merger would have given the merged firm control over the supply of alginate fibre to a number of downstream firms with which the merged firm competed in the supply of alginate fibre medical dressings. The OFT found that the merged firm would have the ability to engage in a range of foreclosure strategies and there was plausible evidence that such strategies would have been profitable for the merged entity. Ultimately, evidence as to Convatec's post-merger incentives and as to the extent of

---

[31] In practice of course, firms tend not to engage in conduct that would not be profitable in the short-run. We must however admit of the possibility that a firm might use the kind of conduct being discussed above in a predatory way to eliminate competition: ie, conduct that might be profitable in the long run. Accurately foreseeing the risks of such conduct is difficult.

[32] This was relevant to the OFT's decision in *Clearnet/London Clearing House*. The OFT concluded that there were no strong incentives to allow favour the Euronext stock exchange in the making of strategic decisions about how to handle transaction clearing business from rival European exchanges. Also important was the governance structure of the merged entity, which would give customers and other exchanges protection against any attempt to favour Euronext. See OFT decision of 11 Aug 2003 concerning the *anticipated merger of Banque Centrale de Compensation SA and the London Clearing House*.

[33] See OFT decision of 12 Feb 2004 concerning the *anticipated acquisition by Convatec Limited of Acordis Speciality Fibres*. The reference was laid aside by the Competition Commission when the parties restructured their transaction.

other constraining factors (such as customer switching or new entry) was too mixed to be relied upon as sufficient to discipline Convatec's behaviour.

IV.18. Similarly, although the OFT concluded in *Synopsys/Avant!* that the merged firm might well have the ability to foreclose, it also concluded that the incentives weighed against following that strategy. There were several indicators that such a strategy was unlikely to be profitable. First, there was a significant risk that designers might choose other design solutions to the Synopsys product. Secondly, there was a prior example of customers and competitors forcing a rival firm (Cadence) to give up its proprietary interface in order to defeat what was said to be an attempt at a similar foreclosure strategy. Thirdly, to implement such a strategy, Synopsys would have had to close the interface between its products and all other types of EDA tools their customers used (not just the two downstream EDA tools where the foreclosure might have been intended), thereby placing at risk its entire product range. Fourthly, anti-competitive conduct could face consequences under anti-trust law.

IV.19. Similar points arise when assessing whether, if a merged entity began sourcing all of its needs of inputs (or a key input) from its own internal production facility, foreclosure concerns might arise on the part of the acquired/acquiring firm's former suppliers. Thus, the OFT might investigate the following points.

- Is there a minimum efficient scale? In other words, will the loss of business affect the long term viability of upstream rivals which may lead to their exit or diminish their ability otherwise to compete?
- A key part of the incentives analysis in this sort of case is the proportion of the downstream market that would be foreclosed if the merged firm sourced the input(s) exclusively from its own upstream capacity.[34]

IV.20. Perhaps most importantly, the merger must be instrumental in changing the parties' incentives to engage in the particular competitive activity being considered (though note that this may be because the merger gives the merged entity a greater incentive to engage in that sort of behaviour). This was a central point in *Eastman Kodak/Bell & Howell Company*.[35]

---

[34] This question arose in the OFT's assessment of *Westbury Processing Plant joint venture*, which concerned a joint venture among a number of milk cooperatives to acquire further processing capacity. The OFT concluded that the transaction would not eliminate from farmers an important choice of milk purchaser—they would retain access to a choice of potential purchasers. See OFT decision of 26 Feb 2004 concerning the *completed acquisition by Milk Link Ltd, First Milk Ltd and Dairy Farmers of Great Britain Ltd of assets of United Milk, namely the Westbury Processing Plant.*

[35] See advice of the Director General of Fair Trading of 24 May 2001 concerning *the completed acquisition by Easman Kodak Company of the services and micrographics businesses of Bell & Howell Company.*

Concerns related to post-merger competition in the servicing of micro-graphics equipments and scanners, where it was said that the merged entity would be able to deny its competitors access to spare parts.

> ... on balance I do not consider that the merger is likely to be detrimental to compe-tition provided competitors have continued access to spare parts. In this regard, evidence of sales of spare parts to third parties, including independent service providers, indicates that Kodak does supply spare parts for its machines. In these circumstances, I consider that recommending a merger reference to the Competition Commission on the grounds of a theoretical possibility of Kodak limiting access to spare parts after the merger would be disproportionate.

IV.21. From the available evidence in that case, it was unclear how the merger changed existing incentives. In those circumstances, a reference would have been made on theoretical grounds only: there being insufficient evidence to conclude that there was a sufficient risk of the anti-competitive outcome to warrant a reference. The points discussed above concerning the Court of Appeal's judgment in *IBA* and their relevance to vertical and conglomerate mergers echo the approach taken by the OFT in *Kodak/Bell & Howell*.

IV.22. An argument often advanced in relation to vertical merger analysis (and perhaps more so in relation to conglomerate mergers) concerns the constraining effect of antitrust laws relating to abuse of market power (whether framed as abuse of dominance or monopolization). Parties frequently assert that the presence of such laws effectively deters firms with market power (and specifically them) from using that power anti-competi-tively. This question is particularly acute in relation to vertical and conglomerate mergers since some of the theories of competitive harm involve predictions of future conduct that may infringe other aspects of competition law.

IV.23. It should be recognized that the risks of punishment if caught infring-ing antitrust laws must play some role in incentives analysis. However, reliance on antitrust law enforcement does need to be tempered by recog-nition of its imperfect nature. For this reason, the importance of antitrust law enforcement in incentives analysis may well vary according to the nature of the anti-competitive conduct being alleged, the characteristics of the market and the firm(s) concerned. For example, where the alleged conduct would be highly visible and third parties well placed to observe it and bring such conduct to competition authorities' notice, this might more easily be taken into account in merger analysis. There are also more funda-mental reasons why antitrust laws are not a panacea for all mergers which are discussed in more detail later.

D. *Conclusions on vertical merger analysis*

IV.24. hree overarching points can be derived from the above explanation of OFT vertical merger analysis.

- First, purely vertical mergers are rarely problematic, and most initial concerns can be dismissed;
- Second, assessment of ability is not enough: assessment of economic incentives is central to the analysis;
- Third, that said, the OFT does refer vertical mergers to the Competition Commission where the evidence raises a sufficient probability of an anti-competitive outcome that the OFT believes that 'it is or may be the case' that an SLC may be expected to flow from the merger.

V. THE OFT'S ANALYTICAL FRAMEWORK FOR CONGLOMERATE MERGERS

V.1. Chapter 6 of the Guidance addresses conglomerate mergers: ie, mergers involving firms that operate in different product markets. Conglomerate mergers could involve products which are weak substitutes, complements (in which case this may have a beneficial impact on pricing incentives) or completely unrelated products. The Guidance states:

Such mergers rarely lead to a substantial lessening of competition as a result solely of their conglomerate effects. In a small number of cases, usually where the products acquired are complementary to the acquirer's own products, potentially adverse effects can be identified related to so-called portfolio power.[36]

V.2. This approach limits the potential application of conglomerate merger theories by the OFT. It implicitly recognizes that many conglomerate mergers are efficiency-enhancing or at least neutral in terms of competitive impact: even possibly those entered into by dominant firms that might otherwise be prohibited from expanding into different product areas by acquisition.

A. *What is the theory of competitive harm?*

V.3. The Guidance focuses on 'portfolio power', arising when 'the market power deriving from a portfolio of products is greater than the sum of its parts'. The Guidance goes on to explain that such portfolio effects may have anti-competitive consequences in three possible situations: (a) where they directly affect market structure; (b) increase the feasibility of entry

---

[36] Guidance, para 6.1.

deterrence strategies; or (c) eliminate the competitive constraint imposed by firms in neighbouring markets.[37]

V.4. Many of the points made above concerning the theory of competitive harm in vertical merger analysis apply equally here, such as the importance of describing the precise analytical framework being considered in the case.[38] In *Arriva/Wales and Borders Rail Franchise*, the OFT's decision sought to identify clearly the foreclosure theory that was being advanced.[39]

V.5. Of particular note are the points relating to evidence gathering. Placed in the context of the earlier discussion in this paper concerning the test for reference in the wake of the *IBA* appeals, it is possible to argue that it is now both harder and easier to refer conglomerate mergers to the Competition Commission. On the one hand, given the greater complexity of conglomerate theories of harm (certainly relative to horizontal mergers), it may be expected to be harder to refer given the Court of Appeal's emphasis on well-reasoned and evidence-based decisions. On the other hand, the Court of Appeal has suggested that the bar for reference may fluctuate according to the scope and quality of the evidence available to the OFT when reaching its belief. Given the complexity and difficulty of many conglomerate merger cases, they may be said to be particularly vulnerable to this sort of consideration.

B. Conglomerate mergers directly affecting market structure

V.6. The Guidance describes a class of conglomerate merger in which the merged firm will control a group of complementary products that customers have incentives to buy from a single source. This theory of harm is not of course dependent on pre-existing market power, or indeed merger-related market power in a single product (though this may of course root a theory of anti-competitive effects more solidly). Rather, it is the very existence of the portfolio of products that gives rise to market power because other non-portfolio competitors do not/cannot constrain the merged firm.

---

[37] The theories of potential competitive harm in conglomerate merger cases are much wider than this. The OFT is not ruling these out entirely through non-inclusion in the Guidance. The Guidance focuses on the most likely potential concerns given past experience.

[38] By way of comparison, see the European Commission's description of commercial bundling as a facet of conglomerate merger analysis in *General Electric Company/Amersham plc.* (Case No COMP/M.3304, at para 37). The Commission describes a four-step analysis: (i) the merged entity must be able to leverage pre-merger dominance in one product to another complementary product; (ii) rivals must not be able to respond competitively; (c) rivals must be marginalized by their inability to respond in a way that forces them to exit the market; and (d) once they have exited the merged firm needs to be able to implement unilateral price increases, sustainable in the long term.

[39] OFT decision of 16 Mar 2004 in *Arriva/Wales and Borders Rail Franchise*.

That may not of itself be an anti-competitive effect of the merged firm's conduct: it may simply be a function of the merged firm's efficiency. But it may be anti-competitive where the evidence shows an expectation that the absence of any effective constraint would allow the merged firm to increase prices profitably, reduce output or reduce service levels/product quality/innovation.

V.7. For example, in *Capital/Virgin* the acquisition was thought to deprive competitors of a rival bundle for radio advertising in London.[40] In practice, this type of analysis is akin to horizontal merger analysis which at heart focuses on the options of customers that might seek to switch away from the merging parties.

V.8. In analysing mergers of this type, it is important to avoid the dangers of identifying portfolio effects simply with firms that offer a wide range of products. In *iSOFT/Torex*, one complaint related to alleged conglomerate effects, but the evidence advanced to support this proposition was limited to assertions that the merged firm would have a broad range of products.[41] This was not found to be a sustainable ground for a portfolio power argument: such arguments need at the least to demonstrate that the broad range of products is likely to give customers an incentive to buy all of their needs from one supplier *and* that this would be to customers' disadvantage, at least in the long run.

C. Conglomerate mergers increasing the feasibility of anti-competitive strategies

V.9. The Guidance then considers a range of circumstances in which the merger may increase incentives to engage in anti-competitive strategies, such as bundling/tying, where rivals are unable to offer a competing bundle. The Guidance notes three possible circumstances in which such concerns might arise.[42]

- Tying or bundling concerns might arise where the merged firm controls complementary goods and where rivals could not provide competing bundles. In this circumstance, they might be unable to constrain the commercial behaviour of the merged firm;
- A conglomerate merger may give rise to predation concerns where a firm can use profits earned in one market to subsidize short-run losses in another: this would only be anti-competitive if the long-run outcome is a

---

[40] See MMC report on *Capital/Virgin*.
[41] See OFT decision of 24 Mar 2004 concerning the *completed acquisition by iSOFT Group plc of Torex plc*.
[42] Guidance, paras 6.4-6.6.

more concentrated market. This theory likely depends on the existence of market power in one of the products in the bundle;

• Finally, a conglomerate merger may in rare instances facilitate coordination where the merged firm's rivals in one market are also rivals in other markets, and if factors pointing to coordination are present in these markets.

V.10. he practical application of these principles can be seen in the OFT's analysis in *Scottish Radio Holdings/Scottish Media Group*, involving the merger of two media groups with interests across a range of advertising products (TV, radio, posters, and newspapers) which have all been found to comprise distinct relevant markets.[43] The concern related to potential bundling of these products to gain market power over media agency customers. Ultimately, the OFT concluded that the risks of any portfolio power outcomes did not warrant reference to the Competition Commission:

• The products involved disparate production, distribution and marketing processes and thus no clear significant economies of scale or scope would be realized (not that this would necessarily be a problem, but that the theory of harm would require this as a necessary condition);
• There was no evidence that customers had a preference for purchasing all their advertising requirements from one source: SMG was already active across five media sectors and had not integrated its sales teams;[44]
• A refusal to supply was not considered plausible given the competitive position in each individual advertising market;
• In any event, recognising the generally pro-competitive nature of conglomerate mergers, the transaction was more likely to be beneficial than detrimental to customers.

V.11. Cases such as *Scottish Radio* above, and other such as *First/Scotrail*[45] and *Arriva/Wales and Borders Rail*, raise again the question of whether the merger is really vertical or conglomerate in character, and whether any distinction is sensible. The 'conglomerate' issue concerned complaints that single-operator multimodal tickets might be used by First to exclude competing bus companies on those routes which terminate at a rail

[43] See Director General of Fair Trading's advice of 21 June 2001 concerning the *completed acquisition by SMG plc of a 29.5 percent shareholding in Scottish Radio Holdings plc.*

[44] The OFT recently rejected a conglomerate effects complaint in *Axciom/Claritas* on the grounds that, although the merger would enable the merged firm to offer a wider range of services, it did not seem plausible that the merged firm would tie services together: there was no evidence that customers purchased services in this way. See OFT decision of 11 Mar 2004 concerning the *completed acquisition by Acxiom Corporation of Claritas Europe Group, including Claritas (UK) Ltd.*

[45] See OFT decision of 26 Mar 2004 concerning the *anticipated acquisition by First Group plc of the Thames Trains rail franchise.*

station.[46] What is clear is that the competitive analysis in *Scotrail* and *Arriva* followed a basic foreclosure analysis, irrespective of the characterisation of the case. Central to the assessment in both *Scotrail* and *Arriva* was review of the parties' respective incentives to engage in the sort of commercial conduct alleged.[47]

V.12. Similar themes have resounded in older OFT conglomerate merger cases. In *Hilton Group PLC/British Sky Broadcasting Group Plc (Hilton/BSkyB)*,[48] the OFT investigated a proposed joint venture between the dominant provider of premium sports channels in the UK and a leading bookmaker (the JV). The JV was to develop a fixed odds betting business linked to Sky Sports (the main premium sports channel in the UK) through digital satellite. It would have exclusive rights to betting associated with Sky Sports channels and the Sky Sports internet site for a period of five years. The joint venture brought together two firms for the purposes of developing a new product in the UK.

V.13. The main concerns which arose were, given that BSkyB had dominant position in premium sports channels and the exclusive nature of the JV, there was a danger that development of competition within such betting services might be impaired in view of the length of the exclusivity provisions. The overall theory of harm was foreclosure by denying rival bookmakers access to the most popular digital satellite platform in the UK. This needed to be weighed against the potential benefits the joint venture would bring:

First-mover advantage alone is not usually a reason for viewing a merger as potentially anti-competitive, since it can be a proper reward of risk or innovation. Investments to develop new services are generally to be encouraged, as they should benefit consumers, but there is a question whether the degree of protection afforded by the five-year period of exclusivity in the case at hand may be excessive and restrictive of competition.[49]

V.14. The pro-competitive aspects of this case were clearly recognized but

---

[46] Interestingly, the Competition Commission has recently published its provisional findings on this case. Rather than addressing the issue as a vertical or conglomerate point, it has defined broader 'public transport network markets' on which the parties may be expected to use single-operator multi-modal ticketing and other techniques to foreclose competition.

[47] In contrast, such concerns were rejected in *First Group/Thames Trains*, where the OFT concluded that the possibility of First engaging in a foreclosure strategy appeared remote. This was due to the limited take-up of existing schemes for multi-modal transport ticketing in the areas of overlap, the conditions imposed by one of the regulatory bodies (the Strategic Rail Authority), and the lack of competitor concerns.

[48] See Director General of Fair Trading's advice of 27 Sept 2001 concerning the *proposed joint venture between Hilton Group plc and British Sky Broadcasting Group plc*.

[49] *Hilton/BSkyB*.

needed to balanced against the potential anti-competitive effects. The concerns were judged sufficient to warrant a reference.

D. *Conglomerate mergers affecting barriers to entry*

V.15. Finally, the Guidance also raises the possibility that, simply through creation of a portfolio of products, this may in itself represent a strategic barrier to entry that might limit the ability of competitors to extend their own product portfolios or enter new product markets.

V.16. This is a concern that has arisen only rarely in the OFT's experience. In *Hilton/BSkyB*, the OFT believed that the transaction had the potential to reinforce BSkyB's market position: betting revenues from the JV were forecast to be substantial and the ability for rival channels to bid for premium sports rights might be curtailed by their inability to implement rival betting services. But even in this respect, the OFT was cautious in balancing the possibility of anti-competitive effects against the potentially strong customer benefits of the transaction:

The proposed joint venture presents a dilemma. In some respects it may enhance innovation and competition in the wider betting market. But its exclusivity provisions pose possible risks to the development of competition in interactive betting (which is forecast to be a large market within the next few years) and in the acquisition of sports rights. These risks require a more thorough examination, which the Competition Commission is best placed to undertake.[50]

V.17. Further, in *BSkyB/Manchester United*,[51] ownership links between the UK's dominant supplier of premium sports channels and one of the UK's leading football clubs gave rise to concern about raising barriers to entry into premium sports channels and pay TV more generally.

V.18. This analytical framework is somewhat unusual in the context of other theories of anti-competitive effects in conglomerate (and vertical) mergers. This is because there is no real assessment of incentives in such mergers. Quite simply, the very fact that the transaction raises barrier to entry so substantially may have anti-competitive effects because it protects the merged firm from future competition from firms outside of the defined market.

---

[50] *Hilton/BSkyB*
[51] See MMC report: *British Sky Broadcasting Group plc and Manchester United PLC: A report on the proposed merger*, Cm 4305, Apr 1999.

E. Conclusions on conglomerate merger analysis

V.19. The analytical framework for assessment of conglomerate mergers lacks much of the clarity of its horizontal merger cousin. This extends not only to matters of practical application, but also into the underlying principles of conglomerate merger analysis. Indeed, the lack of clarity extends so far as the meaning of 'conglomerate merger': where is the line to be drawn between horizontal, vertical, and conglomerate mergers?

V.20. This lack of clarity is reflected in most sets of merger guidelines that touch on conglomerate mergers: because of the variety of theories loosely grouped together as 'conglomerate', guidelines providing a broad outline of those theories run the risk of appearing unfocused. In reality, they likely do no more than restate the principles underlying general practical experience of assessing mergers that do not fit a traditional horizontal or vertical analysis. It is difficult to identify a set of coherent principles that underpin all conglomerate merger cases.

VI. WIDER ISSUES IN THE ASSESSMENT OF VERTICAL AND CONGLOMERATE MERGERS

VI.1. The discussion above has, in large part, focused on the OFT's approach to analysis of vertical and/or conglomerate mergers. In relation to other authorities the OFT appears to be somewhere between the EC and US approaches. The EC has investigated a number of transactions using conglomerate theories and reached prohibition decisions in some cases using those theories.[52] Although the US competition authorities have not litigated a case on the basis of a conglomerate merger theory for many years,[53] they have accepted consent decrees that are based largely—if not entirely—on conglomerate merger theories.[54] The OFT recognizes that vertical and conglomerate mergers may result in harm to competition (and ultimately consumers). However, this recognition is balanced against: (a) a conceptual approach that appreciates vertical and conglomerate mergers only give rise to anti-competitive effects in less direct ways than horizontal mergers, and (b) the knowledge that, in order to show a positive belief that such effects may arise from a particular merger and the merger thus warrants reference, a coherent story and factual evidence are needed.

---

[52] See, for example, *Guinness/Grand Metropolitan*, M.938; *Tetra Laval/Sidel*, M.2416; and *General Electric/Honeywell*, M.2220.

[53] '*Liability has not been found in any case on this theory since the 1970s*', American Bar Association, Antitrust Law Developments (5th edn), vol 1, ch III.C.3, 368.

[54] See, eg, *AOL/Time Warner*, see <http://www.ftc.gov/opa/2000/12/aol.htm>. The FTC's investigation of the *Pepsi, Inc / Quaker Oats Company* merger might also be seen in some respects as a conglomerate investigation: see <http://www.ftc. gov/os/caselist/0110059. htm>.

VI.2. Further, a higher degree of commonality exists among competition authorities' approaches to vertical and conglomerate mergers than might have been implied elsewhere.[55] This might extend so far as the requisite standard of proof. This remains a serious question: as discussed above, given the efficiency enhancing nature of vertical and conglomerate mergers and the inherent uncertainty as to their potential anti-competitive effect, what level of proof is required before they are challenged? This informs the OFT's own experience that initial vertical/conglomerate concerns rarely stand up to the initial assessment against the facts of the case. However, the OFT does not shy from referring a case if the facts suggest that a more in depth investigation was warranted. The institutional framework for merger enforcement in any given jurisdiction may well have an important bearing on the answer to this question.

VI.3. The discussion above raises the question of whether—and if so to what extent—competition authorities should take account of antitrust laws relating to abuse of market power when seeking to decide whether, in the merger context, a firm would have sufficient ability and incentive to engage in, say, a foreclosure strategy. Is *ex post* control (in the UK, via enforcement of the Competition Act 1998) a preferable method of addressing these issues to *ex ante* merger control? Protecting an industry structure that provides incentives to compete rather than engage in anti-competitive conduct is always preferable putting aside issues of imperfections in detection and demonstration of abuse of market power. In this context, John Vickers, OFT Chairman, said:

merger regulation is ex ante intervention to maintain competitive incentives by preventing anti-competitive structural changes in markets. That is very different from ex post intervention to curb and penalise abuse of dominant market power, and the threshold for the latter kind of intervention should be considerably higher than for the former.[56]

VI.4. The OFT's approach in this connection seeks to draw a balance between merger control and other competition law provisions. On the one hand, *ex ante* merger control is adopted because reliance on *ex post* competition law enforcement may not be sufficient to address all aspects of possible competition harm. On the other hand, since analysis of vertical and conglomerate mergers involves assessment of firms' incentives to engage in certain types of behaviour, it cannot be the case that assessment of those incentives should entirely ignore the existence of competition legislation

---

[55] See, eg, extensive press comment comparing the EC's prohibition of the General Electric/Honeywell merger with the US's disposal of the case.

[56] J Vickers, 'How does the prohibition of abuse of dominance fit with the rest of competition policy?', Paper for the eighth annual EU competition law and policy workshop at the European University Institute, Florence, 6 June 2003.

prohibiting the abuse of market power. Accordingly, the OFT does not rely wholly on competition law enforcement (particularly as regards abuses of market power) as a countervailing factor in vertical and conglomerate merger assessment.

VI.5. Overall, the discussion in this paper, and in relation to the three specific points above, points to continuing uncertainty about the way in which vertical and conglomerate merger theories (the latter particularly) are applied by competition authorities. Part of this uncertainty clearly stems from the difficult task of balancing concerns over anti-competitive effects against customer benefits. One alternative approach relies on taking a tougher look at the fundamental principles of many vertical and conglomerate merger theories: ie, they concern firms who already hold significant market power and further erosion of the constraints they face may be particularly harmful. In this circumstance, whilst the likelihood of anti-competitive effects arising from such mergers is remote, the impact they may have is dramatic.

VII. CONCLUSION

VII.1.Vertical and conglomerate mergers raise a broad range of significant issues in merger assessment: what theories of competitive harm are appropriate; what standard of proof needs to be met to demonstrate that the theory is likely to be reflected in practice; how should a competition authority balance expected pro-competitive and anti-competitive effects; and what is the appropriate relationship between *ex ante* and *ex post* competition law enforcement?[57]

VII.2. First, the principal theories of competitive harm in both vertical and conglomerate mergers rely on the ability and incentive of the merged firm to engage in a foreclosure strategy. However, there are strong reasons to seek to categorize the transaction in question (even as between vertical and conglomerate mergers). This is not only because of the useful intellectual discipline that such an exercise brings to merger investigation and assessment, but also because there are underlying conceptual and practical differences between foreclosure theories in vertical and conglomerate mergers.[58] For example, foreclosure via bundling in a conglomerate merger is a very different story from foreclosure via refusal to supply in a vertical case.

---

[57] Some of these issues also apply to assessment of horizontal mergers, which is beyond the scope of this paper.

[58] Foreclosure here covers the wider range of activities than just refusal to supply or tying, but may cover raising barriers to entry or raising rivals costs to diminish competitive constraints.

VII.3. Guidance as to how the OFT approaches such cases is published, although admittedly short. This in part reflects the continually evolving economic literature and rareness of cases in this area. There is, however, a growing decisional practice that will inform firms and their advisers. The OFT practice of publishing reasoned advice in each decision is valuable in this context.

VII.4. Secondly, given that there are a number of accepted theories explaining why vertical and conglomerate mergers might have anti-competitive effects, it is not appropriate for a competition authority to rule out completely pursuing a vertical or conglomerate merger. However, given the complexity of many vertical and/or conglomerate theories of competitive harm, the OFT considers that, as a general matter, more evidence is needed in vertical and conglomerate cases to reach the same standard of proof as applies in horizontal merger cases.[59]

VII.5. Thirdly, the OFT uses the balance between the pro- and anti-competitive effects of vertical and conglomerate mergers in a number of ways. Most obviously, efficiency gains can be used as part of the SLC analysis, and customer benefits can be used to offset the anti-competitive effects of a transaction. But this balance also informs the OFT's approach to the evidential burden in vertical and conglomerate cases. In addition to seeking more probative evidence to refer on the basis of a vertical and conglomerate theory because of the inherent complexity/uncertainty of such theories, the OFT believes this approach to be appropriate because it also reflects some of the balance between the pro- and anti-competitive effects of vertical and conglomerate mergers.

VII.6. Fourthly, the OFT does take into account the existence of broader competition rules when considering the incentives of the merged firm to engage in, say, a foreclosure strategy. However, the OFT also takes into account the fact that *ex ante* merger control exists because of the imperfections of *ex post* competition law enforcement. Accordingly, the OFT does not rely wholly on competition law enforcement (particularly as regards abuses of market power) as a countervailing factor in vertical and conglomerate merger assessment.

VII.7. In sum, this paper sets out the OFT's broad approach to vertical and conglomerate merger analysis. It recognizes the importance of rigorous analysis in such merger cases. Indeed, the importance of a robust and carefully-applied analytical framework in vertical and conglomerate merger

---

[59] The standard and burden of proof remain in principle as they do for horizontal merger cases. The standard of proof and burden of proof are set by the EA02 and do not change according to the type of merger under investigation.

cases is perhaps greater than it is in horizontal merger cases. This is because horizontal merger analysis is better understood and explained than vertical and conglomerate merger cases. Moreover, some of the more exotic theories of vertical and/or conglomerate competitive harm need careful explanation and without a rigorous and systematic analysis there is a danger that the authority is led more by complainants then by the facts of the case.

VII.8. The OFT has said before that: '*In the end, merger analysis is about the rigorous application of economic theory to fact, operating within a defined legal framework.*' This applies as much to vertical and conglomerate mergers as it does to horizontal mergers.

ANNEX A: STATISTICS

References to the Competition Commission under the Enterprise Act (as of 10 May 2004)

Merger	Qualification	Classification	Notes
Archant/London Regional papers of INM plc	Share of supply of local newspapers in East London	Horizontal	Ongoing CC inquiry
Unum Ltd/Swiss Life (UK) plc	Turnover exceeded £70 million	Horizontal	Merger abandoned
AAH Pharmaceuticals Ltd/ East Anglia Pharmaceuticals Ltd	Turnover exceeded £70 million	Horizontal	Merger abandoned
National Milk Records plc / Cattle Information Services	Share of supply of authentic milk recording services	Horizontal	Merger abandoned
Convatec Ltd / Acordis Speciality Fibres	Share of supply of alginate fibre	Horizontal & Vertical	Merger abandoned
Stena AB / P&O	Share of supply of ferry services for freight from Great Britain to Northern Ireland and the Republic of Ireland	Horizontal	Partial prohibition
Drager Medical AG&Co KgaA / Air Shields	Share of supply of neo-natal warming	Horizontal	Ongoing CC inquiry (Provisional findings found an SLC)
Carl Zeiss GmbH/Bio-Rad Microscience Ltd	Share of supply in advanced 3D microscopes	Horizontal	Ongoing CC inquiry (Provisional findings for unconditional clearance)
First Group/ScotRail	Section 66(3) of the Railways Act 1993 and section 23(1) of the Enterprise Act 2002	Horizontal & Conglomerate	Ongoing CC inquiry (Provisional findings found an SLC)
iSOFT Group plc / Torex	Turnover test and share of supply of (a) the supply of Patient Administration Systems to National Health Service hospitals in the UK and the supply of Laboratory Information Management Systems to NHS hospitals in the UK	Horizontal & Vertical	Undertakings in lieu of a reference to the CC accepted.

Annex A *continued*

Merger	Qualification	Classification	Notes
Arriva plc / Wales and Borders Rail Franchise	Section 66(3) of the Railways Act 1993 and section 23(1) of the Enterprise Act 2002	Horizontal & Conglomerate	Undertakings in lieu of a reference to the CC accepted.
Tesco plc / Certain Co-operative Group's stores	Share of supply of one stop shopping in groceries	Horizontal	Undertakings in lieu of a reference to the CC accepted.
Ivax International GmbH / 3M Company's asthema products	Share of supply of salbutamol sulphate and beclomethasone dipropionate inhalers in the UK	Horizontal	Undertakings in lieu of a reference to the CC accepted.
Sibelco Minerals & Chemicals Ltd / Tarmac Central Ltd	Share of supply of silica flour, dolomite, high purity silica sand and feldspar.	Horizontal	Merger abandoned

CHAPTER 11

Abuse and Monopolization—Contrasting Approaches to Pricing

A. Derek Ridyard*

I will introduce the little exam question that I've set the panellists. It's based on a firm called Domco who you might have come across before now and again. Briefly, Domco is a UK producer, has more than a 95 per cent market share in the UK and is clearly regarded as being a dominant company. Domco has large fixed costs. It actually has a big bank loan to pay off: a million pounds per annum repayments on that bank loan which will take place whether or not it produces anything. And its variable costs are very, very simple. Just £1 per unit produced. So a very simple cost structure but nevertheless one which is maybe not that unusual for firms who find themselves accused of dominance, and we have here Domco's trading result in the UK. It sells two million units at a price of £3 per unit. The average cost comes down as output increases as those fixed costs get spread across a bigger and bigger sum of outputs. Charging £3 a unit, selling two million units, it makes a nice profit margin of £1.50 for every unit it sells and a total profit of three million pounds. That's Domco as a dominant company.

Now we introduce the prospect of competition from Compco, no less. Compco starts trying to sell into the UK market from France which means that Compco can reach some of the customers in the UK, but not all of them. It can reach the customers in the south of the UK cost-effectively but not those located in the north. To sell into the UK, Compco has to incur some costs in setting up an import terminal in the UK and because it has some extra transport costs Compco's variable costs are £1.50 including transportation to those Southern customers and Compco's proposition to the market is a price of £2 to undercut Domco's £3. But that competitive offer is only made to customers based in the south of the UK. So then the question is what should Domco do about this new competitive threat? There are three strategies that have been identified as possibilities for Domco. One is to do nothing. If Domco does nothing and just carries on charging £3 a unit, it is going to lose possibly all of its sales in the south of

* RBB Economics.

England but will carry on making the sales in the north. If it does that, if it loses half of its sales, the profits fall from three million pounds to one million pounds. Strategy two is a bit more clever and that is a selective price reduction. So let's imagine that Domco chooses to cut price from £3 to £1.50 but just to those customers in the south, whilst keeping the price at £3 for those in the north. That has much better potential for Domco because it retains those customers in the south at a price which is still above Domco's variable cost and means its profit falls to 1.5 million pounds—not as good as £3 million but better than under strategy one. The third strategy which Domco is considering is altogether much cleverer and complicated. It would consist of some sort of bundled discounts identifying the fact that many of its customers buy both in the north and the south and what Domco is considering doing under strategy three is to go to those customers individually and put together a price offer for them. The bottom line is they get a discount which could be 20 per cent or 30 per cent or whatever across all of the customer's purchases as long as these national customers choose to buy everything from Domco, and the way these numbers are set up is such as to ensure it makes an attractive offer to customers even though the price levels, the effective prices that have been charged for the customers in the south, are still above Domco's variable costs in all cases, but enough to ward off the threat of the importer. So that very briefly is the case study scenario which we are going to address and I've posed six main questions to the panellists, some of which they will try to answer.

The first question very basically is regarding strategies two and three, which involve some sort of price discrimination: is that price discrimination objectionable or anti-competitive under competition law? Secondly, what about efficiencies? Is there some sort of valid efficiencies defence to this kind of pricing that we are postulating for Domco? Thirdly, is there competitive harm, that is to say, is there damage to consumers arising out of this form of price competition? Fourthly, focusing on the third strategy I identified, which is this idea of bundling prices and taking advantage, if you like, of the fact that some of Domco's customers have more options on some of their purchases and more options to shop around than others, do different rules somehow apply to the fact that the practice involves some kind of leveraging of Domco's strength in the north against its competitive weakness in the south? My fifth question is; does the fate of Compco matter to any of this? By that I mean to ask whether we are just talking about what is right for Domco or whether we need to bother about whether Compco succeeds or fails in its quest to make sales in the UK? And the final question, which is perhaps particularly apposite given the range of speakers we have; would Domco be better off or would it have an easier time if, instead of European law being applied, the law was Canadian law or American law and, equally, what about consumers? Would consumers be better off if this whole scenario was being played out in an American context or in a Canadian context than a European one? So having set up the problems for you I will invite the first of our speakers, Greg Werden, to give his views on what the answers are.

B. Gregory Werden[*]

The price discrimination issue is relatively easy under US antitrust law. The Supreme Court's *Brooke Group* decision[1] mandates that Domco's pricing be evaluated using a two-part test for predatory pricing. That Domco's pricing is discriminatory matters very little under that test, and the complainant in a private proceeding or the competition agency in a government case must establish that both parts are met. The first part is that 'the prices complained of are below an appropriate measure of its rival's costs'. At some point the courts may resolve the issue of what cost measures are appropriate, but for now we have only some general ideas. The second part of the test is slightly different in cases arising under the Robinson-Patman Act, which relates to price discrimination, than in cases arising under section 2 of the Sherman Act, which relates to exclusionary conduct that threatens to create or maintain a monopoly. *Brooke Group* was a Robinson-Patman Act case, and in such a case, the second part of the test is that 'the defendant had a reasonable prospect . . . of recouping its investment in below-cost prices'. As most of you know, the second part of the test has not been adopted in Europe.

In the United States, Domco's discriminatory prices would not have required an efficiency justification, so I turn to the third question, which relates to consumer harm and social welfare considerations. For the US perspective on these issues, I again turn to the *Brooke Group* decision. In that case, the Supreme Court pondered the implications under the US legal system of alternative policies toward predation. The Court explained that mistaken inferences of predation impose a substantial social cost 'because they chill the very conduct the antitrust laws are designed to protect'. The Domco hypothetical and the *Brooke Group* case both involve charging low prices to attract customers away from rivals, and the Court noted that is the essence of competition. The Court recognized that price-cutting can go too far and that at some point it becomes anti-competitive, but the Court was seriously concerned about chilling legitimate price-cutting and reluctant to

[*] US Department of Justice (Antitrust Division).
[1] *Brooke Group Ltd v Brown & Williamson Tobacco Corp* 509 US 224 (1993).

declare any price-cutting unlawful. The Court ultimately concluded that 'the exclusionary effect of prices above a relevant measure of cost' either 'represents competition on the merits, or is beyond the practical ability of a judicial tribunal to control without courting intolerable risks of chilling legitimate price cutting.'

I understand the Court to have reasoned along the following lines: intense price competition greatly benefits consumers, although some competitors may lose out. While price-cutting is not always legitimate competition on the merits, it is quite difficult to identify the exceptions, because competition on the merits and exclusionary conduct look so much alike. Beneficial price competition would be significantly chilled if the courts adopted a rule declaring price-cutting to be unlawful under a wide range of circumstances, or if they adopted an open-ended rule entrusting the critical determination to juries. So the Court laid out its two-part test, and since then, no complainant has won a predatory pricing case in the US.

It has been suggested that this hypothetical case could be analysed as 'leveraging', but under US law, that rubric has no special significance. The Supreme Court made clear just this year in the *Trinko* decision that monopoly leveraging violates the antitrust laws only if it involves anti-competitive conduct with a dangerous probability of success in monopolizing a second market.[2] In other words, the metaphor of leveraging adds nothing to the analysis of the case under section 2 of the Sherman Act.

The hypothetical does appear to involve injury to a competitor, as do most cases under section 2 of the Sherman Act, but that fact does not advance the analysis far. US antitrust law draws a sharp distinction between injury to competitors and injury to competition. That Compco was obliged to exit the UK market would be far from sufficient to establish a violation of US antitrust law. As stated by Judge Easterbrook of the Court of Appeals for the Seventh Circuit: 'Competition is a ruthless process. A firm that reduces costs and expands sales injures rivals . . . . These injuries to rivals are byproducts of vigorous competition and the antitrust laws are not balm for rivals' wounds'.[3] This view is mainstream antitrust jurisprudence in the United States, where the courts for some considerable time have recognized that legitimate competition hurts rivals just as exclusionary conduct does. US courts care only whether consumers are harmed, and in most cases, competitors' losses are consumers' gains.

[2] *Verizon Communications Inc v Law Offices of Curtis V. Trinko* 124 S Ct 872 (2004).
[3] *Ball Memorial Hospital, Inc v Mutual Hospital Insurance, Inc* 784 F.2d 1325, 1338 (7th Cir 1986).

Several distinct analyses of Domco's pricing might be used in US courts, and they are not mutually exclusive. First, as I already suggested, the prices would be tested under the *Brooke Group* rule. Secondly, because the practice here is bundled pricing, it might be evaluated under what has been referred to as the 'equally efficient competitor test'. And finally, Domco's conduct would be examined in the light of the most recent relevant decision in the United States in the *LePage's* case.[4]

Applying the *Brooke Group* rule leaves open some questions, particularly how best to compare price and cost in this context. Most likely, a court would look at the bundled price and compare it to the average variable cost for each of the components, summed up over all of them. In this hypothetical case, Domco charges at least £2 per unit, while its average variable cost is £1 per unit, so Domco is pricing above cost per this application of the *Brooke Group* rule. In the bundled pricing context, alternative calculations have been suggested. Treating the incremental portion of the bundle as a separate transaction, Domco is charging £1.75, so it is also pricing above cost per that application of the test. Thus, it appears that no application of the *Brooke Group* rule would find Domco's pricing exclusionary.

US law also suggests that bundled pricing is unlawful if an equally efficient rival could not profitably make consumers an offer they might accept. Here Domco could be bested by Compco's counter offer of £1.75, which is above Compco's average variable cost, so it appears that Domco's pricing is lawful under the equally efficient competitor test. The fixed costs of serving in the UK likely would be irrelevant under this test, because an equally efficient competitor would not incur those costs.

The *LePage's* case involved a monopolist in transparent tape and a rival producing private label tape, which was a substitute for 3M's branded tape, but not a close substitute. 3M offered several different rebate schemes to different classes of customers, including a bundled rebate scheme to certain customers with rebates based on purchases across six product lines. The jury awarded LePage's $68.5 million after trebling on a claim of unlawful maintenance of monopoly. There were other claims in the case, but they were either withdrawn or the jury held in favour of 3M on them. The verdict was reversed initially by the court of appeals, but after rehearing by the full court, the jury verdict was reinstated.

The court rejected 3M's argument that its conduct should be assessed solely under the *Brooke Group* rule. 3M contended that the challenged conduct was price-cutting, and therefore that *Brooke Group* provided the relevant test. LePage's countered that the case was not about price-cutting at all, and

---

[4] *LePage's Inc v 3M* 324 F.3d 141 (3d Cir 2003).

prices actually rose. The court held that the jury was entitled to find that the long-term effects of 3M's pricing were anti-competitive, but it did not explain why. The court held that 3M's bundled pricing could have excluded efficient rivals, but it did not explain what evidence showed that was true. The case is still pending before the Supreme Court, to which 3M petitioned for review. The United States will soon file a brief giving our views on whether the case should be heard.[5]

3M's petition for review repeats its argument that the case is about price-cutting and should be treated as a predatory pricing case. LePage's opposition to 3M's petition disagrees and explains that economic theory has shown that bundled pricing can be used as a price-raising device, even while excluding competitors, so from theoretical standpoint it is wrong to treat this as a predatory pricing case. Of course, a *Brooke Group* type test might make some sense from a policy standpoint simply because it avoids the risk of chilling legitimate bundling conduct.

The Third Circuit analogized the conduct to tying, and 3M's petition for review argues that a tying analysis would be the only possible alternative to a predatory pricing analysis. 3M, however, posits only a traditional tying analysis, which does not fit the case. LePage's legal theory depends crucially on its private label tape being a *substitute* for 3M's branded tape, whereas traditional tying analysis generally is based on the assumption that the tied products are *complements*. Because branded and private label tape are substitutes, they also might not be considered separate products, which is required for an unlawful tie in the United States. In addition, treating 3M's bundling as tying, and analysing it under the rule of reason, is somewhat problematic because there is not a well-developed rule of reason analysis for tying in US antitrust law.

In the *Trinko* case, the Solicitor General argued that, when the claimant asserts that the defendant was under a duty to assist a rival, which of course is the case in this hypothetical scenario, 'conduct is not exclusionary or predatory *unless* it would make no economic sense for the defendant but for the tendency to eliminate or lessen competition'. While the Solicitor General only advocated that test in the context of asserted duties to assist a rival, the Department of Justice has relied on this test in a series of cases not presenting that scenario: *American Airlines, Microsoft* and currently on appeal of Third Circuit, the *Dentsply* case. This is not necessarily a test that is useful in the *LePage's* case because economic analysis has demonstrated that bundled pricing can make good sense even absent any tendency to

---

[5] That brief, which is available at <http://www.usdoj.gov/osg/briefs/2003/2pet/6invit/2002-1865.pet.ami.inv.html>, recommended that the Court not hear the case, and on 30 June, the Court announced that it would not.

exclude. Bundling often is profitable because it effectively works as price discrimination. But that would not appear to be the case in this particular hypothetical, so it may very well be that the 'no economic sense test' could be applied to determine whether this conduct is unlawful under US antitrust law.

C. Denis Waelbroeck*

Well I think Mr Chairman in your case, you ask us essentially two questions. First, you ask us to state what the law is in relation to bundled discounts, and secondly you ask us what the law should say in relation to meeting competition, and you expect us to do that in 10 minutes which is of course a challenge! This is why I gave a written response to give a more complete view. To keep it brief in the 10 minutes you have given me, if you look at the law, the response in Community law is relatively simple in particular in the light of recent judgements of the Court of Justice. To sum it up, it is I think more or less exactly the opposite to what we just have heard about the United States. In a nutshell I think that EC case law has solved in a very simple matter a very complex problem by simply saying that more or less everything that Domco may do in your case study would probably be illegal. Everything except of course possibly if Domco kept its prices at a high level across the board for all its clients, because if it kept its prices at a high level, I suppose that then it complies with its special responsibility as a dominant undertaking to allow competition on the market and therefore it is not infringing Article 82 of the Treaty. That is essentially how I read Article 82 of the treaty and the current case-law, although I accept that it is in some respects confused and obscure.

Now I will address that briefly in relation to your various questions. As regards question number one (ie the legality of a strategy of selective or price cuts in the south of England by Domco), the answer must be given I believe in two steps. First, at the theoretical level, in principle, meeting competition is not prohibited per se under competition law. But in practice the case law has become increasingly strict in relation to meeting competition and I'm not sure that meeting competition is still allowed at all. If we look at the judgments in *Irish Sugar* and *Compagnie Maritime Belge*, it is clear that even if the price cut is done above the costs of the dominant company, and above the costs of the new entrant of Compco, and even if the dominant company is just matching the prices of the new entrant and not seeking to undercut the new entrant's price, and even if this is done

---

* Ashurst.

purely in a defensive manner—that is replying to requests from customers to reduce the price in order to meet the prices applied by a competitor—and even if this is done in a non-discriminatory manner as happened in the *Compagnie Maritime Belge* case, where the CFI emphasized there was no discrimination, but only a reduction of the price across the board, this does amount to an infringement of Article 82 of the EC Treaty. So I repeat, the only solution for Domco is probably to continue to apply the higher prices. Now you will say in *Compagnie Maritime Belge* there was some inflammatory language used by the company saying that it wanted to get rid of competitors and that it was using 'fighting ships', but I am not sure what the relevance should be of the language used by the company when deciding on the legality of its behaviour. *If* the prices are above cost and *if* the company thereby cannot exclude competitors, it is very difficult to see why this behaviour should be prohibited.

Question number two relates to the legality of bundled discounts. Here again, the answer is very simple. Most recently in *Michelin* and in *British Airways/Virgin* the Court found that any type of rebate, be it fidelity rebates, growth rebates, target rebates, bundled rebates and any form of direct or indirect exclusivity, is prohibited more or less per se whatever the form the exclusivity takes. This is so even if there are efficiencies, even if the client wants to have the rebate, even if the competitors provide similar rebates, and even if the practice has and can have no effect on the market. Dominant companies may only resort to linear quantitative rebates and this moreover only if they can establish these linear quantitative rebates are cost justified.

The third question is whether there is a valid efficiency defence under Article 82. Again I have to answer in two steps. If I look at the definition of the abuse, if I go to the basics, ie to the *Hoffmann-La Roche* case law, we have a definition of the abuse which is really comprised of two elements. First you have to demonstrate that the incriminated behaviour is not competition on the merits and secondly you have to demonstrate that the behaviour has an effect on the structure of competition. So in theory if you look at the definition of the abuse given by the case law there is indeed an efficiency element in the definition of the abuse but, in practice, the Court of Justice was always very reluctant to accept any form of efficiency defence under Article 82. For example, in the *British Plasterboard* case[6] the exclusivity agreements entailed a number of efficiencies and the Court of First Instance said 'Yes it is correct, exclusivities are desired by the customer but if you are dominant you have a special responsibility so any form of exclusivity is prohibited more or less per se.' When the CFI's decision was chal-

---

[6] C 310/93P *British Plasterboard* [1995] ECR I-865 [1997] 4 CMLR 238.

lenged on appeal to the ECJ, the Court of Justice in its judgment said for the reasons given by the Advocate General, they would reject this argument and didn't even address it. Now that may be changing, because to some extent in the *Microsoft* decision, a certain element of efficiency defence is taken into account.

In question four, you ask how far the effect of the practice should matter. Here again I think you have to distinguish theory and practice. If you look at the theory, if you go to basics, ie to *Hoffmann-La Roche*, there it is clear that you have to demonstrate an effect of the behaviour. If you look at the case-law of the Court of Justice, most recently in *Michelin* or *British Airways*, the market shares fell from 50 to 40 per cent during the relevant period, the market share of the competitors increased, new competitors entered the market, prices decreased, etc and the Court of First Instance said this was irrelevant because there is a special responsibility for dominant companies.

So, to come to the last question, would Domco be better off in the US? Well I don't know. To be frank, I'm not sure whether the law in the EU has not become so much out of touch with reality that many dominant companies no longer comply with the rule in the Community. In this situation, the advantage of being in the Community is however that you have very little private enforcement while in the US you have more private enforcement, so I don't know whether that is such an advantage to be in the US and that the UK has such an advantage in becoming the 51st state of the US! To conclude I would just say that you have to go back to the definition of what is an abuse. There is clearly a problem because you have a definition in *Hoffmann-La Roche* which, as I said, comprises of two elements—competition on the merits and effects on the market—and you have a case-law which simply does not take these elements into account. So even if the Commission is willing to reform Article 82, in the end it is for the Court to define what the rules are going to be and the Court has in this respect, as we have seen in practice, taken a very strict view and it will be very difficult to reform it.

D. Neil Campbell*

Good afternoon. Thank you Derek and Philip for the invitation to come and participate on this panel in a really quite fascinating topic and with a most intriguing hypothetical. The printed version of Derek's hypothetical,

---

* McMillan Binch.

in order to internationalize it, says it is set in the future where the UK is considering becoming the 51st state, and that's an opportunity to broaden the perspective. I can only conclude that I was invited to be on the panel because Canadians have spent a century or two thinking about the pros and cons of being the 51st state, so I think I am here more for that reason than any particular knowledge of economics or law. In any event, I have given you a paper that talks about the Canadian approach to predation, which is an area in which we have some movement. If I was giving this talk 10 years ago, I think I would more or less have said that we had bought into the *Brooke Group* model that Greg Werden described for you, but I think we are sliding a little bit away from that. But that's not precisely the subject of Derek's hypothetical and so let me try to tackle that as quickly as I can.

I come from a country which, in these matters, is statute rich, but case-law poor and so we don't have the depth of decided cases from which to draw, but on the other hand I have five separate statutory provisions that could apply to the parts of this hypothetical.

I'll talk first about a criminal offence which we typically refer to in practice as predatory pricing although the offence is actually selling at prices 'unreasonably low', whatever that means, and then there is a further requirement that you do one of four things. You must have either the intent or the effect of either 'substantially lessening competition', an old phrase that we all know well, or 'eliminating a competitor'. So to un-bundle that and link it to this case, we think that 'unreasonably low' is probably a price-cost test and the standard might effectively be variable costs. We have been using avoidable costs, which in this hypothetical is going to be a relatively simple calculation based on Domco's variable cost structure. You would find pricing above cost in the scenarios here and you would conclude that it is not a problem, and that would be the end of the analysis. But I do note that our Act says unreasonably low pricing and that does leave open the possibility that a private complainant, or in theory our Competition Bureau, could take a case, which might look at the fact that there was undercutting rather than merely meeting the entrant's pricing and might look at the potential exclusionary impact in assessing the reasonableness of prices. We haven't really seen enough cases to know whether that could happen, but I think it's not beyond the realm of possibility. And if that were the case then I think there is a risk, although the hypothetical is not fully fleshed out, that you do have either an intent or an effect of eliminating a competitor or substantially lessening competition. I think that we are in an environment where our Competition Bureau recognizes the challenge of enforcing criminal law in the context, as Greg Werden said, of what is generally pro-competitive consumer beneficial behaviour in the short term and the Bureau would be cautious about intervening unless there is a clear long-term risk that prices will in fact be elevated and that the incumbent will be able to maintain and exercise market power.

Now we have a second criminal offence which is called geographic price discrimination or geographic price predation, and it is even less actively enforced than our predatory pricing criminal offence. Indeed, Derek, your hypothetical is the only time in my life that I've actually encountered a geographic price predation scenario. It doesn't really arise in day-to-day life, but it would arise in the facts that you have pitched because it basically says that if you were to sell in one area of Canada at a price lower than you are selling in another area of Canada—read north and south in this context of your strategy number two—you have met one element of an offence which then has the remainder of the elements I just talked about on predatory pricing, namely intent or effect of 'substantially lessening competition' or 'eliminating a competitor'. And I think on these facts there is actually a risk under Canadian law that Domco could be offside, assuming that if your facts were fleshed out its conduct would have either of those intents or effects. Again I think it is unlikely that that's the way this case would be dealt with in Canada because it's a little known criminal provision and because I think that the Competition Bureau tries to exercise that discipline that Greg talked about in terms of allowing scope for pricing which is short-term beneficial to customers.

The third thing I need to refer to is a statutory price discrimination offence, which is a variation on the US Robinson–Patman Act, dating I think from around the same time period. In simple terms it says, without any competitive effects test whatsoever, that it is illegal in Canada to give an advantage to one purchaser which is not available to competing purchasers of like quantity and quality. The hypothetical doesn't really indicate whether all the purchasers are competing purchasers but, to the extent that they are, Derek, then the price discrimination strategies here, if the North customers compete with the South customers, or in strategy three, if competing purchasers of like quantity were getting tailor made discounts, then Domco is going to go offside unless it's prepared to make available the discounted pricing to the others. So I think our price discrimination rules create some discipline on Domco, albeit under a law which is essentially lacking in a competitive effects test. It is also a criminal law that is viewed as not altogether economically rational and not aggressively enforced.

At this stage you are probably wondering whether Canada is indeed living in the dark ages. In fact, I think that where this conduct would be dealt with is in a much more modern and well-functioning part of our Act which contains some provisions that we call 'Reviewable Practices'. Reviewable Practices basically are remedial in nature. They are typically focused on vertical non-price restraints. They include tied selling, exclusive dealing, territorial restrictions, a specific provision dealing with refusals to deal and then an overarching umbrella provision, which we refer to as abuse of dominance. This reflects a little bit of European influence but not the full manifestation of Article 82. I'll skip over exclusive dealing because I think it would just roll up into the same kind of analysis that we would give this under our abuse of dominance practice. And here there are three basics: first you need a firm that is in a dominant position—roughly defined as a firm with some market power. Clearly Domco would be in that category. Second, you need a practice of anti-competitive acts. There is clear case law that exclusivity provisions or practices which are predatory or entry-deterring will quality as a practice of anti-competitive acts, indeed the whole focus of our abuse of dominance regime is to identify conduct that has that predatory, exclusionary or entry deterring quality to it. Here I think you would find that Domco is at risk of being found to be engaging in that kind of activity.

The final element of that practice is whether or not competition 'is likely to be lessened or prevented substantially'. Here again, Derek, I think it depends ultimately on the long-term impact of how Compco responds to Domco's strategy two or strategy three and whether those strategies actually allow in the long term for Domco to raise prices or maintain prices above a competitive level. Were that the case, I think you would find that this would be pursued under our abuse of dominance regime. The Bureau has not taken a huge number of cases, but they have not hesitated to use that provision when they see it, including cases involving foreign entrants seeking to get into a market in Canada where they are facing exclusionary barriers. A famous case involving AC Nielsen Marketing Research, which adopted various practices that impeded IRI, Nielsen's major US competitor, from trying to enter the market, is one of the leading cases.

To very quickly comment on efficiencies, the answer is that we have no formal efficiency defence in any of these areas. We have a mild reference under our abuse provisions to something called 'superior competitive performance'. It is simply an opportunity to show that something you were doing was not an anti-competitive act, but really just the result of superior foresight or something like that. So there might be some scope for an attempt to argue that. But it's not really a defence, at best it has the effect of neutralizing some of the intent elements of the conduct. In light of the time running on, I am going to leave the other questions.

I think I've dealt with the core of them and I will add only that our basic approach is to think about protecting competition rather than just competitors. I think there is in practice a mild populous resurgence in our system at the moment. Both in the policy-making stage and to some extent in the agency and courts there is particular attentiveness where the companies who are facing difficulty are small and medium-sized businesses. Thank you very much.

E. Petri Kuoppamaki*

Sticking to the house order, I shall jump to my conclusions. I think rebates are in the interest of customers in most cases and rebates should be encouraged. Also as regards dominant companies, now my comments relate to EC competition law, but I think we have a situation where a strict policy may indeed harm price competition. You get sticky prices. What happens sometimes is basically that you don't implement an aggressive rebate regime and also then of course smaller competitors can have higher prices in the shadow of the monopoly, so I think we have an issue here and generally speaking also non-linear rebates should clearly be allowed. Of course I would not go as far as proposing to reduce Article 82 in a way that would cut off all the case law concerning prices abuse. It's clear that pricing is a viable competitive weapon to exclude competitors, but yet it is clear that the more economics-based approach is needed and so I would very much welcome the Commission considering rebates issues when the modernization of Article 82 is discussed.

As for the law I don't think I have much to add. Denis covered that area from an in-house counsel's perspective. If you look at cases like *Hoffmann-La Roche*, *Michelin*, *British Airways*, you don't really have much of a choice as to what you would advise your client, your business people. Why is that so? Well, looking from pricing perspective, we have of course an issue that if you allow price discrimination, you may enhance output, but on the other hand what you do in EC law is you look at the customers as well and that is maybe a reason not to discriminate against those clients up in the north who don't get the rebate and this might indeed lead to exclusion and keep the concentrated market structure. That's how you analyse this in Europe. So a lot should depend on what the effects on pricing are which is of course a difficult issue to find out.

But I am somewhat more optimistic concerning the meeting of competition defence. I think it's not just theory. You need to have three elements. First, it needs to be punctual, that means it's an overall pricing campaign to exclude competitors. Secondly, it must not be predatory as far as your cost pricing, and thirdly it needs to be defensive. In this case I would say that the

* Nokia.

price cuts would be defensive. They would not be predatory, but it looks pretty much like a scheme to exclude competitors under the EC jurisprudence, so I agree with Denis that it would not help in this case. So my conclusion is pretty much the same as those reached by the previous speakers, or at least Denis, that we would need to give a greater margin as far as pricing is concerned.

I think it is relevant under EC law whether you know the effects of a practice will exclude companies. Of course it should not be relevant unless there is an abuse but the case law at the moment does not appear as such to prohibit the 'checking' of another guy like in ice hockey, but if the bigger guy checks the smaller guy you get quite an easy penalty, so we would need to address that issue more. Of course it's an interesting question whether this harms consumers or not. A negative decision would be based on the premise that the price cut is temporary and prices go up once Compco is excluded from the market. Yet you could think of a limit pricing type of situation where Compco remains a competitive threat and so the prices don't go up and in that situation prohibiting the price cut would not be in the interest of consumers. So we come back to the question as how to then find out what the result would be and I think there, one question is a legal standard and the second question we need to look at is methodology and how to analyse these pricing cases? So to conclude I think there's a lot of work to be done. It does not mean that the kind of case-law would have to be turned upon but we need to include efficiency analysis and efficiency defence under Article 82, which we do not really have to date. Thank you.

[DEREK RIDYARD]

Thanks Petri. Right, let me open it up to the floor. If anyone has any questions or comments they'd like to make?

F. Discussion

[JOHN KALLAUGHER, *Latham & Watkins*]

I have two questions really. The first one is really to the EU panellists in particular and, if it's correct according to the hypothetical that Domco can maintain a £1.50 price differential between northern Britain and southern Britain for any length of time, doesn't that suggest that there are two geographic markets? And if so, under *United Brands*, is it not the case that there is no price discrimination if the price is different by a dominant firm in one geographic market compared to another? That's my first question. My second question is for Greg Werden: where our complainant is not

Compco, but rather a customer in Glasgow who uses the Domco product as an input and now can no longer compete with a rival who is purchasing the input who is based in the south of England—in other words, we have a secondary line entry—how would the situation be under US law as far as that is concerned? Thanks.

[DENIS WAELBROECK]

An interesting question. I think part of the response may be found in the *cellophane fallacy* and the problem of defining properly the market when you have a company that is already applying above marginal cost pricing at the beginning. Can we really claim under the SSNIP test that we have two geographical markets simply because price differences are that big? I think essentially what we are striving at is how we define properly the market and I express some scepticism about the possibility of defining two geographical markets simply because someone enters a part of your market and not yet all if it. That was certainly not the view of the view of the Commission and the Court in *Irish Sugar* for example, but I admit that—given the facts of the hypothetical—it would certainly have to be looked at carefully. That would be my reply but it's partly for the economists to try to find the right test for the defined market.

[DEREK RIDYARD]

One curiosity with the way you've asked the question, John, is that an economist would say price discrimination is where you can charge different prices to two sets of customers, and if you are saying that whenever you can do that they must be separate markets since how then could you charge different prices to them, you've defined price discrimination out of existence.

[JOHN KALLAUGHER]

But in fairness if you have two different areas and if there is a significant price difference between the two, what you would expect to happen is that arbitrage would lead the prices to become uniform and if that doesn't happen, something is going on which suggests that there are two different geographic markets. That's the way I would analyse it.

[GREG WERDEN]

It appears to me that there are two markets. Your second question concerns what is termed 'secondary line' injury under the Robinson-Patman Act, a subject on which I do not know a great deal, since the Department of Justice does not enforce the Robinson-Patman Act. Based on my limited knowledge of the relevant case law, there could be a violation of the Act because the Glasgow manufacturer was put at a competitive disadvantage vis-à-vis some competing manufacturer in the South. However, several defences and limitations also may apply.

[BERT FOER, *American Antitrust Institute*]

I don't think I heard an answer to the question of whether it matters if the new entrant disappears, and in the US lately we are talking more and more about Darwin and less and less about gentlemanly competition whether domestically or internationally. The only thing that was said is that antitrust is to protect competition, not competitors. That doesn't answer this type of question where it appears that if you don't protect the new entrant, there will be no competitors. At a certain point, competition is synonymous with having competitors, so if we are talking as Dr Röller said about dynamic consumer orientation, don't we have to think about the longer term effects including whether anybody else will ever invest in new entry, if we let this go down the tubes?

[GREG WERDEN]

As Dr Röller would tell you, figuring out the dynamics is difficult (read: impossible). To make antitrust workable requires principles that make the application of the law tractable. One of those principles is that there must be a rigorous definition of exclusionary conduct. Some conduct is deemed not to be exclusionary as a matter of law, because it is exactly the conduct expected in competitive markets, or it is quite similar and firms must be given some leeway. We must be quite confident that firms are doing what they should not be before we bring the great machinery of justice to bear, precisely because of these long-term incentive effects you are talking about. We have to consider the incentives of the innovators who may become the monopolists of the future: they won't do the innovation from which consumers would benefit tremendously if they are not going to be able to keep any monopoly profits. That is what the Supreme Court told us in the *Trinko* case. In a very important sense, monopoly is a good thing: the hope for a monopoly is what fuels the engine of competition. We also have to put limits on what monopolists can do, and of course we do that. The *Microsoft* case surely put limits on what Microsoft could do, even though we could not prove beyond any doubt that Microsoft's conduct had any real market-place effect over the long term. That the conduct was likely to have an effect was enough. And the case was not about protecting competitors, but rather about protecting consumers. From an antitrust perspective, they would be the injured parties from Microsoft's exclusionary conduct.

[NEIL CAMPBELL]

Bert, I think under the Canadian law we would analyse first in terms of the effect of the entrant on market power and we would look at prevention scenarios where you keep an entrant out. *Nielsen v IRI* is a good illustration of that, where the concern was making sure you facilitate the entry. But in addition, we do have a couple of quirks—those provisions that I talked about earlier about eliminating a competitor being a discrete branch of our predation concept, irrespective of whether there's a substantial lessening of competition. So there actually is a path under Canadian law. It's a tough one with a strong burden of proof, but there is a built-in provision in our law to worry about that. We actually also have a purpose clause in our Act that creates a separate little 'endorsement' of the role of small and medium-sized businesses and their equitable opportunity to participate in the economy. This most recently has been used by the Competition Bureau in explaining a decision in a merger case and has also been recently endorsed by the Competition Tribunal in interpreting our efficiency defence, and I actually think that we are moving into an area where we may see in Canada more of an emphasis on the participant as part of the analysis.

[JOHN PHEASANT, LOVELLS]

Just a quick comment on the whole issue of linear discounts and dominant companies. Our last speaker said that a non-linear discount should certainly be permitted. I think from the practitioner's point of view, one of the most difficult things when dealing with companies/clients who are held to be dominant or may be in a dominant position is actually giving them sensible advice on the rebates position under European law. Now I just wonder whether the Chief Economist and his team have any projects in mind to look at the effect of the present position under European law and whether in fact it is making markets more competitive where there is a dominant player. A great concern that I have, and which I think other practitioners have, is with the tendency of the Commission to define markets ever more narrowly. You have an increasing number of companies that may be dominant and if they are all expected to comply with these linear rules, even leaving aside the difficult question of matching, it seems to me that we are creating a real minefield and I think some real economic analysis is required to explore the present position.

G. Canada's Post-Chicago Approach to Predation*

A Neil Campbell and Lisa Parliament**

I. INTRODUCTION

In 1992, the United States Supreme Court accepted the 'Chicago School' economic analysis of predation; that aggressive prices are generally pro-competitive and consumer-welfare enhancing, except in rare situations where the predator has sufficient market power to recoup its losses through long-term, supra-competitive prices achieved after its rivals have been disciplined or eliminated.[1] In that same year, Canada's Competition Bureau issued enforcement guidelines[2] indicating that it would approach Canada's broadly worded criminal offence of 'unreasonably low pricing' (ie predation)[3] in a similar manner. However, the Competition Bureau has moved towards a more interventionist approach in proposed revisions to its guidelines and in recent enforcement activity in the airline industry.

One of the primary goals of the *Competition Act* is to 'maintain and encourage competition in Canada' in order to ensure that consumers are provided with 'competitive prices and product choices'.[4] Price reductions are generally considered to be one of the results of competitive markets that are of particular benefit to customers.[5] The classic predation scenario, on the other hand, involves a dominant firm pricing below cost in the short-term so as to reduce long-term competition in its market. The tension that has arisen out of the difficulty in distinguishing between price reductions resulting from vigorous competition in a market and those resulting from anti-competitive predatory practices has resulted in uncertainty for policy-makers, enforcement officials, and judges. This tension is exacerbated by another express goal of Canadian competition policy: ensuring that 'small and medium-sized enterprises have an equitable opportunity to participate in the Canadian economy'.[6]

---

* Paper presented at the British Institute of International and Comparative Law Competition Conference, 10–11 May 2004, London.
** McMillan Binch LLP.
[1] *Brooke Group, Lt v Brown & Williamson Tobacco Corporation* (1993) 61 USLW 4699.
[2] Competition Bureau *Predatory Pricing Enforcement Guidelines* (Consumer and Corporate Affairs Canada Ottawa 1992) [PPEGs].
[3] Competition Act RSC 1985, c C-34, s 50(1)(c).
[4] ibid s 1.1.
[5] J Church and R Ware *Industrial Organization: A Strategic Approach* (Irwin McGraw-Hill San Francisco 2000) ch 2. See also P Bolton et al 'Predatory Pricing: Strategic Theory and Legal Policy' (2000) 88 Geo LJ 2239 at 2241.
[6] ibid.

The development of an appropriate response to predatory conduct has been the focus of a significant body of academic literature and policy debate. Much of the debate is focused on articulation of a price-cost test for predation, but the relevance of ability to recoup short-term losses through long-term gains is also a recurring theme.

From a relatively unsophisticated focus on price-cost comparative analysis in the 1970s and 1980s, Canadian competition policy moved towards more complex assessment of the price-cost relationship in parallel with the consideration of the potential for recoupment. The Competition Bureau's 1992 *Predatory Pricing Enforcement Guidelines* (PPEGs) accepted that market power and the potential for recoupment was a core test for identifying whether to take enforcement action in response to low pricing.[7] However, this has been eroded in a draft version of the *Enforcement Guidelines for Illegal Trade Practices: Unreasonably Low Pricing Policies*[8] released for comment by the Competition Bureau in March 2002. They also substituted a somewhat abstract 'avoidable cost' test for the prior references to old-fashioned accounting concepts of average variable and average total costs. In its annual report, the Bureau stated that the Draft Guidelines were meant to reflect changes in economic thinking about low-pricing behaviour.[9] Although the move to the avoidable cost test can find support in modern economic literature,[10] the Bureau's new ambivalence towards recoupment is on questionable ground.

II. THE ECONOMIC THEORY OF PREDATION

1. Definition of Predation

From an economic perspective, predatory pricing has been defined in a number of ways. For example:

- a firm's deliberate aggression against one or more rivals through the employment of business practices that would not be considered profit

---

[7] See (n 2) para 2.1— The first stage of the Bureau's approach involves an assessment of whether the alleged predatory has market power, meaning an ability to unilaterally affect pricing in the relevant market. The Bureau's analysis is directed towards determining if after the period of low pricing the alleged predator would be able to raise prices and recoup losses or foregone profits.

[8] Competition Bureau *Enforcement Guidelines for Illegal Trade Practices: Unreasonably Low Pricing Policies* (Industry Canada Ottawa 2002) online: Strategis, Industry Canada <http://strategis.ic.gc.ca/pics/ct/ct02339e5.pdf> [*Draft Guidelines*].

[9] Competition Bureau 'Annual Report 2003—Interacting with Canadians', online: Strategis, Industry Canada <http://strategis.ic.gc.ca/epic/internet/incb-bc.nsf/en/ct02763e.html>.

[10] WJ Baumol 'Predation and the Logic of the Average Variable Cost Test' (1996) XXXIX (1) JL & Econ 49 ['Logic of the Average Variable Cost Test'];

maximizing except for the expectation either that: (1) rivals will be driven from the market, leaving the predator with a market share sufficient to command monopoly profits; or (2) rivals will be chastened sufficiently to abandon competitive behaviour the predator finds inconvenient or threatening;[11]

- pricing in a way that sacrifices profits in the short term with a view to excluding rivals, or preventing or deterring entrants, and thereby earning higher profits in the future in the absence of competition (either in the very market in which the pricing conduct occurs, or in other related markets);[12]

- the reduction of price in the short run so as to drive competing firms out of the market or to discourage entry of new firms in an effort to gain larger profits via higher prices in the long run than would have been earned if the price reduction had not occurred;[13] and

- a situation where a dominant firm charges low prices over a long enough period of time so as to drive a competitor from the market or deter others from entering and then raises prices to recoup its losses.[14]

However as Bolton, Brodley, & Riordan have stated, merely defining the concept is not stating an operational legal rule.[15] The development of sound enforcement policies is dependent upon being able to articulate legal rules with measurable factors that are supportable by reference to economic theory. The ability to recoup is one test that serves a particularly important role in reminding that short-term low prices are generally pro-competitive in the absence of longer-term increases.

2. Economic Models of Predation

One of the earliest economic models of predation is that described as the 'long purse' theory.[16] This theory suggests that a firm with easy access to unlimited capital is able to drive out a competitor by pricing below cost.

[11] RH Bork *The Antitrust Paradox: A Policy at War with Itself* 2d. (Maxwell Macmillan Canada Toronto 1993) 144.
[12] G Edwards 'The Perennial Problem of Predatory Pricing' (2002) 30 Aust Bus Law Rev 170 at 171, online: <www.necg.com.au/pappub/perennial_problem_of_predatory_ pricing. pdf>.
[13] PL Joskow and AK Klevorick 'A Framework for Analyzing Predatory Pricing Policy' (1979) 89 Yale LJ 213.
[14] See the Executive Summary of the PPEGs (n 2).
[15] See (n 5) 2243.
[16] For early discussion of the long purse theory, see L Telser 'Cutthroat Competition and the Long Purse' (1966) 9 Journal of Law and Economics 259. For a discussion of the long purse theory and the varied responses to long purse theorists, see M Trebilcock et al *The Law and Economics of Canadian Competition Policy* (University of Toronto Press Toronto 2002) 290–5.

The exit of the competitor from the market means that the surviving predator firm can then raise its prices to recoup its losses.[17] However, economic commentators challenged the long purse theory of predation by performing analyses that emphasized the irrationality of predation strategies.[18] For example, an early empirical study by John McGee concluded that the irrationality of predatory pricing made firms less likely to rely on predation than on other strategies, such as mergers.[19]

Over time, economic theorists began to challenge the very existence of predation as a market strategy.[20] Predation was a particular target of Chicago School critics of traditional antitrust policy, who regarded it as generally implausible.[21] For example, Bork argued that pursuant to the long-purse theory, the success of predatory strategies would depend on the existence of significant entry barriers. He also noted that in a price-cost comparison, the long-term benefits to the predator would be much less significant than might be expected because they must be discounted to account for the time-value of the money. [22]

Challenges to the simple predation theories prompted more sophisticated models that suggested the strategy of predation could be profitable where it would generate reputational effects which can deter potential market entrants.[23] This could make it feasible to recoup initial losses and increase or protect market power,[24] providing a potential explanation for seemingly irrational low pricing strategies.[25]

Despite the considerable disagreement among academics as to whether predation was a viable business strategy in pure economic terms, examples of apparent predation continue to occur.[26] Complaints about this type of market behaviour spurred the development of even more sophisticated

[17] Telser (n 16).

[18] See Trebilcock et al (n 16) 290–95; see generally RA Posner *Antitrust Law: An Economic Perspective* (University of Chicago Press Chicago 1976) 184–8; and see eg, FH Easterbrook 'Predatory Strategies and Counterstrategies' (1981) 48 U Chi L Rev 263.

[19] JS McGee 'Predatory Price Cutting: The Standard Oil (NJ) Case' (1958) 1 JL & Econ 137 at 140–1. McGee argued that the predator selling at a loss is more likely to suffer greater losses than the target, and any increase in market share for the predator only meant that the predator would have an increasingly disproportionate share of losses.

[20] See the discussion in Trebilcock et al (n 16) 288–93.

[21] See eg Posner (n 18); RH Bork *The Antitrust Paradox: A Policy at War with Itself* (Basic Books New York 1978) 144; and see generally, J Tirole *The Theory of Industrial Organization* (MIT Press Cambridge 1988) ch 9. For a general discussion of the Chicago assault on the rationality of predatory strategies, see Church and Ware (n 5) 645–7.

[22] See (n 11).

[23] See, eg, B Yamey 'Predatory Price-Cutting: Notes and Comments' (1972) 15 J of Law & Econ 129.

[24] See discussion in *Draft Guidelines* (n 8) 13–14.

[25] ibid; see also Bolton, et al (n 5) 2299–310.

[26] See, eg, Church and Ware (n 5) 654.

theories that included the possibility that parties may be acting pursuant to imperfect information.[27]

Thus modern economic theory accepts that, given the existence of certain factors, predation can be a rational business strategy.[28] Recoupment plays a significant role in virtually all such theories.[29] For example, Bolton, Brodley, & Riordan note that recoupment could be based on actual price increases, increased concentration and entry barriers after competitor exit, or other relevant market conditions that would support recoupment in the future, as well as welfare-expanding dynamic efficiencies.[30]

3. Economic Tests for Predation

Along with general economic theories designed to explain the phenomenon of predation, a significant body of literature has developed to identify predatory behaviour. These tests have evolved over the years but continue to focus on two key issues: (i) the comparison of prices to some measures of costs; and (ii) the potential for recoupment.

(a) Price-Cost Comparative Analyses

In an analysis that became well known to both academics and courts, Areeda and Turner proposed that illegal predation should be judged by determining whether a firm sells at a price below marginal cost.[31] To operationalize this economic test in situations involving real world accounting data, they suggested substituting average variable cost for marginal cost.

The Areeda–Turner rule has been criticized on the basis that is both under-inclusive and over-inclusive.[32] It is under-inclusive because pricing below marginal cost can be unrelated to predatory activities. It is also over-inclusive in that it is possible to conceive of situations where a dominant firm is able to take advantage of predatory strategies despite the fact that, due to its economies of scale, it has been pricing above marginal cost. In addition, the use of variable costs as a proxy presents challenges, including those related to the difficulties inherent in attempting to distinguish fixed from variable costs, which are not normally segmented in financial accounting records.

---

[27] See the discussion in Bolton, et al (n 5) 2243–62, where the authors describe in some detail the evolution of economic theory and legal policy with respect to predatory pricing; and see also Church and Ware (n) 644–54.   [28] ibid.

[29] Bolton et al (n 5) 2263; and see generally Church and Ware (n 5) 644–5.

[30] See (n 29) 2263–4.

[31] P Areeda and DF Turner 'Predatory Pricing and Related Practices Under Section 2 of the *Sherman Act*' (1975) 88 Harv L Rev 637.

[32] See, eg, Bolton et al (n 5) 2252; and see generally the discussion of the challenges to the Areeda-Turner rule in Trebilcock et al (n 16) 303–6.

(b) The Move Beyond Simple Price-Cost Tests

Several commentators recognized that tests based on comparisons between accounting-based measures of costs and prices were unable to properly distinguish between legitimately competitive behaviour and undesirable predation.[33] Alternative approaches were proposed that involved more contextual considerations.

One of the earliest alternatives to a pure price-cost approach was proposed by Joskow and Klevorick.[34] This approach was structured as a two-stage predation analysis, in which price-cost comparisons were the second step. The first stage involved the assessment of whether appropriate market conditions exist for predatory pricing to occur. Relevant considerations include whether the predator has market power and whether there are significant entry barriers.

Posner developed an alternative test that is based on comparisons of costs and prices; however, it incorporates the element of anti-competitive intent into the concept of predation.[35] In Posner's model, predatory pricing only results where there is pricing below long-run marginal costs that is designed to eliminate a competitor. The introduction of the concept of long-run marginal costs (which effectively involves examining average balance sheet cost items over time) and the requirement to show anti-competitive intent, result in this test being relatively difficult to implement in practice.

In what he viewed as a sharpening of the test proposed by Areeda and Turner, Baumol suggested that average avoidable cost is a better measure for predation.[36] He argued that mere comparison of price and marginal cost is inadequate to distinguish between legitimate business practices and anti-competitive predation. Baumol theorized that any price not below average avoidable cost cannot be predatory, and that therefore it is the assessment of average avoidable cost, not marginal cost, that is critical.

Baumol has also proposed an approach to predation that would require a dominant firm to maintain for a specified period any price cuts that resulted in competitors exiting the market.[37] This requirement would significantly lessen the potential for recoupment, thereby reducing the profitability of

---

[33] See the discussion of the criticism of early price-cost approaches in Bolton, et al (n 5) 2250–62.

[34] Joskow and Klevorick (n 13) 242–70.

[35] Posner (n 18J) 188–9.

[36] Baumol 'Logic of the Average Variable Cost Test' (n 10) 53.

[37] WJ Baumol 'Quasi-Permanence of Price Reductions: A Policy for Prevention of Predatory Pricing' (1979) 89 Yale LJ 1 ['Prevention of Predatory Pricing'] 4–6.

any contemplated predatory strategy. However, it would not address competition that is lessened by weakening or disciplining rivals which do not exit. In addition, the practical application of this approach would require the price benchmark to be adjusted to take into account cost changes or other developments that might occur during the five-year period. More fundamentally, Baumol's formula has the potential to suppress future pro-competitive practices.[38]

In response to what they considered to be a failure of the courts to develop an approach to predation that was consistent with the results of empirical studies and with generally accepted economic principles, Bolton, et al proposed an enforcement policy based on modern strategic theory.[39] They suggested that five elements need to be present:

- a facilitating market structure;
- a scheme of predation and supporting evidence;
- probable recoupment;
- price below cost; and
- absence of a business justification or efficiencies defence.[40]

The initial three factors are viewed as a first-tier that operates as a screening mechanism. Where present, examination of the remaining two factors determines whether the predatory pricing strategy was in fact anti-competitive.

In summary, most approaches now go beyond a basic price-cost analysis and share a common principle: the relevance of the probability of recoupment, broadly defined, to the evaluation of whether low prices are pro-competitive or anti-competitive.

III. THE CANADIAN LEGAL FRAMEWORK GOVERNING PREDATION

Predatory pricing is a criminal offence in Part VI of the Competition Act.[41] In addition, such conduct can be addressed under the broad 'reviewable practice' of abuse of dominance.[42] There is relatively little judicial interpretation

---

[38] For a more detailed critique of Baumol's temporal approach, see Bolton et al (n 5) 2251–2. Despite these challenges, other theorists have also proposed models focus on prevention of recoupment through prohibiting significant changes in price or product after competitor exit or entry. See eg OE Williamson 'Predatory Pricing: A Strategic and Welfare Analysis' (1977) 87 *Yale LJ* 284; and AS Edlin 'Stopping Above-Cost Predatory Pricing' (2002) 111 Yale LJ 941.

[39] Bolton et al (n 5).

[40] ibid 2264.

[41] See Competition Act (n 3) ss 50(1)(b) and (c), which are reproduced and discussed below.

[42] ibid s 79. A reviewable practice is a non-criminal provision that authorizes the Commissioner to apply to the Competition Tribunal, a specialized body composed of judges and lay members, for prohibition orders or other remedies.

of these provisions, which makes the enforcement guidelines issued by the Competition Bureau particularly important.

1. The Competition Act Provisions

a) The Offence of Predatory Pricing

The criminal offence of predatory pricing occurs when a firm:

engages in a policy of selling products at prices unreasonably low, having the effect or tendency of substantially lessening competition or eliminating a competitor, or designed to have that effect.[43]

It is notable that the legislation does not contain any specific reference to costs. However, price-cost comparisons are one natural mechanism for assessing whether prices are 'unreasonably' low.[44]

The offence contains an impact requirement with four alternative permutations. The firm's policy of selling[45] products at unreasonably low prices must:

- have the effect or tendency of substantially lessening competition;
- have the effect or tendency of eliminating a competitor;
- be designed to have the effect of substantially lessening competition; or
- be designed to have the effect of eliminating a competitor.

Although the statutory language of section 50(1)(c) does not mention recoupment, it could be considered as part of a substantial lessening of competition analysis (but not the alternative branches involving elimination of a competitor).[46] Alternatively, it is possible to interpret 'unreasonably

---

[43] ibid s 50(1)(c) There is also a little-used companion offence of geographic price discrimination (s 50(1)(b)) which occurs when a firm: 'engages in a policy of selling products in any area of Canada at prices lower than those exacted . . . elsewhere in Canada, having the effect or tendency of substantially lessening competition or eliminating a competitor in that part of Canada, or designed to have that effect.'

[44] This has occurred in the case law: see the discussion below under the sub-heading 'Significant Cases in the Canadian Law of Predation'. The alternate benchmark under the geographic price discrimination offence is the alleged predator's prices elsewhere in Canada (see s 50(1)(b) above), but this has rarely been used in practice.

[45] The requirement that there be a 'policy of selling' creates some scope for ad hoc low pricing, but the courts have held that relatively modest duration and scope may be sufficient to constitute a policy.

[46] 'Substantial lessening of competition' is a test used in several provisions of the *Competition Act*, and has consistently been interpreted to mean the creation, protection or enhancement of market power: see, eg *Canada (Director of Investigation and Research) v Hillsdown Holdings (Canada) Ltd* (1992), 41 CPR (3d) 289 (Comp Trib) (mergers); *Canada (Director of Investigation & Research) v. NutraSweet Co* (1990), 32 CPR (3d) 1 at 56–60 (Comp Trib) [*NutraSweet*] (exclusive dealing and abuse of dominance); *Canada (Director of Investigation and Research) v. Tele-Direct Publications Inc* [1997], 73 CPR (3d) 1 (Comp Trib) (tied selling and abuse of dominance); and, more generally, AN Campbell *Merger Law and*

low' in a long-term context that involves consideration of whether recoupment through supra-competitive pricing is likely to occur.

b) The Reviewable Practice of Abuse of Dominance

The reviewable practice of abuse of dominance (Canada's general provision dealing with monopolization issues) occurs when:

(a) one or more persons substantially or completely control, throughout Canada or any area thereof, a class or species of business,
(b) that person or those persons have engaged in or are engaging in a practice of anti-competitive acts,[47] and
(c) the practice has had, is having or is likely to have the effect of preventing or lessening competition substantially in a market.[48]

'Anti-competitive act' is defined in a non-exhaustive manner to include 'selling articles at a price lower than the acquisition cost for the purpose of disciplining or eliminating a competitor,'[49] which is a very narrow application of a general price-cost test to a simple reseller context. However, the Tribunal has recognized that other predatory price (and non-price) conduct can also constitute anti-competitive acts.[50] It remains to be seen what cost standard would be employed to identify whether prices are predatory for purposes of an abuse of dominance proceeding.

The requirement of a dominant market position has been interpreted to mean that the firm has market power in a relevant market.[51] When such a firm engages in a practice of anti-competitive acts, a substantial lessening of competition will likely be found to occur assuming that such acts materially enhance or protect the firm's market power. Thus recoupment would be expected to be a central issue in determining whether low pricing constitutes an abuse of dominant position.

Practice: The Regulation of Mergers Under the Competition Act (Carswell Scarborough 1997) ch 5.

[47] The requirement that there be a 'practice', rather than merely an isolated anti-competitive act, is normally not a significant hurdle. The term 'practice', like 'policy of selling', has been interpreted as arising after a very modest duration or scope of authority. See, eg, *Nutrasweet* (n 46) 58–9.

[48] Competition Act (n 3) s 79.

[49] ibid s 78(1)(i). The Act and accompanying regulations also provide a customized regime dealing with predatory pricing or capacity deployment in the airline industry: see ibid s 78 (1)(j) and 78(2)(a), and the Regulations Respecting Anti-Competitive Acts of Persons Operating a Domestic Service, SOR 2000/324 [Airline Regulations].

[50] See, eg, *NutraSweet* (n 46) 56, 57, 59–80.

[51] See, eg, *Canada (Director of Investigation and Research) v Laidlaw Waste Systems Ltd* (1992), 40 CPR (3d) 289 (Comp Trib) [*Laidlaw*]; *Canada (Director of Investigation and Research) v The D&B Companies of Canada Ltd* (1995), 64 CPR (3d) 216 (Comp Trib)

(c) Proposed Amendments to the Predatory Pricing Provisions

In June 2003, the Canadian government requested public comment on a wide-reaching package of proposed changes to the Competition Act.[52] The proposals included the decriminalization of predatory pricing and its explicit inclusion in the civil abuse of dominance regime. Decriminalization of predation would be consistent with the economic theories outlined above, as it recognizes that low pricing is normally advantageous to consumers unless recoupment is likely. However, some of the support for this approach was contingent on two other general changes that are much more controversial: transformation of reviewable practices such as abuse of dominance into civil offences (through the introduction of potentially substantial 'administrative monetary penalties') and/or competition torts (by the introduction of private rights to recover damages).

Stakeholder consultations conducted by the Public Policy Forum found that there was general support for decriminalization of pricing provisions (although the reasons in support varied from chilling of competitive behaviour to increased efficacy of enforcement).[53] However, there was considerable disagreement among the intervenors regarding the desirability of administrative monetary penalties or damage remedies. It therefore remains to be seen when and in what form any changes will be brought forward in legislative amendments.

2. Case Law on Predation

Canadian court and Competition Tribunal cases examining predation are relatively rare.[54] Historically, despite numerous complaints alleging predatory practices, few cases have proceeded to the point where prosecutions

---

[*Nielsen*]; and Enforcement Guidelines on the Abuse of Dominance Provisions (Industry Canada Ottawa 2001) Appendix IV, online: Competition Bureau <http://www. competition.ic.gc.ca/epic/internet/incb-bc.nsf/en/ct02220e.html>. For further discussion see AN Campbell 'Canada's Well Balanced Approach to Monopolisation' (Canadian Bar Association Competition Law Conference Sept 2001) online: McMillan Binch <http://www.mcmillan-binch.com/AboutUs.aspx?Section1=AboutUs&Section2=LawyerPopup& BioID=32ba0445>.

[52] 'Options for Amending the Competition Act: Fostering a Competitive Marketplace' (Government of Canada, 20 June 2003) online: Public Policy Forum < http://www. ppforum. ca/competitionact/dp2003.pdf>.

[53] Public Policy Forum 'National Consultation on the Competition Act: Final Report' 20, online: Public Policy Forum http://www.ppforum.ca/competitionact/final_report.pdf>.

[54] See the discussion in CS Goldman QC and JD Bodrug *Competition Law of Canada* loose-leaf (Juris Publishing Inc New York 2002–) §4.05[1]. A review of the decisions referenced on the Competition Bureau's website reveals only a limited number of cases that have considered predation and even fewer that have actually addressed the appropriate approach or test for assessing predatory strategies.

are initiated and indeed only a modest number of formal inquiries.[55] The VanDuzer Report has speculated that this enforcement record may be a reflection of various factors, including the prioritizing of enforcement objectives, unnecessarily high standards for the test for predation, sporadic enforcement, the evidentiary difficulties in establishing the elements of predation, and the difficulty in designing legal rules for predation.[56] However, the more likely explanation is that there are few cases where firms utilize genuinely predatory strategies. An examination of the cases discussed below suggests the considerable difficulties encountered by courts in their attempts to define and articulate a test for predation that does not encompass what is merely intense competition.

(a) Early Decisions

In the first significant Canadian judicial analysis of predatory pricing,[57] the Court in *R v Hoffman-La Roche*[58] assessed a scheme in which the firm was giving away a branded drug (Valium) to doctors as part of a pre-emptive strategy to respond to legislative changes that implemented a compulsory licensing regime permitting other companies to manufacture and sell competing brands. In interpreting 'unreasonably low', the Court held that the test for unreasonableness is objective, and that intention was irrelevant to this aspect of the analysis.[59] The Court also rejected the argument that a price–cost analysis was always determinative on the basis that, while prices above cost are never unreasonable, prices below cost may or may not be considered unreasonable depending on the circumstances.

The following factors were considered to be significant to the assessment of the predatory nature of the practices:

(i)   the magnitude of the difference between price and cost;
(ii) the length of the period during which sales take place at the low price;
(iii) the circumstances of the price cutting; and

---

[55] JA VanDuzer and G Paquet 'Anticompetitive Pricing Practices and the *Competition Act*— Theory, Law and Practice' (22 Oct 1999) online: Competition Bureau <http://competition. ic.gc.ca/epic/internet/incb-bc.nsf/en/ct01656e.html> [VanDuzer Report].

[56] ibid 12.

[57] There are earlier cases on predatory pricing; however, these provide little substantive analysis on the many issues raised in modern predatory pricing complaints. See eg *R. v Eddy Match CoLtd* (1951), 17 CPR 17 (Que KB) aff'd (1953), 20 CPR 107 (Que CA); and *R v Safeway Ltd* (1973) 14 CCC (2d) 14 (Alta TD) [*Safeway*].

[58] (1980) 109 DLR (3d) 5 (Ont HCJ), aff'd (1981), 125 DLR (3d) 607 (Ont CA) [*Hoffman-La Roche*].

[59] Intent was relevant to the issue of the substantial lessening of competition, as policies that are designed to substantially lessen competition (or eliminate a competitor) are explicitly addressed in s 50(1)(c), the criminal prohibition: Competition Act (n 3).

(iv) the long term benefits that could ensue to the accused company as a result of the price cutting (ie recoupment).

In the result, the Court convicted Hoffman-La Roche. Shortly after the case, however, a substantial number of competitors entered the market, demonstrating that given the market characteristics, recoupment was not possible.[60]

The *Consumers Glass*[61] case was decided soon after *Hoffman-La Roche*. It arose from a price-cutting war between two competitors which each had the capacity to meet market demands. The incumbent firm was eventually pushed out of the market, but was later charged with predatory pricing. The Court acquitted the firm, finding that at all relevant times price was above average variable cost and that the firm was merely attempting to maximize profits in the face of entry. It was therefore not necessary to consider recoupment.

The Competition Tribunal examined predation issues and the Areeda-Turner analysis in *NutraSweet*,[62] in the context of a broadly-based case pursuant to the abuse of dominance provisions. While it held that the practice of 'selling below acquisition cost' for the purpose of eliminating or disciplining a competitor was inapplicable outside a resale context, the Tribunal also assessed generally the practice of predatory pricing and its composite elements. It concluded that capacity was relevant to the price-cost analysis:

• where a firm was operating below capacity, the appropriate test was to compare price and average variable cost;
• where a firm was operating at full capacity, it was more appropriate to compare price and average total cost.[63]

Boehringer Ingelheim (Canada) Inc v Bristol-Myers Squibb Canada Inc[64] involved a motion by Boehringer for an injunction based on allegations that included unfair competition, predatory pricing, libel and slander, among others. The Court found that price-cutting below cost in an effort to match a competitor's prices could not be considered predation.[65] Accordingly, it did not have any reason to address the role of recoupment.[66]

---

[60] As discussed further in Trebilcock et al (n 16) 321–2.
[61] *R v Consumers Glass Ltd and Portion Packaging* (1981) 124 DLR (3d) 274 (Ont HCJ) [*Consumers Glass*].
[62] See (n 46).
[63] ibid The Tribunal also noted that in this market, recoupment of lost profits was unlikely, even though there may have been a desire to eliminate competition. This discussion was largely *obiter*, however, as the Competition Bureau had not asked for any remedy concerning prices other than a prohibition of pricing below 'acquisition cost, a concept that the Competition Tribunal found irrelevant.
[64] [1998] OJ No 4007 (Gen Div) (QL).   [65] ibid para 30.
[66] In *obiter*, the court rejected the argument that they should decide a reasonable selling

Although it was a tort case rather than a *Competition Act* case, the Court in *Ed Miller Sales and Rentals Ltd v Caterpillar Tractor Co*[67] made some important observations regarding the relevance of intent to injure in the context of intense competition and aggressive targeting of competitors. In determining that there was no liability for the tort of interference with contractual relations, the Court noted that competitors often dislike each other, and almost always want to hurt each other's business.[68] The Court stated that driving another competitor out of a market is in itself perfectly legal,[69] and if hating a competitor and wishing it were out of business were part of the tortious offence, competition would be stifled.[70] However, under the intent branch of the existing predatory pricing offence, such motivations would be illegal if connected to a policy of unreasonably low prices. This underscores the importance of incorporating a recoupment concept into the unreasonably low prices' element of the offence rather than only considering it as part of a 'substantial lessening of competition' analysis.

(b) Recent Developments

In July 2003, the Competition Tribunal issued its decision in Phase I of the proceedings in *Commissioner of Competition v Air Canada*.[71] Shortly after the case was initiated, the Tribunal ordered that the application would be heard in two phases: (i) Phase I would address the application of the avoidable cost test, including the identification of the appropriate unit or units of capacity, what types of costs are avoidable and when they become avoidable; and (ii) Phase II would deal with the balance of the application which would focus on the competitive effects of Air Canada's practices.[72]

In its Phase I decision, the Tribunal adopted Baumol's avoidable cost test and attempted to apply it to the complexities of a network industry:

The avoidable cost test for predation determines whether a firm's revenue (price) is above or below its (average) avoidable cost. As discussed by Dr. Baumol, the multi-product enterprise will rationally continue to produce a given product as long as the

price, suggesting that the reasonableness of a price can be volatile, controversial, and can change over an extended period of time: ibid para 34.

[67] [1996] AJ No 722 (CA) [*Caterpillar*].

[68] ibid para 56.

[69] The court also indicated that not wanting to hurt each other's business might even infringe the *Competition Act*: ibid. This would be an overstatement unless there was an actual conspiracy in restraint of trade or joint abuse of dominance: see Competition Act ss 45 and 79.

[70] *Caterpillar* (n 67) para 56.

[71] 2003 Comp Trib 13 [*Air Canada*].

[72] Phase II will address issues such as whether Air Canada was dominant in the market and if it engaged in a practice of anti-competitive acts in a manner that substantially prevented or lessened competition in the market.

revenue from the sale of that product exceeds the product's avoidable costs. If the cost-savings achieved by exit exceed the revenue foregone, then the firm will terminate production of that product. Since no enterprise will rationally set the price per unit of any of its products below their respective (average) avoidable costs in the pursuit of maximum short-term profits, deviations from this rational pricing behaviour may be predatory.[73]

Two important concepts were incorporated into the avoidable cost test. The Tribunal accepted the relevance of redeployment, which extended the scope of costs that were viewed as avoidable. It also included the concept of passenger recapture as a means of redeployment, which again had the effect of broadening the scope of avoidability.[74]

The *Air Canada* decision can be contrasted with a similar case involving competition between American Airlines and various low cost carriers in the United States.[75] The district court granted a motion for summary judgment on the basis that the government failed to establish that American had engaged in pricing below a legal level or that there was a significant risk of recoupment.[76] The test used in the case compared the additional revenue generated with incremental cost, but without the extent of adjustments for recapture and redeployment accepted by the Tribunal in *Air Canada*. This decision was upheld on appeal,[77] although the court declined to dictate average variable cost (or any other test) as the appropriate proxy for marginal cost in every case.[78]

The extent to which the *Air Canada* decision has broader relevance remains to be seen. As the relevant regulatory provisions refer specifically to the avoidable cost test, it is possible that the Tribunal's decision could be restricted to predation in the airline industry.[79] However, the decision may well influence the Tribunal and courts to adopt an avoidable costs test as the appropriate price-cost test for the predatory pricing and abuse of dominance provisions generally. If this occurs, the implications for other non-network industries will depend on how avoidability is assessed in such settings.

---

[73] ibid para 80.   [74] ibid para 333.

[75] *United States v AMR Corporation et al*, Memorandum and Order, United States District Court for the District of Kansas, No 99–1180-JTM [*American Airlines (District Court)*], aff'd *United States v AMR Corporation et al* United States Court of Appeals, Tenth Circuit, No 013202 [*American Airlines (Court of Appeals)*].

[76] *American Airlines (District Court)* (n 75).

[77] *American Airlines (Court of Appeals)* (n 75).

[78] It should be noted that the reasoning in the *American Airlines* decision necessarily focused on the application of the test for summary judgment, as opposed to setting out general principles of predation.

[79] The Tribunal was interpreting industry-specific provisions to determine the issue of Air Canada operated or increased capacity at fares that do not cover the avoidable costs of providing the service, within the meaning of paragraphs 1(a) and 1(b) of the *Airline Regulations* (n 49).

3. Competition Bureau Guidelines

Given the limited jurisprudence on predation, the issuance of the PPEGs in 1992[80] and the recent publication of the Draft Guidelines[81] provide important insight into the Competition Bureau's approach to aggressive pricing.

(a) The 1992 Guidelines

The Competition Bureau published the PPEGs with the intention of ensuring that market participants would not restrain from engaging in price competition as a result of uncertainty regarding the criminal prohibition of predatory pricing.[82]

The approach articulated in the guidelines is a two-stage analysis:

(i) considering market characteristics such as seller concentration and entry conditions, which are indicative of the existence of, or the potential for establishing, market power; and

(ii) confirming that prices are indeed unreasonably low by evaluating the relationship between the alleged predator's prices and costs.[83]

Only if predatory prices could plausibly be recouped in the particular market is there resort to the second stage. Where entry or expansion by other firms would likely constrain recoupment by the alleged predator, the Bureau will normally close its investigation without any detailed price-cost analysis.

In general terms, the PPEGs are consistent with, and supported by, modern economic theory, with the central focus placed on an appropriate market power/recoupment test. However, the second phase used average variable and average total cost to evaluate price-cost relationships. These measures are not necessarily the best approximations for marginal cost.[84]

(b) The New Draft Guidelines

In March 2002, the Bureau released the Draft Guidelines for comment.[85] These guidelines were intended to clarify paragraphs 50(1)(b) and 50(1)(c) of the Competition Act, and to update the PPEGs. The most significant changes contained in the Draft Guidelines are: (i) the shift to a test of avoidable cost rather than average variable cost; and (ii) the demotion of recoupment from an essential screening criterion to merely a non-essential factor for consideration.

---

[80] See (n 2).   [81] See (n 8).   [82] HI Weston, preface to the PPEGs (n 2).
[83] ibid Part II.   [84] Bolton, et al (n 5).   [85] See (n 8).

The first change is consistent with modern economic theory and with recent case law on predation, as avoidable costs in principle should better address the underlying economic issues relating to the identification of price levels which are predatory.[86] However, the decision to reduce the significance of the recoupment of losses test does not have a solid theoretical foundation. The preface to the Draft Guidelines indicates that the proposed alterations are based on changes in economic thinking and changes in the economy.[87] The authority upon which the decision that there is no need to show recoupment is based is not clear.

The response to the release of the Draft Guidelines has been mixed.[88] Although many commentators considered the change to the avoidable costs measure as a positive move to a more appropriate (although less well understood) price-cost standard, the erosion of the recoupment standard was met with considerable (and justifiable) opposition.[89]

IV. CONCLUDING REMARKS

If the Draft Guidelines are evidence of future Canadian competition policy, it seems that there continues to be an evolution in the understanding and development of certain aspects of predation, such as the price-cost relationship. With respect to other elements, however, including recoupment, recent developments are not consistent with an understanding of modern economic theory. If, as modern economic theory suggests, predation without the potential for recoupment is economically irrational, it is questionable whether this type of predation is appropriately the focus of competition policy.

It would be desirable for Canada to decriminalize predatory pricing, since distinguishing between beneficial aggressive pricing and predation is too difficult to justify the use of criminal laws and penalties. Regardless of whether this occurs, the Bureau's move to downplay recoupment as an essential element in the legal framework and enforcement policy should be reversed.

---

[86] Bolton, et al (n 5).

[87] See (n 8).

[88] M Sullivan 'Draft Enforcement Guidelines on Illegal Trade Practices: Unreasonably Low Pricing Policies: The Way Ahead' (Competition in Difficult Times Conference, Toronto, Ontario, 12 Nov 2002) online: Competition Bureau <http://strategis.ic.gc.ca/epic/internet/incb-bc.nsf/en/ct02490e.html>.

[89] Unfortunately, the draft has been placed on hold pending completion of the *Air Canada* case, which leaves considerable uncertainty for firms and their advisers.

H. Exclusionary Pricing and Price Discrimination under EC Competition Law

Denis Waelbroeck*

Dominant companies are subject in the EC to a heavily regulated regime. Pricing policies of dominant companies are prohibited by EC Article 82(2)(a) if they are 'unfair' or 'exploitative'. They can be prohibited by Article 82(2)(b) if they are 'exclusionary' (eg predatory prices or fidelity rebates) or by Article 82(2)(d) if—through bundle rebates—they constitute an incentive to buy several products together. Finally, EC Article 82(2)(c) prohibits price discrimination by dominant companies, ie 'applying dissimilar conditions to equivalent transactions with other parties, thereby placing them at a competitive disadvantage'. The provision requires in principle 'secondary line injury' insofar as it is conditioned on a competitive disadvantage suffered as a result of the discrimination by the trading partner being discriminated against.

Discrimination between the undertaking itself and its competitors or 'primary line competition' is not affected by Article 82(2)(c) (but it may be affected by the more general rules of EC Article 82).

Without pretending to be exhaustive, it is envisaged to discuss hereafter briefly the extent of the rule in relation to the two types of behaviour envisaged by the case-study and to reply thereby also to the main questions which panellists have been asked to address, ie:

- The 'meeting competition defence': should a selective price reduction designed to meet a competitor's prices be allowed? (I)
- 'Fidelity' and 'bundle discounts': Should they be per se prohibited? (II)
- The 'cost justification defence': How should price relate to cost? Are other justifications than cost differences acceptable? (III)
- The 'efficiency defence': How it applies to discriminatory pricing? (IV)
- Effects of the practice: Should they be taken into account and how? (V)

In our reply, it is assumed—as suggested in the case-study- that the practice is non-predatory.

* Ashurst.

I. THE 'MEETING COMPETITION DEFENCE': SHOULD A SELECTIVE PRICE
REDUCTION DESIGNED TO MEET A COMPETITOR'S PRICES BE ALLOWED?

A. Introduction

In theory, non-predatory 'meeting competition', ie a practice where, under a dominant company –when faced with competition- selectively reduces its prices to adapt them to those of the competitor while still making profits, can raise two different concerns:

- It can in exceptional circumstances be *exclusionary*, particularly where the costs of the dominant company are lower than those of its competitors and the dominant company is undercutting its competitor's prices;
- It can also be potentially discriminatory vis-à-vis those customers who continue to pay the higher price, and therefore be regarded as *exploitative*.[1]

Beyond these two concerns, it is difficult to prohibit a practice which is normally the essence of competition. Even where dominant, a company should not be prohibited to compete on prices and thus meeting competition, such behaviour being on its face a reasonable reaction to lower prices charged by a competitor.

In *Compagnie Maritime Belge*,[2] Advocate General Fennelly expressed the problem of a above cost meeting competition as follows (at paragraph 117 of his opinion):

It is natural to approach this latter problem with reserve. Price competition is the essence of the free and open competition which is the objective of the Community policy to establish on the internal market. It favours more efficient firms and it is for the benefit of consumers both in the short and the long run. Dominant companies not only have the right but should be encouraged to compete on price.

At point 132 of his opinion, the Advocate General therefore concluded that:

normally, non-discriminatory price cuts by a dominant undertaking which do not entail below-cost sales should not be regarded as anti-competitive. In the first place, even if they are only short-lived, they benefit consumers and, secondly, if the dominant undertaking's competitors are equally or more efficient, they should be able to compete on the same terms. Community competition law should thus not offer less efficient undertakings a safe haven against rigorous competition even from dominant undertakings.

---

[1] Strictly speaking, the imposition of excessive prices is not anticompetitive, as it only acts as an incentive to stimulate market entry. It is condemned, however, by the Treaty as being an abuse of monopoly power.
[2] ECJ joined cases C-395/96 P and C-396/96 P *Compagnie Maritime Belge* ECR I-1371.

Unfortunately, EC case-law on 'meeting competition' does not provide so far any clear principles on the legality of the practice, other than that it is not per se abusive.

B. *The EC Court's case-law and Commission practice*

The principle that a dominant company may be allowed to react to price competition on the market was for the first time set out by the ECJ in the *United Brands* case[3] where the Court held

> that the fact that an undertaking is in a dominant position cannot disentitle it from protecting its own commercial interests if they are attacked, and that such an undertaking must be conceded the right to take such reasonable steps as it deems appropriate to protect its said interests (paragraph 189).

The ECJ found that 'the density of competition' could justify price differences between Member States (paragraphs 227 and 228), but as in the case at hand the products were sold ex-Rotterdam and differences were made as to the place where the products were to be resold, it was regarded as illegal. This was because 'the interplay of supply and demand should [...] only be applied to each stage where it is really manifest'. Since *United Brands* did not 'bear the risk of the consumer's market', it could rely on the differences in the competitive situation in the Member States only to 'a limited extent' (paragraph 228).

1. *Akzo*:[4] defensive v offensive meeting competition

In the *Akzo* case, both the Commission and the Court accepted the legality of '*defensive*' meeting competition (ie lowering prices vis-à-vis an existing customer base) as opposed to 'offensive' selective discounts (ie designed to win customers away from competitors).

In its Decision, the Commission thus objected to 'offensive' discounts whereunder *Akzo* granted its competitor's customers selective discounts that its own customers did not benefit from.

In its judgment, the ECJ notes (at paragraph 134) that the Commission 'does not in principle, dispute the right of a dominant undertaking to effect alignments of prices', and (at paragraph 156) that the Decision does not prohibit Akzo 'from making defensive adjustments, even aligning itself on ECJ's prices, in order to keep the customers which were originally [Akzo's] own'.

---

[3] ECJ case 22/76 *United Brands* [1978] ECR 207.
[4] Decision of the Commission of 14 Dec 1985 [1985] OJ L374 at 1; ECJ case C-62/86 *Akzo v Commission* [1991] ECR I-3359.

It should be stressed however that Akzo's meeting competition prices were predatory, and it is unclear therefore whether the prohibition of 'offensive' meeting competition would have applied otherwise.

2. *Hilti:*[5] meeting competition allowed provided it is not 'designed purely to damage the business of, or deter market entry by, its competitors'

In this case, Hilti was accused of having offered its competitors' customers special rates 'going far beyond Hilti's normal discounts in order to entice them away' from the competition (see paragraph 46.3 of the Decision). The Commission found these rates not to be 'a direct defensive reaction to competitors', but to reflect 'Hilti's pre-established policy of attempting to limit their entry into the market' (paragraph 80). The Commission –although accepting that 'an aggressive price rivalry is an essential competitive instrument'- found that 'a selectively discriminatory pricing policy by a dominant firm designed purely to damage the business of, or deter market entry by its competitors, whilst maintaining higher prices for the bulk of its other customers is both exploitative of these other customers and destructive of competition' (paragraph 81).

Nevertheless, the Commission still accepted undertakings by Hilti to apply a non-discriminatory pricing policy subject to various exceptions, including 'meeting a competitive offer'.

The difference between 'meeting competition' as allowed by the Commission and Hilti's previous practice is unclear, although it may reside in its 'defensive' nature as opposed to the 'offensive' nature of the previous practice which was designed '*to* damage the business of a competitor' (see below however on the limited value of this criterion of 'intention').

3. *Napier Brown:*[6] 'Meeting' but not 'beating' competition?

In the *Napier Brown* case, concerning a margin squeeze, the Commission did not object to British Sugar meeting Napier Brown's prices, but to its undercutting them.

Given the impact of a margin squeeze, ie of an upstream supplier also active on the downstream market, not allowing its customer and downstream competitor prices sufficient to survive on the downstream market, it is unclear whether the Commission would equally object to a dominant

---

[5] Decision of the Commission of 22 Dec 1987 [1988] OJ L65 at 19; CFI case T-30/89 *Hilti* [1991] ECR II-1439.
[6] Decision of the Commission of 18 July 1988 [1988] OJ L284 at 41.

company undercutting its rival's prices where it was not at the same time the supplier of the basic product.

4. *BPB Super Schedule A:*[7] the right to meet a competitor's price but 'not systematically'—extension of the discounts to the whole geographical zone

In the *BPB* case, the Commission accepted the right for *BPB* to grant discounts so as to meet competition from importers, who were particularly active in Southern England, on the ground that there is no suggestion that these prices 'were in themselves predatory, nor that they were part of any scheme of systematic alignment' (paragraphs 132–3).

Essentially, the discounts in question were being offered to existing *BPB* customers, and were therefore of a 'defensive' nature. The Commission stresses that the discounts in question were small, that the competitor itself was also applying discriminatory prices, and that the level of *BPB's* offer was 'broadly equivalent to or slightly below' those of the competitor.

The Commission moreover also makes the point that the offer was 'open to all customers albeit in a fairly limited geographical area' (as will be seen, however, in the *Irish Sugar* case geographically targeted border rebates to meet competitor's prices were condemned precisely because they were limited to a narrow geographical area).

5. *Tetra Pak II:*[8] undercutting prices and eliminatory intent

In this case, Tetra Pak was accused of offering large price reductions to win customers away from its competitors. The prices were found to be made at losses and moreover so far below the competitors' price levels that the only intention could be to eliminate competitors: '[C]ontrary to its assertion, Tetra Pak never followed Elopak's prices but on the contrary increased the price difference in response to increases by Elopak' (paragraph 151 of the CFI judgment).

The Commission in its Decision found that:

Tetra Pak shall not practice predatory or discriminatory prices and shall not grant to any customer any form of discounts on its products or more favourable payment terms not justified by an objective consideration. Thus discounts on cartons should be granted solely according to the quantity of each order and orders for different types of cartons may not be aggregated for that purpose.

---

[7] Decision of the Commission of 5 Dec 1988 [1989] OJ L10 at 50.
[8] Decision of the Commission of 24 July 1991 [1992] OJ L 72 at 1; CFI, case T-83/91 *Tetra Pak v Commission* [1994] ECR II-755.

The Decision does however not state clearly whether meeting competition precludes an argument of discriminatory pricing.

6. *Compagnie Maritime Belge*:[9] Meeting competition precluded for 'super-dominant' players?

In this case, the Commission—although recognising dominant companies' right to take 'reasonable steps' to protect their interests when attacked—condemned a dominant conference for matching a competitor's prices, without making losses or even without the competitor itself incurring losses when prices were charged at this level.

It did not matter that the rates were essentially 'defensive' in nature, ie granted to existing customers in response to their expectations, following lower rates granted by the competitor.

It was also accepted that the rates were non-discriminatory. The practice was nevertheless condemned because of its alleged exclusionary character.

This was so although the prices were—undisputedly—both above the dominant player's costs, and also above the new entrant's cost (as recognized by the latter) and moreover, the dominant conference's market share decreased during the relevant period.

The absence of exclusionary effect was found by the courts to be irrelevant as long as there was eliminatory intent. The CFI found that—whilst a dominant undertaking can take *reasonable* steps to defend its commercial interests where these are threatened, 'such behaviour cannot be allowed if its real purpose is to strengthen this dominant position and thereby abuse it' (paragraph 146). The eliminatory intent was established by the language used in internal notes (referring to 'fighting ships', 'getting rid' of the competitor, etc).

Also the ECJ in its judgment relied on two elements to condemn the applicant, ie (i) the eliminatory intent and (ii) the dominant group's market share, said to be around 90 per cent. Where these circumstances are not met, the ECJ did however expressly make the point that it did not exclude that meeting competition could be legitimate.

7. *Irish Sugar*:[10] systematically meeting competition not allowed for super-dominant players?

The *Irish Sugar* case also leaves a confused answer as to the legality of the

---

[9] Decision of the Commission of 23 Dec 1993 [1993] OJ L34 at 20.
[10] Decision of the Commission of 14 May 1997 [1997] OJ n° L258 at 1; CFI, case T-228/97 *Irish Sugar v Commission* [1999] ECR II-2969.

meeting competition defence. In this case, Irish Sugar applied lower prices along the border with Northern Ireland in the context of a 'selective coordinated programme to take account of the most vulnerable area'.[11]

Since the discounts were systematic and greater than in the case of *BPB*, the CFI found them to be abusive, adding that there was discriminatory pricing, that the selective pricing policy was deliberate and that the applicant suspected it was illegal. The fact that the border rebates were defensive did not change the analysis. As the rebates were 'aimed at confronting competition', that amounts 'to acknowledging that the rebates were aimed at preventing such competition from developing'.

The Court also repeatedly refers to the special circumstances of the case throughout its reasoning, apparently alluding to the high market share of *Irish Sugar* (88 per cent).

8. *Digital*:[12] defining conditions under which meeting competition is legitimate

In the *Digital* case, the Commission initially objected in a Statement of Objections to meeting competition by a dominant company. It then however accepted an undertaking by *Digital* under which prices could be selectively reduced 'to meet comparable service offerings of a competitor', as long as

no allowance [...] be offered until Digital has completed an internal review process designed to verify that the proposed Allowance shall be offered in good faith as a proportional response to real or (based upon information from the customer or other reliable sources) reasonably anticipated competitive offerings and will not result in a foreclosure or distortion of competition for the servicing of Digital System in any Member State.

If one may venture a conclusion from the above, it is at most that above-cost meeting competition is not per se illegal in EC law. It can be done in response to a competing offer or to a reasonable anticipation of such offer (based upon information from the customers or other reliable source). It can take place through discounts, but also through enhanced services free of cost (*Digital*). But:

- Meeting competition will be harder to justify for 'superdominant' companies than for others (in *Compagnie Maritime Belge* and *Irish Sugar*: roughly 90 per cent of the market), although why this should be

---

[11] See Dolmans and Pickering *The 1997 Digital Undertaking* [1998] ECLR 108; Commission press release IP/97/868 of 10 Oct 1997.
[12] ibid.

so is unclear. As long as the price charged is profitable for the dominant firm, it should be possible for an equally efficient firm to enter the market and compete effectively with it. Similarly, the Court's insistence in *Irish Sugar* that small firms need special protection is misguided, as the latter are not necessarily less competitive and certainly do not deserve special protection. As to the question whether the competitor is a new entrant or an established competitor, it should be equally irrelevant.

- Meeting competition should preferably be done following an *internal review* verifying that it is *'proportionate'*, made in *'good faith'*, and based upon *'reliable sources'* (*Digital*). This seems to reflect US law requirements under the Robinson-Patman Act that, in order to rely on the meeting competition defence, a company has to show that it:
  — received reports of similar discounts from customers;
  —was threatened with a termination of purchases if the discounts were not met;
  —made efforts to corroborate the reported discounts by seeking documentary evidence, or by appraising its reasonableness in terms of available market data; and
  —had past experience with the customer.[13]

However, it is unclear what rules apply under EC law, since collecting information from customers of competitors on the prices that the latter are charging has also been perceived in some cases as an abuse, ie as part of a strategy to eliminate a competitor.[14] In our view, 'meeting competition' is competition on price and should not be conditional on internal reviews such as indicated here above.

- meeting competition should apparently preferably be 'defensive' and not 'offensive' (*Akzo, Hilti*); a 'defensive' ie 'share-protecting' pricing policy seems to respond better to the Court's acceptance of the right of a dominant company to defend its commercial interests where these are threatened than an 'offensive' ie 'share stealing' policy. How far this distinction promotes competition or on the contrary merely constitutes a substitute for pure market-sharing, is open for discussion. Competition law should in principle not be designed to protect competitors but competition. Moreover, if prices are lowered to all, then they could well lead to a growth in demand resulting in an overall positive effect on welfare. If however the meeting competition offer is purely defensive (ie is limited to existing customers of a dominant firm), then any increase in output can only come from the new entrant if the latter finds new marginal

---

[13] See *Continental Baking* 63 FTC 2071 (1963); see also U Springer 'Meeting competition: Justification of Price discrimination under EC and US Antitrust Law' [1997] 4 ECLR 251.
[14] Commission Decision in *Tetra Pak II*, para 165; ECJ judgment in Akzo, para 104.

customers and, if this does not occur, the only benefit is reduced prices. Thus where selective discounts lead to an increase in the volume of the market ('share creation'), they should clearly be seen as increasing over-all welfare by allowing an output at a volume higher than normally achieved by application of a single price to all transactions.

- Mere 'meeting' competition (matching a competitor's prices) seem generally to be viewed as preferable to 'beating' competition (undercut-ting a competitor's prices) (*Napier Brown*), although the case-law does not exclude occasional undercutting (*BPB*). In *Akzo*, the right to effect 'alignments of prices' was recognized. In *BPB*, prices were 'broadly equivalent to or slightly below' those of a competitor. In *Tetra Pak II*, prices were said to be far below those of the competitors. In *Digital*, discounts had to be 'proportionate'. Again, how far this distinction promotes competition or rather leads to umbrella pricing is subject for discussion. In our case study, if Domco chooses to reduce its prices, it has arguably the possibility to price Compco out of the market, even without making losses (since its own costs are lower than those of Compco, which has to ship its products from France, and has presum-ably in any case rarely the same economies of scale as a dominant company). But if the incumbent is able to price more efficiently than the new entrant, then should he not be allowed to do so? Should competi-tion law be there to protect less efficient players or to force higher prices on the market? True, once Compco is gone, Domco can raise its prices again, at least until a new company comes along. Consumers will bene-fit in the short run, but in the long run, Domco will be able to increase its prices again (unless there are no clear barriers to re-entry). If Domco is allowed only to match (not undercut) Compco's prices, Compco could then possibly stay in the market and both parties would essentially be forced to compete. However, if 'beating competition' is prohibited, they could do so only on the basis of non-price factors which is not exactly the result one would expect from a proper application of competition rules.

On a number of other issues, the case-law is also particularly inconclusive:

- In some cases, the non-systematic nature of the practice of meeting competition has been seen as a justification for the practice (*BPB* or *a contrario Irish Sugar*). At the same time, the practice was however occa-sionally found to be justified precisely because it was systematic, ie open to all operators concerned in a specific geographic area (*BPB*). This latter approach seems to reflect the US approach where the Supreme Court found that 'territorial price differences that are in fact responses to competitive condition' do not infringe Section 2(b) of the

Robinson–Patman Act.[15] Also the FTC held that 'if a seller has a good reason to believe that competing firms are charging lower prices in a particular market, it may respond with comparably lower prices on a territorial basis [that is throughout the market rather than on a customer-by-customer basis]'.[16] It is clear therefore that the fact that the lower price is effectively open to competing buyers within the geographical zone concerned is key to the application of the Robinson–Patman meeting competition defence.[17]

- As to the intentional nature of the behaviour, the case-law repeatedly stresses that abuse is an objective concept[18] and that dominant companies should be encouraged to enter into an 'aggressive price rivalry', but at the same time finds that a mere intention to out-compete new entrants is sufficient to establish the abuse. This is so even if the practice was unsuccessful (*Compagnie Maritime Belge, Hilti, Irish Sugar*). It is more than questionable what relevance mere 'intention' should have when deciding objectively on the merits of a practice. The very purpose of competition rules is to encourage competitive conduct and thus competitive intent and not the opposite.

- As to the fact that the practice leads to a 'reduction of profits' (but not to losses- as it otherwise would be potentially predatory), it was sometimes regarded as evidence of the abusive nature of meeting competition (*Compagnie Maritime Belge*). However, any meeting competition necessarily entails reduced profits (unless it is offensive). The purpose of competition rules is not to force companies to increase profits but rather the reverse.

- As to the importance of the price cut, it should not have any relevance either on the legality of the behaviour, contrary to what the CFI appears to indicate in *Irish Sugar*.

From the above, we believe it can be concluded that most restrictions on meeting competition are simply unjustified. Prohibiting meeting competition is prohibiting price competition. In our view,[19] the purpose of competition rules is not to protect companies from price competition from their competitors. As long as meeting competition is not predatory, we see no reason why competition rules should be used as a shield to protect weaker competitors from lower prices applied even by dominant companies.

---

[15] See US Supreme Court *Falls City Industries v Vanco Beverage* 460 US 428, 448 (1983).

[16] FTC *International Tel of Tel Corp* 104 FTC at 435; emphasis in original.

[17] *FTC v Morton Salt Co*, 334 u5 37, 42 (1948); *Caribe BMW v Bayrische Motoren Werke*, 19 F 3d at 751–2.

[18] See, eg, ECJ case 85/76 *Hoffmann-La Roche v Commission* [1979] ECR 461, at para 91.

[19] See D Slater and D Waelbroeck 'Meeting competition: Why it is not an abuse under Article 82'; Liber Professorum, College of Europe PIE—(Peter Lang Brussels 2004). See also on the subject M Waelbroeck 'Meeting competition: is this a valid defence for a firm in a dominant position?' in *Studi in onore di Francesco Capotorti* (Giuffré 1999) 489.

II. 'FIDELITY' AND 'BUNDLE DISCOUNTS': SHOULD THEY BE PER SE PROHIBITED?

In the same way as for 'meeting competition', rebate policies can justify competition related concerns:

- if they are exclusionary, or
- if they are exploitative (in the sense that only some customers benefit from them but not others).

Although the issue of discrimination has occasionally been raised (see on this issue below under III), it is their exclusionary character which has been the focus of most attention so far.

There are many forms which rebates can take, bundle rebates being only one of them. All forms of rebates, be they quantitative rebates, or loyalty rebates, target rebates, growth rebates, etc have some form of loyalty enhancing effect.

In essence, the question is whether dominant companies should react to competitive pressure by applying mere price reductions on individual products, or whether they may also conceive rebate schemes—as do their competitors-which are meant to act as incentives for customers to buy their own products.

Since discounts fundamentally promote competition and benefit consumers, even if they are designed—as any competitive move—to gain more customers, the question is whether they should still be prohibited even when they have no exclusionary effect.

In the current EC case-law, most recently in *British Airways* and *Michelin*, the point is made that companies can apply rebate schemes but (i) only strictly linear quantitative rebates, and (ii) if they can show that they are cost justified.

However, not only it is doubtful that for any company, cost justification will lead to linear across-the-board price structures, but moreover it is unclear why only linear price cuts can achieve efficiencies. It is in this regard generally recognized that for any company, be it dominant or not, there is a need to recover fixed costs and that the best way to achieve this is often in a non-linear way. Moreover, it is clear that fidelity discounts are not necessarily anticompetitive. According to the OECD report on fidelity discounts for instance, it is stated that

because fidelity discounts have potentially significant pro and anticompetitive effects, and both are highly dependent on specific features of the discounts and the markets they are found in, a case by case approach to fidelity discounts seems warranted.[20]

---

[20] OECD report on loyalty and fidelity discounts and rebates. DAFFE/COMP (2002) 21.

Nevertheless, the EC Courts position on these rebates has been increasingly strict over the years. Most recently, the Court in *Michelin* reversed the rule hitherto applicable that rebates are 'presumed' to be cost justified if they are merely quantitative and linear. Henceforth, the burden of proof is no more on the authority but on the defendant company to prove that its rebate scheme is linear and that it is also reflecting economies of scale. Moreover, the effect or absence of effect on the market of the practice is irrelevant.

This raises the question as to how price should relate to cost and whether other justifications than costs are acceptable.

III. THE 'COST JUSTIFICATION DEFENCE': HOW SHOULD PRICE RELATE TO COST? ARE OTHER JUSTIFICATIONS THAN COSTS ACCEPTABLE?

Beyond the difficulty of (i) defining a proper methodology for measuring costs in each industry,[21] (ii) deciding how the cost savings can be attributed to each customer[22] and (iii) laying down what the appropriate time period for recovery shall be,[23] etc it is clear that the cost justification defence is

---

[21] What this methodology is will depend on the industry. In the telecoms sector, for example, it is explicitly noted that marginal costs are not a particularly helpful reference point due to the high fixed costs and low marginal costs in the industry. Thus, the reference figure is long run incremental costs ('LRIC'—ie the average of costs over a period where *all* costs are variable; see Oftel guidelines 7.6). Where there are common costs, once an initial LRIC calculation is made in relation to each service sharing these costs, these services' LRIC will be grouped and added to the common costs. However, LRIC are not always used. For example, in the *BSkyB* decision the reference point taken by the OFT were the *avoidable* costs of the industry (Decision of the OFT under section 47 relating to Decision CA 98/20/2002, BSkyB of 29 July 2003).

[22] In the *BT UK-SPN call service* case, the cost stack of the downstream operator was comprised of the costs of the (a) regulated services provided by BT (call origination and termination) (b) the non-regulated services (call transit over ex-private network acquired by BT). Costs of the latter were calculated using the LRIC formula (see *BT/BSkyB Broadband Promotion* case). Costs of the former were set at the regulated charges. These included the LRIC of call origination and termination services but also of the common costs associated with these services. The price-cost margins were then calculated and averaged out for all customers. The average margins were positive and although for some individual customers they were negative (ie BT was pricing below cost), the degree of difference was considered small enough to fall within the possible margin of error which is *necessarily found in such cost calculations based on assumptions*.

[23] In the *BT/Bsky Broadband Promotion* decision of 15 May 2003, it was alleged that BT was subsidising its broadband service offered at a discount to Sky subscribers. The OFT looked at discounted cash flow cost and revenue forecast information relevant to the deal as a whole and 'The Director was then able to assess BT's assumptions underpinning this information, including the appropriate time period of cost recovery' (point 15 of the decision). The decision continues stating that 'the director used a long run incremental cost (LRIC) base as the cost floor against which to measure the incremental (per broadband customer) revenues obtained via the deal' (point 16 of the decision). Thus, here, cost-justification is not looked at on an individual transaction basis but rather costs are calculated on an averaged out basis over long time periods (the decision states that several time periods were taken into account ranging from x to y years—not specified in the decision for reasons of confidentiality). The Director

necessarily wider than a mere calculation of differences in costs for each transaction. The fact that cost justification can come in the form of a more efficient recovery in the long run of fixed costs is recognized among others in the above referenced OECD report on fidelity discounts.[24]

As a result of the above, the UK general guidelines seem to accept that as long as prices are above marginal cost in the long run, there should be no concern under competition rules:

In general, undertakings will need to set prices above their incremental costs so that common costs, for example, can be recovered. Price discrimination between different customer groups can be a means of achieving this; it can increase output and lead to customers who might otherwise be priced out of the market being served. In particular, in industries with high fixed or common costs and low marginal costs (…), it may be more efficient to set higher prices to customers with a higher willingness to pay. [25]

As we have seen, this is not necessarily a view shared by EC authorities. In EC law, both selective price cuts and bundle discounts have repeatedly been condemned by the EC courts on account of 'discrimination',[26] ie because firms were charging different price-cost margins to different customers.

In our view, this is an excessively strict approach. In practice, companies— even where they are not dominant—will often charge different prices for reasons entirely unrelated to cost differences but which may nonetheless be legitimate.[27]

---

then looked at whether common costs associated with provision of the broadband services would be recovered over a range of retail services (*'combinatorial cost recovery test'*), which he found to be the case (ie indicating that in calculating the LRIC, common costs are excluded thus lowering the floor). Since cost was below price there was no proof of predation or cross-subsidization.

[24] Which moreover notes—beyond recovery of fixed costs—other cost efficiencies such as reducing supplier's sales variability thus allowing economies in smoothing its production and reducing its inventories.

[25] Guideline 3.8.

[26] See eg for selective price cuts: *Hilti* or *Irish Sugar* and for bundle discounts: ECJ 29 Mar 2001 *Portugal v Commission* case C-163/99, paras 52–53, [2001] ECR I-2613.

[27] D Ridyard 'Exclusionary Pricing and Price Discrimination Abuses under Article 82—an Economic Analysis' [2002] ECLR 286: 'price differences that cannot be fully explained by differences in the costs of supply are an extremely pervasive phenomenon in real world markets […] there is almost no plausible cost function that would make [a volume based] discount scheme "cost related"' in the sense that the differences in price were explained by differences in the costs of supply'. Even if some cost savings did result from serving larger customers, it would require a huge coincidence for such saving to be mirrored exactly by a crude discount structure such as postulated here. Indeed stepped volume rebates of the kind described here involve discrete negative prices at the key threshold points in the discount scale. See also Bishop and Walker *The Economics of Competition Law* 201–2: 'If the Commission wants discounts to be cost justified, the most that economic theory suggests should be meant by this is that incremental prices should be above incremental costs. Provided discount schemes or rebates do not lead to incremental prices below incremental cost of supply, they

It is striking in this regard that discrimination is prohibited for dominant companies whilst simultaneously recognized to form part of normal business life for non-dominant companies. Discrimination being an economic reality for undertakings, the Commission even found that preventing them to discriminate through an industry wide agreement infringes EC Article 81.[28]

The OECD report on fidelity rebates notes in this regard that different cost-price margins will often result from exercise of buyer power (in reaction to a more credible switching threat):

Standard volume rebates tend to be a comparatively blunt instrument for encouraging customers to increase their purchases. Their existence is as much a reflection of large buyer power rather than any seller objective or initiative. Large buyers expect to obtain better terms than smaller buyers, and they can often recognise that the seller's fixed cost recovery problem translates to a negotiating weakness when it comes to large buyers. For suppliers, even those who enjoy significant market power, who have low marginal costs of supply and high fixed costs, any threat of withdrawal of purchases or goodwill by a large buyer carries a significant business risk. Volume discounts are often a reaction to this risk.[29]

Different prices hence mostly reflect different elasticies in demand. The question is therefore whether pricing policies taking into account different elasticies in demand are discriminatory.

In *United Brands*, the ECJ itself found that a difference in elasticity of demand ('density of competition') could justify a different pricing (see above). It is a different treatment but of different situations.

The fact that a firm charges different price–cost margins on different transactions is thus not necessarily a form of discrimination even in EC law.

Since companies need to recover their costs, and in particular fixed costs, they will have to do so over a number of different transactions, each of which occurs in different demand conditions. Customers have each their own demand elasticities, in other words, depending on their particular circumstances and willingness to pay, they will have their own demand curves. For the supplier however, each customer then can contribute positively to fixed cost recovery is attractive, even if that entails in some cases, granting substantial discounts.

---

should be considered cost justified. A key point here is that, for firms with low marginal costs, even big price rebates can be "cost-justified" in the only sense that really matters from the point of view of economic efficiency, since they still tend to exceed the marginal costs of supply.'

[28] See Commission decision of 15 May 1974, and 15 July 1975, *IFTRA*.

[29] OECD report on loyalty and fidelity discounts and rebates. DAFFE/COMP(2002)21 at 7.

In our case study, this can be illustrated as follows as regards the various options open to Domco:

	Units sold	Turnover	Cost	Profit
—Strategy 1: do nothing	1 mio	3 mio £	2 mio £	1 mio £
—Strategy 2: cut price across the board to 1,50£	2 mio	3 mio £	3 mio £	0
—Strategy 3: cut price in South only to 1,50£	2 mio	4,5 mio £	3 mio £	1,5 mio £

A strict definition of 'discrimination' as prohibiting any difference that is not justified by differences in costs would outlaw Strategy 3 although customers in the South benefit of lower prices than even Compco would offer and although Domco can ensure through this strategy a more rapid recovery of fixed costs. Strategy 3 however merely takes into account different elasticities in demand as appears to be legitimate under the *United Brands* case law.

This example shows that higher efficiencies and increased output are often achieved where higher price–cost margins can be charged to customers than to others depending on their elasticity in demand. Since different customers will inevitably have different demand elasticities, any attempt to impose a uniform price will arguably result in a suboptimal output.[30] For this reason, it seems to us that creating a constant price–cost ratio over all transactions should not be attempted.[31]

In its September 1999 guidelines on Assessment of Individual Agreements and Conduct, the OFT rightly stresses that:

Price discrimination raises complex economic issues and is not automatically an abuse. There are many areas of business where it is a usual and legitimate commercial practice. For example, it might be objectively justified in industries where there are large fixed costs and low marginal costs.

Also, the EC Commission accepts in its recent guidelines on the application of Article 81(3) of the Treaty, at paragraph 25, that:

---

[30] See also the principles often described as 'Ramsey pricing' which justifies cross subsidizations from product A to product B, and hence price discriminatory as leading to higher economic welfare

[31] See D Ridyard 'Exclusionary pricing and Price Discrimination abuse under Article 82— an Economic Analysis' [2002] ECLR 286: 'A per se prohibition on price discrimination—ie a requirement that dominant firms should earn equal price-cost mark ups on all their transactions—would be unduly restrictive and almost certainly lead to grossly inefficient outcomes in the context of fixed cost recovery industries.'

In markets with high fixed costs, undertakings must price significantly above their marginal costs of production in order to ensure a competitive return on their investment. The fact that undertakings price above their marginal costs is therefore not in itself a sign that competition in the market is not functioning well.

IV. THE 'EFFICIENCY DEFENCE'—HOW IT APPLIES TO DISCRIMINATORY PRICING?

Although there is no equivalent in Article 82 to Article 81(3), it seems to us excessively strict to exclude the efficiency defence in Article 82 cases. Even in horizontal mergers, the Commission has accepted that the efficiency defence applies.[32]

Indeed, competition on the merits is even one of the key elements of the definition of the abuse given by the Court. It is therefore regrettable that any form of 'efficiency defence' has so far been read out of EC Article 82,[33] except possibly in the Commission's recent Microsoft Decision.[34]

A. As to meeting competition

Price competition is the essence of free competition and the basic purpose of competition rules. Prohibiting meeting competition amounts to prohibiting price competition and hence economic efficiency. Dominant companies should be obliged to compete and not prevented to do so.

Should dominant companies however, where they face competition in certain areas but not all, extend the lower prices to all their customers? Or in other words how far can competition rules be used to force companies to apply prices '*as if*' there was competition also in areas where there is none?

When a dominant firm lowers its prices to meet competition, it is indeed— at least partly—responding to a particular competitive context. To what

[32] See Commission guidelines on the assessment of horizontal mergers under the Council Regulation on the control of concentrations between undertakings, OJ no C31 5 Feb 2004 5 at paras 76–88.

[33] See eg CFI case T-65/89 *British Gypsum* [1993] ECR II-389 at paras 65 et seq where the Court accepts that systems of promotional payments are 'standard practice' which is 'in the interest of both parties', as 'the supplier thereby seeks to secure its sales by ensuring loyalty of demand, whereas the distributor for his part, can rely on security of supply and related commercial facilities'. But the Court found that those considerations 'which apply in a normal competitive market' are not valid in the case of companies in a dominant position. That is because 'where, as in the present case, an economic operator holds a strong position in the market, the conclusion of exclusive supply contracts in respect of a substantial proportion of purchases constitutes an unacceptable obstacle to entry to that market'.

[34] Decision of the Commission of 24 Mar 2004, in case COMP/C-3/37.792 *Microsoft*, not yet published.

extent can such a transaction be considered 'equivalent', in the sense of Article 82(c) to another transaction where, in the absence of such a particular competitive context, the dominant firm does not lower its prices?

If meeting competition was in itself discriminatory, the very concept of meeting competition should be prohibited altogether. We have seen that this is not the case, both in the EC and in the US, where meeting competition is at the very least not per se illegal. Moreover, the ECJ has repeatedly accepted that varying intensity in competition can justify different prices even for a dominant company.[35]

In many meeting competition cases, the charge of discriminatory pricing was even not expressly levelled at dominant firms accused of following this practice (eg *Compagnie Maritime Belge*).

The fact that meeting competition is not necessarily anti-competitive is also supported by economic theory, as indicated above.[36]

B. As to 'bundle discounts'

Any form of discounting ought normally to be encouraged by competition law, and not only if it is the result of cost savings. Problems ought to occur only where the discounts are predatory or have exclusionary effects. In applying EC Article 81, the Commission has repeatedly emphasized the potential efficiencies of exclusivities and exclusivity enhancing rebate schemes.[37] We conclude that it should do the same in the context of Article 82. Indeed, the Court repeatedly accepted that exclusivity contracts and the like (fidelity rebates etc) are a standard practice in most markets and are concluded in the interests of the two parties.[38] Logically, they should therefore normally not either be prohibited as a matter of principle[39] and the per se prohibition of such practices in *Michelin, British Airways*, and others appears therefore in our view unwarranted. In the vertical guidelines, the *Commission* explicitly accepts at paragraph 141 that even dominant companies can justify such practice for reasons of efficiencies.

---

[35] See *United Brands* above and implicitly in CFI case T-229/94 *Deutsche Bahn* [1997] ECR II-1689, para 91

[36] In any event, it seems to us that competition authorities that are wary of foreclosure should think twice: indeed, requiring across the board price reductions in a strict non-discriminatory manner—rather than mere local meeting competition—may often have a much more devastating exclusionary impact in the market than selective price competition may have.

[37] See, eg, vertical guidelines, OJ no C291/1, 13 Oct 2000, paras 116, 153 et seq.

[38] See CFI case T-65/89 *British Gypsum* [1993] ECR-389, para 65.

[39] See, eg, CFI case T-65/98 *Vanden Bergh Foods v Commission* 23 Oct 2003, para 159

V. EFFECTS OF THE PRACTICE: SHOULD THEY BE TAKEN INTO ACCOUNT AND
HOW?

A. Measuring foreclosure and assessing its competitive impact: EC law

In applying EC Article 81, a classic distinction is made between restrictions 'by object' and 'restrictions by effect'. Restrictions 'by object' are hardcore restrictions such as cartels, which are condemned per se without regard to their effects. Exclusivity or single branding clauses are however only viewed as restrictions 'by effect'. Their prohibition requires the demonstration of negative foreclosure effects in the market, as shown, for example, by the *Delimitis* judgment or more recently by the *VandenBergh Foods* case. Moreover, there are 'safe harbours' within which such practices are per se allowed, without there being any need to look at the effect of the practice (see Article 5 of Regulation N°2790/1999).

As regards EC Article 82, the situation is much more confused.

In *Hoffmann-La Roche*, and ever since, the Court defined an abuse as being a competitive behaviour: (i) not based on the merits; (ii) which has the effect to affect negatively the structure of competition on the market, or to use the words of the Court:

the concept of abuse is an objective concept relating to the behaviour of an under-taking in a dominant position which is such as to influence the structure of the market where, as a result of the very presence of the undertaking in question, the degree of competition is weakened and which, through recourse to methods differ-ent from those which condition normal competition in products or services on the basis of the transactions of commercial operators, has the effect of hindering the maintenance of the degree of competition still existing in the market on the growth of that competition.[40]

However, when looking at concrete behaviour, the Court repeatedly dismissed any evidence that the alleged abused had not had the effect of harming the structure of competition on the market as being irrelevant, thus discarding entirely one of the two elements of its own definition of an abuse as contained in *Hoffmann-La Roche*.

This is so both for selective price discounts designed to meet competition, and for bundle discounts. In fact, the very wording of EC Article 82(2)(c) requires the demonstration of an effect on the market (ie that the other parties are placed 'at a competitive disadvantage').

In *Compagnie Maritime Belge*, both the CFI and the ECJ rejected the rele-vance of the applicant's assertion that the practice had no negative effects,

---

[40] See *Hoffmann-La Roche*, para 91, emphasis added.

and that its own market share had fallen in the relevant period to the benefit of the competitors.

In *Michelin* and *British Airways*, similar evidence was similarly rejected by
the CFI.[41] In both cases, the Court prohibited rebates schemes even where
they were to the benefit of consumers (and thus were not exploitative) and
did not harm competitors (and thus were not exclusionary).[42] However,
and paradoxically, in *VandenBergh Foods* which was decided simultaneously by the same court, great pain was taken to show the foreclosure effect
of the practice.[43] The difference in approach is striking particularly as in
Michelin and *British Airways*, market shares were much lower than in
VandenBergh Foods (40 per cent in the first two cases as against 89 per cent
in the third one), and as the exclusivity in *Michelin* and *British Airways* was
less coercive than in *VandenBergh Foods* (mere rebates as against contractual exclusivity).

This tends to show that—at least so far—where foreclosure effects are
shown to exist, they will be used in support of a finding that the practice is
abusive but, for whatever reason, not the opposite.[44]

Moreover, whilst there was a 'safe harbour' for certain types of rebates
(mere quantitative rebates which were 'presumed' to reflect cost savings)
before *Michelin*, henceforth such rebates are only allowed where the defendant can show that they were cost justified.

In other cases, the Commission accepted however—rightly in our view—
that effects was an important criteria. In *Digital*, the Commission for
instance accepted an undertaking including some provision that meeting
competition by a dominant company should be accepted provided it did not
result in any foreclosure or distortion of competition. The same effects-
related approach was taken in *Microsoft*.

Given the scarcity of EC case-law on the subject, it is interesting to briefly
examine how the issue of the effect of the practice is addressed in jurisdictions such as the US and the UK.

---

[41] See CFI case T-203/01 *Michelin v Commission* of 30 Sept 2003, and case T-219/99
British Airways v Commission 17 Dec 2003.
[42] See *RBB Brief* of Feb 2004: 'The special responsibility of dominant firms under Article
82: don't compete on price.'
[43] See CFI case T-65/98 *Vanden Bergh Foods v Commission* 23 Oct 2003, paras 98 et seq.
(concerning Art 81), and para 160 (concerning Art 82 and concluding that the practice had a
foreclosure effect).
[44] See, eg, Decision of the Commission in *Irish Sugar* at para 129.

B. Measuring foreclosure and assessing its competitive impact: US law

The US approach to exclusive dealing contracts or contracts which have the same effect[45] has changed considerably over the years. From the passage of the Clayton Act[46] in 1914 and the stricter control of exclusive dealing agreements, until the 1990s, focus was on foreclosure.[47] Foreclosure was measured in different ways over the years. In early cases under the Clayton Act focus was on the market share of the defendant,[48] then moving to the percentage of the market covered by the exclusive contracts.[49] In the *Standard Oil Co (Cal)* case, the Supreme Court adopted a clear quantitative test finding violation of section 3 of the Clayton Act where 'competition has been foreclosed in a substantial share of the line of commerce affected'.[50]

The ruling in *Tampa Electric*[51] in 1961 continued the focus on foreclosure but indicated that a broader analysis of competition may be necessary. From 1982 and the FTC decision in *Beltone*[52] the emphasis on other factors besides market share progressively increased. *Beltone* applied the rule of reason to exclusivity contracts and judged that the foreclosure effect was outweighed by the pro-competitive effects of the agreements (market penetration, avoiding free-rider problem, increased inter-brand competition, etc).

From more recent case-law, it is clear that conduct will not be prohibited without ample evidence of anticompetitive effects or to put it differently, US courts maintain a heavy presumption against finding anticompetitive effects from vertical restraints. In *Gilbarco*,[53] on appeal, exclusive contracts for petrol distribution covering 38 per cent of the relevant market for sales 'appeared significant' but were legally insignificant because alternative

---

[45] Exclusive dealing analysis applies also where exclusivity is the practical effect of the practice under examination see *Tampa Electric v Nashville Coal Co* 365 US 320 (1961).

[46] Section 3 of the Clayton Act outlaws exclusive dealing arrangements where the effect of the arrangement 'may be to lessen competition substantially or tend to create a monopoly in any line of commerce'.

[47] Prior to the passage of the Clayton Act, the courts had taken an extremely permissive approach under common law (see eg *Chicago, St Louis and New Orleans Railroad Co v Pullman Southern Car Co* 139 US 79 (1891).

[48] *Standard Fashion Co v Magrane-Houston Co* 258 US 346 (1922).

[49] *Standard Oil Co (Cal) v United States* 337 US 293 (1998).

[50] In that case the contracts in question affected 6.7 per cent of the relevant market and similar contracts with Standard Oil's six largest competitors covered 42.4 per cent. Exclusivity has been condemned in cases involving contracts covering very low percentages of the market for example *Brown Shoe Co v FTC* 384 US 316 (1966) involving only one per cent of the retail shoe market.

[51] *Tampa Electric Co v Nashville Coal Co* 365 US 320 (1961).

[52] *Beltone Electrics Corp.* 100 FTC 68 (1982).

[53] *Gilbarco* 127 F 3d at 1162.

means of distribution existed and 'these alternatives eliminate substantially any foreclosure effect Gilbarco's policy may have'. Short duration of the agreements was also emphasized. In response to the plaintiff's claim that Gilbarco had tied up the most efficient distributors, the court judged that 'the antitrust laws were not designed to equip [retail gasoline dispenser competitors] with Gilbarco's legitimate competitive advantage'. It moreover pointed out that the evidence demonstrated 'increasing output, decreasing prices and significantly fluctuating market shares'.[54]

CDC v IDEXX concerned a company having 80 per cent of the market for the manufacture of equipment for blood analysis. IDEXX had tied up 50 per cent of 'distributors' (in fact only middle men who put the manufacturers and vets in contact). However, because the 'distributors' were not strategically important, exclusive arrangements were terminable on short notice and there were low barriers to entry the case was dismissed.

The Eighth Circuit held in *Concord Boat Corp v Brunswick*, that a fidelity rebate scheme (one per cent discount for 60 per cent requirements, two per cent for 70 per cent, and three per cent for 80 per cent of requirements) with a one year reference period did not confer any ability to charge supracompetitive prices. It was not economically difficult for customers to switch and there was evidence of switching. Moreover the agreements were easily terminable and there was an absence of barriers to entry.

The US approach to exclusive dealing contracts is to focus on consumer harm. This harm not only consists of creation, enhancement or protection of market power (to increase prices, reduce output, diminish quality or restrict choice) but also of harm to rivals ability to constrain competition. In the latter case, the percentage of the market 'foreclosed' by an exclusive arrangement 'is rarely determinative and often not even interesting'.[55]

There is no standard test to distinguish wrongful impairment of a competitor's ability to compete from plain hard competition but the following factors need to be considered, ie first is there a prima facie case of exclusionary conduct, and second is there a justification for it.

There is a prima facie case of exclusionary conduct in US law only if the defendant has market power and there is an effect on consumers. In this regard, it is important to distinguish between the treatment of monopolists as against the treatment of companies that merely have market powers.[56] For monopolists, it must effectively be shown that the restraint materially

---

[54] Although the third, dissenting judge came to the opposite conclusion.
[55] Jacobson 'Exclusive Dealing, Forclosure and Consumer Harm' 70 ALJ 311 at 349.
[56] See appeal of the US department of Justice in *United States v Dentsply* <http://www.usdoj.gov/atr/cases/indx102.htm>.

impairs rivals, so that the exclusive arrangement may allow the defendant to increase prices or otherwise cause consumer harm. In the case of non-monopolists, a greater quantum of effect is likely to be required. As regards monopolists, if rivals continue to be able to restrain the defendant's market power, harm has not been shown. Impairment of rival's ability to compete will require proof of at least (a) raising of rival's costs by blocking access to distributors (or some other impairment of ability to compete); (b) that cost increase cannot be avoided (eg by competing for the exclusive contract or developing other means of distribution); (c) that there are barriers to entry by suppliers using different distribution methods; (d) that cost increase is not simply a manifestation of the need to compete more vigorously.

Other factors include the significance of the foreclosed distribution resource to competition (see, eg, *IDEXX*); the duration of contracts (see eg *Gilbarco*); the practical ability to terminate agreements (see, eg, *Appleton*); as well as the question whether there is competition for the contract (If so this is an indication of legality especially where the customer has sought such a tender process; see, eg, *Paddock Publications*).[57]

It is however necessary to show—in addition to a harm on competitors—that the impairment allows the defendant to harm consumers, ie to raise prices, reduce output, quality or choice or harm the consumer in some other way; a fact which does not automatically follow from the finding of impairment.[58] There is no automatic link indeed between exclusion of competitors and anticompetitive effects or harm to consumers, as stressed in the OECD study on fidelity discounts: '[E]xcluding competitors through the use of fidelity discounts need not harm consumers.'

Indeed: 'It is axiomatic in competition policy that harm to competitors does not automatically translate into harm to competition and therefore into a reduction in economic welfare.'

One situation which is identified by the report in which fidelity discounts are anticompetitive are where there are 'asymmetries' in the market—the example given being that of a market where one product is a 'must-stock' but not rival products and this asymmetry is combined with a fidelity discount.

Finally, even if there is a prima facie case of exclusionary conduct, this can still be justified by efficiencies.

Justifications may be accepted where rebates may or will promote compe-

---

[57] *Paddock Publications Inc v Chicago Tribune Co* 103 F 3d 42 (7th Cir 1996).
[58] See, eg, *RJ Reynolds Tobacco Co v Philip Morris Inc*, 199 F Supp 2d 363 (MDNC2002), appeal docketed, N° 02.1595 (4th Cir June 2002). In a very short unpublished opinion, the district court decision was upheld in appeal.

tition.[59] This could be for example avoiding free riding, reliable supply assurance, or volume commitments for scale economies.

The plaintiff may then however rebut the defendant's justification by for example showing that it is untrue or that the same efficiencies can be achieved through substantially less restrictive means.

C. Measuring foreclosure and assessing its competitive impact : UK law

As a preliminary point it should be recalled that section 60 of the Competition Act 1998 requires consistency between the application of EC and domestic competition law, thus EC law is highly relevant for the application of the Competition Act 1998 Chapter II prohibition of abuse of dominant position.

1. Guidelines

The Guidelines on Assessment of Individual Agreements and Conduct contain a number of indications as to how the OFT views exclusivity, rebates and foreclosure. The main provisions of the guidelines are discussed below.

The OFT considers that discounting is generally to be encouraged. Where discounts *reflect* cost savings they do not raise any competition concerns.[60] Discounts will *only* be problematic where they are anti-competitive including where prices are predatory or used to foreclose a market.[61]

According to the OFT: 'Foreclosure can occur where discounts are conditional on customers buying all or a large proportion of their purchases from the dominant undertaking (fidelity discounts) or where they are conditional on the purchase of tied products.'[62]

---

[59] *National Society of Professional Engineers v United States* 435 US 679 (1978).
[60] Guideline 5.1.
[61] The OFT report on switching costs states in that in regard in relation to discounts: 'Another means of creating switching costs is through non-linear rebate schemes [...] non-linear schemes could potentially cause customer lock-in, although they may have other justifications in terms of recovery of fixed costs and increasing marginal sales. Such schemes can make it costly for customers near one of the thresholds for a rebate or discount to switch purchases to another firm and can mean that such incremental sales are sold below marginal cost. It is important to note that only non-linear discounts may cause problems—a linear discount (eg 1p back for £1 spent) is equivalent to a simple price reduction and, as long as it is not predatory, should not cause any foreclosure. However, a non-linear scheme, when practised by a dominant firm, can potentially exclude competitors competing for marginal sales. The analysis of the effects of such schemes is complicated, particularly where the product has high fixed costs.'
[62] Guideline 5.2.

Foreclosure occurs when fidelity rebates

restrict appreciably the ability of new competitors to enter the market or the ability of existing competitors to expand their market share [...] they can discourage a retailer from stocking the products of new manufacturers [they make a retailer] reluctant to stock and promote the products of a rival manufacturer.

Markets are foreclosed when undertakings are unable to enter the market either completely or partially. A market might be partially foreclosed if, for example, undertakings had a much lower market share than they would in the absence of the vertical restraint, or if smaller undertakings are prevented from entering the market. Partial foreclosure often results when the vertical restraint raises rivals' costs, thereby raising entry barriers or forcing existing competitors out of the market. Vertical restraints can foreclose markets at either the manufacturer or retailer level.[63]

In assessing whether there is foreclosure, it must be asked what level of competition exists between retailers, whether manufacturers can avoid the restrictions by using other retailers, setting up their own operation (including assessing barriers to entry at the retail level), whether there are opportunities to renegotiate contracts. The supplier's market power must also be assessed. In this regards the guidelines state that:

a dominant manufacturer foreclosing all potential retail outlets—unless the first two factors above indicate otherwise [in other words unless there are barriers to entry at the retail level and few opportunities to renegotiate contracts]—is likely to be found to be behaving in an abusive way.

The effects of foreclosure are not only forced exit of competing manufacturers or the creation of significant or absolute barriers to entry but also the dampening of competition ie a reduction in inter-brand competition which can lead to higher prices or lower quality products and is caused, for example by the tying of retailers to certain products.

The guidelines list benefits of vertical restraints such as overcoming the free-rider problem and state clearly that such benefits may constitute an objective justification preventing the restraint from being considered as an abuse of dominance.

2. Case-law

The guidelines show that in ascertaining the existence of foreclosure and measuring it, market analysis and actual effects are key.

The insistence on an effects based approach in the UK in the specific case of pricing abuses can be seen from various decisions of the OFT. For exam-

---

[63] Guideline 6.10.

ple in the *BSkyB* decision the OFT stated that in order to decide whether behaviour of a dominant company was abusive the authority 'in line with [the *Michelin* I, *Hoffmann La Roche*, and *Irish Sugar*] judgments' must determine whether the dominant company has '(i) ceased to compete on the merits and (ii) whether such deviation [has] adversely affected competition'.[64]

In that decision, it was concluded that (i) avoidable costs for the bundled items were above the incremental price charged (ii) pricing above that level is consistent with normal competition (iii) there was therefore no foreclosure.[65] For the sake of completeness, however, the OFT did go on to make an economic analysis of whether there had been foreclosure.

In this regard the OFT states that it

accepts that BSkyB's mixed bundling is likely to have some effect on the ability of new entrants to enter the wholesale market. However, to find an abuse of the Chapter II prohibition, it would not be sufficient to show that the wholesale pricing structure affected entry to some degree. For bundled pricing to be abusive, it should exceed that which would occur in conditions of normal competition.[66]

The OFT then refers back to the fact that the pricing policy of *BSkyB* was not '*abnormal*' since the incremental price always exceeded the incremental costs.

The OFT further 'characterised departure from conduct that would prevail in conditions of normal competition as [...] deviation from a strategy that would maximise profits absent benefits deriving from entry deterrence'.[67]

The above reasoning related to the market for premium sports channels. The OFT's reasoning concerning alleged foreclosure on the premium film channels market began by noting that here incremental avoidable costs were most of the time *above* incremental prices for additional film channels. However, although *BSkyB* was unable to show that this pricing strategy was profit maximizing, the OFT considered that it did not have sufficient evidence to show an abuse. Moreover, the OFT considered that there were other barriers to entry to the market—vis-à-vis too few film studios were free to construct a viable premium film channel—and that in those circumstances 'even if BSkyB mixed bundling had the hypothetical ability to fore-

---

[64] Decision of the OFT under s 47 relating to Decision CA98/20/2002, BSkyB of 29 July 2003. See also Case No 1009/1/02 *Aberdeen Journals* [2003] CAT 11 para 350.
[65] This also indicates that the burden of proof falls squarely on the authority alleging the abuse.
[66] Decision of the OFT under s 47 relating to Decision CA98/20/2002, *BSkyB* of 29 July 2003 at point 192.
[67] Decision of the OFT under s 47 relating to Decision CA98/20/2002, *BSkyB* of 29 July 2003 at point 194.

close, the particular circumstances of the upstream market means that the bundling did not produce this effect during the period investigated'.[68]

Interestingly the OFT also notes that the fact that BSkyB has been offering film channels in mixed bundles since 1991 is consistent with its claim that mixed bundling is an efficient distribution method rather than a method of deterring entry.

Also as regards the margin squeeze, the OFT states that 'it is possible for BSkyB to offer different profit margins on different packages without necessarily infringing the Chapter II prohibition'.

In the *BT/BSkyB Broadband Promotion* decision, the OFT looked inter alia at foreclosure caused by allegedly discriminatory low prices charged for BT broadband subscription to customers who also had a BT telephone line and a BSkyB subscription. The Director looked at the actual number of potential triple-pay customers (ie the ones who were eligible for the BT promotion and may have seen the applicant's triple-pay service as a substitute) who had taken BT up on its offer. The decision concludes that 'the Director does not consider that a material number of potential customers have been foreclosed from cable or other operators, or services providers as a result of this promotion'. It should be noted that the decision does, just before coming to this conclusion, note the rapid expansion of the market (one million customers growing at 25,000 per week).

Also in the *BT UK-SPN call services* case, it was decided there was no adverse effect on competition as a result of the margin squeeze concerned because in the quarter preceding the decision the volume of calls affected by the alleged violations constituted only one per cent of the calls provided by competing service providers. On biggest estimates this figure could only rise to eight per cent. There was also a comparison between the prices of the UK-SPT services and competitors services. Such figures needed to be handled carefully as low prices by the incumbent could be constraining the pricing policies of competitors. 'The relatively low volumes realised by BT's UK-SPN service, however, does not provide support for the plausibility of this interpretation'.[69]

In the *BSkyB* decision, the applicants had suggested that any rebate or discount offered by a dominant firm has a tendency to restrict a buyer's choice as to his sources of supply and is therefore prima facie an abuse

---

[68] In other decisions, the OFT also found pricing at a level that could not be matched by competitors before going on to see if there were any effects on competition see eg Decision of 11 July 2003, *BT Broadband*.

[69] At point 48.

requiring objective justification.[70] This approach was rejected by the OFT[71] (to be compared with the recent view of the CFI in *Michelin*).

VII. CONCLUSION

The application of EC Article 82 to pricing practices is a complex area. Dominant companies have a special responsibility not to affect negatively a structure of competition which is already weakened. However, this ought not to prevent them to compete on prices or to adopt other normal behaviour as to be found in virtually all competitive markets.

This is so *a fortiori* since any rebate scheme can have pro- and anti-competitive effects, and the former will normally outweigh the latter. Also discrimination can be positive to overall welfare or bad and should therefore normally not be prohibited unless it causes demonstrable harm to competition. It is the effect of the practice that determines its legality, as rightly recognised by the ECJ in the very definition of the abuse given in *Hoffmann-La Roche*.

The rejection by the EC Courts of the effect criterion in *Michelin, British Airways, Compagnie Maritime Belge*, etc, has the unsatisfactory result that any pricing behaviour of a dominant company is per se bad, unless the price is applicable—without rebate schemes—in a non-discriminatory manner across the board. This conclusion is excessive, leads to the promotion of inefficiencies and does not take economic realities into account.

It would appear that dominant companies –as all other companies- are entitled to fairer and clearer rules, a 'safe harbour' within which they may operate without risk of being sanctioned.

Overall, it seems that a distinction should and could be made—as it is done already for Article 81—between behaviour that is per se allowed, even for dominant companies (eg meeting competition, linear quantitative rebates) and other behaviour that ought only to be prohibited if it is shown to have a negative effect on the market (some other forms of rebates).

---

[70] Decision of the OFT under section 47 relating to Decision CA98/20/2002, *BSkyB* of 29 July 2003, at point 170.
[71] ibid point 178–81.

CHAPTER 12

Roundtable with the Authorities

[JOHN VICKERS]

This session is called Roundtable with the Authorities. We have here some authorities of the very highest distinction. We have Hew Pate from the Department of Justice in the US and Philip Lowe from Brussels, so we've got Washington and Brussels here and representatives from three Member States which, in terms of their longevity as Member States, range from the old, the medium, and the extremely new. So we have Fred Jenny from the *Conseil de la Concurrence* in France, John Fingleton, Chair of the Irish Authority, and Andrej Plahutnik from Slovenia. This session will in a way be led by our question master, Mark Clough QC of Ashursts. Since we have a panel and question master I have not been entirely clear what my role is. I now know! I think it is to be a kind of hybrid of—for those of you who watch British television—David Dimbleby, Chris Tarrant, and Desmond Lynam, but that will unfold as the session progresses. The agenda has been developed from a very profound lunch which Mark had with Dr Philip Marsden. There are six broad topics and Mark will lead the questioning on those in turn. The topics are first of all questions about trans-Atlantic convergence/divergence: very fitting given the overall theme of the conference. Second, the new ECMR. How does SIEC relate to SLC and questions of that kind. Third, the role of economics. Fourth, the European Competition Network, now 10 days old in some sense. How is all that going to work? How will it operate with the courts? Fifth, criminalization, and finally the sixth topic asks more globally, how does the work of the competition authorities fit with developments at ICN, OECD, WTO? The format will be Mark asking questions under those six headings, not every question to each of the panellists of course but those people will come in. I want to keep at least 20 minutes at the end for plenary questions but for the first 50 minutes or so it will be Mark and the panel, then we will open it up to everybody. So with that, I hand over to you.

[MARK CLOUGH QC]

Thank you very much Mr Chairman. It's a great honour for me to address our notable regulators, as we like to call them, who are in front of you today. I'm going to ask questions, as John has kindly invited me to. They will be fairly straightforward questions. They are questions that the protagonists have not heard before, although they have heard about the general areas that we at the British Institute believe the audience here would like to hear about and indeed we hope they are topical. So the first question is this and I would like to put it to Hew Pate if I may. Are US businesses harmed by the state of divergence between the competition regimes across the Atlantic?

[HEWITT PATE, *US Department of Justice, Antitrust Division*]

Well your question implies that you are wondering whether US firms are harmed in some way because they are US firms and if that's the implication, I think the answer to that is no. The question is, what are some of the fundamental underpinnings of the attitude the authorities are going to take to firms holding a dominant position or having a monopoly? That's come out in the context of the *Microsoft* case, which is very important. There are plenty of things to say about that and I'll say some of them, but, in terms of convergence and divergence there's a very broad range of things that we enjoy looking at within our very close working relationship, whether it be the technology transfer block exemption, merger analysis, cooperation on particular mergers to make sure that parties don't run afoul with unnecessary procedural divergence, so to a great extent I think that's the picture.

To the extent that you would like to provoke a little *Microsoft* discussion, I am more than happy to oblige and again I think what it comes down to is simply a difference of view as to what the right approach is to unilateral firm conduct. The majority view here appears to be that once a firm is in dominant status there should be gentlemanly competition, to take the phrase of an EC official who recently visited us, versus—to take Bert Foer's phrase which Judge Posner used in a recent panel in the US—a more Darwinian approach. With respect to the *Microsoft* decision itself, we placed great emphasis on going after affirmative misconduct by Microsoft to prevent that in the middleware space not just in the web browser that was the topic of the case.

[JOHN VICKERS]

Philip, do you want to come in on this?

[PHILIP LOWE]

Why not! You can point to the real concepts which seem to be divergent, the procedures which are divergent like criminalization which we will come back to, or indeed to some of the interpretations of what we would regard as abuse of market power, but people seem to forget that historically US law

influenced German law and influenced EU law. We are talking about fundamental concepts which are the same, and often what we are differing on is
not law as such but the interpretation of how markets work. Take, for
example, the expectancy as to whether competition will naturally come to
contest the situation of a monopolist or whether some regulatory intervention is necessary at all, and, as I've said many times, the general US view is
optimistic on that point. The EU view is somewhat conservative and
cautionary, in the sense that it will say, well are there any potential competitors or actually competitors on the horizon anywhere? If not, no one is
going to look out for the poor consumer except regulatory intervention
providing it is successful and effective of course.

Now on the *Microsoft* case, this is a typical example where there would be
divergence between us but there are several elements of convergence in our
Microsoft decision. First of all, we would regard the interoperability part of
our decision as an extension of the same concepts applied by the DOJ in the
area of server to servers away from PC to servers and we don't see a fundamental difference in the type of information, for example, which we
requested from Microsoft than was requested with respect to interfaces
between PC and the server. Now on the tying question, of course in the
States the US decree was not about tying; it was essentially about monopoly maintenance. In fact if I remember rightly the judge, Judge Kollar-
Kotelly, actually said that if there had been a tying case, then an unbundling
remedy might be appropriate. I am paraphrasing here, but I think that was,
as they say in English, the gist of what she said. Yes we do have a view
about foreclosure through tying and we looked carefully at the exceptional
situations which would be, can be defined, in order to say, well without
action against that kind of tying there will be ultimately elimination of
competition for certain products and that's the sense of our decision. I
won't go any further than that. There is a divergence there. Are we chilling
innovation through this or not? Well we would argue that if we don't act
then the monopolist will chill innovation and there is an expression I've
seen recently, which I believe is a quotation from someone in the US
Supreme Court, about the monopolist aggressively competing on the merits.
Well it's very difficult to imagine how a monopolist can compete with
anyone on the merits if there is no one to compete with but I'm exaggerating a little just to make it more interesting.

[MARK CLOUGH QC]

To widen this question a little, I thought in the supplementary category I
might see if this wonderfully peaceful situation that we've just had
described to us might actually have some fundamental flaws of a legal

nature such as the difference, as I think you touched on Philip, between Article 82 and abuse of market power and the Sherman Act approach to monopoly and whether in fact we can never foresee a marriage of the substantive law in the areas of abusive pricing, the predatory pricing aspect of that, the compulsory licensing in the context of *IMS* and *Magill* and the case you have been talking about this afternoon, and that sort of general area that we hear repeatedly at our annual conferences here. The American approach and the EC approach never seem to meet and I wonder if they ever can?

[JOHN VICKERS]

John, you've a westerly position. Any thoughts?

[DR JOHN FINGLETON]

Yes, our deputy Prime Minister famously asked the question as to whether Ireland was closer to Boston or Berlin and got himself into endless trouble everywhere else in Europe for that question. I think it is interesting to note that even within the United States there's huge divergence in the outcomes of court cases. If you take for example the ninth circuit, the California circuit I think, and the seventh circuit, the DC circuit, you get very differing outcomes in antitrust cases, so I'm not sure that the level of difference between the EU and the US on these 'difficult to reason' cases is any more different than the differences that exist either within the EU or within the US. I think that on these very difficult to reason cases two reasonably well-informed people can reach opposite conclusions. I also think that that probably answers Mark's second question which is that even in the US where the statute is the same, different circuits interpret it differently. There are lots of really good examples why the statute may not make a difference provided it's drawn widely enough to include everything. I think competition authorities historically have tended to be very good about narrowing what they go after so as to go after the things that are very harmful, and usually we don't have the resources to go after everything, which is also a good discipline for that.

[JOHN VICKERS]

The Irish Deputy Prime Minister at European Competition Day last week, a week or two ago, also said that monopolies are like children. Other people's aren't very nice, but oh if you get one of your own!

[Mark Clough QC]

Perhaps I can move on to the second question, which is not totally divorced from the first one, and that is a substantive question about merger control. Very simply, what is the difference between the SLC test and the SIEC test or perhaps more precisely the substantial lessening of competition and the significant impediment to effective competition?

[John Vickers]

Fred, I know you've thought about these merger test questions quite a bit. Would you like to comment?

[Frédéric Jenny]

I've thought about the difference between SLC and dominance quite a bit, but this question is quite difficult. I remember when the significant impediment to effective competition came out there were several press releases from several countries in Europe saying: 'Finally our test has been adopted', even though they had different tests. The French was one of the countries claiming that its test had been adopted. I don't personally think, at least in the case of France, that there is a big difference between, in the substantial lessening of competition and the significant impediment to effective competition tests. For all practical purposes, at least in the French context, the two tests are the same. I see that Philip is raising his hand and wants to immediately argue that it is different.

[Philip Lowe]

I'd just like to say that we regard, at last, achievement of this new test as consolidating the consensus on what the target of merger control is: the anticompetitive effects of mergers, which are not limited, at least in theory if not in practice, to cases where you have a creation and strengthening of dominant position, and in particular we were concerned about situations where, even though none of the firms were dominant or became dominant, competition could be significantly impeded. Therefore we needed to clarify the power which should exist for the Commission and indeed whoever else applies our Merger Regulation one day perhaps to go after situations of this kind. Now fortunately, I think, the Court of Justice's decisions and the Court of First Instance's decisions complement this approach because they have always in their decisions adopted a fairly result-oriented approach to the original two-limbed aspect of the dominance test, those limbs being the creation of strength from a dominant position, which significantly impedes effective competition in a single market, and that's why we chose the words which we did in the final compromise in the Council. It seems to us that this is a very solid basis on which we can build consensus and convergence globally about what are the economic targets of merger control, what are the situations of harm to competition which we want to look at, but we're basing it on the European side of case law vis-à-vis dominance which is why we have in particular creation and strengthening of a dominant position in the test. But frankly from the point of view of international convergence this is a good thing. It is a good thing for US firms and it is a good thing for European firms. We've actually got a test upon which we can build the same sort of modelling of economics which we need to find out what will or can or is very likely to be the result for competition, whichever test the Court of First Instance has imposed upon us.

[JOHN VICKERS]

Could I ask, Andrej, stepping back from the SLC versus SIEC specific question, what are your reflections on the debate that we've had in the last couple of years when you've been an imminent member? Your country has now, of course, from 1 May 2004 been a member and the new Merger Regulation is in force. I ask that also partly because the economic structural conditions in the accession countries is different, inheritance is somewhat different in the rest of Europe, and does that fact influence your perspective on these debates too?

[ANDREJ PLAHUTNIK]

First of all I would like to say that perhaps from the beginning of this feeling process back in 1998, what I was missing really in the accession countries or the new Member States was the creation of the Commission policy. We were talking mostly about the Commission Regulation and we were talking about following the ideas of Brussels, so we sometimes wanted to be diligent pupils and we never, or hardly ever, thought about what would be good. We always thought about what would Brussels say and that is the original mistake and the mistake goes on unfortunately. Why? I believe that after the signing of the accession agreement back in Athens last year we are still in the same position. I believe that it is in the interest of the old Member States, if I may say so, that the new Member States are active in negotiations, in providing new ideas, in order to get to the better outcome at the end of the day. I wouldn't like to say that the outcomes in the past were not good, not at all, but that is my opinion. The fact was that sometimes we were not thinking about what we really needed at the end of the day and if we could have been able to think about that then really we would see, I am sure at least for Slovenia and I believe also for the other new Member States, that our goals would just simply coincide with the requirements of the existing Member States, not of the Commission. I think that it was for a lot of time that we proceeded from the wrong perspective. We always tried to think about what the Commission would say. The Commission is just the reflection of the conclusions of the 15 and now 25 Member States.

[JOHN VICKERS]

And so do you like it when some of the children in the class are rowdy and argumentative like John is sometimes? Do you like these debates?

[ANDREJ PLAHUTNIK]

Yes of course. It is necessary; it's competition between the countries and that I think is very innovative.

[FRÉDÉRIC JENNY]

I would like to come back to the question concerning the difference between the SLC test and the SIEC test. I organized a roundtable among competition authorities at OECD on the SLC and the dominance test. At the time all the countries which had the dominance test, including the EU, argued that it would make absolutely no difference if they moved to another test because when examining mergers they were in fact looking for possibilities of reduction in competition due to the transaction. If this is true I've got a difficult time understanding why it is good for convergence if we move away from the dominance test to another test. However, what was also interesting at OECD was that all the countries which didn't have a dominance test said, 'oh yes having a dominance test does make a difference', and they argued that countries which have a dominance test tend to define the market in a different (and narrower) way etc. So I think there are two levels. On one level clearly the new wording is a bit closer to what an economist would like to write. Not quite there, but getting close. Whether it has a real meaning or not is difficult to assess. But as I said I am caught in between an excellent EU contribution to this roundtable saying it's not going to change anything because the EU have got it all figured out and the dominance test can accommodate the collective dominance issue, and the feeling expressed by a number of competition authorities that the change in the European test for mergers will make a difference.

[PHILIP LOWE]

I think it has changed because we are actually concentrating on an analysis of the potential effects of the merger whereas the tendency from time to time at least with dominance was to regard it as a per se test which you had to prove and then all you had to do was to negotiate remedies or ban it.

[FRÉDÉRIC JENNY]

I suspect that you are right.

[PHILIP LOWE]

So although I am very happy with people saying that they may or may not believe in a gap, I think that this is a real convergence in practice and has actually changed, and will actually change the way in which we apply the law. You can see that in the way we've written the guidelines, which have been influenced not just by US and other practices but national practice in the EU, which is very important.

[MARK CLOUGH QC]

Mr Chairman, perhaps we'll put that to the proof with the next question.

[JOHN VICKERS]

I think perhaps Hew's perspective on this might be interesting and then we'll go forward.

[HEWITT PATE]

Even though I have just spent the last five minutes writing down more things to say about Article 82, on this one I think I'll just agree with Philip. I think it was argued that there was not necessarily a need for a change: we are very comfortable in a system where fundamental change can occur through common law constructions and enforcers' attitudes toward a text that hasn't changed for a long time. Moving away from construction, if changing from the dominant position causing lessening of competition test to the SIEC test has removed an opportunity for divergence, then I suppose that's a good thing because it certainly does seem to me to clarify the ability of the Commission to go after merger cases based on unilateral effects, which is something we are very familiar with. While we've spent a good deal of time in the last couple of years reinvigorating coordinated effects in the United States, as you can tell from our current docket, unilateral effects are very important throughout theories of enforcement as well, so we've spent a good deal of time talking about the test and how it is likely to be applied. Perhaps it is seen as a virtue over here not to have adopted a test that has the same wording as the American test. Nonetheless, I agree with Philip that it seems to me to cement a continuing convergence on the merger front if you like to look at it that way.

[MARK CLOUGH QC]

Just before I move on, perhaps I can provoke the Chairman into commenting later by saying that I think we should recognize France's role in this solution of the converged test in that my understanding is that the French merger system has dominance and SLC available, if you like, on demand.

Moving on to a related question, we heard from Philip about the effects and we are all delighted to see European competition law moving into the direction of economics. What about economics? How can you have a merger decision based on economic findings if there is no independent economist responsible for that decision?

[PHILIP LOWE]

That's an interesting question. If there was such an independent animal, I would be very careful to control him via due process of law and particularly on his own. If there was a panel of them maybe it might be less dangerous, but as you know we are operating on the basis of law, first of all. We work out it from the law and the law sets up proof to be brought. It empowers and obliges authorities to investigate cases, to build up a view as to what they believe would happen with or without intervention from the public authorities and in that process, yes economic analysis is necessary. Economic analysis on its own however would be deficient because we have to look, as I say, at the burden of proof to be brought vis-à-vis the parties. We have to take due account of the interests of the parties and we have to therefore come to a conclusion which is based on the law, but nevertheless exploits what economic evidence can be made available, and economic evidence starts off with alternative models and then with data. Frequently the data is not available even though the models are available, so I don't think we are living in a perfect world where if you've got the right number of economists you automatically get the right answer. What you need to be able to do is to test the alternative theories of competitive harm using what tools are available through economics and econometrics. There are various arguments as to how many economists we have on our staff. No one asks the same question of John and Hew and elsewhere, but some people say we have got too few. We were discussing this earlier today; there are 169 out of the 320 professional administrators in DG Competition who have got an economics qualification. Now of course eliminate half of those as irrelevant, they are just macro-economists, people who wouldn't understand how firms behave, but I think the figure is more or less something like 80 out of the total, who can apply micro-economics and who are invaluable on our case teams. In fact, as some of the colleagues in the room know, some of the cases we lost before the Court of First Instance were actually majority case teams composed of economists, so be careful before one generalizes about the two disciplines.

[MARK CLOUGH QC]

Perhaps I can just elaborate that question before we move on to some of the other views. I understand that in the US there is an independent court-going economist who represents the FTC in court in effect to defend the economic decision in parts of the merger cases that are being brought. In that context, that economist is not fully internal. Now I may be exaggerating that a tiny bit and it may be a misunderstanding on my part, but it's in that context that this question is directed. What with the quality of the economists in DG Competition, in the OFT here, or indeed in the Irish competition authorities, Slovenian, French, for that matter, does it make a difference if you have somebody who is truly independent in their assessment before the administrative decision is made, because they have to give expert evidence in court to defend that?

[HEWITT PATE]

Well, we do and it makes a great deal of difference to me and I wouldn't want to try any of this without having the independent voice of the economists. It's a little bit different from what I think you have in mind. We don't have independent court-going economists who decide to bring things to court independent of the agencies' legal structure, but we've just hired a few—Greg Werden could tell me the exact number—and we're well above 50 PhD economists, probably heading towards 60 right now. Obviously there are others with some degrees who work in the division with economics qualifications of other sorts, they work with our case teams but are not a part of them nor do they report through them. The Deputy Assistant Attorney General for Economics is fond of pointing out he's not an attorney and he's not a general and he's not sure if he assists anybody, but he does, and he is a deputy. He is, and my legal case teams would confirm this vehemently, very independent of the legal analysis that goes on and I think that really adds a lot of strength to what we do. Interestingly, although from time to time our economists testify in court in our cases, it is more often the case that we engage outside economists. Perversely, there is a perception on the part of American judges in some cases that an economist who does not work for the agency is somehow more likely to give independent conclusions unshaped by the client's position than would be the case for the internal economist. I know that the reverse of that is true just as all of you who engage expert witnesses who consult and testify for a living know this, but that's the way we tend to do it. We've had very good success when our economists do testify but they are not court-going economists in the way I think you might have had in mind.

[JOHN VICKERS]

Can I ask, John, what is your position on this issue and what would it be if you were not an economist?

[DR JOHN FINGLETON]

In our agency, we've about 30 lawyers and economists. About two-thirds are economists and about one-third are lawyers. I think it is approximately 10 lawyers and 20 economists. When we bring a case to court we always go to an external expert. There was one case recently where I did the expert work. That was the first criminal case and we did that for a very specific policy reason as we were trying to talk economics out of our criminal cases, so I gave the evidence in order to make that point. But normally we go to an external expert and in several cases the external expert, and the advice that person has given, has resulted in us deciding not to bring a prosecution, because we think that the cases aren't strong enough and so it is a useful test of our own analysis.

[PHILIP LOWE]

Just a small comment. I don't want to repeat what Lars-Hendrik Röller already said to this excellent audience, but he has an independent role according to his mandate and I definitely think it influences the way in which we listen to him inside the department because his opinion, if different from our own, will go straight up to the College of Commissioners. The fact that whichever Chief Economist you have has almost certainly been working for all the parties you have been dealing with before, sometimes makes it more difficult to put him in court because there is now quite a constituency of economic consultants and faculties who have been hired by people who have got cases with us. I am looking forward to the day when my Chief Economist is in court.

[MARK CLOUGH QC]

May I just quickly add to Philip's consideration and perhaps Professsor Jenny's? One of the constant discussions that goes on in the context of the British Institute and indeed this morning was the session on vertical mergers and vertical and horizontal mergers. I understand that in the US there is a period of time during which the merger will be looked at which might be described as short term, two years, whereas in the European merger assessment it's likely to be a little looser than that and go on for further time. Now it's in that context that having an independent economist who can defend a case in court, whether it is in the Irish Court or in the US, may be something worth further consideration in Europe. I just throw that up. There does seem to be a difference in the substantive result in the decision-making based on the procedural role of the economist. True or false?

[FRÉDÉRIC JENNY]

In France we have a different process. We don't go to court for mergers. The *Conseil* gives an opinion and then the Minister makes a decision, so it is a slightly different process. We were talking about 'the economist' as if there was an independent economist who knew everything and therefore could tell the court unambiguously what the truth is. It may not be so. I remember that we once had an OECD roundtable with judges at OECD and the issue was how does one get economic expertise into the courts, and there was an Australian judge who commented on how difficult it is for them to listen to an economist because amongst other things they don't even know what question to ask the economist; they don't know economics. What they do is to have economists on both sides cross-examine each other and they see what's left at the end and there usually is not much because the economists know what the weaknesses of their fellow economists' reasoning are.

[JOHN VICKERS]

Your question about the time horizons. I'm not so sure that's a big issue or one that this economics point plays into so much. I think we need to be careful what is meant by 'independent economist'. All agencies should get high quality independent economic advice in some sense. It's partly an organizational question of whether that needs to come from a separate bit of the organization from that which does the case work and there are pros and cons of doing that. I think one of the dangers of that way of thinking is that those who are not in the economics bit think they don't have to do any economics thinking and that could be disastrous. I think one thing that you have in the US much more strongly than here is this 'law and economics all hyphenated tradition' where antitrust lawyers, and a growing number on this side of the Atlantic, are very as knowledgeable, but intuitively knowledgeable about the economic issues. So I think bedding out the economics, including among them non-economists, is a very important part of it rather than having this hermetically sealed pure group who just come in perhaps at the end. Nobody's going that way, but I think we need to think about the other side of it too.

[Mark Clough QC]

Thank you. Perhaps I should move on to a different area now: modernization, decentralization, the first of many revolutions. And the question is this. How is the ECN going to maintain uniform application of competition law in the EU? Are the provisions of the new Regulation 1/2003 on cooperation between the Commission, the national authorities and the courts sufficient?

[John Vickers]

Can we ask first Philip and then Andrej, who could give a new Member State's perspective?

[Philip Lowe]

I don't want to give the impression to Andrej that we are speaking again from the Vatican, but it seems to me this system which is set up by Regulation 1/2003 of parallel competence puts an end to the type of hierarchy which you are imagining was the case when we were negotiating with you. When we are negotiating with new Member States, by the way, everyone says that the best instrument we should use as negotiators is to have 'wing mirrors' so we can see the expressions on the faces of 15 national experts behind us, and it is absolutely certain that the European Union as a whole has been one of the instruments by which competition law and institutions to enforce it have been thrust upon many of our neighbours including those who have joined the European Union, but also many members of the ICN. In fact we wouldn't see so many had we had all those negotiations with third countries on that point.

Now on the issue of uniformity and coherence; yes there is uniformity and coherence without abandoning a notification system with parallel application of the law, but there must be a certain number of measures taken at the beginning and during the process by the Commission and by the courts to ensure uniformity. The first thing is that we've tried to launch a package of

Notices which give guidance both to authorities and to courts on how we have so far as a Commission interpreted the law. Those Notices are binding on us. They are not binding on the national authorities and the national courts but they are certainly binding on us as an indication as to how we think the law should be applied and we've also made clear in them what procedures should be followed. Secondly, we have established—it certainly works electronically, but we have to see how the process can be given life on the basis of individual cases—an electronic system of exchange of information which is the basis upon which we can start work to ensure coherence. Thirdly the Regulation says that we need to intervene where we believe that a case which is being dealt with by one authority which may not be the best place to handle it and so maybe we or another authority should be handling it; this is the first stage at which we can intervene to ensure that the way a case is investigated is going to lead to the right result. Then there is the intervention of almost last resort where 30 days before a decision is about to be taken at national level, the Commission can also intervene again. Now in between that there are all sorts of other issues like *amicus curiae* briefs, guidance asked for by either courts or by parties which places quite a lot of burden on us to provide a service to our colleagues in the national authorities and national courts. However, it's quite possible that Andrej or his courts will disagree with the Commission about their interpretation of Article 81(3) and certainly the Commission's job isn't to try to deliberately to intervene in a court process in a way which tries to establish primacy of its view. If a court finally disagrees with us then there are courts in Luxembourg which can be seized in order to provide the right answer if we've got it wrong.

Now does that mean there will be uniformity overnight? No, but I do think that over time with 26 competition authorities applying the same law we will get much better enforcement, we will get much more informed decisions closer to realities on the ground and we'll get probably better notices finally from the Commission, informed by the work and experience and exchange we have with all the authorities operating in parallel applying the same law.

[ANDREJ PLAHUTNIK]

I would say that if effective competition is a pre-condition for the internal market then we have to apply the same rules or apply the rules under the same standards. That is why I found the so-called reform of European policy in the field of antitrust very useful. Not only because we shall be forced really to apply the law as we would have to do it but also it is a kind of discipline for the national courts. The problem as I see it is not within the institutions but within the courts. At least in my country, and I believe in the majority of the new Member States and some existing Member States, the courts are too legalistic. I would be very happy if the courts would enter into the economic substance. Usually it all ends up with the formal questions and the courts try to find out how to return the case back to the authority for so-called formal mistakes. It might happen sometimes that there could be feelings of a lack of original independent or regional competence but it's the agreement and you take the pros and cons of the agreement as a whole, so I'm very fond of the new ECN. I believe that the first results shall be seen somewhere by the end of the year if not before. The most important thing is that during the working group the people that cooperated found out that they can cooperate also in this so-called probation period. That's my personal impression.

[JOHN VICKERS]

Now we had a huge amount of preparation before it, but we are literally 10 days into the new system. Hew, you've had in your country over a century of some similar issues within the federal system. I wonder what your perspective is on the challenges that we face and what are the main lessons that we can learn from the US experience?

[HEWITT PATE]

Well, 10 days into it and you are miles ahead of us, because we really don't have a system where we've done what I think Philip and his colleagues have done which is, at the outset of the cooperative relationship, tried to figure out what to do with these cases that are Community-wide, sometimes even of global interest. So I think it is very commendable and something that we can draw lessons from to think about in what instances does the central authority need to step in? Maybe it doesn't need to be the Vatican, but a Quaker meeting isn't necessarily a great model for antitrust either, where we have authorities springing up to give whatever answer they are moved to give. If you are on the extreme edge of US antitrust law and think the more intervention the better, then perhaps you like that sort of thing in the sense that Tim Muris has discussed—a race to the bottom approach—where, if you can simply find a regulator with respect to a nationwide or global product who is willing to impose measures, then that conduct is changed nationwide. If you have any sensitivity to the fact that sometimes too much medicine is a bad thing and can actually hurt competition and consumers, you need to be very hesitant about that model, so I think in this respect it's good to really try to think through these issues. We are not there. During the *Microsoft* case we were asked by Microsoft to file a brief. The court ended up asking us to file a brief on Microsoft's assertion that because of the tremendous resources we had put into the case, the States should not be able to come in under section 16 of the Clayton Act to take a different approach. While that certainly would have made life a lot easier from a policy point of view, that is not the law in the United States and we informed the court of that. But it's a discussion that I think you are to be commended for trying to take up at the outset.

[JOHN VICKERS]

Of course a distinguished European advocate has compared modernization with the reformation because before 1 May 2004 for your agreement you needed to go to Philip's Commissioner for a papal indulgence. Now you have to work it all out for yourself. Andrej raised or emphasized the point about the courts and I think there are many open questions about our litigation work: where the agencies should be in relation to the courts, where the courts would like the agencies to be. Is there any sense in these issues?

[JOHN FINGLETON]

Ireland, as of 10 days ago now, has at least 10 competition authorities because all of our courts up to the Supreme Court have been designated as competition authorities with the competence to implement the Regulation and we are somewhat watching with amusement to see how it's going to work within the Irish system. I do know that amongst the judges that I've talked to there's a sense that something more formal will need to be done to help them. Most judges at least in our system tend to operate pretty much in isolation. They don't have large offices and staff and executives to help them so if they communicated with another judge or agency, it would be they themselves picking up the call and that's not usually acceptable for judicial independence. I think there are questions there about completing the network at the judicial level.

Within Ireland, however, I don't see the sort of requirement of the courts to apply Article 81(3) as a big deal because our courts have been applying Article 82, and more or less similar questions arise. I see that as no big deal. There are going to be very few cases in court. They are very expensive to mount and the courts have dealt with them pretty well in Ireland, *Masterfoods*—in which I was an expert on the wrong side—notwithstanding. One of the wonderful ironies about this of course is that the only email system that the network operates with is Microsoft Outlook so Microsoft has got 40 new accounts coming from the Irish competition authority thanks to this leverage. I think that one of the difficulties for a small competition authority is, and bearing in mind that most of the competition authorities in the Member States qualify as small, the resources to deal with this. The original motivation behind this great idea is to prioritize the resource allocation and to move at least some of the enforcement to the Member State levels. Now if it is not to displace existing domestic enforcement in principle it requires some increase in domestic resource allocation, even operating the network for a small competition authority like ours which has about 16 people doing enforcement in total. If you were to put one person full-time just doing network work you're actually reducing the amount of domestic enforcement without having any increase. We're just keeping track of what's going on and I think that's going to be an issue probably for a lot of the smaller competition authorities, and at European Competition day I argued that if this type of move toward subsidiarity was going to be effective—and I think it is right that things that affect Ireland should be done in Ireland—we shouldn't be looking to Brussels to force us to do things. I think we are going to have to strengthen our domestic competition authorities and our domestic policies as well in tandem and so I see this as the beginning of a project which still has a lot of steps to be taken.

[FRÉDÉRIC JENNY]

I think that the modernization process is an extraordinarily important exercise because to the best of my knowledge it is the first attempt to find a framework allowing a large number of competition authorities to cooperate in a practical way on solving common problems, and for reasons which have to do with the globalization and international scene. This process may teach us many useful lessons to solve competition problems raised by the globalization of markets. In the EU modernization process, when it comes to my own agency, the first difficulty is really to identify the cases where we should apply European law because we haven't been used to doing that.

The second difficulty is similar to what John identified: implementing the new regulation requires a lot of manpower the manpower. The only difficulty on the substance I can foresee for us comes from the fact that we have a different way in French law of looking at the domestic equivalent of Article 81/83. We have a competitive assessment first and then if overall on balance competition is impaired, we look at whether or not there is going to be progress. We are going to have to change this. Altogether, I think that the biggest challenge is really the human resources required to just keep track of what's on the network and to look at the cases so we are going to have to find resources for that.

[JOHN VICKERS]

OK. Mark, let's take your last two topics, just a few minutes each, then we can open it up.

[MARK CLOUGH QC]

Absolutely. I was going to say that there are a number of issues that arise out of modernization although I would like to take the opportunity to personally congratulate the Commission on its guidelines; I think it's done an admirable job on with the assistance of the ECN over the last 12 months. But there are questions such as, for example, does it matter that there are only nine of the 25 Member States with leniency policies, which you may want to raise in the discussion session.

Let me move on to the second to last question area, which is criminalization, and my question here is, is there any reason why criminalization of cartels in Europe is largely restricted to island States?

[JOHN FINGLETON]

I think that Ireland and the UK have both been in the very fortunate position in the last five or six years to have carried out a fairly fundamental re-examination of what competition policies were for. Not just from the point of view of looking at Articles 81 and 82 and trying to implement them domestically but, asking from the point of view of an economic policy, what is it we want these policies to achieve? Coming at it from that angle it goes back to something that Fred said earlier. He said that at the OECD when we discussed SLC versus dominance, everybody who had dominance argued for that and everyone who had SLC argued for something different, but we actually had a public interest test as the UK did and we'd asked a different question. We said which test should we have, dominance or SLC and the committee of lawyers came up with the dominance test because the EU has that. Then when I arrived at the agency four years ago I made the argument that an SLC test would be a better test from an economic policy point of view and that argument was persuasive of the government. Similarly the approach to criminalizing hard core cartels is, I think, a one of going back to first principles and asking what do we want to achieve, and in our case a lot of influence came from partly our legal system being like the US one in that we can't impose administrative fines, and partly because of the positive experience of the US which had really come on stream just at the time that we were looking at these questions. Jim Griffin and Margaret Bloom came to Dublin three and a half years ago and talked about leniency just as our legislature was preparing our law and so forth so we just hit at the right time. So I think it has probably got more to do with where we were at in economic policy at a particular point in time than that we are island states.

[JOHN VICKERS]

May I just enlarge that question perhaps for the benefit of other panellists? Does criminalization of hard core cartels assist public enforcement or does it make it too complicated?

[FRÉDÉRIC JENNY]

We do have both administrative sanctions and criminal sanctions against cartels in France. We are not terribly happy with the criminal sanctions. In fact the *Conseil* first gives administrative sanction and then it can refer the case for criminal violations. Most of the criminal cases end up with a dismissal by the judge because the standards that are applied by the criminal courts are so different from the standards applied by the *Conseil*. So we are not asking to have more criminalization of cases, as for us it probably would make things more difficult and there are a couple of countries I know of which have abandoned criminal sanctions (Chinese Taipei, Ireland). Criminal proceedings also often take much longer than administrative proceedings and that's also an important issue. Criminal sanctions seem to be more severe, so that's why they look good on paper, but I think there are plenty of innovative ways of punishing violators, including some that are being considered in Australia right now (such as banning executives for life from participating in businesses or being directors of businesses which is a kind of professional death penalty), which are probably good substitutes for criminal sanctions.

[JOHN VICKERS]

Before bringing on Hew, I'd like to underline what John said about US experience, the, if you like, combined stick and carrot of the criminal regime with serious consequences for individuals, not just companies potentially, and the leniency arrangements. They've visibly worked and all of us in Europe as consumers have benefited hugely from what you've done with one international cartel after another, so I think a lot of it is learning from what was successful. I think that was a big influence on the discussions here in the UK and I think that had a big effect too on the way the EU leniency policy has gone in Philip's area but Hew, how do you see our European issues?

[HEWITT PATE]

I won't say anything surprising. We think obviously it makes a tremendous difference to have a criminal sanction. We see time and time again that some of the individuals who get involved in this sort of criminal conduct may be quite ready to give up some of the shareholders' money in the form of a fine, but that it really sharpens their attention when the question is whether they are going to be subject to a prison sentence. For our part, if you internalize an attitude to competition that says this hard core collusion is the supreme evil of antitrust—we have a hard time seeing why it's any different from fraud or other sorts of white collar offences where criminal sanctions are thought of as being pretty non-controversial—it does work particularly in conjunction with an amnesty policy. Does that mean that we can't work effectively with our colleagues and other enforcement agencies in countries who pursue, as the Commission does, a very vigorous fine-based approach, and then also couple that with leniency? Obviously we are doing that. There can be some problems in terms of reciprocal information sharing because one system may be criminal and civil, but there are ways of working with that. Part of what was at issue in the *Empagran* case we just had is that we think the way to go is to have a network of government enforcers, using a combination of harsh penalties on the one hand and leniency on the other, and that's the way these cases are cracked, that's the way it's brought to light. As John suggests, once that happens, once the cartel is exposed, then consumers immediately benefit in all the countries where the cartel has been operating.

[MARK CLOUGH QC]

I don't know if you would like to open it up to the floor now or would you like me to ask my last question? I can ask it later if necessary. It's quite light-hearted in tone. Let me ask it and see what happens. The question concerns the global approach to competition law enforcement and indeed the main-tenance of divergent national merger control regimes. Is the maintenance of the national divergent merger control regimes just an excuse for businesses to fund regular meetings of the ICN in exotic destinations rather than getting on with having a WTO/OECD common standard solution?

[JOHN VICKERS]

Well thank you for that question! What I suggest we do is this. We have 10 or 15 minutes of questions and comments from the floor. We have, I think, at least a couple of microphones, so whilst one question is being asked if the other microphone can be being put into the hands of somebody with the next question. If questioners could say who they are then that will give us six or eight comments and/or questions. Then we'll have on the panel a minute or two each to pick up anything you like coming out of that and the extraordinarily perceptive question that Mark put just a moment ago.

Questions and Comments

[MICHAEL HUTCHINGS, *Competition Law Forum*]

It's a remark more than a question. Going back to the issue of convergence in the dominance/SLC and so on test, does it really matter or is it just a desire amongst all of us for a sense of neatness that we share terminology? What I am getting at is that I think we've spent a vast amount of time today and at previous conferences on this subject and I particularly allude back to a comment that Bill Kovacic made this morning that really what we need to do now is move on and say 'is merger policy working?' We need to look more at decisions that have been taken over the previous years and see whether they've actually been the right decisions so that in the future we make decisions informed on the basis of what's happened in the past rather than spending too many resources on the fine-tuning of the wording.

[JAMES KANTER, *Dow Jones*]

Mr Delrahim this morning voiced some concerns about the unbundling portion of the EC's *Microsoft* decision. He also enumerated some benefits like buy-ins for negotiated solutions and the kinds of cases that touch on a company's IP rights. In light of those remarks, I wonder what the desirability or likelihood might be of an interim negotiated solution in the *Microsoft* case, perhaps brokered by the Court in Luxembourg pending a final ruling by the CFI?

[MARGARET BLOOM, *Kings College and Freshfields*]

In terms of modernization, we will all be applying the same substantive law but of course there are national procedures. How significant is that? Should we now move to modernization two, so that we have the same procedures throughout Europe? Mark, the good news is, in terms of leniency regimes, according to the Commission website there are now 14 out of the 25 national authorities that have leniency regimes—well actually it says 13 but they haven't added Ireland, which should be there.

[NOREEN MACKEY, *Irish Competition Authority*]

I'd like to address a question to Philip Lowe particularly, and it is in relation to a comment he made about the powers of the Commission under Regulation 1/2003, to intervene at various stages, if necessary, in the national authorities' procedures. In particular he mentioned that there is an intervention of last resort 30 days before a national authority adopts a decision requiring an infringement to be brought to an end or accepting commitments. Now as John Fingleton said, in Ireland and indeed in at least one other Member State, the national courts have been designated as national authorities so in certain situations it's the national court in Ireland that would be adopting a decision requiring an infringement to be brought to an end and notifying the Commission 30 days in advance. Does the Commission envisage treating the situation any differently where it is the national court that is actually the designated authority from a situation where the designated authority is the national competition authority of the country? In other words, would the Commissioner envisage taking the case away from the national court 30 days before it made its decision?

[GEORGE N ADDY, *Davies Ward Phillips & Vineberg*]

Half facetiously, I'd like to get back to the cartel and leniency questions and to put it shortly: is too much success a bad thing? The leniency programmes and the cooperation amongst the various agencies are making it increasingly expensive for people to take advantage of a leniency policy. Is there any concern first that the take-up rate is going to decline or second, is there any move to establish some cooperation or at least recognition amongst the authorities for the amounts coughed up in one jurisdiction being taken to account in another?

[CHRISTOPH STADLER, *Hengeler Mueller*]

I would also like to address a question to Mr Lowe on the cooperation between the national courts and the Commission. The courts, or rather the Member States, are now under an obligation to send copies of written judgments to the Commission. My question is, what will the Commission do with these judgments?

[PETER ROTH QC, *Monckton Chambers*]

A question about modernization. One of the provisions of course is the ability for national authorities to intervene in proceedings before a national court, private proceedings. I wonder what sort of plans or anticipation each of you has for your national authority respectfully to intervene in private proceedings in national courts? I'm not quite sure how that would work in Ireland where as I understood it, the national courts are themselves national authorities, but I suppose the judges might intervene in each others' proceedings?

[ADAM ALDRED, *Addleshaw Goddard*]

Sir David Edward was talking this morning about onus of proof. I just wanted to know what role Article 81(3) will have as far as the regulators are concerned in dealing with infractions of Article 81(1) and perhaps when deciding on whether or not to file?

[JOHN VICKERS]

Thank you. So that's a rich set of topics. We certainly won't be asking everybody on the panel to respond to every question, so it is fine to be selective. I wonder if I could ask Andrej to go first. He was one of those at the ICN conference in Korea so is very well-placed to respond, amongst other things, to Mark's question which I took to be a slightly sceptical question about the value added of such enterprises, but Andrej on that and any other points that you'd like to pick up, please?

[ANDREJ PLAHUTNIK]

First of all, concerning the exotic places, the next ICN conference is in Bonn. Bonn is not very exotic! That's the first point. The second is that the ICN together along with the Global Competition Forum, which takes place also once per year, is the only forum in which different authorities or the people from the different authorities with totally different level of knowledge, of know how, of enforcement can come together, exchange their views, learn from each other and I know that it is the primary task. That is one point. I would like to just tackle the question of intervening at private litigation at a court. First of all I would not like to have the private litigation at a Slovenian court because the level of competition awareness, the level of competition culture is still too low.

[JOHN VICKERS]

Philip, there are a number of modernization questions. There was also a Microsoft question. Any thoughts on those?

[PHILIP LOWE]

Well just on the reference to *Microsoft*, I think the comments you made

James were about the two different aspects of the same decision. One was on bundling and the other was IP rights and I'm not going to comment on that. I've made a statement on our approach to both issues and why we believe that one is complementary to what the US has done. As for the other, we have taken a view in exceptional circumstances of the media player: we would propose an un-bundling solution and we think that the market established by the OEMs to provide the final integrated product to the consumer should develop. Now if the OEMs don't develop that market and the media player vendors don't develop it either, well maybe that will be some sort of market failure, but if we'd gone further and tried to impose a more intrusive remedy we would have been certainly accused of industrial engineering. That's our view on the way in which we've proposed a decision on un-bundling.

I'm not going to comment on the subsequent procedures because Microsoft is appealing before the Court of First Instance and the Commission doesn't comment on the work of the Court of First Instance. I hope you understand that. I think it is pretty normal. On the issue of when and if we intervene with courts, yes we will have to intervene where we believe that there is a genuine inconsistency and incoherence in the application of law and we'll hopefully be having our requests for a stay of execution before a decision heard by a court and hopefully by the court whom we would address. It is not the law that we should talk to any of the parties. Our dialogue would be only with the court. Hopefully we would be able to put up our views if we believe that there is a genuine inconsistency. The hope is that over time we will be able to develop a database which will be useful both for practitioners and for the network but don't expect that to be overnight. The fact is that this is a very, very big project and we've carried quite a lot of the administrative burden of creating the electronic network and getting this guidance out. Hopefully we will not be surprised by too many of the decisions down the line which we haven't heard of earlier through the network itself and through prior interventions.

What is the language which we intend to deal with? Almost certainly at the beginning we will, where possible, use a language which is the language of the ECN, which happens to be English, but you are quite right to point to the fact that there is a limited resource out there in relation to reading documents where the original of which is in one of the languages of the 25 Member States. Now we've counted on Monday again the number of people who speak for example the languages of the new Member States on our staff. There are precisely 57 of them and 10 trainees. Now most of those are in fact working on State aid cases. This morning we discussed a system whereby we would effectively cover any obligatory reading and translation of case work which came up in a merger and antitrust field through networking these 60 odd people inside DG Competition, but you can see it is a very scarce resource and so this is a plane which will take off when the resources are available to it but don't expect it to act like a jumbo jet. It's going to be a fairly strained organization at the beginning to provide the sort of service which you are thinking of in terms of availability of texts to practitioners.

I agree with Margaret totally on procedures. This is a challenge. It would have been nice to have actually had the modernization programme include a one-stop shop for leniency applications. I do think we will move to a 'modernization two' package where probably facilitating private enforcement will be one of the major parts of it. The other major part of it will be trying to agree at least to some degree of approximation on our deadlines and procedures. What frightens me the most is the incoherence which may occur between the dates on which we have to take decisions in our system and the reality in some cases that one competition authority, for purely procedural reasons, will have to take a decision before some others have decided what is the right way to go, so that puts even more of a burden on us to ensure that we are doing the job properly. I think that's enough from me. On the ICN well I far prefer to drive to Bonn and get the job done but the fact is that the merger work has been very, very good in promoting best practices not just on procedures but on substance, and we ourselves have changed our Regulation on notifications to conform to an ICN Best Practice. So yes, it is a very expensive way to discuss things. There isn't a beach in Seoul though! There is only a conference room and a lot of competition authorities talking about competition.

Perhaps I could tell you something which has happened today as a result of the new Merger Regulation, which I think is a very positive thing for Europe, and that is we have received the first application from a firm which has told us that it would have to proceed to 13 separate national filings for a merger and they have requested under the new Regulation to all 13 authorities and ourselves that it should be dealt with by the Commission or by a limited number of the national authorities. That's Europe working properly.

[JOHN VICKERS]

Now time is marching on. I want Hew, who has travelled the furthest, to have the last word, but if Fred could go first and then John with any quick comments on the questions that have been left hanging, please?

[FRÉDÉRIC JENNY]

I just have a quick comment on whether convergence is so important. I must say that I am personally troubled by this question because it is not obvious to me that we should all converge, or that there is a necessity that we should converge, and yet we behave as if convergence was the ultimate goal. Competition law and antitrust law are the product of economic reasoning turned into a legal rule through a political process. Now the economic reasoning tends to be pretty much the same everywhere. The national legal systems are quite diverse and so are the political processes. I don't see anything wrong with the fact that the EU wants to unify the market even though many competition laws/ antitrust laws would not have this as an objective. I don't see anything particularly wrong with Japan and Germany having had a traumatic experience with dominant integrated firms and being particularly sensitive to the dominance aspect, or with South Africa using the fact that integration into the economics field for minorities is something that contributes to economic progress. I think that competition authorities tend to want to converge because it reassures them or maybe because convergence offers them some psychological strength against the evil forces (economic lobbies, politicians, etc) which try to prevent them from doing their work. But we should face the fact that some of the differences among national competition laws are perfectly acceptable and perfectly healthy even if they are not directly derived from economic analysis.

[JOHN VICKERS]

Thank you. John?

[JOHN FINGLETON]

Just on ICN: the reduction of merger filing fees, while a very useful outcome from ICN, is not the only objective. I think that it's done a lot of useful work in advocacy and other areas and I know that when we were framing our own competition law we don't have in our small economy the critical mass of expertise, for example that you saw in the UK when you were doing the Enterprise Act, to actually write detailed policy papers on what the law and policy should be, and we relied heavily on international thinking particularly at that time with the OECD. One of the wonderful things about ICN is that it is more than the usual suspects. It's not just the OECD and it does, as John said, bring in much greater private sector participation than the OECD can manage to do. So I think in that sense the ICN, if it gets into substantive issues particularly as it is doing, can be a great resource, partic-

ularly to the many small economies and those are the ones for whom the
benefits can be the greatest. So I think on a cost benefit basis ICN has a lot
to offer relative to what it will cost.

[HEWITT PATE]

Well this is a very innovative format. It allows the audience to think it has
been allowed to ask pointed questions and then allows us to say whatever
we want. So to try to sort it all out, first, does the wording of the merger
standard make a difference? We hope not and I think it will not. Secondly,
the WTO? No, it is not time to move to dispute resolution on competition
questions before the WTO; the ICN does a terrific job. It's very cost effective and does many things. Don't forget the great work that Frédéric Jenny
does and the Competition Committee and the OECD. All of these things are
complementary. Thirdly, cartels. Yes, we are paying a lot of attention to try
to make sure that you don't have such a great morass of costs when you
come in and report so that instead you'll hunker down and try to just keep
avoiding detection. That's the whole point I was making at our Supreme
Court the other day in the *Empagran* case. But if you do get exposed by a
good leniency programme and there are a lot of costs that are incurred
because of that, well, it's your own fault. You shouldn't fix prices!

Margaret, I am not sure about your point. I don't remember what you said
but it must have been insightful. Regarding *Microsoft*, it's none of my business to answer your question, but as it relates to our settlement I'll take it
as a hook to respond to a little of what Philip had to say and note that there
is a lot of complementarity in the server to server remedy part of what we
did and what the Commission did, so on policy there is also a good deal of
overlap. Bear in mind though, ours was a remedial use of mandatory licensing following a finding of liability based on aggressive affirmative anticompetitive acts. Although there is no valid basis for such claims in the United
States, it remains to be seen in Europe whether a refusal to licence can itself
be the basis of liability. As to the tying comments, Judge Kollar-Kotelly of
course was speaking in the context of a review of a settlement that we had
reached. Beyond that, on the rule of reason approach, I think it is true that
there was a reason why our case wasn't brought as a rule of reason case
originally, and after the court threw it out as a per se tying case we did not
pursue that part of it. Rule of reason is, I think, as we look at it, going to
be somewhat different than what seems to be seen in the decision here, in
the sense that we are trying to drive down to look at the effect on
consumers. There seems to be a good deal of attention to answering that
question by reference to market share of the competitors and with respect
to the innovation and the adjacent markets, all anyone can seem to talk

about on the business pages in the United States is the Google IPO. I think the evidence anecdotally is that there is plenty of incentive for folks to innovate in adjacent markets.

There are things that are very measured about the EC *Microsoft* case. I think one of them though has a little bit of a thirteenth chime aspect about it in the sense that a large part of the decision was driven by the view that people wouldn't buy additional browsers if they'd already got one free. We think that's a commendable recognition that you don't want to do that sort of market outcome driving, but rather than say that indicates the intervention is modest, I might point out that it could, in our view, undermine the question of whether the whole enterprise is sustainable, and I just think in a comparative legal context you need to ask whether you really can stand some of the authorities making distinctions between product improvement and anti-competitive activity where you are in a system that has a much lower threshold for abuse of dominance than the US system.

[JOHN VICKERS]

Thank you very much. Well finally I thank you for all your questions and comments, to the maestro Mark Clough and to the whole panel for what I hope has been a very interesting session. Thank you.

CHAPTER 13

Compulsory Licensing

A. John Kallaugher

This panel deals with the issue of compulsory licensing particularly in the context of dominant firms or firms with monopoly power. This is a very important issue for Trans-Atlantic relations. It's not so widely remembered today that 60 years ago now the United States was involved in its first forays into the international application of antitrust law. The main issue that concerned them was the use of intellectual property rights as a tool for building international cartels. And as any student knows, the interface between intellectual property law and antitrust law or competition law is now without doubt the most complex area of competition law wherever you are practising. And then we put it into another difficult and important area: the whole question of how we deal with monopoly power. This is probably the biggest single area of substantive difference between the laws of the United States and the laws of the European Union and the Member States of the European Union. You put those together and you have the issue of when is it an abuse of a dominant position under Article 81, or monopolization under section 2 of the Sherman Act, for a firm with market power to refuse to give licences under its intellectual property. We also add to that the fact that in the last six weeks we've had major developments here in the European Union dealing with precisely this issue. Most of you are familiar by now, if only from the press, with the *Microsoft* decision of 24 March 2004 and of the judgment of the Court of Justice on 29 April 2004 in the *IMS Health* proceeding.

Given the topicality and the importance of this issue from a trans-atlantic perspective, we are very fortunate to have a very distinguished panel here to discuss these issues. Immediately on my right is Makan Delrahim who is the Deputy Assistant Attorney General, United States' Department of Justice, in the Antitrust Division. He is responsible for international appellate and policy issues, so he has to deal directly with the issues that we have to talk about today. We have then at the far end John Temple Lang, who has had a very distinguished career. He was for many years in the Legal Service of the Community and then in what used to be DG IV, now DG Comp, as the leading expert, I think it is fair to say, internally on issues of what used to be Article 86, now Article 82. He is the one Briton really responsible, more than anyone, for developing the Commission's thinking on essential facilities and related issues and someone who, since he has moved into private practice at Cleary Gottlieb, has been active in these issues, most notably as an advisor to IMS in their ongoing disputes. And then, rounding off the panel, another very distinguished practitioner, Thomas Vinje who has been involved in IP related issues for many years. First in his old shop at Morrison and Foerster LLP and more recently now as a strong addition to the team at Clifford Chance in this area. I am looking very much forward to what they have to say about these topics and I am going to ask John Temple Lang to start first.

B. John Temple Lang

You may be surprised to hear that, after having put before you a fairly condensed paper of 25 or 30 pages, I am going to suggest to you that the law is actually rather simple. It can be summarized as I've tried to summarize it on the first page of my paper and, as I am going to try to summarize it for you now, as essentially three propositions. First there is a rule in Article 82 about discrimination, and the result of that may be that you are obliged to give a second or a subsequent compulsory licence to a licensee who wants it, if you have already given one in equivalent circumstances. That's the first proposition. Not very controversial, and it is rather surprising perhaps that it hasn't given rise to more case law. The second proposition is that Article 82(b) prohibits dominant companies from limiting the production, marketing and so on of their competitors. It may be contrary to that provision if a dominant company acquires technology and then refuses to allow that technology to continue to be available to its competitors. For example the *Tetra Pak* exclusive licensing case: not very surprising and not, in my view, very controversial.

How do I deal with all of the other cases? All of the other cases, I think, can be and should be dealt with by saying that, as the Court of Justice has repeatedly said, it is never an abuse of a dominant position to refuse to licence an intellectual property right in itself. It may, however, be appropriate as a remedy, as a result of other conduct constituting an independent abuse, to require that the intellectual property right be licensed in order to remedy the other abuse. It is only in this sort of situation, where you have an obligation to give a compulsory licence for the first time, that you have substantial transaction costs. That is one reason why, of course, competition authorities tend to stay away from ordering this.

Let me give you two examples of where this principle is obviously right and where the remedy explanation, although the Court has never given it, is in fact a good description of the state of the law. In *Volvo AB v Erik Veng (UK) Ltd*,[1] it was said in passing that a compulsory licence might be appropriate if the dominant company was charging excessive prices contrary to Article 86 (as it was then) paragraph (a). Now that clearly is not an essential facility situation. And the only explanation is that a compulsory licence is an appropriate market-based remedy for dealing with the excessive pricing in a way that does not necessitate continued supervision by the competition authority. The other simple case, again not a conventional essential facility case, is a case like the *Dell* computer decision of the Federal Trade

---

[1] (1989) 4 CMLR 122.

Commission of the United States.[2] A company was found to have failed to
disclose to a standard setting authority at the right moment the fact that it
had patents which read on the standard as it was subsequently developed,
then later claimed royalties. In those circumstances, it may be appropriate
as a remedy to order either what is in effect a compulsory royalty free
licence by preventing the company from obtaining royalties at all, or alternatively to moderate the level of royalties as a kind of punishment and
deterrent for the company involved for not having disclosed its patents at
the right time. If you accept my explanation that compulsory licences are
remedies for the other abuse and not the refusal to licence, I think you will
find on reflection that this is a better explanation of the law.

[JOHN KALLAUGHER]

Thomas Vinje may have a somewhat different view of this.

---

[2] *Dell Corporation VL Bus patents*: this was an important case, involving a zero royalty
non-exclusive license to use the Dell VL Bus patent for personal computers. This did not
involve a merger, but was based upon 'unfair or deceptive acts' by Dell—encouraging PC
manufacturers to adopt this technology while the patent was pending. The order prohibited
Dell from enforcing its patent rights against any PC manufacturer using the VL Bus.

C. Thomas Vinje

Well John, I would suggest that there is a great deal of room for agreement amongst all of us on the panel and perhaps indeed in the room as well. We have come a long way from the days when intellectual property was inherently suspect and I think we could probably all agree today that antitrust agencies and courts must be cautious when adopting compulsory licences as a remedy for antitrust infringements. There is a potential for harm to innovation if agencies or courts are too liberal in granting compulsory licences, but one needs to be careful to avoid going too far in the other direction. Let me make two introductory points. First, while intellectual property certainly has some characteristics that are different from other forms of property, it is still property, and I would suggest that compulsory access to intellectual property should, in principle, be subject to the same analysis as compulsory access to other forms of property. The second basic point is that in the vast majority of cases, and I would emphasize vast majority, it would be in my view entirely inappropriate to deem a refusal to license to constitute an abuse, just like it would be inappropriate in most cases to find a refusal to share any other sort of property, like a factory or a transportation infrastructure, to constitute an abuse. But there are certain cases where refusals to licence intellectual property should be deemed to be abusive and I would suggest that this is especially true in certain information and communication technology markets that are subject to network effects and interoperability constraints on the ability to compete. Sometimes it is useful, perhaps, to descend a bit from the lofty heights of theoretical considerations and consider a few concrete cases in evaluating what the law should say on a particular topic.

I suggest taking at one end of the spectrum, a concrete case concerning pharmaceutical patents. I would submit that it is difficult to imagine as an antitrust matter, leaving aside other public policy questions, any concrete case involving a refusal to licence a pharmaceutical patent where the requisite extraordinary circumstances would be found to exist that are necessary to deem a refusal to license to constitute an abuse. But let's take a couple of concrete cases in the IT sector where I would suggest that refusals to license have appropriately been deemed abusive. Now I could say a fair amount about the *IBM* case.[3] I spent a fair amount of time representing clients involved in that case who obtained a lot of information pursuant to the 1984 Undertaking, but let me simply say that the Undertaking which IBM

---

[3] *IBM Personal Computer, Re* (Commission Decision 84/233) OJ L118, 4.5.84, 24, [1984] 2 CMLR 342.

entered into in 1984 and which it clearly would not have entered into absent the threat of an adverse Commission decision, had great benefits for competition and for consumers in key markets, and there is no evidence, I would submit, that the effectively forced disclosure of interface specifications diminished IBM's incentives to innovate. I represented, again, several companies who obtained specifications vital to their ability to compete, pursuant to that undertaking and while disputes arose regarding what the undertaking meant, what should be paid under it and the like, although it was not always an easy path, it worked pretty well. I would suggest that it was an example of the Commission taking the lead and doing something effective for competition and for consumers.

A few words about the *Microsoft* case. Some of you may know that I am involved in that case or rather, our firm is involved in that case, representing those adverse to Microsoft. Again, it is not clear whether it really is a case, as was the *IBM* case, of compulsory licensing of intellectual property. I will not be going into that in detail, but whether interface specifications are protected by copyright is highly doubtful in my view, certainly under US law and to the extent that there is any European law on it I would suggest it is doubtful as well. Microsoft raised patent issues only very late in the process and has had really rather little to say on that front, and whether trade secrets constitute intellectual property under European law is a question certainly at least under Article 295. In any event, the Commission decision assumes that its order may involve compulsory licensing in intellectual property and let's simply assume the same for today's discussion.

So, is it appropriate to deem Microsoft's refusal to disclose and to licence the relevant interface specifications to constitute an abuse? Let's stand back, for just a moment, and consider what we have here in terms of the concrete facts. We have a company that has a 95 per cent market share in the desktop operating system, the omnipresent desktop operating system. That effective monopoly is protected by network effects, the applications barrier to entry. That monopoly has been shown to be highly durable. Microsoft has been deemed conclusively by the US courts to have illegally maintained its desktop monopoly. There are clear technological inter-dependencies between the desktop operating systems and low end server operating systems. Low end server operating systems provide services such as file, print and group and user administration services to client PCs in a network. A work group server operating system must implement certain interface specifications in order to be able to interoperate with those omnipresent PCs in order to be able to draw on the functionality of those PCs and to provide the services that are expected of a workgroup server operating system. In other words, the ability to achieve that sort of interoperability between a workgroup server operating system and those omnipresent client

PCs is indispensable to the ability of a workgroup server operating system vendor to compete. Indeed there is a risk of elimination of competition by virtue of Microsoft's refusal to provide those interface specifications and that risk of elimination of competition is demonstrated, as the decision points out, by the market shares that we have seen evolve. Microsoft entered this market rather late. It began restricting information flows upon entering the market. It moved from 24.5 per cent of the market in 1996 to 64.9 per cent in 2002, and I won't mention the figures, but the corresponding declines in the market shares of competitors are equally dramatic. Moreover, there are various internal Microsoft communications showing that it intentionally engaged in this conduct. It purposefully intended to eliminate competition by restricting the flow of interface specifications.

So what do we have? We have two clearly separate markets. We have interface specifications necessary to achieve interoperability which is necessary to compete in the workgroup server market. Microsoft's refusal to disclose those specifications is, in the words of the *IMS* decision, 'capable of excluding all competition'. There is no objective justification offered, and finally, the decision requires only disclosure and licensing of specifications, not source code. So this will not, in the words again of the *IMS* decision, allow 'duplication' of Microsoft's products but instead it will allow existing independently developed software with functions equivalent to those provided by Microsoft software to be made interoperable with Microsoft's monopoly desktop operating systems. In other words, the competitors have already developed this functionality; indeed they were the pioneers in such technology and many believe their products' functionality to be superior to the Microsoft functionality, but they need to be able to interoperate with the desktops. So that is all that is at issue. Under those circumstances, I would suggest there is no reason to believe that the order in this case will diminish Microsoft's incentive to innovate, but rather it will allow competitors to continue to exist in the market and to innovate, and indeed that might encourage Microsoft itself to continue to innovate. I would suggest that this is the kind of case where there is an appropriate order for compulsory licensing. I should leave it at that in light of time.

There are plenty of other questions that we can discuss and we can respond to Makan. One thing perhaps we could come back to, which I know will be raised later, is the question of unilateral refusals to deal which is, I believe, a fundamental difference between US law and European law. I would suggest that Europe has it right and that in certain circumstances it would be appropriate to enter a compulsory licence in a unilateral refusal to deal context, and maybe we could come back to a concrete case where I would suggest that that would be appropriate. But I do believe that we want to have time for discussion and so I shall stop there. Thanks very much.

[JOHN KALLAUGHER]

Well thank you for that Thomas. We've heard the two speakers from the European side talking about these issues; let's drill a little bit deeper into some of the issues that are raised under Article 82, particularly in light of *Microsoft* and *IMS*. We've heard John suggesting, if I understand him correctly, that it's really not a question of refusal to licence at all, it is other abuses, and the obligation to licence is simply a remedy. And Thomas is taking a different tack as I understand him. He is really saying that there is a 'refusal to licence' abuse and it has come right down to when there are exceptional circumstances, and if I understood that correctly you are not going to limit what exceptional circumstances are to those three factors that were expressly identified in the *Magill* judgment back in 1995.[4] Now I wonder if each of you would feel comfortable maybe making a brief direct comment on the approach that the other one has taken without necessarily having to go into facts of your own cases if you feel uncomfortable in doing that.

[THOMAS VINJE]

Well, I don't have any fundamental objection to John's approach. Actually, I find it a very interesting one, one that is thought provoking and worthy of further development, certainly. I don't think it necessarily excludes the approach I'm suggesting, at least in the intermediate term. On your question of whether the factors noted in *IMS* and in *Magill* would be deemed appropriate for finding the exceptional circumstances necessary to find an abuse, it is difficult to say exactly what the *IMS* judgment means on that score. I've read it quite carefully, as I am sure everyone else at this table has read it carefully a number of times. It seems to me that the court, appropriately in my view as you intimate, is leaving open the possibility that these may not be the only factors relevant to determining whether exceptional circumstances exist and I would suggest that that really is an extraordinarily sensible thing to do. They cannot tell what sort of cases are coming down the road and for the court to tie its hands and say these are the only circumstances in which exceptional circumstances might exist would strike me as rather unwise.

[JOHN TEMPLE LANG]

I don't find the phrase 'exceptional circumstances' at all helpful. No doubt it is true, but it doesn't provide you with any sort of test. If my theory about

---

[4] Joined Cases C-241/91 P and C-242/91 P.

compulsory licensing being appropriate for a remedy for the other abuse is right, you can have a variety of different situations depending on how many other kinds of abuse you can have. If you look at the case law of the ECJ and in particular at the examples that were given in *Volvo AB v Erik Veng (UK) Ltd*, there are a number of situations where the Court said a compulsory licence might be appropriate. I don't want to talk about the *IMS Health* judgment as such but I do think that it has an effect on one of the examples given in *Volvo AB v Erik Veng (UK) Ltd*. In *Volvo AB v Erik Veng (UK) Ltd* it was said that it would be appropriate to grant a compulsory licence if the use of the intellectual property right resulted in monopolization of a second market, without any other test or requirement being proposed. Since the Court of Justice in the *IMS Health* judgment has said that the *Magill* requirements are cumulative, I take it that that bit of *Volvo AB v Erik Veng (UK) Ltd* has now been overruled.

[THOMAS VINJE]

Maybe it is possible to marry the two concepts. I am not sure that they are really inconsistent. John, if I understood your paper correctly, you have said that the circumstances that had been identified in *Magill* and *IMS* would not in your view necessarily be the only circumstances under which a compulsory licence would be appropriate. I also agree that the term 'exceptional circumstances' in itself does not really tell you anything, but what I think needs to be done is the system needs to go through enough cases where these issues arise, so that a body of law begins to grow that has some coherence. Whether they are analysed under the current approach of extraordinary circumstances requiring a compulsory licence or under your approach, I am not so sure at all that there is an inconsistency there.

[JOHN KALLAUGHER]

Well we could obviously carry this conversation on and I'd like to come back to some of these points, but first I think it would be appropriate, given that this is a comparative trans-atlantic conference, to hear what Makan has to say.

D. Makan Delrahim

Thanks John. I want to thank, particularly Philip and the organizers of the conference for putting such a distinguished first panel together, clearly to make sure everybody gets here before our panel and I think that I express those thanks on behalf of everyone on our panel.

I am going to try to describe some of the history and policy and practical implications of the compulsory licensing and as suggested in compliance with the 'Jenny rule' last night, I am going to get to my conclusion first and that is, compulsory licensing in the United States is a remedy that has been used in the area of remedy for mergers. It is relatively non-controversial in the United States in appropriate cases; however there are differences and there is some debate in the area of liability in the non-merger cases, and I will get to more detail on that. In the United States, compulsory licensing as a remedy in the antitrust cases has gone back and forth, as mentioned in the paper, with the different US Supreme Court decisions over the last century. Compulsory licensing itself as a remedy was, I think, endorsed back in 1902 when the courts first started dealing with intellectual property and antitrust, but more clearly endorsed as a remedy in *Besser Manufacturing* in the 1950s and more recently in the several *Microsoft* cases, particularly the most recent one prior to the Appellate Court which approved the consent decree and tried the non-settling states case there. They've recognized it as necessary in the cases and appropriate, so we operate based on that.

As an antitrust remedy it can be divided in the two types: those related to mergers and those related to non-merger cases, as I mentioned. As a point of structure I am going to get to the history of compulsory licensing in the US and EU but I'm not going to touch on the EU since we have two experts who have gone into that and most of you are already familiar with the cases we are going to discuss today. But I'll look at the differences between the US and EU approach as we see it across the Atlantic. When we start talking about compulsory licensing I think any discussion of that starts with the US's antitrust IP guidelines jointly put out by the DOJ and the FTC. These state that the enforcement agencies will attempt to apply the same general antitrust principles to the conduct involving intellectual property rights that they apply to conduct involving any other form of tangible or intangible property. If we start from that principle—that an antitrust agency can certainly demand divestiture of physical assets in a merger case—we would expect that it would certainly be appropriate to apply it to intellectual property assets. In fact, if you take that one step further, compulsory licensing is often less burdensome than outright divestiture and one should expect the agencies to be able to use that as a potential remedy in merger cases where the merger would otherwise result in a substantial lessening of competition. The reason it is uncontroversial in the United States in the merger context, as I mentioned before, is perhaps due to the fact that they mostly appear in consent decrees between the parties and they involve usually a grant to another single licensee rather than just a broad compulsory licence to anybody who wants to have access to the technology. This is our way of just merely preserving the number of competitors in the market. It is also crucial to remember that that licence has to be as narrow as possible to avoid collusion among the competitors in the market not affected by the proposed merger. That is, I think, an important distinction which we keep in mind among the enforcement agencies and it's an important one that guides how we approach that, as indeed our Supreme Court recently stated in the *Verizon Communications v Trinko* case.

Now turning to the non-merger remedy cases, compulsory licensing has had a long but contradictory history and as at the turn of the century it's gone back between the policies of how the courts have favoured and viewed patent law and antitrust law. Early on in the century, the courts seemed to side with the Patent Act and basically say that once you had exclusive rights—the right to exclude anybody in that marketplace—you had been granted a monopoly and you couldn't take that away with the antitrust laws. That was the mode of thinking then but the pendulum began to change a little bit during the period of the New Deal and by 1952, in the case of *Besser Manufacturing* dealing with a cartel of concrete block manufacturers, the Supreme Court described compulsory licensing as 'a well recognized remedy where patent abuses are proved in antitrust actions and it is required for effective relief'. They repeated that same sentiment in the *General Electric* case and what they did was, in effect, to just take away GE's intellectual property rights by issuing free licences to all its competitors. The Supreme Court has also endorsed compulsory licensing in the 1973 case of the *Glaxo Group* which involved the antibiotics case and it was more of a patent pooling arrangement there, so again you had a concerted action rather than a unilateral action in that case, but some observers believed that it began to swing in the other direction. In the 1980 *Dawson Chemical* case, the Supreme Court criticized compulsory licensing saying 'compulsory licensing is a rarity in our patent system and compulsory licensing of patents often has been proposed but it has never been enacted on a broad scale'. That was a general statement made by the Court but some observers have viewed that the Court's view, with respect to compulsory licensing, has changed in that regard. Until more recently, I think, we have not seen since 1980 many Appellate Court decisions in the

United States that addressed compulsory licensing and the most recent one mentioned is the *Microsoft* case. This is itself unique because it involves both a consent decree, involving the consent decree with the United States Justice Department, as well as a fully litigated court-ordered remedy, which was as a result of several of the states who were party to the case not joining on with that settlement and instead proceeding through the District Court. Now the case is pending decision in the DC Circuit Court of Appeals but the District Court did endorse, as I mentioned at the very beginning, the two consent decrees. Both the one imposed by the court as well as the one negotiated with the Justice Department are very similar in almost all respects. That is somewhat interesting in the sense that one was negotiated, which is often the preferred way of imposing a compulsory license and the one that is usually more effective because you have the buy in from the parties, but one that was also imposed by the courts in that case. So we do have a bit of a confusing record in the United States where you have compulsory license in connection with non-merger cases.

As I mentioned, I will not concentrate on the EU cases, *Magill* and the *IMS*, but I do want to talk a little bit about them because of the US comment earlier, as it alludes to the distinction between the liability and the remedy: is compulsory licensing viewed as a remedy to antitrust violations or does it operate itself as a cause for liability in an antitrust case? Tom mentioned that and that gets us to what we call in the United States 'the unilateral refusals to deal'. A lot of the commentators' quarrel has not necessarily been with compulsory licensing in the remedy phase of each case. It has been mostly with the liability. It is an important point and in over a century of antitrust decisions in the United States only one appellate case, the *Kodak* decision in the Ninth Circuit, has ever found liability and even that is arguable amongst the scholars who commented on that case regarding this theory of unilateral refusal to licence. It is one that even in the United States, even among or within the agencies, generates significant debate as to whether or not it should be a separate form of liability under the US antitrust laws.

The other problem or concern amongst the commentators with *Magill* and the *IMS* case is the fact that they involved certain copyright claims where in the United States both of those might be viewed as un-copyrightable subject matter. In the United States some years ago, our Supreme Court decided in what was called the *Feist*[5] decision that databases and certain kinds of information are not copyrightable and I think that might be the better way to address these types of policy issues rather than through the instrument of the antitrust laws by using the copyright act or the patent laws to address

---

[5] *Feist Publications Inc v Rural Telephone Service Co* 499 US 340 (1991).

issues of policy with respect to the issuance of intellectual property in those areas. So I think some of the differences as far as the views in the US on the *IMS* and the *Magill* case, and perhaps to some extent the *Microsoft* matter, should be animated by the fact that some copyrighted works that have been the subject of those cases, are not copyrightable under the US regime. When you have uncertainties, and I think the Commission's approach suggests that there may have been some, the courts may have become constrained by the absence of harmonized intellectual property laws within the EU and perhaps that's why they went towards that approach. I think that when you do that you create uncertainty in both the competition law as well as the intellectual property regime you are under. From more than just a theoretical standpoint the increase in uncertainty creates disincentives for innovation which should be the ultimate goal of both the intellectual property laws and the competition laws.

Let me just mention the *Microsoft* case which is certainly a work in progress and we await the judgment of the European courts as well as our own courts. Our antitrust division has had a number of concerns about one aspect of that decision of the Commission, which has been the unbundling portion of the Commission's view. But in terms of the interoperability remedy which requires Microsoft to licence technologies used by Microsoft server software to communicate with other Microsoft software on a network, I think there is considerable overlap with the United States' remedy on that issue. Like the US decree, the EC decision appears to focus on providing competing software developers with the opportunity to build products that communicate and interoperate with Windows-based PCs. There is ongoing dialogue between us and the EU and I will just leave it at that. On the decision and any other concerns I will defer to Hew Pate, who you will be hearing from both later today as well as tomorrow and any questions should be addressed to him on that matter. I don't get paid enough to do that!

So what are we left with? There is a history without a great deal of consistency. How do we explain this, and particularly the fact that so many of these decisions seem to be all-or-nothing results? Again I think there is a way of taking a look at the difference between intellectual property law and competition law and whether or not those two have the same or conflicting goals. Is it, as the US believed in the early part of the last century, where one policy grants monopolies and one takes it away, or is it that they both serve the same goal of promoting innovation and competition? The latter is, I believe, the antitrust division's view, and I think it is not a bad view for others to consider as they are developing their competition and intellectual property regimes across the Atlantic.

This brings me to a list of some objections to compulsory licensing on both policy and the practical grounds and these policy concerns I think caused us to be more cautious when considering compulsory licensing as a remedy. Most important of these is the concern that an improperly-designed license can stifle competition, for example, where the Iridium satellite phones seemed to have locked up all intellectual property related to that technology. But in 1998 and 1999 and certainly before the stock market crash, or the bubble bursting in that area, you had a massive increase in mobile phone use and new technologies that we developed which basically made the Iridium satellite phone network obsolete, although it required a lot of investment and you certainly don't want to consider the lock up of all the intellectual property which that consortium had and say that there were no other alternatives and that we should have imposed compulsory licensing, because there should be maximum incentive for those types of technologies to develop as much as they can, given the enormous amount of research, development, and infrastructure investment required for that. So we should be careful not to take competitors' or plaintiffs' claims about so-called dominant firms at face value and I think governments are well served to permit systems that reward innovations. The patent system in the United States does this well when we allow it to work, so it is imperative the antitrust enforcers approach that system with some humility.

I think another related problem is the cost of false positives, which is a concept that combines the fear of stifling innovation with concerns over costs to both the government and the defendant, and again I'll mention the Supreme Court's most recent decision on section 2 in the United States; the *Trinko* case. I know there has been some debate and discussion in the United States on the *Trinko* matter and the decision there but I think it is important to remember that it was a unanimous 9-0 Supreme Court decision that discussed that, and what Justice Scalia said was:

The cost of false positives counsels against an undue expansion of section 2 liability and can chill the very conduct the antitrust laws are designed to protect. No court should impose a duty to deal that it cannot explain or adequately and reasonably supervise. The problem should be deemed irremediable by antitrust law when compulsory access requires the court to assume the day-to-day controls characteristic of a regulatory agency.

I think these are, by and large, the principles the agencies have followed. They have tried not to become regulatory agencies themselves and to recognize the limits of the antitrust courts, as well as the agencies to try to remedy areas where it might be policy considerations within the intellectual property areas. The benefit, I think, of consent decrees is in the United States: we have found the great majority of the licenses are from consent decrees and I'll just quickly mention some of them as the input from the interested parties. Usually you have the various parties who are involved: the competitors or reinforcement agencies. The more of those you have, the more creative solutions you can reach as far as how best to structure the licence. You also have the buy-in by the various interested parties. When there is their consent, you have the feeling that there is some ownership to the solution, to the licence, and I think there is less criticism both from the parties—who are the beneficiaries of the licence—as well as the defendant, who is less likely to criticize the remedy and will probably be more willing to comply with it. Then there is the focus on future conduct and what I think every agency is looking at are the considerations for drafting a compulsory licence when one is warranted. That means ensuring the terms are clear enough: what is it that is being licensed exactly? Are there restrictions? Are there certain fields of the patent or is it becoming too broad? Will it require oversight? Is it difficult to administer, which is a particular concern in the area where know-how is required along with the patent, and what happens to the future patents in the pipeline? In some areas it makes a lot of sense because the value of the compulsory license would evaporate if you had future blocking patents or improvements that would make the prior licence obsolete, but on the other hand you also don't want to harm innovation and incentives because if the current defendant does not have an incentive to improve on the patents they may not invest the R & D to do so. Finally what is the proper level of royalties that should be imposed and should it be royalty-free? Should it be reasonable and if so, what is reasonable? Thanks again and I look forward to the discussions.

[JOHN KALLAUGHER]

Thank you very much for that Makan. I think that what you have succeeded in doing is showing that the development of this law is much more complex than people who just read the summaries of it on this side of the Atlantic sometimes think. And also an important point is that it's not just antitrust law, it is also a lot of IP cases in the US where you have had patent misuse or other intellectual property misuse principles involved which of course is something that we don't see in the case law here. Now that aspect brings me to a question that I would like to put to Thomas and to John, which is this interesting suggestion of yours that, if I can mis-characterize it, is along the lines of what we do in the US if we've got something wrong with the IP laws, which is that we fix it. If you think that the Irish law for copyright of television listings is too broad, why don't you change the Irish law for heaven's sakes? Why do you try to use Article 82 to deal with these problems? I wonder if John and Thomas might want to comment on that aspect your presentation.

E. Discussion

[THOMAS VINJE]

It is extremely difficult to say to what extent the courts may have been influenced in *Magill* or *IMS* by the thin nature of the copyright. I think that is simply not possible to say and I don't think those here who might know something about that would be willing to say something about it. But I would like to give an example of where it is difficult to achieve the result you are suggesting, although I wholeheartedly endorse the proposition that, to the extent possible, the balancing should be done in the formulation of the law itself. However, a recent example shows how difficult that is to achieve and how, on occasion, it may simply be left to the antitrust laws to clean up the mess, so to speak, and that is the example of the pending software patent directive. In that pending directive, the European Parliament proposed an article, Article 6A, which effectively provided that it would not constitute infringement of a patent if implementing that patent was necessary to achieve interoperability. Obviously that was intended to address a competition concern. As I sit here now, I am not personally endorsing that article. There are problems with its formulation, but nonetheless, it is there, its purpose being to address a competition concern in the context of the intellectual property legislation. Objections were raised on the part of certain bodies in industry to that provision and the approach taken by the Irish Presidency and by the Commission has been to delete Article 6A and to replace it with recital 17 if I remember correctly, which refers to Article 81 and 82 and says these issues will be addressed under the competition law. So, if that is the ultimate result, I am afraid people have missed the opportunity to address these competition concerns in the context of the IP law itself and forced the Commission and the courts to address those concerns in the context of antitrust law.

[JOHN TEMPLE LANG]

I think it is obvious that Makan is right to say that one should not try to cure what are said to be defects in intellectual property law by trying to use Article 82. It is unsatisfactory to try to produce ad hoc *ex post* remedies even if you think there is a problem. The fact is that neither the Court of Justice in either the *Magill* or the *IMS Health* judgments, nor the Commission in the *IMS Health* decision made any reference to the nature of the intellectual property right. This has been a comment made repeatedly. I am not sure there is any justification for it. I don't see, myself, any possible legal basis for either the Commission or the Court of Justice saying that certain national copyright rules are in some way unsatisfactory, inadequate, and unjustified. That is simply not something that Community law gives either institution the power to do.

[JOHN KALLAUGHER]

Do you want to come back on that, Makan, at all?

[MAKAN DELRAHIM]

No, I think the debate is a healthy one both here and in the United States because there are some even in the United States who think that antitrust should remedy some of the short-comings of intellectual property law. We've seen that with those two kinds of competing Court of Appeals decisions in the United States, one in the federal circuit Court of Appeal and one in the Ninth circuit Court of Appeal. I mentioned the *Kodak* case, but there is a CSU case and that has gone in completely the opposite way with respect to the unilateral refusals to license as a matter of policy. The Supreme Court has not had the opportunity to comment on that, but as far as *Magill* or *IMS*, some of the commentary may be based on the fact that the claims of copyright were alleged and therefore the decisions are viewed as whether or not it is copyright material, whereas the copyright itself and whether or not it should have been copyrighted material wasn't challenged, and that's what we have in the United States in several cases. I think the *Dawson Chemical* case in 1980 was one that involved patent invalidity and enforceability. The Court, commenting on whether or not antitrust is an effective way of getting to that, ultimately decided on patent misuse doctrines which are now statutory in the patent code in the United States, but as that develops it will be something of interest as new regimes under intellectual property are implemented.

[JOHN KALLAUGHER]

What I would like to do now is take advantage of having the panel here to ask what I think is the most difficult question emerging from this current set of decisions and judgments and that is the idea of the un-met consumer need. This is the lynchpin, I think, of *IMS* as we see it and John, I expect, doesn't want to talk about the case, but I think that IMS would certainly argue that in their case there is no un-met consumer need and certainly that is what they argued before the court and therefore the Commission was wrong to bring all these cases up. I wonder, without having to necessarily address *IMS* directly, whether Thomas and John could talk to us a little bit about their view of what an un-met consumer need is because this obviously depends a great deal on how broad the unilateral obligation to license really is post-*IMS*.

[THOMAS VINJE]

Having not been involved in the case at all I guess I am free to speak about it as I please. Perhaps paragraph 49 of the *IMS* judgment is the most interesting paragraph in this regard and there it says:

The refusal by an undertaking in a dominant position to allow access to a product protected by copyright, where that product is indispensable for operating on a secondary market, may be regarded as abusive only where the undertaking which requested the license does not intend to limit itself essentially to duplicating the goods or services already offered on the secondary market by the owner of the copyright but intends to produce new goods or services not offered by the owner of the right and for which there is potential consumer demand.

Now I would not, but one could go to one end of that spectrum and say that this paragraph would apply only when the party requesting the license will produce an entirely new good or service for which there is no equivalent at all already in the market. That would be one end of the spectrum. The other end of the spectrum would be what I think John would say is the case in *IMS* in which they did essentially intend to duplicate the product. There was, as far as I can tell, really no difference between that which IMS marketed and that which new competitors marketed. In the middle, one might place Microsoft where you do have IBM, Novel, and a number of companies which do market workgroup server operating systems. Indeed they did very well before Microsoft entered that market and they do have functionality which, broadly speaking, is similar to Microsoft products, but it certainly is not identical and certainly the license would not in any way allow them, or be for the purpose of allowing them, to duplicate the Microsoft products because they already have those products which many would say are significantly better than Microsoft products. They certainly do innovate. In many ways they provide many things for which there is consumer demand in terms of security features, in terms of speed of processing, and of all sorts of things. Now within the language of this paragraph, I would suggest that those companies, IBM and the like, do not intend essentially to duplicate the services or goods already on the market. I am sure this will be a matter of debate soon in Luxembourg.

[JOHN KALLAUGHER]

Well thank you. I think we could again go on another bit because there is certainly some room for different interpretations there. You won't reconsider your decision to be silent on this, John?

[JOHN TEMPLE LANG]

No.

[JOHN KALLAUGHER]

That's what I was afraid he was going to say. I'd like to open the questions here up a little bit because I think that Thomas would like to get back to his unilateral refusal to deal point, but before we do that I'd like to, I don't want to cut off discussion from your side. Is there anyone on the floor who has a question that they'd like to put to the panel on these issues?

[GEORGE N ADDY]

My question is to Makan on the *Trinko* decision and perhaps some parts of it that you didn't talk about. I wanted to follow up on that on the basis of what influence it might have on the agencies' enthusiasm to undertake these types of remedies? As I read the decisions, Scalia was saying that part of the fundamental nature of the capitalist system is to reward innovators by allowing them to reap some sort of monopoly rents until their competitors catch up, and also that the courts and agencies haven't been that successful in judging market outcomes. Now I guess I am reading it right, but I'm not as close to the jurisprudence there as you are obviously, and secondly if I am, is that signalling to the agencies to exercise a greater degree of caution or temperance in trying to achieve these types of mandatory licensing remedies or access remedies?

[MAKAN DELRAHIM]

I think, certainly speaking for the Justice Department, but not necessarily for the Federal Trade Commission, since I don't know if their view would be different, the *Trinko* decision goes on not just in this but generally in section 2 in the United States by claiming the *Aspen Skiing*[6] decision stands for the essential facilities doctrine at least at the Appellate Court level, even though the Court had an opportunity to either overturn it or affirm it. It did not. It mentioned it. In the way it mentioned it was in the outer limits of section 2 liability and I think the decision about whether or not antitrust authorities are the proper ones is characterized in that false positives

---

6 *Aspen Skiing Co v Aspen Highlands Skiing Corp* 472 US 585 (1985).

concern that the Court expressed. As I mentioned, I don't think that means the compulsory license is inappropriate for all times. I think it says, 'be careful where you do this to make sure you don't have, especially in the non-merger areas, a limit or a curtailing of the incentives for innovation and make sure that it's narrowly tailored and done properly to limit any kind of adverse consequences on competition and innovation.' So I think your observation is right but I don't think it says that it is out of the question, I just think it says, 'think hard about this'.

[JOHN KALLAUGHER]

Thomas, this almost gets to your unilateral point doesn't it? Do you want to just address this quickly here?

[THOMAS VINJE]

I want to repeat what I said before. I think Europe has been going down the right path with respect to finding unilateral refusals to deal with respect to offering licences to intellectual property, on rare occasions, as constituting an abuse. Maybe I could again use a concrete example looming in the near future where I would suggest it would be appropriate to find a refusal to licence constitutes an abuse and that concerns the mobile software sector. Let us say that there is a company that has a 95–96 per cent market share with respect to desktop operating systems and let us also say that there have been companies who have been developing mobile software for email, calendaring, and the like, on mobile devices. Consumers use those devices to synchronize with and to access data from their desktops and also from servers. Let's say that there is also a dominant position with respect to the email server software by this same company and the market is converging and you have a situation where there never has been interface specifications provided to those producers of mobile software because it's a new thing, but you have a situation where there are clearly two separate markets. The interface specifications between the monopoly desktop and the dominant email server software and that mobile software are essential to competition in that mobile market. In other words, the lack of access to those interface specifications would risk the elimination of competition by those initial developers of mobile software and they have currently been obtaining the information through engineering. Then the dominant company enters the market. It produces its own mobile software which works perfectly with its monopoly and dominant products, and it refuses to provide the interface specifications to the developers of mobile software. Obviously there are all sorts of other considerations that should be taken into account there. That's a simplified picture but I would suggest that if all the 'i's are dotted and the 't's are crossed, that that may very well be a situation where a unilateral refusal to license should be deemed to constitute an abuse.

[JOHN KALLAUGHER]

And just to put it into this comparative context, you are willing to take the risk, I take it, of the false positives in that context?

[THOMAS VINJE]

Yes, I would be very surprised to see those risks realized in reality, put it that way.

[JOHN KALLAUGHER]

Well I think that that sums up or provides a useful conclusion for what I think has been a very interesting panel discussion. What we've seen, I think, is first of all, yes, as we knew at the beginning, there are quite significant differences between the American approach to these issues and the European approach, and indeed that there are differences within the European approach: from people who may be more inclined to protect, to take a restrictive view of what is allowed under Article 82 in terms of requiring people to provide intellectual property, to people who might be inclined to take a somewhat more expansive view of that, and I think without coming to a conclusion on what we have heard from two articulate spokesmen, you can say there is an argument to be made either way. Then there is the American perspective, which is different not just as a matter of policy, but is different institutionally. It is different because of the fact that intellectual property law is federal law and not state law. It is different because of the way in which intellectual property law is enforced in comparison to the EU. All of these things are different, and then there are underlying differences between the two systems and they all come out here today. I think the great thing is that we are able to discuss it in a civilized and comprehensible way. I want to thank the panel for helping us in that direction. Thank you.

F. Forcing Firms to Share the Sandbox: Compulsory Licensing of Intellectual Property Rights and Antitrust

Makan Delrahim*

I. INTRODUCTION

It is a pleasure to be here today to discuss an issue at the forefront of antitrust and intellectual property law: compulsory licensing as a remedy in antitrust cases. Compulsory licensing of intellectual property rights, for good or bad, has been a potential remedy to a whole host of antitrust liability theories, from consummated mergers to refusals-to-deal. Today, I will focus on compulsory licensing purely as a remedy in antitrust matters and not in relation to any particular cause of action.

From the US Supreme Court's decision in *Besser Manufacturing*,[1] to the district court's decision 50 years later in *United States v Microsoft Corporation*,[2] courts have recognized that compulsory licensing can be a necessary remedy in some cases. Compulsory licensing, however, also has the real potential to harm innovation. My goal today is to illustrate the policy and practical issues posed by compulsory licenses, to advise caution when using this remedy, and to suggest ways to use compulsory licensing, when required, that place a minimal burden on innovation and future competition.

As an antitrust remedy, compulsory licenses can be divided into two types: those related to mergers and those related to non-merger cases.[3] Compulsory licensing as a merger remedy is a well-established tool and has not been particularly controversial. Non-merger compulsory licensing imposed by an agency or the courts, though, should be a rare beast.

---

* Deputy Assistant Attorney General, Antitrust Division, US Department of Justice. This paper was presented at the British Institute of International and Comparative Law, London, England, on 10 May 2004.

[1] *United States v Besser Mfg Co*, 343 US 444, 447 (1952) (imposing compulsory licensing on a 'fair' and, apparently, nondiscriminatory basis).

[2] 231 F Supp d 144, 190 (DDC 2002) (decision conditionally approving the consent decree). The consent decree at issue in that reported decision, and currently in effect, is available at http://www.usdoj.gov/atr/cases/f200400/200457.pdf.

[3] Statutory compulsory licenses also exist. See, eg, 7 USC § 2404 (patents necessary for the nation's food supply); 42 USC § 2183 (patents necessary for national atomic energy needs); 35 USC § 203 (patents developed through the use of government research funding); 17 USC § 115 (copyrights in certain musical works). While these clearly qualify as compulsory licenses, they are not remedies—a private or governmental demand for such licenses does not require proof that the owner has violated any law.

As a point of structure, I will turn first to the history of the compulsory licensing remedy in the US and the EU. Next, I will discuss the policy and practical issues raised by compulsory licensing, particularly in the non-merger, non-consent context. Last, I will mention those limited situations where I believe such licensing is the most appropriate, and I will suggest some key items for making a compulsory license potentially less problematic. With that in mind, let's turn to the history of the remedy in the United States.

II. A BRIEF HISTORY OF COMPULSORY LICENSING AS A REMEDY

A. *United States*

Any discussion of licensing in the United States must start with our *Antitrust Guidelines for the Licensing of Intellectual Property*, which state that the United States enforcement agencies attempt to 'apply the same general antitrust principles to conduct involving intellectual property rights that they apply to conduct involving any other form of tangible or intangible property.'[4] That statement is an excellent introduction into my discussion of compulsory licensing in the context of mergers. If we start from the principle that an antitrust agency can certainly demand divestiture of a physical asset in a merger case, we would expect, from the principle articulated in the *Guidelines*, that the agency would also be able to demand divestiture of an intellectual property asset. Taking this one step further, since compulsory licensing is often less burdensome than outright divestiture, one should expect an agency to be able to use compulsory licensing as a potential merger remedy in some situations where, without the license, the merger would result in a substantial lessening of competition. And this is exactly what does, in fact, occur. In the United States, appropriately narrow compulsory licensing is an established remedy in the context of mergers that otherwise would violate the law and can serve as a less-restrictive and more efficient alternative to divestiture.[5] This remedy is relatively uncontroversial, perhaps due to the fact that most such cases appear with the consent of the parties and involve consent decrees and most involve grants to only a single licensee, which is a way merely to preserve the same number of

---

[4] See 1995 Department of Justice & Federal Trade Commission *Antitrust Guidelines for the Licensing of Intellectual Property* § 2.1, available at http://www.usdoj.gov/atr/public/guidelines/ipguide.htm.

[5] See, eg, USDOJ/NK AK Steel consent decree, press release available at http://www.usdoj.gov/atr/public/press_releases/1999/2646.htm; USDOJ/3D System Corp consent decree, press release available at http://www.usdoj.gov/opa/pr/2001/August/414at.htm; USFTC/Dow Chemical Co consent decree, analysis available at http://www.cptech.org/ip/health/cl/uscl/ftc-010212-dow.html; USFTC/Boston Scientific consent decree, analysis available at http://www.cptech.org/ip/health/cl/uscl/ftc-010212-dow.html.

competitors that existed pre-merger.[6] But it is crucial to make such a license as narrow as possible to avoid collusion among competitors in markets not affected by the proposed merger. This is an important point to remember. As the US Supreme Court acknowledged in its recent *Trinko* decision, 'compelling negotiation between competitors may facilitate the supreme evil of antitrust: collusion.'[7]

Turning now to non-merger remedy cases, compulsory licensing has a long but contradictory history. At the turn of the last century, the dominant mode of thinking was to view patent law and antitrust law as opponents – one granted monopolies and one took monopolies away. That mindset required courts to choose sides in a patent-versus-antitrust struggle. In the early 1900s, courts sided with the Patent Act.[8] Compulsory licensing was nearly unknown. But legal thinking gradually changed during the trust-busting period and the New Deal, and by 1952, the pendulum swung back to the point where courts consistently chose the 'antitrust' side. A case in point is *Besser Manufacturing*,[9] which broke up a cartel involving concrete blocks. The Supreme Court in *Besser* described compulsory patent licensing as, I quote, 'a well-recognized remedy where patent abuses are proved in antitrust actions and it is required for effective relief.'[10] A year later, 1953, saw perhaps the most famous compulsory licensing case, *General Electric*,[11] where a district court broke up a light bulb cartel and required GE to issue 'free' licenses to its competitors, the effect being essentially to wipe out GE's light bulb patents.

The Supreme Court also endorsed compulsory licensing in the 1973 case of *Glaxo Group*, stating that compulsory licensing was an accepted remedy.[12] But the pendulum, as some observers call it, again began to swing in the other direction. Just a few years later, in the 1980 case of *Dawson Chemical*

---

[6] Id (patent license to a single competitor; preserved two-competitor market).
[7] *Verizon Communications Inc v Law Offices of Curtis V Trinko, LLP*, 124 S. Ct. 872, 879 (2004).
[8] See, eg, *E Bement & Sons v National Harrow Co*, 186 US 70, 92 (1902) ('The general rule is absolute freedom in the use or sale of rights under the patent laws of the United States. The very object of these laws is monopoly . . . The fact that the conditions in the contracts keep up the monopoly or fix prices does not render them illegal.'); *United States v General Elec Co*, 272 US 476, 493-494 (1926) (holding that patent owner may condition a license to manufacture a product on the fixing of the first sale price of the product); *see generally* R Hewitt Pate *Refusals to Deal and Intellectual Property Rights* (2002) 10 Geo Mason L Rev 429, 441.
[9] *United States v Besser Mfg Co*, 343 US at 447.
[10] Id.
[11] *United States v General Electric Co*, 115 F Supp 835, 843-46 (DNJ 1953).
[12] *United States v Glaxo Group Ltd*, 410 US 52, 64 (1973) ('Mandatory selling on specified terms and compulsory patent licensing at reasonable charges are recognized antitrust remedies.')

v Rohm & Haas,[13] the Supreme Court sharply criticized compulsory licenses, saying, '[c]ompulsory licensing is a rarity in our patent system . . . Compulsory licensing of patents often has been proposed, but it has never been enacted on a broad scale.'

United States appellate decisions since 1980 have been almost silent on the subject of compulsory patent licensing. But I will get to that and clarify further in a little bit. The courts have dealt more frequently with copyright compulsory licensing; however, usually these cases only involve music sharing, not antitrust issues.[14] The exception, of course, is the compulsory license imposed in *United States v Microsoft Corporation*.[15] That license is interesting because it involves not only a consent decree, due to the fact that Microsoft settled with the federal government, but also a fully litigated court-imposed decree, due to the fact that Microsoft did not settle with some of the states. Ultimately, the two decrees were similar in many respects. More importantly, although as yet there is no appellate decision about that remedy, the District Court strongly endorsed the compulsory licensing relief in that case. To quote the District Court, the remedy was 'closely connected with the theory of liability in this case and [will] further efforts to ensure that there remain no practices likely to result in monopolization in the future . . . As a result, the provisions plainly fall within the public interest.'[16] I will return to this later in my comments today.

So what we have in the United States is a bit of a confusing record. Before I try to make sense of this history, let me also mention the EU experience.

B. European Union

There are three high-profile compulsory licensing cases in the European Union, and as in the United States, the precedent is not a model of clarity. I will start with the *Magill* case involving television listings in Ireland and

---

[13] *Dawson Chem. Co v Rohm & Haas Co*, 448 US 176, 215 (1980). The Court noted that '[a]lthough compulsory licensing provisions were considered for possible incorporation into the 1952 revision of the patent laws, they were dropped before the final bill was circulated.' Id at 215 n 21, citing House Committee on the Judiciary, Proposed Revision and Amendment of the Patent Laws: Preliminary Draft, 81st Cong, 2d Sess, 91 (Comm Print 1950). The Court characterized antitrust law and patent law as equivalents in importance: 'The policy of free competition runs deep in our law . . . But the policy of stimulating invention that underlies the entire patent system runs no less deep.' Id at 221.

[14] Eg, *ABKCO Music, Inc v Stellar Records, Inc*, 96 F d 60 (2d Cir 1996); see also 17 USC § 115 (statutory compulsory license for some types of musical works).

[15] Available at INK http://www.usdoj.gov/atr/cases/f200400/200457.pdf and http://www.usdoj.gov/atr/cases/f200400/200457.pdf.

[16] 231 F Supp d 144, 190 (DDC 2002) (decision conditionally approving the consent decree).

Northern Ireland.[17] In *Magill*, several local television stations had each published their own program guides. A publisher, the Magill company, wanted to publish a joint guide. The stations refused and asserted a copyright in their listings. Magill responded with a competition complaint, and the European Court of Justice eventually upheld a compulsory copyright license imposed by the European Commission in favor of Magill.

The second major European case involving a compulsory license is *IMS Health*. In 2001 the European Commission sent a Statement of Objections to IMS, charging that IMS's refusal to license its 'brick structure' for dividing the German market into 1,860 geographical units—used for purposes of collecting and marketing pharmaceutical sales information—was an abuse of dominance, despite IMS's argument that the brick structure was protected under German copyright law. Shortly thereafter, the Commission adopted an 'interim measure' decision ordering IMS to license the brick structure to its two competitors in Germany, pending the Commission's final decision in the matter.[18] The Commission withdrew its interim order last August.[19] The national court of Germany asked for clarification of the relevant competition law standard and, in the most recent pronouncement on this issue in Europe, on 29 April 2004, the European Court of Justice issued a reply.[20] The ECJ's decision stated that while a copyright owner's refusal to license 'cannot in itself' constitute an abuse of a dominant position, such a refusal will be considered abusive if three additional factors are met:

- first, the refusal prevents the emergence of a new product for which consumer demand exists;
- second, the refusal is not justified by any objective considerations; and
- third, the refusal excludes competition in a "secondary market," which appears to mean a market different from the copyright owner's primary product line.[21]

It will be interesting to see how the German court applies this three-part test to the facts of *IMS Health*. Although the ECJ did not specifically say this, the decision strongly implies that dominant firms can lawfully refuse to license any competitor who would operate in the same 'primary market' as the copyright owner. Such a rule would be a significant step away from the

---

[17] *Radio Telefis Eireann v Commission*, Cases C-241 & C-242/91P (1995), ECR I-743, 4 CMLR 718 (1995), 1 CEC 400 (ECJ).

[18] *NDC Health/IMS Health: Interim Measures*, Case COMP D/338.044 (3 July 2001), available at http://europa.eu.int/comm/competition/antitrust/cases/decisions/38044/en.pdf.

[19] *See* Decision, 2003/741/EC, Case COMP/D 38.044, at L 268/71, available at http:// europa.eu.int/eur-lex/pri/en/oj/dat/2003/l_268/l_26820031018en00690072.pdf.

[20] *IMS Health GmbH & Co OHG*, Case C-418/01, available at http:// www.curia.eu.int/jurisp/cgi-bin/form.pl?lang=en.

[21] Id at ¶¶ 34, 38, 53.

Commission's interim measure decision and would bring the state of European law much closer to where US law is today.

As you may be aware, many United States commentators disagreed with *Magill* and the Commission's interim measure decision in *IMS Health*. What may be less obvious is that these commentators' quarrel was not with compulsory licensing in the *remedy* phase of each case. The quarrel was with the *liability* phase, which in essence involved the theory known in the United States as 'unilateral refusal to deal'.[22] Thus is a subtle, but important, distinction. In over a century of antitrust decisions in the United States, only one appellate case, known as the *Kodak* decision,[23] has ever found liability even arguably on this theory, and the prevailing scholarly view in the United States is that *Kodak* was wrongly decided and that the unilateral refusal to deal theory is extremely difficult, if not impossible, to view as an antitrust violation. Compulsory licensing certainly exists in the United States, but it is quite separate from antitrust liability for the refusal to license intellectual property. This may amount to a significant difference between the United States and European Union experiences.

United States commentators had another problem with *Magill* and *IMS*: each case involved a weak copyright in what might well have been considered uncopyrightable facts in the US. A major part of both decisions seems to have been the concern that the underlying intellectual property was questionable.[24] In the United States, a better way to address the copyright issue would have been to do it directly, through the copyright laws themselves, rather than through the blunt instrument of the antitrust laws. I recognize that the European Commission and courts were constrained by the absence of harmonized intellectual property laws in the EU, but if I may, I would sound a note of caution. The Commission's approach could lead to unclear precedent under both bodies of law, antitrust and copyright alike. When uncertainty increases, innovation often decreases, which is exactly the opposite of what should be the long-term goal of competition law. But regardless, I believe that the *Magill* and *IMS Health* cases may provide little precedent for a future case that features undisputed software rights, for example, or strong patent rights.

---

[22] In the context of patents, a unilateral refusal to deal occurs where a patent holder refuses to grant rights in the patent to a potential licensee, but does so without making this refusal conditional on conduct by the licensee and without basing the refusal on an agreement with other third parties.

[23] *Image Technical Services v Eastman Kodak Co*, 125 F 3d 1195, 1225 (9th Cir 1997); cf *In Re Independent Service Organizations Litigation*, 203 F 3d 1322, 1327 (Fed Cir 2000) ('CSU') (finding no liability for refusal to deal in a situation nearly identical to that in *Kodak*).

[24] Cf generally *Feist Publications, Inc v Rural Telephone Service Co*, 499 US 340 (1991) (telephone listings not protected under the Copyright Act, even where a defendant engaged in wholesale copying to create a competing telephone directory).

The third and last EU case I will mention is the Commission's recent decision against Microsoft Corporation. That case is very much a work in progress and we await the judgment of the European courts. Suffice it to say that the Antitrust Division has a number of concerns about the unbundling portion of the Commission's decision. But in terms of the interoperability remedy, which requires Microsoft to license technologies used by Microsoft server software to communicate with other Microsoft software on a network, there is considerable overlap with the United States' remedy. Like the US decree, the EC decision appears to focus on providing competing software developers with the opportunity to build products that communicate and interoperate with Windows-based PCs. Beyond that, for now, I will rely on the statements by Assistant Attorney General Hew Pate in March and April 2004, which are available on the Antitrust Division's website.[25]

What we are left with, in both the US and the EU, is a history without a great deal of consistency. How do we explain this, and particularly the fact that so many of these decisions seem to be all-or-nothing results? I submit that these binary outcomes from the past were the inevitable result of an incorrect, binary way of thinking about the antitrust and patent laws; either the intellectual property laws win, or the antitrust laws win, but never both. The Antitrust Division's view and, I submit, the correct and modern view, is that there is no conflict: antitrust law and intellectual property law serve the same goal of promoting innovation and competition, and we should bear this in mind in the remedy phase just as we do in the liability phase of a case.

This brings me to a list of possible objections to compulsory licensing on both policy and practical grounds, and it also brings me to some thoughts about how the remedy can be used correctly in the future, in those limited situations where it is appropriate.

III. POLICY ISSUES RAISED BY COMPULSORY LICENSING

There are important policy reasons to cause us to be cautious when considering a compulsory licensing remedy. The most important of these is the concern that an improperly-designed compulsory license can stifle innovation.

Some of the risks being taken by today's innovators are massive, with rewards systems that may be very fragile and that could potentially be destroyed by over-aggressive antitrust remedies. As an example I would

---

[25] See http://www.usdoj.gov/atr/public/press_releases/2004/202976.htm; http://www.usdoj.gov/atr/public/speeches/203088.htm.

offer the Iridium satellite telephone network. You may remember that this was a network of satellites shot into space, capable of bringing telephone service worldwide, like no other network, created at a massive cost. It was a stock-market darling in 1998 but unprecedented growth in plain old mobile phones drove the company into bankruptcy just a year later, in 1999.[26] If an antitrust enforcer had looked at Iridium's intellectual property in 1998, wouldn't Iridium have seemed so dominant that rivals needed a compulsory license to compete? If the stock market was so wrong, are we certain that antitrust enforcers or courts would have gotten it right?

Or take the example of Xerox and Kodak, which were the target of compulsory license demands in the Independent Service Organization cases in 1997 and 2000.[27] Xerox was a money-losing company during this period and nearly went bankrupt in 2002. And when you need something photocopied, do you turn to your secretary and say, 'Please go Kodak this for me?' I think we need to be careful not to take competitors' or plaintiffs' claims about so-called dominant firms at face value. Assuming that you think copier innovations are good things, or the development of satellite phone networks is a good thing, you have to permit systems that reward such innovations. The patent system does this well, when we allow it to work, so it is imperative that antitrust enforcers approach that system with some humility. We don't want to kill the goose that lays the golden egg.

Another, related problem is the 'cost of false positives', which is a concept that combines the fear of stifling innovation with concerns over costs to both the government and the defendant. I mention this point due to its prominence in this year's Supreme Court decision in *Trinko*. Let me just quote Justice Scalia, writing for the unanimous Court, who in turn quoted largely from Professor Areeda:

The cost of false positives counsels against an undue expansion of §2 liability [and can] chill the very conduct the antitrust laws are designed to protect . . . No court should impose a duty to deal that it cannot explain or adequately and reasonably supervise. The problem should be deemed irremedia[ble] by antitrust law when compulsory access requires the court to assume the day-to-day controls characteristic of a regulatory agency.[28]

Trinko implies that courts can impose a duty to deal – and by extension, have the power to order a compulsory license – but should be very careful before doing so.

---

[26] See http://news.com.com/2100-1033_3-229816.html. Iridium's stock price peaked at $70 per share in May 1998, followed by a bankruptcy filing in August 1999.

[27] *Kodak,* 125 F 3d at 1225; CSU, 203 F 3d at 1327.

[28] Trinko, 124 S.Ct at 882, quoting PE Areeda 'Essential Facilities: An Epithet in Need of Limiting Principles' (1989) 58 Antitrust LJ 841, 853.

This quote from the *Trinko* decision may not be as broad as it appears, since the case involved the local telephone service industry. That industry is already highly regulated in the United States. But the Supreme Court's warning leads me nicely into my last set of points, which relate to the practical difficulties of compulsory licensing.

IV. PRACTICAL ISSUES RAISED BY COMPULSORY LICENSING

A. *Benefits of the Consent Decree Approach*

Drafting a compulsory license is a difficult process, even for intellectual property licensing lawyers. For antitrust enforcers, licensing is not what we would call our 'core competence'. In the United States, the great majority of compulsory licenses arise out of consent decrees. There are many reasons to prefer this approach, but I will mention only four:

- **Input from interested parties:** A consent decree results from a negotiation, which can involve the full spectrum of interested parties. This includes the government, the defendant, and competitors who may have been harmed. More heads at the table can make for a longer negotiation process, certainly, but can lead to more creative ideas.
- **Buy-in by interested parties:** When parties negotiate a decree, the natural tendency is for them to feel some ownership and to give them an incentive to try to make it work. This can benefit enforcement.
- **Improved enforcement:** Again, if a defendant agreed to a remedy that included a licensing program, it is much more difficult for the defendant to criticize that remedy at a later time.
- **Focus on future conduct:** Parties negotiating a consent license focus less on past harm and more on future competition and future innovation. This clearer focus tends to reduce the chances of "false positives" or other harm to future competition, which was the Supreme Court's concern in the *Trinko* decision.

B. *Considerations for Drafting the License*

Whether the license is by consent or by litigated judgment, certain features will always be difficult. I will mention four of the most challenging, then I will suggest a checklist for drafting a license.

First, we must define the terms of the license. The traditional definition of a compulsory patent license is: 'The granting of a license by a government to use a patent without the patent-holder's permission',[29] but that simple

---

[29] SM Ford 'Compulsory Licensing Provisions under the TRIPS Agreement: Balancing Pills and Patients' (2000) 15 Am U Int'l L Rev 941, 945 (discussing compulsory licensing related to AIDS medications).

definition is next to useless when it comes down to creating a document. Is the scope of the intellectual property, particularly if it is a patent, clear? Is the license only a negative prohibition, meaning simply that a patent owner is barred from suing for infringement? Or does the patent owner have to provide know-how and technology support? Is this an implied license, such as a naked covenant not to sue, or is it a full written license, with normal license terms? Who gets to set field-of-use restrictions or geographic restrictions? Can the patent owner ever terminate for misconduct by the licensee? And this list does not even get into licensing boilerplate such as the term of the license, conditions for payment, accounting, or even indemnities to the licensor or licensee.

Second, a compulsory license will inevitably require some oversight, making it difficult to administer. The oversight difficulty increases as you impose a royalty, and it increases even more if you impose a transfer of 'know-how' and the trade secrets, or at least trade skill, needed to commercialize the patent.

Third, what about future patents in the development pipeline? Some of the old cases, notably the 1953 *General Electric* case, imposed a compulsory license on future patents as well as already-issued patents. On the one hand, this makes sense because the value of a compulsory license would evaporate if a monopolist could come out the very next day with a new blocking patent. But on the other hand, the license could potentially harm innovation by taking away or at least reducing the incentives to invest in future research and development in that field.

Fourth, is the license royalty-free, or if there are royalties, how do you set a reasonable royalty? There is precedent for doing this under patent infringement law, using what United States lawyers call the *Georgia-Pacific* factors.[30] But the *Georgia-Pacific* factors use historical information for past infringement, whereas a compulsory license focuses on the future. As the market changes, would we periodically alter the rate, and if not, why not? A well-known commentator on IP-antitrust issues, Professor Carl Shapiro of the business school at the University of California at Berkeley, has expressed the opinion that when we impose compulsory licensing, we transform the courts into price regulators.[31] It is desirable to reduce the regulatory role, if possible.

---

[30] *Georgia-Pacific Corp v US Plywood Corp*, 318 F Supp 1116, 1120 (SDNY 1970), *modified on other grounds*, 446 F 2d 295 (2d Cir 1971). The fifteen factors include previous royalty rates for licensing of the patent in suit, rates paid by the licensee for the use of other patents comparable to the patent in suit, and the established profitability of the product made under the patent.

[31] See US Department of Justice & Federal Trade Commission Hearings on Intellectual Property and Antitrust, 1 May 2002 Hr'g Tr, The Strategic Use of Licensing: Is There Cause

There is no one correct way to draft such a license, and each case will differ. But I propose that if you conclude that a compulsory license is necessary, ensuring that it has the following elements will address some of the most significant practical problems:

- **Less is more:** To minimize the policy objections and the practical concerns, an overriding goal should be to use the simplest, minimum necessary combination of transfer of rights and government oversight.
- **Objective, verifiable criteria:** Along the same lines, try as much as possible to make the benchmarks for compliance clear. If you do not, ancillary litigation is almost inevitable.
- **Narrow scope:** The coverage of a patent or copyright itself can be a matter of debate, so try to avoid that question by making the scope of the license narrow and clear as to field of use, products, or geography. Consider the question of future intellectual property, but also consider the negative consequences to innovation if future developments will automatically be licensed.
- **Avoid 'know-how' if possible:** Transferring know-how requires ongoing collaboration, which increases the chances of ancillary litigation. Avoid this if you can have a successful license without it.
- **Time-limited:** There should be a sunset provision or at least a mechanism for reconsidering the license as market conditions change, particularly if future patents are involved.
- **Clear royalty:** The royalty term usually will be a 'reasonable and nondiscriminatory' ('RAND') royalty. Be careful, however, to consider whether the defendant will try to make 'reasonable' equate to 'prohibitive'.
- **Clear status of licensees:** In merger cases we often have specific, named licensees. In non-merger cases, we usually have nondiscriminatory licensing to any willing party. Consider which best fits your remedial goals, and make the choice as clear as possible.

V. PREFERRED USES FOR COMPULSORY LICENSING

I hope I have explained why I think this remedy should be avoided where another, simpler remedy is available. That said, I can identify three circumstances where compulsory licensing is particularly likely to be appropriate, although I do not mean to suggest that this is a comprehensive list.

First, a compulsory license is a useful tool in a merger case. If a divestiture is required, a compulsory license can be necessary for the success of one of the divested entities. The narrowness of this license is its virtue—the license typically would apply only to the one divested entity—this remedies the 'supreme evil of antitrust' to use the words of *Trinko*.[32]

A second circumstance is to use compulsory licensing as an alternative to divestiture. For example, the Antitrust Division applied this remedy in 1999 in the AK Steel merger case, where AK Steel sought to acquire the only other competitor that had patent rights to make a type of specialty automotive steel.[33] By a consent order, AK Steel licensed relevant patents to another competitor named Wheeling-Nisshin Inc, and thereby avoided the need to divest part of the combined entities' physical and patent assets or to block the merger completely. This type of remedy shows that compulsory licensing can serve not as a burden, but as a less-restrictive means of accomplishing a competitive result.

And finally, compulsory licensing may be used in a non-merger case when other, less restrictive remedies would most likely fail to address anticompetitive conduct by a defendant. Before imposing the remedy in this type of case, we would look for an extraordinary level of market dominance and a demonstrated history of monopolization and resistance to reform. In other words, we would look for a situation where the chief objections to compulsory licenses evaporate, because monitoring the defendant's behavior has *already* been demonstrated to be a problem and the harm to *other* innovation, by *other* competitors, trumps the alleged harm to the defendant's innovation incentives. But even if compulsory licensing is justified in such a case, the antitrust authorities should draft the license as narrowly as possible. We should adopt the medical principle of 'first, do no harm'. If a defendant has placed a cancer on innovation, cut out the cancer, but be careful not to kill the patient.

In conclusion, compulsory licensing presents many policy and practical issues. I believe, however, that the remedy is appropriate so long as antitrust authorities carefully consider the potential harm to innovation, and draft the license as narrowly as they reasonably can. Thanks for your time today and I look forward to the comments of my distinguished co-panelists on this important topic.

[32] 124 S Ct at 879.
[33] See http://www.usdoj.gov/atr/public/press_releases/1999/2646.htm.

G. Mandating Access: The Principles and the Problems in Intellectual Property and Competition Policy

John Temple Lang*

I. SUMMARY

Two clauses of Article 82 can require mandatory access to intellectual property rights. Article 82(b) prohibits conduct limiting the markets, production or technical development of competitors of the dominant company, if harm is caused to consumers (ie, foreclosure). Article 82(c) prohibits imposing different conditions in equivalent transactions, if a competitive disadvantage is caused (discrimination). Foreclosure is creating a competitive disadvantage vis-à-vis the dominant company itself, which would not exist if it were not for the unlawful conduct. Discrimination is creating a competitive disadvantage vis-à-vis another downstream competitor.

Mandatory access to an intellectual property right can be ordered under Article 82 only if an abuse has been committed. Refusal to licence an intellectual property right is never an abuse in itself. But it can be unlawful if it is connected with a separate abuse, and in those circumstances a compulsory licence may be an appropriate and more effective remedy than merely ordering termination of the abuse. Like any other remedy, it can be ordered only if it is appropriate, proportionate, and effective. In practice a compulsory licence on non-discriminatory terms may be ordered to prevent foreclosure due to termination of access or worsening of the plaintiff's previous terms of access (or any other kind of foreclosure), or to prevent discrimination ('essential facility' cases).

II. EC CASES: MANDATORY ACCESS TO INTELLECTUAL PROPERTY RIGHTS

The question of mandatory access to intellectual property rights has arisen very seldom in European antitrust law. One of the first relevant cases was

* Cleary Gottlieb Steen and Hamilton, Brussels and London; Professor, Trinity College, Dublin; Visiting Senior Research Fellow, Oxford. This paper was delivered at the Fourth Annual Conference on International and Comparative Competition Law, British Institute of International and Comparative Law, May 2004. Some of the points made here are explained in detail in Temple Lang 'Anticompetitive non-pricing abuses under European and national antitrust law' in Hawk (ed) *2003 Fordham Corporate Law Institute* (New York 2004) 235-340.

ungesser,[1] in which the Court said that under Article 81 restrictions on the licensor and other licensees would be justified if, without them, a rational licensee would not take the licence and competition would not be increased at all. Competition authorities should not presume that a licence would have been granted even without the restriction which they criticise.

In *Salora v IGR Stereo Television,*[2] German manufacturers of television transmission and receiving equipment pooled their patents for a stereo television system, and their system was approved by the German authorities. They refused to licence Salora, a small Finnish company, until after most viewers would have bought new sets. The Commission ordered the German companies to grant Salora an immediate licence without quantity limits. No formal decision was adopted. The Commission dealt with the *Salora* case under Article 81 (then 85), but it could have been dealt with under Article 82 (then 86). It has always been accepted that a duty to licence on non-discrimination grounds can arise under Article 81.

The Court of Justice in *Volvo v Veng* and *CICRA v Renault*[3] ruled that the freedom of the owner of an intellectual property right to refuse to licence was the core of the exclusive right, and that therefore the refusal in itself could not be contrary to Article 82. Refusal could be an abuse only if there was some additional 'abusive' conduct, eg, the refusal to supply spare parts to independent repairers, or stopping sales of spare parts for models still in widespread use, or charging excessive prices for the spare parts.

In *Tetra Pak I* (BTG Licence)[4] the Commission decided that the acquisition by a dominant company of an exclusive licencee of the principal alternative technology was contrary to Article 82.

In *Magill,*[5] the television programs case, the television companies in Britain and Ireland each published weekly program magazines listing their own programs. They refused to give lists of their next week's television programs to an independent weekly TV magazine Magill, which wanted to publish all the programs on all the channels for the whole week in one magazine. The

---

1 Case 258/78, *Nungesser*, [1982] ECR 2015.
2 European Commission, Eleventh Competition Policy Report (1981), at 63. The duty to supply under Art 81 is wider than the duty under Art 82(b), which normally arises only if there is *no* other source available, and because under Art 81(3) non-discriminatory licensing may be necessary to avoid the parties having the possibility of eliminating competition in respect of 'a substantial part' of the products in question. A basis of comparison is available if the parties have received licences, and a refusal to licence can amount to a collective boycott. See also Case 22/78, *Hugin* [1979] ECR 1869 and OECD, Competition policy and intellectual property rights, DAFFE/CLP(98)18, (1998).
3 *Volvo v Veng*, Case 238/87, [1988] ECR 6211; Case 53/87, *CICRA v Renault*, [1988] ECR 6039.
4 OJ No L-272/27, 1988; Case T-51/89, *Tetra Pak* [1990] ECR II-309.
5 Case C-241/91P, *RTE and ITP v Commission*, [1995] ECR I 743.

television companies claimed that their programme lists were copyright. The Court confirmed that normally refusal to licence an intellectual property right is lawful. However, the television companies were ordered to give Magill the information, on the basis of Article 82. The Court gave three reasons for ordering disclosure:

• The information was indispensable for the production of a comprehensive TV program guide covering all the TV channels, a new type of product for which there was a clear and unsatisfied consumer demand.
• The TV companies, by refusing to provide essential information, were monopolising the separate market for TV program magazines.
• There was no objective justification for the refusal.

The essential points to note are:

• What Magill magazine needed was the information. The copyright issue had been raised *only* as a defence, by the television companies.[6] The control of the information was not based on the validity of the copyright. The problem would have been the same if there had been no copyright, and the companies had simply refused to give Magill the information.
• Although the Court did not say so, the only provision of Article 82 which could be applicable is Article 82(b).
• The Court did not say whether the two conditions for a compulsory licence (preventing the sale of a new kind of product for which there was

---

[6] In *Philips Electronics v Ingman and Video Duplicating*, High Court London 13 May 1998, CH.1997 P.No 4100, Mr Justice Laddie said (para 52) about *Magill*:

'Even if Irish copyright law did not protect the type of low-level information which Magill wanted to publish, the television companies were the only source of it. If they chose not to distribute the information at all, it was not obtainable elsewhere. Similarly, if they chose to distribute the information in small packages and only at the last possible moment, it might have crippled Magill's nascent business. The information was the raw material from which television guides were made. The television companies therefore held a dominant position both in the information itself and in the guides made from it quite independently of any copyright they might own. It was that dominant position which was being abused. The copyright was merely the tool used to effect the abuse.'

Later he went on (para 55):

'Furthermore on the basis of *CICRA v Renault* and *Volvo v Veng*, I do not accept that the defendants have pleaded an arguable case of abuse . . . the proprietor of an intellectual property right is entitled to go as far as refusing to licence even if it is offered reasonable terms. Based on the cases referred to above it is not an abuse of a dominant position to refuse to licence an intellectual property right on reasonable terms. Even if the royalties sought by the plaintiff are objectively unreasonable and have the effect of destroying the competitiveness of the defendant, it is not an abuse of a dominant position defined by reference to the existence of the intellectual property right. Indeed the proprietor may offer terms which no reasonable competitor could accept. It is difficult to see how that can be worse, or commercially different, to offering no terms at all—i.e. to refusing a licence—a course the rights owner is entitled to take.'

an unsatisfied demand, and monopolising a second market) were alternative or cumulative.[7]

• The copyrighted information was of no literary or artistic value in itself (although the timetables were no doubt the result of planning and market research).

Ladbroke[8] claimed that French horse racecourses were unlawfully refusing to licence Ladbroke to transmit live pictures of French races in its betting shops in Belgium. The Court said the refusal was lawful because, first, the French racecourses were not on the separate Belgian market, so they were not discriminating in favour of their own operations on that market, and second, Ladbroke was on the Belgian market, and so live pictures could not be essential to be present on that market.

An important judgment on 'essential facilities' (*not* concerned with intellectual property) is *Bronner.*[9] A newspaper publisher which had the only home delivery service for the whole of Austria refused to provide delivery services for a competing newspaper. The Court said that the refusal would be unlawful only if it would eliminate all competition by the plaintiff, without objective justification, and if the service was indispensable because there was no actual or potential substitute. There were alternatives to home delivery, and it was possible to develop a competing home delivery system. It had not been shown that it would be uneconomic for competitors, acting jointly if necessary, to set up a second system on a scale similar to the existing system.

III. THE BASIC LEGAL PRINCIPLES

The subject of mandatory access involves several legal principles stated in the Treaty:

[7] See Case T-184/01R, *IMS Health v Commission*, [2001] ECR II 3193, para 104. The *Magill* judgment should be understood as requiring a new kind of product (a comprehensive weekly television programme magazine, as distinct from one limited to one broadcaster), and not merely one more product of the same kind as that already available (which would lead to a duty to licence in every case, if the other conditions were fulfilled). This implies that the demand for the new kind of product must be unsatisfied as well as clear. The more explicit phrase is used in this paper.

[8] Case T-504/93, *Ladbroke*, 1997 ECR II 923: the Court (para 131) said: 'The refusal to supply the applicant could not fall within the prohibition laid down by Article 86 unless it concerned a product or service which was either essential for the exercise of the activity in question, in that there was no real or potential substitute, or was a new product whose introduction might be prevented, despite specific, constant and regular potential demand on the part of consumers.' The Court does not seem to be suggesting that either of these alternatives are sufficient conditions for a duty to supply, it is merely saying that one or the other is a necessary condition.

[9] Case C-7/97, *Bronner v Mediaprint* [1998] ECR I 7791; see also joined cases T-374/94 and others, *European Night Services*, [1998] ECR II 3141.

—Article 4 (competition is an EU objective)

—Article 98 (Member States accept the principle of an open market economy with free competition).

—Article 81 (a duty to provide access on a non-discriminatory basis, as a condition for fulfilling Article 81(3)).

—Article 82(b) (a duty to provide access, to prevent foreclosure).

—Article 82(c) (a duty to provide access, to prevent discrimination).

—Article 295 (the Treaty does not affect national rules on ownership of property).

Mandatory access to intellectual property rights under Article 82 is regarded as an example of the 'essential facility' principle, although the Court of Justice has not used the phrase. It is therefore convenient to summarise the rules on essential facilities, and then to discuss the special rules on intellectual property rights which are said to be essential facilities.

An intellectual property right creates a legal monopoly, but does *not* necessarily create a dominant position. The scope of a patent is not necessarily co-extensive with the scope of the relevant product market. There may be unpatented products or processes which are substitutable for the patented product or process, and there may be other patents protecting products or processes which are substitutable for the patent in question. Though intellectual property rights cost a lot to produce, they can be used at very low marginal cost, so a price above marginal cost does not indicate market power.

Dominance, in itself, is never illegal. It is only abuse of a dominant position which is prohibited. European competition law gives no power to break up a legally acquired monopoly. A dominant enterprise is allowed to compete, as long as it does not use exclusionary or exploitative methods. Doing nothing has never been held to be an abuse.

At least in practice, a distinction must be drawn between a dominant company which acquires the patent or other right from another company, and a dominant company which creates the intellectual property right itself. It is in the former cases that competition law is most likely to intervene. It is legitimate and procompetitive for even an already dominant company to develop or acquire intellectual property rights, and to exercise them in cases of infringement, even if the intellectual property rights give it an important competitive advantage. 'The fact that a dominant trader has, by virtue of his dominance, a competitive advantage over competitors is not an abuse.'[10]

---

[10] Mr Justice Laddie, in *Getmapping v Ordnance Survey*, judgment dated 31 May 2002, High Court, England, HC 02C 00521, [2002] EWHC 1089 (Ch).

Competition law should not be used to try to correct what are said to be defects in intellectual property law.

IV. FORECLOSURE UNDER ARTICLE 82(B) AND DISCRIMINATION UNDER ARTICLE 82(C)

Under Article 82(b), there is a duty to grant access if refusal of access would harm consumers by 'limiting' the production, technical development or marketing of competitors,[11] in a way in which it would not otherwise be limited. Under Article 82(c) there may be a duty to grant access to the facility to a second or subsequent licensee, on non-discrimination grounds. This distinction is important because:

- There can be a duty to give access for the *first* time only under Article 82(b), which expressly requires harm to consumers as an element essential for illegality.[12]

---

[11] Joined cases 40-48/73 *Suiker Unie and others* (*Sugar Cartel*) [1975] ECR 1663, paras 399, 482-483, and in particular paras 523-527; Case 41/83, *Italy v Commission* (*British Telecommunications*), [1985] ECR 873; Case 311/84, *Telemarketing CBEM* [1985] ECR 3261, para 26; Case 53/87, *CICR and Maxicar v Renault* [1988] ECR 6039; Case 238/87, *Volvo v Veng* [1988] ECR 6211; joined cases C-241/91P, *RTE and ITP* ("*Magill*") [1995] ECR I 743 at para 54; Case C-41/90, *Höfner and Elsner* [1991] ECR I 1979 at pp. 2017-2018 in particular para 30; Case C-55/96, *Job Centre* [1977] ECR I 7119 at pp. 7149-7150 paras 31-36; Case C-258/98, *Carra*, [2000] ECR I 4217; Temple Lang, Abuse of dominant positions in European Community law, present and future: some aspects, in Hawk (ed.), Fifth Annual Fordham Corporate Law Institute (1979) 25-83, 52, 60. This point is not mentioned in Faull & Nikpay, The EC Law of Competition (1999) 194, but is correctly stated in eg, Bellamy & Child, European Community Law of Competition (5th edn 2001) 754-755 and in Ritter, Braun and Rawlinson, EC Competition Law—a practitioner's guide (2nd edn 2000) at 362-363; and in Waelbroeck & Frignani, European Competition Law (1999) at 551 ff and in Mercier, Mach, Gilliéron & Affotten, Grands principes du droit de la concurrence (1999) 260-265, among others. In *Arkin v Borchard Lines and others*, High Court, London, 10 Apr 2003, Colman J said (at para 293) 'quite simply, an undertaking in a dominant position must not reduce or attempt to reduce the ability of other participants in the market or of the would-be entrants into the market to compete. This principle palpably underlies the reasoning of the European courts in all the authorities . . .'
See also Gyselen, Abuse of monopoly power within the meaning of Article 86 of the EEC Treaty: Recent developments, in Hawk (ed), 1989 Fordham Corporate Law Institute (1990) 597-650 at pp. 613-617, 635-636; Kauper, Whither Article 86? Observations on excessive prices and refusals to deal, in Hawk (ed.), 1989 op cit 651-686 at 668-685.
The US Supreme Court has recognised that it is sometimes difficult to 'distinguish robust competition from conduct with long-run anti-competitive effects' *Copperweld Corp v Independence Tube Corp*, 467 U.S. 752 (1984), 767-768.
A short-term sacrifice of profits by the dominant company does not necessarily 'limit' the possibilities available to competitors, and may be legitimate to maximise profits in the long term. A downstream price squeeze may not involve any sacrifice of profits at all. Exclusionary conduct may be profitable immediately. But deliberate sacrifice of profits may be evidence of exclusionary intent, unless otherwise explained.
[12] There are strong reasons for saying that harm to consumers is also necessary for an abuse under Article 82(c), but the question has not been decided. A second or subsequent licence of an intellectual property right is not necessarily 'equivalent' to the first arm's-length licence.

- Article 82(b) provides a useful test of exclusionary conduct: does it 'limit' possibilities otherwise open to competitors?
- There can be a duty under Article 82(c) only if the transactions are 'equivalent'. If they are not equivalent, there is no duty to give access under that clause, even on adjusted terms.
- A duty arises under Article 82(c) only if the discrimination would create a 'competitive disadvantage'. So if the companies being treated differently are not in competition with one another, Article 82(c) cannot apply.
- Under Article 82(c), the refusal to licence itself may constitute the abuse, if it is discriminatory. Under Article 82(b), the refusal to licence may constitute the abuse only if, as a result of some other factor, it illegally causes foreclosure which would not otherwise have occurred.
- It is a defence under Article 82(c) to show that the dominant company is offering different terms to meet competition, but such a defence would be inapplicable or irrelevant in foreclosure cases under Article 82(b).
- If both Article 82(b) and Article 82(c) apply, the remedy is not necessarily a duty to grant access on the terms already given to a third party. To avoid foreclosure, it might be necessary to give access on the more favourable terms given to the dominant company's own downstream operations, even if the transactions were not 'equivalent'.[13]
- The dominant enterprise must be present in the relevant market for Article 82(b) to apply: that is not necessary under Article 82(c).

It seems that, in the case of a second or subsequent licence of an intellectual property right under Article 82(c), it is *not* enough to show that a licence has already been granted, and that the transactions are 'equivalent'. It has never been suggested that if a dominant company grants one intellectual property licence, whether voluntarily or compulsorily, it is thereby obliged to grant an indefinite number of other licences on the same terms in 'equivalent' cases. Any such obligation would discourage and seriously complicate granting of first licences, and might even discourage the dominant company from using its own technology, which would be clearly anticompetitive. It seems therefore that even in the case of a second or subsequent licence of an intellectual property right, there is a duty to licence *only* if the conditions for a *first* compulsory licence under Article 82(b) are fulfilled. But this remains to be confirmed.

V. THE FIRST PRINCIPLE: ESSENTIAL FACILITIES UNDER ARTICLE 82(B)[14]

Until 2001, EC competition law on the 'essential facility' principle was clear

---

[13] The law must not allow a dominant company to rely on the fact that it has granted a licence at such a high royalty rate that the licensee's activity is unprofitable, in order to say that it need only grant subsequent licences at the same rate.

[14] Parts of this paper are revised versions of testimony given as a witness at the Hearings of

in most respects. This principle is based on Article 82(b). There is no other provision of Article 82 which makes a refusal of first access unlawful.

Normally, it is pro-competitive to allow companies to keep for their own exclusive use assets which they have acquired or constructed, and to expect other companies to acquire or build corresponding assets for their own use, if they need them to compete. However, if there is an exclusionary abuse contrary to Article 82(b), where a dominant company owns or controls something access to which is essential to enable its competitors to compete, it may be pro-competitive to oblige the company to give access to a competitor, if (but only if) its refusal to do so has sufficiently serious effects on actual or potential competition. This obligation arises, once the abuse is proved, *only* if the competitor cannot obtain the goods or services in question elsewhere and cannot build or invent them itself, and if the owner has no legitimate business justification for the refusal. In other words, the exception applies when *only* 'downstream' competition is possible, and when *that* is possible only if access to the facility is given. The rationale is that one competitor in a downstream market must not be able to get control over the only source of supply of an input which is essential in that market, and monopolise the market by shutting off supply to its rivals, because the two actions would constitute foreclosure. The possibility of having to share a facility, the cost of which is *ex hypothesi* substantial, must always have *some* effect of discouraging investment.

The characteristic of an 'essential facility' case is that the appropriate remedy for the abuse, once the abuse has been identified, is mandatory access on non-discriminatory terms to the input which is necessary in the downstream market. The rules on essential facilities, as they have been understood, say that there is a duty under Article 82(b) to contract on non-discriminatory terms when all the following conditions are met:

1. A company is dominant on the market for the supply of a product or service which is essential for competitors operating on a second (downstream) market.
2. There is no other actual or possible source of the essential product or service, or of a satisfactory substitute for it: competitors could not produce it themselves.

the Department of Justice and the Federal Trade Commission in Washington DC in May 2002 on antitrust law and intellectual property. See Temple Lang, Defining legitimate competition: companies' duties to supply competitors, and access to essential facilities, in Hawk (ed), 1994 Fordham Corporate Law Institute (1995) 245-313; Temple Lang 'The principle of essential facilities in European Community competition law—the position since Bronner' 1 Journal of Network Industries (2000) 375-405; Doherty 'Just what are essential facilities?' 38 Common Market Law Review (2001) 397-436; see generally OECD, The Essential Facilities Concept, OCDE/GD(96)113 (1996).

3. Objectively, competitors cannot offer their products on the second market without access to the product or service.

4. A refusal to supply the product or service would create, confirm or strengthen the company's dominance on the second market[15] (as a seller on that market, and not merely because of its control of an essential factor of production), by 'limiting' or reducing *existing* competition in some way in which it would not otherwise have been restricted, or by preventing the emergence of a new type of product or service offering clear advantages for buyers (not merely one more competitor)[16] which would compete with the dominant company's product. In other words, there must be an identifiable abuse for a duty to contract to arise. Such an abuse can arise when an existing contract is terminated or modified to the prejudice of the other party, or when the dominant company refuses to contract even on the terms on which it normally sells in the downstream market (because such a refusal can only be explained by a wish to squeeze out the other party), or under Article 82(c). *There cannot be a duty under Article 82(b) to contract for the first time unless there has been an identifiable abuse.*[17] It is not an abuse to refuse access merely because the applicant would be better off if it was given access. But there may be a duty to make a second or subsequent contract, on non-discrimination grounds under Article 82(c), with a company with which the dominant company has never previously contracted.

5. There must be scope for substantial non-price competition on the second market, that is, it must not be merely resale or distribution of products or services, and a refusal to contract would prejudice consumers. More competition must be promoted by a duty to contract than would be discouraged by taking away the incentive of the parties to improve the facility or to develop a new facility (apart from the unavoidable effect of discouraging investment in general).

---

[15] If the dominant enterprise is not present on the second market, there can be no foreclosure in its favour, and so only Art 82(c) can apply; Case T-504/93, *Ladbroke* [1997] ECR II-923.

[16] In *Magill*, and in *Sea Containers-Stena Sealink* OJ No L-15/8, 1994, there were new kinds of product or service for which there was a clear and unsatisfied demand, which could be met only if the proposed supplier was given access to the facility (information or harbour). The *Sea Containers* case would be better regarded as coming under Art 82(c), as access was already being given to a third company, or as an abuse against consumers, and *Magill* as primarily an abuse against consumers. If this type of case is regarded as coming under Art 82(b), it would extend the usual principle that a dominant company's conduct is unlawful only if it limits rivals' possibilities in a way in which they would not otherwise be limited (an issue of causation). The extension would be limited to situations in which the dominant company is clearly seeking to protect its product from competition.

[17] All of the cases in which compulsory access has been ordered have involved an identifiable previous abuse, either discrimination, cutting off supply, or depriving consumers of a new kind of product for which there was a clear demand, to protect the incumbent from competition.

6. There is no objective justification for refusal to contract.[18]
7. The Commission has not been compelled to consider the rate of payment which is appropriate in the case of the first compulsory access to an essential facility.
8. At least when a licence of an intellectual property right is asked for, the refusal to licence is unlawful *only* if there is some 'abusive' conduct or element, in addition to the refusal to licence, the effect of which would be exploitative or anti-competitive in some way not merely resulting from the refusal to licence or the exercise of intellectual property right itself.[19]

Because the essential facilities rule is based on Article 82(b), it is subject to the constraints of that clause: there must be some 'limitation' of rivals' possibilities, which harms consumers, ie, exclusionary conduct.[20] The 'essential facility' label does not create a different kind of infringement or different rules. Nor does it create an abuse where no abuse would otherwise exist.

In European competition law, an 'essential facility' may be a product such as a raw material, an intellectual property right, a service, information, infrastructure or access to a physical place such as a harbour or an airport,[21] or a part of a telecommunications network, or a software interface. It is convenient to refer to all these as 'facilities'. The principle now called 'essential facilities' has been applied in Europe in a variety of different industries.[22]

---

[18] Some possible justifications for refusing to contract are listed in Temple Lang 'The principle of essential facilities in European Community competition law—the position since Bronner' 1 Journal of Network Industries (2000) 375-405, at 385-388. Not all of these would be relevant to intellectual property rights.

[19] In non-intellectual property cases, the dominant company may not discriminate in favour of its own downstream activities. But if the essential facility is an intellectual property right, it may licence its own downstream activities without licensing rivals': the difference in treatment is not "additional abusive conduct." Otherwise there would always be a duty to licence rivals if the dominant company was using its own intellectual property.

[20] It was decided in joined cases 40-48/73 *Suiker Unie* [1975] ECR 1663, pp. 1983, 2004 that Art 82(b) prohibits 'limiting' *rivals'* possibilities. Commission decision *British Telecommunications*, OJ No L 360/36, December 21 1982, para 34: Notice on the application of the competition rules to access agreements in the telecommunications sector, OJ No C 265/2. August 22, 1998, para 88. Case 85/76 *Hoffmann La Roche* [1979] ECR 461 and Case 322/81 *Michelin* [1983] ECR 3461 should be regarded as based on Article 82(b). When the Court describes a particular type of conduct as contrary to Article 86, it often does not say which paragraph it is contrary to, because it may be contrary to more than one: joined cases C-395/96P, *Compagnie Maritime Belge*, [2000] ECR I 1365 paras 112 ff.

[21] Advocate General Jacobs in case C-7/97 *Bronner v Mediaset* [1998] ECR I-7791 at 7806-7807.

[22] The phrase 'essential facilities' was first used by the Commission to summarize the previous case law in its decision in the *B&I–Sealink* case, 1992 5 CMLR 255 (a discrimination case), and in its decision in *Sea Containers–Stena Sealink* OJ No L 15/8, 1994. The

If a duty to give access arises, it is a duty to give access on non-discriminatory terms, that is, on terms corresponding to those given to the owner company's downstream operations (because less favourable terms would cause some degree of foreclosure contrary to Article 82(b)). If there are no such operations but Article 82(c) applies, the terms must be sufficient to comply with the requirements of Article 82(c).

VI. MANDATORY ACCESS TO INTELLECTUAL PROPERTY RIGHTS UNDER ARTICLE 82(B)[23]

Mandatory access to intellectual property rights has been regarded as a

Commission referred to judgments based on the same legal principle, Cases 6 and 7/73, *Commercial Solvents*, 1974 ECR 223. Case 311/84 *Telemarketing* [1985] ECR 3261: C-271/90 *Spain v Commission (Telecommunications services)* [1992] ECR I-5833, para 36.
   Port of Rødby, OJ No L 55/52, 26 Feb 1994.
   ACI–Channel Tunnel OJ No L 224/28, 30 Aug 1994.
   Night Services, OJ No L 259/20, 7 Oct 1994; annulled, Cases T-374/94, *European Night Services*, [1998] ECR II 3141.
   Eurotunnel, OJ No L 354/66, 31 Dec 1994.
   Ijsselcentrale, OJ No L 28/32, 2 Feb 1991: see 1992 ECR II 2417.
   Irish Continental Group CCI Morlaix-Port of Roscoff, EC Commission, Twenty-fifth Competition Policy Report (1996), para 43.
   Port of Elsinore, May 1996, Commission press release, IP/96/456.
   Cases C-241/91 P and C-242/91 *RTE and Independent Television* [1995] ECR I-743 ('*Magill*') is the only case of compulsory licensing of an intellectual property right so far upheld by the Community Courts. See also the Merger Regulation decision *WorldCom/MCI*, M.1069, OJ No L-116/1, 1999, para 126 and Commission decision Aug. 28, 2003 *Ferrovie dello Stato* (duty of a dominant railway company to enter into an international grouping with a new entrant, for which it was an obligatory partner, to provide traction and allow access to the track). Case T-65/98, *Van den Bergh Foods* [2003] ECR II, 23 Oct 2003 is *not* an essential facility case: para 161.
   The Commission in its Guidelines on the application of EEC competition rules in the Telecommunication sector (OJ No C 233/2, 6 Sept 1991) said that refusal to provide reserved services (ie services for which a telecommunications company still has a monopoly) would be unlawful when it would make it impossible or difficult for competitors to provide non-reserved services. Companies need access to the networks of the main national telecom operators, and the essential facilities principle is therefore important.
   In the Austrian *Firmenbuch* case, companies were required to provide basic information about their statutes, officers, shareholders, date and form of incorporation, limitation of liability etc. The authorities merely held this information on a business register and made it available to interested parties, without processing it or adding to it. The Austrian court held that the authorities had a legal duty to make it generally available to companies to combine with information not on the register, such as credit ratings etc. The authorities had no copyright in the Firmenbuch information, since it was merely what the companies concerned had told them, although some limited database protection was available: Austrian Supreme Court, judgment dated 9 Apr 2002, Geschäftszahl 40bl7/029 (*Firmenbuch*).
   [23] Cp. Faull & Nikpay, The EC Law of Competition (1999) 633. Article 21 of the Regulation on the Community Patent provides that 'in a situation in which it is necessary to remedy a practice which has been considered anticompetitive at the end of a judicial or administrative procedure, the use of a Community patent may be authorised.' It is not clear whether this adds anything to the legal position already existing under Community competition law. Indeed, because it only applies to 'anticompetitive' practices and not to exploitative practices,

special example of the essential facility principles. The generally accepted principles produce these results:

1. If there is only one market,[24] and the dominant enterprise uses its intellectual property right in that market, no compulsory licence could be ordered.

2. If there is only one market, and the dominant company does *not* use its intellectual property right, no licence can be ordered under antitrust law (a compulsory licence might be possible under patent law exceptionally, eg, on public health grounds).[25]

   A compulsory licence might be ordered if the dominant company had bought the right and then used it to suppress competition, to protect an existing product of its own which was not protected by the right, at least if there was an unsatisfied demand for a new kind of product to which the unused right related.

3. If there are two markets, and the vertically integrated dominant company does *not* use its intellectual property right in the downstream market, there is no duty to licence, because, if the dominant company is not in the downstream market, it has no duty to licence under Article

---

it may not even apply to a compulsory licence given as a remedy for excessive prices or other exploitative abuses contrary to Article 82(a).

Lipsky & Sidak, 'Essential facilities' 51 Stanford Law Review 1187-1249 (1999), at 1218-1220.

The UK Office of Fair Trading, Intellectual Property Rights, a Competition Act 1998 Guideline merely says 'the refusal by a dominant holder of IPR to licence its IPR is not in itself an abuse. It may however be that in certain situations the exercise of the exclusive right in refusing to licence the IPR may infringe' the UK equivalent of Article 82. 'This may occur if there is no objective justification for the refusal and the IPR:

- relates to a product or service which is essential for the exercise of the activity in question, because there is no real or potential substitute; or
- relates to a new product or service whose introduction might be prevented, despite specific, constant and regular potential demand on the part of consumers.'

The Guideline was based on Case T-504/93, *Ladbroke*, [1997] ECR II-923, para 31. It does not suggest that either of these is a sufficient condition for an infringement. It was published by the Office of Fair Trading after the *IMS Health* decision was adopted, very shortly after that decision was suspended: Case T-184/01R, [2001] ECR II 2349 and 3193, and before the suspension was upheld: Case C-481/01P(R), [2002] ECR I 3401.

A national antitrust authority would have no power to order a compulsory licence of an intellectual property right given under the law of another Member State, and Reg. 1/2003 does not alter this.

[24] 'Market' is here used in its normal sense of a demand for and a supply of a product or service. It does not include the mere possibility of granting licences of the intellectual property right. If there is such a right, it is always in principle possible to licence it. But that does not create a market for the purposes of the essential facility principle, and it could not do so, without making every intellectual property potentially right subject to compulsory licensing. The conclusions of the Advocate General in Case C-418/01, *IMS Health v NDC*, are open to this criticism.

[25] See Case 434/85, *Allen & Hanbury* 1988 ECR 1245.

82(b).[26] If it is in the downstream market, but is not using the right, that shows that the right is not 'essential'. However, if the effect of the refusal to licence is that nobody can produce in the downstream market, this may be unlawful abuse if the effect is to force buyers to buy the dominant company's product in the upstream or another market.

4. If there are two markets, and the dominant company uses the intellectual property right in the downstream market, there can be a compulsory first licence if there is a distinct identifiable abuse. An abuse has been said to occur in these situations (but the list is not exhaustive):

   (i)   If by refusing the licence the dominant company is both monopolising the downstream market and preventing users getting a new kind of product for which there is an unsatisfied demand (*Magill* judgment).[27] A company may commit an abuse if it owns the intellectual property right for a desirable new product and neither uses it nor licences it, to protect its existing products from competition. This implies that it is a defence if the dominant company will produce the new product.

   (ii) If the dominant company (or the previous owner of the intellectual property right) had previously given licences, and let its licensees build up downstream activities on that basis, it cannot then terminate their licences, so that it could integrate forward without competition (*Commercial Solvents* judgment,[28] which however did not involve intellectual property rights). (But if the dominant company owned the intellectual property right initially and built the downstream market on it without granting licences, it has normally no duty to licence: it can keep the downstream market to itself).

   (iii) If the dominant company is refusing to supply or licence the production of spare parts, in order to create or extend its dominance in the separate repair services market. This was said to be unlawful, in *Volvo v Veng*.[29]

---

[26] Case T-504/93, *Ladbroke* [1997] ECR II 923.

[27] Case C-241/91P, *RTE and ITP* [1995] ECR I 743; Case T-198/98, *Micro Leader*, [1999] ECR II December 16, 1999.

[28] Cases 6 and 7/73 *Commercial Solvents* [1974] ECR 223; see also Case T-51/89, *Tetra Pak* [1990] ECR II-309.

[29] Case 238/87, *Volvo v Veng* [1988] ECR 6211; Case 53/87, *CICRA v Renault* [1988] ECR 6039. Case 311/84 *Telemarketing v CLT and IPB* [1985] ECR 3261; Case C-260/89 *ERT* (Greek television) [1991] ECR I-2927; Case T-65/89 *British Gypsum* [1993] ECR II-389, paras 92-93; Case T-83/91 *Tetra Pak II* [1994] ECR II-755, at paras 114-116; Cases C 241/91, 242/91 *RTE and ITV* [1995] ECR I-743. These cases show that in cases not involving intellectual property rights, using power in one market to strengthen the dominant company's position in a related market by lessening or eliminating competition in the second market may be unlawful. But this cannot apply directly to intellectual property rights, which inherently limit competition.

(iv) The refusal is combined with refusal by the dominant company either to produce or to allow others to produce, eg, a spare part for one of its old products, so that users will be forced to stop using that product and to buy its new product.[30]

(v) The refusal is combined with prices charged by the dominant company for its products which are so excessively high as to be 'unfair' and prohibited by Article 82(a). This case is discussed separately, below.

(vi) A widely recognised situation, not mentioned specifically by the Court, is where a dominant enterprise acquires important competing technology which it intends to leave idle, and which cannot be invented around ('suppressing patents').[31]

(vii) Where an abuse of 'tying' or 'bundling' of two products which need to be compatible has been prohibited, the dominant company

---

It has been suggested that the *RTE Magill* judgment was influenced by the view that the copyright in the list of weekly television programmes was not the result of creative effort and was therefore of lesser value. But even if there had been no copyright, the TV companies could have refused to provide the information. The case did *not* depend on there being a valid copyright. Also, neither EC law nor national law distinguishes between intellectual property rights of lesser or higher value. There is no legal basis in EC law for saying that some intellectual property rights are second-class rights and can be overridden more easily than others. The EC institutions have no legal power to distinguish between 'good' and 'less good' copyrights. The idea that some copyrights have less value is not suggested in the Commission's decision in *Magill*, nor is it suggested in the judgments of the Community courts in *Magill*. It was not suggested by the Commission in *IMS Health*, and it could not justify the suggestion that a compulsory licence can be ordered when no abuse (other than the refusal to licence) has been committed. The Commission's Notice on the application of Art 81(3) says 'it is only in the precise framework of Art 81(3) that the pro- and anticompetitive aspects of a restriction may be weighed', and the same must be true under Art 82. In any case, an apparently banal list of programmes may be the result of considerable planning and market research into peak viewing hours and viewers' preferences and habits.

Nor is it clear why there might be a distinction between, eg, patents and copyright. A copyright is of less value than a patent, but does not confer a monopoly of anything except the mode of presentation, so is less likely to create a need for a compulsory licence. There would be obvious dangers if a competition authority claimed to decide which intellectual property rights were undesirable or unjustified or insufficiently robust as there would be no legal basis and no criteria for doing so.

[30] Under the 'spare parts' clause in Art 8 of the EC Regulation 6/2002 on Community designs, OJ No L-3/1, January 5, 2002, a Community design right cannot be obtained in features of the appearance of a product which are solely dictated by its technical function, or in features which must necessarily be reproduced in their exact form and dimensions to permit the product to be mechanically connected to another product to perform its function.

[31] Art 82(b) also prohibits limitation by the dominant enterprise of its *own* production or technical development, to keep prices up or to protect an existing product line, but there are no cases of this kind. It would be possible to prove this only in an extreme case, unless suppressed technology had been bought. See Case T-51/89, *Tetra Pak* [1990] ECR II-309 ('*Tetra Pak I–BTG licence*'). If the technology acquired is the only available alternative technology, it is in effect an essential facility even though the dominant enterprise has a second technology.

must provide interface information because without it the remedy would be ineffective.[32]

The mere fact that the dominant company has licensed its own downstream operations and refuses to licence a competitor's is *not* discrimination or foreclosure which amounts to 'additional abusive conduct' which makes a compulsory licence necessary (otherwise there would always be a duty to licence).

If the comment in *Volvo v Veng* in (iii) above is correct, it implies that monopolising a distinct second market may be unlawful even when intellectual property rights are used, and that the two requirements in *Magill* (see (i) above) might be alternatives and not cumulative. This conclusion would follow only if there was no abuse other than limiting competition in the second market. If this is correct, it would apply only when the second market is distinct from the primary market, eg, when a compulsory licence could be ordered for the second market without affecting the value of the dominant company's activities on the upstream market, as in *Magill*. But a vertically integrated dominant company is entitled to use its intellectual property right in any market to which the intellectual property right applies, although the right does not entitle it to commit a distinct abuse against consumers. There is no basis in competition law for saying that an intellectual property right can be used to monopolise one kind of market but not another kind.[33]

The solution can be seen from the words of Article 82(b). The duty to grant a *first* licence of an intellectual property right arises, even if all the other conditions are fulfilled, only if there is some abuse or abusive conduct or effect which is not merely the result of the exercise of the right, and only if the refusal to licence harms consumers. If the refusal prevents the development of a new kind of product for which there is a clear and unsatisfied demand, there is both harm to consumers, which is not merely the result of the refusal to licence, and additional abusive conduct. The same effect can constitute both the abuse and the consumer harm. So in *Magill* both conditions were fulfilled.

If harm to consumers arises *only* because the refusal to grant a first licence prevents competition from developing in the downstream market, there

[32] This was in essence one of the issues in the IBM case: Commission, Fourteenth Report on Competition Policy (1984) paras 94-95.

[33] In cases not involving intellectual property rights, it is contrary to Art 82 to use power in one market to limit competition in another: see eg, C-260/89, *ERT* (*Greek Television*) [1991] ECR I 2927; Case T-65/89, *British Gypsum*, [1993] ECR II 389, paras 92-93; Case T-83/91, *Tetra Pak II* [1994] ECR II 755, paras 114-116. In two-market essential facility cases, there can be a contract for access to the downstream market without otherwise affecting the dominant position in the upstream market.

must also be some other additional abuse which is distinct from the refusal to licence. If there is no additional abuse, there cannot be infringement of Article 82(b). Monopolising the downstream market might harm consumers, which is necessary for an infringement of Article 82(b). But since that is or may be a natural result of the refusal to licence, it cannot also constitute the additional element which is necessary in an intellectual property case. The refusal adds nothing to the situation resulting from the existence of the intellectual property right. Therefore, two elements are always needed. Any other view would deprive owners of intellectual property of a significant part of their rights. So foreclosure may lead to a duty to licence only if the foreclosure is *not* due merely to exercise of intellectual property rights.

VII. ADDITIONAL ABUSIVE CONDUCT

The basic principle is that a dominant company which owns an intellectual property right is not obliged, merely because it is dominant, to licence the right, even if the right contributes to or causes the dominance. Mere refusal to grant a licence of an intellectual property right is *not* unlawful under Article 82. Any other rule would be inconsistent with the concept of intellectual property, and with the principle that Article 82 can apply only if an abuse is being committed. It would also be inconsistent with Articles 4 and 98 EC, which must allow a dominant enterprise to compete, and to invest in intellectual property in order to do so.

Refusal is unlawful only if it is combined with some additional 'abusive conduct'.[34] An intellectual property right is not a valid reason for refusing to contract, if the refusal is linked to a separate abuse, eg, by making it possible, or reinforcing it.[35] A wholly unrelated abuse would not affect the

---

[34] The phrase 'abusive conduct' was used in Case C-241/91P *RTE and ITP* [1995] ECR I, at p. 823.

[35] There are a number of cases under Art 82 in which conduct which might have been lawful in isolation was unlawful because it was combined with other behaviour making up an exclusionary strategy: Case 27/76, *United Brands*, 1978 ECR 207; Case 53/87, *CICRA v Renault*, [1988] ECR 6039, 6073; T-83-91, *Tetra Pak* 1994 ECR II 755 and 1996 ECR 5951; T-65/89, *British Gypsum* 1993 ECR II 389; T-228/97 *Irish Sugar* 1999 ECR II; C-395/96P, *Compagnie Maritime Belge*, March 16, 2000.

Commission Merger Regulation decision *Microsoft/Liberty/Telewest*, Thirtieth Report on Competition Policy (2000) at 186-187 (the Commission argued that Microsoft regularly set up working groups to influence buyers' choice of software).

In predatory prices cases under the second *Akzo* rule (price between average variable costs and average total costs, and evidence of intention to exclude a competitor) the evidence will necessarily be cumulative.

In *Pitney Bowes v Francotyp–Postalia* (1991 FSR 72) the UK court held that the owner's ability to enforce its intellectual property right could be limited if the right created or strengthened the dominant position which was being abused. See also *Rensburg GEMA v Electrostatic*

lawfulness of the refusal to licence. The other abuse may be outside the market to which the intellectual property right primarily relates, and the abuse is relevant only (because of Article 82(b)) if the harm to consumers is serious enough. As already mentioned, the characteristic of 'essential facility' cases is that when an abuse has been identified, the remedy may be to order mandatory access to the facility, not merely to stop the abuse.[36]

The question arises, because the list of examples of 'additional abusive conduct' in *Volvo v Veng* and in *Magill* is not exhaustive, what kinds of other conduct might be sufficient.

The additional element must be an abuse prohibited by Article 82. It must be something done by the dominant company, or which is the effect of something done by it, or for which it is responsible. It must involve effects which are not merely the normal result of enforcing the intellectual property right in the market in which it primarily applies. The additional element cannot be merely an economic monopoly, because that is, at least

---

Plant System [1990] FSR 287; *IBM v Phoenix International* [1994] RPC 251; *Chiron Corporation v Murex Diagnostics* [1994] FSR 187. But if the intellectual property right creates the dominant position which is being abused, a compulsory licence might put an end to the dominant position as well as to the abuse, and this would normally be disproportionate. The compulsory licence should only be the appropriate remedy for the 'additional abusive conduct', as it was in the *Magill* case.

[36] See concerning copyright, Case 158/86 *Warner Brothers Inc. and Metronome Video ApS v Erik Viuff Christiansen* [1988] ECR 2605 ¶¶ 12-13; and concerning patents, Case 19/84 *Pharmon B.V v Hoechst AG* [1985] ECR 2281 ¶ 26.

In *Volvo*, the Court stated: "It follows that an obligation imposed upon the proprietor of a protected design to grant to third parties, *even in return for a reasonable royalty*, a licence for the supply of products incorporating the design would lead to the proprietor thereof being deprived of the substance of his exclusive right" (Case 238/87 *AB Volvo v Erik Veng (UK) Ltd* [1988] ECR 6211, ¶ 8).

The Commission has reached the same conclusion in a case concerning a request for compulsory licensing of intellectual property (relating to hepatitis) in the market to which it primarily relates: 'it is highly doubtful whether one could impose an obligation upon a dominant firm (in an eventual EC bulk intermediate Hep B market), as a remedy to ensure the maintenance of effective competition in the national Hep B markets, to share its intellectual property rights with third parties to allow them to develop, produce and market the same products (ie multivalent containing the Hep B antigen) which the alleged dominant firm was also seeking to develop, produce and market' (Complaint by *Lederle-Praxis Biologicals*, XXIV Competition Report, 1994, point 353).

Venit and Kallaugher 'Essential Facilities: a comparative law approach' in Hawk (ed) Fordham Corporate Law Institute, International Antitrust Law & Policy (1995), 337.

This led the court to reject an essential facilities claim in the UK case CH 1997 P No 4100 *Philips Electronics NV v Ingman,* 13 May 1998; see Treacy 'Essential facilities – is the tide turning?' 1998 European Law Review 501-505.

Lipsky and Sidak 'Essential Facilities' 51 Stanford L Rev (1999), 1187, at 1219. This led the authors to conclude that essential facilities principles should not apply to intellectual property under US law.

Bishop and Walker *The Economics of EC Competition Law* (1999) 119-120; Ridyard 'Essential facilities and the obligation to supply competitors under UK and EC competition law' 8 European Competition Law Review (1996) 438-452 at p. 446.

temporarily, often the result of enforcing an intellectual property right. It must bring about some other effect which is anticompetitive or exploitative, and which harms consumers. There must be some link between the refusal to licence and the 'additional conduct' which makes the refusal unlawful and which explains why a compulsory licence is appropriate in the light of the additional conduct, or as a remedy for the additional conduct. Usually the refusal must make the other conduct possible, or reinforce or worsen its anticompetitive or exploitative effects. Presumably the link must be such that merely putting an end to the other abuse would not be a sufficient or an effective remedy.[37] So it would be 'additional abusive conduct' if the dominant company refused to licence except on anticompetitive terms (eg, on condition that the licensee did not challenge its intellectual property rights) or on exploitative terms (eg, if it insisted on a royalty-free licence of the licensee's rights), or if it refused to licence an intellectual property right which it had committed itself to licence for the purposes of an agreed standard.

Elements which confirm or are relevant only to the company's dominance cannot be regarded as 'additional abusive conduct': the conduct in question, whatever it is, must constitute the abuse. Features of the market which cause the legal monopoly given by the intellectual property right to lead, temporarily or permanently, to an economic monopoly may explain dominance but cannot constitute abuse. So the fact that the intellectual property right is unique, valuable, difficult to duplicate or to 'invent around' or creates an unbeatable competitive advantage cannot amount to 'abusive conduct'.

The view that the 'additional abusive conduct' must be in itself an identifiable abuse, contrary to some provision of Article 82, makes the law clear. Unless 'additional abusive conduct' means 'a separate abuse', it is not easy to see what it could mean. If it does mean 'a separate abuse', there is no reason why it should be limited to any particular type of abuse, whether exploitative or exclusionary. But if it is exclusionary, it must be something more than the mere exercise of intellectual property rights.

VIII. THE SECOND PRINCIPLE: MANDATORY ACCESS ONLY AS A REMEDY

What has been said above does not explain the comment of the Court and the Advocate General in *Volvo v Veng* that a refusal to licence may be illegal if it is combined with excessive prices which are contrary to Article

---

[37] On the relationship between trademark rights and a related unlawful agreement which was contrary to Art 81, see Cases 56 and 58/64, *Consten and Grundig*, [1966] ECR 299 at 345.

82(a).[38] This comment appears hard to understand, because excessive prices have nothing to do with essential facilities, and would be an abuse in the same market as that for which the compulsory licence would be granted. This is inconsistent with the well-established principle that in essential facility cases there must be two markets.

So there is a second principle, which applies to exploitative abuses, and which may be a general principle which provides an overall explanation of the cases, although it is not how the Court has explained them. This principle is that it is *never* an abuse to refuse to give a licence of an intellectual property right, (and there is never a duty under Article 82 to give access to a facility *merely* because it is essential), but that if the dominant company has committed an abuse, mandatory access may be the appropriate remedy. Even if this principle does not replace the existing case law, it provides a useful guideline in future cases, in parallel with the existing case law on essential facilities.

There are a number of arguments for this way of looking at the subject:[39]

- It provides a rational, coherent and comprehensive basis for the relevant legal and economic principles, which should be broadly acceptable to both competition lawyers and intellectual property lawyers, since it does not regard the two bodies of law as conflicting.
- It confines the concept of 'abuse' under Article 82 to the three correct, useful and traditional areas under European competition law: exploitative abuses (Article 82(a)), foreclosure of competitors (Article 82(b)), and unjustified discrimination between companies not otherwise associated with the dominant company (Article 82(c), which is primarily to prohibit protectionist discrimination by State enterprises).[40]
- It answers the question: if refusal to give access is only illegal when linked to a separate abuse, why not simply prohibit the separate abuse? The only answer is: because mandatory access, when appropriate, is a more effective remedy.

---

[38] See also Case 78/70, *Deutsche Grammophon v Metro*, [1971] ECR 487.

On the view suggested in the text, essential facility cases would be a sub-set of the cases in which compulsory access or a compulsory licence is the appropriate remedy, not vice versa. But it seems simplest to accept that there are two parallel principles.

[39] See judgment of Mr Justice Laddie in *Philips Electronics v Ingman and Video Duplicating*, High Court London 13 May 1998 CH. 1997P No 4100 para 37: 'The existence of the intellectual property rights may facilitate anti-competitive behaviour, but such behaviour consists of abusive interference with the market for a product . . . In prohibiting the conduct the court may have the power to intervene in the manner in which the intellectual property rights are exploited by the proprietor. This is to ensure that the proprietor does not continue the abusive conduct in relation to the products by the back door route of using the intellectual property rights.'

[40] Temple Lang and O'Donoghue 'Defining legitimate competition: how to clarify pricing abuses under Article 82 EC' 26 Fordham International Law Journal (2002) 83-162.

- It involves no new rules or concepts.
- It encourages use of a market-based remedy requiring little antitrust supervision, which would be particularly useful in excessive pricing cases.
- It creates a rule with built-in limiting principles: there would be no new concept of abuse and, as in the case of any other remedy for an abuse under Article 82, it would be necessary to consider whether compulsory access was an appropriate, proportionate and effective remedy to put an end to the abuse. This question arises on any view of the law.
- It provides a basis for distinguishing cases where the dominant company developed the property itself (normally, no duty to licence except under Article 82(c)), and cases where it acquired the property and then deprived its competitors of access to it (a duty to licence is appropriate if the dominant company is restricting existing competition, or foreclosing potential competition by protecting itself against a new kind of product for which there is a clear and unsatisfied demand).
- It gives the phrase 'additional abusive conduct' a clear meaning, that of 'abuse'.
- It confirms that, in principle, it is never illegal in itself to refuse to licence an intellectual property right, as the Court has repeatedly said.
- It would *not* provide a basis for protecting competitors rather than competition.
- It provides a rationale for saying what almost all lawyers believe is the law, that a dominant company has no duty to facilitate companies which wish to add on or imitate devices unless it has taken steps to exclude them or create difficulties or handicaps for them.
- It would provide a solution to the problem of the after-effects of abuses on the market (because the remedy can take away the improperly acquired proportion of the dominance, if that can be estimated).
- It allows a variety of justifications for refusal to licence.
- It seems to be an approach on which European and US law could agree.
- It allows a distinction to be drawn between a compulsory licence in a single market situation (eg, excessive pricing), which can be appropriate only if the abuse is in that market, and which requires a strong justification, and a compulsory licence in a second distinct market, which is more likely to be proportional.
- It does not involve trying to use competition law to correct any defects which may exist in intellectual property law.

IX. THE TERMS FOR MANDATORY ACCESS

In most compulsory licence cases, the transaction costs will be small because the licence terms will be the same as or similar to existing licences (in Article 81(3) and 82(c) cases) or to a recently terminated or modified licence (in Article 82(b) cases). Substantial transaction costs, due to the serious difficulty of determining the appropriate rate of royalty and conditions, arise only under Article 82(b) where there is no pre-existing licence and the duty to licence is based on an abuse other than the termination of a licence or worsening of previous licence conditions.[41] This problem arose in *Magill*, and was settled by a compromise. Even for a regulatory authority there are no established principles for doing this, and competition law provides none. The only principles which it seems possible to state at present are that, in order for the licence to be appropriate, proportionate and effective (in addition to the rules on essential facilities summarised above):

1. The dominant enterprise is entitled to a royalty if the intellectual property licensed is valuable in itself (there may be no right to a royalty if the licence only concerns interface information).

2. The dominant enterprise is not entitled to be compensated for loss of profits which were obtainable only through charging excessive prices, contrary to Article 82(a), or for loss of immunity from competition in other respects. Neither avoidable costs (incremental costs for the owner by providing access: these would be zero or marginal in the case of most intellectual property rights) nor fully compensatory costs (including compensation for loss of monopoly profits) would be an appropriate basis for a royalty.

3. The dominant enterprise never has a duty to make a loss on the licence contract, to subsidise a competitor, or to make inefficient entry possible, or to allow market entry which would make both companies uneconomic.

4. A compulsory licence can be ordered to end the abuse, but not to end the dominance (unless the dominance was unlawfully obtained). Therefore a compulsory licence should not be ordered if it would be irrational for the owner ever to grant a licence, eg, a license of the licensor's principal competitive advantage to a direct competitor in the same market. Also, a compulsory licence should not be ordered on terms so favourable to the licensee that the dominance is ended. However, if the dominance is not due to the intellectual property right, there is more flexibility.

5. It is unlikely to be appropriate to order a licence of an intellectual property right to a product for the first time as an *interim* measure, because the Treaty does not alter the national law on property ownership,

---

[41] Where there was a previous licence, the risk of discouraging competition and investment by ordering a compulsory licence is very much less.

Transaction costs of a first licence are less if the royalty and other terms are fixed under regulatory powers, allowing new and precise obligations to be created on policy grounds.

interim measures are primarily for preserving the *status quo* pending a definitive decision, and because a licence once granted is likely to have irreversible effects.[42] This difficulty is *not* overcome by fixing a provisional royalty rate in the interim decision.

6. In intellectual property cases, marginal cost is <u>not</u> an appropriate benchmark for assessing excessive prices, inter alia because companies must be allowed to obtain an adequate return from investment in innovation.

7. The need for continuing regulatory supervision should be minimised as far as possible.

X. CONCLUSION

The need for general principles on mandatory access is not merely theoretical, or the result of tidy-mindedness. If there is no clear general principle, there is *always* a danger that any competition authority will adopt decisions in intellectual property cases on the basis of a static analysis which increase competition in the short term, but reduce it in the long term by discouraging innovation, either by the parties, or generally. Such decisions might be correct in any particular case. But if there are no clear general rules, the case law is likely to develop through a series of short-term decisions which will erode the value of intellectual property rights. It is not possible to confine the disincentive effects of compulsory licensing to an individual case. This risk is particularly likely to arise because cases involving intellectual property rights usually begin with complaints from competitors, and a persuasive competitor can sometimes obtain a competition decision which protects it *against* competition from the dominant company. That is not what competition law is intended to do.

Another serious consequence of not having any clear and generally accepted rule is that every case is likely to be analysed, in effect as if it was a regulatory policy issue, on the basis of pragmatic, *ad hoc*, arguments for or against action under competition law in the light of the particular facts. This would be inevitably time-consuming, complicated, and uncertain (because the results of weighing up arguments cannot be satisfactorily anticipated). It would be expensive in time and legal fees.[43] It greatly increases the complexity of the law. The lack of a clear general rule is also anticompetitive, because the uncertainty discourages companies from

---

[42] Case T-184/01R, *IMS Health v Commission*, Order of the President of the Court of First Instance, [2001] ECR II-3193, paras 91, 128-132, 143-144; Temple Lang 'Defining legitimate competition: companies' duties to supply competitors, and access to essential facilities' in Hawk (ed) 1994 Fordham Corporate Law Institute (1995) 245-313, at 292-293.

[43] See eg, *Intel v Via*, Court of Appeal, London 20 Dec 2002.

procompetitive behaviour because of the fear that it might be regarded as illegal, or at least that it will result in litigation. This increases the risks of gradual erosion of the incentive to innovate.

For these reasons I propose four general principles, on foreclosure, discrimination, exploitative abuses, and the remedies for them:

- Article 82(b) prohibits conduct by which the dominant company 'limits', restricts or eliminates a competitor's possibilities of marketing, production or technical development when harm to consumers results. (This is clearly established).
- A compulsory licence of an intellectual property right is available *only* as a remedy for an identified abuse which is contrary to Article 82, and only when that is an appropriate and proportionate remedy. Mandatory access should not be ordered unless an abuse has been committed. (This seems a correct summary of the existing law).
- Compulsory licences may be required under Article 82(c) and Article 81(3), on non-discrimination grounds. (This is clearly established).
- A second or subsequent compulsory licence should be ordered on non-discrimination grounds under Article 82(c) only if the conditions for a first compulsory licence of the intellectual property right under Article 82(b) are also fulfilled. (This awaits confirmation).

XI. APPENDIX

The IMS Health case

Since the judgment of the Court of Justice in the *Magill* TV programmes case in 1995, the European antitrust law principles were generally regarded as well-settled and clear in most respects, except the rate of royalty in first licence cases. However, in 2001 the Commission adopted a decision in *IMS Health*, which put a number of these principles into question.[44] If the decision is ultimately upheld, it is not clear what the implications would be.

There are several reasons why it is difficult to write about this decision. It is at present *sub judice*, on appeal in the Court of First Instance.[45] Several issues which are essentially similar to those in the Court of First Instance have been raised in case before German courts, which are also *sub judice*.[46] The decision is an interim measures (interlocutory) decision, and therefore not as fully considered and explained as a final decision normally would be. The Commission seems to have changed its legal position in the course of

[44] OJ No L-59/18, 28 Feb 2002; withdrawn, OJ No L-268/69, 2003.
[45] Case T-184/01, *IMS Health v Commission*.
[46] Case C-418/01, *IMS Health v NDC Health*: opinion of Advocate General Tizzano, 2 Oct 2003, judgment dated 29 Apr 2004.

the *IMS Health* case, even before it withdrew the decision. Some lawyers defend the deciison on grounds not mentioned or relied on by the Commission. Last, my law firm, Cleary Gottlieb Steen and Hamilton, is representing IMS Health in both Community Courts.

IMS Health provides pharmaceutical companies with information on sales of pharmaceutical products in Germany, among other countries. This information is used, in particular, as the basis for paying sales representatives. Since these representatives talk to doctors and not to patients or pharmacists, and since patients who get prescriptions from doctors may buy the prescribed drugs from pharmacies where they live or work and not from pharmacies in the neighbourhood of the doctor, collecting and presenting the information in a way that best allows the pharmaceutical companies to measure the effectiveness of their sales representatives is complex and difficult. European data privacy laws do not permit sales data to be presented in a way which would allow readers to identify the sales of any individual pharmacist. IMS Health solved this problem by producing a map of Germany divided into areas, drawn so as to group together in each area as far as possible a full range of specialist doctors and the pharmacists to whom their patients are likely to go to have prescriptions made up. IMS Health then collects sales data from wholesalers which sell to the pharmacists, and supplies the data to pharmaceutical companies on the basis of each area. These areas are then used as the basis of the representatives' sales territories. When it appeared that competitors of IMS Health were using the area structure which IMS had developed, (in which Germany was divided into 1860 areas), IMS sued for copyright infringement, and the German courts accepted that the map of 1860 areas was copyright. The competitors complained to the European Commission, arguing that because the pharmaceutical companies insisted on using the 1860 map, the use of IMS's structure was essential for them to supply sales information to pharmaceutical companies.

The Commission, by an interim measures decision in July 2001, ordered IMS to grant a copyright licence to its two competitors. IMS appealed against this decision, and in October 2001 the decision was suspended by Order of the President of the Court of First Instance.[47] This Order says that a judge should

---

[47] Case T-184/01R, [2001] ECR II 2349 and 3193. See Schwarze 'Der Schutz des geistigen Eigentums im europäischen Wettbewerbsrecht' Europäische Zeitschrift für Wirtschaftsrecht 3/2002, 75-81; Pitovsky et al 'The essential facilities doctrine under US Antitrust Law' 70 Antitrust Law Journal 443 (2002); Marquardt and Leddy 'The essential facilities doctrine and intellectual property rights: a response to Pitovsky, Patterson & Hooks' 70 Antitrust Law Journal (2002) 847-873; Derclaye 'Abus de position dominante et droits de propriété intellectuelle dans la jurisprudence de la Communauté européenne: IMS survivra-t-elle au monstre du Dr. Frankenstein?' 15 Les Cahiers de Propriété Intellectuelle (2002) 21-55; Koenig,

normally treat with circumspection a Commission decision imposing, by way of interim measures . . . an obligation . . . to licence the use of [an] intellectual property right . . . The Commission's provisional conclusion that the prevention of the emergence of a new product or service for which there is a potential consumer demand is not an indispensable part of the notion of 'exceptional circumstances' developed by the Court of Justice in *Magill* constitutes, at first sight, an extensive interpretation of that notion . . .

The Order added that the requirements in *Magill* may be cumulative. In April 2002 the President of the European Court of Justice dismissed an appeal against the Order of October 2001, substantially confirming all the findings made in the earlier Order.[48] Also in 2001, the German courts, which had concluded that European antitrust law did not entitle the competitors to copyright licences or prevent IMS from claiming its rights under copyright law, referred to the Court of Justice several questions intended to resolve the conflict between the judgments of the German courts and the decision adopted by the Commission.

By decision dated August 13, 2003, the Commission withdrew its interim measures decision (but not retroactively), giving as the reason that NDC had made contracts with some big customers. But NDC had always been free to offer any structure which did not infringe copyright and unfair competition law, and had argued that only by using IMS Health's 1860 structure could it get customers to contract with it.

In his Conclusions in the case referred by the German court, given on 2 October 2003, Advocate General Tizzano accepted, first, that there must be two markets for a compulsory licence, and said, secondly, that there could

Bartosch and Braun *EC Competition and Telecommunications Law* (Kluwer 2002) 133-134, 151-157; Baches Opi 'The application of the essential facilities doctrine to intellectual property licensing in the European Union and the United States: Are intellectual property rights still sacrosanct?' 11 Fordham Intellectual Property, Media and Entertainment Law Journal (2001) 409-506; Hull, Atwood and Perrine 'Compulsory Licensing' European Antitrust Review (2002) 36-39. Casper 'Die wettbewerbsrechtliche Begründung von Zwangslizenzen' Zeitschrift für das gesamte Handelsrecht und Wirtschaftsrecht, 166. Band, Dezember 2002, 685-707; Gitter 'The conflict in the European Community between competition law and intellectual property rights: a call for legislative clarification of the essential facility doctrine' 40 American Business Law Journal (2003) 217-300; Dolmans & Ilan 'A health warning for IP owners: the Advocate General's opinion in IMS and its implications for compulsory licensing' 11 Competition Law Insight (2003) 12-16; Narciso 'IMS Health or the question whether Intellectual Property still deserves a specific approach in a free market economy' [2003] Intellectual Property Quarterly 445-468; Derclaye 'Abuses of dominant position and intellectual property rights: a suggestion to reconcile the Community Courts case law' 26 World Competition (2003) 685-705; Lebrun '*IMS v NDC*: Advocate General Tizzano's Opinion' [2004] European Intellectual Property Review 84-87; Aitman and Jones 'Competition law and copyright: Has the copyright owner lost the ability to control his copyright?' [2004] European Intellectual Property Review 137-147.

[48] Case C-481/01P(R), [2002] ECR I 3401. See also Case C-418/01, *IMS Health v NDC Health*, the case referred by the German court.

be a duty to licence only if the licensee intended to provide a new product or service with different characteristics, which would meet an unsatisfied need. However, he said that a 'potential' upstream market would be enough: it would be enough if there was a need and a demand for the input, even if it had never previously been licensed. He did not state any limiting principles or consider eg, the implications of his conclusions for process patents or non-intellectual property competitive advantages. The implications of the 'potential market' concept and the 'different characteristics' concept, if either or both were adopted without limiting principles, would be far-reaching.[49] Every process patent is an input. New functions can always be added to software. A compound medicine is always a product different from its component medicines. Many patents, in particular software patents, are for 'follow-on' inventions. The law could hardly impose a duty to share important internally-generated competitive advantages with direct competitors, on demand, merely on the basis of their intention to offer a product with some new characteristics. It would be unsatisfactory if a dominant company had to decide whether it was legally free to refuse a licence merely on the basis of a competitor's allegations about the degree of novelty of a product which the competitor was not yet in a position to produce, and which it would certainly be unwilling to describe in detail.

The Court of Justice in its judgment on 29 April 2004 confirmed that refusal to licence cannot in itself be an abuse. For an abuse, the product or service must be indispensable for carrying on a business, the company seeking the licence must intend to offer new products or services, not offered by the copyright owner, for which there is a potential consumer demand, the refusal must reserve the market to the copyright owner by eliminating all competition on that market, and the refusal must not be justified objectively. This confirms that the *Magill* requirements are cumulative, and that there must be new products which are not being offered, rather than merely products with different characteristics. The Court also said that there must at least be two different stages of production, so that the upstream product is indispensable for supply of the downstream product. The refusal must prevent the development of the secondary market to the detriment of consumers. A 'potential' market might be enough. This may merely mean that it would not necessarily be a defence that the company had never sold the upstream product, if there was a real upstream market in other respects. If it means more than that, it will cause difficulties, since no limiting principles are stated.

---

[49] In *Philips Electronics v Ingman and Video Duplicating* (High Court London 13 May 1998), Mr. Justice Laddie said (para 53): 'Whenever an intellectual property right exists there is a correlative potential market in licences to exploit it. It is the ability to grant or refuse such licences which constitutes the right in the first place. This is only an alternative way of saying that the proprietor owns exclusive rights which he can exploit, if he wishes, by licensing.'

The judgment however did not explicitly discuss whether a product can ever be 'indispensable' merely because customers insist on it (which would imply that customer preference could make an essential facility out of a competitive advantage), or whether a licence could be 'indispensable' or a market could be 'reserved' when competitors are free to offer their products, but customers prefer those of the dominant company. The Court merely said, commenting on the *Bronner* judgment, that the existence of 'alternative solutions, even if they are less advantageous' exclude a duty to licence.

On the legal issues, the Commission in its pleadings emphasised that pharmaceutical companies helped IMS Health to develop its 1860 structure (though they had not made a legal claim to own the copyright jointly and they never agreed to use it or to treat it as an industry standard) and that they have cost reasons for not wanting to switch from the 1860 structure. Even on this basis, the Commission's decision against IMS Health appears to go further than the *Magill* television programmes case in several respects:[50]

1. The Commission says that a licence of the IMS Health copyright is an 'essential facility' *only* because pharmaceutical companies do not want to use any map except the IMS 1860 structure, although competitors can develop and offer their own structures or maps.
2. Apart from the refusal to licence the copyright, there is no 'additional conduct' by IMS which could be unlawful.
3. The Commission says that the 'exceptional circumstance' which justifies a compulsory licence, *even if there is no abuse*, is that, since customers want to use only the IMS copyright, if there is no compulsory licence, there is no competition.
4. The Commission says that there is no need for two separate markets in compulsory licence or essential facility cases: it is enough if there are separate stages of production, and that any distinct input, or apparently any intellectual property right, could be an essential facility if it is valu-

---

[50] Other differences include the facts that in *Magill*, the information about next week's programmes was owned by the TV companies, in *IMS Health* the sales data was freely available from wholesalers; in *Magill*, nobody could produce a substitute for the programme list, while in *IMS Health* the plaintiffs had produced their own brick structures; in *Magill*, the TV companies had discriminated, because they had given programme information to daily newspapers and foreign magazines, but IMS Health had never licensed its brick structure anywhere to a competitor except when it sold a business; in *Magill*, the TV stations could make a profit from supplying valuable information while still allowing a comprehensive magazine to start up; licensing in *Magill* did not affect the TV companies' core broadcasting activities, they still needed to produce programme listings; the plaintiff in *Magill* had not infringed copyright rights; *Magill* was a final decision, not an interim measures decision; in *Magill*, if the information could have been given without a copyright licence, the magazine would have got all it needed.

able enough. The Commission apparently says this even if the input is a competitive advantage of a kind which has never previously been marketed or licensed by any company, and which it would never be economically rational to licence to a direct competitor.

5. The Commission said (but the Court of Justice rejected the argument) that it is enough if the proposed licensees would offer substantially the same product or service as the intellectual property owner, apparently without any assurance of a lower price, and that they do *not* need to offer a new kind of product or service.

Taken together these principles[51] would apparently imply that:

- Customer preferences, if strong enough, can make a competitive advantage into an essential facility which the dominant owner must share with rivals.
- A monopoly or near-monopoly position can be made the subject of compulsory intellectual property licensing, even if no abuse or additional abusive conduct has occurred: in other words, dominance without abuse would be illegal.
- A refusal to licence an intellectual property right, without more, is prohibited by European antitrust law if the right is so valuable that it leads to a monopoly or near-monopoly.
- A compulsory licence can be ordered to oblige a dominant company to share its principal competitive advantage with its competitors. This would end its dominance, even though no abuse had been committed.
- All process patents, if they are valuable enough, would be subject to compulsory licensing.
- Neither of the two requirements stated in *Magill* is necessary for a compulsory licence of an intellectual property right (the Court has rejected this view).

Although the validity of the copyright was contested in the German courts, which upheld it, the Commission has never suggested that it has power to declare the IMS Health copyright invalid,[52] or that the compulsory licence is justified because the copyright is in any respect unusual or unsatisfactory.

In short, there are a number of surprising and controversial features of the Commission's decision. If the Community Courts in due course uphold the validity of the Commission's decision, whatever the grounds might be,

---

[51] The *IMS Health* decision is also open to the objection that it would be impossible in the circumstances of the case to determine a satisfactory rate of royalty for the licence envisaged by the Commission, but this question was not dealt with in the decision.

[52] In another case, the Commission has purported to decide that a licence of an existing patent was not essential to comply with a standard, but the Commission has no power to make such a determination, under competition law or otherwise.

European antitrust law would go much further than the *Magill* television programs case in the direction of compulsory licensing.

Microsoft

In contrast to *IMS Health*, in the European *Microsoft* case the company was refusing to licence interoperability information, limiting technological development to the detriment of consumers, and discouraging investment by other companies in PCs, low-end servers and online music players. There is clear additional conduct apart from a refusal to licence and there are clearly separate markets. The *Microsoft* case is not an essential facility case. Microsoft's conduct is putting existing competitors out of the market, and the products which the competitors produce are different from Microsoft's. There are tying and bundling issues and network effects, none of which were present in *IMS Health*. The Commission's decision requires Microsoft to offer a version of its Windows OS without Windows media player and to separate its media player from Windows. The Commission also wants Microsoft to give its competitors in the server market the interface information needed for full interoperability with Windows PC and servers, which is a logical consequence of the unbundling order. A compulsory licence in the *Microsoft* case would not go to the essence of the intellectual property right, since Microsoft would be required to licence only the information needed for a satisfactory interface and not the rights needed to make a product. In the *IMS Health* case, a compulsory licence was claimed precisely to enable the competitor to present the same data in the same format as IMS Health, that is, to produce the same product. Whatever the merits of the *Microsoft* case may be, therefore, none of the objections to the *IMS Health* decision are applicable to the *Microsoft* situation.

CHAPTER 14

Modernization—Avoiding the Ice Cream Trap; ECN Cooperation; Case Allocation; and Parallel Actions

A. Kris DeKeyser*

1 May 2004 was really a historic day not only because of accession, but also for the antitrust community, because of the entry into force of Regulation 1/2003. And, as was said yesterday, it is not yet the jumbo jet, it's a plane taking off gradually. As you all know, during the celebration of the new system we have seen an unprecedented number of policy discussions among authorities, academics, councils, and companies from literally all over the world. And a lot has been said and written about this. Everybody will remember the heroic debate triggered by the business community about the abolition of the notification system which is replaced now by this directly applicable exception system. There has also been a lot of debate about the harmonization of the substantive rules through the introduction of Article 3 which creates, basically, a single common standard for the assessment of agreements by all enforcers in the Union and a level playing field for the business communities throughout Europe. The same is true for the slightly increased powers of investigation of the Commission which, for instance, can now do also inspections at non-business premises, which had been commented on a lot. Not least of course, a lot has been said about this greater involvement of the Member States through national competition authorities and courts.

But having said all this, the time has come now for the theoretical debate to leave the scene and to let things develop in practice and that is why during the panel discussion of this morning we would like to concentrate really on a number of practical issues which are being raised with regards to the implementation of Regulation 1/2003. The first question which immediately comes to mind relates to the consistent application of Articles 81 and 82 in this decentralized enforcement system. The issue is not completely new because the question came up already under the old regime of Regulation 17 more particularly in the *Ice Cream* case and you all know that in that case, the Irish High Court found that Unilever's practice of

* European Commission.

freezer exclusivity in Ireland was found compatible with Articles 81 and 82, while the Commission came to a different view. Then the Irish High Court asked for a preliminary ruling and the Court basically came to the opinion that national court decisions cannot run contrary to Commission decisions, even if the Commission decision conflicts with a decision given by a national court in first instance, and then some further details were given as to the procedures. The legislator has now basically inspired itself on this *Masterfoods* case-law and it's led to Article 16 of the new Regulation, and on top of that we have also Article 15 of the Regulation which sets up some specific mechanisms for cooperation between the Commission and the national competition authorities on the one hand and the national courts on the other hand in order to help to ensure a consistent application of the law by the courts of different fora.

At the level of the competition authority, of course consistency is managed through a completely different scheme. It is managed through this newly set up European Competition Network and through the mechanisms set up in Article 11 which as you said yesterday, also includes Article 11(6) which is, I would call, the atomic bomb because it allows the Commission basically to take a case and make it impossible for the national competition authority to continue. As a neutral chair, I would personally therefore take the view that these provisions should ensure a high level of coherency and consistency in the application of Articles 81 and 82 by the different enforcers, but I am looking forward to hearing whether Matthew and Christoph share this view and I would ask them to give a reply to the one billion dollar question: will consistent application of the law indeed be maintained in the new regime? So Christoph will look in more detail into the issue of coherence under administration in the new system. Did we go far enough for ensuring such a consistent and coherent application? Matthew will look into the issue raised by that question, while Christoph will focus on specific features of parallel procedures before the Commission and national courts and whether judges indeed fear and endure intrusion by the Commission in cases pending before it? But the issue of consistency and coherency is of course not the only challenging area for the practical implementation because cooperation between competition authorities in the ECN at the earlier stages of the procedure is also crucial for the success of the new regime. First of all we must come to an efficient division of work within the Network, otherwise we will not be spending our scarce resources in an efficient manner and we would certainly not achieve our objective of increased enforcement in the Union. A lot of negotiations took place in two days and a lot of discussions within the Network which resulted in the Network notice and we will tackle questions such as, how will this work in practice, which criteria are decisive, is there a risk of forum shopping and so on? Finally, also during the fact-finding phase, Regulation 1/2003 has brought significant changes compared to the previous regime. There are Articles 11 and 12 which provide a huge exchange of information within the Network. At the same time, it is clear that these powerful tools cannot be applied blindly and without any guarantees and I will ask John then to look at these guarantees more particularly in view of the rights of defence and protection of confidentiality. And finally, Lynda will look into one particular issue which comes up in this respect, because when we exchange information within the Network we should be extremely careful not to undermine our leniency programmes, and I would ask Lynda whether indeed we have been able, within the Network, to maintain the trust of potential leniency applicants in our respective leniency programmes?

B. Neil Feinson*

Well Kris has asked me to talk about work-sharing within the European Competition Network, which is the network of national competition authorities. I'd like to start by stressing two fundamental points about modernization and the purpose of this network. Firstly, modernization is not a one-stop shop, so unlike the ECMR, where only the Commission applies Community law, it is a system of parallel competences where the Commission and Member States together enforce competition articles of the EC Treaty. The second point I would like to make is that the purpose of the Network is to coordinate the use of this parallel competence and coordination with the goal of achieving an efficient and effective enforcement of the Treaty articles. It is not a mechanism to produce formal binding unique case allocation decisions. It is a subtle distinction, but I think it is quite an important one in understanding how we will go about doing this.

So how will case coordination work in practice? When opening a case, authorities will complete an electronic fiche on an intranet which is going to link the national authorities so that we can notify each other and the Commission of the key details of the case. Now we will do this for two purposes. One is to identify actual or potential multiple proceedings and the second one is to allow an authority to indicate an interest in a case that is being taken by another authority without perhaps necessarily wanting to open proceedings itself. This might be useful when the authority indicating the interest itself has a case with the same parties in the same market or perhaps dealing with the same issues, perhaps a margin squeeze case for example. So where there is a possibility of actual or potential multiple

---

* Office of Fair Trading

proceedings in the same case, there are three, I suppose, main possible outcomes. The first, and the most traditional, is that up to three national authorities will proceed in parallel. There may possibly be one authority that takes the lead, whether intellectually or in terms of investigation, but up to three acting in parallel. Alternatively, one or more of the national authorities may suspend or close their own proceedings because they believe action by another authority is capable of addressing their concerns and thirdly, where more than three national authorities are well-placed to pursue a case or where it interests more than three Member States the Commission could take the case. Thus the process is less one of actively deciding who is best placed uniquely to take this particular case, but rather and I think it is put rather nicely in the Network notice, a division of labour where some authorities abstain from acting. So I think it is that idea of abstaining from acting, of self denial almost if you like, which is the key to understanding how we will coordinate our cases. So it is important to see national authorities are not prevented from bringing multiple proceedings, and the Network notice does set out what are, in effect, guidelines for efficient enforcement. In particular the two key ones; that no more than three national authorities will act in parallel in any one case, and, that national authorities may desist from action if a fellow authority can address the problem adequately.

Now I suppose some of you may be a little sceptical about this idea of a self-denying competition authorities and I agree, I think you can see that national authorities may well become over-stimulated, over-excited when they see this plethora of cases across Europe on their intranet and that they will want to get involved in all of them whether or not they are well-placed to do so and whether or not somebody else has got the competition problem sorted, and I have heard it suggested that the vogue for quantitative performance targets in the public sector could be something that would push them to do this. In reality however, I would say two things. Firstly there is a strong presumption, as set out in the Network notice, that authorities will collaborate to streamline a number of proceedings and secondly, I suspect that most national competition authorities will be keen to focus only on cases with real national interest and where their efforts can bring real added value, because simply put, resources in most national authorities are just too scarce for any other approach, so that's certainly the OFT's perspective.

And finally just a word from the point of view of parties, from an undertaking's point of view, in many cases the authority which first opens proceedings in a case will continue to take the case through to the end. If there are any changes to that, whether it is an additional authority also bringing a case or whether it is a decision that actually another authority is better placed to take the case, the undertakings concerned will be informed of that and that decision will normally be taken within the first two months of the proceedings. And finally just to touch on forum shopping. I suppose a complainant can always make a complaint to whichever jurisdiction they consider will be most advantageous to them but the process is always the same. All of the authorities will take a look at the case and all will consider whether they might be well placed to act. If the recipient of the complaint doesn't feel there is a material link between the complaint and its territory, it may well simply reject the case. So I think although it is not quite a 'fire wall', there is a discontinuity I would say between decisions over who takes the case, or decisions to abstain from taking the case, and decisions by undertakings as to who they should notify of a complaint. I will leave it there and pass on to the next speaker.

[Kris DeKeyser]

Thank you Neil. It is always good to hear that for once competition authorities do give their blessing to a coordinated practice, albeit between authorities themselves, in order to come to an efficient division of work. Let's now try to move from the beginning of the case to the investigative phase and I would ask John Schmidt to start.

C. John Schmidt*

Thank you. I will look at information exchange between the authorities and, in particular, how that impacts the rights of the parties that are subject to the investigation. First I will give an outline of the basic framework of the information exchange, which is relatively straightforward and relatively easy. Information can be exchanged not just between the Commission and the national competition authorities (NCAs), but also amongst NCAs. Typically that is done in the course of an ongoing investigation, the idea being that you have not quite a real time exchange of information, but as close as possible to real time exchange of information, that all ECN members are brought up to speed and can therefore act when they consider they need to act, and the information that can be exchanged is effectively not limited. The scope is for investigations under Articles 81 and 82. It also extends to the scope of investigations under national law, the application of national law equivalences of Articles 81 and 82, and there are certain limits to the use of the information that is being gathered or exchanged, but on the whole those limits are not in relation to the gathering of the informa-

* Shearman & Sterling LLP.

tion, but are largely in relation to the use of the information once it has been obtained and once it has been exchanged within the ECN. The first one is quite a known concept, professional secrecy, contained in Article 28 that is now transposed also to Member States so that the concept of safeguarding business secrets isn't confined to the Commission anymore, but must be safeguarded by Member States, the authorities and Member States, and the civil servants within those authorities. The second limitation is that the information that is gathered and that is exchanged can only be used for the specific subject matter of the investigation for which it was gathered. Again that is not a novel concept. I'll come back to that later. Finally in relation to natural persons, the information can only be used in order to impose sanctions of a similar kind that are available under Articles 81 and 82 and the underlying idea there is to draw a distinction between criminal sanctions and non-criminal sanctions, but potentially also within criminal sanctions perhaps between custodial and non-custodial criminal sanctions.

I have now chosen three particular issues that I think may come to the fore in future. I don't think that the issues are necessarily novel issues, but they haven't been rectified in the Regulation and they may even be exacerbated once we multiply the regime from one to 26 or multiplied by 26. The first relates to what information can be gathered. Effectively I think all information can be gathered and information that is gathered can be exchanged, and that includes information both for the application, as I said, of Articles 81 and 82, but also for the application of the national equivalent, and I think that is where you already start having a problem with the procedural rules particularly of Member States and in essence of privilege rules, and in particular in-house privilege rules where if the authority applies national law there may be a different rule for privilege; it may exclude certain documents and then there is an issue for the party on how those documents are excluded in the transmission. Can the parties prevent those documents from getting into the hands of the authority whose national rules are designed to prevent those documents from falling into the hands of those authorities? The next question is whether simply all information will be exchanged within the ECN or whether there will be some prioritization of information that will be exchanged? I think that Article 11 sets an obligation on the Commission to inform the Member States and to transmit only the most important documents to the Member States. I think there you already get into issues of how do you identify what the most important documents are? How do you classify relevant information and for third parties I think the key issue is to ensure that all the important facts for the parties are put to the Member States, also attenuating facts and other facts that the third parties regard as relevant and important. So there are particular access issues there.

The next point I have is language, which is again probably quite a normal problem already. The documents, I suspect, will be exchanged in the language in which they have been drafted and that may not present any issues in relation to languages of the larger Member States, but if you then get into the more exotic languages it can present an issue particularly for the parties, and I suspect also for the authorities, in order to make sure that it is clear what the document says and that the translation is done accurately so that the contents and gist of the documents are translated into the local language appropriately, and for third parties obviously they want to ensure that this is done adequately in the same way that the authorities want to ensure that if they rely on those documents the decision becomes as appeal-proof as possible. So in that relation, although it is a similar point to the first point on which information is exchanged, do third parties have an ability to see that the full picture is transmitted to the individual and Member States? I think that in this area probably the interests are more aligned between the parties and the authorities.

The final topic I think is, in terms of substantive issues, perhaps even more interesting, and that is the limitation to the subject matter of the investigation. Again I don't think that is a novel issue, but I've listed four scenarios which I think could give rise to various levels of issues in future. And the first one is what I call a 'creeping cartel'. The Commission investigates a cartel, say in Denmark. It has suspicion that there is a Danish cartel in operation. It goes into Denmark and then finds in its fact-gathering exercise that the cartel actually extends to other Member States, to the rest of Scandinavia, possibly even Germany or France. In that case, I think, certainly in terms of the past practice, the Commission has found it quite easy to bring that within the definition of 'subject matter of the investigation' just because of the wide drafting of the Commission's authority. I think the issue then becomes trickier when you look at what I call a 'cartel cluster'. The Commission investigates the Danish cartel, finds that it either exists or doesn't exist, but in the process stumbles across information that discloses a cartel by the same Danish company in another Member State, perhaps with other members in the cartel, but those other Member States are separate geographic markets not linked to Denmark. In that case I think it would be much more difficult to bring that within the subject matter of the investigation. But, I think as a result of the manner in which the Regulation has been drafted, once the information is in the hands of the Commission, it is perfectly entitled to exchange that information with the other NCAs, although the other NCAs are not entitled to use that information in order to impose sanctions and you can see where I am going with that.

Other issues may include investigations such as merger investigations, where you have potentially parallel merger investigations that look at

Article 81 agreements, Article 81 issues: can the Commission use that information in a parallel cartel investigation? Is there any difference if the merger involves Article 2(4) issues where there is in fact a live Article 81 investigation in parallel with the cartel investigation? And the final point is really my key question, does it all matter? Are the procedural safeguards really effective because all those limitations can effectively be circumvented relatively easily by the authorities since if the Commission finds out that it has in another file, or information that it is aware of, it can simply then re-request the information under Article 18? If Member States have received information which they cannot use in order to impose sanctions, but they are aware of the existence of that information, can they simply re-request that information under their national equivalent fact gathering powers, and does that then entitle them to use that information in imposing sanctions?

The final issue concerns leakages and I don't want to spend too much time on it except to just quickly address the question of whether there is a concern from the petitioner's point of view on leakages, and whether in future that concern is exacerbated. My position is that there is already a certain amount of concern. I think that the Commission has an extremely high reputation in terms of keeping information, or keeping business secrets, secret; keeping confidential information, confidential, but currently there are issues already at Commission level. Only a few weeks ago there was the judgment in the *Carbon* cartel where the Court identified that there was apparently a tip-off by one of the Commission case handlers to one of the alleged cartelists just before the dawn raid. I think in merger cases it is becoming more common to find the content of discussions between the parties and the Commission reflected in the press relatively quickly after those discussions have taken place. I don't want to make too big a point of it but there are, despite the very high reputation, issues already and I think they will be exacerbated if you multiply that by 26 and add the number of Member States to that. Again it is not a new issue, but I think that will be an issue of concern in future and in a way, all those issues lead nicely to Lynda's topics because all the issues that I think I've raised really come to the fore in relation to leniency applications and in particular in the interface where one Member State or a number of Member Sstates have leniency programmes in place and other Member States do not.

D. Lynda Martin Alegi*

Thanks very much John. In a case where leniency presents itself as an

<hr>

* Baker & McKenzie.

option, you are basically looking at whether you are going to go for the 'confess and cooperate' route or the 'deny and defend' or better maybe 'stop, wait and see if you catch the case early'. US criminal sanctions very often dictate which way that balance will tip, but where the decision depends on the European outcomes, I think these new rules and the exchange of information provisions that John has discussed will have a real impact. In favour of leniency, modernization promises more resources to stamp out cartels so you will have less chance of escape, but against it, modernization may make it significantly harder to be certain of avoiding sanctions and more likely that a leniency application will create a new risk of sanctions in other jurisdictions. Of the 26 authorities with power to sanction violations of EC competition law, only DG Comp and 13 of the NCAs have leniency policies at all. That leaves 12 black holes and of course not all the national policies offer full immunity or great certainty. The Competition Law Forum is one of the bodies that have pressed DG Comp to be the central recipient and coordinator of all leniency applications under Article 81. In my view there is a good argument that DG Comp must and will play that role and I encourage it to do so. In other words I encourage us to recognize that we actually already have an efficient system hiding somewhere behind the apparent complexities. The Commission's leniency notice is binding on DG Comp. Where the threshold conditions in paragraph 8 are met, the Commission is committed to grant immunity subject to continued cooperation. The European Court of Justice has of course established that once the Commission has made such a commitment, as to its exercise of discretion in the notice, it will be bound by that notice. Then you can press DG Comp to initiate proceedings—it's not entirely clear to me whether a decision under paragraph 15 of the Leniency Notice in itself will be an initiation of proceedings—so that the NCAs are relieved of their ability to apply Article 81, and also I would suggest that a reading of Article 11(6) with Article 3(1) means that national authorities are also unable to apply their national law at that point. Alternatively, even if the Commission is not inclined to initiate proceedings, I would say that since leniency is a Community interest measure, NCAs must facilitate and not jeopardize the Community leniency policy and so parties will be able to point to Article 10 of the Treaty and ensure that NCAs cannot impose sanctions that would undermine the leniency policy.

Unfortunately this very simple effective system is not endorsed by the ECN notice. Paragraph 83 envisages that a leniency applicant needs to file applications with all relevant NCAs. An impossible task of course, because of the 12 black holes and it won't necessarily be appropriate for companies to challenge and try to force the Commission to initiate proceedings or ensure compliance with Article 10 given the nature of leniency cases. So we do need to look at the issues under the ECN notice at least until my brave new world is clearly established. The first issue with the ECN notice, and I've got three issues that I'm going to point to with it, asks whether companies can rely on the rules at all? Can we rely on self-denial in cartel cases which of course are the very most important ones that all of the NCAs want to pursue? Against DG Comp, yes, we can rely on the notice, but against the 23 NCAs who have signed the statement saying that they will comply, it is not so clear. Paragraph 4 of the notice expressly says that the consultations and exchanges within the Network and matters between the NCAs and public authorities don't alter rights for companies. Of course there is also no question of relying on the ECN notice against the two NCAs who haven't yet signed up, but I presume they will do soon. The second critical point is whether that first notice under Article 11 of Regulation 1/2003, which I've referred to as a tip-off, will lead to NCAs being tipped off to start a case on their own and ultimately sanction. Under paragraph 42 of the ECN notice, DG Comp will only pass Article 11 notices to those NCAs which are committed to comply with the ECN notice and are committed not to use that sort of tip-off to start their own investigations, but as I've just pointed out, as a company thinking of leniency you cannot necessarily rely on that, and in any event the NCA can use information from other sources. So, if your cartel should become public at a subsequent time as a result of the information you have produced, that presumably is information from other sources that an NCA could use and rely on. The third important issue is confidential information and here I think the notice is somewhat more satisfactory because paragraphs 40 and 41 provide that information will be passed on under Article 12 only with the applicant's consent in leniency cases. But even here, consent is going to be encouraged so since you have an obligation to cooperate, you may be under pressure to agree. There are exceptions where the receiving authority has received a leniency application or has committed not to use the information to apply sanctions to the applicant. That commitment is copied to the applicant and so there I think you would have a much stronger argument that you can rely on it.

So there are cracks in the ice cream parlour of leniency, and as to how to avoid them, there is no magic scoop.

Some practical suggestions when considering leniency. You will obviously be weighing the sanctions that you are mitigating against. I would suggest that you should always apply to DG Comp first. Try to get them to be the first authority and to apply the ideal approach. You may want to use the hypothetical basis where it is not absolutely apparent that DG Comp will be best placed. You should ask DG Comp to initiate proceedings. They can do that at any time. You should though, I suggest, apply simultaneously to all NCAs with jurisdiction, not just those that are well placed if there is any doubt, particularly if there are any criminal sanctions, and you can refer to their own leniency policies and if none, then to Article 10. You should be reciting reliance on the NCA's commitment to abide by the ECN notice where you are relying on it and finally you should confirm, where appropriate, that you don't consent for the notice or confidential information to be passed to NCAs who haven't signed up.

So there are still some traps. Watch out for the drips of ice cream, but there is an efficient system lurking in there somewhere. Thank you.

[KRIS DEKEYSER]

Thank you very much. These are of course very interesting issues and I would be very tempted to reply, but unfortunately that would not be fair towards our other speakers so I will give the floor to Matthew and Christoph. I would ask you to do it in as a condensed way as possible as to allow us also to have some discussion on the issues. Thanks.

E. Matthew Levitt*

So is there coherence in the new system? Will the ice cream trap be avoided in the future? Well there are two basic ways in which the Regulation attempts to achieve coherence.

There are some legal principles empowering and requiring the Member States to apply EC competition law. The Regulation asserts the supremacy of European competition law over national competition law. That is expressly stated in Article 3 of the Regulation and the reality is, I think, that it also asserts the primacy of the Commission and the European Courts over national competition authorities and national courts to apply European competition law. Those are the legal principles aimed to achieve coherence.

There are also some practical measures. I won't go into these in any detail at all, but we have heard quite a bit over the last two days about the system of information sharing, principles of case allocation, modalities for intervention in national courts by the European Commission, and indeed also by the national competition authorities.

Will all this be enough? In my view, the risk of ice cream traps occurring in the future will not be eliminated. There is always going to be that possibility. I don't think the Regulation does totally exclude that.

---

* Lovells.

First, and I want to make five points really going to that theme, what is the scope of Article 16 of the Regulation? Article 16 of the Regulation is entitled Uniform Application of Community Competition Law, and I will just read a bit of it. It says: when national courts rule on agreements, decisions or concerted practices under Articles 81 or 82 of the Treaty which are already the subject of a Commission decision they, ie the national courts, cannot take decisions running counter to the decision adopted by the Commission. And there is a similar provision in relation to national competition authorities: they must not act in a way which is counter or which conflicts with what the Commission has already decided. The question though is, what exactly is the scope of that obligation? Does it mean that, if the Commission has taken a decision or is contemplating a decision relating to a set of agreements between two parties, a national court or an NCA cannot look at that agreement between those two parties in that market? Or does it go beyond that? If one is talking about exclusive purchasing agreements, is it sufficient to fall within the scope of the obligation in Article 16 that the supplier is the same? If we are talking about a different national market, is that sufficient to create potential conflict and therefore trigger the obligation of deference in Article 16? I think this may well be a topic of a reference to the ECJ in the not too distant future because it is obviously rather crucial and it goes to the heart of the way in which the Regulation is intended to ensure coherence. Depending on what answer the ECJ might give to that question about the scope of Article 16, there may well be a need to supplement Article 16 of the Regulation with the more fundamental obligation in Article 10 of the Treaty, which is the article about mutual cooperation and respect between Commission and Member States and which itself provided the basis for the Court's judgement in *Masterfoods v Unilever*. In other words, there may be a need beyond the black letter of Article 16 of the Regulation to define more broadly the circumstances in which coherence and harmony need to be achieved on the basis of Article 10 of the Treaty: because of course it is not sufficient that an NCA and the European Commission achieve the same result if they are looking at the same agreement between the same parties in the same market. Coherent application of European competition law throughout the Union requires more than that as there needs to be harmony in the application of competition law throughout.

The second point is that the Commission's Notice on cooperation with national courts itself admits of the possibility that a national court can proceed, either if there is no reasonable doubt about what the Commission's decision may be or if the Commission has already decided on a similar case to the case which the national court is looking at. So there are circumstances in which a national court can itself look at the dispute that it has got before it and say, 'Well I think it is pretty clear what the Commission would do in this case'; or it might look at a similar decision by the European Commission and say, 'Well, I can go ahead'. I don't disagree with that in principle but already it allows for some sort of blurring of the edges of the obligation in Article 16 of the Regulation.

The third point is the specificities of individual cases—that is, the conflict, or the difference, between fact and law. In a sense it is easier to say what the law is in the abstract than to apply the law in the abstract to the concrete case before the national courts, and that is of course particularly true of competition law. It is probably true of most commercial disputes but competition law, as we all know, has to be applied in the factual and economic context of the case at hand. The ECJ in *Masterfoods* says that, where the outcome of the dispute before the national court depends upon the validity of a Commission decision, then the national court ought to stay its case. But how obvious is it always going to be whether the outcome of the national dispute actually does depend on the validity of a Commission decision? The answer will always depend on a mixture of what the law might be and the way in which it applies to the facts in hand before the national court. I would say that involves quite a bit of subjective judgment which ultimately will be for the national court to evaluate and decide whether this is the sort of case where we do decide to stay, because our answer to this dispute depends on the validity of a Commission decision? And a related point to that, on this theme of fact versus law, I think comes back to a point that Sir David Edward was making yesterday morning about the limitations of the reference procedure, the Article 234 procedure under the EC Treaty, because that procedure is not explicitly meant to get the European Court to give the answer on the application of the law to the facts in the national dispute. As we all know, the questions which are put to the ECJ are rather abstract. They are the questions that need to be answered in order to determine the national dispute—but the answer that the ECJ gives in most cases is a rather abstract answer given *in the context of* the dispute. It doesn't answer the dispute. It doesn't provide the answer 'yes' or 'no' to the claim which might be before the national court. So there is an inherent limitation in the ability of the ECJ reference procedure to ensure that you will always get the right outcome at national level.

The fourth point is the role of the Commission. What will be its basis for determining whether it ought to intervene in national litigation? Will it know whether it should intervene? When a judgment has been delivered, it will get a copy under the ECN system and therefore it will have the ability to intervene if there is an appeal. But there may not be an appeal. If there is, it could intervene, but up until the point of delivery of the judgment the Commission may not be informed about the case going on at the national level. Will it have the resources to intervene? Will it be reluctant to take a position against an NCA in national litigation? In the way the ECN is structured, there is a kind of brotherhood of national competition authorities and the Commission, and one gets the impression from reading the notices that there is a kind of solidarity between the Commission and the NCAs. Would it be reluctant, I wonder, to intervene against an NCA if it felt that it has taken the wrong position? Would it intervene against the NCA in a national court case?

The final point concerns the hierarchy which the Regulation achieves. It is a structure with the Commission and the European Courts at the top and the ECN, the NCAs, and the national courts below it. The Regulation is focused on ensuring that sort of vertical consistency and coherence. But I think it doesn't do so much to ensure there is coherence horizontally at the national level. As Neil was saying before, the Regulation and the notices recognize that up to three different Member States may look at the same dispute simultaneously without the Commission becoming the best placed authority. Suppose the three NCAs do look at the case, suppose there are three judicial reviews, so the three cases go to national courts within each of the three Member States. What is the mechanism in the modernization system to ensure that those three national courts all come to the same and correct outcome?

So I think there are certainly gaps in the system. Maybe it doesn't matter so much because I think my concerns are more directed at national litigation than conflict in the application of the law between the Commission and the national competition authorities. I think in relation to that, the problem is not so great but in relation to national private enforcement I think the risk is greater. At the moment there isn't a lot of that going on in Europe, but, if as Philip Lowe said this morning there ought to be more of it, and I agree there ought to be more of it, then the problem could become more intense as the years go by.

F. Christoph Stadler*

Thank you. I would like to distinguish two situations within the ice cream trap. The first situation would be where a complaint is submitted first at the Commission level. The Court cannot avoid the ice cream trap by simply not accepting the claim. It has to accept the claim and start proceedings, but it may stay the proceedings if need be and it may even be under an obligation to stay the proceedings. Now in the other situation where the claim at

* Hengeler Mueller.

national level is put in first, the Commission has a choice of whether to open proceedings or not. In the *Ice Cream* case it did open proceedings. Certainly at national level, at the level of national courts, this might be seen as a way by which the Commission could take the case away from the national courts. I would submit that the Commission is going to exercise this power quite prudently. The important thing in Article 15 of the Regulation is that the Commission has other options. It doesn't need to open a case but it can also intervene and take part in the national proceedings and that is what I am going to focus on within the next 10 minutes.

The next point is what I would call the universe of Article 15. First, how does the Commission learn that there is an Article 81 or 82 case pending? As you know there is an obligation on the Member States to send written judgments to the Commission which also means that the Commission will not usually intervene in lower level court cases. It simply will not know about the case. This problem has been solved differently here in the UK where the parties are under an obligation to inform the national competition authorities, the UK competition authorities of any claim they bring under Articles 81 and 82 which is quite clever indeed. So the parties may wish to address the Commission with a request to make observations even in lower level court cases. My expectation would be however that the Commission will hardly be inclined to do so, given the limited resources it has. The court may ask for transmission of information in the Commission's possession. Now what kind of information is this? In the Commission notice on cooperation between the Commission and national courts, it specifies that the court may ask whether certain cases are pending, whether a decision is likely to be taken, when it is likely to be taken, whether the Commission has initiated the proceedings. These basically are questions to avoid the ice cream trap. The court wants to know whether the Commission has already started a proceeding or whether it may have to stop and stay its own proceedings.

The Court may ask for the Commission's opinion on questions concerning the application of the Community competition rules. Section 27 in the notice specifies that this can be an opinion on economic, factual and legal matters. One question arising from this respect is whether the court can avoid a lengthy Article 234 procedure if it has before itself a legal issue which may be crucial for the outcome of the case. The Commission has suggested that it may be able to provide answers of written opinions within four months. The clear answer is no. If the legal issue is indeed crucial for the outcome of the case and if the court's decision cannot be appealed, there is an obligation to submit the crucial issue to the European Court of Justice, which means that the judges in the highest courts might sometimes face a rather difficult decision of whether they ask the Commission for an opinion or whether they will have to go beyond and put the question to the ECJ. What will these opinions look like? The notice says that the Commission will limit itself to providing the national court with the factual information or the economic or legal clarification asked for without considering the merits of the case. Well I submit that this might be difficult at times, but at the same time I would suggest that there is no problem in this because the Commission's opinion is not binding on the court.

The fourth possibility exists where the Commission or the national competition authorities may submit written observations to the court. There is no limitation with respect to the NCAs, whereas the Commission can only submit written observations where the coherent application of Articles 81 or 82 so requires. So the question is: when does the coherent application of Articles 81 or 82 require the Commission to submit written observations? Certainly that would be the case where diverging precedents exists in the various countries of which the Commission would be aware. Also I would suggest the Commission would be entitled to submit these written observations when a novel question is to be decided. I think that would be in the interest of a coherent application if the Commission were able to do so. I would also suggest that these possibilities, these rights of the Commission, should be construed widely in order not to force the Commission to open its own case in this matter, but to use the other instruments Article 15 provides for. What are the contents of these written observations? Again the notice says that the Commission will limit itself to an economic and legal analysis of the facts underlying the case. Well an economic and legal analysis of the facts underlying the case is basically what the judge does too. But again I would submit it is not a problem as these written observations are not binding on the national court.

The last possibility consists of oral observations. These are only foreseen with permission of the national court and that is true for the NCAs and for the Commission. Now I had the pleasure of sitting for three days in the British Court of Appeal last year where one party labelled Articles 81 and 82 arguments as European defences and I could see that it might be difficult for some British judges to allow a European regulator or enforcer to plead in his court. I was told by the Federal Cartel Office that the Germans are the only Member State with some experience in the field because the Federal Cartel Office (FCO) has been pleading in the German courts for many years now. I will just briefly explain how it works. The FCO makes oral observations in about every case at the level of the Federal Supreme Court, usually not at lower courts. The FCO rarely expresses itself in writing; instead representatives go to the oral hearing and plead. They rather tell the court how, in the FCO's opinion, the case should be decided. They provide a practical solution and pride themselves on doing this. Now the court, of course, is entirely free as to whether to adopt this solution or not. I have noticed that the UK practice guidelines have required the Commission or the national competition authorities or the UK authorities to give reasons why they would want to orally plead. The German solution is quite different. Our law as it is currently, since there is a new law in the pipeline, foresees that the national competition authorities may plead irrespective of permission of the court.

Finally I have a number of issues for discussion. I will only address one of these issues and that is the one of judicial independence. Is judicial independence threatened by the new instruments foreseen in Article 15? I would say clearly not. These are all non-binding instruments. The court is free to listen to the Commission, to read what the Commission has to say or the national competition authorities, and decide differently and I am sure that will be done. The more serious point may be the one that I raised at the beginning where the Commission may be seen to take away cases from the national courts in specific situations.

[KRIS DEKEYSER]

Thank you very much. I am happy with the gist of the last point that the Commission did well in preserving the independence of the judiciary. Unfortunately it is a very frustrating exercise here because we have a very wide range of issues and lunch is approaching and I would be very happy to, at least, participate in replying to all of these issues, but I am afraid it will not be possible, so I have to say to Philip that you should probably organize another conference on modernization. Although we thought that we had already a wide range of conferences and we had exhausted the topic, that is certainly not the case. But I would like to give you the floor now to pick up here one or the other issues which you would like to have further discussed by the panel.

G. Discussion

[PETRI KUOPPAMAKI, NOKIA CORPORATION]

I think this modernization is a big leap forward and as regards substance of the law I would anticipate that we will see a kind of convergence of national rules to a larger extent as a result of this cooperation. However, my question relates to the court structures. Decisions of the national authorities are sometimes appealed. In some countries courts take part of the first instance decision, for example, the decision on fines or prohibitions. Now looking at the court structures in EU countries, in some countries we have administrative process law, in some countries we apply civil process law, and in some countries criminal process law is applied. How do you see how this will affect the functioning of the Network and should there be more harmonization? I can think of three alternatives. One way is harmonization of the procedural rules. A second alternative would be not to harmonize on national level, but to change Regulation 1/2003 in a way to make it easy to play the role of a Supreme Court like you have at the national level: cases can go along various roads and you don't care so much because you have that supreme level where all cases eventually meet. And the third alternative would be some kind of court structure at national level to tackle these issues.

[KRIS DEKEYSER]

Thank you. On the harmonization we have heard yesterday and also this morning that indeed there might be a need for a modernization based exercise. We are not yet there and we are very well aware so with this first exercise we have done harmonization of the substantive law, but as far as the procedural issues are concerned we are far from there, so this might give rise indeed to a couple of difficulties in practice. We have our objectives now to try to see how it works and find out what the difficulties will be and then to take further steps if necessary. The ideas you have launched are very interesting ones and of course we will reflect on these once we have some further experience. It is indeed true that as far as the courts are concerned there is quite a different picture in each of the Member States as you said, for example in Finland. We have the court involved in the decision-making process in order to allow the administrative authority to impose fines, so it is really very different in Ireland. We have a particular situation. We have, in Estonia, a very difficult situation, it is true and we are very well aware of it, but we think it is too early yet to go a step further now. It is however certainly something we had on the books, let's say. Somebody else from the panel want to add something?

[NEIL FEINSON]

Just a short remark. Some of the procedural rules will be derived from Regulation 1/2003 directly, which I think would be directly applicable so the Commission's possibility to make observations, for instance, or the court's right to request an opinion from the Commission probably in my view doesn't even need to be transposed into national law before it can start.

[KRIS DEKEYSER]

Thank you. If there are no further questions then I would like to thank the panel for their very interesting presentations.

H. Modernization: Cooperation within the Network—Some Thoughts on Leniency

Lynda Martin Alegi*

I. THE LENIENCY PROMISE

Leniency procedures allow a competition violator[1] to secure favourable treatment for the corporate and any individual wrong-doers as an encouragement and reward for providing information and cooperating in detection and termination of the unlawful behaviour. The wrong-doer also accepts at least the possibility of compensating customers and consumers.

II. LENIENCY: THE BALANCE

A company considering whether to apply for leniency needs to weigh the pros and cons of the confess/cooperate leniency route against the alternative of deny/defend (better described as 'stop, wait and see').

In favour of an immediate application for leniency will typically be a desire to be the first to cooperate and secure maximum benefit, to avoid or minimize sanctions for the corporation, to avoid criminal and/or civil sanctions for individuals and to minimize reputational risk. Weighing against the leniency option will typically be the risk that admitting to a violation in one jurisdiction will create the risk of sanctions being imposed elsewhere, where leniency is not available. The leniency route will make investigation a virtual certainty and so rule out the possibility that the cartel could be terminated and go undetected. Leniency will also encourage, indeed virtually guarantee, civil damage claims and will inevitably lead to at least some reputational damage.

In favour of the 'stop, wait and see' approach is the hope that it may be possible to escape detection and/or conviction and so avoid the investigation process, sanctions, damages, and reputational risk entirely. Against the 'stop, wait and see' approach is the risk that a co-cartelist may apply for leniency first and thus full or only moderately reduced civil sanctions, and criminal penalties where applicable, will be applied. Reputational risk may also be greatest in this situation.

---

* Baker & McKenzie, London.
[1] In the EC case limited to cartelists, although RPM is also subject to leniency under the OFT's procedures.

From the viewpoint of competition authorities, considering the way in which companies will balance the leniency option, the authority can encourage more leniency applications by:

- Maximizing the sanctions applicable for breach;
- Maximizing the reduction in the sanctions, up to full immunity, available to the first leniency applicant. This will include ensuring that the reduction to be obtained can be ascertained with certainty and relied upon;
- Avoiding creating additional sanctions risks in other jurisdictions;
- Lightening the investigational risk for cooperators;
- Reducing the civil damages risk for cooperators, while ensuring that consumers are compensated;[2]
- Reducing the reputational risk for cooperators;
- Enhancing the risk of detection (including by encouraging leniency applications).

A successful leniency programme thus creates a virtuous circle for competition authorities.

III. LENIENCY POST-MODERNIZATION

One of the objectives of the Modernization programme is to enhance the rate of detection of unlawful cartels by freeing DG COMP resources to focus on serious violations of competition law. This objective suggests that the leniency programme needs to remain effective. In practice, the most important factor which will determine whether leniency continues to be effectively encouraged in the post-Modernization world will be whether the reduction in sanctions, including full immunity, can be secured with certainty and without creating additional sanctions risks elsewhere.

The effectiveness of a European leniency programme is also impacted by the availability and effectiveness of third country regimes and the extent of sanctions which can be avoided by applying for leniency elsewhere such as the US, Canada, and Australia. It is also affected by the risk of civil damages, currently treble damages, in the US. These aspects are beyond the scope of this brief note.

IV. MAXIMIZING LENIENCY POST-MODERNIZATION—THE BACKGROUND AND CHALLENGES

DG Comp and 25 NCAs can now apply Article 81, each with their own procedures and sanctions.

---

[2] In this regard note the current proposals to de-treble damages payable by successful leniency applicants in the US–H Pate presentation to the antitrust section of the ABA, 12 Aug 2003, followed by legislation currently before the US Congress.

Currently only DG Comp and 13 NCAs have a leniency policy (Belgium, Cyprus, Czech Republic, France, Germany, Hungary, Ireland, Latvia, Lithuania, Netherlands, Slovakia, Sweden, and UK).[3] The Finnish programme is in draft with enactment imminent and a leniency programme is under active consideration in Italy.[4]

[3] Note that special considerations apply to Scotland.
[4] Source: DG Comp website:

Austria
No leniency programme

Belgium
Conseil de la Concurrence's Leniency Programme (2004) Press Release only: <http://mineco.fgov.be/organization_market/competition/press_releases/press_release_300420 04_fr.pdf>

Cyprus
Commission for the Protection of Competition's Cartel Immunity and Reduction of Fine Programme (2003): <http://www.competition.gov.cy/competition/competition.nsf/All/A439D27C48FC3CD8C225 6CBB003A15B9/$file/CARTEL%20_MMUNITY_AND_REDUCTION_Of_%20A_FINE_P ROGRAMME.pdf?OpenElement>

Czech Republic
Office for the Protection of Competition's Leniency Program (2002): <http://www.compet.cz/English/Leniency/Leni_eng.htm>

Denmark
No leniency programme

EU
European Commission's Notice on immunity from fines and reduction of fines in cartel cases (2002): <http://europa.eu.int/eur-lex/pri/en/oj/dat/2002/c_045/c_04520020219en00030005.pdf>

Estonia
No leniency programme

Finland
Finnish Kilpailuvirasto's Leniency Programme (still in draft but its enactment is imminent) Bill introduced before Finnish parliament in Feb 2004, see Press Releases: <http://www.kilpailuvirasto.fi/cgi-bin/english.cgi?luku=news-archive&sivu=news/n-2004-02-19> <http://www.kilpailuvirasto.fi/cgi-bin/english.cgi?luku=news-archive&sivu=news/n-2003-10-24>

France
Law No 2001-420 of 15 May 2001 on 'New Economic Regulation' (Art L464-2 III of the French Commercial Code): <http://www.legifrance.gouv.fr/WAspad/VisuArticleCode?commun=&code=&h0=CCOM-MERL.rcv&h1=4&h3=14>

Germany
Bundeskartellamt's Notice 68/2000 on the guidelines relating to the setting of fines (2000) <http://www.bundeskartellamt.de/Bonusregelung-E.pdf>

Greece
No leniency programme

Hungary
GVH's Leniency Policy (2004): <http://www.gvh.hu/index.php?id=3009&l=e>

Ireland
Competition Authority's Cartel Immunity Programme (2001): <http://www.tca.ie/documents/cartelimmunityprogramme.pdf>

The 14 existing policies are not identical as to their scope or conditions and not all provide for complete immunity or for certainty to the applicant. Beyond checking the countries on the list, an adviser will need to check that the relevant policies are adequate and applicable in relation to the specific case at hand.

Italy
No leniency programme but under active consideration
Note: On one occasion the Italian Antitrust Authority did not impose a fine on a member of a cartel, to take account of its co-operation with the IAA. The IAA specifically referred to the European Commission's Leniency Notice.
Latvia
Konkurences Padome's Procedures for Calculation of Fines (Cabinet Regulation No 468) (2003):
<http://www.competition.lv/Alt/ENG/E30norma/E_mkn468.htm>
Lithuania
Konkurencijos Taryba's Leniency Programme
 No further details available (source: European Commission list, see below)
Luxembourg
No leniency programme
Malta
No leniency programme
Netherlands
NMa's Leniency Guidelines (2002):
<http://www.nmanet.nl/en/Images/14_8180.pdf>
Poland
No leniency programme
Portugal
No leniency programme
Spain
No leniency programme
Slovakia
Protimonopolny urad Leniency Programme
No further details available (source: European Commission list, see below)
Slovenia
No leniency programme
Sweden
Konkurrensverket's General Guidelines on Leniency (2002):
<http://www.kkv.se/engwebb/eng_doc/com_leniency.htm>
UK
Civil: Office of Fair Trading's Competition Act 1998 Guidance as to the Appropriate Amount of a Penalty (2000) (New Guidance to be issued June/July 2004)
<http://www.oft.gov.uk/NR/rdonlyres/eiscwggjiniljc5a45kahes3xvmpqqpcbev3teeocuif-shkxnoypdhrqbdhvilmtuswgjo7zpo3febc7l7ouydkjbca/oft436.pdf>
Criminal: Office of Fair Trading's Criminal Immunity for Individuals: Guidance on the Issue of No-Action Letter for Individuals (2003):
<http://www.oft.gov.uk/NR/rdonlyres/eazysgycabnnrtafmfec4qturdtgjkvsdr6cwbktyxwze-myvgncir6g4l4e6fj7qihc5byj73opxmyf5ssmp3lhqyuf/oft513.pdf>
European Competition Authorities
Principles for Leniency Programmes, Dublin (2001):
<http://www.tca.ie/eca.pdf>
European Commission list of leniency programmes
(NB: Ireland's programme is missing from list)
<http://europa.eu.int/comm/competition/antitrust/legislation/authorities_with_leniency_progr amme.pdf>

Modernization is designed to allow DG Comp to concentrate on cartels, but it has more cartel cases than it can currently handle and is reviewing all pending files. While the intention of DG Comp is undoubtedly to be able to handle the serious cartel cases for which it is well placed in accordance with the Notice on Cooperation within the Network of Competition Authorities (ECN Notice), there a risk DG Comp could be tempted to decline to handle some such cases in the future.

New cases will be publicised within the network which may give rise to a 'tip off' effect. In particular DG Comp must transmit 'the most important documents' to NCAs under Article 11.2 Regulation 1/2003 but there is no firm timeframe. Without delay after commencing a formal investigation under Article 81, an NCA must inform DG COMP and DG COMP/the NCA may then inform other NCAs under Article 11.3 Regulation 1/2003.

In addition confidential information may be exchanged under Article 12 of Regulation 1/2003, but note that:

- Such information can only be used 'in respect of the same subject matter' although this includes the application of national law where this 'does not lead to a different outcome'. It is arguable that since Article 3.2 of Regulation 1/2003 already precludes different substantive outcomes under national law and Article 81, this language should include a different outcome in terms of leniency. But paragraph 28(b) of the ECN Notice interprets Article 12.2 as referring only to a different outcome 'as regards the finding of an infringement';
- The information can only be used to impose sanctions on individuals if:
  (i) Both the transmitting and receiving states' laws have a similar kind of sanction or
  (ii) The rights of defence were protected at the same level by the transmitting authority when it collected the information as would apply under the receiving authority rules.

A final challenge is that international cooperation and various performance-related pressures appear to be increasing the rivalry between NCAs to maximize their own prosecution rates and cumulative fines totals. These pressures may encourage a suboptimal allocation of cartel cases and a short term view of leniency.

V. AN EFFECTIVE POST-MODERNIZATION LENIENCY PROGRAMME: A SUGGESTION

The Commission's Leniency Notice[5] provides the rules under which the

---

[5] Commission Notice on immunity from fines and reduction of fines in cartel cases OJ C 45 of 19 Feb 2002 at 3.

Commission will grant an undertaking immunity from fines which would otherwise have been imposed. One of the objectives of the 2002 Leniency Notice was to provide additional certainty to companies and the Notice accordingly seeks to limit the Commission's discretion. Where the threshold conditions referred to in paragraph 8 are met then, subject to continued compliance with the on-going conditions of cooperation set out in paragraph 11, the Commission is committed to grant immunity.[6]

Once the company has been granted conditional immunity from fines by the Commission, it is submitted that there are two possibilities. The first is that this grant of provisional immunity itself amounts to or is accompanied by the 'initiation by the Commission of proceedings for the adoption of a decision',[7] in which event under Article 11.6 of Regulation 1/2003 the NCAs are relieved of their competence to apply Article 81. Reading Article 11.6 together with Article 3.1 of Regulation 1/2003, since an NCA may only apply national competition law to an agreement which may affect trade between Member States where it also applies Article 81, presumably the NCA is also no longer able to apply national competition law. Alternatively, even if the grant of immunity by the Commission is not held to be a formal initiation of proceedings, the better view is that once the Commission has decided to apply the leniency policy, NCAs' duty under Article 10 of the Treaty establishing the European Community to facilitate achievement of the Community's tasks and to abstain from any measure which could jeopardize the attainment of the objectives of the Treaty kicks in.[8] Once a company has qualified for immunity from the Commission it would jeopardize the Community's competition policy for a fine, nevertheless, to be imposed by an NCA and so no such fine may be imposed.

Unfortunately, this suggested, simple approach is not adopted in the ECN Notice. Should DG Comp refuse to grant conditional leniency or fail to act on a leniency application, an action before the Court of First Instance would be available in theory, but in most circumstances could not be brought without prejudicing the company's overriding requirement for confidentiality.

Until the situation is resolved, whilst it would appear essential to apply to DG Comp in all leniency situations involving cartels, which may affect

---

[6] It is clear law that the Commission may not depart from such rules that it has imposed on itself—see, eg, Case T-7/89 *Hercules Chemicals v Commission* [1991] ECR II 1711 para 53.

[7] This requires an official act on the part of the Commission indicative of its intention to proceed to a decision—see Case 48/72 *Brasserie de Haecht v Wilkin* (No 2) [1973] ECR 77 para 16.

[8] See J Temple Lang 'The Implications of the Commission's Leniency Policy for National Competition Authorities' [2003] 28 ELRev June 430.

trade between Member States, it would be equally appropriate to follow the suggestion in the ECN Notice paragraph 38 to file leniency applications with all relevant NCAs simultaneously as well. The problems and complexities of the ECN Notice process are examined next.

VI. MAXIMIZING LENIENCY POST-MODERNIZATION: THE PROCESS

Where a cartel has an effect on trade[9] and has effects sufficient to establish local jurisdiction in four or more Member States, the ECN Notice suggests that the Commission is particularly well-placed to act. If all of the Member States concerned have adequate and applicable leniency programmes, some inconvenience, but relatively few real problems should arise. A leniency application should be submitted first to DG COMP since the first authority to deal with a matter will generally remain in charge of it.[10] It would be advisable to ask DG Comp to agree that it is best placed, to accept the case and to initiate proceedings, which it may do at any time.[11] Article 11.6 of Regulation 1/2003 will then apply to relieve NCAs of their ability to apply Article 81 and, as discussed above, arguably also national law. Until the new procedures are well-settled it would, however, in any event be cautious to consider applying at the same time to any NCA whose regime imposes high risks in the circumstances, particularly if there is a risk of criminal prosecution of individuals. Indeed if there is any doubt it would at this stage be appropriate to apply for leniency in all Member States concerned at the same time.[12] The cautious view would suggest that all NCAs which could have jurisdiction to apply Article 81 or their national law should be approached. In addition, the leniency applicant should make clear to DG Comp and all NCAs approached that the company does not consent to notice regarding the opening of the case or confidential information disclosed to be passed on to other NCAs.[13] Each leniency application should recite that the applicant is relying on the NCAs' commitment to abide by the ECN Notice.[14]

If not all of the Member States concerned have satisfactory leniency programmes, a company considering leniency could be well-advised to

---

[9] Note that where a cartel has no effect on trade, only national law will apply and only national leniency, if any, will be available. This situation is not impacted by Modernization.

[10] Para 6 ECN Notice.

[11] See Art 2.1 Regulation 773/2004.

[12] Note that para 38 of the ECN Notice merely refers to it being in the applicant's interest to apply to all NCAs which are well-placed to deal with a case.

[13] See discussion of paras 39–42 of the ECN Notice below.

[14] This may help in establishing a legitimate expectations argument. It is by no means clear that a company can rely on an NCA's declaration that it will abide by the ECN Notice—see in particular the discussion below of para 4 of the Notice.

apply initially to DG Comp on a hypothetical basis.[15] If there is any doubt as to whether DG Comp will accept the case and initiate a procedure, the balance of advantage in favour of leniency may need to be reconsidered. This will include considering whether withdrawal of evidence under paragraph 17 of the Leniency Notice will be effective in practice.

The most difficult situation for the would-be leniency applicant is probably that where the cartel has an effect on trade, but has effects in three or fewer Member States. There is a greater risk that DG Comp will not agree that it is best placed to handle the matter in this situation. Nevertheless, if any leniency applications are being made, an application to DG Comp is in any event to be recommended to preserve the arguments referred to in section 5 above and to avoid the risk and complications of another cartelist applying to DG Comp first. If all of the Member States concerned have adequate, applicable leniency programmes then certainly if DG Comp has not agreed to initiate proceedings and probably in any event, the applicant will need to consider applying to all NCAs simultaneously. As suggested above, it should be made clear that there is no consent to passing on of information to other NCAs. If not all of the Member States concerned have adequate applicable leniency programmes, the benefit of avoiding sanctions in some might be outweighed by the increased risks elsewhere. This in turn depends on how the discretion regarding tip-off and exchange of confidential information described briefly in Section 4 above will operate in practice. The ECN Notice paragraphs 39–42 attempt to deal with this and attempt to protect a leniency application from the risk that a non-leniency NCA may be tipped off to start a case or be given confidential information and impose its own sanctions.

Some protection, but certainly no guarantee is available. A threshold issue before considering the procedures is the extent to which they will be binding on NCAs. NCAs have been invited to make a declaration acknowledging the principles of the ECN Notice and declaring that they will abide by them. According to the list published on the website of the European Commission, authorities in each of the Member States, save for Greece and Spain, have already signed the statement.[16]

Looking at the notification of the start of an investigation, which risks acting as a tip-off to other authorities about the existence of a cartel for which leniency has been requested, paragraph 42 of the ECN Notice states that DG Comp will only pass on information regarding commencement of

---

[15] Following the procedure in para 13(b) of the Leniency Notice.
[16] But note that the list should be checked in each case and it should be confirmed, in particular, that no additional authority could have jurisdiction in any Member State in question. See also the discussion of para 4 below.

its own or an NCA case to other NCAs who have committed to respect the principles of the ECN Notice.[17]

Paragraph 39 of the ECN Notice goes on to state that in leniency cases

information submitted to the network pursuant to Article 11 will not be used by other members of the network as the basis for starting an investigation on their own behalf whether under the competition rules of the Treaty or, in the case of NCAs, under their national competition law or other laws.

Whilst an NCA which has declared its intention to abide by the principles in the Notice can be expected to do so, it is less clear that a leniency applicant can rely on this. Paragraph 4 of the ECN Notice expressly states that 'consultations and exchanges within the network are matters between public enforcers and do not alter any rights or obligations arising from the Community or national law for companies'. The position is even less comfortable when the fact of an investigation becomes public knowledge or is otherwise communicated to another NCA since paragraph 39 is expressly without prejudice to the NCAs' power to open an investigation on the basis of information received from other sources.

As regards confidential information, paragraphs 40–1 of the ECN Notice provide that a leniency applicant's confidential information will only be passed on under Article 12 of Regulation 1/2003 with the applicant's consent. However:

- Consent will be 'encouraged'. It will be important to consider the implications of this for any obligation to co-operate under the national leniency programme rules;
- There are exceptions which apply where the receiving authority has also received a leniency application from the applicant and where the receiving authority has given a written commitment[18] that it will not use the information transmitted, or any information it receives subsequently to impose sanctions on the leniency applicant or its employees.

VII. CONCLUSIONS

The ECN Notice reflects substantial work on the part of DG COMP and the NCAs in attempting to achieve a workable system for effective leniency in the post-Modernization world. However, the result as set out in the Notice is far from clear and satisfactory. It is submitted that the most

---

[17] But note that para 42 does not bind transmitting NCAs. Hence the importance of obtaining their agreement not to provide the Art 11.3 Notice to other NCAs.

[18] Copied to the applicant and therefore presumably a source of legitimate expectations for the applicant.

appropriate approach to leniency is that suggested in this paper, for DG Comp to fulfil its commitment to grant leniency to any applicant who fulfils the condition and to require NCAs to recognize this either by initiating proceedings and taking charge of the case or by reference to the Treaty. Unless and until this approach is adopted, would-be leniency applications will be well-advised to consider carefully the balance of factors in favour of a leniency application on the one hand or a 'stop and wait and see' approach on the other. This note has attempted to give some guidance on steps which can be taken to maximize the effectiveness of leniency applications where this is the chosen route.

I. Benefits and Challenges of Leniency Programmes in the Context of EC Modernization

Margaret Bloom*

I. INTRODUCTION

In recent years quite a few jurisdictions have introduced leniency programmes[1] for uncovering cartels. This significant growth reflects their considerable benefits as the most effective tool in the fight against cartels. However, there are a number of challenges in devising and operating effective programmes. This paper considers the possible implications of EC Modernization for leniency programmes. It also considers, briefly, a second topical issue for leniency programmes for international cartels, which is the impact of some recent actions by the US plaintiffs bar in claims for treble damages. These actions could adversely affect applications to European leniency programmes—as well as to the US and other jurisdictions.

Before discussing benefits and challenges, it is useful to consider the current position on where leniency programmes exist and the necessary elements of an effective programme.

II. WHICH COUNTRIES HAVE A LENIENCY PROGRAMME?

The longest standing programme is that operated by the Antitrust Division of the US Department of Justice, which dates from 1978. Important changes were made to the programme in 1993 to widen its application and make the grant of amnesty (ie 100 per cent leniency) certain provided that the necessary conditions were satisfied.[2] On this side of the Atlantic Ocean, a Leniency Notice was introduced by the European Commission in 1996.

* King's College, London; and Freshfields Bruckhaus Deringer. I gratefully acknowledge comments received from Richard Whish, Jon Lawrence, Paul Lomas, Samantha Mobley, Eddy De Smijter, Neil Feinson and Emma Scaife. However none of them bears any responsibility for the final text. This paper was prepared for the VI Treviso Conference 'Antitrust between EC Law and National Law', 13–14 May 2004.
    [1] The term 'leniency programme' is used in this paper to describe all programmes which offer either full immunity (sometimes called amnesty) or a significant reduction in penalties which would otherwise have been imposed on a participant in a cartel, in exchange for the freely volunteered disclosure of information on the cartel which satisfies specific criteria prior to or during the investigative stage of the case, and does not cover reductions in the penalty granted for other reasons.
    [2] The 1993 US programme is available at <http://www.usdoj.gov/atr/public/guidelines/0091.htm>.

This, too, has been revised—in 2002.[3] The revisions to the EC Notice increased the rewards that a successful applicant would receive and the degree of certainty and transparency of the programme.

Outside Europe and the US, other countries with leniency programmes include Canada, Australia, Brazil, Korea, and South Africa. Within Europe, 14 of the Member States of the enlarged EU currently have programmes: Belgium, Cyprus, Czech Republic, Finland, France, Germany, Ireland, Hungary, Latvia, Lithuania, Netherlands, Slovak Republic, Sweden, and UK. Norway and Switzerland also have programmes. A number of countries are developing programmes.

III. KEY ELEMENTS OF A SUCCESSFUL PROGRAMME

Predictability and certainty are key. There are other important elements which have been well summarized in the latest OECD Competition Committee report[4] on cartels and leniency:

The US and EC experiences are instructive as to the necessary elements of a successful leniency programme. They could be summarized as follows:

- Complete immunity from sanctions should be awarded to the first applicant. This maximizes the reward for cooperation;
- Only the first to apply should receive complete immunity, and if the programme is extended to subsequent applicants, the gap in the rewards should be substantial. This maximizes the incentive to be the first to defect, thus destabilizing the cartel. If the returns to the second applicant approximate those that would accrue to the first, then the result may be that no one would apply;
- The programme should have maximum transparency and certainty. Would-be applicants should be able to predict as accurately as possible what the outcome of their application will be;
- The programme should be available in circumstances in which the competition agency has already begun an investigation. If the members are aware of an investigation and of the possibility that one of them could benefit from leniency, the stability of their agreement is likely to be severely eroded;
- The competition agency should accord confidentiality to leniency applications and the information resulting there from to the maximum extent possible.

---

[3] Official Journal of the European Communities 2002/C 45/03. The 2002 Notice is also available at <http://europa.eu.int/eur-lex/pri/en/oj/dat/2002/c_045/c_04520020219en 00030005. pdf>.

[4] 'Hard Core Cartels—Recent progress and challenges ahead' OECD 2003.

In addition, if a leniency programme is to be effective at tackling and deterring cartels the competition authority needs effective sanctions for those participating in cartels and effective powers of investigation to bring cases to successful infringement decisions or prosecutions.

As the OECD report stated, '[e]xperience has shown that a properly structured leniency programme can dramatically increase the success of an anti-cartel effort'.

IV. BENEFITS

Broadly, there are four important benefits of an effective leniency programme:

- A much increased ability to uncover cartels;
- Faster investigations;
- An increased ability to meet the standard of proof necessary for a successful infringement decision or prosecution, and hence reduced risk of a successful appeal; and
- Greater deterrence to cartels.

Given the considerable harm caused by cartels, these benefits are of very real value. While it is not possible to calculate precisely the overall damage caused by cartels, the OECD 2003 report estimated the harm caused by 16 large cartels. Typically, the unlawful gain to the cartel members was between 15 and 20 per cent of the volume of commerce cartelized. This gain was, of course, an equal loss to consumers. However, in addition to these higher prices, output was reduced and there was a loss of other benefits of competition such as innovation and increased quality. The OECD Competition Committee concluded that 'the total harm from cartels is significant indeed, surely amounting to many billions of dollars each year'.[5]

1. A much increased ability to uncover cartels

Competition authorities with leniency programmes are clear about their value for uncovering cartels.

In the US, James Griffin, Deputy Assistant Attorney General, US Department of Justice Antitrust Division, considers that their 1993 programme is their most effective investigative tool. '[T]he Leniency Program is the Division's most effective generator of international cartel cases and it is the Department's most successful leniency program'.[6]

---

[5] See (n 5).
[6] The Modern Leniency Program After Ten Years, 'A Summary Overview of the Antitrust Division's Criminal Enforcement Program' speech to American Bar Association Section of Antitrust Law, 12 Aug 2003. Available at <www.usdoj.gov/atr/public/speeches/201477.htm>.

Its success is dramatically illustrated by the rate of applications:

The revised Corporate Leniency Program has resulted in a surge in amnesty applications. Under the old policy, the Division obtained roughly one amnesty application per year. Under the new policy, the application rate has jumped to more than
one per month. (In the first six months of this fiscal year (October 2002–March
2003), amnesty applications jumped to three per month, an all time high.) As a
result of this increased interest, the Division frequently encounters situations where
a company approaches the government within days, and in some cases less than one
business day, after one of its co-conspirators has secured its position as first in line
for amnesty. Of course, only the first company to qualify receives amnesty.[7]

In the EU, Olivier Guersent, Head of the Scrutiny and Coordination Unit in
the DG Competition of the EC, considers the EC leniency programme to be
a key measure in the European Commission's fight against cartels. The
other two key measures are EC Modernisation and the creation in 1998 of
a dedicated 'Cartel Unit':

The second key measure (the first one in terms of actual impact so far) is no doubt
the adoption in 1996 of the Leniency Notice and the implementation of the
Leniency Program since then. For the first time, the Commission introduced the
granting of immunity and/or reduction of fines into the range of its investigative
tools. The results are well known: the Notice has proven to be a formidable tool to
detect and prosecute cartels. Not only did it enable the Commission to uncover individual cartels, but the fear that one member could go to the authorities and obtain
immunity proved to de-stabilise cartel activity in general. As a result, since 1996, the
Leniency Program has been the most effective generator of important cases. About
100 companies have filed leniency applications under this program and, since 1996,
the Commission has taken 24 formal decisions in cartel cases in which companies
co-operated with the investigations. . . . Already the new instrument is very successful. Since 19 February 2002, the date of publication of the new Notice, more than
50 new leniency applications have already been submitted,[8] amongst which 44
applications [were] for immunity [ie 100 per cent leniency]. These include a number
of simultaneous applications in both the US and the EU (and some simultaneous
applications in Canada), which allowed in a number of cases, for close co-operation
and/or simultaneous investigative measures.[9]

Between 1996 and 1998, none of the on-site inspections[10] carried out by
the European Commission were based on a leniency request. However, as
the EC policy became more widely known, the position changed dramatically. Between 2001 and 2003 nearly two-thirds of inspections were based

---

[7] See (n 7).
[8] 33 of the 53 applications for leniency were granted.
[9] 'The Fight Against Secret Horizontal Agreement in the EC Competition Policy', speech
to Fordham Corporate Law Institute 30th Annual Conference, Oct 2003. The statistics cover
the period up to 1 Oct 2003.
[10] Each inspection concerns a different case and involves numerous companies inspected.

on leniency requests. Another striking fact is that throughout the eight-year period to 2003 there were generally three or four inspections a year that were not based on leniency requests.[11] But inspections based on leniency applications rose steadily from one in 1999 to 14 in the first nine months of 2003. This demonstrates the strong ability of leniency programmes to uncover cartels. Almost all the Commission inspections since 1996 have resulted in decisions.[12]

The immunity and/or leniency that has been granted in EC cases under the 1996 EC Leniency Notice is set out in Table 1. The cases cover infringement decisions from 1998 to 2003. The first case in which immunity—that is 100 per cent leniency—was granted was in the Vitamin Cartel with the decision in 2001. However, the first application which led to 100 per cent leniency was in the Carbonless Paper Cartel with the decision later in 2001.

Table 1: EC 1996 Leniency Notice Cases[13]

Year	Decision	Reduction of fine and number of companies
1998	Stainless Steel	40 per cent: 2 companies, 10 per cent : 4
1998	British Sugar	50 per cent: 1, 10 per cent: 3
1998	Preinsulated Pipes	30 per cent: 5, 20 per cent: 3
1998	Greek Ferries	45 per cent : 1, 20 per cent : 6
1999	Seamless Steel Tubes	40 per cent : 1, 20 per cent : 1
2000	Lysine	50 per cent : 2, 30 per cent: 2, 10 per cent : 1
2001	Graphite Electrodes	70 per cent: 1, 40 per cent: 1, 30 per cent: 1, 20 per cent: 2, 10 per cent: 3
2001	Sodium Gluconate	80 per cent: 1, 40 per cent: 2, 20 per cent: 3
2001	Vitamins	100 per cent: 1, 50 per cent: 2, 35 per cent: 3, 30 per cent: 1, 15 per cent:1, 10 per cent: 1
2001	Brasseries Luxembourg	100 per cent: 1, 20 per cent: 3
2001	Brasseries Belges	50 per cent:1, 30 per cent: 1, 10 per cent: 4
2001	Citric Acid	90 per cent: 1, 50 per cent:1, 40 per cent:1, 30 per cent:1, 20 per cent: 1
2001	Zinc Phosphate	50 per cent: 1, 40 per cent: 1, 10 per cent: 4
2001	Carbonless Paper	100 per cent: 1, 50 per cent: 1, 35 per cent: 1, 20 per cent: 1, 10 per cent: 3
2002	Methionine	100 per cent: 1, 50 per cent: 1, 25 per cent: 1
2002	Industrial & Medical Gases	25 per cent: 2, 15 per cent: 2, 10 per cent: 2
2002	Fine Art Auction Houses	100 per cent: 1, 40 per cent: 1
2002	Plaserboard	40 per cent: 1, 30 per cent: 1
2002	Methylglucamine	100 per cent: 1, 40 per cent: 2
2002	Food Flavour Enhancers	100 per cent: 1, 50 per cent: 1, 40 per cent: 1, 30 per cent: 1
2002	Rond à Beton	20 per cent: 1

[11] In 2002 there were six and in the first nine months of 2003 there were seven.
[12] See (n 10) for the facts in this paragraph.
[13] See (n 10). The original table has been updated for this paper.

Table 1: *continued*

Year	Decision	Reduction of fine and number of companies
2002	Speciality Graphites	100 per cent: 1, 50 per cent:1, 35 per cent: 6
2003	Sorbates	100 per cent: 1
2003	Carbon and Graphite Products	100 per cent: 1, 40 per cent: 1, 30 per cent: 2, 20 per cent: 1
2003	Organic Peroxides	100 per cent: 1, smaller per cent: 5
2003	Industrial Copper Tubes	50 per cent: 1, 30 per cent: 1, 20 per cent: 1

The UK is one of the Member States that has introduced a civil leniency programme in recent years. This is already delivering real benefits in uncovering cartels despite the fact that a programme needs time to become most effective as greater awareness of it develops among business and their advisers. The operation of the UK civil leniency policy by the Office of Fair Trading is illustrated in the following extract from an article on the UK Competition Act 1998:

Informants remain the key to uncovering cartels including applicants for leniency. By the end of April 2003 we had granted leniency—to at least one of the parties—in 19 cases since the Act came into force [in March 2000]. Some of these involve resale price maintenance. Our civil leniency policy applies to horizontal cartels and any form of price fixing including resale price maintenance. So far, three of these cases have concluded with infringement decisions. . . . Two of the 19 cases are the result of leniency plus. This applies where a party has 50 per cent leniency or less—may be none—if they inform us of another cartel or price fixing agreement and qualify for 100 per cent leniency in that, they can also have some or additional leniency for the first one. Of course, 100 per cent leniency is only available to the first applicant in any case. Our leniency plus policy is based on the amnesty plus policy of the US Department of Justice which uncovers between a quarter and a half of their cartel cases.[14]

2. Faster investigations

Clearly, the better the information that a competition authority has about a cartel and the faster this is obtained, the faster the investigation can move forward. In some cases the leniency applicant provides high quality documentation including diaries and emails. In other cases the evidence provided may be largely oral. Generally, the national or regional cartels that are tackled by national authorities are less well documented by the members of the cartels than the international cartels that are tackled by the US and

[14] M Bloom 'Key Challenges in Enforcing the Competition Act' (2003) Competition Law Journal, Jordans.

European Commission. Whatever the position on documentary evidence, information from those granted leniency should enable the investigation to be completed sooner subject to the workload and priorities of the competition authority. This has been evident from the early experience with the UK civil leniency programme:

Even when leniency applicants come in after we have started an investigation, they can deliver real value. For example, in one case the information provided cut the investigation time by about a half.[15]

3. An increased ability to meet the standard of proof necessary for a successful infringement decision or prosecution

In proving a cartel infringement, competition authorities must satisfy the requisite legal standard for their jurisdiction whether this is 'beyond reasonable doubt' for a criminal regime, a 'firm, precise and consistent body of evidence' required by the community courts,[16] 'strong and compelling evidence' required by the UK Competition Appeal Tribunal[17] or such other standard required in national rules. Rightly, these are tough standards to satisfy and the evidence provided by a leniency applicant may be crucial to meeting the necessary standard. Following EC Modernization, the national competition authorities will continue to apply national rules on the standard of proof to their cases under both EC and national law as stated in recital 5 of Council Regulation (EC) 1/2003 of 16 December 2002.

4. Greater deterrence

The above benefits mean that jurisdictions with a leniency programme—and effective powers of investigation and sanctions against cartels—are much more likely to uncover and successfully prohibit or prosecute cartels. This will deter cartels from forming in the first place.

V. CHALLENGES

This paper now considers the possible implications of EC Modernization for leniency programmes and, briefly, the impact of some recent actions by the US plaintiffs bar.

[15] See (n 15).
[16] Cases 29-30/83 *Compagnie Royale Asturienne des Mines SA and Rheinzink v Commission* [1984] ECR 1679, paras 16 to 20; Cases C-89/95 etc *Ahlström Osakeyhtiö and others v Commission* [1993] ECR I-1307, para 127.
[17] *Napp Pharmaceutical Holdings Ltd and Subsidiaries v The Director General of Fair Trading* (Case No 1001/1/1/01)[2002] CompAR 13, paras 91–113.

1. Possible implications of EC Modernization

A key aim of EC Modernization is to enable the resources of the European Commission and the national authorities to be targeted more effectively on significantly harmful anticompetitive behaviour. Cartels are clearly significantly harmful. However, some have commented—forcefully at times—that the current arrangements for handling the EC and national leniency programmes under Modernization are likely to deter leniency applicants. Are these concerns valid? More importantly, could changes be made to strengthen the effectiveness of leniency under Modernization?

The main concerns can be summarized as follows:

• Only some Member States have national leniency programmes. Does this mean that cooperation within the European Competition Network (ECN) will be difficult on cartel cases with leniency? Specifically, how will any reallocation of cases work where leniency is involved and not all the authorities have leniency programmes? Also, how will information provided by leniency applicants be kept confidential and—in particular—not passed to an authority that does not have a leniency programme?
• Even if all Member States introduce leniency programmes, different members of a cartel might obtain immunity from different Member States. How would this be handled?
• Some Member States have criminal enforcement powers. Will this be an additional complication in handling cartel cases within the ECN?

As discussed above, predictability and certainty are key to an effective leniency programme. Those raising these concerns fear that—unless changes are made—Modernization will reduce predictability and certainty and hence discourage applications for leniency. Are they right?

2. Only some Member States have leniency programmes

While only 14 of the 25 Member States of the enlarged EU currently have leniency programmes, it is likely that more will be introduced. A central and up to date list of Member States with programmes and contact points for leniency applicants would be useful. I welcome the recent publication on the European Commission website[18] of a list of those authorities that operate a leniency programme. Hopefully, in time, this list can be developed to provide either contact points or links to these on NCA websites.

---

[18] See <http://europa.eu.int/comm/competition/antitrust/legislation/authorities_with_leniency_programme. pdf>.

When most Member States have such programmes (with similar conditions) any reallocation of cases should not be a problem as far as leniency is concerned. Until then, I should expect that neither Member States nor the Commission would readily transfer a case where one or more of the undertakings has leniency to a Member State that does not recognize leniency. Any case reallocations will be at the outset of proceedings—and will be exceptional as explained below. However, it would be useful to have more explicit guidance in the Commission Notice on Cooperation within the Network of Competition Authorities on whether leniency cases might be reallocated and in what circumstances—not least given that this concerns regulatory practice rather than legal protections. It might appear that paragraph 40 of the Notice[19] covers this situation, stating that information provided by a leniency applicant will not be transmitted to another ECN member without the consent of the applicant. Does this mean a case involving leniency would not be reallocated without the permission of the applicant? Not as such, because there are some exceptions to paragraph 40. Paragraph 41 of the Notice[20] allows leniency information to be transferred to another authority without the permission of the leniency applicant, provided that the information is not used to impose sanctions on the applicant. Hence, a leniency case could be reallocated without the consent of the applicant, but the reallocation should not harm the applicant. The Notice makes it clear that re-allocation of a case will be exceptional—ie where the original authority considers that it is not well placed to act or where other authorities consider themselves also well placed to act. This statement covers reallocation in general—it is not particularly directed at leniency cases.

The current leniency programmes operated by national competition authorities (NCAs) differ to some extent. It is clearly desirable that all programmes—existing and new ones—should be as similar as possible. This is particularly important in terms of the conditions to be satisfied.[21] But it is also desirable for the degree of leniency granted. The Competition Law Forum of the British Institute of International and Comparative Law has proposed that a Regulation or Directive should be adopted to ensure harmonized leniency programmes throughout the EU.[22] It would have been

---

[19] See below for the text of para 40.

[20] See (n 25) for the text of para 41.

[21] On the coverage of programmes, the UK civil leniency programme is unusual in that it includes leniency for vertical price fixing in addition to the more traditional leniency for horizontal cartels. The wider scope of the UK programme has been beneficial for a number of OFT cases.

[22] Competition Law Forum contribution to the public consultation on the 'Modernisation Package'. Available at: <http://europa.eu.int/comm/competition/antitrust/legislation/procedural_rules/comments/competition_law_forum_en.pdf>.

desirable if Regulation 1/2003 could have provided a legal basis for leniency programmes for all ECN members. Although most leniency programmes are based on administrative practice rather than on formal legal powers, such a power in the Regulation should have provided useful backing for Member States seeking to introduce programmes—and particularly for those facing objections to such programmes. Better still would have been provision in the Regulation for a single EU programme operated by all ECN members. However, that would almost certainly have been too big a step to take at the same time as the other Modernization changes given the number of Member States without a programme.

As indicated above, the Cooperation Notice addresses the issue of confidentiality of information provided by leniency applicants by restricting the use that can be made of such information and restricting its transfer within the network.[23] Importantly, the Cooperation Notice states that other members of the ECN will not start their own investigation if they are informed of a case initiated by another member as a result of a leniency application. But does this restriction fall away once an investigation becomes public? Of course, this would be no different from the position prior to Modernization where an NCA could start an investigation as a result of published information in another Member State.

The Cooperation Notice makes it clear that only limited details of a case will be transmitted to other authorities under Article 11 such as: the authority dealing with the case, the product, territories and parties concerned, the alleged infringement, the suspected duration of the infringement, and the origin of the case. The Notice explains that a standard form will be used for these details which are required to detect multiple proceedings and to ensure that cases are dealt with by a well placed competition authority. The key paragraphs on leniency in the Notice are as follows:

Paragraph 39—As for all cases where Articles 81 and 82 are applied, where an NCA deals with a case which has been initiated as a result of a leniency application, it must inform the Commission and may make the information available to other members of the network pursuant to Article 11(3) of the Council Regulation (cf paragraphs 16 *et subseq*). The Commission has accepted an equivalent obligation to inform NCAs under Article 11(2) of the Council Regulation. *In such cases, however, information submitted to the network pursuant to Article 11 will not be used by other members of the network as the basis for starting an investigation on their own behalf whether under the competition rules of the Treaty or, in the case of NCAs, under their national competition or other laws.* This is without prejudice

---

[23] The 'Commission Notice on the cooperation between the Commission and the courts of the EU Member States in the application of Articles 81 and 82 EC' also states, in para 26 that '[t]he Commission will not transmit to national courts information voluntarily submitted by a leniency applicant without the consent of that applicant.'

to any power of the authority to open an investigation on the basis of information received from other sources or, subject to paragraphs 40 and 41 below, to request, be provided with and use information pursuant to Article 12 from any member of the network, including the network member to whom the leniency application was submitted. [Emphasis added]

Paragraph 40—Save as provided under paragraph 41,[24] *information voluntarily submitted by a leniency applicant will only be transmitted to another member of the network pursuant to Article 12 of the Council Regulation with the consent of the applicant. Similarly other information that has been obtained during or following an inspection or by means of or following any other fact-finding measures which, in each case, could not have been carried out except as a result of the leniency application will only be transmitted to another authority pursuant to Article 12 of the Council Regulation if the applicant has consented to the transmission to that authority of information it has voluntarily submitted in its application for leniency.* The network members will encourage leniency applicants to give such consent, in particular as regards disclosure to authorities in respect of which it would be open to the applicant to obtain lenient treatment. Once the leniency applicant has given consent to the transmission of information to another authority, that consent may not be withdrawn. This paragraph is without prejudice, however, to the responsibility of each applicant to file leniency applications to whichever authorities it may consider appropriate. [Emphasis added]

Although the Cooperation Notice has been prepared jointly by the Commission and the Member States, it only binds the Commission. However it states, in paragraph 42, that:

---

[24] Para 41. 'Notwithstanding the above, the consent of the applicant for the transmission of information to another authority pursuant to Article 12 of the Council Regulation is not required in any of the following circumstances:
(1) No consent is required where the receiving authority has also received a leniency application relating to the same infringement from the same applicant as the transmitting authority, provided that at the time the information is transmitted it is not open to the applicant to withdraw the information which it has submitted to the receiving authority.
(2) No consent is required where the receiving authority has provided a written commitment that neither the information transmitted to it nor any other information it may obtain following the date and time of transmission as noted by the transmitting authority, will be used by it or by any other authority to which the information is subsequently transmitted to impose sanctions:
  (a) on the leniency applicant;
  (b) on any other legal or natural person covered by the favourable treatment offered by the transmitting authority as a result of the application made by the applicant under its leniency programme;
  (c) on any employee or former employee of any of the persons covered by (a) and (b).
A copy of the receiving authority's written commitment will be provided to the applicant.
(3) In the case of information collected by a network member under Article 22(1) of the Council Regulation on behalf of and for the account of the network member to whom the leniency application was made, no consent is required for the transmission of such information to, and its use by, the network member to whom the application was made.'

Information relating to cases initiated as a result of a leniency application and which has been submitted to the Commission under Article 11(3) of the Council Regulation will only be made available to those NCAs that have committed themselves to respecting the principles [of this Notice, including the principles relating to the protection of applicants claiming the benefit of a leniency programme.] The same principle applies where a case has been initiated by the Commission as a result of a leniency application made to the Commission.

A list of those authorities that have signed a statement declaring that they acknowledge these principles and will abide by them has been published on the website of the Commission.[25] Time will tell whether business is sufficiently reassured by these passages in the Notice and the commitment to abide by them—or requires some greater protection if leniency applications are to be fully utilized. Greater protection will be necessary if one or more of the authorities fails to commit publicly to the Notice unless it is very clear that they will be excluded from all Article 11(3) information relating to cases initiated as a result of a leniency application.

3. Different cartelists might obtain leniency from different Member States

Even if all Member States introduce leniency programmes, it would be possible—at least in theory—for different members of a cartel to obtain leniency from different Member States. If the cartel relates to more than three Member States, it would be expected to be handled by the Commission. The Notice says the Commission would be 'particularly well placed' to deal with a case with effects on competition in more than three Member States. This is not, of course, a commitment that the Commission will handle all such cases. But I should expect that to be the position for cartel cases—or for almost all of them—given that action against cartels is a Commission priority The key leniency question then would be which of the undertakings, if any, has applied for and obtained leniency from the Commission? Taking a different example, if the cartel involves, say, three Member States it may be handled jointly by all three NCAs. Or one or two of the NCAs could handle the case on behalf of all three. When fines are imposed, leniency should be applied against the fines in relation to the jurisdiction of each Member State as appropriate. Some Member States—including the UK—can impose fines in respect of effects in other Member States as long as the other Member States agree. The outcome in this example might depend on the extent to which the NCAs handling the case can impose fines in respect of other jurisdictions. If they can, I should expect

---

[25] <http://europa.eu.int/comm/competition/antitrust/legislation/list_of_authorities_joint_statement. pdf >. See also para 72 and the Annex of 'Commission Notice on cooperation within the Network of Competition Authorities'.

them to take full account of any leniency that has been granted by the other NCAs—this might be a condition of agreement to fining for effects in other Member States. Another possibility would be for the Commission to take the case—even with less than four jurisdictions involved—if there are difficult issues with leniency. While any such difficulties would not be the result of Modernization as such, business may reasonably expect a more 'joined up' system with Modernization. It would be valuable to have more guidance on how leniency would be handled in such situations in the Cooperation Notice.

The Competition Law Forum (CLF) has proposed that an application to any Member State should count as 'first' for leniency in all Member States which have leniency programmes where the cartel has effects.[26] Presumably this would also be subject to meeting the substantive criteria of each Member State concerned? While this should secure certainty and predictability for leniency applicants such arrangements could be difficult to operate in practice. Practitioners with experience of leniency applications have mixed views as to whether such arrangements would be workable given the lack of harmonization of Member States' conditions for leniency and the challenge of coordinating any multiple applications made to different authorities at the same time in the same case.

Applications for leniency in the same cartel may well come in very close to each other. If multiple applications were made at the same time to different NCAs could the true 'first' be clearly established? This should be possible if there is a precise definition of what is required. However, currently, different NCAs might have different views about what is required from an applicant to establish the 'first' position. Authorities might fear that there would be an incentive for members of the cartel to agree that simultaneously each should make an application to a different NCA in the hope that all would be judged as 'first'! In practice, cartel members would probably not trust each other to act simultaneously in this way. But an EU wide system would need very close coordination between authorities. Probably closer than it is possible to deliver currently given the differences in procedures and conditions to be satisfied. Until a harmonized leniency policy for all NCAs or uniform approach to first contact is introduced, the CLF proposes that the Commission should act as the central recipient and coordinator of all leniency applications for breaches of Article 81. Whatever their difficulties these proposals reflect real concerns that the uncertainty of current arrangements will discourage leniency applicants. The ideal solution would, of course, be a single EU leniency programme which applied throughout the Union operated by the Commission and the NCAs, hence providing a

---

[26] See (n 23).

completely uniform approach to first contact, conditions, procedures etc. The relative roles of the Commission and the NCAs would need to be carefully defined.

4. Some Member States have criminal enforcement powers

In some jurisdictions—including the UK—there are criminal sanctions for cartels. Experience in the US is that a criminal regime is a powerful incentive to apply for leniency. In a lecture at King's College London in February 2004, James Griffin, Deputy Assistant Attorney General, US Department of Justice Antitrust Division, illustrated this point with two anecdotes:

Senior Executive: 'As long as you are only talking about money, the company can take care of me—but once you begin talking about taking away my liberty, there is nothing the company can do for me'.

In 25 years of prosecuting individuals engaged in cartels, I have never had one lawyer for an executive I was prosecuting tell me that his client would spend a few extra days in jail for a reduction in the recommended fine.

However, some have suggested that executives may be more cautious about applying for civil leniency from the European Commission if there is also likely to be a criminal trial in, say, the UK. Their argument is that the application to the Commission opens up the risk of the criminal trial. But there is a criminal leniency programme in the UK to which the executive should apply at the same time as going to the Commission—and there must be a real risk that another cartel member might make an application under the UK criminal leniency programme. If so, this opens up the risk of criminal trials for the other members of the cartel. Hence the existence of the criminal regime in the UK seems more likely to increase than reduce applications for leniency for the reasons indicated by James Griffin. In addition to the deterrent impact of criminalization the UK Enterprise Act (2002), also introduced powers for company directors to be disqualified for breaches of the competition prohibitions. This is a further deterrent to cartels—and no application for a Competition Disqualification Order will be made against a director whose company has benefited from leniency under the UK or European Commission programmes or who has been granted immunity from UK criminal prosecution under the criminal leniency programme.

5. The impact of actions by the US plaintiffs bar

In recent years members of the US plaintiffs bar have sought—with some success—disclosure of corporate leniency statements made by undertakings to the European Commission for use in US treble damages actions. They have also sought to use the US Foreign Trade Antitrust Improvements Act

1982 (FTAIA) to obtain treble damages through the US courts for injuries to foreign plaintiffs for conduct outside the US. The scale of US treble damage awards—for example, totalling billions of dollars in the case of the vitamins cartel—is such that potential applicants for leniency for international cartels may decide not to come forward if the risk of very large private action awards is increased by these recent developments. This may particularly discourage potential applicants in international cartels with mainly European effects and only very minor effects in the US. It could reduce the effectiveness of leniency programmes at the same time as Modernization is implemented.

What are the solutions?

6. Corporate leniency statements

There is a tension between the US oral approach and the EC document based approach. However, progress has been made in devising an oral approach for leniency applications in Europe. But various issues remain, including whether the undertaking should receive a copy of the tape recording of its oral leniency statement to the Commission and what, if any, signatures are required from the undertaking. As long as the Commission holds the only copy of the recording and the undertaking does not sign to acknowledge it is a correct recording, the material is expected to be safe from US courts requiring disclosure. But the Commission may wish to have a stronger link between the undertaking and its statement, as the latter is likely to be an important part of the evidence of the cartel. Similar concerns are being raised in respect of some applications to national authorities.[27] Further work is necessary to develop a workable solution. Some leniency applicants settle with private litigants before there is any possibility that such companies will be able to request or use the evidence given under leniency. But this may only be practical in some cases.

7. FTAIA

F Hoffmann-La Roche Ltd v Empagran, SA, currently before the US Supreme Court, will determine whether FTAIA does allow claims for conduct outside the US to be made in the US. The Goverments of the US,[28] Belgium, Canada, Germany, Ireland, Japan, Netherlands, and the UK, as well as various US and international business organizations have sent briefs to the Supreme Court in support of the petitioners' argument that FTAIA

---

[27] This issue needs to be resolved for applications to NCAs as well as for those to the Commission.
[28] Brief for the United States as amicus curiae supporting the petitioners, Feb 2004. Available at <http://www.usdoj.gov/atr/cases/f202300/202397.htm>.

does not so apply. The US 'is concerned that the court of appeals' holding [that FTAIA allows foreign plaintiffs injured by anticompetitive conduct to sue in the US] will substantially harm its ability to uncover and break up international cartels and undermine law enforcement relationships between the United States and its trading partners'.[29] Similar concerns are reflected in most of the other briefs. This Supreme Court case is of great importance to the future of effective leniency programmes for international cartels. It is of at least as great importance for the future of private antitrust litigation in Europe. If the Supreme Court confirms that claims for conduct outside the US can be made in the US, the expected development of private antitrust litigation in Europe will be frustrated.

In a separate initiative, legislation has been introduced to the US Congress which includes detrebling as part of the US Department of Justice Antitrust Division's amnesty programme. Hewitt Pate, the Division's Assistant Attorney General, personally commended this concept prior to the introduction of the legislation:

One concept that is favoured by a number of experienced antitrust prosecutors would involve amending the antitrust laws to limit the damage recovery from a corporation that meets the strict criteria of our amnesty program, *and* that also cooperates with the consumers victimized by the cartel in their suits to recover damages from the remaining members of the cartel, to the actual damages caused by the corporation. A carefully limited detrebling concept of this type could address a major disincentive that currently confronts companies who are contemplating exposing cartel activity to the Division—the threat of treble damage lawsuits with joint and several liability. A concept of this type could be carefully drawn to ensure all other conspirator firms would remain jointly and severally liable for treble damages caused by the conspiracy, so the full potential for victims to be compensated civilly would remain. Of course, without detection, the potential compensation to consumers harmed by antitrust crime is zero, and fraudulent anticompetitive conduct will continue. In my personal view, it would be worthwhile to consider whether a carefully crafted provision of this type could enhance detection, and thereby enhance overall punishment and deterrence of cartel activity.[30]

The Senate has approved the legislation and it is currently before the House of Representatives. Hopefully the detrebling provision can be implemented soon—and the Supreme Court will decide that the jurisdiction of the US courts is not extended to apply to injuries that result from purely foreign commercial transactions. If so, two potential threats to leniency programmes will have been resolved.

---

[29] See (n 29).

[30] H Pate 'Vigorous and principled antitrust enforcement: priorities and goals' speech given before the Antitrust Section of the American Bar Association Annual Meeting, 12 Aug 2003. Available at <http://www.usdoj.gov/atr/public/speeches/201241.htm>.

VI. CONCLUSION

The benefits of leniency programmes clearly outweigh the challenges. However there is scope to strengthen these benefits through resolving more of the challenges.

My main conclusions on the impact of EC Modernization on leniency programmes are:

- The worst concerns are unlikely to be experienced in practice. However there are changes that could and should be made to improve certainty and predictability. At least more guidance should be provided. All Member States should have programmes and these should have identical terms. Without that, the ECN should consider what changes can be introduced to increase harmonization between Member States. The ultimate objective should be a single EU leniency programme operated jointly by all members of the ECN. A Council Regulation might be the most effective way to achieve that;
- Until there is a single EU leniency programme, applicants for leniency should continue to apply to all those authorities who may end up taking a cartel case against them. If it is not possible to do this simultaneously—not least because applications may also be required to the US—the order of application should take account of the severity of punishment likely following action by an authority, including potentially imprisonment.

As for the challenges from the US plaintiffs bar, further work is necessary to resolve the discovery issue. The *Empagran* case is key to resolving the FTAIA challenge.

CHAPTER 15

Human Rights Issues in Competition Cases

[Philippa Watson, *Essex Court Chambers*]

Good afternoon. It is my pleasure and privilege to chair this session this afternoon on the very interesting and vital topic of human rights, or what I prefer to call the fundamental rights, in competition law. We have two speakers. Richard Wainwright needs no introduction, but I would just mention that he is, I would say, the Commission's chief legal adviser on competition matters, a job which carries an enormous amount of responsibility and an enormous number of obligations, so we are very pleased to have him here with us this afternoon. Dr Renato Nazzini has done a huge amount of work on fundamental rights, procedural guarantees, prior to moving to the Office of Fair Trading where I presume he is putting all that he has learned into practice to guarantee our rights won't appear in front of the OFT. Richard has produced a paper on which he says he is going to pick up a few points. Renato, I think, is going to speak briefly about double jeopardy and then hopefully we will have time for a few questions and we might even stick to our allocated time frame.

A. Richard Wainwright*

Thank you Philippa. Just a few words of introduction: as Philippa has said, another expression used here is the fundamental rights. We are not talking about the cruel and unusual punishments which DG Competition inflict on leniency applicants in the basement of their building in Brussels, we are talking about things like rights to a fair trial, a right to respect for private life, or the right not to be tried or punished twice. As you will see, if you have had a chance to look at my paper, or you will already know no doubt, there is nothing about human rights or indeed fundamental rights in the original treaties, the Treaty of Rome, Paris or whatever, but since the early 1970s the Court of Justice has held that fundamental rights as derived from the constitutional traditions of the Member States and as set out in the European Convention on Human Rights, constitute general principles of

---

* European Commission.

Community law. So, across a whole range of areas, I think originally very often in the agricultural field, they have applied the principles, particularly, of the European Convention on Human Rights. Now I have got a limited time, as Philippa has said, so I am going to just concentrate on two topics from my paper. I raised eight topics and there are one or two more, which I thought about since then which I could have put in, but I am going to talk about the right to a fair trial as it is expressed in Article 6 of the Convention on Human Rights. In the terminology of the Court of Justice, that is usually called the rights of the defence. We do have these terminological problems. When I was practising English law—I don't know whether it still exists— we used to call those the principles of natural justice and I think in American legal parlance it is called due process. And I am particularly going to talk about two aspects of the right to a fair trial, rights of the defence. I am going to talk about the privilege against self-incrimination and I am also going to talk about legal professional privilege.

Let's start with the privilege against self-incrimination. As you will know the Regulation 17/62 Article 11, and now it is another Article in Regulation 1/2003, gives the Commission powers to require, in other words to ask and then if they don't get it to order, undertakings on pain of being fined to provide them with all the necessary information in order for them to carry out their duties, and this is done in writing. The so-called Article 11 letters are addressed to those undertakings suspected of being part of a cartel and the Regulation says they are required to answer them. Back in the late 1980s the issue was raised in a case called *Orkem*, which many of you will have heard about, as to whether the Commission was allowed to use these powers which provided for, in the Regulation, effectively to require people to incriminate themselves, and the *Orkem* case set out a division between the sort of things based on the Convention on Human Rights and those based on the idea of the privilege against self-incrimination, as to what sort of questions could be asked and what could not. Basically the division is that the Commission is entitled to require the production of pre-existing documents. It is entitled to require what was called factual information— that is to say if there was a question about meetings, where you present at such a meeting? What was the subject matter? And so on and so forth, but it was not entitled to require the undertakings to incriminate themselves, or in other words to say, 'I was there and we talked about raising prices or keeping prices up or fixing quotas' or whatever, and this provision in *Orkem* was dealt with again in subsequent case-law in *Mannesmann* where it was confirmed, even though in the meantime, particularly in the *Saunders* case under the Convention on Human Rights, the Court of Human Rights in Strasbourg had suggested that the privilege against self-incrimination also included the right to remain silent, part of the presumption of innocence. So the issue remains, and in fact it went up to the Court of Justice in one case where they managed to avoid dealing with the issue but they said that it still remains an outstanding issue as to whether the privilege against in self-incrimination goes further than we have in the current case, further than *Orkem* and further than *Mannesmann* and actually would allow, in effect, a party who receives an Article 11 request for information to effectively refuse to reply at all. There was a very recent judgment, on 29 April, in a case that's usually called the *Graphite Electrodes* cartel where this issue was raised, as one of a whole number of issues raised before the Court of First Instance, and the Court of First Instance effectively agreed with the argument of the Commission that the right to silence was something that was a reasonable presumption in relation to an individual. There were other arguments as well, but in relation to an undertaking, a non-legal person wouldn't necessarily, couldn't necessarily, be argued by them. And so we have a situation where so far the Court of First Instance has held firm, if that's the right expression, and has refused to allow companies to plead the right to silence. They must answer to these Article 11 requests for information. It is almost certain that this case will now be appealed before the Court of Justice and we may well then have a final judgment from the Court of Justice, which of course wouldn't necessarily mean the end of the story because as we've seen in another case, *Senator Lines*, it would even then perhaps be possible, in theory at any rate, for the parties to take the matter further on to the Strasbourg Court claiming that the system set up by the European Community Treaties doesn't effectively adequately protect their human rights. I should just add in this, and I know we don't have very much time, that this distinction is of course important for one aspect of what we call our leniency programmes, because we give reduction of fines for what we call cooperation and cooperation includes basically giving information which you are not required to give. In other words if you agree, if you tell the Commission, 'Yes I was at this such and such a meeting and we did discuss prices and we did discuss market sharing' then you will get a reduction of the fine for cooperation, but, of course, if you have a right to silence all along then logically at any rate you should get some sort of reduction for simply speaking at all. So there could, at least one day, be a spin-off from this litigation which is still pending in relation to our leniency programmes.

Now the other thing I want to mention today, and the second of some eight topics I raised in my paper, is also an issue which arises in relation to a right to a fair trial, and in this case it is the aspect of the right to a fair trial under Article 6 where you have a right to legal representation, and it is the issue of legal professional privilege, which is also very much being litigated before the European courts at the moment. I hesitated before I came to this when I spoke to Philippa as to whether I should talk about that. She says she thinks you might be rather interested, so I will speak about what is happening in the case with a certain amount of circumspection. Just to set the background, apart from the right to request written information, the Commission has a right to make inspections. These are what are usually called dawn raid inspections because they tend to be made rather early in the morning, with the cooperation of national authorities, where they go into the offices of the firms concerned and they open files, take copies, and so on and so forth. And back in the late 1970s, in a case called *AM&S*, the question arose, in the context of one of these dawn raids, as to whether or not there was, under EC law, a confidentiality—to use the expression of the court—of the communications between lawyer and client or, if there wasn't such a confidentiality, the alternative would be of course that the Commission would be entitled to take a copy of these communications and to put them on their file. In fact, John Temple Lang was counsel for the Commission in that case, and David Edward was acting for the CCB, the European Bar Association. The result of the case, I have to be very short on this, was that the Court held that the confidentiality of written communications between lawyer and client is protected, provided on the one hand their communications are made for the purposes and in the interests of the clients' rights of defence, so they have to be in context of some sort of litigious context, and on the other hand that they emanate from independent lawyers, and there has only been one other case of the Court which relates to this, the so-called *Hilti* case, where the scope of this privilege was extended also to notes which reported the content of the communications between outside lawyer and client. Perhaps as a detail to this I should add for the benefit of our trans-Atlantic friends that the Court limits itself to considering independent lawyers as lawyers who qualify to practise in the States of the European Union, although I believe it is a matter of practice at DG Competition to accept that lawyers practising in other jurisdictions can also benefit from this privilege, but it is not in the case-law.

In a sense it is quite odd that this case-law remained as it was. There has been a certain amount of agitation particularly about the restriction of the privilege to independent lawyers, in other words the exclusion of advice from in-house counsel. There was even an attempt by the European Parliament during the course of the modernization exercise to introduce a provision which would have extended that to in-house counsel (which didn't succeed), but we now have two pending cases which came up last year. First, *AKZO*, which is actually a famous client of the Community courts, operating in the chemical industry which tends to often be the subject of interest from DG Competition and again, because of the constraints of time, without going into too much detail, suffice to say that in the course of an inspection on *AKZO*'s premises, the issue of legal professional privilege was raised in relation to two types of documents which are not covered by the current *AM&S* criteria, or if you like, standards. One was documents which were prepared in-house with a view to obtaining advice from outside counsel, which are not covered under the present standards, and the other type of documents were communications within the firm with in-house counsel, and in one case the Commission actually refused categorically to recognize any type of privilege and took the copies and went home with them and put them on the file, and in another case they said, 'Well there might be' and they put them in an envelope following at least partly the *AM&S* procedure, and sealed the envelope and took it home and put it in the safe. *AKZO* attacked the Commission's refusal to return these documents, take them off the file and return them or take them out of the envelope and return them, and there was an interim measures hearing by Judge Vesterdorf last year in which he, and again I summarize, said, 'Well I cannot exclude the possibility that legal professional privilege mightn't be an evolving issue, but there may be something legal in what they say', so in fact he had the envelope himself and he kept it. He was the only one who had actually seen inside it, and so he ordered that the Commission couldn't open the envelope, indeed he kept it himself, pending of course the decision of the Court in the final decision of the Court, but he did say as far as the other documents were concerned that were on the Commission's file, there was nothing he could do about that. He couldn't take away the knowledge that they had. He noted an undertaking which we gave during the hearing that we wouldn't disclose the contents of these documents to any third parties in the context of any access to file procedure and on that basis he made his order. That order has been appealed by the European Commission, there has been a cross appeal by *AKZO* and there we are. So whatever view one might have of the merits or demerits of this action, it is very much before the Court of First Instance and indeed before the President of the Court of Justice, who now has to deal with the appeal and the cross appeal.

I am going to stop there because I know I would like you to have a chance to ask some questions and my colleague, Dr Nazzini, has something to say. I am afraid I am finishing with my conclusions rather than starting with them, I am sorry about that, but I would like to recall something that Sir David Edward said at the beginning of this conference yesterday morning, which seems like a real age ago. He said that we must never forget what we are trying to do is to get a good decision or, if not the best decision, at least a good decision, and when we are talking about human rights issues in general and particularly rights of defence, I think we have to remember that it is always a balancing exercise: we have the rights of the individual, which have to be protected, but we also have the general interest of the public and of the Community institutions in carrying out their job as efficiently and as speedily as possible. It is of course exactly these sorts of balances which have to be made both by the Commission and by the Court in an issue where we have a human rights argument. Thank you very much.

[Renato Nazzini's remarks were superceded by a paper which he prepared subsequently. It is at D. of this chapter—Editor's Note]

[PHILIPPA WATSON]

We have time for a few brief questions. Is there anybody who would like to start?

B. Discussion

[ALAN RILEY]

My question is more a comment, because I suspect that the Commission won't give me a real answer. Traditionally the Commission have said, in relation to *Saunders* and the rule against self-incrimination, that we must understand we're not like the Americans. These Americans have got electronic surveillance, they can put wire taps on, they can probably even ask the CIA to use their spy satellites. They can get loads of information whereas we, the poor Commission, only have the dawn raid power and the power to obtain information in Article 11 of Regulation 17/62 now Article 18 of Regulation 1/2003. My question, which I invite you to answer, is whether or not that approach, that argument which would be very powerful before the Court, is in fact quite significantly undermined by leniency. My understanding is that now the Commission under the new February 2002 leniency notice has received around 100 leniency applications. I understand the Commission has so many leniency applications it can't cope with them. Now when you have this embarrassment of riches of information, can the Commission so easily maintain the argument that it needs to obtain 'test me' evidence if necessary by compulsory powers? Thank you.

[RICHARD WAINWRIGHT]

Well, I'll say two things. One is the bureaucratic answer. We have a

Council Regulation which gives us this power and it is normal that we should exercise the powers we were given. The second point, I think, is in relation to the right to silence and I don't want to be too polemical about this, but just to say that I understand the situation in the United States is also that corporations—ie, legal rather than human persons—don't have the right to plead the Fifth Amendment either, and so at least the argument of the Commission, which so far has been accepted by the Courts, but may well not be accepted right at the end, is that we are not quite in the same situation on right to silence as we are when an individual finds himself up in criminal court facing possible imprisonment and so on. We don't have the right to imprison as you know. Maybe that is too our advantage for the time being, but I think that is all I can say for the time being.

[JULES STUYCK, *Katholieke Universiteit Leuven*]

I have a short question for Dr Nazzini, at least I hope he will have a brief answer and depending on his answer, I might have a second brief question. The question is; at the end of your talk you said something about *Walt Wilhelm* and you said it was a different setting because it was national law and EC competition law, and my question is whether in view of the evolution of the case-law in the European Convention, the Charter and Regulation 1/2003, whether *Walt Wilhelm* would still hold and that there would be no *ne bis in idem* in relationship of national and European competition law?

[RENATO NAZZINI]

Thank you Professor Stuyck. My short answer is that I think that *Walt Wilhelm* stands. The reasons are the following. As regards the principle of *ne bis in idem*, one should make a fundamental distinction, which was implicit, I think, in what I said, between the finding of infringement and the punishment. There are two different dimensions to the double jeopardy principle. One is that the same person cannot be prosecuted or tried twice for the same infringement and the second is that the same person cannot be punished twice for the same infringement. These two levels of protection are based, of course, on the same broad policy, but I think here they are clearly distinct levels of the same principle or even, perhaps, two different principles. As regards the prohibition of a second finding of guilt, this protection is more intense and, therefore, its application is narrower. It is confined to the application of the same legal provisions within the same legal system, including, of course, the Community legal order. As regards the rule against double punishment for the same, or substantially the same, offence, this protection is less intense because it only applies to the punishment and not to the finding of guilt. Its application is therefore broader and extends to punishment for the same, or substantially the same, conduct under different legal provisions in different legal systems. I think *Walt Wilhelm* does stand because the *ne bis in idem principle* does not bar a second prosecution and trial in relation to infringements of different legal provisions. However, the double jeopardy principle prevents double punishment. It is true that Regulation 1/2003 has brought about a 'revolution' in the relationship between national competition laws and EC competition law. However, national competition laws have been preserved and may be applied in parallel to EC competition law under Article 3 of the Regulation. One could even argue that if the double jeopardy principle prevented a finding of guilt under EC and national competition law, the possibility of parallel application under Article 3 of the Regulation would be in breach of a fundamental right. This is not to say that the *ne bis in idem* principle does not apply to the concurrent application of national and EC competition law. It applies in its second dimension relating to punishment. When it comes to punishment, then the *Walt Wilhelm* case does stand because the same person cannot be punished twice for the same behaviour albeit under different legal provisions as a matter of 'natural justice', as the Court of Justice said in that case. Thank you.

[MATTHEW HEIM]

I just wanted to ask a brief question on the Charter of Fundamental Rights. To what extent do you think the Charter has or will change the behaviour of the Commission, or for that matter a national competition authority, following its proclamation by the Member States and the institutions bearing in mind it is not legally binding and more importantly bearing in mind the fact that it enshrines the ECHR as interpreted strictly by the Court in Strasbourg?

[RICHARD WAINWRIGHT]

I'll just say one thing, but I think Renato might like to add to it. I like the Charter very much because it has provisions which go well beyond the Convention on Human Rights, for example, provisions against treating elderly people worse than younger people, which I think is a very good idea, but as far as competition law is concerned, as far as I can see the only significant effect of the Charter—and here I get into the territory of Renato—is that Article 50 of the Charter, as you know, extends the principle of double jeopardy beyond double jeopardy in one Member State or *ne bis in idem* in one Member State to *ne bis in idem* in all the Member States of the Union, and indeed I think in my paper I quote some suggestion by the Secretariat to the Charter, which suggests that they think already whatever the Member States have said about the Charter is already expressed as a general principle.

[RENATO NAZZINI]

If I may I shall perhaps just add one thing from the point of view of the national competition authorities, of course in a personal capacity. The Charter doesn't change much for national competition authorities insofar as national competition authorities in the EU are already bound by the European Convention on Human Rights unlike the Commission. Therefore even the binding or non-binding force of the Charter, as long as the Charter reinstates rights in the European Convention on Human Rights, is not really an issue. Where further rights are protected by the Charter, as is the case for the principle of *ne bis in idem*, as Richard rightly pointed out, then the position is exactly the same as for the European institutions.

[OLIVER BRETZ, *Clifford Chance*]

One of the things that's been quite shocking to some of us who have been on the receiving end of dawn raids at our clients' premises is really the use that the European Commission makes of the computers of the lawyers, and in particular, lawyers who are responsible for competition law and policy inside the organization. I was really just going to ask whether there will be some new guidance being issued in the light of the *AKZO* decision considering the very significant risks that you might actually get hold of information which you are not supposed to have.

[RICHARD WAINWRIGHT]

I think Serge Durande could say something about this. Do you want to? We've got the Hearing Officer here and he would be very well-placed to say something about that.

[PHILIPPA WATSON]

We've got the Commission's Hearing Officer and we would like to benefit from his presence if he is willing to give us his wisdom.

[SERGE DURANDE, *European Commission*]

I feel like giving an answer for the times when I was on the giving end of the dawn raids you see, not as the Hearing Officer. Honestly, it is a question of knowing the facts, finding the evidence and if the evidence is in the computers, it is in the computers. What specifically the question is, I am not sure. You cannot simply say that I am not looking into a place where I know the evidence is.

[OLIVER BRETZ]

Sorry; it was a question about legal privilege.

[PHILIPPA WATSON]

And access to lawyers' computers, wasn't it?

[SERGE DURANDE]

You have to take the evidence where it is, whether it is in a computer or on a piece of paper or in a book or anywhere. You have an inspection and you take the evidence. This is very clear. Now you have to take it respecting the rights of defence. Rights of defence as far as you are concerned, as a lawyer, are expounded in *AM&S* and Richard Wainwright talked about it a few minutes ago. We have to wait for what the outcome of the present case in front of the Court now. We don't know more than that but today your computer is, as a start, in itself privileged if you are an in-house lawyer.

[RICHARD WAINWRIGHT]

Can I just complete on that? I think, Serge, that is the official position of the Commission. The only other thing I would add is that we've had interesting questions raised in relation to information on computers which apparently is alleged to be stored in servers outside the European Union, and the question has been raised as to whether we have jurisdiction over that to suck out that information. Of course we have said that we have. We haven't been sued yet!

C. Human Rights:* What Have they to do with European Competition Law?

Richard Wainwright**

I. SOURCES

European Convention on Human Rights (ECHR) (1950)

1. The Court of Justice has held in judgments going back to the early 1970s that fundamental rights, as derived from the constitutional traditions of the Member States and as set out in the ECHR, constitute general principles of Community law.[1]

Treaty on European Union (Maastricht 1992)

2. 'The Union shall respect fundamental rights, as guaranteed by the European Convention for the Protection of Human Rights and Fundamental Freedoms signed in Rome on 4 November 1950 and as they result from the constitutional traditions common to the Member States, as general principles of Community law'.

Charter of Fundamental Rights of the European Union (Nice, 2000)

3. The Charter was 'proclaimed' by the European Council at Nice, but is not yet legally binding. It is referred to by the CFI (eg T-54/99, max mobil) and by A-Gs (eg A-G Mischo in C-20 and 64/00 Booker Aquaculture). With the exception of Article 50 (*ne bis in idem*)[2] the Charter does not appear to go further, for the purposes of competition law, than the analogous provisions of the ECHR.

II. RIGHT TO A FAIR TRIAL[3] (ARTICLE 6 ECHR)

A. Hearing by 'an independent and impartial tribunal'

4. The position of the Commission as investigator, prosecutor, and judge in competition cases has been criticized.[4]

---

* Otherwise known as 'fundamental rights'—see Watson: 'Fundamental Rights and Competition Law' [2003] Comp Law, 22.
** Principal Legal Adviser, European Commission. Any opinions expressed are personal to the author. Paper presented at the British Institute of International and Comparative Law, 10–11 May 2004, London.
[1] See, eg, Case 4/73 *Nold*.   [2] See part IV below.
[3] Generally referred to in the case-law of the Court as 'the rights of the defence'. In English legal terminology, it is normally called 'the principles of natural justice', and in American, 'due process'—see Jacobs 'The Right to a Fair Trial in European Law' [1999] EHRLR/issue 2.
[4] See Waelbroeck and Fosselard 'Should the Decision-making power in EC Antitrust Procedures be left to an Independent Judge?' [1994] Yearbook of European Law 14.

5. The European Court of Human Rights has held that the prosecution of offences which are 'criminal' within the wider meaning of Article 6 ECHR can be entrusted to administrative authorities, provided that the persons concerned are able to challenge any decision before a judicial body that provides the full guarantees of that article.[5] This has been applied by the CFI, noting that the judicial control exercised by the CFI over the Commission under Article 230 satisfies the requirements of Article 6 ECHR6.[6]

6. There may however be a case, other than on human rights protection grounds, for the separation of the adjudicative function (CFI/ECJ) from the investigative/prosecutorial function (Commission) in cases brought under Articles 81 and 82 EC.[7]

B. *Privilege against self incrimination*

7. The powers of investigation of the Commission are subject to certain limitations which flow from the privilege against self incrimination.

8. In *Orkem* (374/87), the Court held that the Commission was allowed to use its mandatory powers of investigation to secure factual information, such as the circumstances in which meetings of producers were held or the subject-matter of measures taken by the undertakings concerned, and that the Commission could also require the disclosure of documents in the undertaking's possession, but that the Commission could not require an undertaking to answer questions relating to the purpose or the objectives of measures taken which would compel it to admit participation in a violation of EC antitrust law.

9. In judgments posterior to *Orkem*, the European Court of Human Rights has confirmed that the privilege against self-incrimination forms part of a fair procedure under Article 6 ECHR.[8] This privilege respects the right to remain silent of an accused person, but allows the use in evidence of compulsorily acquired documents.

10. In *Mannesmann* (T-112/98), the CFI repeated the terms of the judgment in *Orkem*. Subsequently in *PVC II* (C-238/99P etc) the ECJ left open the questions as to whether *Orkem* is still good law insofar as it allows the Commission to use mandatory powers to require answers to factual questions.[9]

---

[5] *Bendenoun v France* A/284 (1994).   [6] Case T-348/94 *Enso Espa_ola.*
[7] See Wils 'The combination of the investigative and prosecutorial function and the adjudicative function in EC Antitrust enforcement' (2004) 27(2) World Competition.
[8] See *Saunders v UK* (1996).
[9] See Wils 'Self-incrimination in EC Antitrust Enforcement' (2003) 26(4) World Competition.

11. The issue of the 'right to silence' of an undertaking (a 'legal person')[10] may be decided in a series of pending cases in SGL (T-239/01 and Carbide Graphite (T-252/01) (graphite electrodes cartel).

C. *Legal professional privilege*

12. In *AM & S* (155/79) the Court held that

> he confidentiality of written communications between lawyer and client [is protected] provided that, on the one hand, such communications are made for the purposes and in the interests of the clients' rights of defence and, on the other hand, they emanate from independent lawyers, that is to say lawyers who are not bound to the client by a relationship of employment.

In *Hilti*, (T-30/89) the CFI expanded the scope of legal professional privilege to include internal notes 'confined to reporting the text or content' of communications between lawyer and client.

13. In two linked pending cases, *Akzo* (T-125/03R and T-253/03R), the issue is raised as to whether the *AM & S* criteria are not too restrictive in the light of further developments under the ECHR and in the Member States—in particular insofar as they exclude from privilege: (1) internal documents drafted with a view to seeking legal advice from outside lawyers, and (2) communications with in-house lawyers.

14. In an order of 30 October 2003 (*Akzo*, T-125/03R and T-253/03R) the President of the CFI held that, prima facie, such an extension of the *AM & S* criteria could not be excluded. This order is now the subject of an appeal by the Commission and a cross-appeal by Akzo (C-7/04P(R)).

15. The scope of legal professional privilege in Community law is therefore still at issue.

D. *Fines and bank guarantees*

16. The issue of the compatibility with Article 6 ECHR of a requirement to provide a bank guarantee for a fine pending the result of an appeal was raised in *Senator Lines* (T-191/98R and C-364/99P(R)). Both the President of the CFI and of the ECJ rejected a request to suspend this requirement on the grounds that, although the company itself could not provide a bank guarantee, recourse could be had to the assets of the group to which it belonged.

---

[10] In the United States, corporations are not protected under the Fifth Amendment privilege against self-incrimination (*US v Whit*, 322 US 694 (1944)).

17. The company then brought an action before the European Court of Human Rights against the Member States (Application 56672/00 *Senator Lines v Austria*), arguing that the Member States were responsible for the acts of Community institutions and that by dismissing the requested interim relief, the EC Courts were allowing an administrative body to force the company into liquidation, in violation of the rights to a fair hearing, effective access to judicial recourse, and the presumption of innocence.

18. On 30 September 2003, in Cases T-191/98 and T-212/98 to T-214/98, *Atlantic Container Lines et al*, the CFI quashed the fines on Senator Lines and the other addressees of the Commission decision.

19. In these circumstances, on 17 March 2004, the European Court of Human Rights decided that the application was inadmissible since the applicant company could no longer claim to be a 'victim' of a violation of its ECHR rights.

20. Mention should also be made of a pending case, *Cementir Cementerie del Tirreno* (138/04), in which the applicant challenges the practice of the Commission in calculating interest due on fines not paid, pending an ultimately unsuccessful appeal. The Commission practice, Interbank (now European Central Bank) rate at the date when the fine was originally due plus 1 per cent, discourages appeals. It is argued that it is contrary to the principle of Article 6 ECHR, in a situation of declining interest rates.

21. The question of the compatibility with the ECHR of EC practice and case-law, regarding bank guarantees for fines pending appeals and regarding interest due on those fines, therefore remains open.

E. Obligation to act within a reasonable time

22. It is constant case law that Article 6 ECHR requires that decisions adopted following administrative proceedings in competition matters must be adopted within a reasonable time.[11] This time runs from the notification of the Statement of Objections which is considered to be the time when 'the person is charged' in ECHR terms. This principle also requires that judicial proceedings on an appeal from a competition decision be conducted within a reasonable time (C-185/95P *Baustahlgewebe*). Breach of this principle may affect the legality of the

---

[11] See in particular *PVC II* (Joined Cases C-238/99P etc Limburgse Vinyl et al, para 167) and Joined Cases T-5/00 and T-6/00, NFVGEP and T-67/01, JCB Service, where this requirement is considered to be an element of the right to good administration under Article 41(1) of the Charter.

Commission or judicial decision. It may also be taken into account in any reassessment of the fine imposed.

III. RIGHT TO RESPECT FOR PRIVATE AND FAMILY LIFE (ARTICLE 8)

23. Regulation 17, Article 14 (now Regulation 1/2003, **Article 20**), confers on the Commission investigatory powers, including powers to examine business records, take copies, ask for oral explanations, and enter premises, land and means of transportation of undertakings. Where an undertaking refuses to submit to an investigation, Member States are required to offer the Commission officials the necessary assistance.

24. In *Hoechst* (46/87 and 227/88) it was held that before granting any assistance to an investigation amounting to a measure of constraint, the body responsible under national law (usually a court) must satisfy itself: a) that the Commission's decision is authentic and b) that the measures of constraint applied for are not 'arbitrary or excessive'. However, it must not substitute his own assessment for that of the Commission on the need for the investigation.

25. In *Roquette* (C-94/00) the French cour de Cassation questioned whether *Hoechst* remains good law in the light of developments under the ECHR, in particular the judgment of the European Court of Human Rights of 16 December 1992 in *Niemitz* and of 16 April 2002 in *Colas* where that Court held that Article 8 of the ECHR may also protect certain professional business activities or premises.

26. In the *Roquette* judgment of 22 October 2002, the ECJ confirmed the basic principles of the *Hoechst* judgment. It added that the Commission must provide to the national court all the information which that court needs to carry out its review as to whether the coercive measure sought are not 'arbitrary or disproportionate'. However the national court may not demand that it be provided with the evidence in the Commission's file.

27. The *Hoechst* and *Roquette* caselaw is now codified in Article 20 paragraphs 7 and 8 of Regulation 1/2003. Note also, Article 21 of this Regulation, which expressly authorizes inspections, on reasonable suspicion, of other premises (including houses and cars of directors managers and staff of undertakings)—subject to prior authorization from a national court. The question as to whether authorization from a national court is required for a 'forced entry' into business premises is left to national law.

28. The issue could still arise therefore in those Member States, where a

court authorization is not required for entry into business premises, of compatibility of national law with Article 8 ECHR, in particular in the light of the *Colas* judgment. This could put into question a Community investigation in those Member States.

IV. RIGHT NOT TO BE TRIED OR PUNISHED TWICE (ARTICLE 4 OF PROTOCOL 7 ECHR)

29. The right not to be tried or punished twice under the jurisdiction of the same State is usually called the principle of '*ne (or non) bis in idem*' ('double jeopardy' in common law terminology). In *PVC II* (already cited), the ECJ confirmed that the principle of *ne bis in idem* is a fundamental principle of Community law also enshrined in Article 4(1) of Protocol 7 to the ECHR and that it 'precludes, in competition matters, an undertaking from being found guilty or proceedings being brought against it a second time on the grounds of . . . conduct in respect of which it has been penalised or declared not liable by a previous unappealable decision'.[12]

30. The CFI has held that the *ne bis in idem* principle does not prevent the European Commission from imposing fines on undertakings which have already been fined by the US and Canadian authorities for involvement in the same cartel. Nor is the Commission required even to take into account in its own fine calculation the amount of the fines already imposed by those authorities. This is because the fines imposed pursue different ends (competition within the European Community and competition on the markets of those third countries).[13]

31. Article 50 of the Charter of Fundamental Rights of the European Union restates the principle of *ne bis in idem* to apply not only within the jurisdiction of one State, but 'within the Union', that is between the jurisdictions of several Member States.

Although, pending the possible transformation of the Convention into

---

[12] At para 59, the Court nevertheless confirmed the legality of the re-adoption of a decision, which had been annulled by the ECJ in 1994, because the Commission had failed to authenticate its decision in the way provided by its own Rules of Procedure (C-137/94P BASF et al).

[13] T-224/00, *Archer Daniels Midland* (amino acids), now under appeal in C-397/03P. See Vesterdorf 'Double jeopardy by parallel international prosecution of cartels—*ne bis in idem* principle in competition matters' 21 (*European Commission v the International Cartel Workshop*, 1–3 Oct 2003) where, basing himself on the principle of Case 14/68, Wilhelm suggests that account should be taken of a third country authority fine/sanction where that authority has based its calculation on the worldwide turnover of the undertakings concerned and/or their worldwide profits on the markets affected.

a new European constitution, the Charter is not yet legally binding, the extension of the *ne bis in idem* principle to apply between the jurisdiction of several Member States 'corresponds to the *acquis* in Union law' according to the Convention Secretariat.[14]

32. As from 1 May 2004 under Regulation 1/2003 national competition authorities (NCAs) will be fully empowered to apply Article 81 and 82 EC.

The Commission and the national competition authorities will form a network for the application of Community competition rules 'in close cooperation'. A number of guidelines have been laid down in a Joint Statement of the Council and the Commission on the functioning of the network[15] made at the adoption of the Regulation and in a Commission Notice on cooperation within the Network of Competition Authorities.[16] These guidelines lay down criteria to ensure that cases should be handled by a single authority which is 'well placed'.

33. However there are possible scenarios where 'parallel action by two or three NCAs may be appropriate where an agreement or practice has substantial effects on competition mainly in their respective territories and the action of only one NCA would not be sufficient to bring the entire infringement to an end and/or to sanction it adequately'.[17]

In such cases, Article 50 of the Charter could be invoked, where an agreement or practice has been sanctioned in one Member State, against subsequent sanctions imposed by the second and third Member States.[18]

V. NO PUNISHMENT WITHOUT LAW (ARTICLE 7 ECHR)

34. Article 15(2) of Regulation 17 (now Article 23(3) of Regulation 1/2003) provides that in setting the amount of the fine which the Commission may impose for infringement of Article 81 or 82 EC (within a limit of 10 per cent of turnover) 'regard shall be had both to the gravity and to the duration of the infringement'. No other criteria are indicated.

---

[14] Council of the EU: 'Charter of Fundamental Rights of the European Union—Explanations relating to the complete text of the Charter' Dec 2000 69.

[15] Council doc 15435/02 ADD 1, available on the Council website.

[16] Available on the website of DG Competition.

[17] Commission Notice, para 12. If there are effects in more than three Member States, the Commission is considered 'particularly well placed' (para 14).

[18] See Wils 'The principle of *ne bis in idem* in EC antitrust enforcement' (2003) 26(2) World. See also Vesterdorf (n 13).

In two pending cases before the CFI (T-43/02, *Jungbunzlauer* and T-279/02, *Degussa*), the applicants question the compatibility of this provision with Article 7 ECHR on the grounds that it lacks legal certainty (*'nulla poena sine lege certa'*).[19]

VI. CONCLUSIONS

35. 'Human rights' points continue to be raised before the European Courts, which examine them with great respect. The present position can be summarized as follows:

—The combination of investigative prosecutorial and adjudicative functions in the Commission is defendable under the ECHR, but there may be the other arguments in favour of a separation of such functions;

—A question mark still hangs over the 'right to silence' in the context of self-incrimination;

—The issue of legal professional privilege, decided in 1982 in *AM & S*, has now been reopened in *Akzo*;

—The requirement of bank guarantees for fines pending appeal is still open to challenge. The calculation of the interest due on those fines is being challenged;

—Both the Commission and the European Courts are obliged to act 'within a reasonable time';

—A Community investigation by 'forced entry' into business premises in those Member States, which does not require a court authorization, could be put into question;

—The principle of *ne bis in idem* might under certain circumstances affect the functioning of the Network of Competition Authorities under Regulation 1/2003;

—The legal basis for Commission fines for breaches of Articles 81 and 82 EC is being questioned before the CFI.

---

[19] The arguments seems to be inspired by the judgment of the German Constitutional Court of 20 Mar 2002 (2 BvR 794/95) declaring a financial sanction of German criminal law (Art 43a of the *Strafgesetzbuchs*) to be incompatible with constitutional principles of legal certainty (Art 103, para 2, of the *Grundgesetz*).

D. The Principle of Double Jeopardy and the Multi-jurisdictional Enforcement of EC Competition Law

Renato Nazzini*

I. INTRODUCTION

This paper addresses the problem of the application of the principle of double jeopardy, or, in the Latin variant, *ne bis in idem*,[1] in the concurrent enforcement of competition law by the EU competition authorities. Following modernization of EC competition law,[2] the problem becomes more acute. The question is, in its essential terms, simple: when is a second investigation into the same or similar facts and against the same person

---

* PhD, Solicitor, Principal Case Officer, Office of Fair Trading and Visiting Fellow, British Institute of International and Comparative Law. The views expressed in this paper are personal to the author and do not necessarily reflect those of the Office of Fair Trading.

[1] In this paper, *ne bis in idem* and double jeopardy are used interchangeably. For an analysis of the general principles applicable to concurrent enforcement of competition law, see R Nazzini *Concurrent Proceedings in Competition Law: Procedure, Evidence and Remedies* (OUP Oxford 2004) ch 5.

[2] At European level, modernization of EC competition law was the most important reform of competition law enforcement since Council Regulation (EEC) 17/62 First Regulation implementing Arts 85 and 86 of the Treaty [1962] JO 13/204, [1959 – 1962] OJ Spec Ed 87 (Regulation 17/62) was adopted. Council Regulation (EC) No 1/2003 on the implementation of the rules on competition laid down in Arts 81 and 82 of the Treaty [2003] OJ L1/1 (Regulation 1/2003) makes Art 81 EC directly applicable in its entirety. It extends the direct effect thus far confined to Art 81(1) EC and Art 82 EC to Art 81(3) EC. As a consequence, there are no more obstacles to a full application of the provisions of Community competition law by national competition authorities. The Commission or the Office of Fair Trading (OFT) may both conduct investigations for the enforcement of Arts 81 and 82 EC. The Commission, under Regulation 1/2003, will retain the power to enforce Arts 81 and 82 EC in cases having a Community dimension or where action by national competition authorities would be ineffective or inefficient. The OFT retains the power to apply UK competition law but, under Regulation 1/2003, has the additional power to apply Arts 81 and 82 EC. The competition authorities of the other EU Member States have concurrent jurisdiction with the Commission and the OFT to apply Community competition law. Cases are allocated on the basis of the principles set out in the Joint Statement of the Council and the Commission on the functioning of the network of competition authorities of 10 Dec 2002 (Brussels 10 Dec 2002 15435/02 ADD 1 RC 22) and the more detailed rules contained in the Commission Notice on cooperation within the network of competition authorities (Commission Notice on cooperation within the Network of Competition Authorities [2003] OJ C101/43). For an analysis of the abolition of the notification procedure and the decentralized enforcement of EC competition law in the new system, see A Riley 'EC Antitrust Modernisation: The Commission Does Very Nicely—Thank You! Part One: Regulation 1 and the Notification Burden' [2003] ECLR 604 and, by the same author 'EC Antitrust Modernisation: The Commission Does Very Nicely—Thank You! Part Two: Between the Idea and the Reality: Decentralisation under Regulation 1' [2003] ECLR 657. See also R Whish and B Surfin 'Community Competition Law: Notification and Individual Exemption—Goodbye to All That' in D Hayton (ed) *Law's Future(s). British Legal Developments in the 21st Century* (Hart Oxford 2000) 135–59.

barred by a previous decision or investigation? The answer is, however, difficult for three reasons.

The first reason is inherent in the very nature of the principle of *ne bis in idem* as an international standard of justice. In its high-level formulation, the principle is clear and widely accepted or, at least, acceptable. When it comes to its application to a specific case, however, there seems to be little guidance as to the set of technical concepts and rules that, in any national legal system, complement the principle of double jeopardy. In the application of any doctrine of double jeopardy in the criminal laws of the 'civilized nations', there is no or little doubt as to the high-level formulation of the principle. The problems, and divergences, arise in its application and, in particular, in the solutions to issues such as the nature, or type, of decisions that give rise to the estoppel and the test to be applied for determining whether the second prosecution relates to the same, or similar offence, or to the same, or similar facts. These problems are solved in the national criminal law systems is ways that are jurisdiction-specific and cannot be imported into the trans-national environment of the concurrent application of Community competition law by the 26 EU competition authorities.

The second reason lies in the novelty of the system of concurrent enforcement of competition law in the EU. It is true that concurrent enforcement of Community competition law was possible before Council Regulation 1/2003 came into force except for the application of Article 81(3) EC. It is also true, however, that in the new system the emphasis on concurrent enforcement is much stronger. The removal of the Commission's exclusive jurisdiction on the application of Article 81(3) EC empowers national competition authorities to apply Community law in full and encourages them to share with the Commission the responsibility of maintaining a system of undistorted competition in the common market. Going even further, Article 3 of Regulation 1/2003 imposes a duty on national competition authorities to apply EC competition law when they apply national competition law and the anti-competitive behaviour has an effect on trade between Member States. Finally, Regulation 1/2003 and the Commission Notice on cooperation within the Network of Competition Authorities[3] contain unprecedented provisions on the cooperation between the Commission and the national competition authorities, thus shaping a system that has concurrency as one of its main pillars. The third reason is that competition law investigations are criminal in nature for

---

[3] Commission Notice on cooperation within the Network of Competition Authorities [2004] OJ C101/43.

the purposes of the application of the principle of *ne bis in idem* but are, and remain, administrative procedures whose structure, function, and effects are very different from those of criminal investigations and trials. Transposing a criminal law concept into this newly developed system of administrative proceedings and sanctions is not easy because of the procedural differences that exist between criminal procedure and administrative investigations in all Member States.

The focus of this paper is on the enforcement of competition law by EU competition authorities, including the national competition authorities and the Commission. This paper does not address the question of whether it is possible to apply administrative, civil, and criminal sanctions in respect of an agreement or practice which has already been subject to previous proceedings. This is because the problem only arises if multiple sanctions of the same nature are imposed on the same person. Generally, criminal sanctions, administrative sanctions, and civil remedies are imposed on, or awarded against different persons and/or for different purposes. In the enforcement of competition law by the EU competition authorities, on the other hand, the same undertaking may be subject to administrative investigations for the same or similar behaviour by more than one authority. Are multiple investigations, and multiple sanctions, barred by the principle of *ne bis in idem*?

This paper is structured as follows. First, it will provide an overview of the principle of *ne bis in idem*. Secondly, the conterminous principles of legal certainty and legitimate expectations will be examined. Thirdly, the paper will go on to analyse the categories of decisions that national competition authorities, and in particular the Office of Fair Trading (OFT), may adopt under Regulation 1/2003 and the *ne bis in idem* implications if a second investigations is conducted by the same or another competition authority. Fourthly, a further dimension to the principle of *ne bis in idem* will be discussed, namely the application of different competition laws to the same, or similar, facts. Finally, conclusions will be drawn.

II. THE TRANS-NATIONAL DIMENSION OF THE PRINCIPLE OF *NE BIS IN IDEM*

The double jeopardy rule originates in the criminal law systems of the States. Its application is generally limited to proceedings that are criminal under national law. Its effect is to bar a second prosecution when the defendant has been already validly acquitted or convicted for the same offence or, in certain circumstances, for an offence based on the same or substantially the same facts. In English criminal law a plea of *autrefois aquit* or *autrefois convict* bars a second prosecution if the defendant has been previously acquitted or convicted of the same offence as that of which he is charged in the second prosecution.[4] Furthermore, under the doctrine of abuse of process, the court is required to stay proceedings if the defendant has previously been acquitted or convicted on the same or substantially the same facts (albeit of a different offence), unless there are exceptional circumstances.[5] Similar rules exist in most legal systems. This concept of the double jeopardy rule is at the origin of a wider principle enshrined in international conventions and in Community law. This broader principle tends to be applied to proceedings that are criminal in nature albeit not criminal under national law. Furthermore, it may have a transnational application, ie may be applied to proceedings taking place in different States. While proceedings against individuals are not barred by proceedings against companies and civil remedies are not barred by proceedings of a criminal nature, the question must be asked as to whether investigations of a criminal nature against undertakings may be barred because the same, or substantially the same, infringement has already been investigated by the same or a different authority in the same or even in a different State.

Article 4 of Protocol No 7 to the European Convention on Human Rights and Fundamental Freedoms states:[6]

No one shall be liable to be tried or punished again in criminal proceedings under the jurisdiction of the same State for an offence for which he has already been finally acquitted or convicted in accordance with the law and penal procedure of that State.

The provisions of the preceding paragraph shall not prevent the reopening of the case in accordance with the law and penal procedure of the State concerned, if there is evidence of new or newly discovered facts, of if there has been a fundamental defect in the previous proceedings, which could affect the outcome of the case.

Protocol 7 has not been ratified by the UK. However, since the rights protected by the Convention are generally regarded as fundamental rights in Community law, Article 4 of Protocol No 7 may indirectly affect the legal position in the UK in the enforcement of EC competition law through the jurisprudence of the Court of Justice.[7] It should also be noted that Article

---

[4] *Connelly v DPP* [1964] AC 1254, 1339–340, HL, per Lord Devlin.

[5] ibid.

[6] Convention for the Protection of Human Rights and Fundamental Freedoms (the European Human Rights Convention) (Rome 4 Nov 1950), Protocol No 7, Art 4.

[7] The European Human Rights Convention, Protocol No 7, Art 4 was referred to by the Court of Justice as reflecting a 'fundamental principle of Community law' in Joined Cases C-238/99 P, C-244/99 P, C-245/99 P, C-247/99 P, C-250/99 P, C-251/99 P, C-252/99 P and C-254/99 P *Limburgse Vinyl Maatschappij NV (LVM) v Commission of the European Communities (PVC No 2)* [2002] ECR I-8375, para 59; WPJ Wils 'The Principle of *Ne Nis in Idem* in EC Antitrust Enforcement: A Legal and Economic Analysis' [2003] World Competition 131, 133. For a general overview of the problems arising from the application of the European Human Rights Convention to administrative proceedings by the Commission, see A Riley 'The ECHR Implications of the Investigation Provisions of the Draft Competition

4 of Protocol 7 only applies to proceedings within the same jurisdiction and does not provide for a principle of transnational *ne bis in idem.*

Article 50 of the European Charter of Fundamental Rights[8] departs from the traditional view that the double jeopardy rule only applies to criminal proceedings within the same jurisdiction and adopts a principle of Community-wide *ne bis in idem.* Article 50 states: 'No one shall be liable to be tried or punished again in criminal proceedings for an offence for which he or she has already been finally acquitted or convicted within the Union in accordance with the law.'

The Charter is not legally binding in itself.[9] It is addressed to the Member States only insofar as they apply Community law.[10] However, it is a highly influential statement of the fundamental rights protected by Community law. Furthermore, its binding effect may follow from its being expression of 'general principles of Community law' under Articles 6(2) and 46(d) of the EU Treaty.

The problem arises because administrative proceedings by the Commission and the OFT are criminal for the purposes of the European Human Rights Convention[11] and, it would appear, for the purposes of the interpretation of the Charter.[12] Protocol 7 to the European Human Rights Convention and the Article 50 of the European Charter provide for the right not to be tried twice for the same offence. This would appear to be a general principle of Community law. However, its extent and application in competition

Regulation' [2002] ICLQ 55–89 and R Wainwright 'What Have They to Do with Competition Law?' Paper presented at the Fourth Annual Conference on International and Comparative Competition Law—The Trans-Atlantic Antitrust Dialogue, organized by the British Institute of International and Comparative Law, London, 11–12 May 2004.

[8] Charter of Fundamental Rights of the European Union [2000] OJ C364/1 (the European Charter of Fundamental Rights).

[9] The Preamble of the European Charter of Fundamental Rights states: 'This Charter reaffirms [. . .] the rights as they result, in particular, from the constitutional traditions and international obligations common to the Member States [. . .].

[10] European Charter of Fundamental Rights, Art 15(1).

[11] The European Court of Human Rights adopted a substantive test for the definition of the autonomous meaning of 'criminal charge' under Art 6 of the Convention in *Engel v Netherlands* (1979/80) 1 EHRR 647. Administrative proceedings under Community law are criminal for the purposes of Art 6 of the European Human Rights Convention: Case C-235/92 P *Montecatini Spa v Commission of the European Communities* [1999] ECR I-4539, paras 175–6. The same applies to proceedings under the Competition Act 1998: *Napp Pharmaceutical Holdings Ltd v Director General of Fair Trading (Napp No 3)* [2001] Comp AR 33, [2002] ECC 3, paras 68–76; *Napp Pharmaceutical Holdings Ltd v Director General of Fair Trading (Napp No 4)* [2002] ECC 13, paras 98–103.

[12] European Charter of Fundamental Rights, Art 53(3): 'In so far as this Charter contains rights which correspond to rights guaranteed by the Convention for the Protection of Human Rights and Fundamental Freedoms, the meaning and scope of those rights shall be the same as those laid down by the said convention. This provision shall not prevent Union law providing more extensive protection'.

law proceedings is not entirely clear. Yet some guidance may be found the case-law of the Court of Justice.

The Court of Justice rejected a broad interpretation of the *ne bis in idem* principle in competition matters. It held in the *PVC (No 2)* case that the principle of *ne bis in idem* only prevents proceedings being brought twice against the same undertaking and in respect of the same anti-competitive conduct when the infringement or non-infringement of competition law has been established in an administrative decision or in a judgment not subject to (further) judicial review or appeal.[13] If the Community courts declare a decision of the Commission void on procedural grounds in a judgment not subject to (further) appeal, there is no final determination of the issue of infringement. Therefore, administrative proceedings can be reinstated by the Commission in respect of the same anti-competitive conduct. The Court went on to say:[14]

The application of that principle therefore presupposes that a ruling has been given on the question whether an offence has in fact been committed or that the legality of the assessment thereof has been reviewed. Thus, the principle of non bis in idem merely prohibits a fresh assessment in depth of the alleged commission of an offence which would result in the imposition of either a second penalty, in addition to the first, in the event that liability is established a second time, or a first penalty in the event that liability not established by the first decision is established by the second.

In Community law the relevant test for the application of the principle of *ne bis in idem* is whether the infringement or the non-infringement has been established in a decision not subject to (further) appeal or judicial review application.

III. LEGAL CERTAINTY AND LEGITIMATE EXPECTATIONS

The principles of legal certainty and legitimate expectations can at times prevent a public authority from acting in a manner which reneges on previous decisions. However, the application of these principles to enforcement proceedings beyond the application of the *ne bis in idem* rule is very limited. If an investigation does not terminate with a final infringement or non-infringement decision that bars further proceedings, there is no reason why launching further proceedings would offend against the principle of legal certainty or legitimate expectations of the parties. In *Klöckner-Werke AG v High Authority* the Court of Justice said:[15] '[. . .] The administrative

---

[13] Joined Cases C-238/99 P, C-244/99 P, C-245/99 P, C-247/99 P, C-250/99 P, C-251/99 P, C-252/99 P and C-254/99 P *Limburgse Vinyl Maatschappij NV (LVM) v Commission of the European Communities (PVC No 2)* [2002] ECR I-8375, para 59.

[14] ibid paras 61–2.

[15] Joined Cases 17/61 and 20/61 *Klöckner-Werke AG v High Authority of the European Coal and Steel Community* [1962] ECR 615.

authority is not always bound by its previous actions in its public activities by virtue of a rule which, in relations between the same parties, forbids them to venire contra factum proprium.'

There is, therefore, no general principle or rule that prohibits a Community institution from reneging on a previously adopted position unless further conditions are fulfilled. In the *Perfumes* cases the Court of Justice considered the legal effect of letters by Commission officials stating that in view of the small market share of the companies concerned and the competitive structure of the relevant market there was no need for the Commission to take action on the basis of the facts in its possession. As a result of this analysis, the file was closed.[16] The Court stated that the letters in question were pure case closure letters based upon the facts known to the Commission at the relevant time. They were not binding on national courts.[17] It followed that such case closure letters did not have legal effects and were not binding on the Commission. However, they gave rise to legitimate expectations for the undertakings concerned that their agreement is compatible with Article 81 EC. Therefore, unless there is a material change of circumstances or the case closure or comfort letter was adopted on the basis of incorrect or incomplete information, the Commission is prevented from reopening the investigation.[18] The same test applies, under the doctrine of legitimate expectations, to any final position adopted by the Commission in a procedure under Article 81 or 82 EC by way of which the procedure is discontinued or terminated on the grounds that the agreement or conduct is compatible with EC competition law. The doctrine of legitimate expectation, therefore, complements the principle of *ne bis in idem*. In certain cases, it can provide a more straightforward answer to the problems raised by the application of the double jeopardy rule.

IV. TAXONOMY OF DECISIONS BY THE COMMISSION AND NATIONAL COMPETITION AUTHORITIES

The following sections will attempt to show how the principle of *ne bis in idem* might apply to the types of decisions that may be made by competition authorities.

---

[16] Joined Cases 253/78 and 1-3/79 *Procureur de la Republique v Bruno Giry and Guerlain SA* [1980] ECR 2327; Case 31/80 *NV L'Oréal v PVBA 'De Nieuwe AMCK'* [1980] ECR 3775, 3805.

[17] ibid.

[18] AG Reischl in his Opinion in the *L'Oréal* case [1980] ECR 3775, 3805; PM Roth (ed) *C Bellamy and G Child: European Community Law of Competition* (5th edn Sweet & Maxwell London 2001) 874–5.

1. Decisions Prohibiting an Agreement or Conduct and/or Imposing a Fine

There is little doubt that decisions prohibiting an agreement or conduct with, or without, a fine preclude a further investigation and/or decision in respect of the same agreement or conduct by the same parties. Under Regulation 1/2003 and the Commission Notice on cooperation within the Network of Competition Authorities a problem arises as to the scope of the infringement decision. If the infringement decision is limited to the effects on competition within the territory of the competition authority dealing with the case, such a decision may not bar subsequent proceedings by another competition authority against the same parties and in respect of the same agreement or conduct but in relation to the effects on competition within the territory of another Member State. Whether or not this constitutes a breach of the principle of *ne bis in idem*, it undoubtedly creates an additional burden for the undertakings concerned that will have to face multiple proceedings in respect of the same infringement. However, if case allocation within the network works well and all material facts are known before the infringement decision is made, the rules on allocation and co-operation should ensure that the case is dealt with by taking into account the effects on competition in all the Member States affected.

2. Decisions Finding that there Has Been No Infringement

According to the *PVC (No 2)* case,[19] decisions finding that there has been no infringement preclude a further investigation and/or decision in respect of the same agreement or conduct by the same parties. The element of uncertainty here is that it is not entirely clear whether national competition authorities may find that an agreement or conduct does not infringe Article 81 or 82 EC. This power is explicitly conferred upon the Commission by Article 10 of Regulation 1/2003. However, Article 5 of the Regulation, which provides for the powers of national competition authorities to apply Articles 81 and 82 EC, simply states that national competition authorities may decide that 'there are no grounds for action on their part' where, on the basis of the evidence before them, the conditions for the prohibition are not met. In the absence of a developed administrative practice and further guidance from the Community and the national courts, it is difficult to say whether decisions under Article 5(2) of Regulation 1/2003 are decisions establishing that an infringement has not been committed, thus barring further proceedings under the *ne bis in idem* principle, or 'case closures' that may only give rise to legitimate expectations in the way described by the Court of Justice in the *Perfumes* cases.

---

[19] See (n 13).

3. Decisions Accepting Commitments or Informal Settlements

The Court of Justice gave some guidance on the issue of *ne bis in idem* with regard to settlements in *Criminal proceedings against Hüseyin Gözütok and Klaus Brügge*.[20] In that case, the Court gave a preliminary ruling on two references raising the same issue on the interpretation of the Convention Implementing the Schengen Agreement, which, in Chapter 3 of Title III, provides for the application of the *ne bis in idem* principle.

Criminal proceedings against Mr Gözütok in the Netherlands had been discontinued following an offer by the prosecution to drop charges if Mr Gözütok agreed to pay a sum of money determined by the prosecution. The German authorities brought a prosecution against Mr Gözütok for the same offence. Proceedings against Mr Brügge raised the same question. The Court held that where the prosecution is discontinued by decision of the prosecuting authority and on condition that the accused performs obligations determined by the prosecution, a second prosecution is barred. However, the Court clarified that a material fact in reaching this conclusion was that under national law further proceedings were definitively barred.[21] Therefore, the consequences of discontinuing proceedings under national law were material to the decision as to whether the discontinuance was a final disposal of the case. The Court also stated that what matters is not the procedure per se, eg whether the discontinuance of proceedings is embodied in a formal judicial decision, but the effect of discontinuing proceedings.

The judgment in the *Gözütok* case does not solve the question of the nature of informal settlements or decisions accepting commitments in competition law proceedings. It does, however, provide some guidance on this point in that it clarifies an important principle, namely that in the application of the double jeopardy rule under the Shengen Agreement the emphasis is on the effect of the settlement/decision under the relevant legal framework and not on the form of the settlement/decision. Under Regulation 1/2003, the competition authorities of the Member States must be able to accept commitments by decision but the consequences of such decisions are left to the procedural autonomy of the Member States. In the UK, section 31B(2) of the Competition Act 1998 provides that the OFT shall not continue an investigation or make an infringement decision if it has accepted commitments. However, the investigation may be reopened in case of material changes of the circumstances,[22] breach of commitments,[23] or submission of incomplete, false, or misleading information leading to the commitments

---

[20] Joined cases C-187/01 and C-385/01 *Criminal proceedings against Hüseyin Gözütok (C-187/01) and Klaus Brügge (C-385/01)* [2003] ECR I-1345.
[21] ibid para 30.
[22] Competition Act 1998, s 31B(3)(a).
[23] ibid s 31B(3)(b).

being accepted.[24] Article 9(2) of Regulation 1/2003 contains similar provisions allowing for the reopening of the case following a commitments decision by the Commission. The conditions for reopening the investigation under the Competition Act 1998 and Regulation 1/2003 probably satisfy the *ne bis in idem* test under Community law and, indirectly, Article 4 of Protocol 7 of the European Human Rights Convention. They are also in tune with the doctrine of legitimate expectations adopted by the Court of Justice in the *Perfumes* cases.

A problem arises as to whether commitments decisions bar proceedings being brought in respect of the same agreement or conduct by another competition authority under the Community law principle of *ne bis in idem*. The question is whether these decisions finally establish the infringement of the relevant prohibition. Article 9 of Regulation 1/2003 strongly suggests that decisions making commitments binding are not final decisions as to whether Article 81 or 82 EC has been infringed. Article 9(1) indicates that the Commission may accept commitments on the basis of 'concerns' following a 'preliminary assessment' of the case. Article 9(2) provides that the Commission may, upon request or on its own initiative, reopen the proceedings, albeit in limited circumstances. Section 31A(2) of the Competition Act 1998 also refers to 'competition concerns' rather than to an infringement of the relevant prohibition. The OFT may reopen the investigation under section 31B(3). Applying the test adopted by the Court of Justice in the *Gözütok* case, it would appear that decisions accepting commitments bar proceedings in another Member State. This is because, under the relevant legal framework, decisions accepting commitments bar the reopening of the investigation albeit not absolutely. The principle of *ne bis in idem*, therefore, demands that a second investigation be barred. However, a literal application of the *PVC (No 2)* case would appear to point in a different direction. Settlements and decisions accepting commitments do not rule on the issue of liability for infringement of competition law. They address 'competition concerns' by way of a negotiated solution. They do not contain a finding of infringement. Therefore, they may bar further proceedings by the same authority under the doctrine of legitimate expectations but do not call for the application of the double jeopardy principle. It may be argued that the apparent conflict between the two judgments should be resolved by giving precedence to the *Gözütok* case because *PVC (No 2)* was not concerned with commitments decisions but with an infringement decision tainted with a serious procedural irregularity. On the other hand, the *Gözütok* case can be distinguished on the grounds that it concerned criminal proceedings against individuals that are very different

---

[24] ibid s 31B(3)(c).

from administrative investigations against undertakings. In any event, neither *Gözütok* nor *PVC (No 2)* is exactly in point and it is possible that the question will have to be clarified by the national or Community courts.

4. Decisions Rejecting Complaints

Decisions rejecting complaints may amount to non-infringement decisions, ie decisions that establish that the relevant prohibition has not been infringed. Under the *ne bis in idem* principle, it would appear that such decisions preclude further proceedings into the same subject-matter unless the are material changes in the circumstances, in which case the agreement or conduct in question would not be the same. However, decisions dismissing complaints may not amount to decisions establishing that no infringement has occurred. For instance, where national competition authorities 'decide that there are no grounds for action on their part . . . where on the basis of the information in their possession the conditions for prohibition are not met' (under Article 5(2) of Regulation 1/2003), this decision may well be construed as not establishing, once and for all, that the relevant prohibition has not been infringed. The same problem may arise with regard to decisions under Article 7 of Commission Regulation 773/2004 relating to proceedings by the Commission pursuant to Articles 81 and 82 of the EC Treaty. Article 7 provides that the Commission may reject a complaint when it considers that on the basis of the information in its possession there are insufficient grounds for acting on the complaint.[25] This appears to suggest that the decision adopted on these grounds is not a final decision establishing that there is no liability for infringements of Community competition law. Paragraph 79 of the Commission Notice on the handling on complaints by the Commission under Articles 81 and 82 of the EC Treaty clearly states that a decision rejecting a complaint does not rule on the question whether or not there is an infringement of Articles 81 and 82 EC even if the Commission has assessed the facts.[26] These are strong arguments to say that such decisions do not have the effect of barring further proceedings under the relevant legal framework and, therefore, the application of the principles in *Gözütok* would suggest that the principle of *ne bis in idem* does not apply. Furthermore, the decisions in question do not establish that the relevant competition law prohibition has not been infringed and, therefore, according to the *PVC (N0 2)* case, they do not preclude the adoption of an infringement decision relating to the same agreement or conduct under the doctrine of double jeopardy.

[25] Commission Regulation No 773/04 relating to proceedings by the Commission pursuant to Arts 81 and 82 of the EC Treaty [2004] OJ L123/18, Art 7.
[26] Commission Notice on the handling on complaints by the Commission under Arts 81 and 82 of the EC Treaty [2004] OJ C101/65, para 79.

In conclusion, as regards decisions rejecting complaints, a distinction must be made between decisions establishing that there has been no infringement and decisions under Article 5(2) of Regulation 1/2003 and Article 7 of Commission Regulation 773/2004. Decisions establishing that there has been no infringement preclude a subsequent finding of infringement against the same parties and in respect of the same agreement or conduct. Decisions by national competition authorities under Article 5(2) of Regulation 1/2003 and decisions by the Commission under Article 7 of Commission Regulation 773/2004 are decisions that there are no, or insufficient, grounds for action on the basis of the evidence before the investigating authority. They do not preclude a subsequent infringement decision under the doctrine of *ne bis in idem* although they may give rise to legitimate expectations of the undertaking concerned.

5. Decisions Based on Lack of Evidence

An acute problem arises with regard to decisions that are based on lack of evidence of infringement after a full investigation has been conducted with the involvement of the parties concerned. In criminal proceedings lack of evidence leads to an acquittal, ie a decision establishing that there is no liability. In civil proceedings the same fundamental principle applies: a party failing to prove his case fails on the merits. If the claimant fails to establish any element of the cause of action the court will give judgment for the defendant. This judgment is a final decision on the merits that bars further proceedings under the doctrine of *res judicata*. However, the same principles may not apply to administrative authorities. It is true that administrative proceedings in competition law matters are criminal in nature for the purposes of the application of certain international or trans-national standards of justice such as the principle of *ne bis in idem*. However, because of their structure, function, and effects, the administrative proceedings in question are very different from criminal and civil proceedings. The uncertainty may be resolved by going back to first principle. The very essence of the double jeopardy rule is to prevent more than one prosecution of the same person when liability has not been established in a first set of proceedings. There may be circumstances in which a second prosecution may be brought, but they are generally very narrowly defined and applied. It would therefore appear that where a full investigation has been conducted with the involvement of the parties concerned and no proof of infringement has been established to the requisite standard, further proceedings are barred under the *ne bis in idem* principles unless exceptional circumstances apply.[27] The

---

[27] See, for instance, the circumstances in which a second prosecution is allowed under Art 4(2) of the European Human Rights Convention, Protocol No 7.

definition of 'exceptional circumstances' will be a matter for the national and Community courts to clarify but one can imagine, for instance, cases in which the undertakings under investigation have deliberately misled the competition authority and material changes of circumstances.

6. Other Case Closure Decisions

There are some decisions that are clearly not infringement or non-infringement decisions. Decisions by the Commission dismissing the complaint on grounds of inadmissibility or lack of legitimate interest of the complainant fall within this category.

In the UK, it would appear that a decision by the OFT that there are no reasonable grounds for suspecting that an infringement of the relevant prohibitions has occurred is not a decision establishing that there is no liability with respect to the alleged infringement if the Office has only conducted a prima facie assessment of the complaint on the basis of the evidence available to it.

After the OFT has established that there are reasonable grounds for suspecting that the relevant prohibition has been infringed and has exercised formal powers of investigation, it may still bring the investigation to an end without any finding of infringement or non-infringement. Such case closures are also unlikely to prevent further investigations under the principle of *ne bis in idem*. They are akin to case closures by way of informal letter by the Commission of the type analysed by the Court of Justice in the *Perfumes* case.[28] However, if they are notified to the undertakings under investigation, they may give rise to legitimate expectations. As a consequence, the case could only be reopened, or new proceedings commenced, if the circumstances materially change or the case closure was based on incorrect or incomplete evidence. If the case closure is not notified to the undertakings under investigation, it is highly unlikely that any form of legitimate expectation may arise.

If the OFT brings the investigation to an end after a full investigation with the involvement of the undertakings concerned because it is not possible to establish proof of the infringement to the requisite standard, further proceedings against the same parties and relating to the same infringement are barred under the principle of *ne bis in idem* unless there are 'exceptional circumstances'.[29]

[28] *Giry and Guerlain* case; *L'Oréal* case.
[29] See the analysis of the decisions based on lack of evidence in the previous section.

V. *NE BIS IN IDEM* IN RESPECT OF MULTIPLE FINING DECISIONS

The same agreement or conduct may give rise to liability to administrative or criminal fines under different legal systems. Community law and national law may both apply to the same anti-competitive agreement or conduct. Legal systems of States outside the Community may also impose sanctions for the same agreement or conduct that may be subject to an infringement decision for breach of Community competition law. The principle of double jeopardy comes into play when the same undertaking is subject to fines for the same or substantially the same facts albeit under different legal provisions in different legal systems.

The Court of Justice has taken a pragmatic approach to the problem of multiple fining decisions under different legal systems. It held in *Walt Wilhelm v Bundeskartellamt* that parallel proceedings under Community and national competition laws are permissible insofar any later fining decision takes into account any fines already imposed on the same person in previous decisions.[30]

In *Boehringer Mannheim GmbH v Commission*, the Court of Justice considered whether the fines imposed by the Commission should take into account any penalties imposed by State authorities outside the European Community. The Court held, on the facts, that the agreements that were the subject matter of the criminal prosecution in the US were different in 'their object and their geographical emphasis' to the cartel investigated by the Commission.[31] As a consequence, no issue of *ne bis in idem* arose.[32]

In the UK, section 38(9) of the Competition Act 1998 provides that in setting the amount of a penalty under Part I of the Act, the Office of Fair Trading, the Competition Appeal Tribunal, and any court to which an appeal lies as to the amount of the penalty, must take into account any penalty or fine imposed by the Commission, or by a court or other body in another Member State in respect of the same agreement or conduct. Therefore, penalties and fines imposed by authorities and courts of third States, ie states that are not Members of the EU, are not taken into account.[33]

---

[30] Case 14/68 *Walt Wilhelm v Bundeskartellamt* [1969] ECR 1, para 11. This rule against double jeopardy in fining decisions follows from a principle of 'natural justice' (ibid).

[31] Case 7/72 *Boehringer Mannheim GmbH v Commission of the European Communities* [1972] ECR 1281, para 4.

[32] ibid paras 5–8.

[33] On this point see the Director General of Fair Trading's guidance as to the Appropriate Amount of a Penalty (OFT423, Mar 2000) para 2.15 and the Draft OFT's Guidance as to the Appropriate Amount of a Penalty (OFT423, Apr 2004) paras 1.15 (as regards penalties imposed by the OFT under national and EC competition law) and 2.18 (as regards penalties imposed by the OFT and by bodies and courts of other Member States or the Commission).

VI. CONCLUSION

The analysis of the application of the principle of *ne bis in idem* to the categories of decisions that may be adopted by the Commission and the national competition authorities shows the difficulties of transposing a concept embedded in the national criminal laws of the Member States into a trans-national context. This type of difficulty is not new in Community law but is more acute in the case of the principle of *ne bis in idem* because of the technical, non self-standing, and context-specific nature of the principle. A comparison can be made with the transposition of the principle of proportionality into Community law.[34] The principle of proportionality is, by its very nature, a flexible standard of judicial review. In its general formulation, it can be applied to any given set of facts through established forms of judicial reasoning without resort to a further set of technical concepts and legal rules necessary for the principle of proportionality to be given full meaning and effect in any given case. It is, therefore, possible to say that the principle of proportionality is self-standing and non context-specific.[35] The contrary is true of the principle of *ne bis in idem*. The principle of *ne bis in idem* is not self-standing. In order for the principle to be given full meaning and effect in any given case, it is necessary to resort to a set of technical concepts and legal rules that necessarily complement the principle, including the definition of acquittal and conviction and the definition of what constitutes the same, or similar, offence. These concepts are context-specific in that they depend on the procedural framework within which they apply. The classical definitions of the national criminal laws of the Member States cannot be easily transposed into the context of concurrent administrative proceedings under Regulation 1/2003. The development of a consistent body of case-law providing the undertakings exposed to multiple infringement proceedings with the desired degree of legal certainty may take some time especially in the light of the fact that the final word on

---

[34] Joined cases 279/84, 280/84, 285/84, and 286/84 *Walter Rau Lebensmittelwerke v Commission of the European Communities* [1987] ECR 1069; Case 138/78 *Hans-Markus Stölting v Hauptzollamt Hamburg-Jonas* [1979] ECR 713; Case 122/78 *SA Buitoni v Fonds d'orientation et de régularisation des marchés agricoles* [1979] ECR 677; Case 66/82 *Fromançais SA v Fonds d'orientation et de régularisation des marchés agricoles (FORMA)* [1983] ECR 395; Case 181/84 *R v Intervention Board for Agricultural Produce (IBAP), ex p E D & F Man (Sugar) Ltd* [1985] ECR 2889; Case 21/85 *A Maas & Co NV v Bundesanstalt für landwirtschaftliche marktordnung* [1986] ECR 3537. See T Tridimas *The General Principles of EC Law* (OUP Oxford 1999) 124–62.

[35] Any legal rule or principle is context-specific and non self-standing in that it is construed and applied within a specific legal system and can only operate in conjunction with other principles and rules within the same system. However, in the 'legal transplant' of concepts and rules from one system to the other, it is possible to say that some concepts and rules can be more easily applied to the relevant facts without the 'medium' of other legal concepts and rules. Thus, the principle of proportionality can be applied to any given set of facts without the necessary filter of a set of further system-specific concepts and rules.

any of the problems highlighted in this papers lies necessarily with the Court of Justice. However, the analysis carried out in the paper with respect to the main categories of administrative decisions that may be adopted by the Commission and the EU national competition authorities demonstrates that a structured approach to the application of the double jeopardy principle is possible under the current law. Overall, the system does not fail to meet the standards of legal certainty that are required for an efficient and fair application of EC competition law under Regulation 1/2003.

CHAPTER 16

Cartels and Leniency

A. Bill Kolasky*

Good afternoon. At these types of conferences we always hear a great deal, especially from the enforcement officials, about what an effective enforcement tool leniency programmes are and how important it is therefore that your company has a strong compliance programme and that you be the first one in the door to obtain leniency. Today's panel is going to focus on the far more difficult question of what you do when one of your co-conspirators beats you to the punch and gets into the agency first. In order to deal with that very practical and very serious issue, we've created a little bit of a hypothetical to provide a case study and I am going to run through that very quickly before I introduce our very distinguished panellists.

This is the airborne freight cartel. The airborne freight industry is a highly concentrated industry with three major international carriers, two of which are European companies. CDL is headquartered in France, ScotsAir is located in the UK, and American Eagle is located in North America, and I've identified the CEOs of these companies; Jacques Cartel in the case of CDL, Sir Jeremy Bright, perhaps not so bright, and finally GB Hangar, I'll let you figure out the initials. In addition there are five regional carriers, two in Europe, Air Italy and Norse Air, and three in Asia. This is an industry in which demand has grown dramatically over the last 15 or 20 years and capacity has always been very tight in the industry so that prices have consistently increased. The double whammy of the dot.com bust in early 2001 and the World Trade Centre attack on 11 September had disastrous consequences for the airborne freight industry. Within a couple of months, traffic dropped off by nearly 25 per cent. All of the carriers cut rates aggressively in order to hold on to their market shares and major customers demanded even larger discounts. By the fourth quarter of 2001, all three major carriers were experiencing substantial losses.

While he was in Europe on business, the CEO of American Eagle, GB Hangar, invited the CEOs of ScotsAir and CDL to dinner at a Michelin two star restaurant in Paris; this was after all a recession. At dinner, Hangar was

---

* Wilmer Cutler & Pickering LLP.

very aggressive in arguing that business was certain to improve and now was the time to begin raising prices. He told the others that he planned to announce a five per cent rate increase the next day to become effective as of 1 February and that he hoped the others would follow. After several bottles of wine he declared loudly that their large corporate customers lied like troopers to get discounts they didn't deserve and he suggested that the three companies should call each other whenever a customer demanded a discount to check to make sure the others were offering such a discount. Cartel and Bright for the most part listened politely, expressed their general agreement that business should begin turning up and that this would provide a better climate for price increases but were otherwise non-committal. However, when they returned to their hotels that evening they sent emails to their vice-presidents for sales, reporting on the conversations and instructing them to 'follow up'. Following the dinner, American Eagle announced a five per cent price increase. Within days ScotsAir and CDL announced similar price increases. These were followed by similar increases in April and June. The April increases were led by ScotsAir, the June increases by CDL. Prior to each increase, the three executives talked to one another. Major customers who tried to negotiate discounts off the new rates generally found that they were unable to do so. What they didn't know was that whenever they asked for a discount, the sales VP of one carrier would check with the other carrier before authorizing a discount. Prices continued to firm up throughout 2002 and 2003, ultimately rising above pre-11 September levels. After the Paris meeting and the first round of price increases, CDL's vice-president of sales, Frederic Bourgeois contacted ScotsAir and two smaller regional carriers in Europe to propose a similar arrangement for regional airfreight service between the UK, France, and Spain. ScotsAir, CDL and the two regional carriers in Europe thereafter coordinated on a series of rate increases for this traffic.

On 7 May 2004, just last week, the Financial Times reported that the US SEC was about to indict Hangar for insider trading based on his purchases of additional shares of American Eagle stock in late January 2002, shortly after the Paris dinner. The same day CDL and ScotsAir received Grand Jury subpoenas in the United States and dawn raids in Europe. On Monday 10 May, earlier this week, the Financial Times reported that American Eagle had received a conditional grant of amnesty from both jurisdictions.

To deal with this situation we have a very distinguished panel. First let me introduce Oystein Meland, who is an attorney from the Wikborg, Rein & Co firm in Norway and an experienced corporate lawyer who has served as general counsel to several Norwegian companies. He will play the role of ScotsAir's general counsel. Next to Oystein are his lawyers. Gary Spratling, from Gibson Dunn & Crutcher in the United States probably needs no introduction. He was a former head of criminal enforcement at the antitrust division in Washington and is now one of the leading cartel lawyers in the United States, if not the world. Next to him we have Diana Good, who is a senior partner at Linklaters here and is one of the leading cartel lawyers in the UK and the EU. Next to Diana we have Margaret Bloom, who served for many years as the deputy director of OFT with responsibilities for cartel enforcement and is now teaching at King's College London and consultant with Freshfields.

We then have the enforcers, beginning first with Stephen Blake, one of the senior cartel enforcers at the European Commission in Brussels; Denyse Mackenzie, head of cartel enforcement for the Canadian Competition Bureau; Jim Griffin, head of cartel enforcement for the Department of Justice in Washington DC; and finally Simon Williams of your own OFT, who heads up cartel enforcement there. Now you may ask why we have eight speakers. The answer is simple. Multinational cartels are very wide-ranging and this is only a small insight into the number of people who would actually be involved in investigating and defending this type of cartel. Because we have so many speakers we've adopted an interactive approach and I've asked each of the speakers to hold themselves to three minutes, and because we have multiple questions for each speaker the discipline is that any speaker who exceeds their quota loses their next question! So with that, let me start off with Jim. Before serving those grand jury subpoenas on these three companies, what preliminary investigation would you have done in order to authorize those subpoenas?

B. Jim Griffin*

The first thing you have to notice is that the first Financial Times article appears on Friday and it was at that point that Grand Jury subpoenas were served on CDL and ScotsAir, and it was the very next Monday that American Eagle announced its acceptance into our conditional amnesty programme. I'm available to give out markers over the weekend, no question about it for people who want leniency or amnesty, but it is highly unlikely that American Eagle came in Friday night and that we did all the prep work and got everything in order for them to get a conditional amnesty letter by Monday, so the assumption here is that I have had a good deal of time to work with American Eagle. Obviously we will have collected all of their important documents including the price notices, any emails back and forth regarding the prices, all internal documents regarding the

* USA OJ

price increases, faxes, emails, I've mentioned travel documents putting Hangar in Paris on the appropriate date, all telephone records that will give some corroboration to the telephone calls that surrounded the price increases and also the policing calls between the Vice President. From our perspective, much more importantly, I'll have had the chance to talk to those Vice Presidents at American Eagle to get their story and maybe Hangar. I say maybe Hangar, because Hangar has a problem that he's going to have to resolve. He's about to be indicted for securities law violations. We can't give him amnesty for that so he's going to have to make a decision. Does he come in with the company, get amnesty for the antitrust crimes that he's committed and cooperate with us? If he does he will get that but he remains exposed for the securities violations.

Next step will be to consensually monitor some conversations. If Hangar is in we will have him make a call or have a meeting with Sir Jeremy Bright and Mr Cartel and we will record those conversations. In addition we will have border watches up to be sure. Going back to the consensual monitoring, we will certainly have, even if Hangar is not in, conversations between the appropriate American Eagle Vice Presidents and their counter parts at the other two companies and we will record those. We will have border watches up so that if Sir Jeremy or Mr Cartel come into the United States and the time is appropriate for us to otherwise go overt, we will confront them at the border, question them and give them Grand Jury subpoenas. We will also be coordinating with Stephen. This is a situation where we will, like our amnesty policy provides, hold confidential the identity and all information provided by an amnesty applicant. We often get waivers from companies to discuss with other enforcement authorities where they have a conditional amnesty agreement and waivers of that confidentiality, restriction, and we will be coordinating with Stephen. It is possible that he has asked me to hold off going overt with our investigation until he has had time to make arrangements with the various national authorities for the dawn raid. It's more likely that I've asked him to hold off on his dawn raids while we do some consensual monitoring and set up some telephone calls.

Finally, for the life of me I cannot understand why American Eagle's lawyer didn't go to Canada, but he didn't and is absent from this meeting because he is meeting with his client trying to explain his way out of that decision; but if he had gone to Canada I would have talked to Denyse and we would have perhaps made arrangements if appropriate or opportune not to consensually monitor conversations, but to wire tap, which can be done in Canada.

[BILL KOLASKY]

Simon now; obviously you would be involved in the dawn raid here in the

UK, but now that the UK has criminalized cartel behaviour would you also open a separate criminal investigation of Sir Jeremy and his subordinates?

C. Simon Williams

The short answer is we might do. I won't stick precisely to the detailed facts and instead I'll talk a little bit more generally about some of the issues that would be on our minds in terms of deciding whether or not to open a criminal investigation. The first would be that the offence provision only came into being from June 2003, so where we are dealing with allegations of behaviour, a significant or substantial proportion of which was prior to June 2003, we might take the view that that wasn't the best sort of scenario in which to use the Enterprise Act to do a criminal investigation. Obviously having said that, if we executed a warrant under the Enterprise Act I would have thought it should be possible to uplift material on any raids that predated June 2003 if we can actually demonstrate that it was clearly relevant to the offence post June 2003.

The second issue would be how did we get the information about the cartel? If we got it as result of leniency, someone would have presumably come to the UK to make a leniency application simultaneously with the US and any of the other relevant jurisdictions. If we get the information from leniency, then it should be possible for us to use that information as a basis for seeking warrants from the High Court for criminal investigation and for doing criminal raids, but of course in relation to the people who actually sought leniency, under our programme if you come in for leniency before there is any pre-existing investigation as a company then your directors and employees who are relevant in the matter can also get what we call a no action letter, meaning that they won't be prosecuted for the criminal offence either. So for those that came in first, where there was no pre-existing investigation, they are not going to be subject to any kind of prosecution, they don't have to worry about criminal investigation as such although the information they have provided will one day be used potentially in evidence if there was such an investigation and they may have to give evidence for us.

But there is another issue. If you give a central player to a cartel immunity from prosecution through a no action letter then you must consider very carefully the ability in English law to be able to successfully prosecute the other individuals involved in the cartel, and it may well be that the Serious

* OFT

Fraud Office, who will probably be responsible for prosecuting this type of case, might take the view that it creates too many complications, especially when we take into account all the other considerations. So that's another thing that we would have to look at. The final issue of course is whether there is sufficient evidence of dishonesty here on the facts to constitute a good case to go forward under the Enterprise Act. So there are a number of factors that would feed in here and I suppose my conclusion at the end of the day is where I started with. We *may* conduct a criminal investigation but we may decide in fact that this case is best done under other legislation.

[BILL KOLASKY]

Thank you. Denyse, as Jim noted, they apparently have not gone into Canada. Now how important is it in terms of Canada's ability to conduct an investigation here whether the carriers have facilities in Canada or merely serve customers there?

D. Denyse Mackenzie*

Well, on the facts it's not that important. We have a policy and we will prosecute cartels that occur effectively where the agreement is made outside of Canada and the activities take place outside Canada, but there are effects in Canada. On the facts of this case of course you have three companies with facilities in Canada, who are doing business in Canada, which is helpful not least because Canada has a provision that would allow us to track the implementation of the cartel activity through the business in Canada and they would be liable for implementing the directives of the cartel. That's section 46. It's a rather unusual provision and there is basically no requirement that the person implementing knew what they were doing in terms of implementing the cartel. The other thing of course, getting down to the basis of enforcement, is that it would make our lives much more difficult particularly given that we don't, at this stage given the facts, have an immunity applicant and that Steve and Jim didn't bother to tell them to come to Canada. But leaving that aside, the challenge is really to the collection of evidence, and there could be some service challenges later on. In terms of our formal powers once an enquiry is underway; we will be able to seek disclosure of documents and oral testimony and we will be able to seek a disclosure of documents in possession of the affiliate, if in fact they qualify as affiliates, and that is the businesses that are carrying on business in Canada, we can seek or require them to produce documents belonging to

* Canadian Competition Bureau

their head office in other countries. That's also a very useful secure or evidence ability that we have.

I guess the only other thing that I would mention is that once we did have sufficient evidence of course we would be trying to search at this stage, given that the cat's out of the bag. It would be doubtful that we would find too much although we do have the ability to do electronic searches and I was interested in the debate earlier on about e-searches. The way our legislation is framed, we can secure any emails or traffic that is on the server wherever it is located, so basically if you can get it through that server we can get it and that is a very useful tool, so we would be able to get the email traffic exchanged. Short answer or long answer is it would make our lives difficult. It would probably be a longer investigation since, given that Jim is not going to give me anything on the confidential information he has received nor is Steve, we would have to get information the hard way and start interviewing clients, customers etc, or wait for a long time until I can get the information through an MLAT (Mutual Legal Assistance Treaty) or other bilateral process from Steve and Jim.

[BILL KOLASKY]

Oystein, after listening to Jim, Simon, and Denyse, I can tell that this is not your best Friday ever. What do you do when the EU and the UK competition officials show up to conduct the dawn raid and after?

E. Oystein Meland

The first thing I would do is cancel my golf weekend. Secondly, I would cooperate by the book with the investigators from the EU during the dawn raid to ensure that all documents seized were properly locked as per the book and that we, the company, received copies of all seized documents in the same order. And of course I would not allow any interviews from any individuals in the company and all questions they may ask should preferably be directed by me or any assistants I may have and be of a factual nature for clarification of the documents they wanted to have, and I would immediately pick up the phone and hire help from our outside lawyers to be present and assist the investigators and oversee that no documents are seized which they are not entitled to seize, such as privileged documents, and I would ensure or at least try to ensure that they stayed away from my computer.

Thirdly, I would immediately engage external qualified legal assistance both in the US and in the EU, probably because of the different procedural rules, and finally I would get on to start an internal investigation assisted by independent lawyers forthwith to find out what has been going on in ScotsAir. Of course I didn't know anything about this! Now this goes both with respect to the worldwide services and to regional business, and I would try to locate my CEO who is probably out there playing golf to recommend that I, who ordinarily would report to the board of directors directly, should establish a special task force, which I would suggest that I should head, completely independent of the CEO, and report to the board directly for purposes of handling the internal investigation. I would also, remembering this is a Friday in May, nevertheless try to convene a board meeting immediately. I would outline for the board the facts as we knew them at that stage and also the relevant rules both in EU on fines and leniency for cooperation, and I assume for this purpose the OFT is not involved.

I would also outline the leniency guidelines to prepare the board as soon as possible to make a decision, even though we know that Eagle Air is there already, on whether we should make contact with DoJ and EU to offer our full cooperation in order to try to secure at least being second in the door, and the reason for this advice to the board is simple. If the company, as the board at that particular Friday would like to think, is innocent, they've nothing to lose by cooperating anyway. On the other hand if the company, as seems by the facts outlined here, is guilty of an offence both in the US and in the EU, the company has everything to gain by cooperating in full and thereby receive the best treatment and reduction in fines even though they were second. The problem is really then how shall we approach them? Whether we will be able to, particularly in the EU, but also in the US, give anything of value to the authorities? That really depends on what we find. I will assume at that stage, because we know that Eagle Air has been granted conditional immunity, that sufficient facts outlining this case have already been delivered to, scrutinized by, and digested enough, by the relevant authorities before the dawn raid and the subpoenas action did take place, and I would also assume that they have had sufficient time to prepare this since it was a coordinated action across the Atlantic. And furthermore I must assume that if we do not act fast, there is a presumption that CDL will and in other words we will be third in the door and have an even less possibility of getting the level of treatment and reduction we otherwise could. Thank you.

[BILL KOLASKY]

Gary, I know you were at an Eric Clapton concert last night and so you couldn't have been happy when your cell phone rang at 5 am Friday morning in San Francisco, but Oystein's on the line, who's been a long time client of your firm. What advice do you give Oystein as to how to handle the US side of this investigation?

F. Gary Spratling

Much of the advice I would give Oystein has already been articulated by him in terms of the steps that would be taken by the company. We know at the time that the dawn raids and search warrants are executed that there is coordination between jurisdictions which oftentimes leads you to suspect that there is an amnesty applicant. We don't know that yet. We don't know that until yesterday when the news comes out in the *Financial Times*, but on Friday we had talked about the necessity of having an emergency board meeting and getting people together. And when I'm talking with Oystein today, Tuesday afternoon, I'm concerned because we are not having this conversation in getting ready to meet with the board yesterday. Yesterday was the day that the news came out that there was an amnesty applicant. CDL now knows the same thing that we do, that is that there is an amnesty applicant. We have got to be prepared to move as quickly as possible. Why do we care that it is Tuesday instead of Monday, because to those of us who do this all of the time, we've lost a day and the Department of Justice frequently tells you, in their speeches and in their papers, about how often the difference between the person giving amnesty and the person coming in number two is less than a day. But what isn't always mentioned, and is equally true, is that there is often less than a day between the person that comes in second and the person that comes in third, especially when there is an announcement of amnesty. And the difference here between the firm that comes in second and the firm that comes in third, as I'll mention in a moment, is enormous. It is night and day. It is everything. It is the ballgame and so we've got to be moving as quickly as possible. We're going to discuss that a little bit.

I'm going to make sure that Oystein has sent out the document preservation notice that we talked about on Friday and that we discussed the draft, because no matter how deep a pile of trouble that this company's executives are in right now, we're going to make sure that it doesn't get any worse by somebody sending out a misguided email that talks about document preservation, but which can be interpreted as a document destruction memo, as we've seen in a couple of recent prosecutions. That is something we could spend five or 10 minutes on. It is an absolutely critical step which can't be missed, no matter what the pressure is to do everything else with respect to the prosecutors. In terms of advice at this point it is pretty easy. One firm of a three-firm cartel has got amnesty in cooperating. Oystein and I do not

need Jim to tell us that they'd been working with the amnesty applicant for
a long time. That is the nature of the game with amnesty and the fact that
the investigations are coordinated, the raids are coordinated, also tells us
that they've been working even a longer time and we can make all the
assumptions, not even hearing what Jim said, with respect to the documents
that they have, the individuals that they talk to, the likely consensual monitors they've engaged in; we know that that evidence is out there and we
know that they've also got a pile of evidence when they came with their
search warrants on us and our competitor, normally a competitor, the other
firm in the cartel, and collected all that information. And there is something
that Jim didn't mention, that the FBI probably pulled these drop-in interviews at the same time as the execution of the search warrants where they
get so much information, and so I would tell Oystein at this point, and he
already knows this because of his experience, that this is the closest thing
to a lay-down case that the DoJ gets.

In my paper I talk about the way you try to figure out. The factors to
consider in whether or not to go in and cooperate, whether it is cooperation after amnesty or before amnesty, and one of the things I talk about, it's
a mouthful but it's really what you do, is called simultaneous relational
analysis of the risk and opportunities that cross jurisdictions. It's a very
complicated process. You have to be schooled in how to do it, but here,
forget that. Throw that away. There is no analysis. Get in and talk to the
Department of Justice. Why? Because an admission by and corroboration
from the number two firm in a three firm cartel is very valuable to the
Department of Justice and will probably get you some substantial assistance
cooperation, but you are valuable only if you are number two. The number
three firm in this cartel that ends up going into the Department of Justice is
going to get hammered, absolutely hammered, so you can't be number
three. So that's our goal and I assume during this discussion that my partner has already talked to Sir Jeremy Bright, enough to find out just the
outlines of what was done, worse that we've got some basis to go in and get
amnesty, and also to explain to him that we now have a conflict of interest
with him and he is better represented by separate counsel which the
company will be happy to recommend and an attorney that we can cooperate with in that matter.

[BILL KOLASKY]

Diana, what about over here in the EU, and in particular what would you
advise ScotsAir with respect to the regional short haul cartel once you learn
about it?

G. Diana Good

OK, well I am very fortunate that I have got a very sophisticated client who's obviously handled the dawn raid pretty well and he's already had some very good US advice, but the situation in the EU does complicate things. I agree with all the advice that has already been given. I agree entirely that we need to get in and be number two in relation to the international cartel as soon as we can, I'll come back to how soon that can be in the EU, but we have the regional cartel which hasn't yet crossed, as we understand it, the doorstep of the relevant authorities and therefore we do have an opportunity in relation to the regional cartel to get in and be number one and get 100 per cent immunity. In the face of the OFT saying that they may pursue criminal charges against individuals, and Sir Jeremy Bright is obviously a particular target although there may be others within a company as well, both the criminal liability for the individuals and the potential for director disqualification orders for up to 15 years are things that are worth ensuring that we, as a company, together with the individuals, if at all possible, apply together to get in as number one in relation to the regional cartel. My strong advice is that the company has to apply for leniency in all relevant jurisdictions and do that simultaneously because it's not entirely clear at this stage which NCA is the one best placed for this case to be allocated to. We have the additional problem that there are some jurisdictions here where leniency doesn't apply, by way of example Spain, but I have to say that although applying for leniency to any and all of the authorities is not going to be a complete magic wand, certainly not vis-à-vis Spain, it's still definitely worth getting in as quickly as possible.

In terms of time and certainty, the EU and the OFT don't, I am afraid, offer exactly the same kind of certainty or speed in terms of the advice that I can give Oystein, because so far as both the EU and the OFT are concerned, we can't go in and make marker applications over the course of the weekend and get hold of Jim during that time. We actually have to turn up with real evidence and we have to turn up with hard documentary evidence, and so far as the international cartel is concerned we don't know what information they already have. We have to come up with information for the EU which is sufficient and in terms of the OFT we have to come up with all information available in relation to the existence and nature of the cartel and the same applies for the individuals. So we have a particular problem that we do need to move fast but we have to investigate and this could take us some serious time. We will do it as quickly as possible. In the meantime we have to give extreme care to questions of privilege. We've already heard earlier on today about the problems with privilege. Privilege is also seriously under attack by our own Court of Appeal here in both the *Three Rivers* case and the recent tobacco litigation case, which actually means that in the context of assisting with this investigation there is no assurance that any communications between us are privileged, so real care has to be given to that.

We can go and make paperless applications when we are ready for leniency, but we have to work out what we are generating in the meantime before we are in a position to do that. We have the additional problem that there is a real tension with the individuals. We need to be able to get the cooperation of Sir Jeremy Bright and other individuals. We want to be able to persuade them that the sensible things is to cooperate and apply together for leniency, but Sir Jeremy Bright may want, and is certainly entitled to, separate representation and it's one of the things that we will have to get into place immediately. He has a very different kind of tension here to the company and it's quite possible that Oystein might not get the instructions he wants to terminate activities in the cartel. My advice to Oystein is going to be you have to apply, you have to take steps to terminate, we have two to investigate and if the board aren't going to accept your advice you may have no alternative but to resign or you may be subject to a disqualification.

[BILL KOLASKY]

Thank you very much Diana. Oystein, are you happy with the advice you have received so far?

[OYSTEIN MELAND]

Yes, but as a client am I allowed to ask a question?

[BILL KOLASKY]

Absolutely.

[OYSTEIN MELAND]

The problem with the EU is that we must give the Commission specific valuable evidence. But how do we then give the evidence? To what extent would you advise me that we can in fact give the evidence by way of oral proffer? And how can we try to assure ourselves that in fact we will be giving them something we think is of added value? We don't know because we don't know exactly what they have already. So how do we get around that and how do we sort that in practice before we sit down with the EU?

[DIANA GOOD]

We are going to need to have trawled the documentary evidence, the emails, we are going to have to have talked to the relevant senior people and we are going to have to then, when we are ready to do that, approach the relevant authorities and the truth of the matter is, experience, and Gary, I am sure you will agree, experience indicates that it is quite a long road to reach a point with the relevant authorities at which you can be satisfied that they are going to be sufficiently satisfied, hopefully, to grant leniency at the end of the day, because that's the other problem, we don't have certainty until the end of the day. All I can say is we are going to have to do as thorough an investigation in as short a period of time as possible and then present that in good faith, and then we are going to have to have some serious discussions with the Commission. We will do all of that on an oral basis, provide an oral statement, but a transcript will be made and there are issues as to whether that transcript is discoverable in subsequent litigation. I'll defend you hard against that.

[BILL KOLASKY]

Stephen, let's assume that after Diana does enough investigation to understand the facts, ScotsAir comes in and applies for a leniency and in the course of doing so, tells you about the regional short haul cartel that it helped to put together. Is that going to help it or is that going to hurt it?

H. Stephen Blake*

It depends; it shouldn't hurt it at all. How you analyse this depends on how you treat this short haul cartel. There are two ways of looking at it. One would be to say that it is a separate infringement, quite independent although linked to the main infringement, in which case immunity could be available still for that infringement. The second would be to say it is not an infringement, it's part of the infringement that is already being investigated, it is a sub-arrangement and in that case, if the Commission does not already know about this regional arrangement, then effectively what will happen is that ScotsAir will get immunity for that aspect of the cartel. The way that that works is that ScotsAir would need to come in, they would need to provide us with evidence of significant added value and of course included in that evidence would be the evidence of this separate arrangement or this related arrangement. If we didn't already know about that arrangement, we would not take that into account when we set the fine.

* European Commission

So in calculating the fine we would have to set a portion of the amount of the fine for the global cartel and for the regional cartel. As far as the global part of the cartel is concerned then ScotsAir could qualify for a maximum 50 per cent reduction if it's the first in after the immunity applicant, and whether it got 50 per cent or 30 per cent would depend on a number of factors, including the degree of its cooperation during the continuation of the investigation and the quality of the evidence that it provides and how quickly it comes in, which is another reason why they would want to come in quickly. But as regards the regional aspect of the cartel it would not be fined for that aspect. So in terms of weighing up the risks, should it tell the Commission about the regional aspect of the cartel or should it not, or rather, should it come in at all, and if it's going to come in would it risk its position by telling the Commission about the regional cartel? If the Commission didn't already know about it, then it's not going to prejudice its position.

Could I just comment on a couple of things that have been said before? It's quite right that there is no marker system in the EU that the evidence has to be provided in order to qualify and if someone else comes in with the evidence first it doesn't matter how many times you have rung up the Commission to say that you are coming, you won't be in first. Here we have the problem of the weekend and certainly if it's an oral application that you want to make and if the evidence, the added value that you can give, is in the form of statements then that's going to pose a problem. If you have written evidence that has not been taken by the Commission during its inspection, then there is always the possibility of faxing that information to a dedicated fax line. Now whether you want to do that or not is something that you would want to think about. The other point that I would make is just to go back to Oystein's advice in terms of how he would receive the Commission officials. Obviously his cooperation is very welcome, but I would make one clarification which is that this dawn raid is taking place under Regulation 1/2003, not under Regulation 17/62, and if the officials wanted to ask questions, they would be entitled under Article 20(e) to ask any representative or member of staff of the undertaking for explanations, not only of the contents of the documents, but also on facts or documents relating to the subject matter and purpose of the inspection and to record the answer. That is actually a wider power than existed under Regulation 17/62 and I would not advise him to refuse that because the fines for this kind of procedural infringement have also been increased under the new Regulation, but Diana would no doubt have told him that.

[DIANA GOOD]

But I was only given three minutes!

[STEPHEN BLAKE]

I know and I have taken six to answer a different question to one that I was asked!

[BILL KOLASKY]

That's a very good lead in to my question to Margaret, which is that this is the first dawn raid at least that I've heard about since 1 May, since modernization. How is that going to change the world in terms of the way this investigation gets conducted?

I. Margaret Bloom

OK, first of all I'll take the main cartel and this would also apply if the regional cartel is part of the main one. In relation to that there are really few changes apart from the obvious one that the EC, I mean Stephen's jurisdiction, now covers 10 extra Member States, so there is that one. There are a few additional powers of investigation. He's already mentioned the one that's rather wider when they do the dawn raids. There is another power which enables the Commission to take statements from individuals if they consent. Now maybe there are one or two either disgruntled current employees or former employees who would like to go off to the Commission and make some interesting oral statements, maybe somebody from American Eagle, ScotsAir, CDL, and there the power might be useful, but its not a compulsory power. They also have an additional ability in terms of premises. They can now raid private homes if books or records are kept there. So maybe Sir Jeremy's home might be an interesting place to go and visit or Frederic Bourgeois', the VP's home. So those are for the main cartel.

On the regional short haul cartel, if it's a separate infringement, so if it's not part of the main one, then you get into the question that was addressed in the ice cream panel. Briefly let me just raise three issues. In this area, modernization has a significant effect on two of them and on the third, well, it is arguable that it should. The first one is the question of who would take the case we've got in the regional short haul cartel. It affects the UK, France, and Spain. Strictly speaking if you read the material, the Commission is only particularly well-placed if there are more than three Member States so they could say, no we are not taking it. They might be able to; Diana or Gary might be able to persuade them that they should take it. If they didn't then it could be one, two, or three Member States who could take it. Some of those Member States, the UK for example, could fine for effects in the other two, if the other two agreed, so that's that question. Secondly on information exchange: this morning they raised the question of safeguards. Some people are asking what happens to the information when it goes into the ECN? I think, personally, the safeguards look pretty good, but I well understand the questions and there are two Member States, one of which is included in these three, who have not yet committed to abide by all the conditions in the Cooperation Notice. Lastly on leniency itself, strictly this one isn't a change from modernization but on the other hand because there's an ECN, the expectation, not unreasonably, is that this should be a more joined-up affair. So although it doesn't actually change, expectations change and as Diana mentioned, Spain doesn't have a leniency regime. Obviously the UK and France do. So that's it, thank you.

[BILL KOLASKY]

Simon, Margaret raised the question of information sharing among the national authorities. Can you comment a little bit further on that and the extent to which the OFT would actually exchange information with other national authorities and what safeguards you have in place to protect the information?

J. Discussion

[SIMON WILLIAMS]

Obviously we are a European Member State and therefore if we are disclosing to other European Member States, it will be through the European Competition Network facility and the rules governing information exchange there are clearly laid out in Articles 11 and 12. There are clearly safeguards for leniency information and generally leniency information of course cannot be disclosed. As far as disclosure to other jurisdictions outside the Community are concerned, such as the United States, we have gateway provisions in our Enterprise Act, section 243 or something like, which basically say that we can disclose to others. We have to be satisfied that they have in their own jurisdiction suitable laws on data protection, preservation of confidentiality, etc. We would like, I think, to conclude MOUs with some of those countries that we are likely to exchange information with on a more regular basis, and I think there is still one in discussion with the United States. So there are provisions available. We can even disclose the information for things other than the cartel situation, for example if it was relevant to a criminal offence in another jurisdiction, but subject to all sorts of safeguards that I won't trouble you with at the moment. We do want to protect the leniency programme so we will do everything we can to make sure that confidentiality during the investigation is protected vis-à-vis third parties, potential litigants, etc, but of course, when we get to the end game, whether it be evidence in a criminal court or an infringement decision under the civil regime, clearly if anything you've given us under leniency is evidentially significant eventually it is going to find its way into the public domain at that stage.

[BILL KOLASKY]

Gary, I think I heard Jim come close to accusing American Eagle's lawyers of malpractice. Would you go into Canada? Would you recommend to Oystein that he go in to talk to Denyse?

[GARY SPRATLING]

Yes, I would recommend that Oystein go into Canada and other jurisdictions as well. The way the hypothetical was set up here, it doesn't present the potential for the type of interesting analysis you can get into in weighing what jurisdictions you should or should not go into and which you do first because, remember we have a situation, a three firm cartel, one firm cooperating with amnesty, compulsory process against the remaining firms, and so you have to. Your game right now is to secure as much protection as you can in the rest of the world. Now that doesn't mean that you go to every jurisdiction but my rule of thumb, which I have said for so many years I think that everybody has adopted it, is that you look at the jurisdiction where you will get hurt most by not having protection and you go there first. That's got to be Canada here. It looks like maybe the amnesty applicant in the other two jurisdictions did not seek amnesty in Canada and that may not be a mistake. There are reasons why occasionally you do not go and seek amnesty in other jurisdictions. It can be for the collateral consequences in that jurisdiction. You may think that there are jurisdictional issues for that enforcement authority. I've seen times when applicants misinterpreted one of the conditions of the Canada amnesty policy about disclosure of any and all offences which put you in the same category as a witness making a disclosure to an omnibus question at the end. There are reasons why the applicant may have not gone in. In this situation it is hard to believe it would have been an irrational decision, but there may be reasons, so you'd go in first and you'd try to get it in Canada.

With respect to the rest of the world and the other jurisdictions where this company does business, the significant ones that you really have to think about are first of all in Asia—Korea and Japan. Korea has an amnesty policy, Japan does not, even though they are much more active now on the enforcement front. At a recent IBA conference in Korea, they talked about these new initiatives that they are undertaking and yet they have no amnesty policy. You would also have to look at Singapore. When you are in this game of the international coordinating counsel you have to keep track of all the jurisdictions where things are happening and the reason Singapore is important is they have just announced a new antitrust policy and we know from the newspapers that Singapore has a tremendous airfreight market because of all the high technology equipment that is manufactured there and air freighted to various jurisdictions. So you would have to talk to counsel in Japan and Singapore about what to do. One caveat with respect to talking to counsel about that and any other jurisdictions, as you begin to get outside of the obvious jurisdictions, Canada, Australia—I didn't talk about that, I don't have time to talk about that I know—but when you get into the other jurisdictions there gets to be a problem when you're in jurisdictions, which are in the majority, where there is no provision for plea negotiations and plea agreements. That could completely change your attitude with respect to whether or not to go in and lay things out because there is the possibility that you will get no credit for it. There is the possibility that there is still a formulaic approach under the criminal sentencing scheme or the civil sentencing scheme as to what the penalty is going to be, so you have to think about that.

[BILL KOLASKY]

Thank you Gary. Denyse, we are now on Wednesday, let's say, tomorrow, looking ahead a day and Gary or his Canadian counterpart has contacted you. Are they in time? Is amnesty still available in Canada?

[DENYSE MACKENZIE]

Well just as a first point it's always available as long as, number one, we haven't already referred to the AG for charges and you are first in. In this case, on the facts that we have, it would look like ScotsAir would be first in, if they came, and frankly I would be happy to see ScotsAir given the percentage of the commerce because it may be that, in fact, they have a smaller amount of the commerce in Canada than one of the others, and that helps when you have a nice deep pocket to go after for a fine.

[GARY SPRATLING]

We'd love to help you out Denyse!

[DENYSE MACKENZIE]

Right! But the other thing that has to happen of course is they have to understand how our system works. Luckily they have guidelines on that that are published and I want to make a few points about those, because I think it is very important that they are published so there isn't any misconception about what's involved. I also want to make the point that our amnesty system is very, very similar by design to the amnesty system that you see in the United States. We have a marker system, there is a one point contact, you don't have to have the whole ball of wax when you come in, we want you in early, but you have to promise to make full truthful complete ongoing disclosure. You cannot be the instigator of the cartel and by that I mean *the chief* instigator, not one of the various instigators, and on the facts of this case it looks to me if you look at February and I think it's April, May, or June, as if they all took their turns in leading the pack. I don't believe we'd find American Eagle and nor in this case ScotsAir as being instigators, so you are covered on that side of things.

The other thing we'd like, if possible, is for restitution to be made as part of the amnesty deal. We've already mentioned confidentiality and we likewise would hold confidential the name of any amnesty applicant and the information provided. Now that can get tricky in this situation because always we want to cooperate with our colleagues. Jim mentioned that we, and certainly I, would have preferred to be able to work in parallel so that if we were going to do any searches we would have done them at the same time. If there were going to be wire taps we could have set that up because we would have got the traffic between the Vice Presidents and that includes the Vice Presidents talking perhaps to the Canadian officers. That would have been very useful information. So those sorts of things are all part of it but at this stage if we have a different amnesty applicant we're going to be restricted to a certain amount as to what we can share with our colleagues. The other thing in Canada that you cannot have is a situation where the applicant is the sole beneficiary in Canada of the cartel. For clear policy reasons we are not about to give amnesty to a participant that has reaped all the benefits in the Canadian market. That said, even when all that is done, and we've talked, and we talk in hypothetical terms, when a marker comes in, it's done in a context of usually the counsel phoning, getting hold of me, and if I'm not there for the day then I've assigned somebody, one of my Assistant Deputy Commissioners (ADCs), who will take the information and they will take it in a hypothetical sense. They will ask whether there has been a marker on 'x' and they will name the industry sector sufficiently for us to check all of our records and we do that quite quickly and get back to them and say that there is no 'x' yet. Then they will come back and tell us that they want to have that marker and at that stage then we set up the disclosure process and that has to take place rather quickly. There can be reasons for more lengthy disclosure but in general we like that to be done within three weeks maximum and as I said it's so rare that if it's going to go over, there had better be a good reason for it.

The other thing about amnesty is you don't have it if you don't do what those conditions require you to do. We can revoke it. It has not been done, we've come close I can tell you, but it has not been done yet, but it could be done and when we recommend to the AG—because it's what we do, we recommend, we don't have at the Bureau the right to grant amnesty; we can just recommend it to the AG—they are then going to take that and proceed with what we call the provisional grant of immunity, and after that there will be, after a full proffer of the information, a letter that confirms all the details and obligations that they have under the programme. They are well known, they are transparent, they are very clear and we do that so there won't be any miscalculations down the way. So, with that said, as I said, we would likely determine that American Eagle is not the instigator, but if ScotsAir came in, likewise they wouldn't be the instigator and if they are first in on that Wednesday then they would have the marker.

[BILL KOLASKY]

Thank you. Diana, Denyse dismissed the idea of American Eagle as the instigator here, but Sir Jeremy has hired Margaret's law firm Freshfields and you have talked to the partner at Freshfields who is working for him and Sir Jeremy is really upset. As far as he is concerned, it was this guy from Texas, GB, who got him into this. Is there anything that they can do to get the authorities in Brussels to take away amnesty from American Eagle?

[DIANA GOOD]

Tempting though it is to go on the offensive in relation to Mr Hangar and clearly there are arguments that can be made, I think the problem here is that even if Hangar hasn't behaved entirely properly, American Eagle have got in there first and have provided information sufficient to enable the Commission and other authorities to do their dawn raids. Therefore I don't think we are going to be able to push Hangar out and then say that we are entitled to the 100 per cent immunity, because we will never have got in there first. So I think really we have to use the arguments more to demonstrate that Jeremy Bright and ScotsAir were not coercers in any way, they were led into this, and use this as an argument to demonstrate that in relation to the international cartel they weren't the main player. Indeed in relation to the regional cartel they weren't the main player either. That was that horrible man Jacques Cartel, or was it Bourgeois? So I think that we do stand on solid ground when we say that we are entitled to a greater reduction in terms of the fines on the international cartel for coming in at number one on the regional cartel. I think we have to use it more to demonstrate that we weren't that bad, rather than really push to get amnesty removed, because I think that could back fire on us.

[BILL KOLASKY]

Jim, Gary talked about advising ScotsAir to get in early so that they could get a substantial reduction in the fine. Let's assume that he has done that. Is there any way that he is going to be able to talk you into not requiring Sir Jeremy and one or two of his subordinates to serve jail time and second, in figuring out how much jail time Sir Jeremy should serve, what impact, if any, does the fact that cartel behaviour is now criminal in the UK have on your position?

[JIM GRIFFIN]

Yes, Sir Jeremy picked the wrong time. First with the agreement with Scots-Air, Sir Jeremy and perhaps others are clearly going to be carved out of the non-prosecution protection of the company plea agreement. Gary's already noted that he's got separate counsel. We will be dealing with separate counsel to either work out a plea arrangement with Sir Jeremy or not. I think that he has a very limited opportunity, depending upon how fast he gets in and provides cooperation with us and the value of that cooperation, for working out a plea agreement that would allow him to argue for no jail time. He's beyond the point where we would agree to a no jail deal for him, but what are the important elements for him? The first one is timing. If he gets in quickly, before there has been any prosecution of any US executive, he's in better shape. Now by that I mean, suppose Hangar had decided not to come in with the company and we've prosecuted Hangar and he's going to jail for some substantial period of time. At that point a similarly situated foreign executive is not going to be given a better deal, but even in this situation, even if that has not occurred, let's say Hangar came in with the company and he's not being prosecuted, we now have the situation where Bright is in early. He's certainly going to get some credit for submission to jurisdiction because we don't have jurisdiction over him, but his leverage there is less than it would have been 12 days ago, right? June 2003 is the key date, six months or a year ago, because the offence is now criminal in the UK and it is an extraditable offence under the new Extradition Act in the UK. That doesn't mean that the UK will automatically extradite him if we indict him and ask that Simon send him over, but he might, and we'll be seeing how that plays out in the future. What is going to happen is we become better positioned to extradite for antitrust offences. You are going to see our position with foreign executives hardening so that we shrink the disparity between foreign executive jail sentences and US executive jail sentences, not by bringing the US executive jail sentences down, but by increasing the foreign executive jail sentences.

[BILL KOLASKY]

Thanks Jim. Well we've been talking about the criminal process but that's only the beginning. Let's move forward now and assume that ScotsAir is about to sign a plea agreement with Jim. Oystein, at this point what steps do you take to prepare to defend the inevitable private treble damage antitrust actions in the United States? I assume that you expect some?

[OYSTEIN MELAND]

I assume for the purpose of this that Gary has scared me stiff, or the client stiff, already, telling me all about it. What I would do is of course, as I did before. I would give all the relevant facts to our US lawyers. I would discuss with him, and agree with him, who are the best civil attorneys available in the States. Maybe it is somebody from his firm, maybe it is himself, I don't know, and I would hire them. I would also get on to, if we have not done that already, the best forensic economist to see what price increase, if any, this cartel activity has led to and thereafter I would approach all major customers because I would assume that there are larger and smaller customers. As regards major customers, I would see to it that somebody high up from the company approaches them directly in person. Depending on the advice I got of course, my inclination in the States would be to fight, first of all, all procedural questions, such as lack of personal jurisdiction and governing law clauses in the contract to see if we could get the cases out of US courts and out of US jurisdiction and over to, for example, arbitration, which is very common in these kind of contracts. I would thereby try to gain time and again try to negotiate settlements with the customers.

[BILL KOLASKY]

Thank you. Margaret and Diana, to what extent does the company need to worry about private damage actions over here either in the UK or in other European jurisdictions?

[MARGARET BLOOM]

OK I'll start on that one. In terms of the UK there have been a number of changes aimed at making it easier to secure redress. First of all the Enterprise Act and Article 16 of Regulation 1/2003 together mean that any infringement decision of either the OFT or the European Commission is binding on the courts here, so they don't have to prove that and the action for damages can start from that basis. The Competition Appeal Tribunal can also award damages and they have a case before them at the minute which is a result of a vitamins decision by the European Commission, and the Competition Appeal Tribunal can also take a form of group actions, brought by certain designated consumer bodies on behalf of groups of consumers. The bad news in a sense, if you are wanting redress, is there haven't actually been any awards of damages from the UK courts, nor yet from the Tribunal. There have been a number of out of court settlements. There is a very interesting case, *Crehan v Inntrepreneur* which is on appeal, so let's wait and see what comes out of that one.

And then a quick comment in terms of other European countries. Last year, in the *Arlanda* case in Sweden, SAS won _100 million and it has been right through the Swedish system, no further appeal, and that was as a result of price discrimination under the Article 82 Swedish equivalent. I think there are very few cases of damages awarded so far within European countries. I am positive of the last point, that if *Empagran* goes the wrong way—wrong way means that if the Supreme Court upholds the DC Circuit judgment—you can forget about any private actions in Europe. Everybody will be crossing the Atlantic to the US.

[BILL KOLASKY]

Diana; anything to add on that?

[DIANA GOOD]

Yes absolutely. In the meantime though, there was an important decision this time last year in the case of *Provimi v Aventis*. I see some of my opponents in the room, so forgive me for saying that we won that case. They lost it. But the importance of that decision, which was a jurisdictional challenge, was that we were acting on behalf of claimants who brought proceedings against members of the Vitamins cartel. There was no doubt that the defendants intended to pursue a policy of divide and rule. We had, I think, a total of 11 potential jurisdictions in which to bring claims, not all within the EU, but the problem with the EU at the moment is although potentially damages were available, there aren't the substantive decisions, and the procedures and rules and timetables are very, very different from one country to another, so we ran as a test case, bringing a claim in the High Court in London. We brought a claim on behalf of a German plaintiff in relation to purchases from a German subsidiary of the Swiss and French parent company cartelists and that's why we faced the jurisdictional challenge. There were a number of hurdles; there were jurisdiction clauses and principles in relation to where proceedings should be brought, it was a complicated case and a complicated decision, but the bottom line is that, provided there is an English anchor, of which there was here because part of the cartel was operated in the UK, UK purchases from a UK company, the fact that claims were brought in this instance say by a Germany company against a German defendant did not mean that the English courts did not have jurisdiction, and the mere fact that a subsidiary of cartel member had implemented the cartel was sufficient. There wasn't a need to prove knowledge and those proceedings could be bought in the UK, so in brief what that means, pending as you say the outcome of *Empagran*, is that in terms of forum, London does look like a very appealing forum at the moment because there is case-law which means that, provided there is an English angle to the cartel, all European losses can be claimed in the English courts.

[BILL KOLASKY]

We've gone about 15 minutes beyond the original concluding time. I wanted to allow some time for questions from the audience.

K. Questions

[CHRISTOPHER BROWN, *Competition Appeal Tribunal*]

I just wanted to perhaps firstly make an observation, which is to the lawyers representing the cartelists. Presumably you also instruct your clients to institute a compliance programme, if they haven't got one already. That'll be a plus point when it comes round to fining. Obviously it will be a minus point if you have already got one. And secondly, on the question of the conflict point that Gary Spratling brought up, at what stage do you say go and get your new counsel, especially if you are looking to coordinate a move towards the authorities?

[GARY SPRATLING]

That's a great question and something to which entire half days are devoted in white collar crime seminars in the United States, but the short answer is the company has the right to find out from its executives what happened. But at the stage that you know that there is a risk of exposure for that individual then my practice, which is not everybody's practice, is to cease questioning the individual because at that point, to obtain information from him which would be to his advantage if he were dealing through separate counsel and that they would offer that information is the time to recommend to him that he get separate counsel. Of course then what you hope to do through a joint defence agreement is to continue to share information so that you have the benefit of the knowledge of that exposure. You won't be able to deliver it to the Department of Justice because you won't have him as a witness, unless it is coordinated nicely, unless it works out, but often you don't have him there and that affects the level of cooperation you can give the Department and in exchange, the deal that they are going to give you. Did that answer the question?

[CHRISTOPHER BROWN]

Yes.

[BILL KOLASKY]

I just wanted to change the facts a tiny bit. American Eagle's conditional grants of immunity becomes rather suspicious. What would the regulators in the panel, or at least those who have been regulators, do about withdrawing immunity? What are the current approaches to that especially in the light of the US current case?

JIM GRIFFIN]

I suppose I should take the first crack at that. I can't say anything about the current case as most of you know we removed an amnesty applicant from the programme and pulled its conditional amnesty agreement, which we are allowed to do under the terms of the agreement. That should not signal any change in the requirements, or how we interpret the requirements, of the amnesty programme. All of the facts in that case will come out eventually. They are not out now. When they are out I think we will be talking about that a good bit, but my point in answering your question, or the point I would like to leave you with is that there has been no change in the US amnesty programme. You must cease the conduct when it is discovered. You must cooperate fully, you must agree, forward-looking, to pay restitution to victims, and you must not have been the leader in the cartel. Those remain the conditions. Those are forward-looking. They are representations which are made to us in the conditional amnesty letter and we now have revoked one.

[SIMON WILLIAMS]

I was just going to comment very briefly on the UK position. We, I don't think, have revoked a single leniency applicant who has actually signed up with us, but clearly we could do so if they miserably failed to cooperate or they totally and utterly designedly mislead us into signing up with leniency in the first place, but it's very rare and it hasn't happened in the UK.

[BILL KOLASKY]

I was going to ask, what about Canada and the EU?

[STEPHEN BLAKE]

The situation in the EU is broadly the same. It has not happened so far. Of course that doesn't mean that it couldn't happen and the conditions, as you know, are slightly different from the conditions in the American policy, but in particular, the key condition which I think we have in common is the requirement to cooperate fully and I think that's the key area where an undertaking could come unstuck if it starts to play silly games with the Commission. As regards the other, if it turned out that they did end their involvement at the time that they made their application or that they had coerced another undertaking, then that could also be a ground for revocation. It's not happened so far and I think that in my own view we've never had to do it. If it became apparent that that was likely or that was going to be the case then I think the Commission would want to inform the undertaking, give them an opportunity to respond and then if the Commission took the view it hadn't complied then it would inform the undertaking accordingly and obviously that would have an effect on its duty to cooperate.

[DENYSE MACKENZIE]

In this factual situation as we have seen today, we had very experienced defence counsel giving advice to their client, which I think was frankly exemplary. That's not always the case. You can have a situation, not that anybody in here would be affected by that, but you can have a situation where perhaps the immunity applicant isn't getting the best advice and before we would revoke immunity, we would, obviously in terms of even due process in our own activities, give them a chance to answer why they haven't complied with what they were supposed to comply with. That being said, a grant of immunity is a tremendous privilege frankly, and so we are going to come down very hard on somebody who would jeopardize our investigation or not give full and frank and truthful disclosure or in any way put our litigators into positions which may really jeopardize their cases and we would revoke. As I said before we haven't done that yet, but we came pretty close.

[BILL KOLASKY]

Don, very quickly.

[DON BAKER, BAKER MILLER PLC]

Well, the quick question is for the counsel to the company, both European and American counsel. What do you recommend doing about the people? Do you keep Sir Jeremy on the job? Do you keep the Vice Presidents who have been doing the price-checking on the job? What do you do?

[GARY SPRATLING]

In this situation it is easy. They are gone!

[DON BAKER]

Do your European colleagues agree with you?

[GARY SPRATLING]

The reason is this is not a tough situation. It would be a much tougher situation if we were the amnesty applicant and you were asking us what happened to Hangar. Now that's a whole different situation, because there the Department of Justice may want you to keep the person round on some sort of different status so you get the benefit of cooperation. If you fire him you can't deliver and you can't get your amnesty. So that's a different situation, but when you are second or third in, it's an easy question; they're gone!

[DIANA GOOD]

Yes I agree with that. The issue with the individual is how to actually achieve a degree of cooperation so that you can make this joint application I mentioned earlier, but you do not achieve that by effectively offering them an amnesty within the company and keeping him on and letting Jeremy Bright go on like that. I'm not saying that there won't be accommodations for the purpose of maintaining a relationship, in terms of paying for attorneys' fees and keeping the severance and all those types of things. There certainly will be accommodations, but you can't leave that person in a position of responsibility. They got the company in that situation in the first place.